Firearms Assembly
The NRA Guide
to Pistols and Revolvers
Revised and Expanded

D1608347

Firearms Assembly

The NRA Guide
to Pistols and Revolvers
Revised and Expanded

Edited by Joseph B. Roberts, Jr.

**A Publication of
the National Rifle Association of America**

BOOK SERVICE

Copyright © 1993
by the National Rifle Association of America

For information, address the National Rifle Association,
1600 Rhode Island Avenue, N.W., Washington, D.C. 20036

ISBN 0-935998-76-4
Library of Congress Catalog Card Number 93-083847
Published March 1993

Printed in the United States of America

Published by the
National Rifle Association of America
1600 Rhode Island Avenue, N.W.
Washington, D.C. 20036

The Cover
The Smith & Wesson Model 59 pistol on the cover
is from the collection of
The National Firearms Museum, Washington, D.C.

Cover Design by Michael R. Bloom
Cover Photograph by Carl B. Neustrand

George Martin, Executive Director, NRA Publications
Lourdes Fleckenstein, Dep. Director & Book Service Manager
Joseph B. Roberts, Jr., Editor, NRA Book Service
Michael A. Fay, Manufacturing Director
Harry L. Jaecks, Art Director
Michael R. Bloom, Design Associate

CONTENTS

Foreword ix
Allen & Thurber Pepperbox 2
Astra Cadix Revolver 4
Astra 357 Revolver 6
Astra Constable Pistol 8
Astra Models 400 & 600 Pistols 10
Ballester-Molina Pistol 12
Beretta Model 90 Pistol 14
Beretta Model 92F (M9) Pistol 16
Beretta Model 950B Jetfire Pistol 18
Beretta Pocket Pistol Model 1934 20
Bergmann Special Model Pocket Pistol 22
Bernardelli Model 60 Pistol 24
Browning Cal. .25 Auto Pistol 26
Browning Model 1910 Pistol 28
Browning .380 Automatic Pistol, Post 1968 30
Browning Medalist Pistol 32
Browning Model 1900 Pistol 34
Browning Swedish Model 1907 Pistol 36
Browning Model 1922 Pistol 38
Browning M35 Hi-Power Pistol 40
Browning Model 1936 Pistol 42
Browning Nomad Semi-Automatic Pistol 44
Charter Arms Police Bulldog Revolver 46
Charter Arms Undercover Revolver 48
Colt Model 1902 Military .38 Pistol 50
Colt (Post-war) .25 Pocket Automatic Pistol 52
Colt Automatic .32 and .380 Pocket Pistol 54
It's Very Easy (Colt .45 Auto Pistol) 56
Colt .22 -.45 Conversion Unit 60
Colt Double-Action Revolver (Model 1877) 62
Colt Model 1878 Double-Action Revolver 64
Colt Double-Action New Army and New Navy Revolvers 66
Colt Deringer No. 3 69
Colt Frontier Scout Revolver 70
Colt Gold Cup National Match Mark III Pistol 72
Colt Woodsman Pistol 74
Colt Official Police Revolver 76
Colt Paterson Revolving Pistol 78
Colt (Pre-war) .25 Pocket Automatic Pistol 80
Colt Single Action Army Revolver 81
Colt Model 1851 Navy Revolver 84
Colt Model 1855 Sidehammer Revolver 86
Crosman Series 130 (Air) Pistol 88
Crosman Series 150 (CO2) Pistol 90
Crosman Single Action 6 (CO2) Revolver 92
CZ Model 27 Pistol 94
CZ Model 50 Pistol 96
Dan Wesson Model W-12 Revolver 98
Deringer's Pocket Pistol 100
Dreyse Model 1907 Pistol 102
Enfield Revolver No. 2, Mk1 and Mk1* 104
Erma .22 Pistol 106
Feinwerkbau M-65 (Air) Pistol 108
French Model 1935-A Pistol 110

Frommer STOP Automatic Pistol 112
Glisenti M1910 Pistol 114
Glock 17 9mm Pistol 116
Haenel-Schmeisser Model I 118
Hammerli Free-Pistol 120
Hammerli-Walther Olympia Pistol 122
Harrington & Richardson Model 922 Revolver 124
H & R Model 929 "Side-Kick" Revolver 126
H & R Self-Loading Pistol 127
H & R Premier Revolver 129
Heckler & Koch P9S Pistol 131
High Standard Victor Pistol 133
Hi-Standard Dura-Matic Pistol 136
Hi-Standard Model D-100 137
Hi-Standard Model HB Pistol 138
Hi-Standard Sentinel Revolver 140
Hi-Standard Supermatic Trophy Pistol 142
Hungarian Model 1937 Pistol 144
Iver Johnson Model 1900 & U.S. Revolver 146
Iver Johnson Model 50 Revolver 148
Iver Johnson Model 66 Revolver 150
Iver Johnson Top-Break Revolver 152
Japanese Type 26 Revolver 154
Japanese Type 94 Pistol 156
Lahti M40 Pistol 158
Le Francais 9mm Browning Long Pistol 160
Le Francais Pocket Model Pistol 162
Liberator Pistol 164
Luger Pistol 165
Liliput 4.25mm Automatic Pistol 168
Makarov Pistol 169
Mauser HSc Pocket Pistol 171
Mauser Military Pistol ("Broomhandle Mauser") 173
Mauser Pocket Pistol Model 1910 175
Mauser W.T.P. Old Model 177
Nambu Type 14 Pistol 178
Ortgies Pocket Pistol 180
Polish Radom P35 Pistol 182
Remington New Model Cal. .44 Army Revolver 184
Remington Double Derringer 186
Remington Model XP-100 Pistol 188
Remington-Elliot Repeaters 190
Remington New Model Pocket Revolver 192
Remington Pocket Pistol Model 51 194
Rossi Princess Revolver 196
Ruger .22 Automatic 198
Ruger Bearcat Revolver 200
Ruger Blackhawk .357 Revolver 202
Ruger's Hawkeye Single-Shot Pistol 204
Ruger Security-Six Revolver 206
Ruger Single-Six Revolver 208
Sauer & Sohn Model 38 Pistol, Cal. .32 ACP 210
Sauer Model 1930 Pistol 212
Savage Model 1910 Pocket Pistol 214
Savage Model 101 Pistol 216
SIG-Neuhausen Pistol 218
Smith & Wesson .35 Cal. Auto Pistol 220

Smith & Wesson Bodyguard Revolvers 222
Smith & Wesson Centennial Revolver 224
Smith & Wesson Escort Pistol 226
Smith & Wesson K-38 Heavyweight Masterpiece Revolver 228
Smith & Wesson Military & Police Revolver 230
Smith & Wesson Model 39 Pistol 232
Smith & Wesson Model 41- 46 Pistol 234
Smith & Wesson Model 52 Pistol 236
Smith & Wesson Model 59 Pistol 238
Smith & Wesson Model 29 Revolver 240
Smith & Wesson New Departure Safety Hammerless Revolver 242
Smith & Wesson No.1 Revolver 244
Star BM/BKM Pistols 246
Star "Super" Model Pistols 248
Star Model BS Pistol 250
Star Model F Cal. .22 Pistol 252
Star PD .45 Pistol 254
Steyr Model 1912 Pistol 256
Steyr Model SP Pocket Pistol 258
Stoeger Luger .22 Pistol 260
Tokarev Pistol 262
Unique Military & Police Pistol 264
U.S. (Navy) Model 1842 Percussion Pistol 266
U.S. (Army) Model 1842 Pistol 268
Walther Model 4 7.65mm Pistol 270
Walther Model 6 9mm Pistol 272
Walther Model 8 Pistol 274
Walther Olympia Rapid-Fire Pistol 276
Walther Model 9 .25 ACP Pistol 278
Walther P.38 Pistol 280
Walther Model PP .22 Cal. Pistol 282
Webley Mk IV Revolver 284
Webley Mk VI Revolver 286
Webley Metropolitan Police Pistol 288
Whitney .22 Automatic Pistol 290
Appendix 292

FOREWORD

Since 1952, when its May issue carried the late E. J. Hoffschmidt's splendid treatment of the Browning Hi Power pistol, the AMERICAN RIFLEMAN has printed hundreds of "Exploded Views" on handguns and long guns. Many artists and writers have contributed and the AMERICAN RIFLEMAN articles have prompted manufacturers and importers to include clear parts representations and disassembly/reassembly instructions in their manuals.

Today such manuals almost always accompany new guns and we wonder how we got along without them before. They are now so much taken for granted that some gunsmiths will refuse to work on a gun for which no exploded view exists.

It would be nice if the AMERICAN RIFLEMAN could claim to have originated as well as popularized the exploded view but that is not exactly the case. During World War I, NRA member Charles Newton, who initiated so many things of interest to shooters, illustrated his catalog with a very modern looking exploded view of his very modern looking rifle. With a nod of thanks to Newton, we have included his drawings in the volume devoted to rifles and shotguns. All of the entries in this book have appeared previously in the AMERICAN RIFLEMAN.

In addition to revising and expanding the previous edition by the inclusion of the most recent and non-duplicative entries, this edition contains a long overdue and very useful Appendix whereby the reader can identify firearms that are not specifically covered, but which can be disassembled using instructions published for other similar firearms — the many variations and aliases of the Colt Government Model pistol come to mind by way of an example.

Over the years the NRA "Firearms Assembly" books have proven themselves accurate, timely and extremely useful additions to the library of any firearms *aficionado* or professional. We are confident that this volume and its companion, FIREARMS ASSEMBLY, *The NRA Guide to Rifles and Shotguns, Revised and Expanded*, will prove worthy successors to the earlier editions.

Pete Dickey
Technical Editor
AMERICAN RIFLEMAN

WHAT THE NRA IS
WHAT THE NRA DOES

The National Rifle Association was organized as a non-profit, membership corporation in the State of New York in November 1871, by a small group of National Guard officers. The object for which it was formed was the "...improvement of its members in marksmanship, and to promote the introduction of the system of aiming drill and rifle practice as a part of the military drill of the National Guard...."

In 1877, its name was changed to the National Rifle Association of America (NRA). During its years of existence, NRA Headquarters has been located in New York, New Jersey and, since 1908, in Washington, D.C.

The NRA represents and promotes the best interests of gun owners and shooter-sportsmen and supports their belief in the ideals of the United States of America and its way of life. It is dedicated to firearms safety education as a public service, marksmanship training as a contribution to individual preparedness for personal and national defense, and the sports of shooting and hunting as wholesome forms of recreation. It stands squarely behind the premise that ownership of firearms must not be denied to law-abiding Americans.

The purposes and objectives of the National Rifle Association of America are:

To protect and defend the Constitution of the United States, especially with reference to the inalienable right of the individual American citizen guaranteed by such Constitution to acquire, possess, transport, carry, transfer ownership of, and enjoy the right to use arms, in order that the people may always be in a position to exercise their legitimate individual rights of self-preservation and defense of family, person, and property, as well as to serve effectively in the appropriate militia for the common defense of the Republic and the individual liberty of its citizens;

To promote public safety, law and order, and the national defense;

To train members of law enforcement agencies, the armed forces, the militia, and people of good repute in marksmanship and in the safe handling and efficient use of small arms;

To foster and promote the shooting sports, including the advancement of amateur competitions in marksmanship at the local, state, regional, national and international levels;

To promote hunter safety, and to promote and defend hunting as a shooting sport and as a viable and necessary method of fostering the propagation, growth, conservation and wise use of our renewable wildlife resources.

ALLEN AND THURBER PEPPERBOX

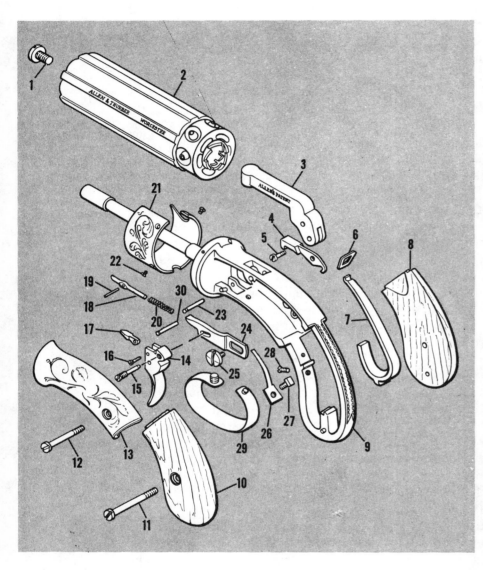

THE pepperbox pistol holds a unique position in American firearms history. It bridged the gap between the single-shot pistol and the revolver with stationary barrel. Pepperbox guns were handy, fairly reliable, and supplied a series of quick shots. They proved popular and were carried West in great numbers during the gold rush era.

While there were flintlock pepperboxes, they were clumsy and expensive. The common pepperbox, as we know it today, came about after development of the percussion cap.

Ethan Allen saw the possibilities of a percussion pepperbox and in 1834 patented his self-cocking gun. A few years later, with the aid of his brother-in-law, he founded the Allen and Thurber Gun Co. They made guns from 1837 to 1842 in Grafton, Mass. In 1842 they moved to Norwich, Conn. Then in 1855 they moved back to Massachusetts and settled in Worcester. During all these moves, a steady flow of pepperboxes were turned out. A wide variety of models was offered. The barrels ranged from 2¼″ to 5½″ in length and in calibers from .28 to .36.

Allen and Thurber guns were well made. The barrels were bored from a block of cast steel. The frame was also cast. Operating parts were machined from bar stock and hardened where necessary. Walnut was used for the grips in most cases and the frames were generally scroll engraved.

The self-cocking lock mechanism was unique for its time. It is fairly simple and contains a minimum number of parts. Lack of shielding between the caps in some of the earlier pepperboxes resulted in occasional multiple discharges. Allen overcame this by putting a snug-fitting shield around the nipple area which kept the caps in place and also helped keep the sparks from igniting the other loaded barrels.

The revolver, with its fixed rifled barrel and compact design, to say nothing of its reduced weight, soon overshadowed the pepperbox design. The invention of the metallic cartridge gave the pepperbox its final kiss of death, since it was impractical to try to convert a pepperbox to fire fixed ammunition.

PARTS LEGEND

1. Barrel retaining screw	11. Grip screw	21. Nipple shield
2. Barrel group	12. Side-plate screw	22. Shield screws
3. Hammer	13. Side-plate	23. Trigger pin
4. Sear	14. Trigger	24. Hand
5. Sear screw	15. Hand operating pin	25. Hand retaining screw
6. Mainspring link	16. Barrel latch screw	26. Hand spring
7. Mainspring	17. Barrel latch	27. Spring retaining screw
8. Right grip	18. Detent pin	28. Mainspring tension screw
9. Frame	19. Detent retaining pin	29. Trigger guard
10. Left grip	20. Detent spring	30. Hammer pin

By EDWARD J. HOFFSCHMIDT

By EDWARD J. HOFFSCHMIDT

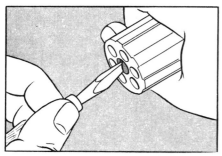

1 The Allen and Thurber pepperbox barrel group rotates around a central pin fixed to the frame. To remove the barrel group, remove the barrel retaining screw (1) and pull the trigger until the hammer just clears the nipple. Then pull barrel group forward off pin. Use a good grade of penetrating oil on all the screw heads and threads.

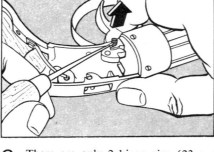

3 There are only 2 hinge pins (23 and 30) in the entire gun, one retaining the trigger, the other retaining the hammer. Since both of these pins are blind pins and do not extend through the frame, a notch was cut in the frame and an undercut was machined into the pins. If a thin screwdriver or pick is inserted as shown, the pins can be easily pried out.

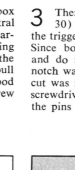
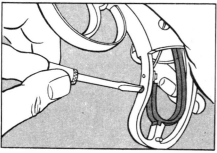

2 The trigger pull can be adjusted to a certain extent by loosening or tightening the mainspring tension screw (28). When this screw is removed, the mainspring (7) can be pushed out of its seat in the frame and lifted free.

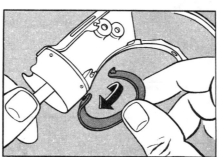

4 Once the side-plate has been removed, internal parts can be easily unscrewed and removed. To remove the trigger guard (29), push rear of the guard forward and pull down on it slightly. When it comes free of the frame, unscrew as shown. ∎

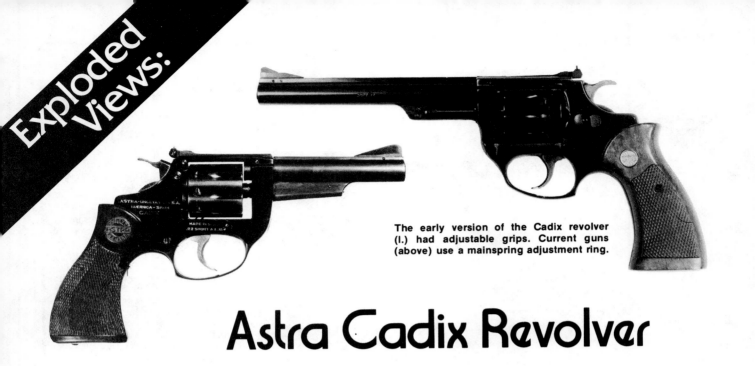

The early version of the Cadix revolver (l.) had adjustable grips. Current guns (above) use a mainspring adjustment ring.

Astra Cadix Revolver

BY PETE DICKEY

THE Spanish gunmaking firm of Esperanza y Unceta was founded in Eibar in 1908. The present factory was built in Guernica in 1913 and a year later the brand name Astra was registered. In 1926, the firm name was changed to Unceta y Cia., and changed again in 1953 to Astra-Unceta y Cia. Here and in Europe it is known simply as Astra.

Semi-automatic pistols formed the bulk of Astra's producton for a half century, and it supplied guns ranging from the Campo Giro to the Junior Colt.

Although well-made S&W type revolvers bearing the Union name were cataloged and sold by Unceta y Cia. in the 1920s and '30s, these were not made in Guernica but in Eibar by a contracting firm. Revolvers did not become a part of Astra's production until 1958.

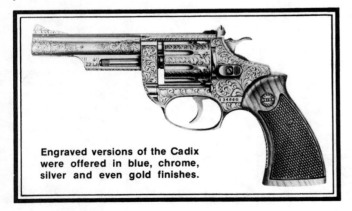

Engraved versions of the Cadix were offered in blue, chrome, silver and even gold finishes.

In January of that year, the first true Astra revolver prototypes were produced and given the name Cadix — the archaic spelling of the Spanish port Cadiz.

The early revolvers were essentially S&W derivations in .22 cal. with shrouded extractor rods, but included some interesting innovations.

The swing-out cylinder held not six but nine .22 Long Rifle (or Short or Long) cartridges; the frame profiling was distinctly different from that of S&W; and the one-piece plastic grip was affixed to a spacer block on the frame tang. This permitted the grip to be adjusted vertically to suit differing hand sizes. 2", 4" and 6" barreled versions were provided.

Despite its large cylinder capacity, the Cadix was small in size and inevitably (1962) a five-shot .38 Spl. version came along, followed by a six-shot .32 and nine-shot .22 Mag. in 1969. The 2"-barreled .38 proved a most popular addition to the line of the U.S. importers of the time, Firearms International Corp., and many Cadix revolvers were sold here. The small .38 dispensed with the adjustable grip feature, substituting a conventional grip frame and two-piece walnut grip panels.

By 1968, the adjustable grip feature had disappeared from all models in favor of a conventional grip and a mainspring adjustment ring as shown in the photographs.

Over 300,000 Cadix revolvers have been made to date, but while they are still in production in carbon and stainless steel versions, Astra's U.S. importer Interarms does not carry these models. Instead, it concentrates on Astra's double-action semi-automatics and magnum-framed revolvers.

A 2" .38 Spl. version of the Cadix, known as the Model 250, is now in use by various units of the Spanish police. ∎

Disassembly Instructions — Either Type

First check that the revolver is unloaded by moving the thumbpiece (10) forward and swinging the cylinder (3) out to the left. The grip (17) or grip plates (A,D) (depending on model), are taken off by removing screws (57) or (G).

Remove the cylinder, its crane (2) and

attendant parts by loosening the front sideplate screw (48) and sliding the opened cylinder assembly forward off the frame (1). Disassembly of the cylinder is accomplished by clamping the extractor rod (55) in a padded vise with two or three empty cartridges chambered to prevent damage to the extractor guide pins. The cylinder is

then turned clockwise to free it from the extractor rod (Fig. 1).

The sideplate (14) can now be taken off to expose the internal parts by first removing its screws (46, 47, 48, 49) and then tapping the right side of the frame with a plastic or wooden mallet to loosen the plate which can then be removed with the fingers. Do not pry with metal tools which can damage the finish or internal parts (**Fig. 2**).

Fig. 1

Fig. 2

With the sideplate removed, the internal parts and their function are apparent. No further disassembly should be required for maintenance.

If it is required that the rebound slide (12) be removed, caution is necessary as it is powered by a heavy spring that could cause injury if released unexpectedly. Eye protection is mandatory.

Compress the rebound slide spring (31) with a screwdriver and lift it over the frame pin which restrains it (**Fig. 3**).

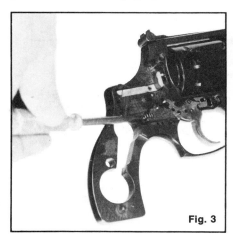

Fig. 3

When replacing the rebound slide, first reinstall its spring and replace the two pieces as a unit.

Reassembly of remaining parts is done in reverse order.

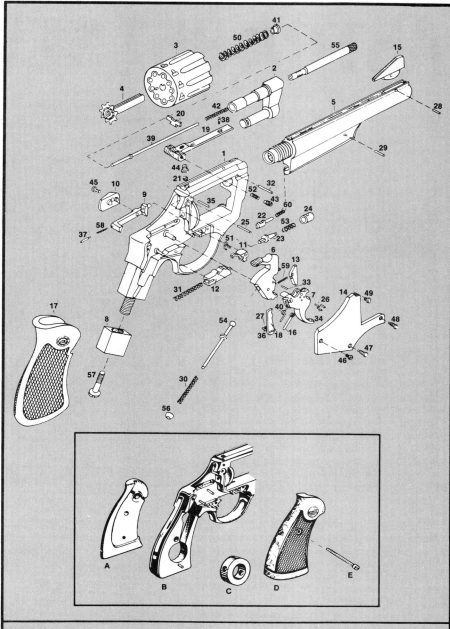

Parts Legend
1. Frame
2. Crane
3. Cylinder
4. Extractor
5. Barrel
6. Hammer
7. Trigger
8. Grip adjusting block
9. Bolt
10. Thumbpiece
11. Cylinder stop
12. Rebound slide
13. Sear
14. Sideplate
15. Front sight
16. Trigger lever
17. Grip
18. Hand
19. Rear sight leaf
20. Sight slide
21. Elevating stud
22. Locking bolt

23. Firing pin
24. Firing pin bushing
25. Firing pin retaining pin
26. Lever spring pin
27. Lever spring collar pin
28. Front sight pin
29. Locking bolt pin
30. Mainspring
31. Rebound slide spring
32. Barrel pin
33. Sear pin
34. Hand spring pin
35. Bushing retaining pin
36. Cylinder lever pin
37. Bolt plunger
38. Sight leaf screw
39. Center pin
40. Hand spring
41. Extractor rod collar
42. Center pin spring
43. Windage screw
44. Elevation screw
45. Thumbpiece screw

46. Flat head sideplate screw
47. Rear sideplate screw
48. Front sideplate screw
49. Top sideplate screw
50. Extractor spring
51. Cylinder stop spring
52. Sight slide spring
53. Firing pin spring
54. Hammer strut
55. Extractor rod
56. Mainspring seat
57. Grip adjusting screw
58. Bolt spring
59. Sear spring
60. Locking bolt spring

Detail
A. Left grip
B. Frame
C. Adjustment ring
D. Right grip
E. Grip screw

exploded views:
ASTRA 357 REVOLVER

BY INIGO DIAZ-GUARDAMINO

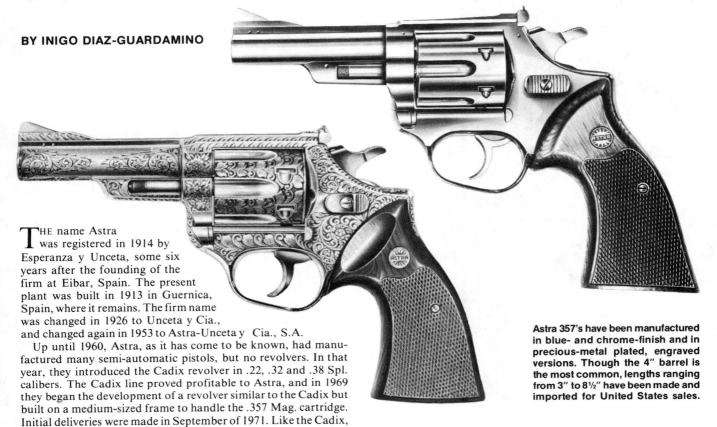

Astra 357's have been manufactured in blue- and chrome-finish and in precious-metal plated, engraved versions. Though the 4″ barrel is the most common, lengths ranging from 3″ to 8½″ have been made and imported for United States sales.

THE name Astra was registered in 1914 by Esperanza y Unceta, some six years after the founding of the firm at Eibar, Spain. The present plant was built in 1913 in Guernica, Spain, where it remains. The firm name was changed in 1926 to Unceta y Cia., and changed again in 1953 to Astra-Unceta y Cia., S.A.

Up until 1960, Astra, as it has come to be known, had manufactured many semi-automatic pistols, but no revolvers. In that year, they introduced the Cadix revolver in .22, .32 and .38 Spl. calibers. The Cadix line proved profitable to Astra, and in 1969 they began the development of a revolver similar to the Cadix but built on a medium-sized frame to handle the .357 Mag. cartridge. Initial deliveries were made in September of 1971. Like the Cadix, the Astra 357 is similar in its internal construction to the modern Smith & Wesson revolver. Internally, the most significant difference is the coiled, music wire mainspring which, around its strut, impinges on an internal ring in the butt of the revolver. This ring has four annular holes which are counterbored to varying depths. The ring can be turned manually after the removal of the grips and mainspring assembly, so that different trigger pull weights can be achieved.

In 1971, the 357 was available with 3″, 4″ or 6″ barrel lengths, and in 1976 an 8½″ barreled version was introduced.

By mid-1979, approximately 55,000 357s had been made and sold in blue, chrome, and engraved versions. Current plans call for the introduction of the 4″ barrel version in stainless steel in the very near future. In addition to the 55,000 unit quantity, over 16,000 similar guns in .38 Spl. caliber have been produced, but are seldom encountered in the United States. The standard version of the .38 Spl. gun is termed the Model 960, and a single-action version with screw-adjustable trigger, designed for competitive shooting, is termed the Match Model. ∎

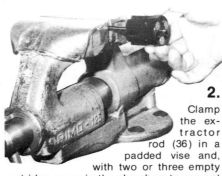

1. To remove the cylinder assembly, back off the front sideplate screw (33). Then, moving the thumbpiece (8) forward, swing out the cylinder assembly and push it and its crane (2) free of the frame.

2. Clamp the extractor rod (36) in a padded vise and, with two or three empty cartridge cases in the chambers to prevent damage to the extractor and its guide pins, turn the cylinder clockwise to free it from the extractor rod.

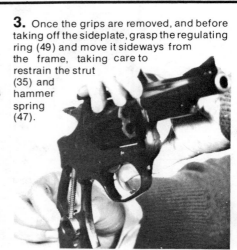

3. Once the grips are removed, and before taking off the sideplate, grasp the regulating ring (49) and move it sideways from the frame, taking care to restrain the strut (35) and hammer spring (47).

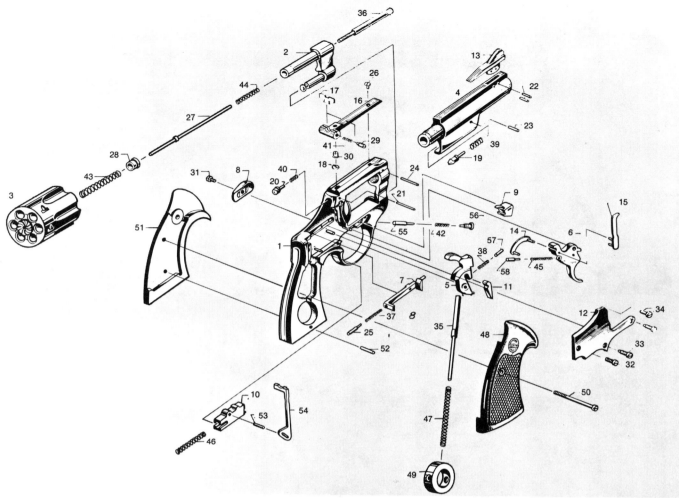

Parts Legend

1. Frame
2. Crane
3. Cylinder with extractor and pins
4. Barrel
5. Hammer
6. Trigger
7. Bolt
8. Thumbpiece
9. Cylinder stop
10. Rebound slide
11. Sear
12. Slideplate
13. Front sight
14. Trigger lever
15. Hand
16. Rear sight leaf
17. Sight slide
18. Rear sight elevator
19. Locking bolt
20. Firing pin
21. Firing pin retaining pin
22. Front sight pin (2)
23. Locking bolt pin
24. Barrel pin
25. Bolt plunger
26. Sight leaf screw
27. Cylinder pin
28. Extractor rod collar
29. Windage screw
30. Elevator screw
31. Thumbpiece screw
32. Flat head sideplate screw
33. Front & lower sideplate screw (2)
34. Top sideplate screw
35. Hammer strut
36. Extractor rod
37. Bolt spring
38. Sear spring
39. Locking bolt spring
40. Firing pin spring
41. Sight slide spring
42. Cylinder stop spring
43. Extractor spring
44. Center pin spring
45. Hand torsion spring
46. Rebound slide spring
47. Hammer spring
48. Right grip
49. Regulating ring
50. Grip screw
51. Left grip
52. Grip pin
53. Safety pin
54. Safety
55. Cylinder stop plunger
56. Cylinder stop screw
57. Sear plunger
58. Hand plunger

4. Remove the sideplate screws (32, 33, 34) and tap the frame lightly with a wooden or plastic mallet at the right side of the grip to loosen the sideplate (12). Do not pry the sideplate from its seat.

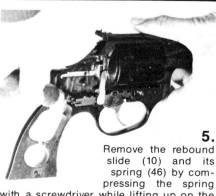

5. Remove the rebound slide (10) and its spring (46) by compressing the spring with a screwdriver while lifting up on the rebound slide and pulling it off the fixed frame pin. Take care that the rebound slide spring is not lost, by keeping a cloth over the gun to trap the spring and prevent injury.

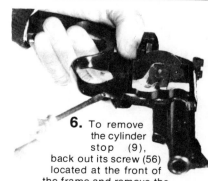

6. To remove the cylinder stop (9), back out its screw (56) located at the front of the frame and remove the cylinder stop spring (42) and the cylinder stop plunger (55). With a screwdriver, push the narrow side of the cylinder stop to force it out of the frame. Reassemble in reverse order.

Astra
Constable Pistol
exploded views:

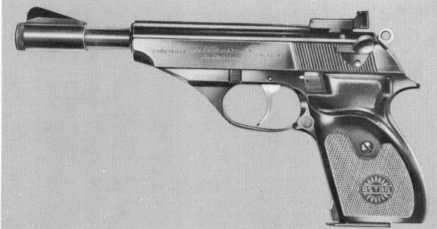

Though appearing to have a double-action trigger, the Astra Constable Sport model is a single-action version made in .22 cal. only and equipped with a removable barrel counterweight. The Sport model is virtually unknown in the U.S.

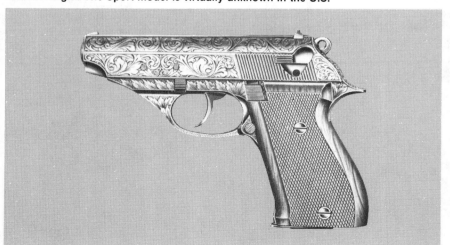

Usually the Constable is encountered in blue finish with plastic grips. Some versions have been imported with wooden grips and chrome, chrome engraved and other deluxe finishes. Two grip screws on each side indicate later production.

BY NRA TECHNICAL STAFF

In the mid-1960s, Astra began the development of their first double-action semi-automatic pistol. It was not until 1970 that the first production models were shipped to the United States.

These original pistols in calibers .32, .380 and .22 Long Rifle were all equipped with plastic grips affixed with a single screw on each side and an integral thumb shelf on the left side. Early guns had fixed rear sights and positive firing pins. The positive firing pin meant that if the pistol, with chamber loaded, were to be carried with the chamber loaded, the hammer fully down and the safety "OFF", the firing pin would impinge on the cartridge primer. Safe carrying the pistol, then, required either that the pistol be carried with the chamber empty, or with the chamber loaded, the hammer down and the safety engaged.

Later pistols were equipped with flat plastic grips lacking the thumbrest, affixed with two screws on each side, and a rear sight adjustable for windage. Still later, positive firing pins were changed to firing pins of the inertia type making it safer to carry the gun. This change in the firing pin was accompanied by minor changes to the safety, the disconnector and the slide retainer. The firing pin change took place in the .380 A.C.P. and .32 calibers at Serial No. 1091101, and in the .22 caliber pistols at Serial No. 1140551.

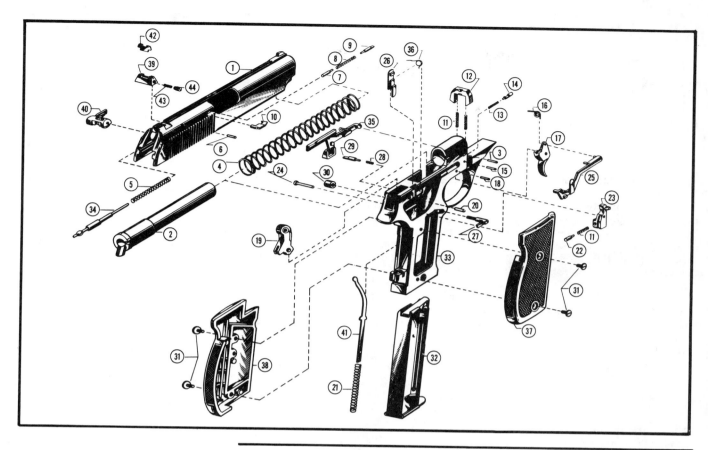

Since that time the Constable has undergone no major change.

Constables were imported by Interarms, of Alexandria, Va. By 1988, Interarms had dropped both the .32 and the .22 Long Rifle guns from their catalogs. The .380 appears in Interarms's 1990 catalog, but not in the 1992 edition.

Astra Constables were, like other Astra products, of good quality and well finished throughout. At various times they have been offered in blue, chrome and chrome-engraved finishes. The Constable Sport Model, in .22 Long Rifle only, was fitted with a six-inch barrel a windage and elevation-adjustable rear sight and a barrel counterweight.

Field Stripping Instructions

Depress the magazine catch button (30) and remove the magazine (32) from the pistol. Retract the slide (1) and release it after checking that the chamber is empty. Leave the hammer (19) at the full cock position. With the thumb and index finger of the left hand, pull down the takedown latch (12) located in front of the trigger and with the right hand pull the slide fully to the rear. The slide may then be lifted clear of the frame (33) and removed by sliding it forward off the barrel. This is all that is necessary to clean and lubricate the pistol. Further disassembly is not recommended.

Parts Legend

No.	Part	No.	Part	No.	Part
1.	Slide	15.	Takedown plunger pin	30.	Magazine catch button
2.	Barrel	16.	Trigger spring	31.	Grips screws
3.	Barrel pin	17.	Trigger	32.	Magazine complete
4.	Recoil spring	18.	Trigger pin	33.	Frame
5.	Firing pin spring	19.	Hammer	34.	Firing pin
6.	Firing pin retainer	20.	Hammer pin	35.	Slide retainer
7.	Safety plunger	21.	Main spring	36.	Disconnector spring
8.	Extractor spring	22.	Sear plunger	37.	Right grip
9.	Extractor retainer	23.	Sear	38.	Left grip
10.	Extractor	24.	Sear pin	39.	Rear sight
11.	Sear spring and takedown yoke spring	25.	Sear bar	40.	Thumb safety
12.	Takedown yoke	26.	Disconnector	41.	Hammer strut
13.	Takedown plunger spring	27.	Magazine catch	42.	Sight slide
14.	Takedown plunger	28.	Magazine catch spring	43.	Sight slide spring
		29.	Magazine button plunger	44.	Windage screw

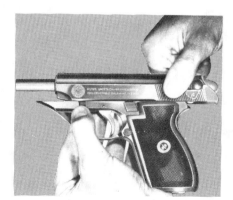

Remove the magazine and cock the hammer. Pull down the latch located in front of trigger and pull the slide fully to the rear.

With the slide now fully retracted it may be lifted and removed from the frame. Further disassembly is not recommended.

Astra Models 400 and 600 Pistols

By E. J. HOFFSCHMIDT

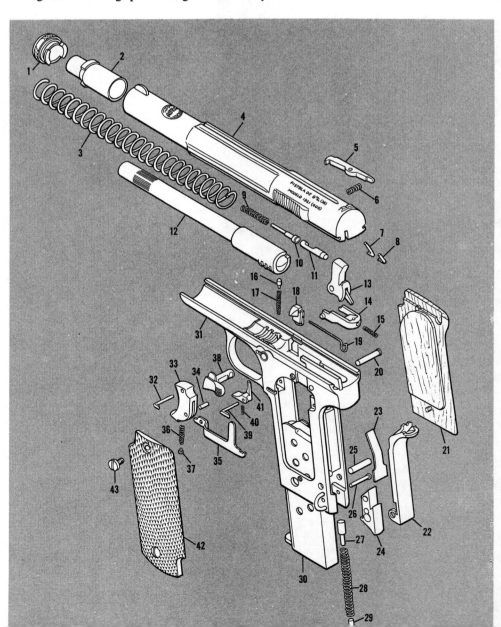

THE Spanish-made Astra Model 400 (Model 1921) semi-automatic pistol is a blowback-operated arm. That is, the breech is not locked in firing. A locked breech is usually considered necessary to handle the more powerful 9 mm. loads, but in the Model 400 pistol the opening of the breech is delayed through the use of a heavy slide and a powerful recoil spring.

The standard Astra Model 400 pistol will fire either the 9 mm. Largo (9 mm. Bergmann) cartridge or the .38 Automatic Colt Pistol cartridge.

During World War II the German Army obtained the Astra pistol in cal. 9 mm. Parabellum (9 mm. Luger). This gun is known as the Model 600 and has the inscription "PIST. PATR. 08" stamped on the barrel opposite the ejection port in the slide. Model 600 pistols used by the German Army have the German Ordnance acceptance mark on the right side of the grip overhang. After World War II, 14,000 Model 600 pistols were sold to West Germany for police use. It is also offered commercially.

There are several safety features in the Models 400 and 600 pistols. A thumb safety locks the trigger and slide, and a grip safety locks the sear. A magazine safety blocks the trigger when the magazine is removed.

Disassembly procedures for the Models 400 and 600 pistols are essentially identical.

Parts Legend

1. Barrel bushing lock
2. Barrel bushing
3. Recoil spring
4. Slide
5. Extractor
6. Extractor spring
7. Firing pin retainer pin
8. Extractor retainer pin
9. Firing pin spring
10. Firing pin
11. Firing pin extension
12. Barrel
13. Hammer
14. Sear
15. Sear spring
16. Safety catch detent
17. Detent spring
18. Slide stop
19. Slide stop spring
20. Hammer pin
21. Right grip
22. Grip safety
23. Grip safety spring
24. Magazine catch
25. Grip safety pin
26. Magazine catch stop
27. Upper spring plunger
28. Hammer spring
29. Lower spring plunger
30. Magazine
31. Frame
32. Trigger pin
33. Trigger
34. Trigger bar pin
35. Trigger bar
36. Trigger bar spring
37. Spring plunger
38. Safety catch
39. Magazine safety pin
40. Magazine safety spring
41. Magazine safety
42. Left grip
43. Grip screw (4)

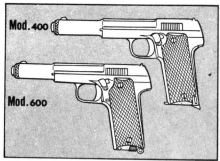

1. Mechanically, the Models 400 and 600 are similar. The Model 600 is ¾" shorter. The front-to-back grip depth is less in the Model 600 because of the shorter cartridge it fires. Most parts are not interchangeable but the takedown sequence is similar.

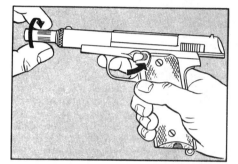

2. To field strip for general cleaning, first clear chamber and remove magazine (30). Pull slide (4) to rear, then rotate safety catch (38) up as slide is moved forward until catch engages slide. Rotate barrel (12) as shown, until it is released from frame (31) and engaged with slide. Release safety catch and move barrel and slide forward off frame.

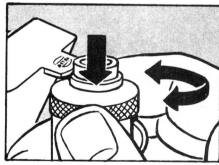

3. To disassemble, first clear chamber and remove magazine. Place pistol, muzzle up, on table. Depress barrel bushing (2) with magazine floorplate or screwdriver. Turn barrel bushing lock (1) either way until it holds barrel bushing. Grip barrel bushing and lock firmly with both hands and turn lock about ¼-turn, releasing recoil spring (3). Remove recoil spring, bushing, and lock. Barrel and slide are removed from frame as in field stripping.

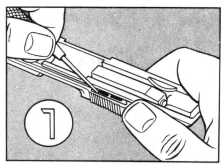

4. L-shaped retainer pins (7 & 8) retain the extractor (5) and the firing pin extension (11). Remove pins by prying up with a small screwdriver or punch. When reassembling firing pin spring (9), firing pin (10), and firing pin extension (11), align cut-out on the firing pin extension before inserting the retainer pin (7).

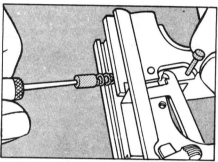

5. Remove the 4 grip screws (43) and the grips (21 & 42). Replace magazine (30) in frame. Insert punch through hole in frame below trigger bar (35). Hold hammer (13) with thumb and pull trigger, allowing hammer to fall until upper plunger (27) stops against punch. Remove magazine. Drift out hammer pin (20) from left side and remove hammer. Hold upper plunger with drift and remove punch. Remove upper and lower plungers (27 & 29) and hammer spring (28). (Model 600 has no lower plunger.)

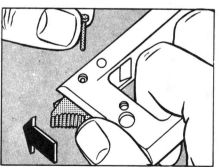

6. Most Model 400 pistols have magazine catch as shown here. Remove magazine catch stop (26). Drift out grip safety pin (25), remove grip safety (22), and push out magazine catch (24) in direction indicated. It is unnecessary to remove side magazine catch on late Models 400 and 600 pistols. ∎

Astra Model 400 Pistol

PISTOL MAGAZINES

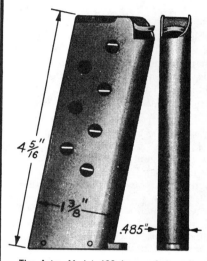

The Astra Model 400 is a unique automatic pistol. It was designed to fire several different cartridges, including the 9 mm. Bergmann-Bayard and .38 Colt Automatic round. Of blowback type, this pistol has a strong recoil spring and a very heavy slide to resist the recoiling forces of powerful cartridges. Unlike some Spanish pistols, the Astras are well made and finished.

Model 400 magazines can generally be recognized by the uncommonly wide cross-section necessary to handle the long cartridges. The Astra trademark, but not the model number, will usually be found on the tip of the magazine floorplate.

The right side of the magazine is cut lower than the left. This allows the tip of the follower to operate the hold-open device that holds the slide back when the last shot has been fired.—EDWARD J. HOFFSCHMIDT

Ballester-Molina Pistol

BY MARK A. KEEFE, IV

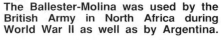

IN 1929 Dr. Arturo Ballester Janer and Ing. Eugenio Molina formed *Hispano Argentina Fabrica de Automoviles S.A.* (HAFDASA) in Buenos Aires for the manufacture of automobiles, trucks, buses and diesel engines for the Argentine market. The firm proved successful and went on to make small arms of several types, but none of its products was to become so well-known throughout the world as its .45 cal. pistol made from 1937-1953.

For the first three years the pistol was marked Ballester-Rigaud (Ing. Rorice Rigaud being the engineer behind the project), but thereafter the more familiar Ballester-Molina marking was standard.

The pistols were issued to Argentine military and police forces to complement their U.S.- and Argentine-made

M1911-type .45s and were sold commercially throughout Latin America. Dr. Tarquino C.A. Darre Nogare, president of the *Asociacion Argentina Coleccionistas de Armas y Municiones*, reports that during World War II the British purchased 10,000 Ballester-Molinas that were issued to the Eighth Army in North Africa, where they gained a high reputation; 5,000 more are said to have been bought by the British and used in other areas, some reportedly in clandestine activities.

In the 1960s surplus Ballester-Molinas began to be imported into the U.S. and, on a sporadic basis, fairly large quantities have continued to come in to be well received by collectors and shooters. A .22 cal. "trainer" version was also made for commercial and military sales (from 1940 to 1953), but is rarely encountered here.

In 1981 the trademark "Ballester-Molina" was registered for pistols by the U.S. Patent and Trademark Office and assigned to Carlos Jose Luis Ballester Molina of Buenos Aires. We found he is a descendent of both the original founders of the firm and is actively seeking international cooperation for the eventual reintroduction of the Ballester-Molinas on the market. Unfortunately, neither he nor our other correspondents in Argentina had definite information on the total quantities of .45 or .22 cal. pistols manufactured in the 1937-1953 period. The Ballester-Molina's slide unit with its inertia firing pin differs from that of the M1911A1 mainly in its serrations, its markings and the absence of a second disassembly notch. Its magazine interchanges with that of the Colt and its frame has the Colt-type plunger tube assembly, but there the parallels end.

The simplified magazine catch and vertically grooved grip plates are distinctive; otherwise the pistol is a near-

Pull the hammer back past the fully cocked position, turn the thumb safety 180° and withdraw it from the frame. The hammer and its pin then can be removed.

Fig. A

The Ballester-Molina was used by the British Army in North Africa during World War II as well as by Argentina.

clone of the Star Modelo P of the 1930s. Star features include: a solid backstrap with no grip safety; a pivoted trigger with its sear bar and disconnector covered by the right grip plate; and a hammer-blocking thumb safety that can be applied with the hammer cocked or fully down.

Disassembly Instructions

Press the magazine catch button (21), remove the magazine (19), retract the slide (33) to assure an empty chamber and release the slide. Push in the plug (24) and maintain control of it while turning the barrel bushing (2) 90° clockwise. Slowly release the plug and remove it, the recoil spring (25) and the barrel bushing.

Retract the slide and push the shaft of the slide stop (34) that protrudes from the right side of the frame (10). Remove the slide stop to free the slide that can now be moved forward off the frame to free the recoil spring guide (26) and barrel (1) with its link and pin (17 & 18). Push the firing pin (7) in with a punch and pry the firing pin stop down to free the pin and its spring (8). The extractor (6)

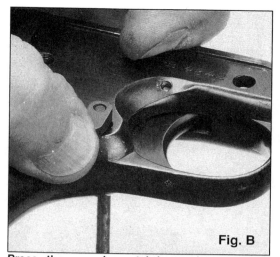

Fig. B

Press the magazine catch button in as far as it will go and then turn the exposed magazine catch off the threaded stem.

scent while pulling the trigger. Drift out the large hammer pin (14) from the right side and remove the hammer with its strut and pin, and the hammer spring and plunger (15 & 16).

Push the magazine catch button (21) in as far as it will go with a punch and turn the now fully exposed magazine catch (20) off the threaded stem of the button (**Fig. B**). If the assembly is so tightly joined that this can not be done, do not depress the button but, with padded pliers turn the magazine catch button (21) counterclockwise to free it from the catch and spring (20 & 22). Drifting out the trigger pin (37) permits removal of the trigger/sear bar assembly (36) through the magazine well, thus allowing the disconnector (3) to be slid down and out of its dovetail in the frame (**Fig. C**).

Drift the combination safety stop/sear pin (28) to the left and remove the sear and sear spring (27 & 29). The ejector pin (5), though tightly fitted, may be removed

to free the ejector (4) if required, but the plunger tube assembly (23), containing a spring and detent plungers for the safety and slide stop, is staked in place and should not be removed. Reverse the above procedures for reassembly. ∎

Drifting out the trigger pin allows removal of the trigger/sear bar assembly through the Ballester's magazine well.

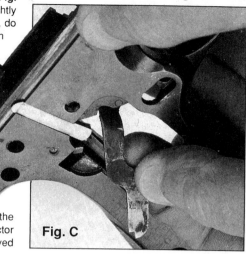

Fig. C

can now be pried from the rear of the slide, completing disassembly of that unit.

Remove the four grip plate screws (12) and grip plates (11). Pull the hammer (13) back past the fully cocked position, turn the thumb safety (35) 180° and withdraw it (**Fig. A**). Grasp the hammer and control its full de-

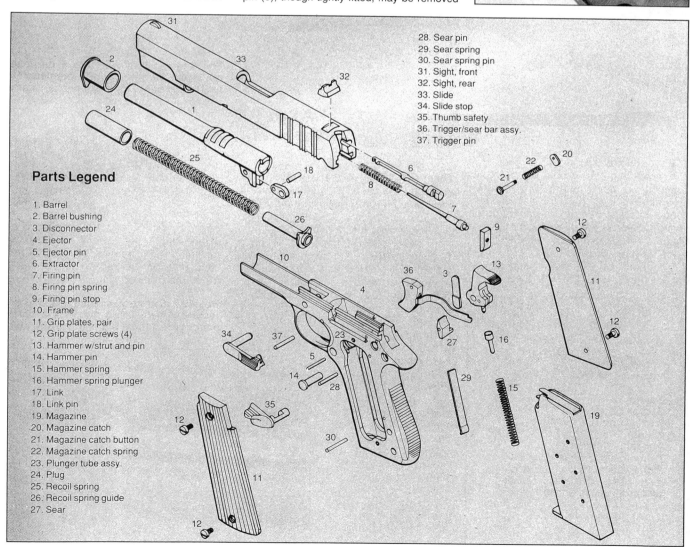

28. Sear pin
29. Sear spring
30. Sear spring pin
31. Sight, front
32. Sight, rear
33. Slide
34. Slide stop
35. Thumb safety
36. Trigger/sear bar assy.
37. Trigger pin

Parts Legend

1. Barrel
2. Barrel bushing
3. Disconnector
4. Ejector
5. Ejector pin
6. Extractor
7. Firing pin
8. Firing pin spring
9. Firing pin stop
10. Frame
11. Grip plates, pair
12. Grip plate screws (4)
13. Hammer w/strut and pin
14. Hammer pin
15. Hammer spring
16. Hammer spring plunger
17. Link
18. Link pin
19. Magazine
20. Magazine catch
21. Magazine catch button
22. Magazine catch spring
23. Plunger tube assy.
24. Plug
25. Recoil spring
26. Recoil spring guide
27. Sear

BERETTA MODEL 90 PISTOL

By DENNIS RIORDAN

The Beretta Model 90 self-loading pistol is a typical, modern pocket handgun. Produced in Italy by the firm of P. Beretta, this blowback-operated arm fires the 7.65 mm (.32 ACP) cartridge and has an eight-shot magazine detached by pressing a catch on the left side of the frame.

Special features of this pistol are its double-action lock mechanism with rebounding hammer, lightweight alloy frame and stainless steel barrel. As in many other self-loading pistols, the recoil spring surrounds the barrel, which is rigidly attached to the frame. the hammer is exposed and a manually operated safety is on the upper left of the frame. When the safety is moved downward into the fire position, a red warning dot on the frame is exposed. When pivoted upward on "SAFE", the safety locks the hammer and slide. It can also be used as a manual slide lock to hold the slide open.

Due to its double-action lock mechanism and rebounding hammer, the Model 90 may be safely carried with the chamber loaded, the hammer down and the safety disengaged. It can then be fired by simply pulling the trigger. This makes it possible to get the pistol into action quickly. Also, in the event of a misfire, additional blows on the firing pin can be given quickly by pulling the trigger.

The hammer is cocked automatically during firing. To make the pistol safe for

Beretta Model 90 .32 ACP pistol.

carrying with the hammer cocked and chamber loaded, it is necessary to engage the safety on "SAFE".

Another safety feature is provided by the extractor which serves as a chamber-loaded indicator. When the chamber is loaded, the extractor protrudes from the slide and is easily seen and felt.

After the last round in the magazine is fired, the magazine follower pushes up the ejector which latches the slide to the rear. This is a highly desirable feature.

The pistol had smooth clean lines. This plus the black anodized finish on the frame, high-luster blue of the slide and a satin chrome finish on the trigger combine to give attractiveness.

Handling qualities are generally excel-

lent. The weight is well distributed and the checkered black Tenite grips are shaped to fit the hand. Barrel length is 3-5/8", and overall length is 6-5/7". Weight, unloaded, is 19-1/2 ounces.

The fixed, square-notch rear and square-blade front sights are well suited for a pocket pistol. Sighting is aided by a wide flat rib integral with the top of the slide. Fine serrations on the rib give a dull non-reflective surface.

Though well designed and reliable, the Beretta Model 90 was discontinued in the early 1980s.

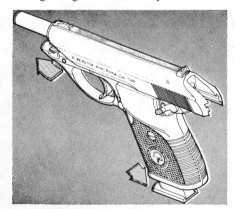

1 To field-strip the Model 90, depress magazine catch (32), and withdraw and unload magazine. Disengage safety (38), and pull slide (4) fully to the rear to clear chamber. Replace magazine and draw slide rearward until it locks open. Grasp serrated fingerpieces of slide catch (17), and pull catch forward and up. Remove magazine.

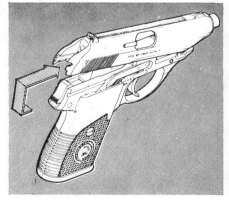

2 Grasp slide firmly, pull fully rearward and lift rear end out of frame (19). Ease slide forward off barrel (21), and remove recoil spring (14). This is sufficient takedown for normal cleaning. Position tightest coil of recoil spring to rear during reassembly. Slide catch closes automatically as the slide moves over it.

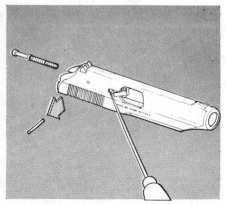

3 For further disassembly, drive out firing pin retainer (6) to free firing pin (8) and spring (7). Depress extractor plunger (2) well into slide with ice pick or awl, pivot extractor (1) toward breech face and remove. Ease out plunger and spring (3).

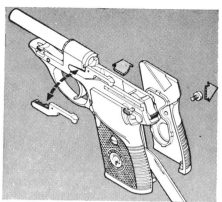

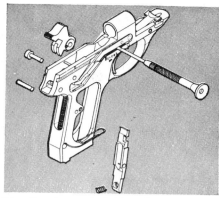

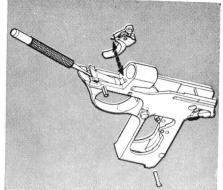

4 Place left thumb against forward portion of ejector (27) so that its spring (26) cannot fly loose. Push rear of ejector to the right, levering forward end out of frame. On replacement, small hooked end of spring must seat into frame notch just forward of barrel flange (arrow). Remove barrel nut (20) with 15 mm. wrench to release barrel. Nylon inserts in barrel nut face toward frame in assembly. Remove right grip screw (10) and insert knife blade between the grips. Pry right grip (9) outward off positioning pin fixed to bottom of left grip (39). Engage safety, and remove left grip.

5 Insert a straightened paper clip through small hole in tip of hammer strut (43), working through the frame tunnel provided. Release safety, pull trigger (29), and lower hammer (42) with thumb. Push out hammer pin (36) and lift out hammer. Push out sear pin (37) to release sear (40) and spring (41). Hold trigger depressed and insert small screwdriver between trigger bar (22) and spring (23). Lever the spring downward free of trigger bar. Then, pry the bar outward and off.

6 Push out trigger pin (30). Pivot trigger assembly forward, and remove from below. On replacement, small hooked end of trigger spring (28) must seat into frame tunnel (arrow). Drift out slide catch pin (18) to remove slide catch, spring (16), and plunger (15). To reassemble slide catch parts, start pin through frame and partially into catch. Position catch in take-down attitude, and install spring and plunger through hole in its forward end. Depress plunger with a thin punch inserted through the frame channel provided, and tap pin to fully seat it.

Parts Legend

1. Extractor
2. Extractor plunger
3. Extractor spring
4. Slide
5. Rear sight
6. Firing pin retainer
7. Firing pin spring
8. Firing pin
9. Right grip
10. Grip screw (2)
11. Magazine bottom
12. Magazine follower
13. Magazine body
14. Recoil spring
15. Slide catch plunger
16. Slide catch spring
17. Slide catch
18. Slide catch pin
19. Frame
20. Barrel nut
21. Barrel
22. Trigger bar
23. Trigger bar spring
24. Safety spring
25. Safety plunger
26. Ejector spring
27. Ejector-empty magazine indicator
28. Trigger spring
29. Trigger
30. Trigger pin
31. Trigger sleeve
32. Magazine catch
33. Magazine catch screw
34. Magazine catch spring
35. Hammer stop pin
36. Hammer pin
37. Sear pin
38. Safety
39. Left grip
40. Sear
41. Sear spring
42. Hammer
43. Hammer strut
44. Hammer spring
45. Magazine spring
46. Magazine bottom plate

7 Cutaway shows relationship between parts. Pistol is cocked. Chamber is loaded, and safety disengaged. Parts are number keyed to parts legend.

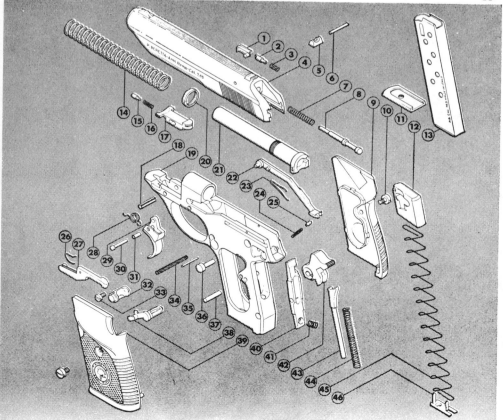

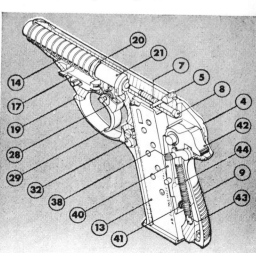

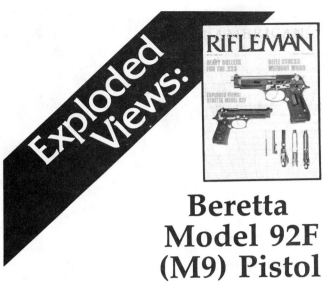

Exploded Views:

RIFLEMAN

HEAVY BULLETS FOR THE .223 — RIFLE STOCKS WITHOUT WOOD

EXPLODED VIEWS: BERETTA MODEL 92F

Beretta Model 92F (M9) Pistol

THE Beretta Model 92SB-F pistol was adopted in 1984 as a U.S. government military standard pistol. Its official designation is the M9 pistol or PDW (Personal Defense Weapon). More recent imports of this Beretta 9 mm are marked as Model 92Fs.

Tracing its ancestry back to the earlier, single-action Beretta Models 1934 .380 and 1951 "Brigadier" 9 mm pistols, the double-action 92F's disassembly instructions may be applied in part to earlier variants of the Beretta Model 92 and the Brazilian-made Taurus 92, although both of these pistols feature frame-mounted sear-blocking safeties instead of the 92F's slide-mounted firing pin block safety. When the safety on a 92F is turned down to the "on-safe" position, the firing pin is physically disconnected from the hammer and the connection between the trigger and sear is interrupted.

An additional blocking device incorporated in the 92F is designed to prevent the firing pin from moving forward to strike a cartridge primer unless the trigger is pulled rearward, even if the pistol is dropped and lands muzzle-first.

Additional information on the Beretta 92SB-F can be found in the August 1985 *American Rifleman*, pp. 48-51. ∎

BY DOUG WICKLUND

Adopted by the U.S. military in 1984 as the M9 pistol, the Beretta 92F 9 mm also has been chosen by many police agencies.

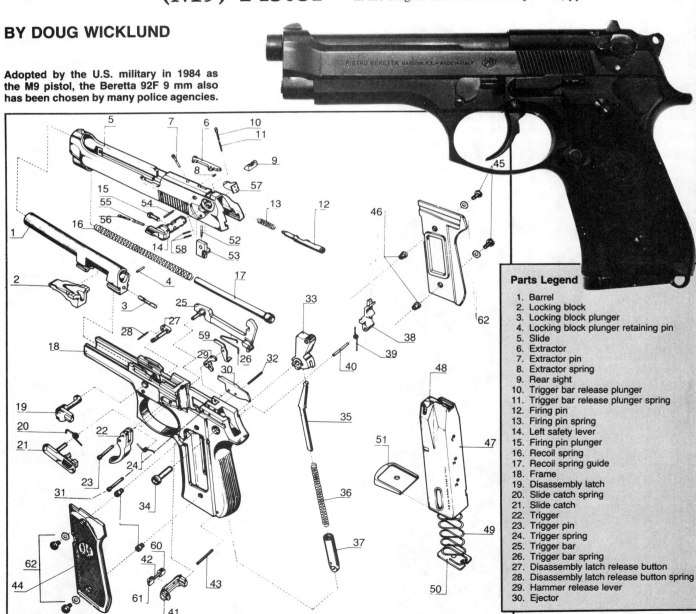

Parts Legend

1. Barrel
2. Locking block
3. Locking block plunger
4. Locking block plunger retaining pin
5. Slide
6. Extractor
7. Extractor pin
8. Extractor spring
9. Rear sight
10. Trigger bar release plunger
11. Trigger bar release plunger spring
12. Firing pin
13. Firing pin spring
14. Left safety lever
15. Firing pin plunger
16. Recoil spring
17. Recoil spring guide
18. Frame
19. Disassembly latch
20. Slide catch spring
21. Slide catch
22. Trigger
23. Trigger pin
24. Trigger spring
25. Trigger bar
26. Trigger bar spring
27. Disassembly latch release button
28. Disassembly latch release button spring
29. Hammer release lever
30. Ejector

Disassembly Instructions

Clear the pistol by removing the magazine, retracting the slide, and checking the chamber and magazine well.

With the slide forward and the hammer down, press the disassembly latch release button (27) and swing the disassembly latch (19) down and forward. Allow the slide assembly to move forward off the frame (18) **(Fig. 1)**. With the slide assembly resting upside down on a firm surface, lift the recoil spring guide (17) from its step on the locking block (2) and, restraining the guide, remove the spring (16) and guide to the rear. Push the plunger (3) at the rear of the barrel underlug (1) to detach the locking block from the slide lugs **(Fig. 2)**. Move the barrel forward to clear the extractor (6) and remove from the slide.

This completes basic field-stripping of the Beretta 92F. Further disassembly is not recommended by Beretta unless performed by a competent gunsmith. Nevertheless, considering the likelihood that the Beretta will be with us in quantity in the forseeable future, we pass along our experience in full disassembly.

Remove the grips (44), taking care not to lose the grip screw washers (62). Press the back of the magazine release button (41) down and away for removal. Reinstalling the magazine release can be done with the button oriented to the left or right.

Depress the upper arm of the trigger bar spring (26) from its groove in the underside of the trigger bar (25) and slowly release the spring out and away to the right. Remove the trigger bar. Pull the slide catch (21) out to remove the catch and its spring (20). The trigger pin (23) can be drifted out to the left, freeing the trigger (22) and its spring (24).

31. Hammer release lever pin
32. Ejector spring pin
33. Hammer
34. Hammer pin
35. Hammer strut
36. Hammer spring
37. Hammer spring cap
38. Sear
39. Sear spring
40. Sear pin
41. Magazine release button
42. Magazine release button spring
43. Hammer spring cap spring pin
44. Grip (LH/RH)
45. Grip screws (4)
46. Grip screw bushings (4)
47. Magazine tube
48. Magazine follower
49. Magazine spring
50. Magazine lock plate
51. Magazine base
52. Firing pin block spring
53. Firing pin block
54. Firing pin retaining spring pin
55. Safety plunger spring
56. Safety plunger
57. Right safety lever
58. Right safety lever spring pin (2)
59. Firing pin block lever
60. Magazine catch spring bush (short)
61. Magazine catch spring bush (long)
62. Grip spring washers (4)

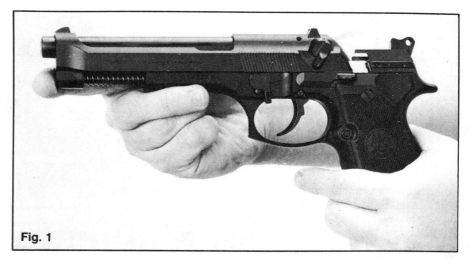

Fig. 1

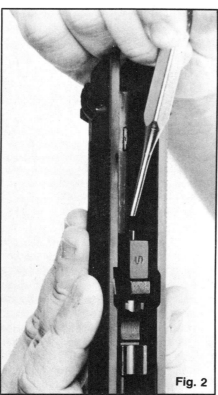

Fig. 2

Drift out the hammer spring cap spring pin (43) to free the cap (37) and slowly release tension on the hammer spring (36) to remove. Tapping out the hammer pin (34) will allow the removal of the hammer (33) and strut (35). Drift out the sear pin (40) to release the sear (38) and its spring (39) into the magazine well. Tap out the hammer release lever pin (31) and the ejector spring pin (32) to free the ejector (30) and the hammer release lever (29) for removal upwards from the frame.

Remove the firing pin block lever (59) by lifting up and out.

With the slide-mounted safety in "on-safe" position, drift out the two right safety lever spring pins (58). Pull the right safety lever (57) to the right for removal. Tap out the firing pin

retaining spring pin (54) to remove the firing pin block (53) and its spring (52). With a punch, dislodge the firing pin plunger (15), depress the rear face of the firing pin (12), and pull the left safety lever (14) up and to the left for removal, taking care not to lose the safety plunger (56) and its spring (55), the trigger bar release plunger (10) and its spring (11). Slowly release pressure on the firing pin to remove it and its spring (13). Drift out the extractor pin (7) and pry out the extractor (6) and extractor spring (8).

To disassemble the magazine, use a punch to depress the stud on the lock plate (50). Release the magazine base (51) by sliding it forward, taking care to restrain the magazine spring (49) and lock plate as tension is released **(Fig. 3)**.

Reassembly is in reverse order.

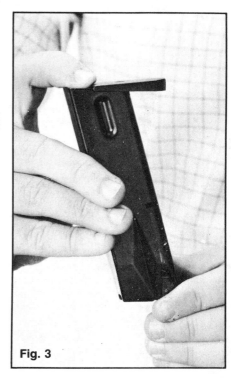

Fig. 3

Beretta 950B Jetfire Pistol

By E. J. HOFFSCHMIDT

MADE by the Italian arms firm of Pietro Beretta, the Model 950B Jetfire cal. .25 ACP semi-automatic vest pocket pistol is a slightly modified version of the Beretta Model 950 pistol introduced after World War II. A similar Beretta pistol, designated Minx, is chambered for the .22 short rimfire cartridge. Except for mechanical changes necessitated by differences in caliber, disassembly and assembly procedures for the Jetfire and Minx pistols are identical.

The barrel of the Model 950B pistol is hinged at the muzzle end so that it can be tipped up for loading or cleaning by pushing a thumb latch on the left side of the frame. This convenient feature makes it unnecessary to retract the slide manually to load or unload the gun. Unloading must be done by tipping up the barrel since there is no extractor in this pistol.

In use, the fired case acts as a piston and blows back the slide until the ejector kicks the case away from the slide and clear of the pistol. The returning slide then pushes a fresh round from the magazine into the chamber. Cocking of the exposed hammer is done automatically by the action of the recoiling slide.

The combination recoil and barrel latch spring of the Model 950B pistol is formed from music wire and is secured in the frame by a cross pin in rear of the trigger. Upper ends of this spring extend beyond the frame and engage recesses in the slide. Adoption of this system eliminated the need for a coiled recoil spring around or under the barrel.

Two music wire recoil springs, one on each side of the frame, were employed in the earlier Model 950 pistol. A separate barrel latch spring was also used in this model.

The Model 950 and Model 950B pistols lack mechanical safeties, but their exposed hammers can be placed in half-cock position.

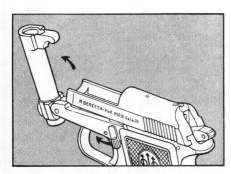

1 The takedown procedure for the Beretta Model 950B Jetfire pistol is simple and easy. First remove the magazine (27), then press forward on the barrel latch (18) to tip up the barrel (14). Now, clear the chamber and then swing the barrel up to vertical position. Cock the hammer (30) and lift the front of the slide (1) slightly, until it is free of the frame (22). Pull the slide forward approximately 1/8″ and lift the slide free of the frame.

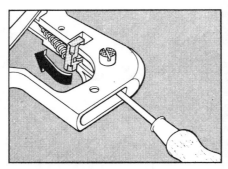

2 Before driving steel pins in or out of an aluminum alloy frame, it is sound practice to relieve the spring tension on the part retained by the pin. Lower the hammer and remove the hammer spring assembly before removing the hammer pin (21). Insert a narrow screwdriver into the magazine well as shown. Push up and outward on the hammer spring retainer (33) until it is free of its recess in the frame. This will relieve the tension on the hammer pin and hammer.

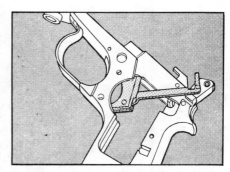

3 After the trigger pin (17) has been removed, the trigger will snap back under the influence of the trigger spring (11). To remove the trigger, lift the tail of the trigger bar (9) up over the sear and pull the trigger assembly out through the cutout in the left side of the frame. Reverse the procedure for reassembly. When the trigger bar is back in its proper place below the sear, rotate the upper portion of the trigger until it lines up with the hole in the frame. Insert trigger pin.

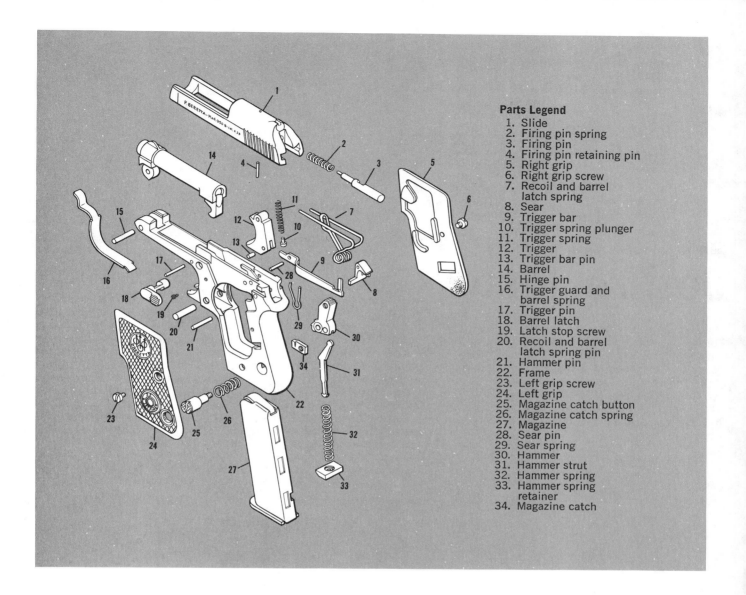

Parts Legend

1. Slide
2. Firing pin spring
3. Firing pin
4. Firing pin retaining pin
5. Right grip
6. Right grip screw
7. Recoil and barrel latch spring
8. Sear
9. Trigger bar
10. Trigger spring plunger
11. Trigger spring
12. Trigger
13. Trigger bar pin
14. Barrel
15. Hinge pin
16. Trigger guard and barrel spring
17. Trigger pin
18. Barrel latch
19. Latch stop screw
20. Recoil and barrel latch spring pin
21. Hammer pin
22. Frame
23. Left grip screw
24. Left grip
25. Magazine catch button
26. Magazine catch spring
27. Magazine
28. Sear pin
29. Sear spring
30. Hammer
31. Hammer strut
32. Hammer spring
33. Hammer spring retainer
34. Magazine catch

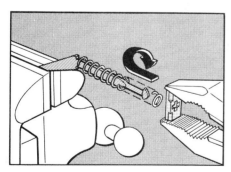

4 The hammer spring (32) and hammer strut (31) are assembled as a unit for easy handling. To disassemble this unit, hold the hammer strut in a padded vise as shown. Grasp the hammer spring retainer (33) with pliers and push toward the spring until the tail of the strut is clear of its seat in the retainer. Rotate the retainer 90° and ease the retainer off the tail of the strut. Be sure to use care in removing the retainer because it is under spring tension.

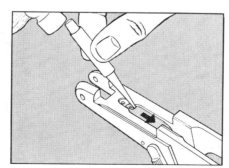

5 In taking down the Beretta Model 950 Jetfire pistol, after the barrel hinge pin (15) and barrel (14) have been removed, the trigger guard can be pulled free of the frame. The barrel latch (18) must be removed in order to further disassemble the gun. To remove the barrel latch, first remove the tiny latch spring screw, and then gently drive the spring rearward out of its recess in the frame. The barrel latch can now be pulled from the frame of the pistol.

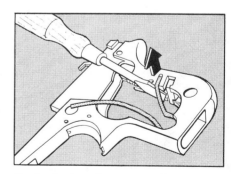

6 In further disassembly of the Model 950, remove both grips to expose the separate recoil springs which must be removed one at a time. Lift the long leg of the recoil spring out of its recess in the frame. Next pry the short leg gently out of its recess as shown. Gently wiggle the spring out of its seat in the curved recess in the frame. The long legs of the springs are ground thinner on one side. This ground side must face toward the frame in reassembly. ■

BERETTA
pocket pistol model 1934

By E. J. Hoffschmidt

THE Italian firm of Pietro Beretta has been in the gunmaking business since 1680. They have manufactured everything from match locks to machine guns and today are noted for their line of shotguns and pocket pistols. Probably the best known product of this Italian firm is the 1934 pistol. This handy little pistol has been an official side arm of the Italian Army

The late E.J. Hoffschmidt was a gunsmith, engineering draftsman and researcher, with a particular interest in self-loading pistols.

and was widely used by Italian police before the end of World War II.

It is best known for its simple design and rugged construction. The gun has surprisingly few working parts and complicated milling machine operations have been virtually eliminated, thereby making the pistol easy to mass-produce. Although the 1934 lacks the more advanced features found on contemporary German pocket pistols, such as double-action, magazine disconnector, and cartridge indicator, it is nevertheless a handy little gun. Model 1934 type pistols are found in either .32 ACP (7.65

mm.) or .380 ACP (9 mm. short).

The Model 1934 resembles a larger, earlier version, the Model 1923. This gun was chambered for the 9 mm. Glisenti cartridge. Like the 1934, it was blowback-operated but had a fiber buffer to prevent the slide battering the receiver when using the more powerful 9 mm. ammunition.

The simplicity of the design is best demonstrated by the disconnector mechanism. The trigger bar has an arm that extends up into a slot in the slide. Unless the slide is fully forward, the arm on the trigger bar will not allow

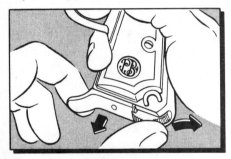

1 Before attempting to field strip gun, remove magazine (18) and retract slide (1) to clear chamber. If magazine is empty and slide open, a good deal of force will be necessary to remove the magazine because slide pressure tends to hold magazine in

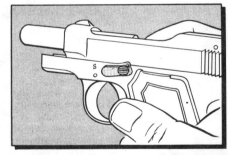

2 To remove barrel, rotate safety catch (30) to safe position and pull slide back as far as it will go. The safety catch will snap into hold-open notch on the slide. Push back or tap muzzle of barrel to free it from receiver grooves

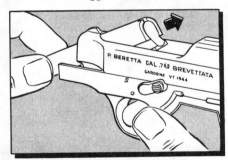

3 After barrel (36) is free of recesses in receiver, push it up and out, through open portion of slide as shown. Next, hold slide and release safety catch (30). Ease slide assembly off front of receiver (33)

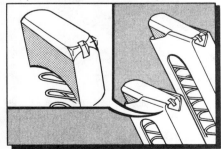

4 To prevent magazine being held in by slide, grind back edge of follower to a slight radius, removing sharp shoulder that holds slide open after last shot. Remove follower before grinding by depressing button on magazine floorplate. At same time, slide plate off to front

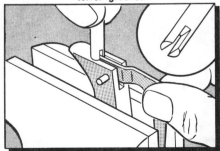

5 In general, the gun is simple to strip—it is merely a case of driving out retaining pins. When it comes to replacing trigger bar (24), the simple tool shown above will hold trigger spring plunger (25) depressed while trigger bar is pinned back into place

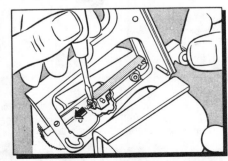

6 After replacing sear lever (12), hammer (10) can be easily lined up with hole in receiver (33) if hammer strut is out of way. To do this, first push hammer strut down from hammer opening. Use a screwdriver or piece of brass to hold it down, as shown, until hammer is pinned into place

the trigger bar to engage the sear plate. This clever device prevents the gun firing full automatic, since it pushes the trigger bar clear of the sear plate every time the slide recoils and allows the sear to be released again only when the slide is fully forward.

Although the gun is reliable, it has one or two serious drawbacks. When the last shot is fired, the slide is held open by the empty magazine follower. The slide cannot be run forward until the empty magazine is removed. Since the magazine must be withdrawn against the pressure of a stiff recoil spring, the operation requires two hands and a good deal of force, or else the slide must be locked back in takedown position by the safety catch, a slow operation either way.

This feature was corrected on some pistols by grinding the back edge of the magazine follower as shown in illustration 4. If this is done, the gun will not remain open after the last shot and the magazine can be removed easily.

Another awkward feature is the position and amount of motion necessary to operate the safety catch. Since the safety catch locks only the trigger, it is theoretically possible for the gun to fire if dropped on the hammer.———■

Parts Legend

1. Slide
2. Extractor
3. Extractor spring
4. Extractor pin
5. Rear sight
6. Firing pin spring
7. Firing pin
8. Right-hand grip
9. Grip screw (see 31)
10. Hammer
11. Hammer strut
12. Sear lever
13. Hammer spring
14. Hammer strut nut
15. Magazine catch spring
16. Spring follower
17. Magazine catch
18. Magazine
19. Magazine catch pin
20. Magazine catch hinge pin
21. Sear lever pin
22. Sear plate
23. Sear plate screw
24. Trigger bar
25. Trigger spring plunger
26. Trigger spring
27. Trigger
28. Trigger bar pin
29. Trigger pin
30. Safety catch
31. Grip screw (see 9)
32. Left-hand grip
33. Receiver
34. Recoil spring guide
35. Recoil spring
36. Barrel
37. Ejector
38. Ejector pin
39. Hammer pin

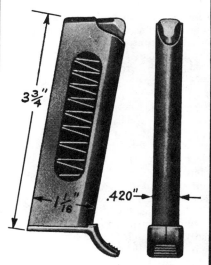

Beretta Model 1934 Pistol

PISTOL MAGAZINES

3 3/4"   1 1/16"   .420"

Many Model 1934 Beretta pocket pistols were brought back by soldiers after World War II. These simple, rugged pistols are found in cals. .380 and .32 ACP. They are generally well made and finished, though later wartime production guns show a marked deterioration in finish and workmanship. Beretta magazines can be identified by the wide, open panel on each side.

The finger-rest floorplate affords a good grip and facilitates removal of the magazine. The cal. .32 magazine usually has a stamped floorplate, while the cal. .380 floorplate is usually machined from steel.

Beretta magazine followers are machined from steel. They must be rugged, since they act as a slide hold-open device when the last shot has been fired. The V-groove cutout on the back strap and the small notch in the follower are good points of recognition.—EDWARD J. HOFFSCHMIDT

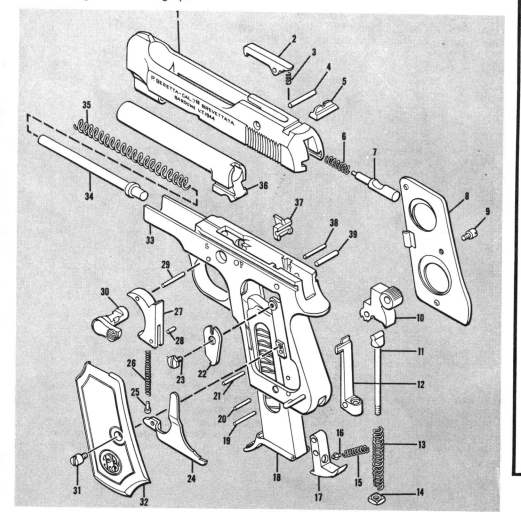

BERGMANN
Special Model Pocket Pistol

By E. J. HOFFSCHMIDT

1 To field strip the Bergmann, first remove magazine and clear chamber. Pull down takedown latch (43) at front of trigger guard. Pull slide to rear as far as it will go and lift it free of frame. Slide (1) can now be run forward off barrel

THEODOR Bergmann was one of the earliest exponents of self-loading weapons. His firm, in Gaggenau and Suhl, Germany, turned out a wide variety of guns, ranging from automatic pistols to light machine guns.

Shortly before World War II, German gun firms were engaged in a double-action pistol race. Walther started the activity with their extremely successful models PP and PPK. To compete, Mauser and J. P. Sauer brought out double-action pistols. Around this time the firm of August Menz started production on a double-action pistol also produced under the Theodor Bergmann trade name.

While resembling the Walther PP, the Menz or Bergmann is different internally. The gun is a maze of small springs and intricately machined parts and has an unusual double-action trigger. On an ordinary double-action pistol, a steady pull on the trigger will cock the hammer and fire the gun. On the Bergmann a steady pull will only bring the hammer back to full cock and hold it there. The trigger must then be released slightly and pulled again to fire the gun. This makes aimed fire much easier but prevents getting the psychological first shot off rapidly.

Safety is unusual

The safety is unusual as it rotates the firing pin out of line with the hammer but does not lock the sear. The firing pin, housed in a cylinder, is rotated by the safety catch. As the firing pin housing rotates, a projection on the end moves into position to absorb the hammer blow. This construction gives an unusual degree of effectiveness to the Bergmann Special safety.

The slide remains open after the last round is fired. When the empty magazine is removed, a short pull on the slide releases the catch and allows the slide to close.

Sales of the cal. .32 Model I began around 1938. The cal. .380 Model II was to be produced a short time later but the beginning of World War II in 1939 put an end to this interesting line of pocket pistols.

Parts Legend

1. Slide
2. Extractor pin
3. Extractor
4. Extractor spring
5. Housing plunger
6. Plunger spring
7. Firing pin housing
8. Firing pin spring
9. Firing pin
10. Safety catch
11. Detent retainer screw
12. Detent ball
13. Detent spring
14. Spring guide
15. Right grip
16. Retainer plate screw
17. Spring retainer plate
18. Trigger bar guide spring
19. Trigger bar
20. Spring retainer pin
21. Trigger bar spring
22. Pin retainer spring
23. Trigger
24. Trigger pin
25. Retainer spring pin
26. Trigger spring
27. Recoil spring
28. Frame and barrel assembly
29. Hammer
30. Sear
31. Hammer strut
32. Sear spring
33. Hammer spring
34. Magazine catch
35. Magazine
36. Left grip
37. Grip screw
38. Sear stop pin
39. Hammer pin
40. Ejector
41. Hold-open spring
42. Hold-open catch
43. Takedown latch
44. Takedown latch spring
45. Takedown latch pin

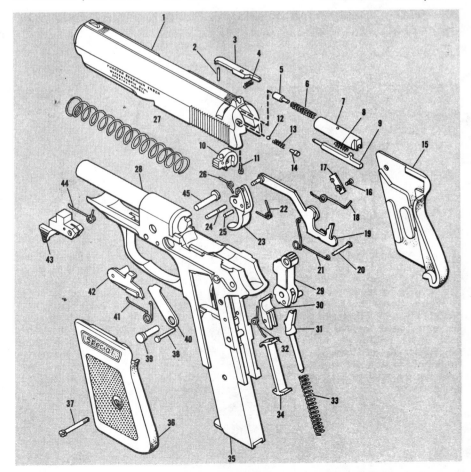

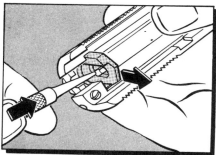

2 Safety catch (10) must be removed to get at firing pin (9). Loosen detent retainer screw (11) and carefully remove detent components. Hold firing pin housing (7) and firing pin forward and free of seat in safety catch, and push up safety catch

3 Last coil of recoil spring (27) fits barrel very snugly and must be pushed free as shown. When replacing spring, be sure large end protrudes off barrel; otherwise gun cannot be reassembled

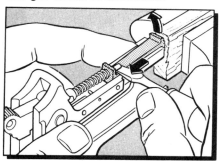

4 Magazine catch (34) hooks over a cross pin in frame and must be pushed back and lifted up for removal. Use a screwdriver to ease it free and to prevent hammer spring (33) from throwing catch. Remove hammer spring and strut (31)

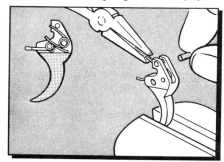

5 Trigger (23) houses 2 springs—trigger spring (26) and pin retainer spring (22). When reassembling gun, use slave pins to hold springs in place. Slave pins should be only as wide as trigger and are pushed out when parts are pushed in ∎

**Bergmann
Double-Action
Special Model
.32 ACP Cal.**

PISTOL MAGAZINES

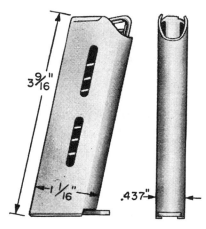

Bergmann double-action pistols are not common but they are interesting. The Special Model was a contemporary of the Walther, Sauer, and Mauser double-action pocket pistols. While the gun contains a few novel features, it did not sell very well. Its mechanism does not seem rugged since it contains 13 wire springs. Another reason for its low sales appeal was its manual double-action mechanism. When the trigger is pulled, the hammer goes to full cock and stays there until the trigger is released and pulled again. While this makes for safer and more accurate shooting, it slows down the psychologically-important first shot.

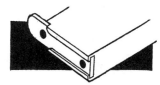

Bergmann magazines can be recognized by the 2 holes in the floorplate and by the way the magazine sides fold over to hold the floorplate. The floorplate is permanently fixed and should not be removed. The long observation slots in the right-hand side also identify the magazine.

The magazine follower is made from a simple steel stamping and can be identified by the depression on the left front edge. This depressed area operates the hold-open latch when the last round is fired.—E. J. HOFFSCHMIDT

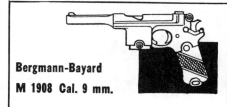

**Bergmann-Bayard
M 1908 Cal. 9 mm.**

PISTOL MAGAZINES

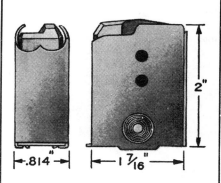

The Bergmann-Bayard is a Belgian version of a German gun that was widely used by the Danish armed forces. Later the Danes manufactured their own guns. The Bergmann is an awkward gun. While the grip is good, the gun is very muzzle heavy. It is a locked-breech recoil-operated gun and fires the 9 mm. Bergmann cartridge. The cartridges look like 9 mm. Luger rounds but are shorter and not interchangeable. The guns are generally well made and finished but are not the best for military use.

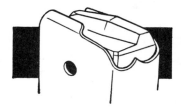

Bergmann-Bayard magazines are as distinctive as the rest of the gun. They are strongly made and hold 8 rounds. The odd multi-angled follower is milled from solid steel.

The detachable floorplate allows the magazine to be cleaned if necessary. The distinctive concentric circles on the sides are for gripping the magazine when removing it from the gun.
—E. J. HOFFSCHMIDT

BERNARDELLI MODEL 60 PISTOL

Illustrations By DENNIS RIORDAN
Text By LUDWIG OLSON

Produced by the well-known firm of Vincenzo Bernardelli in Gardone V.T., Italy, the Bernardelli Model 60 self-loading pistol is designed for informal target shooting and self defense. This modern blowback-operated arm was introduced in 1959. it is made in .22 Long Rifle and .32 ACP calibers and was also offered in .380 ACP.

The model 60 is handsome and of simple construction. It has a 3-1/2" barrel attached rigidly to a black-finished light-weight alloy frame. The slide is blued steel and houses both the barrel and recoil spring. Both sights are integral with the slide which is serrated along the top to reduce glare.

Located on the let side of the frame behind the trigger, the manual safety is convenient to operate with the thumb. Other safeties are a half-cock position of the exposed hammer and a magazine safety which prevents firing when the magazine is removed. What appears to be a safety on the left rear of the frame is actually a takedown latch.

The large, well proportioned black plastic grips are checkered on the sides and rear. A curved piece integral with the black plastic magazine base serves as a rest for the little finger and contributes to ease of handling.

Though well finished and reliable the Model 60 was made unimportable by the 1968 Gun Control Act and was replaced by the similar, but importable, Model 80.

Parts Legend

1. Extractor
2. Extractor spring
3. Extractor pin
4. Firing-pin retainer
5. Slide
6. Firing-pin spring
7. Firing pin
8. Magazine-follower button
9. Right grip
10. Grip screw (2)
11. Recoil spring
12. Frame
13. Barrel pin
14. Barrel
15. Ejector
16. Ejector pin
17. Hammer pin
18. Takedown-catch screw
19. Hammer-spring housing stop
20. Hammer
21. Magazine body
22. Hammer strut
23. Hammer plunger
24. Hammer spring
25. Magazine follower
26. Left grip
27. Magazine safety
28. Magazine-safety spring
29. Magazine-safety pin
30. Trigger
31. Trigger bar
32. Trigger-bar spring
33. Trigger-bar spring screw
34. Sear spring
35. Sear pin
36. Sear
37. Takedown-catch spring
38. Takedown catch
39. Manual safety
40. Manual-safety screw
41. Magazine-catch stop
42. Hammer-spring housing pin
43. Hammer-spring housing
44. Magazine catch
45. Magazine-catch spring
46. Magazine spring
47. Magazine-spring plate
48. Magazine base

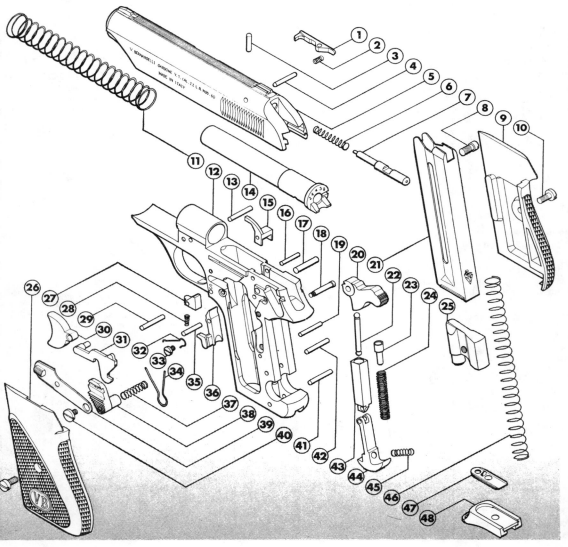

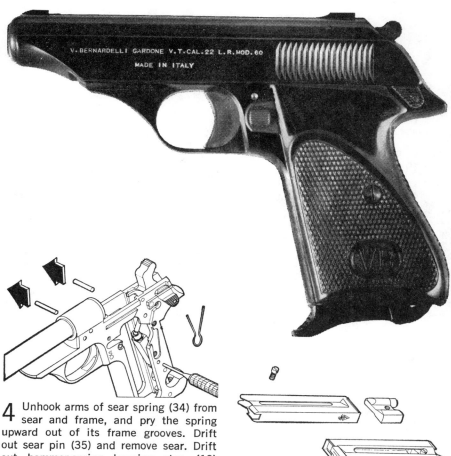

1 Begin field-stripping the Model 60 by moving manual safety (39) up to safe position. Push back magazine catch (44) and remove magazine. Draw slide (5) fully rearward to clear chamber. Hold takedown catch (38) depressed and pull slide rearward ⅝". Then, lift rear of slide and ease forward off frame (12). Remove recoil spring (11). This is sufficient takedown for normal cleaning. Position tightest coil of recoil spring to rear in reassembly.

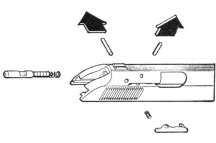

2 For further disassembly, drift out firing-pin retainer (4) to release firing pin (7) and spring (6). Drift out extractor pin (3), and remove extractor (1) and its spring (2). Extractor pin must not protrude from bottom of slide on replacement.

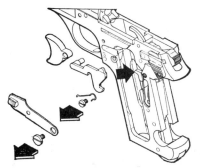

3 Unscrew grip screws (10) and remove grips (9) (26). Remove manual-safety screw (40) and lift off manual safety. Unhook trigger-bar spring (32) from trigger bar (31). Unscrew trigger-bar spring screw (33) and remove trigger-bar spring. Pull trigger-bar from frame. Draw trigger (30) forward and remove through trigger guard. Grasp hammer (20) firmly and push arm of sear (36) to the rear. Ease hammer fully forward.

4 Unhook arms of sear spring (34) from sear and frame, and pry the spring upward out of its frame grooves. Drift out sear pin (35) and remove sear. Drift out hammer-spring housing stop (19) with 1/16" diameter pin punch. Hold hammer-spring housing (43) to rear while removing punch, then allow housing to pivot slowly forward into the magazine well until spring tension is relieved. Remove hammer strut (22), plunger (23), and spring (24).

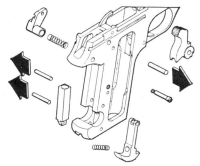

5 Drift out hammer pin (17) and remove hammer. Drift out magazine-catch stop (41) and remove magazine-catch spring (45). Hammer-spring housing and magazine catch are released by removing hammer-spring housing pin (42). Unscrew takedown-catch screw (18) to release takedown catch and spring (37). Reassemble in reverse. Angled cut on spring housing faces toward rear of frame. Assembly of hammer group is eased if hammer spring is tensioned with hammer in full-cock position.

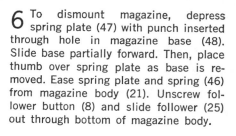

6 To dismount magazine, depress spring plate (47) with punch inserted through hole in magazine base (48). Slide base partially forward. Then, place thumb over spring plate as base is removed. Ease spring plate and spring (46) from magazine body (21). Unscrew follower button (8) and slide follower (25) out through bottom of magazine body.

7 Cutaway indicates relationship between parts. Pistol is shown loaded and cocked. Parts are number keyed to parts legend. ∎

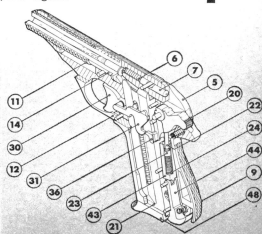

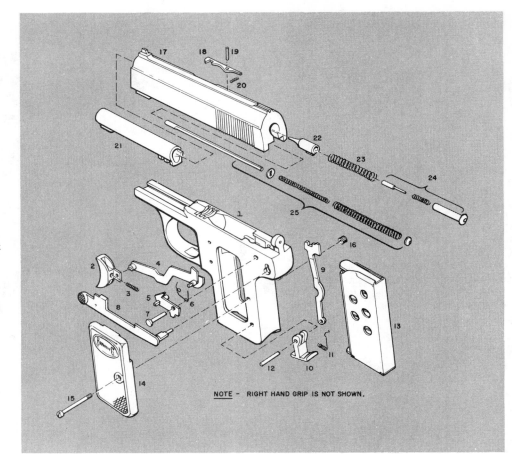

Parts Legend

1. Receiver
2. Trigger
3. Trigger spring
4. Connector
5. Sear
6. Sear spring
7. Sear pin
8. Safety
9. Magazine safety
10. Magazine latch
11. Magazine latch spring
12. Magazine latch pin
13. Magazine assembly
14. Grip, left (right grip not shown)
15. Grip screw
16. Grip escutcheon (contained in right grip)
17. Slide
18. Extractor
19. Extractor pin
20. Extractor spring
21. Barrel
22. Firing pin
23. Firing pin spring
24. Cocking indicator assembly
25. Recoil spring assembly

NOTE – RIGHT HAND GRIP IS NOT SHOWN.

BROWNING Cal. .25 AUTO PISTOL

By JAMES M. TRIGGS

The original cal. .25 ACP (6.35 mm Browning) pocket pistol was invented by John M. Browning in 1905 and patented in Belgium that same year. Initial production in 1905 was by the Belgian arms firm Fabrique Nationale d'Armes de Guerre. The U.S. patent covering this hammerless, blowback-operated, self-loading pistol was granted to Browning on January 25, 1910 (No. 947,478). Production of this pistol in the United States was begun in 1908 by Colt's Patent Fire Arms Mfg. Co., under a licensing arrangement with the inventor. Over a million of these "vest pocket" pistols have been produced by the FN firm, and Colt produced approximately 500,000 before discontinuing the model in 1946.

Redesigned model

In 1954, the Browning Arms Co. of St. Louis, Mo., introduced a redesigned model of this pistol, made in Belgium by the FN firm. It features a magazine disconnector, mechanical safety and cocking indicator, and weighs only 10 ounces in the standard model. A lightweight version weighing 7-3/4 ounces is available.

The Browning .25 Caliber Auto Pistol is offered in Standard and Renaissance grades, the latter featuring a hand engraved, chrome-plated frame and slide, simulated mother-of-pearl grips and a gold-plated trigger. The Standard grade pistol is blue-finished and the grips are of black plastic.

Restrictions imposed by the 1968 Gun Control Act halted importation of the Browning .25 Auto pistol.

Disassembly Procedure

Pull back magazine latch (10) and remove magazine (13) from butt. Draw slide (17) back and check chamber to be sure pistol is unloaded. Replace empty magazine and pull trigger to uncock action. Remove magazine.

Draw slide to rear until forward nose of safety (8) can be pressed up into front notch of slide, holding slide to rear. Turn barrel (21) ⅓-turn clockwise, push down on safety, and release slide from receiver to front.

Remove recoil spring assembly (25) from receiver. Turn barrel ⅓-turn counterclockwise and withdraw it from front end of slide (17). Firing pin (22), firing pin spring (23), and cocking indicator assembly (24) may be removed from rear of slide. Extractor (18) and extractor spring (20) may be removed by drifting out extractor pin (19). Reassemble in reverse.

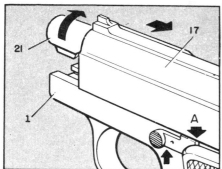

1 To separate slide (17) from receiver (1), pull slide back until forward nose of safety (8) can be pressed up into front notch of slide (17) as shown at "A", holding slide to rear. Turn barrel (21) ⅓-turn clockwise to unlock it from receiver. Push down on safety and draw slide forward off receiver

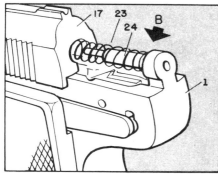

2 In reassembling pistol, replace barrel so that its ribs enter corresponding grooves in slide. Replace recoil spring assembly (25) in receiver and firing pin (22), spring (23), and cocking indicator assembly (24) in rear of slide. Replace slide on receiver so its lugs engage grooves in receiver. Be sure that rear of cocking indicator assembly (24) is seated against spur projecting upward from rear of receiver as shown at "B". Push slide rearward until forward nose of safety can be pressed up into front notch of slide. Turn barrel ⅓-turn counterclockwise, locking it in receiver. Disengage safety, release slide, and replace magazine, completing reassembly ∎

Beretta Model 1915-1919 .32 Cal. Auto

PISTOL MAGAZINES

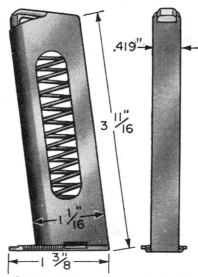

Beretta pistols are renowned for their simplicity and rugged construction. Even though the factory has been in business in Italy since 1680, it is only since World War I that their pistols have become popular in America. The Model 1915 was made in .25, .32, and 9 mm. Glisenti and saw action during the first World War. Later, the slide was redesigned and the gun designated the Model 1915-1919.

While the magazines are rarely, if ever, marked, the 1915 model has the characteristic long open side panels that aid in loading. The floorplate, with its serrated front edge and its movable locking plate, is characteristic of only the 1915-1919 Beretta magazines. Providing the caliber is correct, they can be used in the later Beretta automatics.

The square feed notch and straight feed lips help identify Beretta 1915-1919 magazines. The magazine follower is pressed from sheet steel but is very sturdy. Unlike later Beretta magazine followers, a space can be seen under the follower from side to side.— E. J. HOFFSCHMIDT

PISTOL MAGAZINES

Bernardelli Vest Pocket Pistol

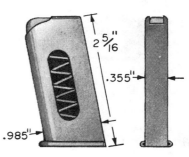

Shortly after World War II, many Bernardelli pocket pistols were imported into the United States. They were manufactured by Vincenzo Bernardelli Armi in Brescia, Italy. The Bernardelli pistol is a modified version of the famous Walther Model 9, and is generally well made and finished. Like the Walther, it is compact and has an excellent grip. Those unfamiliar with the Bernardelli pistol sometimes mistake the takedown button (at rear of frame) for a safety.

Bernardelli magazines follow the usual Italian pattern, having a wide slot on either side. The follower is a contoured stamping that works much more smoothly than the usual flat stamping found on most cal. .25 pistol magazines.

Bernardelli pocket pistol magazines can be recognized easily by the 3 holes in the detachable floorplate.— E. J. HOFFSCHMIDT

BROWNING
MODEL 1910

By JAMES M. TRIGGS

In 1910 John M. Browning obtained a Belgian patent for an improved version of his earlier Model 1900 self-loading pocket pistol. The new pistol, designated Model 1910, featured both magazine and grip safety mechanisms and was striker fired. The recoil spring encircled the barrel which gave the muzzle of the pistol a rather streamlined appearance.

The Model 1910 was first produced by the Belgian firm of Fabrique Nationale d'- Armes de Guerre in 1912, and in the years up to the end of World War II, Model 1910s were extremely popular items on the European market. In 1954, Browning Arms Co., of St. Louis, Mo. introduced the Model 1910 into the United States. Chambered for the .380 ACP cartridge, the pistol was known as the Browning .380 Auto.

Browning .380s sold before the 1968 Gun Control Act halted their importation had fixed sights and a magazine capacity of six rounds. They were offered in Standard and Renaissance grades, the latter having a hand-engraved, chrome-plated frame and slide, simulated mother-of-pearl grips and a gold-plated trigger. the Standard grade guns were blue-finished with black plastic grips.

Following implementation of GCA '68, the Browning .380 was redesigned to meet import criteria. The barrel was lengthened by an inch to 4-7/16 inches. The magazine floorplate was refitted to include a finger extension. Grips were changed to include a thumbrest. And, the sights were changed to a target-style front blade and a windage and elevation adjustable rear. In that configuration Browning .380 Autos qualified for importation and their sale was resumed.

Despite the fact the that Browning .380s, both pre- and post-1968 versions, were well made, accurate, good handling, reliable pistols they have been replaced in Browning's product line by double-action models.

Disassembly Procedure

Remove magazine (30) and check to be sure it is empty. Check action to be sure pistol is unloaded. Replace magazine and pull trigger to release firing pin. Remove magazine.

Pull slide (29) to rear until nose of safety (9) enters front notch of slide. Turn barrel (20) ⅓-turn counterclockwise and

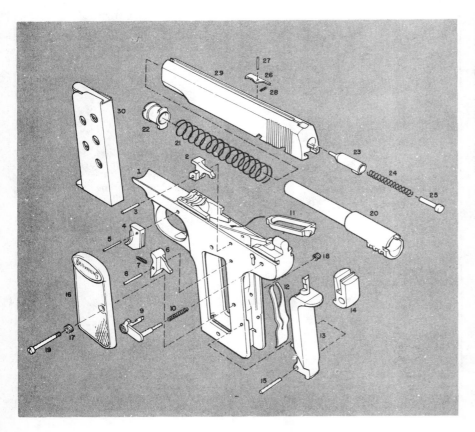

Parts Legend

1. Receiver
2. Sear
3. Sear pin
4. Trigger
5. Trigger pin
6. Magazine safety
7. Magazine safety spring
8. Magazine safety pin
9. Safety
10. Safety spring
11. Connector
12. Sear spring
13. Grip safety
14. Magazine latch
15. Grip safety pin
16. Grips (right grip not shown)
17. Grip escutcheon, unthreaded
18. Grip escutcheon, threaded (contained in right grip)
19. Grip screw
20. Barrel
21. Recoil spring
22. Slide ring
23. Firing pin
24. Firing pin spring
25. Firing pin spring guide
26. Extractor
27. Extractor pin
28. Extractor spring
29. Slide
30. Magazine assembly

press safety down to release slide. Draw slide assembly off receiver to front. Remove firing pin (23), firing pin spring (24), and guide (25) from rear of slide.

With slide upside down, turn barrel ⅓-turn clockwise until its lugs release from slide. Depress slide ring (22) slightly and rotate it ¼-turn counterclockwise until its lugs release from slide. Take care as slide ring is under great pressure from recoil spring (21). Withdraw slide ring, barrel, and recoil spring from slide.

To assemble, replace barrel in slide and turn it so its lugs enter corresponding groove in rear of slide. Replace firing pin assembly in rear of slide. Replace slide on receiver and push back until safety nose engages front notch in slide. Turn barrel clockwise, release safety, and allow slide to move forward until nose of safety can be engaged in rear notch in slide. Replace recoil spring around barrel and place slide ring on spring and press spring back into slide. Position slide ring so its lugs enter corresponding slots in face of slide. When slide ring is firmly seated, rotate ¼-turn clockwise to lock it in place.

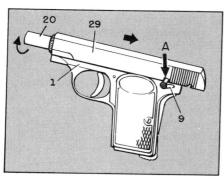

1 To remove slide (29) from receiver (1), pull slide back to position shown. Press nose of safety (9) up into front notch of slide as shown at "A". Turn barrel (20) ⅓-turn counterclockwise. Depress safety (9); draw slide off receiver to front

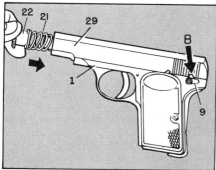

2 In reassembling pistol, after replacing slide assembly on receiver, lock in rear position with nose of safety (9) in forward notch of slide (29). Turn barrel (20) ⅓-turn clockwise and allow slide to go forward until nose of safety can be engaged in rear notch in slide as shown at "B". Replace recoil spring (21) on barrel (20). Place slide ring (22) over end of spring and press spring back into slide as shown. When slide ring is firmly seated against face of slide, turn ¼-turn clockwise to lock in place ■

Bayard Model 1908

PISTOL MAGAZINES

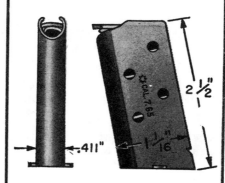

The Bayard Model 1908 is one of the smallest large-caliber pistols made. It was manufactured in cals. .32 ACP and .380 ACP, both with same relative over-all dimensions. Compactness was achieved by keeping the barrel short and limiting the magazine to 5 rounds. Due to the lightweight slide, it was found necessary to provide a buffer spring to snub its recoil. This additional spring allows the use of a lighter than usual recoil spring, thereby making the slide relatively easy for a woman to operate. The lack of projections and compact size make the gun an excellent pocket pistol.

Magazines for these pistols are easily identified. The floorplate has a pair of ear-like projections that assist in removing the magazine. The large cross cut retaining notch in the backstrap is another point of identity.

There is nothing distinctive about the sheet-metal follower, but the magazine can be singled out because of its relatively large cross-section in relation to its size.—EDWARD J. HOFFSCHMIDT

Clement Model 1903 Pistol

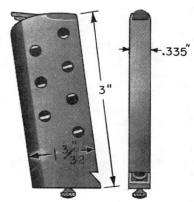

Charles P. Clement of Liege, Belgium, introduced his first automatic pistol in 1903. It is designed to fire an odd bottleneck cal. 5 mm. cartridge. Like many early automatic pistols, the Clement looks like a small version of the Model 1900 Browning pistol. Of straight blowback design, it has no outstanding features other than good workmanship and its unusual cartridge.

Clement cal. 5 mm. magazines are readily identified by the knurled button on the floorplate which facilitates removal of the magazine. The deep retaining groove in the backstrap is a notable characteristic.

Another identifying feature is its rather narrow cross section when compared with other pistol magazines. The sheet-metal follower is half again as thick as the usual follower.—E. J. HOFFSCHMIDT

BROWNING .380 AUTOMATIC, POST '68

Illustrations by DENNIS RIORDAN
Text by LUDWIG OLSON

SEMI-AUTOMATIC pistols designed by the U. S. small arms genius, John M. Browning, and produced in Belgium by Fabrique Nationale (F.N.) have an enviable reputation for simplicity, strength, and reliability. Millions of Browning pistols were produced through the years, and F. N. still manufactures them in various models and calibers.

Among the most popular Browning pistols was the Model 1910 offered in cals. .32 ACP and .380 ACP. Of simple blowback design, this compact pocket arm was an immediate success, and a great many were sold.

In 1954 the Browning Arms Co. introduced a cal. .380 ACP version of this pistol in the U. S. where it was offered for many years as the "Browning .380 Caliber Automatic Pistol". This pocket arm failed to meet requirements of the point system of the Fed-eral Gun Control Act of 1968, and it was redesigned to qualify for importation under the 1968 regulations.

Called the Browning .380 Pistol, the redesigned version introduced in 1971 is basically the same in mechanical design as its predecessor and is chambered for the cal. .380 ACP cartridge. This redesigned pistol has a 4-7/16" barrel and weighs 23 ozs. unloaded. Its combined overall length and height exceed 10" as required by import regulations, and it is fitted with target-style sights. The fully-adjustable rear sight has a wide square notch, while the square-top front sight, which is sloped off at the rear to prevent catching on a holster, is wide and easily seen.

In addition to a thumb-operated safety on the left side of the frame, the Browning .380 has a grip safety, magazine disconnector to prevent firing when the magazine is removed, and a signal pin which extends rearward through a hole in the frame when the firing pin is cocked. Another safety feature is provided by the extractor which projects slightly from the slide to signal the presence of a cartridge in the chamber.

The six-round magazine of this pistol is detached by pressing a magazine latch at the bottom of the frame. Extending from the lower front of the magazine is a curved extension which serves as a finger rest and facilitates magazine removal. The checkered black plastic grips are held to the frame by a single screw, and the left grip has an integral thumb rest.

This well-made pistol with high-luster blue finish possesses generally good handling qualities. Unfortunately it was dropped from production around 1981.

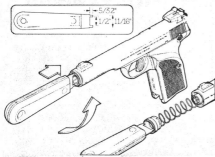

1 To field-strip the Browning .380, remove and unload the magazine (38). Replace the magazine, and draw the slide (19) fully to the rear. Then, check to see that the chamber is empty. Pull the trigger and engage the safety (31). Use a tool to force the slide ring (1) rearward, and rotate ¼ turn. Hold the slide ring tightly and ease it out of the slide. (Removal and replacement of the slide ring is aided by use of a spanner tool fitted to the index cuts. The tool shown was made from a thin-bladed putty knife.) Remove the recoil spring while turning it counterclockwise as viewed from the muzzle.

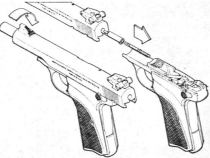

2 Remove the magazine. Release the safety and pull the slide back until the safety can be raised into the forward slide notch. Turn the barrel (17) to the right (viewed from the rear) as far as it will go. Release the safety and move the slide forward off the frame (34). Withdraw the firing pin and signal pin with springs (13) (14) (15) (16) from the rear of the slide. Turn the barrel fully to the left and remove through the front of the slide. This completes field-stripping for normal cleaning.

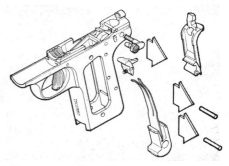

3 If necessary to disassemble further, rotate the safety upward and withdraw the safety and safety spring (32) to the left. Unscrew and remove the grip plate screw (25), and remove the grips (20) (26). Push out the grip safety pin (33) to release the grip safety (37), sear spring (36), and magazine latch (35). Push out the magazine safety pin, and remove the magazine safety (24), taking care to avoid loss of its spring (23). In reassembling these parts, seat the large end coil of the spring in the recess at the front of the magazine safety.

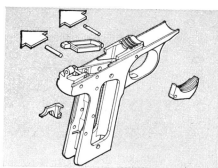

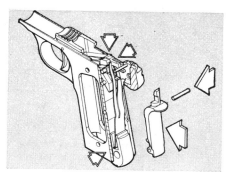

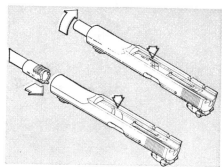

4 Push out the sear pin (27) and withdraw the sear (22) through the rear of the frame. Slide the connector (21) rearward, and lift it out of the frame grooves. After the trigger pin (28) has been driven out, the trigger can be rotated forward and removed through the guard.

5 Reassemble the parts in the frame in reverse order, being careful to avoid deforming the magazine safety spring. The pins for the sear, magazine safety, and grip safety are interchangeable. Install the sear spring with its hooked end seated in the groove at the front of the magazine latch cutout (arrow), split fingers contacting the connector and sear (arrows). The spring is tensioned by insertion of the grip safety.

6 In reassembling the barrel and slide, hold the slide upside down. Insert the barrel with its multiple lugs up, and move the barrel rearward until the lugs align with the recess opposite the front of the ejection port (arrow). Rotate the barrel fully to the right to move its lugs into the slide recess (arrow). The rest of the reassembly is the reverse of field-stripping.

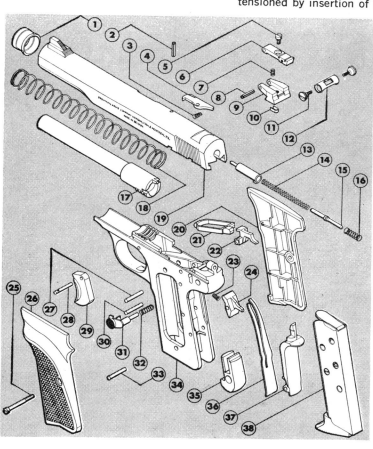

7 Cutaway shows the relationship between the assembled parts. The pistol is shown cocked and unloaded and the safety is disengaged, but the sear is locked by the grip safety. Parts are number keyed to the parts legend.

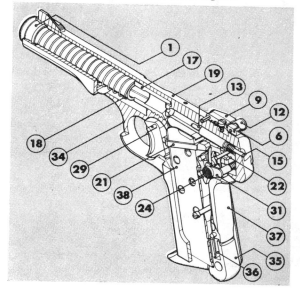

PARTS LEGEND

1. Slide ring
2. Extractor pin
3. Extractor spring
4. Extractor
5. Rear sight adjusting screw, elevation
6. Rear sight leaf
7. Rear sight spring, elevation
8. Rear sight leaf pin
9. Rear sight base
10. Rear sight detent spring, elevation
11. Rear sight adjusting screw, windage (2)
12. Rear sight aperture
13. Firing pin
14. Firing pin spring
15. Signal pin
16. Signal pin spring
17. Barrel
18. Recoil spring
19. Slide
20. Grip plate, right
21. Connector
22. Sear
23. Magazine safety spring
24. Magazine safety
25. Grip plate screw
26. Grip plate, left
27. Sear pin
28. Trigger pin
29. Trigger
30. Magazine
31. Safety
32. Safety spring
33. Grip safety pin
34. Frame
35. Magazine latch
36. Sear spring
37. Grip safety
38. Magazine

safety pin

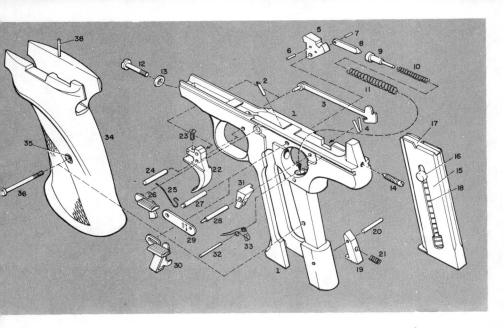

Parts Legend

1. Frame
2. Ejector
3. Disconnector
4. Disconnector spring
5. Hammer
6. Dry-fire pin
7. Hammer link pin
8. Hammer link strut
9. Mainspring plunger
10. Mainspring, inner
11. Mainspring, outer
12. Barrel mounting screw
13. Barrel mounting screw washer
14. Trigger pull adjustment screw
15. Magazine body
16. Magazine button
17. Magazine follower
18. Magazine spring
19. Magazine latch
20. Magazine latch pin
21. Magazine latch spring
22. Trigger
23. Trigger backlash adjustment screw
24. Trigger pin
25. Stop open latch spring
26. Stop open latch
27. Hammer pin
28. Sear pin
29. Click plate
30. Safety
31. Sear
32. Sear spring pin
33. Sear spring
34. Grips
35. Grip screw washer
36. Grip screw
37. Grip screw nut (not shown)
38. Shell deflector

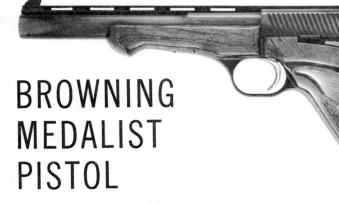

BROWNING MEDALIST PISTOL

By JAMES M. TRIGGS

Parts, Barrel Assembly

A. Barrel
B. Sight blade
C. Sight blade pin
D. Barrel guide pin
E. Rear sight base
F. Elevation screw
G. Detent plunger
H. Detent plunger spring
J. Windage screw
K. Windage screw detent plunger
L. Windage screw detent spring
M. Windage screw nut
N. Elevation spring
O. Fore-end
P. Fore-end screw
Q. Fore-end screw escutcheon (not shown)
R. Barrel weight support
S. Barrel weight screw
T. Barrel weights (3)

Parts, Slide Assembly

1A. Slide
2A. Recoil spring
3A. Recoil spring guide
4A. Extractor
5A. Extractor spring plunger
6A. Extractor spring
7A. Firing pin
8A. Firing pin retaining pin
9A. Firing pin spring

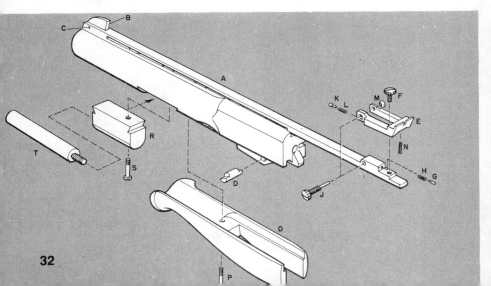

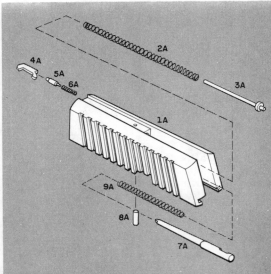

The Browning Medalist, cal. .22 Long Rifle, self-loading pistol was introduced by Browning Arms Co., of St. Louis, Mo., in 1962, and remained a part of the company's sales lineup until 1974. Made in Belgium, the Medalist was designed primarily for target shooting.

It was regularly furnished with a set of hand filling, thumbrest target grips and three accessory, barrel counterweights. The sight rib, which carries both front and rear sights, is permanently attached to the barrel. The rear sight is fully adjustable for elevation and windage.

There is a dry-fire device made in combination with the mechanical safety. By activating this device the shooter can conduct realistic "dry-firing" exercises without retracting the slide to cock the lock mechanism before each shot. Using the dry-fire device the sear can be engaged with the hammer by a light downward thumb pressure against the safety latch. The dry-fire device must be inactivated before the pistol can be fired with live ammunition.

Another interesting feature of the Medalist pistol is the shell deflector pin installed on the upper right side of the grip opposite the breech.

The Medalist's detachable box magazine holds 10, .22 Long Rifle cartridges. The trigger is adjustable for weight of pull and overtravel. The breech of the pistol remains open after firing the last shot.

1 Check action to be sure pistol is unloaded and then remove the magazine. Pistol is shown assembled with the magazine removed.

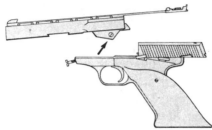

4 Slide barrel assembly rearward and upward to disengage it from the frame as shown.

2 Loosen fore-end screw (P) and remove fore-end (O). Loosen barrel mounting screw (12) until it is felt to disengage from threads in barrel.

5 Press down on stop open latch (26), releasing slide (1A). Pull slide off front end of frame taking care not to allow compressed recoil spring (2A) to escape. Remove spring and recoil spring guide (3A). Further disassembly is not recommended.

3 Pull slide (1A) all the way back and lock back by pressing up on stop open latch (26).

6 Pistol is shown with barrel weight support (R) fastened into dovetail under barrel with one of 3 barrel weights (T) assembled to support. ∎

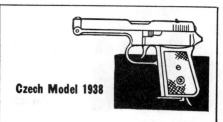

Czech Model 1938

PISTOL MAGAZINES

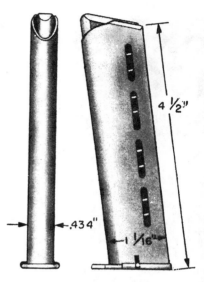

4 1/2"
.434"
1 1/16"

The .380 ACP cal. CZ Model 1938 was manufactured in Czechoslovakia at the government arsenal all during World War II. It is a well-made blowback-operated gun. Its hinged slide and barrel make it easy to clean and service. The design incorporates a rather odd trigger mechanism. Unlike most double-action pistols, the hammer does not stay cocked between shots but follows the slide forward. The trigger must then be pulled all the way to cock the hammer and fire the next shot.

CZ 38 magazines are dead-ringers for the 1910 Mauser magazines except that they are about one-third longer, and have more observation slots in the left side. The floorplate is removable and can be recognized by the cut that retains the tail of the follower spring.

Like the 1910 Mauser, the follower is machined from solid stock. It can be recognized by the milled groove that extends from the backstrap up into the rear of the follower as shown.—E. J. HOFFSCHMIDT

BROWNING 1900

Illustrations by DENNIS RIORDAN
Text by LUDWIG OLSON

In April, 1897, John M. Browning of Ogden, Utah, met Hart O. Berg, commercial director of the F. N. (Fabrique Nationale) armsmaking firm, Herstal, Belgium. This important meeting began a relationship which resulted in F. N. producing a variety of Browning-designed small arms, among them a blowback-operated semi-automatic pistol chambered for the .32 ACP cartridge.

Commonly called the Model 1900, this pistol was first produced in Jan., 1899. It was the first Browning-designed pistol to be put into production and the first arm chambered for the .32 ACP cartridge, which was also a Browning development.

There are various names for this pistol. While it is commonly called Model 1900, it is listed as Model 1899 in the official history of the F. N. firm. A German Burgsmueller arms catalog of 1912 called it the original Browning repeating pistol, large model and did not give a model designation. The Model 1900 designation used in this article is by far the most popular and commonly used for this arm.

The Model 1900 became popular immediately, and was sold in large quantity. In 1900, this pistol was adopted by the Belgian government for arming its officers, and it was also used extensively by police in many European cities. By 1909, 500,000 of this model had been produced, and it was discontinued about 1912 when the Browning Model 1910 pistol was introduced.

Weighing only 22 ozs. unloaded and measuring 6⅜" in overall length, the Model 1900 is an excellent pocket arm. Its detachable magazine which holds seven rounds is released by pressing forward the magazine catch at the lower rear of the frame. Handling qualities of the pistol are generally favorable except that the grip is almost at a right angle with the line of bore, which is not good for natural pointing.

Screwed rigidly into the frame, the barrel is housed in the slide under the recoil spring. The breechblock is fastened to the slide with two screws, and holds the cocking lever, firing pin, and extractor. A V notch in the top of the breechblock serves as the rear sight. The front sight is on the slide.

A very clever and desirable feature of this pistol is that the recoil spring is also used to drive the firing pin. Another clever feature is the method of attaching the checkered hard rubber grips to the frame by means of concealed retainers. After the grip screws are loosened, the retainers can be turned out of engagement with a screwdriver or similar tool inserted in the magazine opening of the frame. The grips are then easily removable to facilitate cleaning.

The safety on the upper left side of the frame is on safe when pivoted upward. With the safety in this position, the sear and the slide and breechblock assembly are blocked, and the marking "SUR" (French for safe) is exposed on the frame. Turning the safety down to fire position exposes the marking "FEU" (fire). The safety can also be used to latch the slide and breechblock assembly to the rear—a very desirable feature.

When the pistol is uncocked, the upper tip of the cocking lever projects above the breechblock in such a manner that it blocks the line of sight. It is thus possible to determine by sight or touch whether the pistol is cocked.

The Model 1900 had such an excellent reputation for sound design and reliability that several of its features were used in other makes of European-produced pistols. Also, many crude copies of the Model 1900 were turned out. These are generally believed to be of Oriental origin, although it is not actually known who produced them. Original specimens produced by F. N. are of high-quality workmanship and finish throughout. Most have blued finish and hard rubber grips, although it was possible to obtain nickel-plated specimens with mother-of-pearl grips at extra cost. ∎

1 Push the magazine catch (25) forward and remove the magazine (9). Release the safety (19). Draw the slide (4) fully to the rear and check visually that the chamber is empty. Release the slide and pull the trigger. Unscrew and remove the breechblock screws (5) (6), and move the slide forward off the frame (26). Lift the forward end of the recoil spring (1) until it snaps free of the frame. Withdraw the breechblock (11) to the rear. This is sufficient disassembly for normal cleaning. Disassemble further only as required.

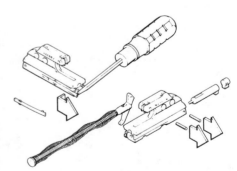

2 Insert a narrow screwdriver blade beneath the hook of the extractor (14). Push the extractor outward until its lug clears the side of the breechblock. Then, pry the extractor forward, bringing its wings into alignment with the disassembly hole. Drift out the cocking lever pin (27), and remove the recoil spring mechanism. Drift out the breechblock plug pin (30) to release the breechblock plug (32) and firing pin (31).

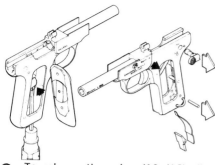

3 To release the grips (10 (16), first loosen the grip screws (15) and turn the grip retainers (17) from horizontal to vertical with a screwdriver inserted through the bottom of the magazine well. Drift out the magazine catch pin (24), and remove the magazine catch (25) and trigger bar spring (29). Pull the forward end of the trigger bar (22) downward into the magazine well and remove. Move the safety midway between safe and fire positions and push out with a punch.

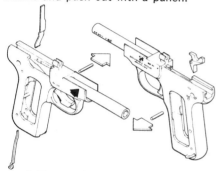

4 Drift out the sear pin (23) and lift out the sear (8). Push the safety spring (28) downward and remove through the underside of the frame. Center the sear spring (7) in the frame with a screwdriver blade, and push upward to remove. Drift out the trigger pin (20), roll the bottom of the trigger forward, and remove through the side of the trigger guard.

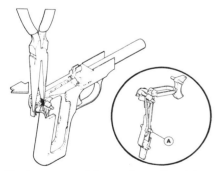

5 In reassembly, replace the trigger and trigger pin, and install the sear spring through the top of the frame. Align the spring vertically, and lever it horizontally against the left side of the frame. Insert the tail of the sear between the sear spring and frame backstrap, and replace the sear pin. Install the safety spring from below, sliding it upward

PARTS LEGEND

1. Recoil spring
2. Recoil spring guide nut
3. Recoil spring guide
4. Slide
5. Breechblock screw (long)
6. Breechblock screw (short)
7. Sear spring
8. Sear
9. Magazine
10. Right grip
11. Breechblock
12. Cocking lever
13. Recoil spring guide pin
14. Extractor
15. Grip screw (2)
16. Left grip
17. Grip retainer (2)
18. Barrel
19. Safety
20. Trigger pin
21. Trigger
22. Trigger bar
23. Sear pin
24. Magazine catch pin
25. Magazine catch
26. Frame
27. Cocking lever pin
28. Safety spring
29. Trigger bar spring
30. Breechblock plug pin
31. Firing pin
32. Breechblock plug

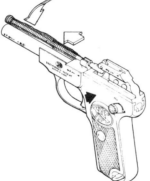

6 Safety must be disengaged to install the breechblock. Depress the trigger and start the breechblock assembly into the frame until resistance is felt, then release the trigger and push the breechblock fully home. Again depress the trigger and pull forward on the recoil spring to release the firing pin from the sear. Grasp the rear of the recoil spring tightly and pull forward over the recoil spring guide (3), until the assembly can be swung down within the frame fork.

against the right side of the frame and behind the sear. Flex the safety spring with padded long nose pliers when installing the safety. Inset shows proper location of springs in the frame. All seat upon the fixed frame pin (A), which is never removed.

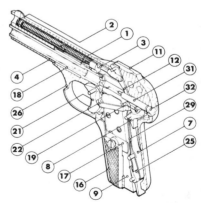

7 Cutaway shows the relationship between parts. Pistol is shown cocked and unloaded with the manual safety disengaged. Parts are number keyed to the parts legend.

BROWNING SWEDISH MODEL 1907 PISTOL

By E. J. HOFFSCHMIDT

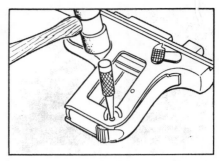

3 Unscrew the grip screw (33), and remove the grips (23) and (32). While holding the hammer (20) firmly, pull the trigger (27), and ease the hammer forward. Drift the grip safety pin (28) out to the right, cock the hammer, pivot the safety upward, and lift it from the receiver. Remove the hammer, ejector (15), grip safety (24), hammer spring (25), sear spring (26), and the magazine catch (29). Drift out sear pin (18); remove sear (17), disconnector (16), and trigger.

THE Swedish Model 1907 semi-automatic pistol was designed by John M. Browning, the U. S. arms inventor. Chambered for the 9 mm. Browning Long cartridge, this well-made blowback-operated pistol was produced by Fabrique Nationale (FN) in Belgium and Husqvarna Vapenfabriks Aktiebolag (Husqvarna Arms Factory, Inc.) in Sweden.

Of concealed-hammer type, the pistol is simple and compact, and has a good grip and balance. It has a detachable 7-round magazine, a manual safety, a grip safety, and a slide stop that holds the slide open after the last cartridge is fired. The grip safety also serves as a cocking indicator, since it projects rearward only when the hammer is cocked.

During World War II, the Model 1907 was superseded in the Swedish Service by Walther and Lahti pistols chambered for the 9 mm. Luger cartridge. However, the Model 1907 was retained for several years as a substitute-standard sidearm.

In the late 1950's, a quantity of Model 1907 pistols was imported into the U.S. and sold as military surplus. Many of these were converted to fire the .380 Automatic cartridge, and were stamped "CAL 380" on the left of the receiver. Converted specimens are accurate but give feeding and ejection malfunctions.

While the 9 mm. Browning Long cartridge is not produced in the U.S., it has been imported by military surplus arms dealers in sufficient quantity for shooting. It has a semi-rim straight case slightly longer than that of the .380 Automatic cartridge. A typical factory load has a 110-gr. round-nose full-jacketed bullet driven at 1000 feet per sec-

ond (f.p.s.) muzzle velocity. The muzzle energy is 244 ft. lbs.

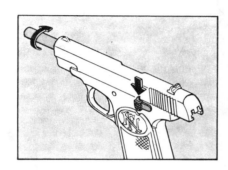

1 To disassemble the pistol, first remove the magazine (30) and clear the chamber. Pull back the slide (1) and push the safety (31) upward to engage it with the forward notch in the slide. Turn the barrel (10) 90° to lock it into the slide. While holding the slide, release the safety from the slide notch, and strip the slide, barrel, and recoil spring (13) off the front of the receiver (34). Also remove the slide stop (19) from the receiver.

2 Remove the recoil spring guide (14), and bushing stop (12). To remove the barrel bushing (11), rotate it 180° as shown and lift it free of the slide. Rotate the barrel to free it from the recess in the slide. Then pull the barrel out forward.

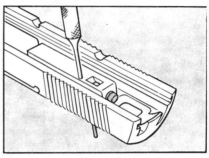

4 The firing pin (8) and firing pin extension (7) are retained by a long pin (3). Drive this pin out of the slide using the correct-size punch. The extractor (5) is retained by a shorter pin (2). When replacing the retaining pins, be sure they are driven in to proper depth so that they do not drag on the receiver and scar it.

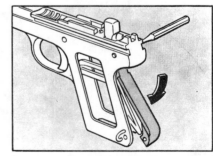

5 In reassembling the lock mechanism, replace the trigger, sear, disconnector, and sear pin. Then install the ejector, engaging the disconnector. Replace the magazine catch, sear spring, hammer spring, and grip safety, and put the hammer in position with the hammer roll behind the hammer spring. Use a punch to align hole in hammer with hole in receiver. Then pull the trigger down, and insert the safety in the receiver part way. Pressing forward on grip safety, align holes in grip safety and receiver using punch and insert pin from right. Cock the hammer, and push safety in all the way.

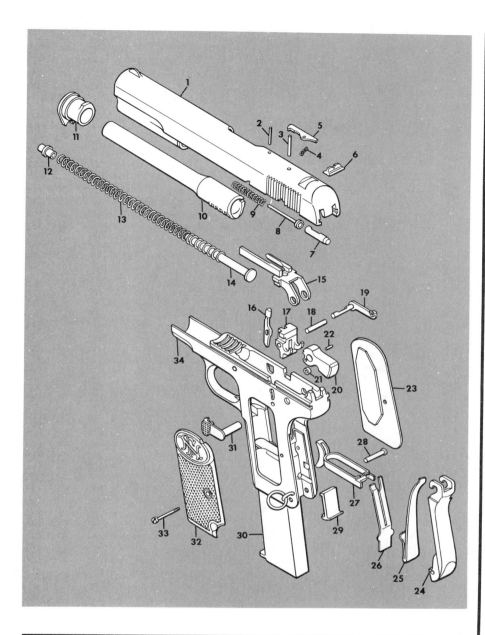

Parts Legend

1. Slide
2. Extractor pin
3. Firing pin retainer pin
4. Extractor spring
5. Extractor
6. Rear sight
7. Firing pin extension
8. Firing pin
9. Firing pin spring
10. Barrel
11. Barrel Bushing
12. Bushing stop
13. Recoil spring
14. Recoil spring guide
15. Ejector and cartridge guide
16. Disconnector

17. Sear
18. Sear pin
19. Slide stop
20. Hammer
21. Hammer roll
22. Roll axis pin
23. Right grip
24. Grip safety
25. Hammer spring
26. Sear spring
27. Trigger
28. Grip safety pin
29. Magazine catch
30. Magazine
31. Safety
32. Left grip
33. Grip screw
34. Receiver

SWEDISH BROWNING MODEL 07

PISTOL MAGAZINES

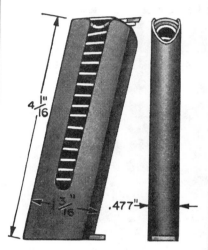

Most of the Swedish Model 07 FN Browning pistols in this country were imported after World War II. Although only an enlarged version of the Browning pocket pistol, it fires the fairly powerful 9 mm. Long Browning cartridge. The gun is unusual in that the hold-open lock is on the right side and has no thumb lever to unlock it. When the magazine is released and the slide pulled back, the lock drops free. Though these guns were in the Swedish service for about 50 years, they are generally in excellent condition and are well made and finished.

The Model 07 magazine is distinctive in that one side has a solid wall, while the other is cut out ¾ of the way down. This long cut allows the follower lip to extend out far enough to lift the hold-open lock when the last shot is fired.

The magazine floorplate is pinned in place and can be recognized best by the squared-off tip on its front end.—E. J. HOFFSCHMIDT

BROWNING MODEL 1922 PISTOL

By E. J. Hoffschmidt

I N the early and mid-1900's, the Mauser firm was arming many countries with Model 1898 rifles. In Herstal, Belgium, Fabrique Nationale d'Armes de Guerre was doing the same with Browning pistols. John Browning's reputation for designing reliable and compact pistols needs no further mention here; it is sufficient to say that FN found the market for Browning pocket pistols so great that they had produced over a million by the middle of 1912.

The compact little Model 1910 was very popular with police forces and was carried far and wide throughout Europe and South America. When the need for a larger military-type pistol arose, the Model 1910 was revised. The barrel was lengthened, as was the grip. The new gun is commonly called the Model 1922. Like its predecessor it was available in cals. 7.65 mm. (.32 ACP) and 9 mm. Browning Short (.380 ACP). The cal. .32 gun has a magazine ca-

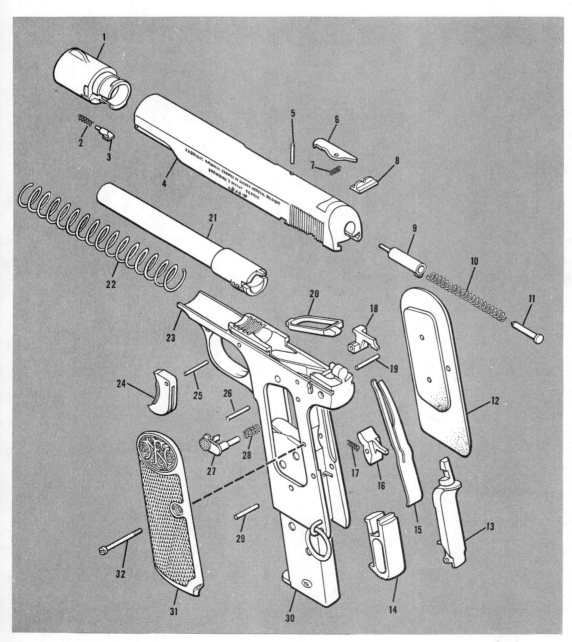

Parts Legend

1. Slide extension
2. Slide extension spring
3. Slide extension catch
4. Slide
5. Extractor pin
6. Extractor
7. Extractor spring
8. Rear sight
9. Firing pin
10. Firing pin spring
11. Spring follower
12. Right grip
13. Grip safety
14. Magazine catch
15. Mainspring
16. Magazine safety
17. Magazine safety spring
18. Sear
19. Magazine safety pin
20. Trigger bar
21. Barrel
22. Recoil spring
23. Frame
24. Trigger
25. Trigger pin
26. Sear pin
27. Safety catch
28. Safety catch spring
29. Grip safety hinge pin
30. Magazine
31. Left grip
32. Grip screw

pacity of 9 rounds and was issued to French, Belgian, Dutch, and Danish officers before World War II. The cal. .380 gun, with 8-round magazine capacity, was even more popular. It was issued to police and army officers in Poland, Czechoslovakia, Yugoslavia, Holland, Sweden, France, and Belgium, and was widely used in Central and South America.

The Model 1922 is a simple and reliable gun. While not a true military arm by American standards, its fine grip and good balance make it an excellent choice for offense or defense. It has a straight blowback action, and the takedown procedure is simple—the gun can be stripped in a matter of seconds. Aside from the difference in calibers and national crests or markings, there are 2 variations: the pre-war gun with fine finish, and the crude revised gun made under German occupation. The Germans apparently liked the Model 1922 and issued all that FN produced.

As the war progressed, the Germans simplified the gun to save materials and machine time. They eliminated the magazine safety and simplified some internal parts. The hard rubber grips with the FN trademark were replaced by crude wooden grips. The trigger was simplified by eliminating the comfortable trigger shoe effect found on pre-war guns. The lanyard loop was dropped and the fine finish and polish eliminated. It is interesting to note that while putting their Ordnance proofmarks on the guns, the Germans allowed the FN firm to mark the pistols with their trade name and not the 'ch' code that had been assigned to FN.

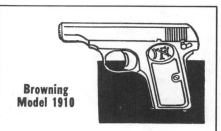

Browning Model 1910

PISTOL MAGAZINES

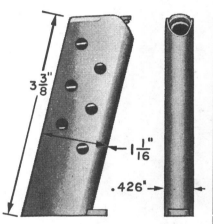

By 1910 John Browning had designed numerous automatic pistols, and the Model 1910 shows the results of this experience. The gun is simple, compact, and extremely well made. It was widely used as a police and service weapon in several countries, including Peru and Japan. While it was manufactured in both cals. .32 ACP and .380 ACP, the former caliber is by far the most common. While the Model 1910 incorporates none of the more modern features such as double-action trigger pull, it is nevertheless a very fine pocket pistol.

Model 1910 magazines are generally well made and can usually be recognized by the (Fabrique Nationale) trademark on the side. They can easily be confused with Browning Model 1922 magazines since the 2 are identical except for length. The Model 1910 is the shorter by about ½".

While the flat, stamped followers sometimes show a tendency to cock, the rest of the magazine is very well made and gives reliable service.—E. J. HOFFSCHMIDT

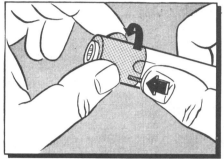

1 To strip the Model 1922, first remove the magazine and clear chamber. Push small serrated slide extension catch (3) forward, until it is clear of slide. Rotate extension about ¼ turn as shown, until it snaps free of slide

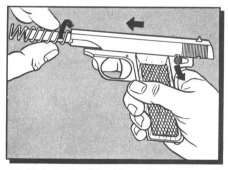

2 Pull back slide (4) until safety catch (27) can be engaged in forward notch. Rotating barrel (21) as shown will free it from recesses in frame. Now release safety catch and pull slide and barrel off front of frame

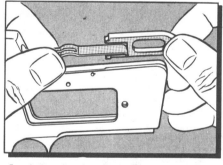

4 If gun is disassembled further, entire sear mechanism can be easily checked by removing the grips and pushing out grip safety hinge pin (29). When replacing mainspring (15), be sure tail is engaged in corresponding notch in magazine catch (14) as shown

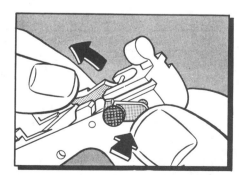

3 To remove safety catch (27), push up as far as it will go and it will snap out. To replace safety, push it in as far as it will go, then snap it down to fire position. Be sure sear (18) is pivoted clear before pushing safety all the way in

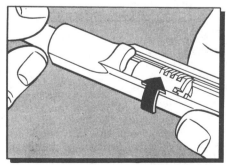

5 When reassembling gun, insert barrel into slide until barrel lugs line up with cut in slide. Then rotate barrel as far as it can go. It is now in position to allow slide to be assembled to frame ■

39

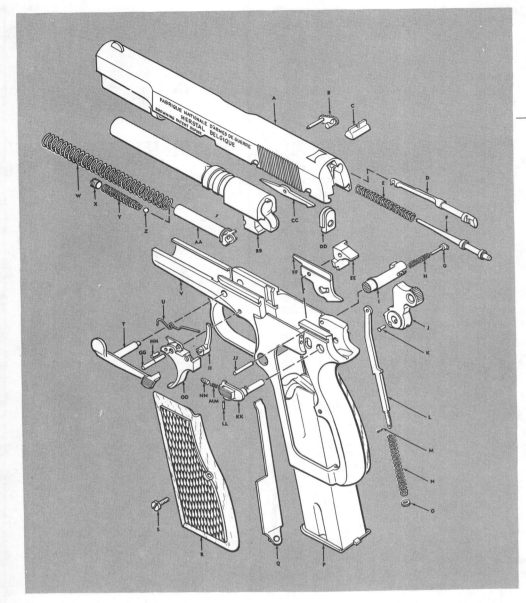

Legend

A—Slide
B—Sear lever retainer
C—Rear sight
D—Extractor
E—Firing pin spring
F—Firing pin
G—Magazine catch spring guide
H—Magazine catch spring
I—Magazine catch
J—Hammer
K—Hammer pin
L—Hammer strut
M—Hammer strut pin
N—Hammer spring
O—Hammer spring support
P—Magazine
Q—Sear spring
R—Left-hand grip
S—Grip screw
T—Slide stop
U—Trigger spring
V—Frame (receiver)
W—Recoil spring
X—Spring retainer
Y—Detent ballspring
Z—Detent ball
AA—Recoil spring guide
BB—Barrel
CC—Sear Lever
DD—Firing pin retainer plate
EE—Sear
FF—Ejector
GG—Trigger pin
HH—Trigger spring pin
II—Trigger lever
JJ—Sear pin
KK—Safety catch
LL—Stud retainer pin
MM—Stud spring
NN—Stud
OO—Trigger

M35 BROWNING HI-POWER

By E. J. Hoffschmidt

THE Browning Hi-Power is an excellent example of what a military semi-automatic pistol should be. It has a large magazine capacity, and is rugged, dependable, and accurate.

The Browning M1935, or the 13-shot 9 mm. Browning Hi-Power as it is better known, was the last pistol designed by John Browning. Although patented in 1927, the gun was not produced until 1935, when it was manufactured by Fabrique Nationale for the French Colonial troops. Later, a shorter 10-shot version was produced by Fabrique Nationale for the Belgian government.

The original large model was also manufactured, under license, by the John Inglis Co. of Canada, which made the gun in 2 models during World War II for the Chinese Government. The first model was a standard holster gun with fixed sights; the second had an adjustable rear sight and was machined to take an attachable holster stock for long-range shooting.

Made in 9 mm. Luger caliber, the M35 Browning Hi-Power has a double-row clip which holds 13 cartridges. It has a barrel of 4⅞" in length and measures 7¾" long over-all. Weight empty is 2 lbs.

M35 Browning Hi-Power

PISTOL MAGAZINES

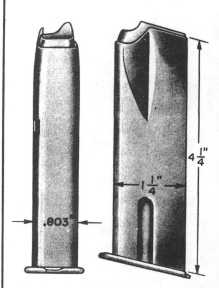

The Browning Hi-Power pistol is one of the best military automatics yet designed. It is rugged, reliable, and has a magazine capacity of 13 rounds. It was the last pistol designed by John Browning and embodies many improvements over the .45 Model 1911 automatic. Brownings were made before and during World War II by Fabrique Nationale in Belgium. During World War II they were also manufactured in Canada for the Chinese and later for the British, Canadian, and Greek armed forces.

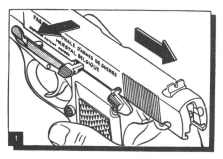

Figure 1—Remove the magazine. Pull back the slide and push the safety catch into the second notch. Push out the slide stop (T—see 'exploded' drawing) from right to left, as shown. Release the safety catch and permit the slide to go forward and off the receiver runners

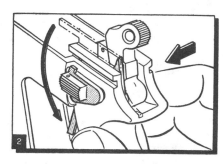

Figure 2—Push the safety catch down to fire position, then push sear pin (JJ) out from right to left. Allow the ejector (FF) to pivot down until it stops. With the ejector in this position, the safety catch (KK) can now be pushed out

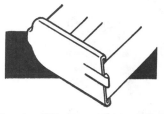

Browning Hi-Power magazines are the largest of the common pistol magazines. They can be easily identified by the fact that they are much wider than the normal 9 mm. magazine and also by the large detachable floorplate.

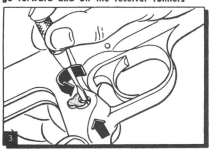

Figure 3—Hold the gun in the left hand and push in the magazine catch (I) until it is flush with frame. Using a ⅛ inch wide screwdriver, turn the magazine catch spring guide (G) ¼ of a turn. This will lock the spring guide to the magazine catch. Then lift out the unit

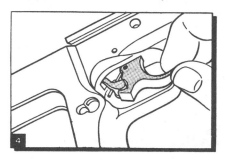

Figure 4—Push trigger pin (GG) out from right to left. Hold the gun with the right side up. With the right hand, pull the trigger forward and upward; this will remove parts (U), (HH), (II), and (OO) as a unit. These parts must be replaced as a unit when reassembling the gun

The followers of the Browning magazines are usually large white metal castings. The magazine feed lips are very strong, since they are stiffened by the long crease in either side of the magazine.—E. J. HOFFSCHMIDT

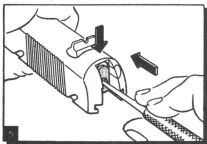

Figure 5—To remove firing pin (F) and spring (E), hold the slide in the left hand. With a ⅛ inch punch, push in the end of the firing pin; at the same time, push down on the firing pin retainer plate (DD). After firing pin and spring have been removed, pry out extractor (D)

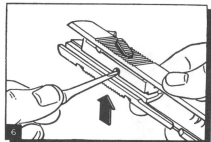

Figure 6—To remove the sear lever (CC), hold the slide upside down in the right hand. Using a small screwdriver, pry up the end of the sear lever retainer (be sure the extractor has been removed before doing this). When the head of the retainer is clear of the slide, pry it the rest of the way from the outside of the slide

The knurled plug in the base of the grip is a combination hammer spring guide and screwdriver

This Browning handgun was never manufactured. Only a few were made, in French 7.65 long automatic, in 1936 for French government trials

The Browning Model 1936

By E. J. Hoffschmidt

THE so-called small version of the Browning HiPower Model 1935 has come to be almost a legend among automatic pistol collectors.

Story has it that the gun was manufactured for the French by Fabrique Nationale of Belgium, and that it is a small scale version of the 1935 HP. But that is where the story ended. Or at least it ended that way until an original test model, serial #7, turned up on this side of the Atlantic.

The pistol pictured here was 'liberated' from the Fabrique Nationale company museum by either German or Allied troops. Ten years later, it turned up in a Washington, D. C., gun shop where it was purchased for a nominal sum by a pistol collector.

A letter to Fabrique Nationale via their American representative, the Browning Arms Co., brought a prompt informative reply:

"This model was actually never manufactured. There were a few made in 1936 for French government trials. The exact quantity is not known. It was designed for the French 7.65 long automatic cartridge (page 28 of *Centerfire Metric Revolver Cartridges* by White and Munhall) which, being considerably more powerful than the regular .32 caliber automatic pistol cartridge, required a locking system.

"FN presented its models at the French trials through FN's subsidiary at that time which was known as the Manufacture d'Armes de Paris and explains the marking on the right-hand side of the pistol.

"The tests were held at Versailles and Chalon; and according to FN, they clearly emerged the victor in the competition. In any case, the pistol gave good results; however, the French considered it too complicated. They then proceeded to make their own pistol at St. Etienne which in some respects was a copy of the FN model and which was never very successful as made by the French.

"The changes made on the mechanism with respect to the present 9 mm. HP model were partly made to satisfy French specifications (caliber, single row magazine, front sight, and angle of grip), and partly for simplification and economy (recoil spring guide, ejector mounting, hammer and sear) and partly as necessary adaptation to the different caliber."

While the 1936 model may look, operate, and field strip like the 1935 HP, the resemblance is only skin deep, for it has many unique and original

The hammer and sear mechanism on the Browning Model 1936 is one unit

features. Probably the greatest point of difference between the 1935 HP and the 1936 is in the hammer and sear mechanism. This new mechanism is a removable assembly, similar to the Swiss Neuhausen SP47/8 or the Russian Tokarev. It is held in the frame by a large-headed pin and the safety catch. A cartridge case is the only tool necessary to remove the large-headed pin. When the pin is pried out, it frees the safety catch so that it can be removed. Then the entire sear mechanism can be lifted out of the frame. This is truly a simple, rugged and compact sear mechanism assembly. It contains the magazine disconnector that prevents the gun from being fired when the magazine is out of the gun. It contains the firing disconnector that prevents the gun from firing before it is fully locked or from shooting full automatic, and also contains the hammer and sear—all in one block and all in relative operating positions ready to be repaired or adjusted.

Another interesting feature is the inclusion of a small screwdriver in the butt. The large knurled plug doubles as a hammer spring guide and a screwdriver. This screwdriver is just the right size to fit the screw slot in the magazine catch. The only rub is that you must have a screwdriver to begin with to remove the walnut grips and get at the pin that retains the screwdriver.

Shooting this pistol is a distinct pleasure. The cartridge is not too powerful and the excellent grip shape gives the pistol a feel that is second to none. It weights 28 ounces empty, is 8-1/8 inches long, and has a magazine capacity of eight rounds, so when we compare this information with the information on the 1935 HP, we see that the so-called 'small model', although thinner and lighter, is actually 3/8 of an inch longer. ◊ ◊ ◊

FIREARMS ASSEMBLY
The NRA Guide to Rifles and Shotguns
Revised and Expanded

A Companion to This Volume

For Ordering Information Write:

National Rifle Association
Sales Department, P.O. Box 5000
Kearneysville, WV 25430-5000
Tel: 1-800-336-7402

PISTOL MAGAZINES

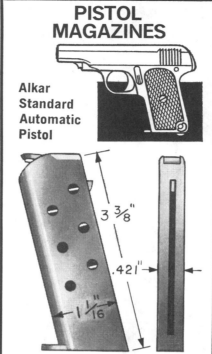

Alkar Standard Automatic Pistol

S. A. Alkartasuna of Spain produced a wide variety of inexpensive copies of Browning pistols which sold mostly under the "Alkar" trademark. From time to time some original ideas were introduced. The so-called Standard Automatic Alkar pistol has one of these features. Unlike most inexpensive pistols, the magazine follower itself does not hold the slide open when the last shot is fired. A projection on the back of the magazine follower pushes up a slide-stop in the frame when the magazine is empty.

Standard pistol magazines are rarely marked, but can be recognized by the long, thin slot down the backstrap. The projection on the follower that operates the stop travels up and down this slot. Aside from this, it resembles most other Spanish cal. .32 magazines.

The Alkar pistol using this magazine can be recognized by the slot cut in the magazine catch. This slot allows the projection on the follower to clear when the magazine is inserted or removed.—E. J. HOFFSCHMIDT

PISTOL MAGAZINES

Alkar Cartridge-Counter Pistol

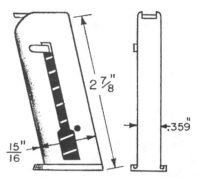

Manufactura de Armas de Fuego of Guernica, Spain, has turned out a variety of pocket pistols under the trade name Alkar, including the little cal. .25 pistol shown. This pistol has a cartridge indicator to show when there is a round in the chamber, and incorporates a grip safety that can be locked out of action.

The cartridge-counter magazine is an unusual feature of the pistol. The left grip has a series of plastic windows molded into its surface. When a fully-loaded magazine is inserted into the gun, the indicator can be seen through the lowest window. As the gun is fired, the indicator moves upward, showing how many rounds remain in the magazine.

The magazine follower is a bent piece of sheet metal, but it is much thicker than those in most magazines. This greater thickness retains the tail of the indicator pointer.

The T-shape slot in the side and the thick, serrated-end floorplate are typical of this magazine.—E. J. HOFFSCHMIDT

Browning Nomad Semi-Automatic Pistol

By THOMAS E. WESSEL

1 Remove magazine (37) and coin-slotted barrel mounting screw (16) located under barrel (1) on front of frame (18). Pull slide (9) rearward and tap muzzle on a padded surface, while retaining slide in rearward position. Push barrel rearward and slightly upward to separate it from frame. Allow slide to move slowly forward and off front of frame, being careful not to lose control of recoil spring (26)

The Belgian-made Browning Nomad self-loading pistol, chambered for the .22 Long Rifle cartridge (both standard and high velocity) was introduced in 1962 and dropped in about 1973. It was a blowback operated and the concealed hammer was of pivoted type.

The frame was lightweight alloy; other parts were steel. The black plastic grip was of one-piece construction and the side panels sharply checkered. The detachable magazine held 10 rounds. The rear sight was fully adjustable for elevation and windage.

The barrel was secured to the frame by a single screw and unique wedge lock arrangement. The standard barrel was 4-1/2 inches long, but a 6-3/4-in. barrel was also offered. This pistol did not have an automatic slide stop or magazine disconnector.

The Browning Nomad was essentially a sports pistol, for the camper or the informal target shooter. It weighed 26 ounces and, with the standard barrel, was 8-7/8 inches overall.

2 Remove firing pin (14) by inserting a small drift into hole on top of slide and drifting out firing pin retaining pin (15). Firing pin and firing pin spring (13) may be removed from rear of slide. Perform this disassembly only when necessary. When replacing firing pin retaining pin, it is necessary to peen over the rim of the pin hole to keep the pin in place

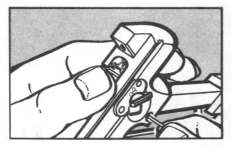

3 Remove grip screw (33) and grip (30). Depress hammer (43) with thumb until upper collar on mainspring plunger (40) is no longer visible through access hole in side of frame. Insert a long, 1/16″ diameter steel brad in this hole to retain mainsprings (38 and 39) fully compressed. Hammer will now move loosely

4 Using tweezers, pluck out disconnector spring (23) from right side of frame and lift away disconnector (22). Drift out trigger pin (20, arrow) and remove trigger (21)

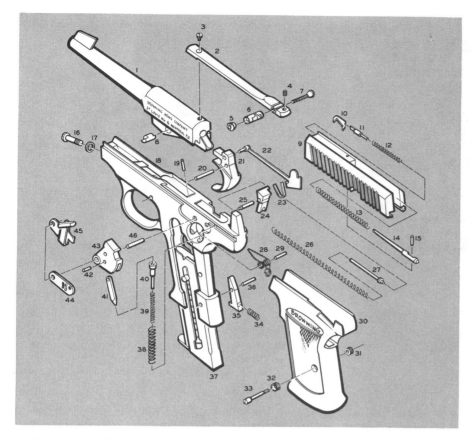

Parts Legend

1. Barrel
2. Rear sight base *
3. Rear sight base mounting screw *
4. Rear sight adjusting screw, elevation
5. Rear sight adjusting screw nut, windage
6. Rear sight
7. Rear sight adjusting screw, windage
8. Barrel guide pin
9. Slide
10. Extractor
11. Extractor plunger
12. Extractor spring
13. Firing pin spring
14. Firing pin
15. Firing pin retaining pin
16. Barrel mounting screw
17. Barrel mounting screw washer
18. Frame
19. Ejector *
20. Trigger pin
21. Trigger
22. Disconnector
23. Disconnector spring
24. Sear
25. Sear pin
26. Recoil spring
27. Recoil spring guide
28. Sear spring
29. Sear spring pin
30. Grip
31. Grip screw nut *
32. Grip screw washer *
33. Grip screw
34. Magazine latch spring
35. Magazine latch
36. Magazine latch pin
37. Magazine
38. Outer mainspring
39. Inner mainspring
40. Mainspring plunger
41. Hammer link strut
42. Hammer link pin
43. Hammer
44. Click plate
45. Safety
46. Hammer pin

* Permanent factory sub-assembly to other major part.

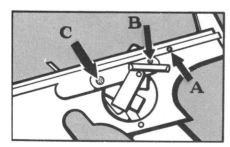

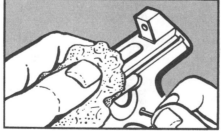

5 Continue by drifting out (A) sear spring pin (29) and remove sear spring (28). Tweezers will aid in lifting spring from slot in top of frame. Drift out (B) sear pin (25) from left to right and remove sear (24). Drift out (C) hammer pin (46) and remove hammer with attached link strut (41). The safety (45) and click plate (44) may now be removed

6 Should it be necessary to remove mainsprings, grasp the frame using clean cotton waste to pad hand, placing thumb over slot in top of frame and over that area where springs will emerge. Withdraw steel brad inserted earlier. Springs and plunger will jump upward into padding. Reassemble arm in reverse ∎

Campo Giro Model 1913-16 Pistol

PISTOL MAGAZINES

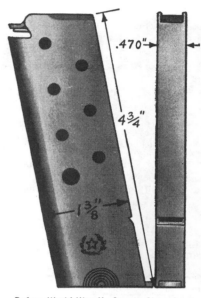

Before World War II, Campo Giro pistols were relatively scarce here, but after World War II a number of these interesting Spanish pistols were imported. Though awkward in design, they are generally well made and finished. Since they fired the powerful 9 mm. Campo Giro (9 mm. Bergmann-Bayard) cartridge from an unlocked breech, a unique slide buffer was incorporated to prevent battering of the frame and of the barrel.

Campo Giro magazines are relatively easy to recognize. The floorplate extends to the rear of the magazine instead of to the front. The circular finger grip cuts, and the star inside the wreath are additional points of recognition.

The magazine lips look like those of most other magazines, but the follower has a bent step which operates the slide hold-open catch when the gun is empty. This is characteristic of the Campo Giro magazine.—EDWARD J. HOFFSCHMIDT

EXPLODED VIEWS:

Charter Arms Police Bulldog

BY CHARLIE GARA

CHARTER Arms Corp., founded in 1964, produced its first revolver in 1965. Called the Undercover, it was a .38 Spl. five-shot with a 2″ barrel and remains part of the Charter line.

Following in close succession through the years were other models in a variety of calibers which included several distinct features. All, however, incorporated the original basic design: lightweight all-steel construction (with the exception of the grip frame and ejector rod head), beryllium copper firing pin,

hammer block safety, and single- and double-action mechanism without a sideplate.

Built on a larger frame, the Police Bulldog was first produced in early 1982. With fixed service sights, this six-shot .38 Spl. is factory approved for use with +P ammunition.

Charter's Police Bulldog is available with 2″ barrel, 4″ tapered barrel, 4″ bull barrel, or 2″ barrel and snag-free pocket hammer.

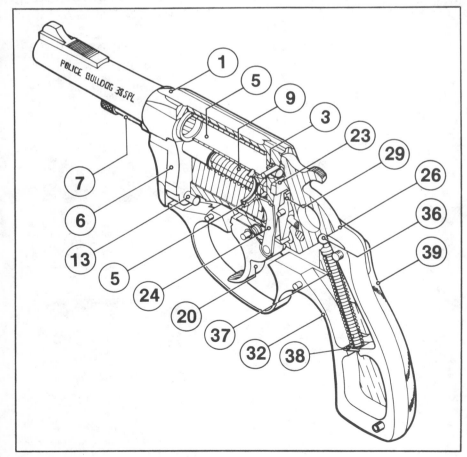

Disassembly Procedure

Before attempting any disassembly, push the cylinder latch (42) forward and swing the cylinder (5) out to be sure that it is unloaded.

To remove grip assembly (39), unscrew grip screw (40) until it protrudes above the left-hand grip surface or on larger grips is completely free. With screwdriver blade in

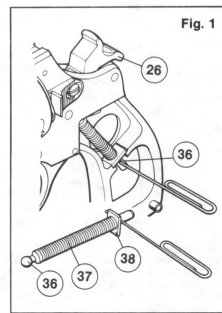

Fig. 1

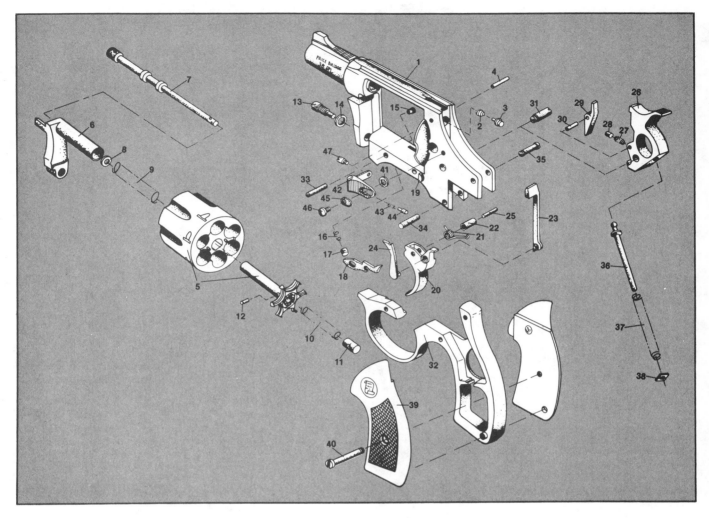

Parts Legend

1. Frame, barrel & sight assembly
2. Firing pin spring
3. Firing pin
4. Firing pin retaining pin
5. Cylinder & ejector assembly
6. Crane assembly
7. Ejector rod
8. Ejector rod washer
9. Ejector rod return spring
10. Ejector rod lock spring
11. Ejector rod bushing
12. Ejector rod assembly pin
13. Crane screw
14. Crane screw washer
15. Cylinder stop bushing
16. Cylinder stop spring
17. Cylinder stop plunger
18. Cylinder stop
19. Ejector limiting stud
20. Trigger
21. Trigger spring
22. Trigger spring bushing
23. Hammer block assembly
24. Hand assembly
25. Trigger pin
26. Hammer
27. Hammer pawl spring
28. Hammer pawl plunger
29. Hammer pawl
30. Hammer pawl pin
31. Hammer screw
32. Grip frame
33. Cylinder stop retaining pin
34. Frame assembly pin
35. Frame assembly screw
36. Mainspring guide rod
37. Mainspring
38. Mainspring seat
39. Grip assembly
40. Grip screw
41. Cylinder latch washer
42. Cylinder latch
43. Cylinder latch plunger spring
44. Cylinder latch plunger
45. Cylinder latch cover plate
46. Cylinder latch retaining screw
47. Cylinder latch release screw

screw slot, tap screwdriver handle inward to loosen right-hand grip. Remove screw (40) and grips (39).

Bring hammer (36) all the way back to cocked postion. Insert paper clip or small pin through hole at bottom of mainspring guide rod (36). Gently lower hammer and remove entire guide rod (36), mainspring (37) and mainspring seat (38) assembly . . . CAUTION: If paper clip is removed from (36, 37, 39) assembly, components under compression could cause serious injury **(Fig. 1).**

Disassemble grip frame (32) by removing frame assembly screw (35) from right side of frame. Then tap out frame assembly pin (34) and cylinder stop retaining pin (33).

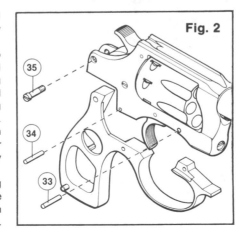

Fig. 2

Carefully ease grip frame from bottom of frame group (1) **(Fig. 2).**

By removing hammer screw (31), from right side of revolver, hammer (26) can be disengaged from trigger (20) and lifted out of frame.

To remove cylinder group, remove crane screw (13) and nylon crane screw washer (14). Push forward on cylinder latch (42) and swing cylinder (5) out. Cylinder, crane assembly and the rest of cylinder group can now be removed from frame.

The preceding disassembly procedure allows for the occasional cleaning of the entire revolver. Further disassembly is not recommended by the factory. Reassemble in reverse order.

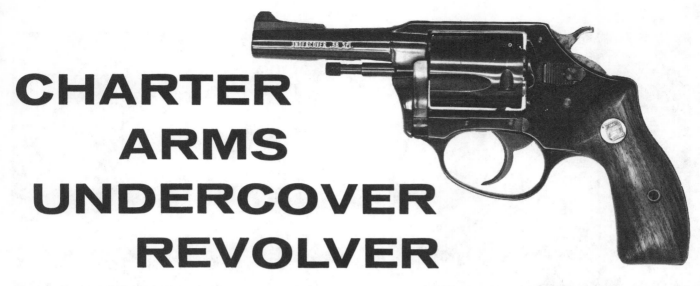

CHARTER ARMS UNDERCOVER REVOLVER

Illustrations by DENNIS RIORDAN
Text by LUDWIG OLSON
Technical Editor
THE AMERICAN RIFLEMAN

DETECTIVES and many other law enforcement personnel require a compact, lightweight handgun suitable for carrying concealed. In addition to being compact and lightweight, such a gun must be reliable, powerful, and quick to get into action. It must also be safe to carry and reasonably accurate.

Most law enforcement officers feel that a .38 Special revolver with a short barrel and small frame best meets these requirements. A good example of such a handgun is the Charter Arms Undercover revolver chambered for the .38 Special cartridge. Introduced in 1966, this double-action revolver with swing-out cylinder is produced by the Charter Arms Corp., Bridgeport, Conn., with choice of 1⅞″ or 3″ barrel length. Weight with 1⅞″ barrel is only 16 ozs., and the overall length is 6¼″. Compactness is aided by the small frame, small round butt, and the five-shot cylinder which is smaller in diameter than a six-shot cal. .38 cylinder.

Despite its light weight, the Undercover revolver handles very well. It fires 148-gr. mid-range, 158-gr. standard-velocity, and 200-gr. loads. Recoil is considerable, especially in firing 158-gr. and 200-gr. loads, but the high position of the oil-finished walnut grips at the rear of the frame helps reduce recoil effect.

Contributing to ease of handling are the natural pointing qualities and favorable balance. Cocking the exposed hammer with the thumb is smooth and easy. The single-action trigger pull is clean and weighs approximately 5 lbs., but the double-action pull is quite heavy.

The cylinder and crane are latched to the frame by the ejector rod projecting from the rear of the cylinder and by the ejector rod collar at the front of the frame. These two points of support give strong latching. The cylinder is unlatched by pressing forward the cylinder latch or pulling the ejector rod forward. All fired cases are ejected simultaneously by a single stroke of the ejector rod.

As with several current double-action revolvers, a transfer bar (called hammer block by the Charter Arms Corp.) transmits the hammer blow to the spring-loaded firing pin in the frame. However, the transfer bar is elevated in line with the firing pin only when the trigger is to the rear. This positive safety system prevents accidental discharge should the revolver be dropped with the hammer down and trigger forward.

Most metal parts, including the investment-cast frame, are blued steel. The butt and trigger guard are a single piece of black-finished aluminum alloy. Coil springs are used throughout, except for the wire torsion-type trigger spring. The fixed sights consist of a ⅛″ width front sight on a serrated ramp, and a square-notch rear sight integral with the frame.

The Undercover revolver is optionally available with nickel-plated finish and checkered walnut grips. It is well suited for its intended purpose of law enforcement and also for guard use and home defense. ∎

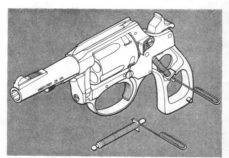

1 Press cylinder latch (37) forward and swing out cylinder (18). Make sure that gun is unloaded. Partially unscrew grip screw (51), and tap with screwdriver handle to loosen right grip (10). Remove both grips, then draw back hammer (33). Insert a straightened paper clip through hole in bottom of mainspring guide rod (42), pull trigger, and lower hammer gently with thumb. Remove mainspring (43), seat (45), and guide rod as an assembly.

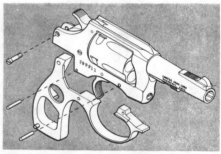

2 Unscrew frame assembly screw (7), and drift out frame assembly pin (6) and cylinder stop pin (8). Butt (28) can now be removed from frame (1).

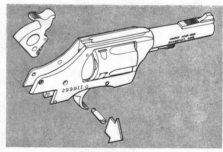

3 Unscrew hammer screw (5), and lift hammer from frame. All moving lockwork parts are now accessible for cleaning and lubrication.

4 To remove fouling from bushing portion of crane (14), unscrew crane screw (19), and remove it along with its nylon washer (20). Then, dismount cylinder from frame. Draw crane forward out

of cylinder to clean the crane bushing.
Further disassembly is not recommended.
Reassemble in reverse.

PARTS LEGEND

1. Frame and barrel assembly
2. Firing pin retaining pin
3. Firing pin spring
4. Firing pin
5. Hammer screw
6. Frame assembly pin
7. Frame assembly screw
8. Cylinder stop pin
9. Trigger pin
10. Right grip
11. Ejector rod head
12. Ejector rod collar spring
13. Ejector rod collar
14. Crane
15. Ejector rod washer
16. Ejector return spring
17. Ejector rod
18. Cylinder
19. Crane screw
20. Crane screw washer
21. Cylinder stop spring
22. Cylinder stop plunger
23. Ejector
24. Ejector rod lock spring
25. Cylinder stop
26. Ejector rod bushing
27. Ejector rod assembly pin
28. Round butt
29. Hammer pawl
30. Hammer pawl pin
31. Hammer pawl plunger
32. Hammer pawl spring
33. Hammer
34. Grip locating pin
35. Cylinder latch washer
36. Cylinder latch release screw
37. Cylinder latch
38. Cylinder latch cover plate
39. Cylinder latch retaining screw
40. Cylinder latch spring
41. Cylinder latch plunger
42. Mainspring guide rod
43. Mainspring
44. Left grip
45. Mainspring seat
46. Trigger spring
47. Hand
48. Trigger spring bushing
49. Trigger
50. Hammer block
51. Grip screw

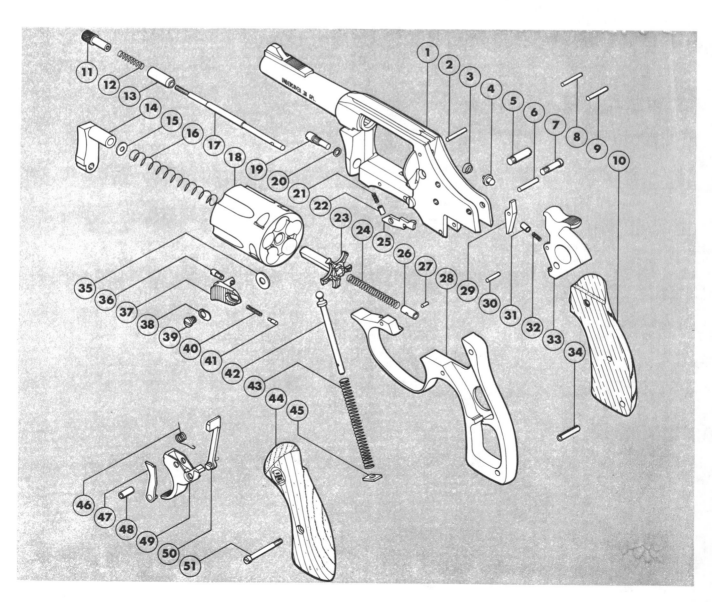

Colt Model 1902 Military .38

**BY
PETE DICKEY**

THE Model 1902 Military .38, made from 1902 to 1929, was one of a number of early Colt semi-automatic (and prototype full-automatic) pistols designed by John Browning. These locked-breech pistols utilize the "parallel-rule" locking system where the barrel, supported by two links, dropped down and back in recoil, with its "up" and "down" bore line axes remaining parallel to the slide's center line.

Disassembly instructions for the Model 1902 Military are also useful for the Model 1900 that had a combination rear sight and firing pin safety but no slide lock; the 1902 Sporting Model, a shorter-gripped seven-shot magazine version of the eight-shot Military; and the 1903 Pocket Hammer Model that was like the 1902 Sporting save for its 4½" vs. 6" barrel and short slide. All were chambered for the early .38 ACP cartridge—NONE should be fired using modern .38 Super or .38 Super + P ammunition.

Early versions of all may be found with a rounded hammer top instead of the spur shown; many will be found lacking the slide stop.

The pistols had half-cock hammer notches and disconnectors that Colt called "safeties" at the time. None, save possible "experimentals," had conventional manual safeties.

The .45 cal. Colt Model 1905 pistols and their variants, also using the parallel-rule locking system, were, except for their caliber and exposed extractor, quite similar to the .38s and can be field-stripped using the same procedures.

The Model 1905 .45s evolved into the M1911 pistol; the .38s, understandably, disappeared soon after the dramatic appearance of Colt's Super .38 with its nine-shot magazine capacity and unrivalled .38 Super cartridge in 1929.

Fuller details on the Models 1900-1905 were given in the December, 1984, *American Rifleman*.

Disassembly Instructions

Push magazine catch (32) forward and remove magazine (34). Retract slide (3), check that chamber is empty and allow slide to close.

Grasp mid-portion of slide/receiver in right hand. With left hand use toe of magazine's floorplate to depress takedown plunger (28). With right index finger push out slide lock (11) from its seat. After complete removal of the slide lock, the slide can be withdrawn from the rear of the receiver. (**Fig. 1**)

The barrel (2) and its dual links (30) are removed by drifting out the long front and rear bottom link pins (29). Note that when the front link pin is fully removed, it frees the takedown plunger (28), and the recoil spring (26) with its guide (27) that are under compression and will be released with considerable force. Separation of barrel, links and their short retaining pins is straightforward.

Receiver stripping, if required, is accomplished by first removing the four stock screws (38) and both stocks (37). After drifting out the ejector pin (24), carefully pry up the ejector (23) from its seat. This frees the slide stop (39) that is removed as a unit with its friction spring (40). (**Fig. 2**)

When the magazine catch pin (33) is driven out, the catch will drop from the magazine well together with the combination sear/disconnector/trigger spring (20). The trigger itself (16) may now be removed.

A single pin (19), when removed, frees the sear (17) and disconnector (18), and it is wise to keep their relative postions in mind for reassembly.

Removal of the mainspring screw (22), lo-

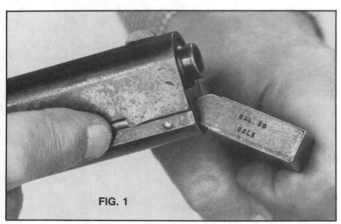

FIG. 1

FIG. 2

FIG. 3

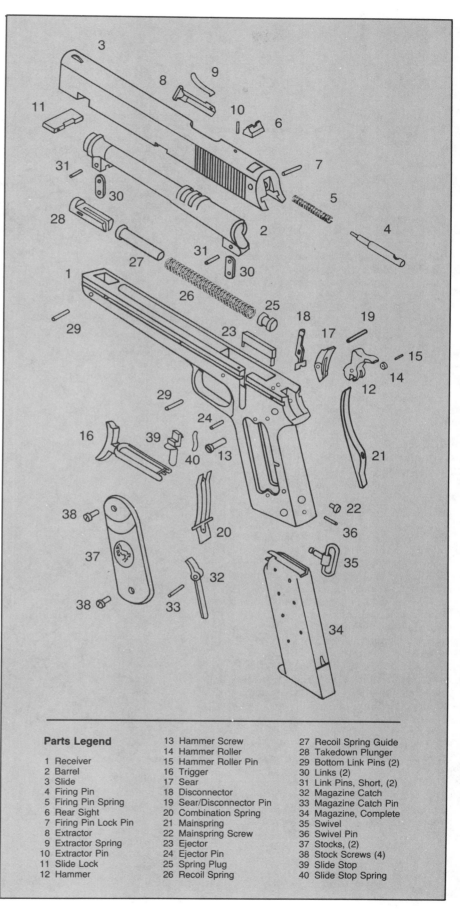

cated on the backstrap, releases the mainspring (21). Removal of the hammer screw (13) and hammer (12) with its roller (14) and pin (15) completes receiver stripping except for the swivel (35) that is held by a pin (36) at the bottom of the backstrap.

The slide may be completely stripped, if required, by first drifting out the rear sight (6) from left to right. The inertial firing pin and its spring (4 and 5) are held by a lateral pin (7) that is also driven from the left and the extractor with spring (8 and 9) are fixed with a small vertical pin (10) that can be drifted down through the top of the slide by a small punch.

Once the extractor pin is removed, the extractor and spring, by means of a small screwdriver, may be pried away from the firing pin hole and forward until they are free of the slide. The spring should not be removed from the extractor unless replacement is necessary.

Reassembly is done in reverse order, with, of course, the rear sight firing pin retainer and slide lock being inserted from right to left.

Various parts are shown in **Fig. 3** where they are placed on top of the receiver for clarity. **Fig. 4** shows a piece of tape used as an insertion aid for the sear and disconnector.

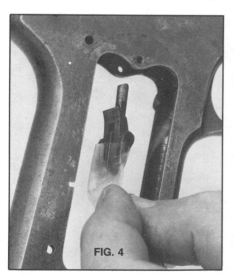

FIG. 4

Parts Legend

1 Receiver	13 Hammer Screw	27 Recoil Spring Guide
2 Barrel	14 Hammer Roller	28 Takedown Plunger
3 Slide	15 Hammer Roller Pin	29 Bottom Link Pins (2)
4 Firing Pin	16 Trigger	30 Links (2)
5 Firing Pin Spring	17 Sear	31 Link Pins, Short, (2)
6 Rear Sight	18 Disconnector	32 Magazine Catch
7 Firing Pin Lock Pin	19 Sear/Disconnector Pin	33 Magazine Catch Pin
8 Extractor	20 Combination Spring	34 Magazine, Complete
9 Extractor Spring	21 Mainspring	35 Swivel
10 Extractor Pin	22 Mainspring Screw	36 Swivel Pin
11 Slide Lock	23 Ejector	37 Stocks, (2)
12 Hammer	24 Ejector Pin	38 Stock Screws (4)
	25 Spring Plug	39 Slide Stop
	26 Recoil Spring	40 Slide Stop Spring

COLT .25 AUTOMATIC PISTOL

Illustrations by DENNIS RIORDAN
Text by LUDWIG OLSON

In the first half of the 20th century, Colt's, of Hartford, Conn., was one of the leading producers of .25 ACP pistols. Their first pistol of this type was developed by John M. Browning, the famous American arms designer, and introduced in 1908. Approximately 50,000 of these excellent, blowback-operated arms were produced.

The 1908 Colt was discontinued in 1946, and Colt did not re-enter the .25 ACP pocket pistol field until 1958, when the introduced the "Junior" Colt. This pistol was made for Colt by Unceta & Cie in Spain.

The 1968 Gun Control Act stopped importation of the Junior Colt, and this Spanish-made was replaced by a .25 ACP pocket pistol introduced in 1970 and called the Colt Automatic Caliber .25. Blowback-operated, like its predecessors, the Colt .25 was made in the United States by another manufacturer for sale by Colt. The pistol weighed only 12-1/2 ounces, measured 4-7/16 inches in overall length and had a six shot detachable magazine. Its front and rear sights were integral with the slide, as was a serrated rib running between them.

A mechanical thumb safety on the left side of the frame also serves as a slide hold-open device. Other safety features are an exposed hammer with rounded spur and a disconnector safety that prevents firing when the magazine is removed. The exposed hammer makes it possible to tell, at a glance, if the pistol is cocked.

Although the hammer has a half-cock notch, a moderate pull on the trigger when the safety is "OFF" will cause the hammer to drop. The firing pin is independent but not of rebounding type. Thus, in the case of original production Juniors and Colt .25s, when the hammer is fully lowered it contacts the primer of a chambered cartridge. It is therefore unsafe to carry the pistol with a round in the chamber and the hammer down. **This condition was cause for a recall in the mid-1980s in which the factory fitted those pistols that were returned with rebounding firing pins.**

The Colt Automatic Caliber .25 was dropped from the company's product line in 1975.

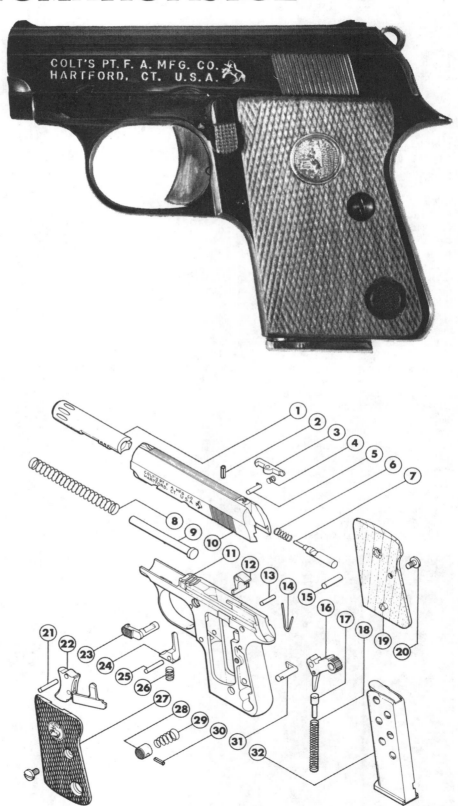

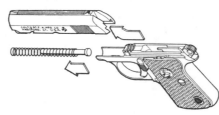

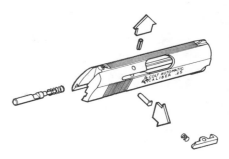

1 Begin takedown by moving safety (23) upward to safe position. Depress magazine-catch button (28) and remove magazine (32). Draw slide (10) fully rearward to clear chamber. Safety will engage slide, locking it open. Rotate barrel (1) ⅜ turn clockwise and pull forward as far as it will go. Then rotate it ⅜ turn counterclockwise and remove from slide.

2 Grasp slide firmly and move safety downward to fire position. Ease slide forward off frame (11). Remove recoil spring (8) and guide (9) from frame tunnel. This is sufficient disassembly for normal cleaning.

3 To disassemble further, drive out extractor pin (2) with a pin punch that closely fits hole in slide. Extractor (3) and its spring (4) may then be lifted out. Pry out firing-pin retaining pin (5) with a narrow screwdriver blade inserted under its elongated head. Removal of the pin releases firing pin (7) and spring (6).

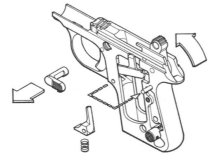

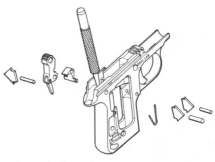

4 Unscrew grip screws (20) and remove grips (19) (27). Rotate safety ½ turn from safe position and withdraw from frame. Drift out magazine-safety pin (25) and remove magazine safety (24) and spring (26). Insert magazine-safety pin in frame hole below disconnector (22). Pull trigger and lower hammer with thumb, until hammer-spring guide (17) stops against the pin.

5 Unhook forward arm of sear spring (14) from sear (12), and remove spring. Drift out hammer pin (15) and lift hammer assembly (16) from frame. Drift out sear pin (13) and remove sear. Depress hammer-spring guide with punch, and withdraw magazine-safety pin. Then, ease out hammer spring (18) and guide.

Parts Legend

1. Barrel
2. Extractor pin
3. Extractor
4. Extractor spring
5. Firing-pin retaining pin
6. Firing-pin spring
7. Firing pin
8. Recoil spring
9. Recoil-spring guide
10. Slide
11. Frame
12. Sear
13. Sear pin
14. Sear spring
15. Hammer pin
16. Hammer w/strut & pin
17. Hammer-spring guide
18. Hammer spring
19. Grip plate, right
20. Grip screw (2)
21. Trigger pin
22. Trigger w/disconnector
23. Thumb safety
24. Magazine safety
25. Magazine-safety pin
26. Magazine-safety spring
27. Grip plate, left
28. Magazine-catch button
29. Magazine-catch spring
30. Magazine-catch pin
31. Magazine catch
32. Magazine

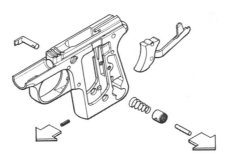

6 Drift out magazine-catch pin (30) to free magazine catch (31), spring (29), and button. Drift out trigger pin (21), releasing the trigger assembly. Reassemble in reverse. Trigger must be rotated forward to fully compress its internally located spring when the trigger pin is replaced.

7 Cutaway shows relative positions of internal parts. Pistol is pictured with magazine and manual safeties released and hammer at full cock. Parts are number keyed to parts legend.

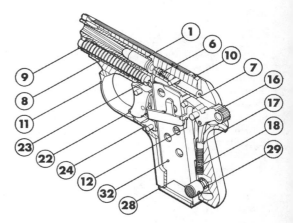

1. Receiver
2. Slide
3. Front sight
4. Rear sight
5. Extractor
6. Extractor spring
7. Extractor pin
8. Front firing pin
9. Rear firing pin
10. Firing pin spring
11. Firing pin lock pin
12. Recoil spring guide
13. Recoil spring
14. Plug
15. Barrel
16. Ejector
17. Ejector pin
18. Hammer
19. Hammer roll
20. Hammer roll pin
21. Slide lock safety
22. Sear
23. Disconnector
24. Sear pin
25. Trigger
26. Depressor
27. Grip safety
28. Sear spring
29. Mainspring
30. Magazine catch
31. Grip safety pin
32. Grips (2)
33. Escutcheons (2)
34. Grip screw
35. Magazine

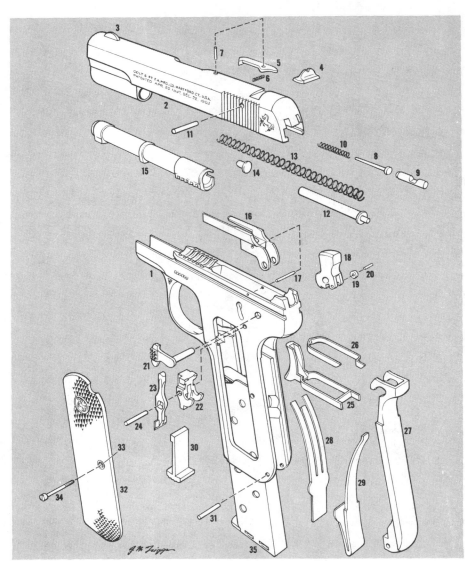

Colt Automatic .32 and .380 Pocket Pistol

By James M. Triggs

Introduced around the turn of the century, the Browning-designed .32 pocket automatic pistol was the first hammerless or concealed-hammer pistol produced by the Colt firm. Early models show the single patent date of April 20, 1897; later models bear the additional December 22, 1903, patent date.

A salient design feature of this excellent pistol is the slide lock safety mechanism which, in addition to its primary function of holding the slide to the rear, also serves as a mechanical safety to block the hammer and as a means of determining whether the hammer is cocked. If the hammer is cocked, the

The late James M. Triggs was a well known writer-illustrator and collector of antique firearms.

slide lock safety can be pushed upward to engage a corresponding cut in the slide. When the hammer is down in fired position, the slide lock safety cannot be pushed upward to engage the slide cut.

The grip safety, which automatically blocks the sear to prevent discharge of the gun unless pressure is simultaneously applied to both trigger and grip safety, is another important and widely copied design feature. It also serves as a cocking indicator by projecting from the rear of the grip only when the hammer is cocked. Later models with serial numbers above 468,097 incorporate a magazine disconnecter device to prevent the gun firing with the magazine removed.

James E. Serven in his fine book, *Colt Firearms 1860-1954*, records that

pistols with serial numbers 1 to 72,000 had four-inch barrels requiring a separate bushing. Pistols 72,001 to 95,800 had 3¾-inch barrels and a small extractor. Pistols 95,801 to 105,050 had 3¾-inch barrels with a larger extractor. Final production from gun number 105,050 to 572,215 had 3¾-inch barrels with integral bushing and a locking lug at the muzzle end of the barrel. There was a change in the slide lock safety at gun number 416,896.

Initially offered in .32 caliber only, the pistol was announced in the additional .380 ACP chambering in 1908. It is possible to convert either model to either caliber by substitution of magazines and barrels. Colt discontinued production of this pistol in both calibers in 1946.

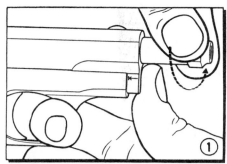

1. Remove magazine and check chamber to insure that it is unloaded. Cock the pistol. Grasp the pistol as shown, lining up the mark and arrow stamped on right side of slide with forward edge of receiver. With fingers of left hand twist barrel to left until its locking lugs disengage from receiver. Withdraw slide, barrel, recoil spring, and guide from receiver. Turn barrel and withdraw it from slide

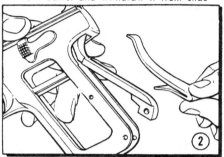

2. Remove stocks and drive out grip safety pin (31). Pull out lower end of grip safety (27) and withdraw the mainspring (29), sear spring (28), and magazine catch (30)

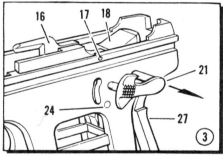

3. Put slide lock safety (21) in "safe" or **up** position and withdraw it from receiver as shown. Hammer (18), ejector (16), and grip safety (27) can now be removed. Sear (22) and disconnector (23) can be removed by driving out their retaining pin (24)

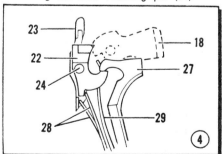

4. Parts may be reassembled in reverse order. Sear and disconnector are assembled in relationship as shown. Insert sear spring so that its leaves engage sear and disconnector. Insert mainspring so smaller leaf faces in toward the magazine well. Hammer must be in forward position to insert mainspring ——————

PISTOL MAGAZINES

Bayard Model 1908 Cal. .25 Pistol

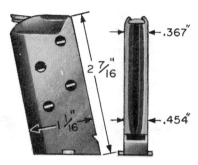

The Bayard Model 1908 pistols in cals. .32 and .380 are among the smallest in those calibers. Virtually the same frame and slide are found on the Bayard cal. .25 pistol, one of the largest cal. .25 vest-pocket-type guns. Workmanship is generally good, but the high sharp-edged rear sight makes it difficult to get the Bayard cal. .25 pistol out of the pocket quickly.

The ear-like projections are the best points of identity for the magazine. Another identification feature of the cal. .25 magazine is the retaining notch in the backstrap.

The magazine is as wide as a normal cal. .32 magazine except that upper portion and feed lips are reduced to accommodate the smaller cal. .25 cartridge. Backstrap is indented to accommodate the shorter round.—E. J. HOFFSCHMIDT

Beretta Model 1915

PISTOL MAGAZINES

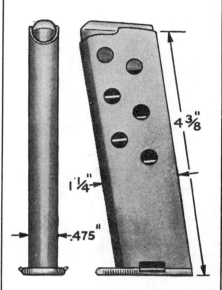

The Beretta Model 1915 pistol fires a 9 mm. Italian pistol cartridge. The cartridge is dimensionally similar to the 9 mm. Luger but lower powered. The gun has a heavy slide to resist the blowback forces. In addition to a strong recoil spring, a short very heavy buffer spring is mounted in the receiver. This takes up the shock of the heavy slide. Although the gun is well made, the grip is too straight and the gun sits too high in the hand for accurate snap shooting.

Unlike most Beretta magazines, the side is pierced with holes instead of the usual long open side. The follower is machined from solid steel and is easily recognized by the notch in the backstrap.

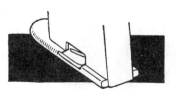

Another point of recognition is the unusual magazine floorplate release. Lift up on the wing like extensions and the floorplate can be pushed free of the magazine for cleaning. — E. J. HOFFSCHMIDT

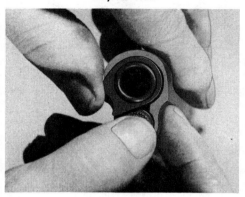

2 With thumb, press inward on knurled end of plug, at same time rotating barrel bushing ¼-turn clockwise to free plug and recoil spring assembly. Rest heel of gun on table so both hands may be used

1 Press magazine catch with right thumb and, at same time, withdraw magazine from receiver. Pull slide to rear and look in chamber to see that gun is not loaded. Close slide and pull trigger so hammer is down

IT'S VERY EASY....

Takedown of the .45 auto pistol may look difficult, but if you do the job step-by-step you will have no trouble

THE fact that the basic U. S. Pistol, Caliber .45, Model of 1911, is still the official handgun of our Service, speaks well for both the Colt firm and the board of U.S. Army officers involved in its selection. Composed of four line officers and one Ordnance officer, this selection board was convened by a Special Order of the Secretary of War dated December 28, 1906. Weapons referred to the board were all of .45 caliber and included autoloading pistols of Colt, Luger, Savage, Knoble, Bergmann, and White-Merrill design, and double-action revolvers by Colt and Smith & Wesson. Also considered was the unique automatic revolver of Webley-Fosbery make.

The evaluation program instituted by the board was designed to simulate rigorous service conditions as much as possible and included endurance, dust, rust, accuracy, functioning, and numerous other tests calculated to reveal design flaws and general service capabilities of the various guns submitted.

Service test revealing

By 1907 the board had completed its work and all but the Colt and Savage entries had been eliminated from consideration. A service test of both the Colt and Savage pistols was then authorized with two troops of U.S. Cavalry assigned for this purpose. This initial service test revealed that neither pistol had reached the desired perfection. Accordingly, the Ordnance Department instituted a series of further experiments and informal tests which eventually resulted in the appointment of a new selection board which convened in March of 1911.

Its superiority noted

The first paragraph of their final report is as follows:

"Of the two pistols, the board was of the opinion that the Colt is superior, because it is more reliable, more enduring, more easily disassembled when there are broken parts to be replaced, and the more accurate."

That, in short, explains why the Browning-Colt .45 Automatic pistol was eventually adopted as an official U.S. Service arm and formally designated as the U.S. Pistol, Caliber .45, Model of 1911. It is recorded that Colt made up nearly 200 experimental pistols before producing the model finally accepted.

Serviceably accurate, readily disassembled without the use of tools, and extremely rugged in every detail, the Model of 1911 has achieved a reputation for combat serviceability unsurpassed by any other military handgun.

It is admittedly a difficult weapon to shoot accurately and during the early 1920's several minor changes were made in an attempt to better its handling qualities. These changes included an arched mainspring housing, shorter hammer spur, Patridge-type sights, short trigger, and longer grip safety horn. These changes eliminated 'pinching' of the thumb web, and men with short fingers or small hands welcomed the shorter trigger. The better sights also improved the sight picture for target shooting purposes. This improved model was designated as the Model 1911-A1.

Not always wanted

Surprisingly enough, many present-day shooters prefer the original long trigger and old-style flat mainspring housing and will invariably 'demodernize' a new gun by substituting old-style parts for the new!

Target shooting with the 'as issued' Service pistol can be disappointing if the various moving parts are not precisely fitted and adjusted. In race-track terminology, the .45 Colt is a 'mudder' designed to function reliably with a good deal of foreign matter in its mechanism. The necessarily wide clearances between moving parts are desirable in a military but un-

3 Remove plug and recoil spring. If spring does not come free easily, rotate plug in counter-clockwise direction to separate plug from recoil spring

4 Rotate barrel bushing counter-clockwise until disengaged from slide. Remove barrel bushing

desirable in a target weapon. Thus, Colt in 1933 introduced their National Match .45, which is the same basic pistol machined to closer tolerances, with specially selected barrel and optional adjustable rear sight, and precision-fitted lock work. It enjoyed considerable popularity, but was discontinued during World War II. It was reinstated in the Colt handgun line in 1957 as the Colt Gold Cup National Match model.

Good scores attainable

Most U. S. marksmen now have their commercial or military .45's 'accurized' by one of the several experienced pistol-smiths specializing in this type of work. Scores obtainable today with such pistols would have been considered fantastic 20 years ago.

A modern variation of this basic Browning-Colt pistol is the Colt Commander, featuring frame and slide of lightweight Coltalloy. With a ¾-inch shorter barrel and weighing 26½ ounces as compared with 39 ounces for the Model 1911, this model was particularly designed for those who prefer lightweight but powerful handguns. Although not at this time an official Service arm, its development by Colt engineers was undoubtedly sparked by the present Service trend towards lightweight and miniature equipment. The demands of modern warfare have stimulated this type of development engineering, and we can be thankful that civilian manufacturers are often independently engaged in such costly research projects. Their unselfish efforts have helped to give the U.S. Serviceman some of the finest combat weapons available in the world today.

5 Slide is pulled to rear until lug on slide stop is opposite clearance notch on slide. Rounded end of slide stop pin protruding on right side of receiver is pushed inward by finger of left hand, which disengages slide stop from slide

6 Remove slide stop

7 Pull receiver group to rear and off slide. Recoil spring guide can now be lifted out

8 Push link forward and remove barrel from front of slide

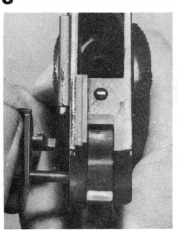

9 With hammer cocked, rotate safety lock almost to "On" position. It can now be pulled to left and away from receiver

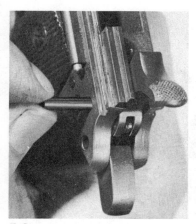
10 Remove hammer pin

11 Lift out hammer assembly

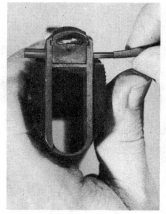
12 Using hammer strut, punch out mainspring housing pin

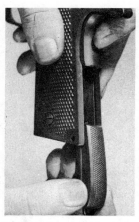
13 Slide mainspring housing off receiver

14 Lift out grip safety

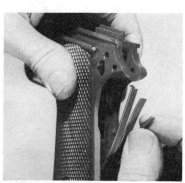
15 Lift out sear spring

16 Remove sear pin

DIRECTIONS FOR ASSEMBLY

To assemble slide: Insert extractor into slide with its flat side parallel to recess wall and push inward until notch near rear of extractor is opposite notch in right side of recess wall.
❪ Place firing pin spring on firing pin and insert assembly into firing pin hole in slide. Depress firing pin with fingertip and at same time insert firing pin stop with its rounded edge up and notch to left. Push upward on firing pin stop until it engages shoulder at rear of firing pin, thus holding firing pin in place within slide. Using hammer strut, depress firing pin to permit movement of firing pin stop upward into final position. End of firing pin should now protrude through hole in firing pin stop. ❪ Assemble link to barrel with link pin. ❪ Insert barrel assembly into slide and engage barrel locking lugs with recesses in slide. ❪ Insert barrel bushing into slide. ❪ Insert recoil spring guide into recoil spring and place assembly in slide with wings on recoil guide toward barrel.

To assemble receiver: Insert trigger. ❪ Insert magazine catch. ❪ Assemble sear and disconnector together with flat face of disconnector against trigger yoke and sear over disconnector, curved section inwards, lugs pointing to bottom. ❪ Insert sear pin from left side of receiver. ❪ Replace sear spring and retain in place with mainspring housing inserted ⅛″ short of final position. ❪ Replace hammer and strut assembly. ❪ Insert hammer pin. ❪ Replace grip safety. ❪ Cock hammer and replace safety lock. ❪ Lower hammer and with end of hammer strut in mainspring cap press mainspring housing into place and insert mainspring housing pin.

To complete assembly of pistol: Cock hammer. While holding both slide and receiver bottom side up and with link tilted forward, slide receiver into the slide assembly and insert slide stop, taking care that slide stop pin engages link. Push forward and inward to engage slide stop. ❪ Engage safety to lock receiver and slide together. ❪ Place plug over end of recoil spring. Push plug into slide until barrel bushing can be rotated into locked position. ❪ Disengage safety. ❪ Insert magazine.

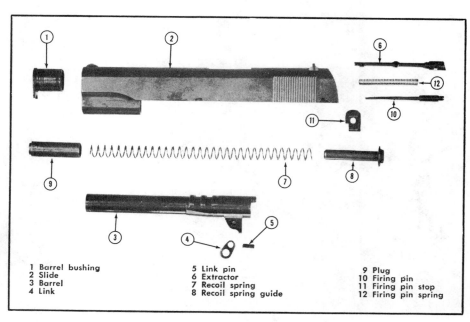

1 Barrel bushing	5 Link pin	9 Plug
2 Slide	6 Extractor	10 Firing pin
3 Barrel	7 Recoil spring	11 Firing pin stop
4 Link	8 Recoil spring guide	12 Firing pin spring

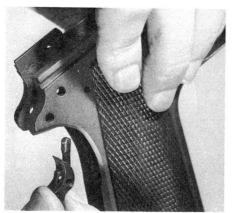

17 Lift out sear and disconnector. Note relationship of these parts to facilitate reassembly

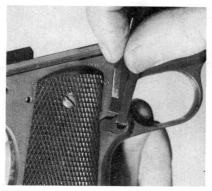

18 Depress magazine catch from left side; at same time rotate magazine catch lock ¼-turn counter-clockwise using lip of sear spring as screwdriver. Magazine catch assembly is then removed from right side of receiver. Catch assembly can be reduced to components by turning lock clockwise ¼-turn. Spring and lock will come out

19 Remove trigger

20 With hammer strut, push out link pin, separating link from barrel

21 With hammer strut, push in on firing pin. At same time place fingernail against top edge of firing pin stop and push downward, freeing firing pin stop from recess in slide

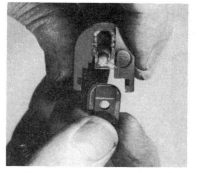

22 Remove firing pin stop. Firing pin assembly can now be removed from slide

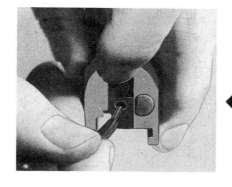

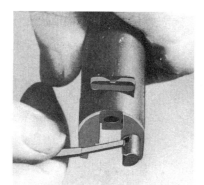

23 With hammer strut, pry out and remove extractor

24 Separate firing pin from firing pin spring

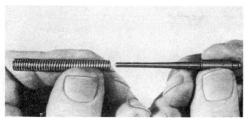

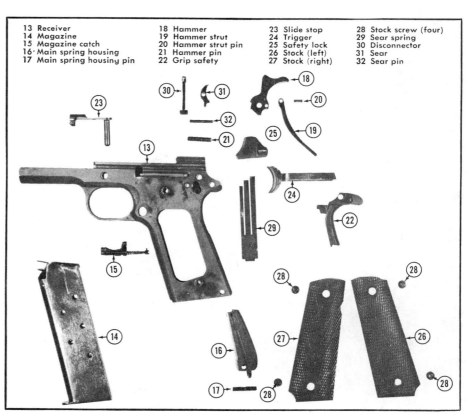

13 Receiver
14 Magazine
15 Magazine catch
16 Main spring housing
17 Main spring housing pin
18 Hammer
19 Hammer strut
20 Hammer strut pin
21 Hammer pin
22 Grip safety
23 Slide stop
24 Trigger
25 Safety lock
26 Stock (left)
27 Stock (right)
28 Stock screw (four)
29 Sear spring
30 Disconnector
31 Sear
32 Sear pin

Colt .22-.45 Conversion Unit

By EDWARD J. HOFFSCHMIDT

In 1938 the Colt firm introduced their cal. .22 long rifle conversion unit for the M1911 cal. .45 ACP pistol.

While the method of converting a cal. .45 pistol to cal. .22 was not revolutionary, the method of attaining a recoil effect similar to that developed by the .45 ACP cartridge was. The Williams floating chamber was the answer. The floating chamber is in effect a movable piston attached to the end of the barrel. When the .22 cartridge is fired, some of the gases are trapped between the barrel and the movable chamber. The gases thrust the chamber back with enough force to operate the slide and thus closely duplicate the recoil of the cal. .45 cartridge.

The Colt conversion unit has been modernized from time to time. The original unit was marked "Colt Service Model Conversion" with "Ace" inside of a triangle. A later model had the Colt rampant and the words ".22-.45 Conversion" added to the slide. This model eliminated the spring wire on the barrel that retained the ejector. The latest model illustrated here has a Micro adjustable rear sight and the serrations on the slide are slanted.

The current .22 conversion unit can be installed on any Model 1911-type pistol as well as the Super .38. But this unit cannot be used on the Colt Commander pistol.

A .45-.22 conversion unit to convert the cal. .22 Service Ace to cal. .45 ACP was manufactured for a few years, but did not prove popular. It was dropped following World War II.

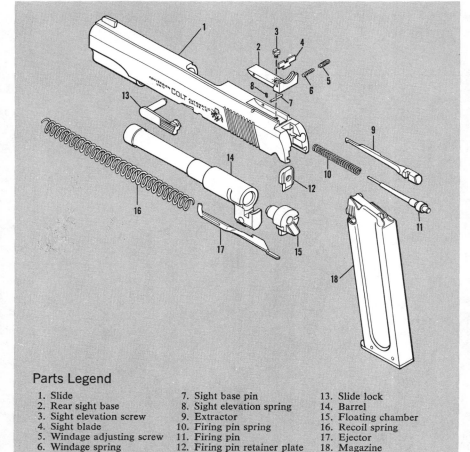

Parts Legend

1. Slide	7. Sight base pin	13. Slide lock
2. Rear sight base	8. Sight elevation spring	14. Barrel
3. Sight elevation screw	9. Extractor	15. Floating chamber
4. Sight blade	10. Firing pin spring	16. Recoil spring
5. Windage adjusting screw	11. Firing pin	17. Ejector
6. Windage spring	12. Firing pin retainer plate	18. Magazine

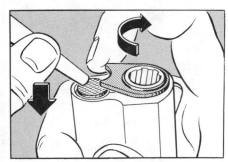

1 Center-fire slide assembly and magazine must be removed prior to installing conversion unit. First remove magazine and clear chamber. Push in knurled end of plug below barrel and rotate bushing ¼-turn clockwise. Ease out plug and recoil spring. Turn bushing counter-clockwise until it can be eased off barrel

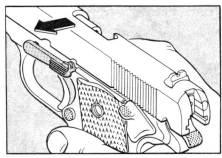

2 Pull slide to rear until smaller recess in lower edge of slide is even with end of slide stop. Press end of slide stop that projects from right side of frame and pull it free from left side. Ease slide and barrel forward off frame. Turn conversion unit upside down. Insert recoil spring guide in conversion unit recoil spring and place assembly in position on barrel. Slide conversion unit on frame. Install slide stop from the conversion unit and bushing of center-fire barrel. Place plug over recoil spring, then depress plug until bushing can be rotated ¼-turn counter-clockwise to secure plug and recoil spring assembly in slide

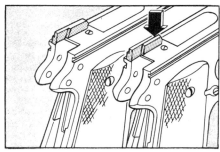

3 If conversion unit binds when installing it on a Super .38 pistol, the ejector may be at fault. To correct this, file a 1/32" wide bevel (arrow) along inside edge of ejector. This alteration to the gun will not affect its operation when firing cal. .38 cartridges

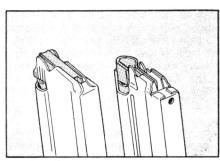

4 Colt Ace (r.) and conversion unit magazines are not interchangeable although they handle same ammunition. Conversion unit magazines are usually marked as such on the base. If not, they can be recognized by the narrow follower as compared with hollow sheet metal follower of Ace magazine. Follower button on conversion unit magazine runs diagonally up the magazine, while follower button of Ace magazine runs parallel to back and front strap

Clement M1907 Cal. .25 Pistol

PISTOL MAGAZINES

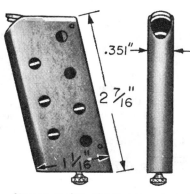

Clement pocket pistols are unique in that they are just the opposite of the usual pocket pistol in design. The M1907 Clement has a light slide and a heavy recoil spring, instead of a heavy slide and a light spring. Although the outline looks awkward, it fits the hand well. The barrel is considerably farther below the line of sight than in most automatic pistols. In general, Clement cal. .25 pistols were well made and finished.

Clement M1907 magazines can be readily identified by the small knob screwed into the magazine floorplate. The knob provides easy magazine removal.

The follower is bent sheet metal. The backstrap is about 3 times as thick as the side walls, making the magazine very sturdy.—EDWARD J. HOFFSCHMIDT

CZ M1950 Cal. .32

PISTOL MAGAZINES

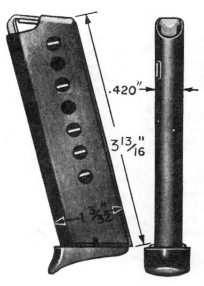

Shortly after World War II, the firm of Ceska Zbrojovka (CZ) brought out a new pocket pistol. While it resembles the Walther PP in outline, it is mechanically very different. The CZ pistol features a double-action trigger mechanism and a very convenient safety.

Like most Czech weapons, the CZ is well made. The magazine is no exception. It can be recognized by the single row of holes in the left side and absence of holes in the right side. Another point of recognition is the large D-shaped hole cut into the right front of the magazine.

The floorplate is removable. Some magazines are found with a plastic extension molded to the floorplate as shown here.—EDWARD J. HOFFSCHMIDT

By James M. Triggs

COLT
Double Action Revolver

ALTHOUGH self-cocking revolvers had been in use for many years prior to 1877, it was not until that year that such an arm was offered by Colt's Patent Fire Arms Mfg. Co., of Hartford, Conn. Designed in 1876 by Colt employee William Mason, the Double Action or DA model was initially introduced in cal. .38 only. Subsequently it was offered in cal. .41, with a small quantity also made in cal. .32. Distinctive features of the DA model are the double hand, birdshead grip, and the absence of the customary bolt locking notches on outer surface of the cylinder.

Collectors commonly refer to this model as the 'Lightning' although this was not a factory appellation, having been apparently coined by B. Kittridge & Co., of Cincinnati, Ohio, who used it in their arms catalogs to identify the original cal. .38 model. The name 'Thunderer', applied to the later cal. .41 version, also stemmed from this firm and was likewise not an official Colt name.

The DA model was offered both with and without rod ejector and in various barrel lengths from 2″ up to 7½″, with the 7″ and 7½″ barrel lengths available on special order only. Manufacture of this model ceased in 1910.

The late Jim Triggs was a writer-illustrator and well known gun collector.

DISASSEMBLY PROCEDURE

Due to the intricacy of the lock mechanism of the Lightning Colt, special care should be taken in disassembling to note the exact relative positions of all parts to facilitate correct reassembly.

To remove cylinder (8), open loading gate (13) and press in cylinder pin lock screw (10). Draw cylinder pin (7) forward as far as it will go. Cylinder may be pushed out of main frame (9) after pulling hammer (29) back slightly. This is sufficient disassembly for normal cleaning purposes.

To disassemble lock mechanism, proceed as follows:

a) Remove grip screw (52) and grips (49). Remove backstrap screws (42) and butt screw (43) and drop backstrap (41) off main frame (9).

b) Loosen mainspring tension screw (47) and remove mainspring screw (40). Disengage top of mainspring (39) from stirrup (33) and remove.

c) Remove rear and front trigger guard screws (45 & 46), pull trigger (18) back slightly, and remove trigger guard (44) from main frame, exposing inside lock mechanism.

d) Remove sear screw (28) and drop out sear (27) and hand and cylinder stop tension spring (35).

e) Remove hammer screw (32) and drop hammer (29) down out of main frame. Disengage trigger strut (25) from its seat in hammer and remove hammer.

f) Loosen trigger spring screw (37) and remove trigger screw (19). Draw trigger (18) out of main frame with hand (17) intact. Cylinder stop (38) may be dropped out of its hole in left side of main frame. Trigger strut spring (22) and hand spring (23) may be removed from trigger (18) by unscrewing hand and strut spring screw (24). Trigger strut (25) and trigger roller (20) may be removed from trigger by drifting out their respective retaining pins (26 & 21).

g) Ejector assembly (2,3,4,5,6) may be removed by unscrewing ejector housing screw (3) and drawing ejector housing (2) forward out of its seat in main frame. Loading gate (13) may be removed by unscrewing loading gate catch screw (16) from underside of main frame. Drop out loading gate catch and spring (14 & 15). Swing loading gate down and pull forward out of main frame.

Reassembly procedure follows the reverse order of the steps outlined above.

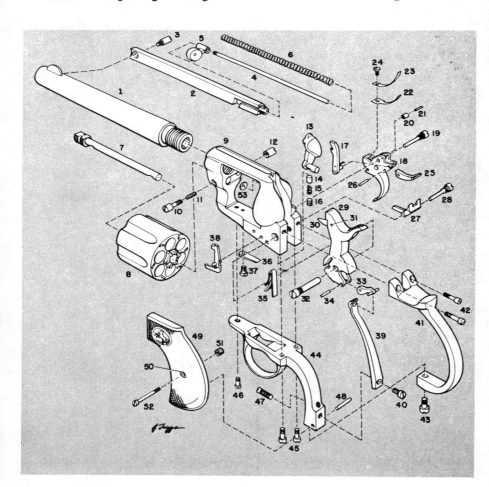

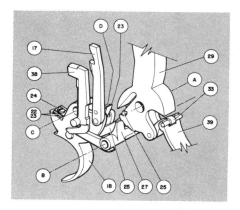

1 This perspective view shows lock mechanism with all parts in proper position as they are when assembled inside the main frame. For greater clarity of detail, hammer screw (32), trigger screw (19), and sear screw (28) are not shown but their respective center-lines are indicated at "A", "B", and "C". Also omitted for clarity is hand and cylinder stop tension spring (35) which is inserted into bottom of frame so its wider, flat arm presses against rear of hand cut in frame and its 2 forward, curving arms press against rear edges of hand and cylinder stop respectively. Trigger spring (36) is also omitted to avoid confusion. "D" indicates the pin of the hand against which hand spring (23) bears

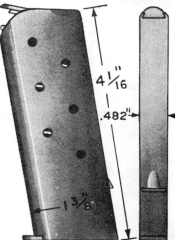

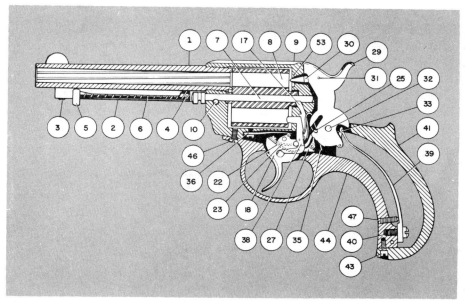

2 This drawing shows entire revolver in longitudinal section and demonstrates proper relationship of all interior parts. Note that hand and cylinder stop tension spring (35) is shown here with its long arm **behind** hammer for clarity only. In assembling the lock mechanism in this position, this spring is on the **left side** of hammer

Parts Legend

1. Barrel
2. Ejector housing
3. Ejector housing screw
4. Ejector rod
5. Ejector rod head
6. Ejector spring
7. Cylinder pin
8. Cylinder
9. Main frame
10. Cylinder pin lock screw
11. Cylinder pin lock screw spring
12. Cylinder pin lock nut
13. Loading gate
14. Loading gate catch
15. Loading gate catch spring
16. Loading gate catch screw
17. Hand
18. Trigger
19. Trigger screw
20. Trigger roller
21. Trigger roller pin
22. Trigger strut spring
23. Hand spring
24. Hand and strut spring screw
25. Trigger strut
26. Trigger strut pin
27. Sear
28. Sear screw

29. Hammer
30. Firing pin
31. Firing pin rivet
32. Hammer screw
33. Stirrup
34. Stirrup pin
35. Hand and cylinder stop tension spring
36. Trigger spring
37. Trigger spring screw
38. Cylinder stop
39. Mainspring
40. Mainspring screw
41. Backstrap
42. Backstrap screws (2)
43. Butt screw
44. Trigger guard
45. Rear trigger guard screws (2)
46. Front trigger guard screw
47. Mainspring tension screw
48. Grip pin*
49. Grips, hard rubber (left hand only shown)
50. Escutcheon*
51. Escutcheon nut*
52. Grip screw*
53. Recoil plate

* Grip pin, grip screw, and escutcheons were not supplied on 'Lightning' revolvers with one-piece hardwood grips.

Colt Model 1878 DA Revolver

BY DOUG WICKLUND

Exploded Views:

More than 50,000 of the Colt Model 1878 (above) and Model 1902 revolvers were produced by 1905. The Model 1902, sometimes erroneously called the "Alaskan" model, was for Filipino police use.

COLT's first heavy-framed double-action revolver was, in some respects, an evolution of its smaller 1877 "Lightning" that was made for cartridges ranging only from .32 to .41 cal.

In contrast to the Model 1877, the Model 1878 had an integral grip frame and was primarily made for the .45 Colt or .44-40 Win. cartridges. Lesser quantities were made in .32-20 and .38-40 for domestic use and for .450, .455 and .476 for the British trade.

Other chamberings, perhaps made on special order basis, have been reported ranging from the .22 rimfire through the 11 mm German Ordnance cartridge; cataloged barrel lengths ran from 3½″ to 7½″.

A removable circular plate on the left side of the frame allowed access to the internal parts, an important consideration due to the intricate construction of the solid-framed Model 1878. Lockup was affected by indexing cuts on the ratchet rather than the periphery of the cylinder, but ejection of spent cartridges still relied on the proven ejector rod system of Colt's Single Action Army revolver.

The first Model 1878s had checkered walnut grip panels, but later examples left the factory with checkered hard rubber panels embossed with the traditional rampant colt motif in an oval cartouche. Checkered walnut, ivory or pearl grip panels were available as options.

Produced from 1878 to 1905, the majority of these revolvers went into the civilian market, but an order for 5,000 revolvers from the Philippine Constabulary forces in 1901 (6″ barrel, .45 Colt cal., hard rubber grip panels) resulted in production of a modified revolver with lengthened trigger and a larger trigger guard. Collectors now call this revolver the Model 1902 Philippine variation; only 4,600 are estimated to have been actually produced.

The total production run for the Models 1878 and 1902 is estimated to have been near 51,210 before manufacture ceased in late 1905.

Disassembly Instructions

Open the loading gate (13) and pull back the hammer (26) to the half-cock position. Rotate the cylinder (8) and check that each of the chambers is empty.

To remove the cylinder, open the loading gate and press in on the base pin catch screw (10). Draw the base pin (6) forward for removal. The cylinder can be pushed out of the frame (9) after pulling the hammer back slightly. For cleaning purposes, no further disassembly is required or advised.

To disassemble the lock mechanism, remove the grip plate screw (28) and the grip plates (42). Remove the mainspring screw (34). Disengage the top of the mainspring (33) from the hammer stirrup (31). Take out the front and rear trigger guard screws (39 & 40).

In reassembly, be sure the longer of the two screws is replaced in the front trigger guard screw hole.

Pull the trigger guard (38) down and out of the frame. To remove the trigger spring (21), disengage the top of the spring from the trigger stirrup (22) and tilt the spring up and out. (**Fig. 1**)

Remove the hammer screw (29) to detach the sideplate (30). Pull the hammer back and out through the frame opening. (**Fig. 2**)

To remove the trigger (18), drive out the trigger pin (19) to the left, then push the trigger up into the frame to free the hand (16). The hand can be pulled up and out through the sideplate hole. Depress the front of the trigger and pull downward for removal.

Drive out the sear pin (25) to the left and lift out the sear (24). To remove the loading gate (13), loosen the loading gate spring screw (15) and using a screwdriver, pry up the loading gate spring (14). Pull the loading gate out toward the barrel for removal.

Note that the firing pin (27) is held in place by a staked-in rivet and should not be removed except for replacement.

The ejector assembly can be removed by unscrewing the ejector tube screw (3) and drawing the ejector tube (2) forward out of its seat in the frame.

To remove the base pin catch screw (10), use two screwdrivers (**Fig. 3**) to hold the base pin catch (12) and unscrew the lock screw.

Reassembly is in reverse order. ■

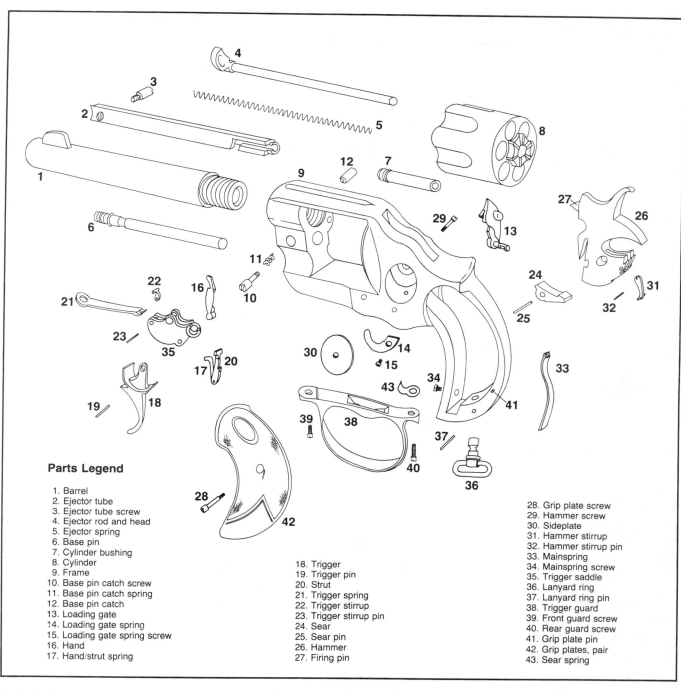

Parts Legend

1. Barrel
2. Ejector tube
3. Ejector tube screw
4. Ejector rod and head
5. Ejector spring
6. Base pin
7. Cylinder bushing
8. Cylinder
9. Frame
10. Base pin catch screw
11. Base pin catch spring
12. Base pin catch
13. Loading gate
14. Loading gate spring
15. Loading gate spring screw
16. Hand
17. Hand/strut spring

18. Trigger
19. Trigger pin
20. Strut
21. Trigger spring
22. Trigger stirrup
23. Trigger stirrup pin
24. Sear
25. Sear pin
26. Hammer
27. Firing pin

28. Grip plate screw
29. Hammer screw
30. Sideplate
31. Hammer stirrup
32. Hammer stirrup pin
33. Mainspring
34. Mainspring screw
35. Trigger saddle
36. Lanyard ring
37. Lanyard ring pin
38. Trigger guard
39. Front guard screw
40. Rear guard screw
41. Grip plate pin
42. Grip plates, pair
43. Sear spring

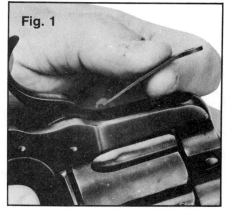

Fig. 1

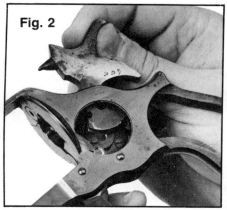

Fig. 2

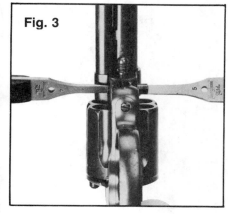

Fig. 3

COLT DOUBLE-ACTION NEW ARMY and NEW NAVY REVOLVERS

By James M. Triggs

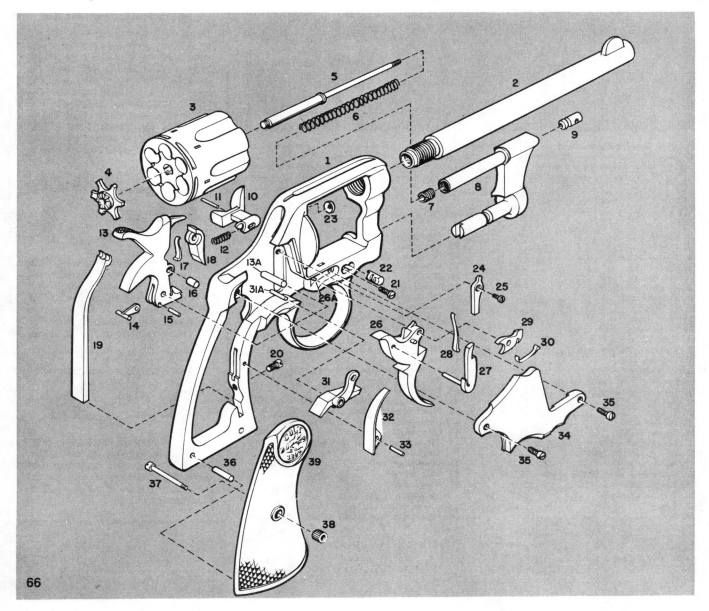

IN 1889 Colt's Patent Fire Arms Mfg. Co., Hartford, Conn., offered their first swing-out cylinder revolver. It was chambered for the Colt cal. .38 long and short cartridges. Almost simultaneously this revolver was adopted by the Navy Dept. The Army at the time was equipped with cal. .45 Colt and Smith & Wesson single-action revolvers.

The War Dept. soon evidenced interest in this new arm. On Apr. 15, 1889, a Board appointed by Brig. Gen. S. V. Benet, Chief of Ordnance, convened at Springfield Armory, Springfield, Mass., to test samples of the cal. .38 Smith & Wesson Safety Hammerless revolver and the cal. .38 Colt Double-Action Navy pattern revolver.

The finding of the board was that both revolvers possessed certain advantages and that a competitive test in service would be required to determine the superior weapon. In 1890 Ordnance purchased 100 each of the Colt and Smith & Wesson revolvers which were then issued to the Cavalry for trial.

On Apr. 25, 1892, S. B. Elkins, Secretary of War, approved the recommendation by the Chief of Ordnance, Brig. Gen. D. W. Flagler, that a cal. .38 Service revolver be adopted in lieu of the cal. .45 Colt revolver then standard. Flagler's recommendation was based upon reports of troop commanders who had tested these revolvers plus the findings of a final selection board convened Nov. 28, 1891, which recommended adoption of the Colt revolver with modifications to correct certain defects encountered during the trials. The board reconvened Mar. 1, 1892, to examine a Colt revolver incorporating certain improvements and recommended its adoption as modified.

The initial contract let to the Colt's Patent Fire Arms Mfg. Co., Hartford, Conn., was for 5000 cal. .38 double-action revolvers of the final pattern approved for adoption by the Secretary of War. This revolver was designated Army Model 1892 and the solid-head reloadable case ammunition for it was produced at Frankford Arsenal. Additional quantities of the Model 1892 revolver were later ordered and issued.

Use of the Model 1892 in service indicated that its design, which allowed operation of the hammer without fully closing the cylinder, could damage the arm. Accordingly, a hammer and trigger lock was devised to correct this condition. Model 1892 revolvers in the hands of troops were recalled and replaced with Model 1894 revolvers obtained under contract with Colt's.

Subsequently the Model 1892 revolvers were reworked by Colt's to conform with Model 1894 specifications.

Various Service models

A summation of the various Service models is contained in the *Description of the Colt's Double-Action Revolver Caliber .38*, published in 1917 by the Government Printing Office, which states: "The Colt's double-action revolvers, caliber .38, in service are marked Army Models 1894, 1896, 1901, and 1903. The first model issued was that of 1892, but all revolvers of that model were altered into model of 1894 by the addition of the locking lever, which is pivoted by its screw in a recess

(Text continued on following page)

DISASSEMBLY PROCEDURE

To remove cylinder and crane assembly, unscrew crane lock screw (21) and withdraw crane lock (22). Press latch (10) back and swing out cylinder. Grasp crane (8) and pull forward out of frame (1). Further disassembly of cylinder and crane is not recommended. However, if this disassembly is absolutely necessary, note

Parts Legend

1. Frame
2. Barrel
3. Cylinder
4. Ejector & ratchet
5. Ejector rod
6. Ejector spring
7. Crane bushing
8. Crane
9. Ejector head
10. Latch
11. Latch pin
12. Latch spring
13. Hammer
13A. Hammer pin
14. Stirrup
15. Stirrup pin
16. Strut pin
17. Strut spring
18. Strut
19. Mainspring
20. Mainspring tension screw
21. Crane lock screw
22. Crane lock
23. Recoil plate
24. Locking lever
25. Locking lever screw
26. Trigger
26A. Trigger pin
27. Hand
28. Hand spring
29. Bolt
30. Bolt spring
31. Rebound lever
31A. Rebound lever pin
32. Rebound lever spring
33. Rebound lever spring pin
34. Side-plate
35. Side-plate screws (2)
36. Stock pin
37. Stock screw
38. Escutcheons (2), right only shown
39. Stocks (2), right only shown

that, after pressing in ejector rod (5), clearing ratchet from cylinder, ejector and ratchet (4) must be unscrewed from ejector rod *clockwise* and a special wrench or spanner will be necessary to remove crane bushing (7).

To disassemble lock mechanism, unscrew stock screw (37) and remove stocks (39). Remove side-plate screws (35). Loosen side-plate (34) by turning revolver over and tapping frame with a fiber or wooden mallet. If it is necessary to pry out the side-plate to any extent, do so most gently and gradually to avoid burring edges of side-plate cut in frame. Remove side-plate, exposing lock mechanism.

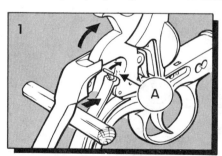

Lift hand (27) out of trigger. Loosen mainspring tension screw (20). Pull hammer to full cock and slip a ½" wooden dowel or handle of a small screwdriver between mainspring (19) and rear strap of frame. Pull trigger, releasing hammer and allowing stirrup (14) to rise clear of its seat in end of mainspring as shown at "A" in sketch 1. Remove dowel and pull mainspring up out of its seat in frame. Rebound lever spring (32) may be removed by drifting out its pin (33). Pull hammer back to almost full-cock position and lift out of frame. With the blade of a small screwdriver, lift bolt (29) up off its pin and remove. Rebound lever (31) and trigger (26) may now be lifted out of frame. Locking lever (24) is removed by unscrewing locking lever screw (25). Latch may be removed by drifting out latch pin (11) with a very thin punch,

withdrawing latch (10) and spring (12) toward the front.

Removal of hammer pin (13A), trigger pin (26A), or rebound lever pin (31A) from frame is not recommended and is seldom if ever necessary.

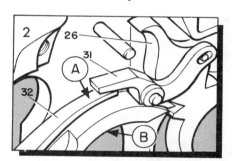

In reassembling lock mechanism, replace latch assembly, locking lever, and trigger first. Replace rebound lever spring and pin. Compress tip of rebound lever spring with pliers, the jaws of which have been taped or otherwise covered to protect the finish of the arm, applied at A and B as shown in sketch 2. Drop rebound lever into place while holding spring compressed fully. A little juggling will be necessary when replacing bolt (29), and bolt spring (30) must be pressed down with blade of small screwdriver or other small tool to clear forward arm of rebound lever before bolt can be pressed all the way down into position on trigger pin (26A).

Pull trigger back and replace hammer. Replace mainspring in its seat and compress with a dowel as previously described. Pull stirrup back until it is in position over its seat in tip of mainspring. Pull trigger releasing hammer and withdraw dowel. Replace hand and push forward into its slot. When replacing side-plate, be sure hand spring slips into the recess milled into reverse of side-plate. Replace side-plate screws and stocks. Replace cylinder and crane assembly. Place crane lock and crane lock screw together and press into frame, tightening crane lock screw as it engages its threads.

in the left side of the frame and prevents the hammer being cocked until the cylinder is positively closed and locked. The models of 1894 and 1896 are identical. The model of 1901 differs from the previous models in having the butt swivel for lanyard. The model of 1903 differs from the model of 1901 in having the diameter of the bore reduced to insure better accuracy and in having a smaller and better shaped handle. The model of 1901 revolvers last made have the thinner stocks".

It is important to note that Service arms are often turned in for repair at arsenals and that replacement parts may differ in pattern from the original. A case in point is use of the .357" groove diameter Model 1903 barrel for rebarreling of Models 1892, 1896, and 1901 revolvers with original .363" groove diameter barrels.

Commercial versions

Concurrent with production of Service revolvers for the Navy and War Depts., Colt's manufactured commercial versions with hard-rubber grips (the Service models had plain walnut grips). These were advertised as New Army and New Navy revolvers and in catalogs and advertisements were given the Service model designations, such as New Navy Model of 1895 or New Army Model of 1894, despite the fact that the guns were substantially identical. The Service revolvers had 6" barrels and were chambered for the cal. .38 Colt long and short cartridges. Commercial models were offered in 3", 4½", and 6" barrel lengths and in several calibers, including .38 Colt long and short, .41 Colt long and short, .32-20 WCF, and .38 Special.

In the spring of 1904 Colt's offered a target version designated Officers Model and chambered for the .38 S&W Special cartridge. It featured adjustable rear and front sights and immediately became popular with target shooters.

The Marine Corps in 1905 adopted a Colt cal. .38 revolver mechanically identical to the Army and Navy arms, but with rounded, narrower butt. The Service version was furnished with butt swivel, but this fixture was not present on the companion commercial model, optionally available in blue and nickel finishes.

In 1908 production of the New Army, New Navy, Marine Corps Model, and 1904 pattern Officers Model revolvers was discontinued. In their stead Colt's introduced the Colt Army Special revolver with greatly improved lockwork, double leaf mainspring, and cylinder revolving to the right. The target version of the Army Special revolver, also introduced in 1908, was again designated Officers Model. ∎

PISTOL MAGAZINES

Colt .38 Military Model Pistol

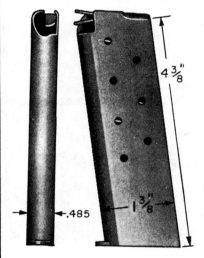

The Browning-designed Colt .38 Military Model pistol was produced commercially from about 1902 to 1928. Commonly called the Military Model 1902, this pistol fires the .38 ACP cartridge and should not be used with the more powerful .38 Super round.

The blued sheet steel 8-round magazine of the Model 1902 resembles that of the Colt .38 Sporting Model pistol, but is ⅜" longer. One of the main identifying features is the bent-down part of the follower that lifts the slide hold-open catch when the magazine is empty.

Another identifying feature is the backstrap notch. The base bears the marking shown or "MIL. COLT .38 CAL." Some bases are unmarked.
—E J. HOFFSCHMIDT

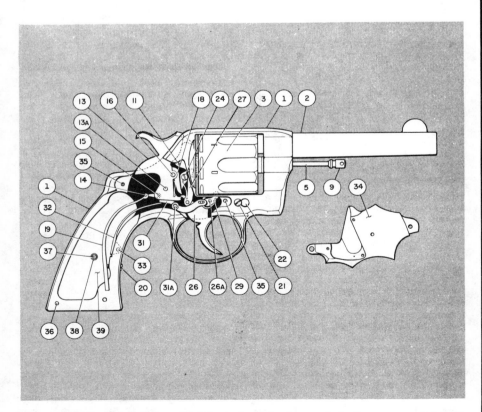

This sectionalized view shows all of the lock mechanism parts in the proper relationship when assembled. Note that the inner (reverse) face of the side-plate (34) is shown here

Colt Deringer No. 3

By James M. Triggs

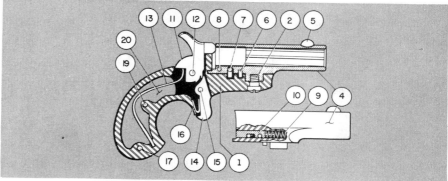

COLT's Patent Fire Arms Mfg. Co., of Hartford, Conn., began manufacture of single-shot cartridge pistols about 1872 after the acquisition of patents and other assets of the National Arms Co. of Brooklyn, N. Y. The National Arms Co., formed about 1863, was the successor to the Moore Patent Fire Arms Co., manufacturer of the single-shot cartridge pistol patented (No. 31,473) Feb. 19, 1861, by Daniel Moore. As made by Colt's, the National Deringer (Moore patent) was offered with both metal and wood stocks in cal. .41 rimfire only. At about the same time Colt's also began production of a small cal. .41 rimfire single-shot pistol based upon Patent No. 105,388 granted July 12, 1870, to Colt employee F. Alexander Thuer. The Thuer pistol was of side-swinging barrel type, similar in appearance to side-swing single-shot pocket pistols manufactured at the time by J. M. Marlin, Hopkins & Allen, Forehand & Wadsworth, and others. The unique patented feature of the Thuer pistol was the automatic ejector which eliminated the necessity for manual case ejection after opening of the breech. As stated in a Colt advertisement of 1872, "The exploded shell need not be touched by the fingers."

The Thuer pistol weighed 6½ ozs. as against 10 ozs. for the Colt-National pistol with metal grips. It was available with silver-plated frame and blued barrel, or with silver-plated frame and barrel. Stocks were optionally of walnut, rosewood, ivory, or pearl. There was a change made in the barrel marking as well as changes in shape of hammer and frame during its period of manufacture, which extended to 1912. Frame of the pistol was always of bronze, with other parts of iron.

Present collectors designate the Thuer-designed pistol as the Third Model whereas the Colt-National metal-grip and wood-grip pistols are designated First Model and Second Model respectively.

In late 1959 Colt's introduced the Colt Deringer No. 4 chambered for the cal. .22 short cartridge. Primarily offered to interest the collector of Colt arms, it features a frame and barrel die-cast from zinc alloy, but is otherwise a close replica of the original Thuer model.

DISASSEMBLY PROCEDURE

To disassemble barrel assembly, remove barrel screw (2) from underside of frame (1). With hammer at half-cock or safety position, swing rear of barrel (4) to right and remove barrel from frame. Remove barrel latch and ejector screw (8) from left side of barrel while pressing barrel latch and ejector in. Withdraw barrel latch & ejector (10) and spring (9) from rear of barrel. Draw barrel latch release pin (7) from left side of barrel. Removal of barrel stop pin (6) is seldom necessary and should not be attempted during normal disassembly.

To disassemble lock mechanism, remove grip screw (19) and grips (20).

Mainspring (13) may be tapped out of its seat in frame and removed. Remove hammer screw (12) from left side of frame and withdraw hammer (11) from top of frame while pressing back on trigger. Remove trigger screw (15) from left side of frame and drop trigger (14) and trigger spring (16) out bottom of frame. NOTE: Trigger spring shown in exploded drawing is of the coil type which rests in a shallow hole at rear of trigger. Earlier types are provided with a flat, V-shaped trigger spring, shown in longitudinal-section drawing. The barrel latch bushing (3) may be removed only by drilling. Reassemble in reverse. ∎

Parts Legend

1. Frame
2. Barrel screw
3. Barrel latch bushing
4. Barrel
5. Front sight
6. Barrel stop pin
7. Barrel latch release pin
8. Barrel latch & ejector screw
9. Barrel latch & ejector spring
10. Barrel latch & ejector
11. Hammer
12. Hammer screw
13. Mainspring
14. Trigger
15. Trigger screw
16. Trigger spring (flat or coil type)
17. Grip pin
18. Escutcheon (2, right & left)
19. Grip screw
20. Grip (2, right & left)

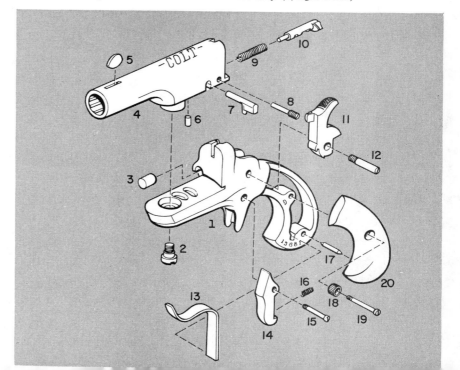

COLT
FRONTIER SCOUT REVOLVER

By Thomas E. Wessel

In late 1957 Colt's Patent FireArms Mfg. Co., of Hartford, Conn. announced production of a new .22 caliber single-action revolver patterned after their time-tried Model P, Single Action Army revolver. Designated the Frontier Scout, it was about 4/5 the size of its progenitor and featured a one-piece aluminum alloy grip frame. The cylinder frame was also of aluminum alloy, but the barrel and cylinder were of steel. Barrel length was originally 4-3/4 inches. Empty weight was 23

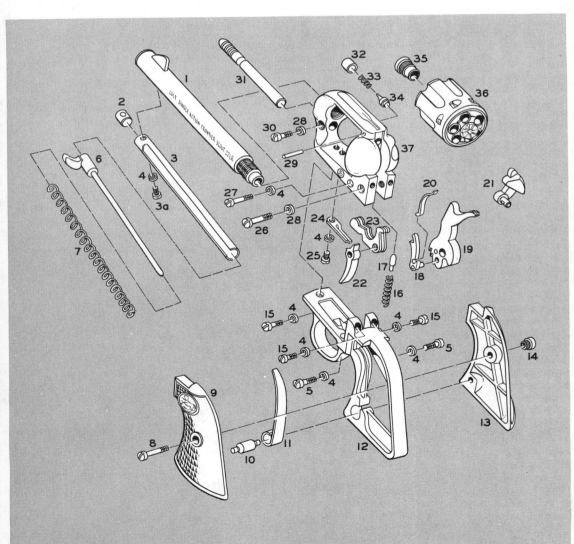

Parts Legend

1. Barrel
2. Ejector tube plug
3. Ejector rod tube
3a. Ejector tube screw
4. Nylon washer, small (8)
5. Backstrap screw, bottom (2)
6. Ejector rod
7. Ejector spring
8. Stock screw
9. Stock, left
10. Stock pin
11. Mainspring
12. Backstrap
13. Stock, right
14. Stock screw nut
15. Backstrap screw, top (3)
16. Gate spring.
17. Gate detent
18. Hand and post
19. Hammer
20. Hand spring
21. Gate
22. Trigger
23. Bolt
24. Bolt and trigger spring
25. Bolt spring screw
26. Hammer screw
27. Bolt and trigger screw
28. Nylon washer, large (2)
29. Recoil cup pin
30. Base pin screw
31. Base pin
32. Recoil cup
33. Firing pin spring
34. Firing pin
35. Cylinder bushing
36. Cylinder
37. Frame

ounces. Initially the Frontier Scout was furnished in dual-tone finish, in which the grip and cylinder frames were bright and the barrel and cylinder were blue. An all blue version was announced in September 1958.

The 9-1/2"-barrel, Buntline Frontier Scout was introduced in July 1958, available in blue finish only. In July 1959 Colt began delivery of Frontier Scout revolvers chambered for the then-new .22 Winchester Magnum Rimfire cartridge.

Colt Industries terminated production of Frontier Scout revolvers in 1970, replacing the revolver with the "Peacemaker" rimfire and then the "New Frontier" version.

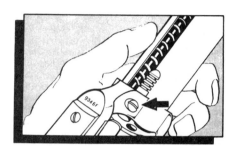

1 To remove cylinder (36), first insure that the hammer (19) is in half-cock position with cylinder free to rotate. Open loading gate (21). Next, using screwdriver, remove base pin screw (30) and washer (28). Withdraw base pin (31). Cylinder may now be removed from loading gate side of arm

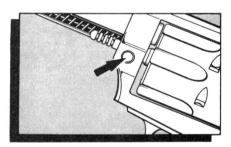

2 Reassemble cylinder into revolver in reverse order. Locking notch in base pin must be properly aligned with base pin screw hole in left side of frame (37), otherwise screw cannot be replaced

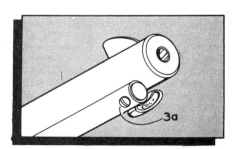

3 To remove ejector rod tube (3) and assembly, including ejector rod (6) and ejector spring (7), unscrew ejector tube screw (3a) holding assembly to right lower side of barrel (1). Entire assembly may now be removed. Reassemble in reverse order, insuring that small nylon washer (4) is replaced

Erma .22 Cal. Target Pistol

PISTOL MAGAZINES

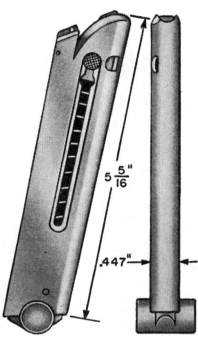

The Erma magazine is almost identical with that of the Luger, or Erma Luger conversion unit magazine, but due to the location of the magazine catch slot it cannot be used in a conversion unit without alteration. Like the rest of the gun, Erma pistol magazines are very well made. They are built of steel at least three times as thick as that used in average pistol magazines.

The Erma magazine aluminum base plug is made and numbered exactly as in the Luger magazine.

Magazine malfunctions are kept to a minimum by the strong feed lips. Since these lips are too thick to spring and free the cartridges, a leaf spring is riveted to the left side of the magazine.—E. J. HOFFSCHMIDT

FRENCH MODEL 1950

PISTOL MAGAZINES

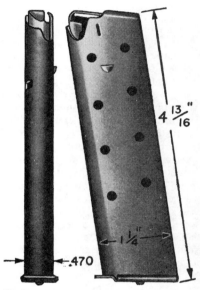

The French Model 1950 pistol is one of the best French pistols put out to date and is an excellent military weapon. The grip is good and the safety catch is very convenient. It fires the powerful 9 mm. Luger cartridge from a Browning-type locked breech. The gun is easy to field strip. With slide removed, the entire sear mechanism can be lifted out.

The magazine is a bit longer than the average 9 mm. magazine since it was designed to hold 9 cartridges in a straight column. The floorplate is detachable and resembles that of the P38 pistol. The plate is generally marked 1950.

The magazine follower is made from a sheet metal stamping but is well designed and functions perfectly. The small louver or dimple which protrudes from the side of the magazine operates the magazine safety and serves as another point to identify this magazine.— E. J. HOFFSCHMIDT

Colt Gold Cup National Match Mark III Pistol

By JAMES M. TRIGGS

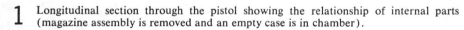

THE Colt Gold Cup National Match Mark III cal. .38 Special semi-automatic pistol was introduced in 1962.

The Gold Cup model was first offered in 1961. Changes in the barrel specifications were made shortly thereafter. After limited production of the modified pistol, Colt's completely redesigned the pistol and designated it Mark III.

The rifling specifications of the barrel were changed to give a nominal bore diameter of .347", with groove diameter of .357". Barrel chamber diameter was reduced .002" and the chamber wall was threaded to increase friction between the cartridge case and chamber walls as a result of the outward pressure from the expanding powder gases. This holds the barrel and slide together until the bullet has cleared the barrel and the pressure drops. The forcing cone, or bullet seat between chamber mouth and origin of the rifling, is much shorter in the Mark III barrel than in barrels of the previous models. The barrel bushing fits the frame tightly and the barrel is ground at the muzzle to give minimum play between slide and bushing when slide is in battery.

A depressor and depressor spring act on the sear to keep the hammer from following as the slide goes into battery.

The Mark III pistol was fitted with Colt "Accro", rear sights and a Patridge front. More recent Colt Gold Cup pistols - the Series 70 and Series 80 - have used Colt-Eliason target sights.

Takedown Procedure

Press in magazine catch (4) at left side of receiver and drop magazine assembly (2) out butt of pistol. Draw slide to rear and check chamber to be sure pistol is unloaded. Pull trigger and let hammer down with thumb. Press inward on knurled end of recoil spring plug (42) and turn barrel bushing approximately 1/4-turn clockwise. (Due to close fit of bushing to slide, a wrench fitted to bushing should be employed to loosen it.) Remove plug (42) and recoil spring (43) from front of slide. Rotate barrel bushing counterclockwise until it disengages from slide and remove to front.

Draw slide to rear until lug at rear end of slide stop (3) lines up with clearance cut on lower left hand edge of slide. Press in rounded end of slide stop pin which protrudes from right hand side of receiver.

Remove slide stop from left side of receiver. Pull slide forward off receiver and remove recoil spring guide (44). Remove barrel from front of slide, taking care not to lose barrel return spring (41).

Slide group. Press in on rear end of firing pin (46) with a small punch until it clears firing pin stop (45). Remove firing pin stop from bottom of slide. Firing pin and firing pin spring (47) may be removed from rear of slide. Extractor (48) may be pried from rear of slide with small screwdriver. Removal of rear sight assembly (39) is accomplished by drifting out rear sight leaf pin (38). Detailed disassembly of rear sight is shown on following page. Reassemble in reverse.

Complete disassembly of rear sight assembly is not recommended except when necessary for repair.

Receiver group. With hammer at full cock position, rotate safety lock (9) toward its "on" position until it can be pulled out of left side of receiver. Drift out hammer pin (8) and remove hammer (27) and hammer strut (29) from top rear of receiver. Hammer strut can be removed from hammer by drifting out hammer strut pin (28). Drift out mainspring housing pin (13) and slide mainspring housing (14) out of grooves at rear of receiver. Mainspring (17), mainspring cap (16), and mainspring housing pin retainer (18) are removed from housing after drifting out mainspring cap pin (15). Lift grip safety (26) out rear of receiver and remove sear spring (19) from rear of receiver. Drift out sear pin (7); drop sear (30) and disconnector (31) with depressor (32) and depressor spring (33) out of receiver. (See Fig. 2 for reassembly.)

Remove stock screws (11) and stocks (12—not shown in exploded drawing) from sides of receiver. Depress magazine catch (4) from left side of receiver and, using a small screwdriver, turn magazine catch lock (6) 1/4-turn counterclockwise from right side of receiver. Remove entire magazine catch assembly from right side of receiver (Note: magazine catch assembly parts are shown at left side of receiver in exploded drawing for clarity. They are assembled in the receiver from hole in right side.) Turn magazine catch lock (6) 1/4-turn clockwise to separate catch lock, spring (5), and catch (4). Remove trigger assembly (20) with trigger stop (21) from rear of receiver. Reassemble receiver group parts in reverse.

1 Longitudinal section through the pistol showing the relationship of internal parts (magazine assembly is removed and an empty case is in chamber).

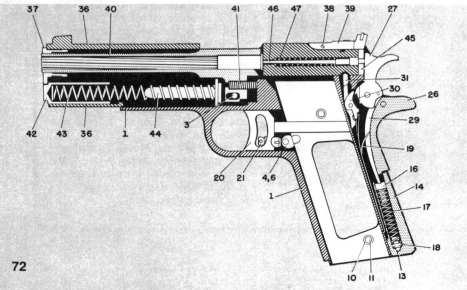

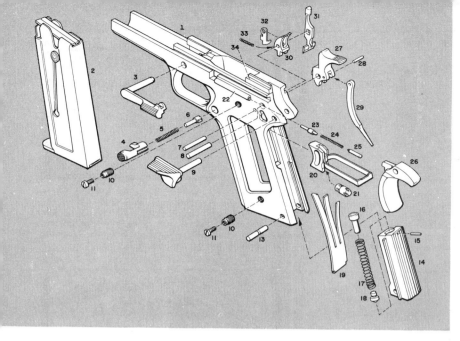

PARTS, RECEIVER GROUP—

1. Receiver
2. Magazine assembly
3. Slide stop
4. Magazine catch

5. Magazine catch spring
6. Magazine catch lock
7. Sear pin
8. Hammer pin

9. Safety lock
10. Stock screw bushing (4)
11. Stock screw (4)
12. Stocks (2, not shown)
13. Mainspring housing pin
14. Mainspring housing
15. Mainspring cap pin
16. Mainspring cap
17. Mainspring
18. Mainspring housing pin retainer
19. Sear spring
20. Trigger assembly
21. Trigger stop
22. Plunger tube (shown assembled to receiver)
23. Slide stop plunger
24. Plunger spring
25. Safety lock plunger
26. Grip safety
27. Hammer
28. Hammer strut pin
29. Hammer strut
30. Sear
31. Disconnector
32. Depressor
33. Depressor spring
34. Ejector (shown assembled to receiver)
35. Ejector pin (assembled to receiver, not visible in drawing)

2 The sear (30), disconnector (31), depressor (32), and depressor spring (33) are shown below assembled in correct relationship. In the view to the left the disconnector has been omitted for clarity. In the view to the right, sear, disconnector, depressor, and depressor spring are shown assembled.

To facilitate reassembly of this assembly in receiver, it is suggested that a short slave pin (A) having a length equal to the width of the sear be employed to hold the parts together correctly. The slave pin will be drifted out when sear pin is replaced through frame.

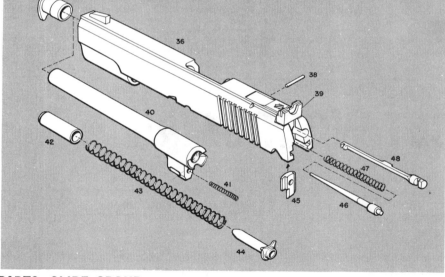

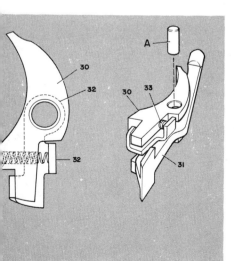

PARTS, SLIDE GROUP—
36. Slide
37. Barrel bushing
38. Rear sight leaf pin
39. Rear sight assembly
40. Barrel
41. Barrel return spring

42. Recoil spring plug
43. Recoil spring
44. Recoil spring guide
45. Firing pin stop
46. Firing pin
47. Firing pin spring
48. Extractor

PARTS, REAR SIGHT ASSEMBLY—
49. Rear sight leaf
50. Elevating screw
51. Detent balls (2)
52. Elevating screw detent spring
53. Elevating springs (2)
54. Windage spring
55. Rear sight blade
56. Windage screw

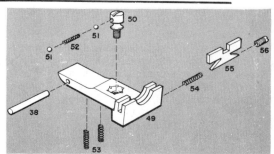

73

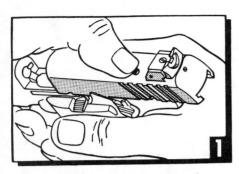

Check the magazine and chamber to be sure the gun is empty. Pull the slide back as far as it will go. Press down the assembly lock plunger (K), depress the slide stop (RR), and push the slide closed by hand, since the recoil spring is locked and cannot return the slide

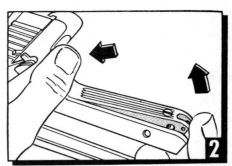

Remove the grips and push out the upper housing lock pin (PP). Pull the trigger to release hammer. Retract the slide about ⅛ inch, then press inward and upward as shown. The main spring housing (GG) will snap out. Remove the slide (P) and magazine (KK)

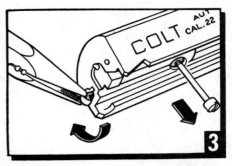

Grasp the end of the extractor (G) with pliers and rotate 180 degrees, then pull it forward. Thread grip screw (NN) into the firing pin stop (N). Pull it out. The firing pin (F), on firing pin spring (E), may then be removed through the rear of the slide

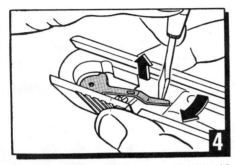

Press forward on recoil spring guide (I) with small screw driver assembly. Assembly lock (J) will disengage. Ease recoil spring (D) and guide (I) out of the slide. Lift end of assembly lock (J) up and turn lock plunger (K) 90 degrees. Work the assembly lock forward out of its grooves in slide

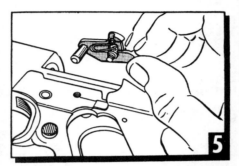

The Woodsman goes back together again easily except for the slide stop spring (TT). A great deal of effort will be saved if the slide stop (RR), the plate screw (QQ), and spring (TT) are assembled as shown before attempting to install them when re-assembling the gun

After all parts, with the exception of the housing (GG) and grips, have been reassembled into the slide (P) and receiver (WW), assemble the frame and receiver together, insert housing into the receiver, and press firmly against a table. The housing will snap into place

COLT WOODSMAN

From its introduction in 1915, as the "Colt Automatic Cal. .22 Long Rifle", to its discontinuance in 1977 the "Woodsman" (so named in 1927) was the .22 rimfire self-loader by which other self-loaders were judged.

The Match Target version shown here is only one of many heavy- and light-barrel target and sporting models once made. It is of the early post World War II variety with a disconnector safety mechanism and an M1911-style magazine release. Earlier and later versions used a magazine release located at the bottom of the grip frame and the disconnector safety was included only from about 1948 until 1955.

Other post-war developments, that continued through the production life of the Woodsman, were an internal extractor and an automatic slide stop. This last feature was not installed in the less expensive Colt Challenger (1950 - 1955) or the Huntsman (1955 - 1976) models

that are otherwise similar in construction to the late Woodsman.

Pre-World War II "Colt Automatic" and "Woodsman" pistols (plus a few of the latter made just after the war) are eagerly sought by collectors as well as by shooters and are easily distinguished from later production by their short mainspring housings and a resultant "pocket pistol" look to the grip frame.

Early pistols of this type, having serial numbers below 83,790, **should not be fired with high velocity ammunition** unless their mainspring housings have been replaced with one of the newer, stronger housings that, in the Woodsman's heyday, were available as replacement parts.

Many of the older pistols were later fitted with strengthened mainspring housings that are distinguishable by horizontal striations, running across the housing where it meets the web of the shooter's hand. Older units, safe (if

otherwise in good condition) only with standard velocity ammunition, have checkering in this area.

Like other .22 rimfire self-loaders the chamber and breech face of the Colt Woodsman must be kept clean. Greased or waxed ammunition leaves deposits that cause extraction troubles and, at times, misfires.

The field stripping procedure for the pistol illustrated is the same as for earlier and later models, with one exception. The grip of 1948-1955 vintage pistols must be removed and the housing lock pin (LL) pushed out of the frame if one wishes to remove the mainspring housing. The housing lock pin was added at the request of Marine Corps shooters to prevent the back strap from being forced inward and pinching the skin between the thumb and forefinger when the pistol is gripped tightly.

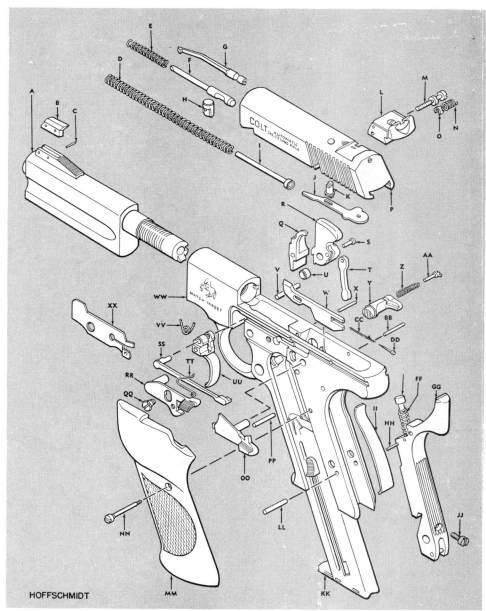

Legend

A—Barrel
B—Front sight blade
C—Sight blade pin
D—Recoil spring
E—Firing pin spring
F—Firing pin
G—Extractor
H—Firing pin stop
I—Recoil spring guide
J—Assembly lock
K—Assembly lock plunger
L—Rear sight
M—Sight windage screw
N—Windage screw detent spring
O—Windage detent
P—Slide
Q—Sear
R—Hammer
S—Hammer strut pin
T—Hammer strut
U—Bushing
V—Trigger pin
W—Ejector
X—Ejector pin
Y—Magazine catch
Z—Magazine catch spring

AA—Magazine catch lock
BB—Ejector pin
CC—Ejector spring
DD—Ejector plunger
EE—Main spring cap
FF—Main spring
GG—Main spring housing
HH—Main spring cap pin
II—Sear spring
JJ—Grip adapter screw
KK—Magazine
LL—Housing lock pin
MM—Left hand grip
NN—Grip screw
OO—Safety catch
PP—Upper housing lock pin
QQ—Side plate screw
RR—Slide stop
SS—Trigger bar
TT—Slide stop spring
UU—Trigger
VV—Trigger spring
WW—Frame (receiver)
XX—Side plate

NOTE: Models produced subsequently to 1955 do not have magazine safety.

By E. J. Hoffschmidt

By James M. Triggs

Colt's Official Police Revolver was introduced in 1908, as an improvement over the New Army and New Navy revolvers. Originally known as the "Army Special", the Official Police given its most recent name in 1928. Production of Army Special/ Official Police revolvers continued without any interruption in serial number sequence. From the time of its introduction until 1935, Army Special/Official Police models were offered in .32-20, .38 Special and .41 Colt. In 1930 the Official Police was offered chambered for .22 rimfire ammunition. In 1935, both .32-20 and .41 Colt versions were discontinued.

During the course of production Army Special/Official Police grips were made from black hard rubber, walnut and reddish-brown plastic. The last guns had checkered walnut grips

During World War II Colt produced a wartime-finish version of the Official Po-

Colt Official Police Revolver

LEGEND

1. Hammer
2. Hammer pin
3. Hammer stirrup
4. Hammer stirrup pin
5. Strut
6. Strut spring
7. Strut pin
8. Firing pin
9. Firing pin rivet
10. Safety
11. Safety lever
12. Hand
13. Trigger
14. Trigger pin
15. Mainspring
16. Bolt
17. Bolt spring
18. Bolt screw
19. Rebound lever
20. Rebound lever pin
21. Crane lock
22. Crane lock screw
23. Sideplate
24. Sideplate screws (2)
25. Latch
26. Latch spring
27. Latch spring guide
28. Latch pin
29. Cylinder
30. Cylinder bushing
31. Ejector and ratchet
32. Ejector rod
33. Ejector rod head
34. Ejector spring
35. Crane bushing
36. Crane
37. Barrel
38. Stock pin
39. Stock screw
40. Stocks (2)
41. Escutcheons (2)
42. Recoil Plate
43. Frame

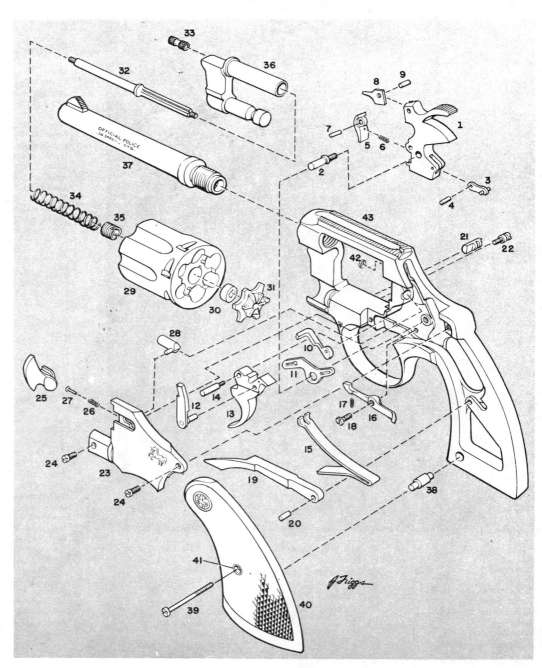

lice revolver, for use by defense plant security personnel and other emergency law enforcement agencies. Known as the Commando model, it was discontinued at the war's end. In addition, Colt Officers Model revolvers, in .22 rimfire, .32 S&W Long and .38 Special were made using the Official Police frame and mechanism, as were the rounded-butt, "Marshal" model revolvers made from 1954 to 1956.

Army Special and Official Police revolvers were serially numbered beginning at "1". The change in designation came at about number 526,000 — there being an overlap between 513,276 and 540,000. "Marshals" were numbered concurrent with the Official Police production. Rimfire Official Police revolvers, Commando Models and Officers Models were numbered separately, beginning with "1".

The Official Police revolver was discontinued in 1969.

Model 1905 Colt

PISTOL MAGAZINES

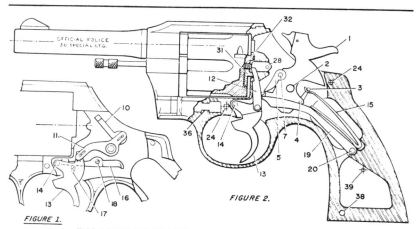

FIGURE 1.

FIGURE 2.

DISASSEMBLY AND ASSEMBLY PROCEDURE

Remove crane lock screw (22) and crane lock (21). Swing out cylinder and remove cylinder and crane assembly by pushing to the front. Disassembly of the cylinder and crane assembly should be undertaken only by a competent gunsmith.

Remove stock screw (39) and stocks (40). Remove sideplate screws (24). Do not attempt to pry out the sideplate (23) but tap the frame and sideplate with the wooden handle of a tool until the plate loosens and can be lifted out. Remove the latch (25) and latch spring and guide (26 and 27) from the sideplate.

To remove the mainspring (15), lay the pistol flat and push the hammer back about ¼″ with the left forefinger. Holding a screwdriver in the right hand, press down on the mainspring near the stirrup (3) with the flat tip of the screwdriver. Push the hammer forward to disengage the stirrup from the mainspring and lift out the mainspring with the fingers.

Remove hand (12) from trigger (13). Drive out the rebound lever pin (20) with a punch or drift pin and remove the rebound lever (19). Remove the trigger by lifting it up off the trigger pin (14). Draw the hammer (1) to its rearmost position and lift it up off the hammer pin (2). Drive out the strut pin (7) from the hammer with a small punch and remove the strut (5) and strut spring (6). Drive out the hammer stirrup pin (4) and remove the hammer stirrup (3).

Remove the safety lever (11) from its pivot around the base of the hammer pin (2) and remove the safety (10) from its slot in the frame. Remove the bolt screw (18) and remove the bolt (16), using care not to lose the bolt spring (17). The latch pin (28) can be dropped out of its hole in the frame.

Removal of the barrel, firing pin, recoil plate, stock pin, trigger pin, or hammer pin should be attempted only by an experienced gunsmith.

The revolver is reassembled in the reverse order. The safety lever (11) should be placed back on its pivot with the slot in its short end engaging the stud on the safety (10). Replace the trigger so that the stud on the right side of the trigger engages the slot on the longer end of the safety lever. This assembly should be tested by moving the trigger back and forth to determine if the safety and safety lever are operating smoothly with the safety in its full "up" position when the trigger is all the way forward. The proper relationship of the safety, safety lever, trigger, and bolt are shown in Fig. 1.

To replace the mainspring (15), grasp the spring between thumb and forefinger of the right hand and slide the slotted end of the spring into position with the hammer stirrup (3), guiding the stirrup into position by moving the hammer on its pin with the forefinger of the left hand. When the stirrup and mainspring have been engaged, lift the bottom of the spring onto the rebound lever (19) with thumb of right hand. Replace hand (12) in its hole in the trigger and press upward on the rebound lever (19) to allow the hand to be fully seated. The sectionalized diagrammatic view in Fig. 2 shows these parts in their proper relationship.

Replace the latch spring and guide (26 and 27) in sideplate (23) and place sideplate in position on frame but do not seat fully. Place the latch (25) in its slot in the sideplate so that the stud on the latch pin (28) engages the hole in the latch. Seat the sideplate tightly and replace the screws (24). Replacing cylinder and crane assembly and the stocks completes the reassembly. —————————

The Model 1905 Colt Automatic pistol was the forerunner of the world famous Models 1911 and 1911A1 U. S. Service pistols. It is the most common automatic pistol of the series of semi-experimental versions that led up to the Model 1911. While the Model 1905 is an effective weapon, it is primarily a collector item today. Except for a few details, the magazines look like Model 1911 magazines. Model 1905 magazines have 6 holes per side instead of the 5 found in the Model 1911.

Model 1905 magazines can be recognized by the extra horn-like projection in the front notch instead of the smooth line found on Model 1911 magazine.

Other points of identification are the retainer protrusion and cut on the back strap.— E. J. HOFFSCHMIDT

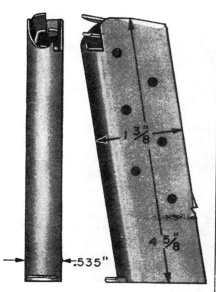

77

Colt Paterson Revolving Pistol

By Thomas E. Wessel

In 1836 a group of financiers in Paterson, N.J. organized the Patent Firearms Manufacturing Co. for the purpose of making percussion ignition, revolving-cylinder, repeating firearms under patents held by Samuel Colt, a young inventor from Hartford, Conn. The group, led by its president, Elias B.D. Ogden, established a factory in Paterson. Dudley Selden, Colt's cousin, was secretary and general manager.

Except for a limited number of revolving *rifles,* very few arms were produced in 1836. The first government trial of the rifles was held in 1837 and the results were unfavorable. In 1838, however, Colt succeeded in selling 125 rifles to the U.S. Army for use in the Seminole campaign. Officers, part of the campaigning force,

also purchased a few of the pistols.

An additional order, for both carbines and pistols, was obtained from the Republic of Texas, in 1839.

During this time Colt did everything possible to promote the sale of his guns, including presentation of a pistol to President Andrew Jackson. Some of his promotional methods may have seemed unorthodox to his conservative cousin Dudley Selden, as friction between the two eventually caused Selden to resign. John Ehlers took over Selden's duties as secretary and general manager.

In 1841, Colt, dissatisfied with the distribution of royalty payments by Ehlers, undertook legal action against the firm. Colt's suit resulted in the company's bankruptcy in 1842 despite a last minute

order from the Army's Ordnance Department for 160 carbines. Luckily, for Colt, he retained ownership of his patents.

Though short-lived, the Patent Firearms Manufacturing Co., made a wide variety of guns; rifles, carbines, pistols, and shotguns. Pistols were sold in calibers from .28 to .36 and with barrels ranging from 2-1/2 inches to nine inches in length. By virtue of their place of manufacture, these early Colt firearms are referred to as "Paterson Colts, or "Patersons"

Paterson guns, especially the pistols, re much sought after by collectors. This desirability plus their relative rarity of causes them to be ranked among the most valuable of antique arms.

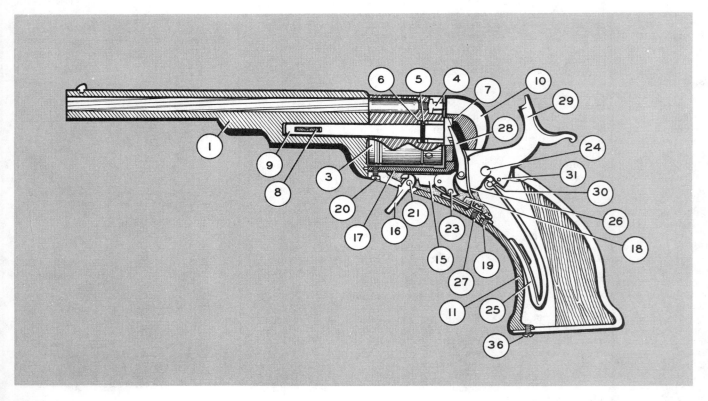

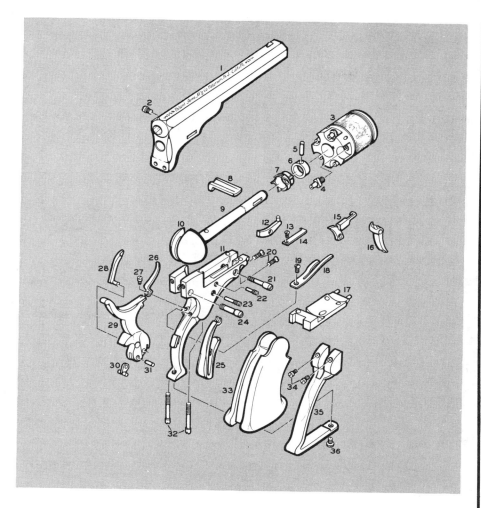

Parts Legend

1. Barrel
2. Wedge screw
3. Cylinder
4. Nipple (5)
5. Ratchet-retaining collar pin
6. Ratchet-retaining collar
7. Ratchet
8. Wedge
9. Cylinder arbor
10. Recoil shield
11. Frame
12. Bolt
13. Upper trigger spring screw
14. Upper trigger spring
15. Trigger actuating bar
16. Trigger
17. Frame plate
18. Bolt and trigger spring
19. Bolt and trigger spring screw
20. Frame plate screw (2)
21. Trigger screw
22. Bolt screw
23. Actuating bar screw
24. Hammer screw
25. Mainspring
26. Hand spring
27. Hand spring screw
28. Hand
29. Hammer
30. Stirrup
31. Stirrup pin
32. Recoil shield retaining screw (2)
33. Grip
34. Backstrap screw (2)
35. Backstrap
36. Butt screw

Disassembly Procedure

Remove wedge screw (2) and tap out wedge (8) from right side using a plastic or rubber hammer. Remove barrel (1) and cylinder (3). Next, remove frame plate screws (20) and lift away frame plate (17). Remove butt screw (36) and backstrap screws (34). Lift away backstrap (35) and grip (33), which may then be separated. All internal working parts are exposed at this point.

Should further disassembly be required, continue by removing hand spring screw (27) and hand spring (26). With the left hand, compress mainspring (25) slightly to relieve tension on stirrup (30) and hammer (29), and remove hammer screw (24) and hammer together with hand (28). Remove bolt and trigger spring screw (19) and spring (18), then remove trigger screw (21), bolt screw (22), and actuating bar screw (23). Remove trigger (16), actuating bar (15), and bolt (12). Removal of the upper trigger spring screw (13) permits removal of the upper trigger spring (14). Drifting out of the ratchet-retaining collar pin (5) permits removal of the ratchet-retaining collar (6) and ratchet (7). Reassemble Colt Paterson in reverse order. ■

Schwarzlose
Blow-Forward
Pistol

PISTOL MAGAZINES

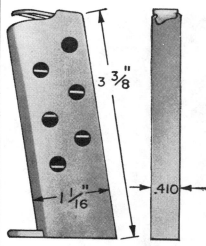

The German Schwarzlose pocket pistol is one of the most unusual ever produced. When the chambered round is fired, the cartridge case remains stationary against the back of the frame. The slide is blown forward off the cartridge case ejecting the fired case and ramming a loaded cartridge into position. When the slide returns to the rear, it slides the chamber over the incoming cartridge, The pistols were not too well made and have little to recommend them.

The backstrap of the magazine is cut down lower on the left side to allow the rammer to clear the magazine. The curved front end of the sheet metal follower is another pertinent feature of the Schwarzlose magazine.

The grip safety is in the front grip strap, necessitating a longer floorplate than usual. —EDWARD J. HOFFSCHMIDT

By James M. Triggs

THE Colt .25 hammerless vest-pocket model pistol was introduced in 1908. Unlike the other Colt 'hammerless' pistols which were really of concealed-hammer design, the .25 was actually hammerless, with a straight-line firing pin propelled by a coil spring behind it.

The gun was made with thumb-operated and grip safeties from the beginning. In 1917, a safety disconnector was added to prevent firing with magazine removed, as a safeguard against accidental discharge by users who failed to realize that removing the magazine did not unload the chamber of the gun. All pistols above serial number 141,000 have that feature.

Manufacture of the .25 was ended in 1946.

The late James M. Triggs was a well known writer-illustrator and collector of antique firearms.

COLT .25 POCKET AUTOMATIC

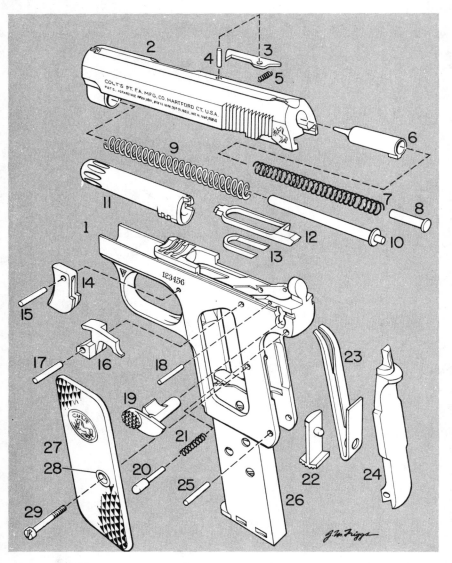

Check the pistol to be sure it is unloaded. Insert magazine and pull the trigger. (Do not attempt to disassemble this gun with the action cocked!) Remove magazine. Holding the pistol as shown, draw the slide back until its front edge is about 1/16th of an inch from the front edge of the receiver. Turn the barrel ¼ turn to the right. The slide may now be drawn forward and off the receiver. Turn the barrel back ¼ turn to the left and drop it out of the receiver from the rear. The firing pin, mainspring, and guide are easily withdrawn from the slide as are the recoil spring and guide from the receiver. The extractor and extractor spring can be removed from the slide by drifting out their retaining pin

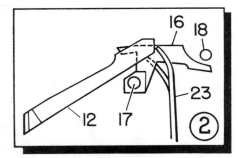

Remove the stocks. Drift out the grip safety pin (25) and remove the grip safety (24) from the receiver. Remove the sear spring (23). Note that the short leaf of the sear spring faces toward the rear of the pistol. Remove the magazine catch (22). Turn the slide lock safety (19) to the "up" position and withdraw it from the receiver. Remove the slide lock safety plunger and spring (20 and 21) from their hole beneath the slide lock safety. Drift out the sear and grip safety pin (17) and remove the sear through the bottom of the receiver behind the magazine well. Normally there is no need to withdraw the sear stop pin (18). The trigger may be withdrawn by drifting out its retaining pin (15). Withdraw the connector (12) from its grooves in the receiver. The depressor (13) is not normally removed but can be withdrawn toward the rear through the connector grooves. Reassemble in reverse order taking care that the sear, connector, sear spring, and sear stop pin are in the proper relationship as shown by the diagram

LEGEND

1. Receiver
2. Slide
3. Extractor
4. Extractor Pin
5. Extractor Spring
6. Firing Pin
7. Mainspring
8. Mainspring Guide
9. Recoil Spring
10. Recoil Spring Guide
11. Barrel
12. Connector
13. Depressor
14. Trigger
15. Trigger Pin
16. Sear
17. Sear and Grip Safety Pin
18. Sear Stop Pin
19. Slide Lock Safety
20. Slide Lock Safety Plunger
21. Slide Lock Safety Plunger Spring
22. Magazine Catch
23. Sear Spring
24. Grip Safety
25. Grip Safety Pin
26. Magazine
27. Stocks (2)
28. Escutcheons (2)
29. Stock Screw

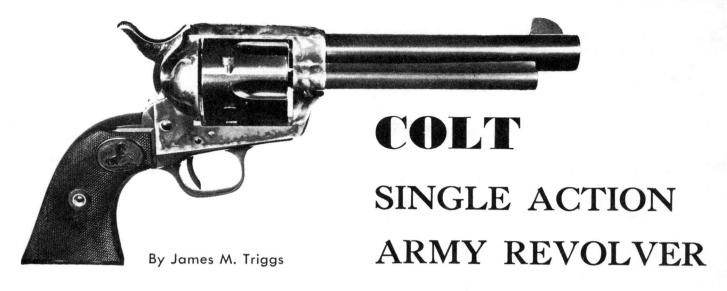

COLT
SINGLE ACTION
ARMY REVOLVER

By James M. Triggs

"A MILITARY weapon extracting the discharged shells singly; combining strength and simplicity of action; not liable to get out of order; readily taken apart and easily cleaned; having entire exchangeability of parts, with a high order of finish. Commended for durability and actual service in the hands of a soldier. . . ."

The above succinct report, by the judges of the Centennial Exposition held in Philadelphia in 1876, is as relevant today as it was over 80 years ago. It is a striking fact indeed that the revolver referred to remains in production as of this date. As such, it can claim the longest production period of any revolver, if not any cartridge firearm, ever commercially produced. Introduced in 1873 as the Single Action Army, it is also known as the Single Action Army and Frontier, Frontier Six-Shooter, Peacemaker, and Model 'P'.

It enjoyed continuous production from 1873 until 1941 when reduced sales and pressure of defense contracts terminated its manufacture. After World War II the demand for Colt Single Action revolvers skyrocketed to the point where collectors often paid from three to four times the pre-war price. In light of this strong demand, Colt's in 1955 decided to resume limited production. Specifications remained unchanged although calibers were restricted to .38 S&W Special and the traditional .45 Colt. Recently Colt's also resumed production of the unique Buntline Special version of the Single Action Army which features a barrel 12 inches long!

It is perhaps significant that only minor design changes have been effected during the years that the Colt Single Action has been produced. Early guns with serial numbers below 165,000 are

The late Jim Triggs was a writer-illustrator and well known gun collector.

in the so-called blackpowder category, whereas those with higher numbers were manufactured after the advent of smokeless powder. The change-over, which occurred in 1896, was reflected in reduced headspace tolerances to accommodate the higher pressures developed by smokeless powder cartridges. The substitution of the spring release for the screw originally used to retain the base pin occurred about the same time as the change to smokeless.

The barrels of early Single Action revolvers were rifled with comparatively narrow lands, whereas those made subsequently have wider lands with lands and grooves of equal width. Some were furnished smoothbored for use with shot cartridges. Barrel lengths varied from three inches up to 16 and 18 inches for the special-order Buntline models. Some guns were produced

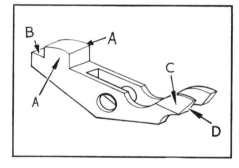

1 The parts most frequently requiring replacement in the Single Action are the hammer, trigger, and bolt which are subject to breakage. These replacement parts are usually a little oversized so careful fitting is in order. This drawing shows the steps necessary in installing a new bolt. First, file sides of bolt cylinder-engaging tip at "A", trying bolt tip in bolt recesses in cylinder until a close fit is achieved. Try fit again with bolt and cylinder installed in frame. Some additional fitting may now be necessary to allow bolt tip to pass smoothly through cut in frame. The height of engaging tip of bolt, as it rises up through frame to engage cylinder, can be controlled by filing forward lip of bolt at "B". Removing metal at this point will allow bolt to rise higher up out of frame. Use care in this operation since, if too much metal is removed, bolt may not lower far enough to allow cylinder to turn. File a bevel at the rear ·tip of the bolt as shown at "C" to allow this tip to slide smoothly over the bolt cam on the hammer. Timing of the bolt fall into its locking recess in the cylinder is determined at "D". If insufficient metal is removed at this point, the bolt will not fall; if too much is taken away, the bolt will fall too soon and a **stripe around the cylinder will result**

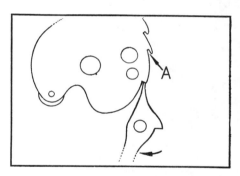

2 Frequently the sear end of the trigger is broken off. This increases the sear thickness and, in effect, forms a wedge which will invariably break the loading notch (A) on the hammer if the trigger is not replaced. If the trigger is replaced after the loading notch is broken, it will be impossible to maintain a true edge on the sear with this rough area existing on the hammer. In this case hammer replacement is mandatory. First, determine that end of new sear will fit snugly into loading notch without any bind, and when installed in frame is not so high that it will not engage full-cock notch in hammer when hammer is pulled back to the cocked position. With end of sear at right height to engage hammer properly, stone proper angle on tip, then hone with Arkansas stone. This figure shows correct relationship of full-cock notch in hammer and sear end of trigger with hammer cocked. Note that angle on tip of sear and notch in hammer are parallel to direction of travel of sear tip when trigger is pulled. If angle is not parallel to this motion, it will result either in a hard trigger pull (because sear must lift hammer slightly to clear notch) or sear can easily slip off hammer notch, a **dangerous condition**

without ejector assemblies. From the collector standpoint, an almost endless number of variations is likely to be encountered, from the plain standard models to those elaborately engraved and ornamented to suit a king's taste. A collection by caliber alone would be imposing, considering that the Single Action has been factory chambered for virtually every American rimfire and center-fire handgun cartridge of significance as well as English, German, and Russian service cartridges. Suffice to say that caliber variations range from the lowly .22 rimfire up to and including the enormous .476 Eley.

Colt Single Action Army Revolver

DISASSEMBLY PROCEDURE

Unload revolver. Remove cylinder (14) by opening loading gate (15) and withdrawing base pin (7) and, with hammer at half cock, press cylinder out of frame to right. The base pin is removed by pressing in base pin screw. On older models below serial number 165,000, base pin is held in place by base pin screw (7A) in front of frame; loosening this screw will free base pin.

Remove stocks (42). Remove backstrap (38) by unscrewing two upper backstrap screws (39) and front backstrap screw (35). Remove mainspring screw (36) and drop out mainspring (37). Remove front trigger guard screw (32) and two rear trigger guard screws (33) and lift trigger guard (31) from frame. Unscrew bolt spring screw (29) and remove sear and bolt spring (28) from underside of frame. Remove hammer screw (30) and trigger and bolt screws (26) and remove trigger (27), bolt (25), and hammer (16) with attached hand and spring (21) from inside of frame.

The loading gate (15) is removed by unscrewing gate catch screw (24) from its hole in underside of frame and dropping out gate spring (23) and gate catch (22). The base pin screw (8), base pin spring (9), and base pin nut (10) can be removed from frame by unscrewing screw from nut.

The ejector assembly is removed by unscrewing ejector tube screw (3) from barrel (1). Lift ejector tube (2) free of ejector stud in barrel and push tube toward front of gun, disengaging rear of tube from its seat in frame. The ejector rod (5) and ejector rod head (6) and ejector spring (4) may be withdrawn from ejector tube from rear.

This completes disassembly. Reassembly is accomplished in reverse order. Removal of barrel or replacement of either barrel or cylinder should only be attempted by an experienced person equipped with proper tools. The accompanying longitudinal section shows relationship of all parts with revolver assembled.

PARTS LEGEND

1. Barrel
2. Ejector tube
3. Ejector tube screw
4. Ejector spring
5. Ejector rod
6. Ejector rod head
7. Base pin
7A. Base pin screw (old style)
8. Base pin screw
9. Base pin spring
10. Base pin nut
11. Base pin bushing
12. Frame
13. Recoil plate
14. Cylinder
15. Gate
16. Hammer
17. Firing pin
18. Firing pin rivet
19. Hammer roll
20. Hammer roll pin
21. Hand (with hand spring)
22. Gate catch
23. Gate spring
24. Gate catch screw
25. Bolt
26. Trigger & bolt screws
27. Trigger
28. Sear & bolt spring
29. Bolt spring screw
30. Hammer screw
31. Trigger guard
32. Front trigger guard screw
33. Rear trigger guard screws (2)
34. Stock pin
35. Front backstrap screw
36. Mainspring screw
37. Mainspring
38. Backstrap
39. Backstrap screws (2)
40. Escutcheons (2, left-hand only shown)
41. Stock screw
42. Stocks (left-hand only shown) ———◼

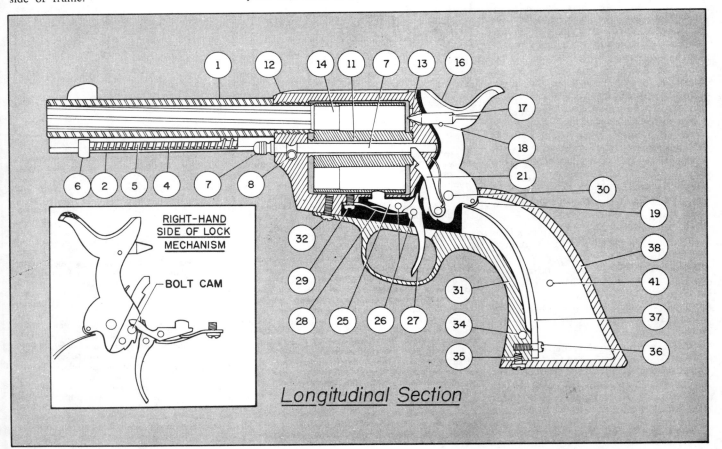

RIGHT-HAND SIDE OF LOCK MECHANISM

BOLT CAM

Longitudinal Section

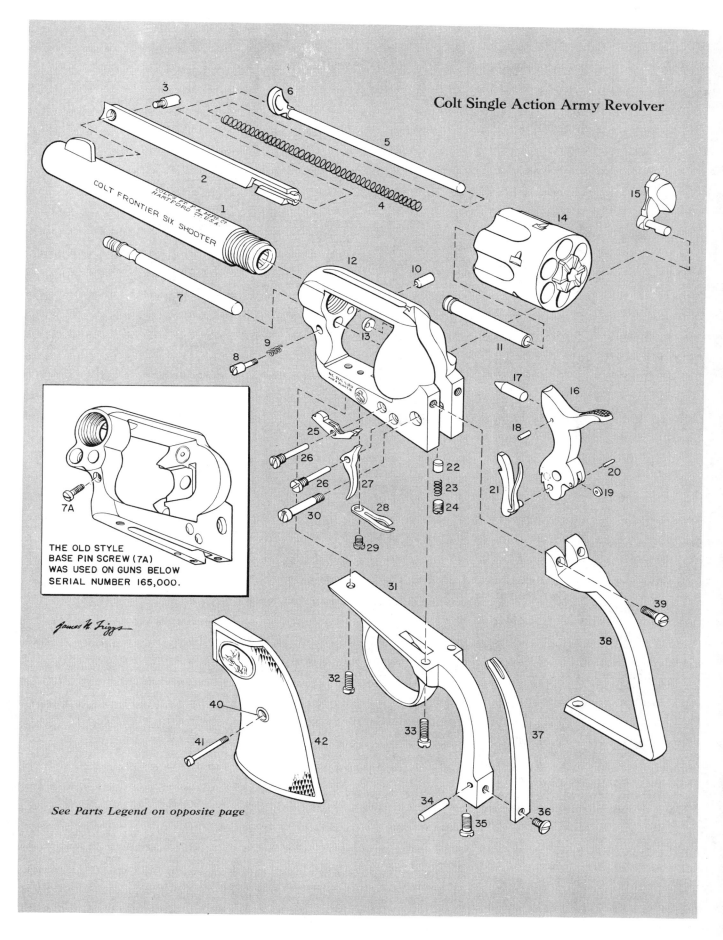

Colt Single Action Army Revolver

COLT FRONTIER SIX SHOOTER

COLT'S PT. F.A. MFG. CO.
HARTFORD CT. U.S.A.

THE OLD STYLE
BASE PIN SCREW (7A)
WAS USED ON GUNS BELOW
SERIAL NUMBER 165,000.

James H. Triggs

See Parts Legend on opposite page

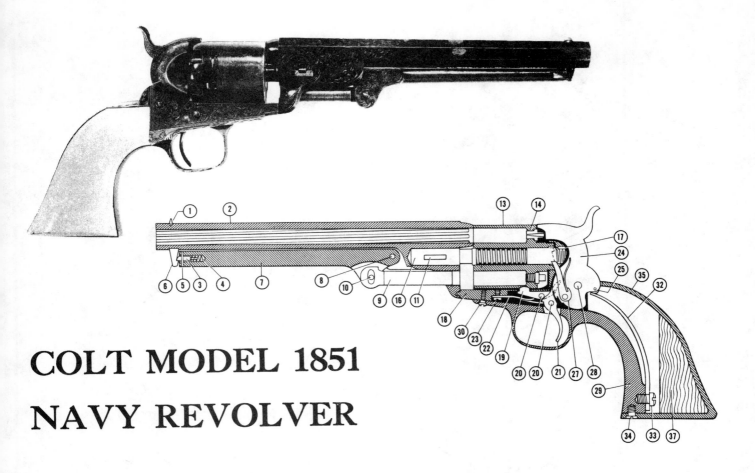

COLT MODEL 1851
NAVY REVOLVER

By James M. Triggs

THE .36 caliber Colt Navy pattern belt pistols, frequently called the Model of 1851, present mechanical features more or less typical of the complete series of percussion ignition open-top Colt revolvers regardless of caliber. Disassembly and assembly procedures are similar regardless of vintage.

When working with antique revolvers such as these, it is imperative that care be taken from the start to prevent damage to old and often hard to replace parts. Marring of original finish must be avoided. Screwdrivers used should be selected to fit precisely the various screws in main frame and barrel. Likewise, the use of a plastic or fiber head hammer is recommended for driving the barrel wedge, or for any other hammering which may become necessary.

Original Colt nipple wrenches are brittle and will break quite easily. Modern nipple wrenches are available at little cost and will prove much more satisfactory for the removal of old nipples which often are rusted in place.

For normal cleaning purposes separation of barrel from frame and removal of cylinder will usually suffice.

DISASSEMBLY PROCEDURE

Separate barrel and frame assemblies by gently driving barrel wedge (11) as far as it will go to the left and pulling barrel (2) off the cylinder pin (16). If barrel wedge has a spring, the right-hand lip of the spring must be depressed where it protrudes from barrel before wedge can be moved. Wedge can be removed completely by unscrewing barrel wedge screw (12).

Remove loading lever screw (8) and pull loading lever (7) and plunger (9) free of barrel. The loading lever latch (3) and spring (4) may be removed by gently drifting out their retaining pin (5). Remove plunger screw (10) and separate loading lever and plunger. The barrel stud (6) is force-fitted in a dovetail milled on underside of barrel and should be removed only if replacement is necessary.

Slide cylinder (13) off cylinder pin (16). If removal of nipples (14) is necessary for replacement, care should be taken that a proper nipple wrench is used.

Removal of cylinder pin (16) from lock frame (18) is not recommended. This cylinder pin, or arbor, was very tightly fitted originally and the firm association of pin and frame over the years is further complicated by a lock pin (17)

which is usually next to impossible to remove and generally must be drilled out, before cylinder pin can be unscrewed from frame.

Remove the two backstrap screws (36) and butt screw (34). Pull backstrap (35) and one-piece wood grip (37) free of lock frame (18) and trigger guard (29). If it is necessary to remove grip from backstrap, use care to avoid chipping or cracking grip since it is usually quite tightly fitted. If gun has two-piece grips held together by a screw, they should be removed before removing backstrap. Remove mainspring screw (33) and mainspring (32). Remove front trigger guard screw (30) and rear trigger guard screws (31) and drop trigger guard (29) off frame.

Remove trigger and cylinder locking bolt spring screw (23) and spring (22). Remove trigger and cylinder locking bolt screws (20) and drop trigger (21) and cylinder locking bolt (19) out of frame. Remove hammer screw (28) and pull hammer (24) and hand and spring (27) gently out bottom of frame. The hand can be lifted out of its hole in the hammer. If replacement is necessary, hammer roll (25) can be removed by gently drifting out its retaining pin (26).

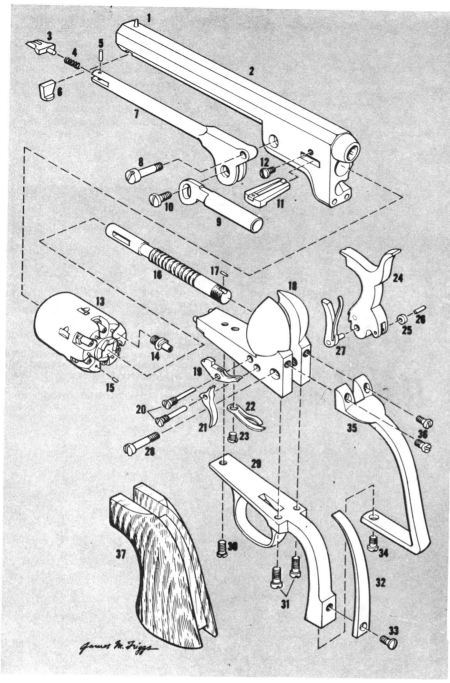

Steyr Cal. .25

PISTOL MAGAZINES

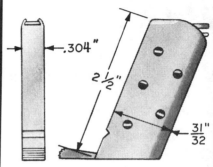

This little Steyr pistol incorporates a number of unusual features. The barrel tips up for easy cleaning or for single-shot loading. With barrel tipped up, the gun can be easily cocked since the slide is then disconnected from the recoil spring. The gun has no extractor and depends upon gas pressure to extract the empty cartridge case. The guns are generally well made and make excellent pocket pistols since they can be easily loaded and unloaded even if one hand is disabled.

The unusual reversed floorplate allows the Steyr magazine to be removed with one hand. The tail of the floorplate is below the magazine catch and can be easily pushed out with the thumb, as the same thumb depresses the magazine catch.

The magazine follower has no outstanding features. It is constructed like the followers of many common European magazines.—EDWARD J. HOFFSCHMIDT

LEGEND

1. Front sight
2. Barrel
3. Loading lever latch
4. Loading lever latch spring
5. Loading lever latch spring retaining pin
6. Barrel stud
7. Loading lever
8. Loading lever screw
9. Loading plunger
10. Loading plunger screw
11. Barrel wedge (with spring)
12. Barrel wedge screw
13. Cylinder
14. Nipples (6)
15. Safety pins (6)
16. Cylinder pin
17. Cylinder pin lock pin
18. Lock frame
19. Cylinder locking bolt

20. Trigger and cylinder locking bolt screws (2)
21. Trigger
22. Trigger and cylinder locking bolt spring
23. Trigger and cylinder locking bolt spring screw
24. Hammer
25. Hammer roll
26. Hammer roll pin
27. Hand and hand spring
28. Hammer screw
29. Trigger guard
30. Front trigger guard screw
31. Rear trigger guard screws (2)
32. Mainspring
33. Mainspring screw
34. Butt screw
35. Backstrap
36. Backstrap screws (2)
37. Grip (one-piece)

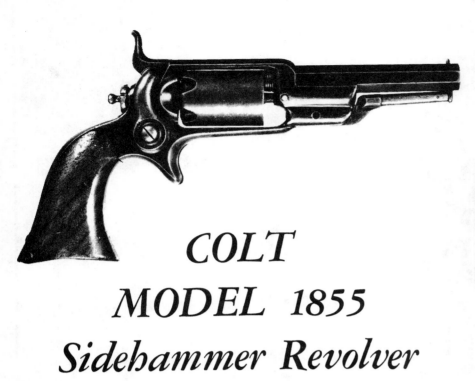

COLT
MODEL 1855
Sidehammer Revolver

By Thomas E. Wessel

F ROM the standpoints of both design and serviceability, the Model 1855 spur-trigger sidehammer pocket revolvers must be considered deficient in comparison with other percussion revolvers regularly produced by Colt's Patent Fire Arms Mfg. Co. Relatively weak and fragile parts resulted in an inordinate number of mechanical failures, but despite this many were sold.

1 Disassembly of the Colt Root should not be attempted, due to the fragile and intricate nature of the parts, unless absolutely necessary. Should disassembly be required, commence by depressing the cylinder arbor retaining latch (33). On some models, a screw is used to retain the cylinder arbor (21). Withdraw arbor from rear of frame (8) and remove cylinder (9). Remove screw (18) and grip (19)

Parts Legend

1. Barrel
2. Loading lever
3. Loading lever latch pin
4. Loading lever latch spring
5. Loading lever latch (ball type)
6. Rammer pin
7. Rammer
8. Frame
9. Cylinder (nipples integral)
10. Hammer
11. Hammer screw
12. Hand pin
13. Trigger spring
14. Trigger
15. Hand spring
16. Hand
17. Mainspring retaining pin
18. Grip screw
19. Grip
20. Mainspring tension screw
21. Cylinder arbor
22. Cylinder arbor sleeve
23. Mainspring
24. Stirrup
25. Cylinder stop
26. Cylinder stop spring
27. Trigger screw
28. Stirrup pin
29. Sear
30. Side-plate
31. Cylinder stop screw
32. Side-plate screw
33. Cylinder arbor retaining latch
34. Arbor retaining latch pin
35. Arbor retaining latch pin spring

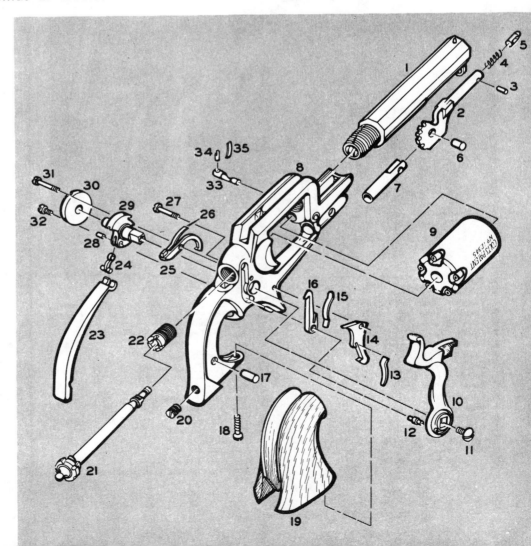

The basic patent covering the Colt Model 1855 revolver was granted to Elisha K. Root on Dec. 25, 1855 (No. 13,999). Root had joined the Colt firm in 1849 and was made shop superintendent. A gifted inventor, he designed many of the machines which made possible the mass production of Colt firearms and had much to do with the design of many Colt arms. Root eventually became President of Colt's upon the death of Samuel Colt in 1862. Root died in 1865.

The Model 1855 revolver, commonly called Root Model by collectors, was made in cals. .28 and .31, and only at the Hartford, Conn., factory established in 1855. None was made in Colt's London factory, although some were made in the Hartford plant for the English trade and were stamped "Address Col. Colt—London".

Barrel styles

According to James E. Serven's *Colt Firearms 1836-1960*, the 4½" barrel revolvers are found only in cal. .31, and always with round barrels. The revolvers with 3½" barrel may have round or full fluted cylinder, round, or octagonal barrel, 3 different devices for holding the cylinder pin, and 2 types of cylinder engraving. Standard stocks were of varnished walnut, but ivory was also used on some guns. Some presentation Model 1855 revolvers have grips made from the famous Connecticut Charter Oak.

Model 1855-type revolvers were the first Colt revolvers to have a top strap over the cylinder and a screw-in barrel. They also were the first use by Colt's of the creeping-type loading lever.

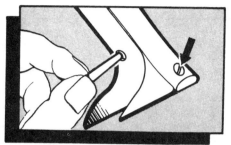

2 Next, remove mainspring tension screw (20—arrow) and drift out mainspring retaining pin (17). This will relieve spring tension on moving parts

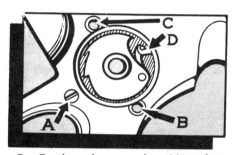

3 Continue by removing (A) trigger screw (27), (B) side-plate screw (32), and (C) cylinder stop screw (31). Tap out side-plate (30), then using a small screwdriver or punch as a lever, flick (D) mainspring free of stirrup (24)

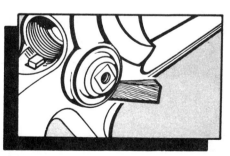

4 Remove hammer screw (11). Insert a narrow, hardwood wedge in small crevice between hammer (10) and frame, and tap gently. This will pry off hammer which is usually hard pressed in place on the sear (29), which may now also be removed from left side of frame. Trigger (14), trigger spring (13), cylinder stop (25), cylinder stop spring (26), hand (16), and hand spring (15) may now be dismounted. Removal of these parts is obvious once the side-plate is off, but removal sequence is important

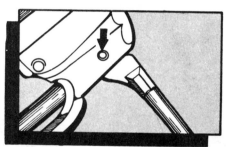

5 Unlatch loading lever (2) and push down until rammer pin (6) is seen through hole in front portion of frame (arrow). Drifting out of rammer pin will permit removal of loading lever assembly and rammer (7)

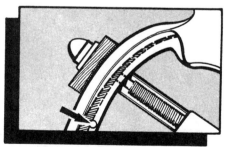

6 Reassemble in reverse order. When replacing mainspring retaining pin, it is necessary to compress mainspring to align groove in spring with pin hole in frame. Accomplish this by placing a small block of soft wood, shaped to contour of backstrap, and felt padded on surface which bears on backstrap. Using a woodworker's clamp, from which the button has been removed, apply to mainspring as shown and compress until pin hole (arrow) is clear, then insert mainspring retaining pin, and replace mainspring tension screw (20) ∎

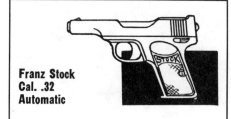

Franz Stock
Cal. .32
Automatic

PISTOL MAGAZINES

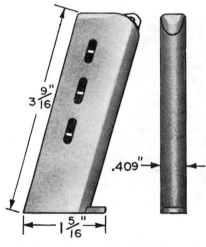

The Franz Stock pocket pistol is one of a number of short-lived makes manufactured in Germany after World War I. When compared with its contemporaries, the Stock pistol is bulky. In spite of its larger size and weight, it was well made and had good pointing qualities.

Except for the 3 elongated slots on the right-hand side of the magazine, there is little to identify Stock magazines. Some will be found with the intertwined F. S. trademark engraved on the floorplate.

Followers of cal. .32 Stock magazines are of sheet metal and they are well finished. Since the follower is guided at the front and rear strap of the magazine, there is little tendency to cock or bind.—EDWARD J. HOFFSCHMIDT

CROSMAN
Series 130 Pistol

By THOMAS E. WESSEL

In 1952, Crosman Arms Co., of E. Bloomfield, N.Y., introduced the Series 130 pneumatic single-shot pistol. Produced in caliber .177-inch (The Model 137) and .22 (The Model 130), this pistol has a rifled barrel and shoots skirted lead pellets.

This pistol is well suited for indoor target practice as in develops relatively low power and makes very little noise. It is cheaper to shoot than a CO_2 pistol as no gas cylinders are required. However, it must be pumped up before each shot, and this requires considerable effort on the part of the shooter. About six strokes are needed for shooting at 25 feet, and up to 10 strokes may be used when additional power is desired.

There have been several manufacturing changes in this pistol since its introduction, the most recent of which resulted in the Crosman Model 1377.

Parts Legend

1. Barrel
2. Lock pin
3. Grip screw (2)
4. Tube plug
5. O ring (breech bolt)
6. Breech bolt
7. Loading sleeve
8. Breech bolt screw
9. Breech plug
10. Sight screw
11. Rear sight
12. Right grip
13. Left grip
14. Front sight
15. Sear block stop
16. Sear spring (for sear block)
17. Tube
18. Breech gasket
19. Front sight pin
20. Valve cap assembly
21a. O ring (valve cap assembly)
22a. Quad ring
23a. Exhaust valve washer
24. Exhaust valve ring
25. Exhaust valve body
26. Check valve spring
27. Check valve
28. O ring (check valve)
29. Check valve body
30. O ring (check valve body, front)
31b. Compression head
32b. Cup washer
33b. Felt retainer
34b. Felt washer
35. Piston
36. O ring (check valve body, rear)
37. Pump lock nut
38. Pump guide
39. Pump guide pin
40. Lever link
41. Lever
42. Lever rivet
43. Trigger
44. Takeup spring
45. Safety spring
46. Safety ball
47. Sear
48. Front frame screw lockwasher
49. Front frame screw
50. Grip frame
51. Trigger pin
52. Safety
53. Sear pin
54. Sear spring head
55. Sear spring (for sear)
56. Frame screw
57. Sear block
58. Bumper

(a) *Components of permanent factory valve cap assembly (20)*
(b) *Permanently assembled to piston (35) at factory*

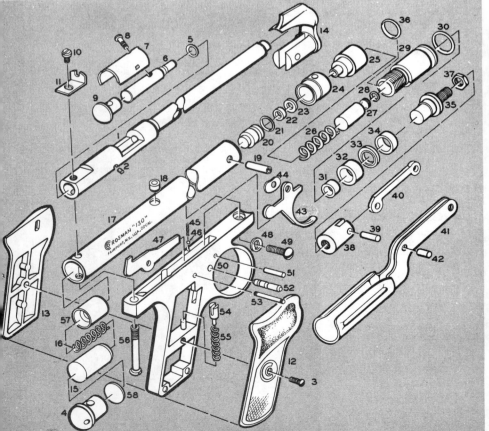

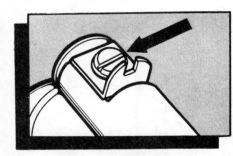

1 Remove sight screw (10), rear sight (11), and frame screw (56)

2 Remove front frame screw (49) and front frame screw lockwasher (48). Grip frame (50) may now be separated from barrel and tube

3 Drift out front sight pin (19) and remove front sight (14). The entire pump assembly, from lever (41) back to and including piston (35), may now be withdrawn from front of tube (17). From rear of tube, withdraw tube plug (4), bumper (58), and sear block stop (15). Sear spring (16) and sear block (57) may also be removed. Insert a ⅜" dowel into rear of tube and push out exhaust valve body assembly

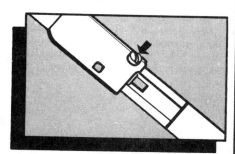

4 Remove breech plug (9) from rear of barrel (1). Remove breech bolt screw (8) and loading sleeve (7). Breech bolt (6) may now be removed from rear of barrel

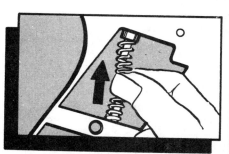

5 Remove grip screws (3) and grips (12) and (13). With thumb and forefinger, lift up on sear spring (55) and remove it. Sear spring head (54) will drop out. Drift out sear pin (53) from right to left and remove sear (47). Drift out trigger pin (51) from right to left, and remove trigger (43) and takeup spring (44). Reassemble in reverse

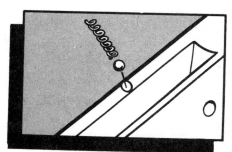

6 When working with grip frame assembly, be careful not to lose safety spring (45) and safety ball (46) ∎

PISTOL MAGAZINES

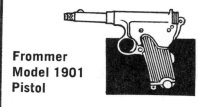

Frommer Model 1901 Pistol

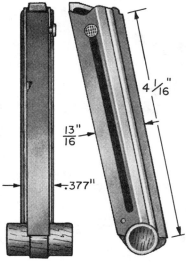

4 1/16"

13/16"

.377"

The Frommer Model 1901 automatic pistol, which shoots the cal. 7.65 mm. Frommer M1901 cartridge, is typical of most early automatic pistols in that it has an extremely complicated mechanism. The magazine, essentially a miniature version of the Luger magazine, is well made, as is the rest of the gun.

The magazine is formed from 2 sheet metal channels that are overlapped to form a stiff rib down either side. The machined follower operates smoothly. A button on the follower extends through the outside of the magazine to facilitate loading.

The floorplate is a piece of turned walnut with knobs on the sides to permit easy removal of the magazine.—E. J. HOFFSCHMIDT

PISTOL MAGAZINES

Galesi Model 1923 Cal. 6.35 mm. Auto. Pistol

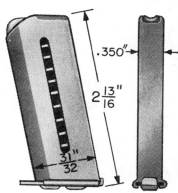

.350"

2 13/16"

31/32"

In 1923 the firm of Industria Armi Galesi, Brescia, Italy, began producing a new model cal. .25 semiautomatic pistol. In outline it resembles the Browning pocket pistol. However, it incorporates a much simpler takedown system and a unique method of retaining the magazine.

The magazine floorplate acts as the magazine catch. When magazine is inserted, the floorplate is pushed to the rear, where it locks in a frame recess. To remove it, push the floorplate forward until it is clear of the pistol frame and then pull out the magazine.

The follower is another point of identification. Made from drawn sheet metal, its upper surface is concaved for rigidity and easier feeding.—E. J. HOFFSCHMIDT

89

CROSMAN
Series 150 Pistol

By THOMAS E. WESSEL

The Crosman Series 150 pistol, produced by Crosman Arms Co., of E. Bloomfield, N.Y., uses carbon dioxide (CO_2) as a propellant and shoots skirted lead pellets. Commonly called a CO_2 "Pellgun", this pistol is of single-shot type and was introduced in 1954. Until 1959 it was produced in .22 caliber (The Model 150) and .177 caliber (The Model 157).

Unlike pneumatic and spring-type air guns this pistol has no pump. Liquid CO_2 is contained in a steel cylinder called a "Powerlet" which is inserted into a tube underneath the barrel. Pulling the trigger releases the hammer which actuates a valve and the valve meters a fixed amount of gas into the barrel to propel the pellet. As soon as any amount of gas is released from the Powerlet more of the liquid turns to gas keeping the pressure constant. In this manner gas pressure from shot to shot remains relatively constant until the Powerlet is almost empty.

The Crosman Series 150 has undergone a number of manufacturing changes in its nearly 40 year production history. The latest version is the Crosman "SSP".

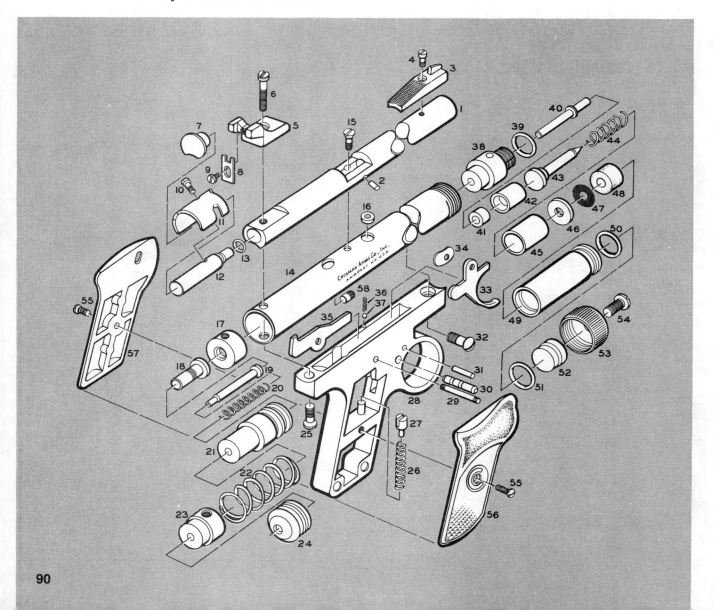

1 Before disassembly, exhaust all gas from pistol by successive cocking and firing. Then remove tube cap (53) and take out gas cylinder. Remove the rear and front frame screws (25 & 32). The barrel and tube assembly may now be separated from the grip frame (28)

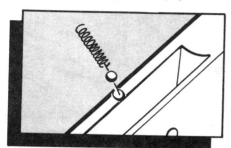

2 During disassembly, take care that safety spring (36) and safety spring ball (37) do not drop out of the grip frame and become lost

3 Remove rear sight screw (6), rear sight (5), and breech plug (7). Remove the breech bolt screw (10) and slide the breech bolt (12) and the loading sleeve (11) off to the rear

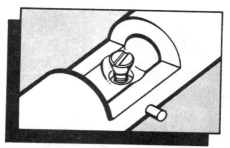

4 Remove hold-down screw (15) and lift barrel (1) off tube (14)

5 From rear of tube, remove hammer assembly consisting of cocking cap (24), tube plug (23), hammer spring (22), hammer (21), cocking spring (20), cocking rod (19), and hammer plug (18). Using a ⅛" rod from rear of tube, push valve assembly out forward. Through screw hole in top of tube, drive out thrust pin (58) and then remove small tube plug (17)

6 Remove grip screws (55) and right and left grips (56 & 57). Lift sear spring (26) off its guide in grip frame, and remove sear spring head (27). Drift out sear pin (29) from right to left, and remove sear (35). Drift out trigger pin (31) from right to left, and remove trigger (33) and take-up spring (34). Prior to reassembly, clean and oil all O-rings. Reassemble in reverse order ■

Parts Legend

1. Barrel	21. Hammer*	41. Exhaust valve washer
2. Lock pin	22. Hammer spring*	42. Exhaust nut
3. Front sight	23. Tube plug*	43. Piercing pin
4. Front sight screw	24. Cocking cap*	44. Check valve spring
5. Rear sight	25. Frame screw, rear	45. Spacer
6. Rear sight screw	26. Sear spring	46. Washer
7. Breech plug	27. Sear spring head	47. Screen
8. Sight blade	28. Grip frame	48. Filter
9. Elevation screw	29. Sear pin	49. Piercing body
10. Breech bolt screw	30. Safety	50. O-ring (piercing body)
11. Loading sleeve	31. Trigger pin	51. O-ring (rest block)
12. Breech bolt	32. Frame screw, front	52. Rest block
13. O-ring (breech bolt)	33. Trigger	53. Tube cap
14. Tube	34. Take-up spring	54. Connecting screw
15. Hold-down screw	35. Sear	55. Grip screw (2)
16. Breech gasket	36. Safety spring	56. Grip, right
17. Small tube plug	37. Safety spring ball	57. Grip, left
18. Hammer plug*	38. Exhaust valve	58. Thrust pin
19. Cocking rod*	39. O-ring (exhaust valve)	
20. Cocking spring*	40. Valve stem	*Permanent factory assembly

Glisenti Model 1910 9 mm. Auto

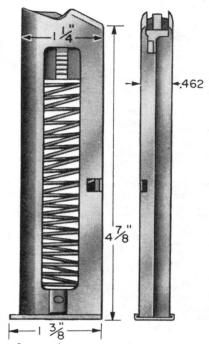

PISTOL MAGAZINES

Once you have encountered a Glisenti magazine, you will probably not forget it, for it is as distinctive as the gun itself. Even though it was used by the Italian army and navy during World Wars I and II, the gun is not too common. While the design is not the best, the guns are usually well made. The gun uses a recoil unlocking system that is very similar to the Italian Fiat M35 ground machine gun.

The open sides are characteristic of Italian magazines, but the Glisenti is the largest of them and is usually chrome-plated. The floorplate can be removed for cleaning by depressing the button in the middle of it and sliding it to the front.

The heavy machined follower with the serrated finger grip on either side is an excellent means of identification. The step or ridge along the backstrap that guides the follower is an obvious feature.—E. J. HOFFSCHMIDT.

Crosman Single Action 6 Revolver

By Thomas E. Wessel

THE Crosman Single Action 6-shot cal. .22 gas-powered revolver was introduced in 1959. It uses Crosman Powerlet CO_2 cylinders as a propellent source and cal. .22 skirted pellets, or Pells, also adapted to air and gas rifles. The lock mechanism is of single-action type requiring hand cocking of the hammer for each shot.

1 To disassemble Crosman Single Action, first exhaust CO_2 gas by pushing hammer (10) forward with thumb and remove empty gas cylinder. Remove grip screw (22) and right and left grips (9 & 23). Support butt and muzzle of gun on wooden blocks to free cylinder (24). Place hammer at half cock and remove hammer screw (7) with lockwasher (6), 2 short frame screws (5), and long frame screw (4). Insert a screwdriver in slot behind trigger (17) and pry off right frame (3). **Caution:** Use care when removing right frame as internal parts are under spring tension. All internal parts may now be lifted away. Oil and clean all O-rings and seals before reassembly

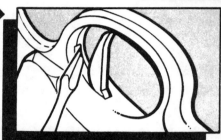

2 Commence reassembly by first assembling plate (25) onto valve assembly, then place valve, with plate in position, into cylinder. Install valve and cylinder assembly into left frame (2). Spot hole in valve fits over pin in frame casting. Place barrel (1) in left frame and locate shoulder of barrel in plate

3 Place cylinder spring (18) and ball (19) into depression in casting. Hold ball and spring lightly with left thumb, then rotate cylinder forward until ball raises slightly and back end of spring drops into depression in casting. Holding ball and spring firmly, turn cylinder backward until spring compresses and lies flat in depression. **Caution:** Cylinder must not be moved or disturbed after ball and spring are in place

Parts Legend

1. Barrel
2. Frame, left
3. Frame, right
4. Frame screw, long
5. Frame screw, short (2)
6. Lockwasher
7. Hammer screw
8. Grip insert
9. Grip, right
10. Hammer*
11. Index spring*
12. Index hand*
13. Index pin*
14. Hammer spring
15. Trigger pin
16. Trigger spring
17. Trigger
18. Cylinder spring
19. Cylinder ball
20. Retaining nut
21. Retaining screw
22. Grip screw
23. Grip, left
24. Cylinder
25. Plate
26. Pell spring
27. O-ring (rear valve body)
28. Valve body
29. O-ring (front valve body)
30. Valve stem
31. Exhaust nut washer
32. Exhaust nut
33. Valve return spring
34. Spacer
35. Screen
36. Filter
37. Piercing body
38. CO_2 seal
* Factory subassembly

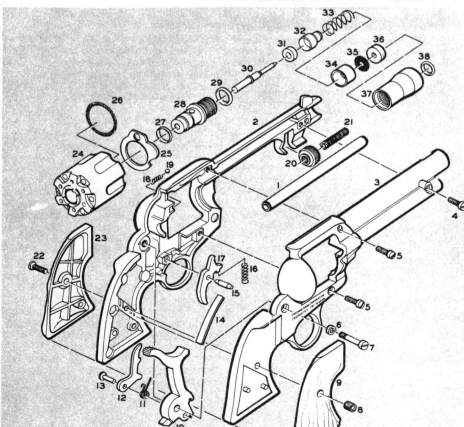

Velocity is about 245 feet per second (f.p.s.) with the 14.3-gr. skirted pellet which gives a penetration of 1″ in hard laundry soap at 5 ft. This pistol is thus capable of inflicting a serious wound and should be employed with the same respect and caution as a cartridge firearm.

This pistol is suitably accurate for informal short-range target shooting.

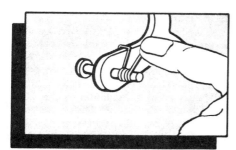

4 Index hand (12) should not normally be disassembled from the hammer (10), since that disturbs the riveted end. Should it be necessary, the hammer group may be reassembled by placing index pin (13) through its hole in hand (12), and placing index spring (11) over pin and hooking it to hand as shown. Next, place other end of index pin in its hole in left side of hammer and catch index spring on hammer boss. Re-rivet or peen end of index pin against right side of hammer. When placing hammer assembly in right frame, hold index hand away from indexing lugs on cylinder lest it be disturbed. Hammer assembly may be held in place with a ⅛″ slave pin

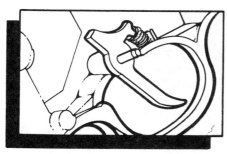

5 Assemble trigger pin (15), trigger (17), and trigger spring (16)

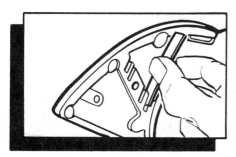

6 Put hammer spring (14) into lower slot in left frame. Place retaining screw and nut (21 & 20) in notch at muzzle end, then place right frame over left and press halves together. Replace frame screws, hammer screw and lockwasher (7 & 6), grips, and grip screw ∎

PISTOL MAGAZINES

Haenel-Schmeisser Model I Vest Pocket Pistol

The Haenel-Schmeisser Model I cal. .25 vest pocket pistol was designed by Hugo Schmeisser and introduced in 1920. It is known for its clean lines and unusual features, including absence of an ejection port. When lock mechanism is cocked, end of firing pin spring guide protrudes beyond end of slide. Design incorporates rigidly mounted barrel.

Magazine can be removed only when the safety catch is in "safe" position. This feature prevents accidental firing of a round that may have been left in the chamber. Upon reinsertion of the magazine, the pistol cannot be fired until safety is moved to "fire" position.

Like the rest of the gun, the magazine is well made. It is distinguished by the semi-circular cutout in the floorplate and backstrap. This cutout is a takedown tool and fits over the recoil spring guide when the slide is retracted.—E. J. HOFFSCHMIDT

Jager .32 Cal. Auto Pistol

PISTOL MAGAZINES

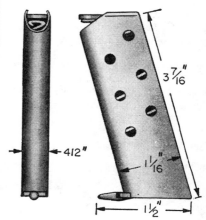

The Jager Automatic, introduced prior to World War I, was a bit ahead of its time. It had a receiver built of sheet steel and castings, thereby doing away with costly forgings and a great deal of expensive machining time. While these are ideals the modern gun designer strives for, they were not to be found in other pistols produced around the same time as the Jager. In spite of the Jager's unique design features, the gun had little else to recommend it. It is heavier and bulkier than most common .32-cal. automatics.

Jager 7-shot capacity magazines are readily recognizable by the spur that extends from the front edge of the floorplate. This spur is really a tool to facilitate field-stripping the gun, and is used to depress spring-loaded pins in the frame.

While the magazine itself is well made, the follower is a simple flat stamping characteristic of the average .32 automatic. The magazine has observation holes on each side.—E. J. HOFFSCHMIDT

CZ Model 27 Pistol

By E. J. Hoffschmidt

THE Czech Model 27 pistol has had a short but intriguing history. During the early 1920's, the newly formed Czech army was seeking a military pistol. Around the same time the Mauser firm was experimenting with a pistol designed by Josef Nickl, who had been an assistant to Paul Mauser. The Nickl design featured a locked slide with rotating barrel, and the hammer was external. Lockwork, frame, and magazine were like that of the Mauser Model 1910 Pocket Pistol. Eventually the Czechs were licensed to manufacture this gun. It was issued in 1922 and revised in 1924 to become the standard military pistol. Although the main topic of this article is the Model 27, the Model 24 must be mentioned because it is often mistaken for the later Model 27 gun.

Like the Mauser prototype, the Model 24 is a locked-breech gun with a barrel that rotates to unlock. This feature was dropped in the Model 27, since a simple blowback system is strong enough for the cal. .32 cartridge.

The Model 27 saw wide service before, during, and after World War II, and thousands were brought back from Europe by U. S. soldiers. There are 3 more or less common variations in markings. Late prewar and early wartime manufactured guns are usually blued and well finished and are usually marked "Bohmische Waffenfabrik AG in Prag" along the top of the slide. As the war progressed, efforts were made to increase production by substituting stamped for machined parts. The side-plate, safety arm, magazine catch, and firing pin retainer were all replaced by sheet metal stampings. The trade name was dropped, and the German code letters "fnh" and "Pistole Modell 27 Kal. 7.65" were stamped into the slide. The fine prewar bluing was dropped in favor of the more durable Parkerized finish. Production was started up again by the Czechs shortly after the end of World War II. These postwar guns are marked "Ceska Zbrojovka-Narodni Podnik" above "Strakonice" which means Czech National Cooperative Arsenal in Strakonice.

As pocket pistols go the gun is simple, compact, and reliable. The sights and grip are good. The efficient Mauser-type safety catch is one of the best features of the gun. Simply cock the hammer and

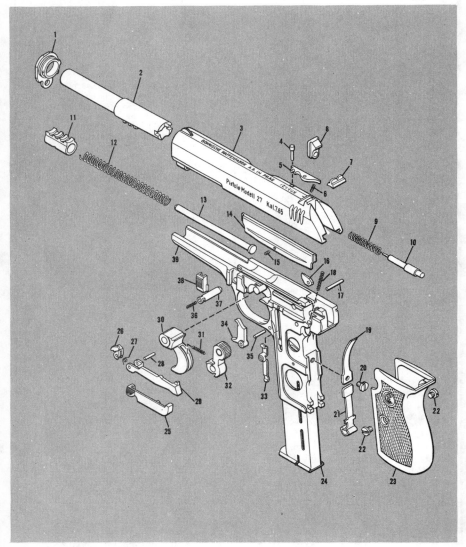

Parts Legend

1. Barrel bushing
2. Barrel
3. Slide
4. Extractor pin
5. Extractor
6. Extractor spring
7. Rear sight
8. Firing pin retainer
9. Firing pin spring
10. Firing pin
11. Barrel retainer
12. Recoil spring
13. Recoil spring guide
14. Side-plate
15. Side-plate screw
16. Ejector
17. Ejector pin
18. Safety and trigger bar spring
19. Hammer spring
20. Spring retaining screw
21. Magazine catch
22. Grip screw (2)
23. Grip
24. Magazine
25. Safety catch
26. Disconnector
27. Disconnector spring
28. Hinge pin
29. Trigger bar
30. Trigger
31. Trigger spring
32. Hammer
33. Safety release
34. Magazine disconnector
35. Disconnector hinge pin
36. Takedown catch spring
37. Takedown cross pin
38. Takedown catch
39. Frame

press down the safety until it clicks. Press the button below the catch and it snaps back to fire position in an instant. Another admirable feature is the simple takedown. The gun can be field stripped in seconds.

From the military standpoint it leaves a lot to be desired. So little of the hammer is exposed that it is awkward to cock if the shooter's hands are greasy or wet. The magazine safety is another debatable feature. If the magazine is lost, the round in the chamber cannot be fired. The gun cannot even be used as a single-shot weapon. When the last shot is fired, the magazine follower holds the slide open. This makes it necessary to remove the magazine against the pressure of the spring-loaded slide, which greatly slows magazine changes. The Czechs too realized the shortcomings of the Model 27 and around 1950 replaced it with a double-action pistol greatly resembling the Walther Model PP.

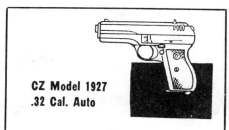

**CZ Model 1927
.32 Cal. Auto**

PISTOL MAGAZINES
One of a series

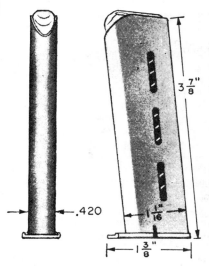

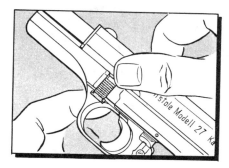

1 To strip Model 24 or Model 27, pull slide back over an empty magazine. Slide will stay open and relieve tension on barrel retainer (11). Push in protruding end of takedown cross pin (37), at same time slide takedown catch (38) down and free of frame

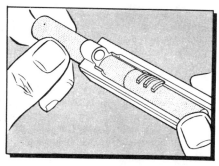

4 To get barrel (2) out of slide, pull it forward until the 3 barrel lugs line up with cut in slide as shown. Rotate lugs into cutout and pull barrel free of slide. On earlier Model 24, barrel can be pulled straight out of slide

Two models of this pistol were brought over by returning GI's—the gray-finished pistol usually marked Model 27 and the blued prewar pistol marked Bohmische Waffenfabrik on the top of the slide. The operating mechanism of this gun bears a close resemblance to the 1910 Mauser. While far from the best .32 cal. automatics, they are interesting and serviceable guns. The main drawback is the fact that when the last shot has been fired, the magazine holds the slide open, making it necessary to withdraw the magazine against the force of the recoil spring.

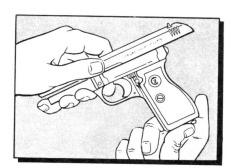

2 After takedown catch assembly has been removed, pull out magazine as shown and ease slide assembly off frame. Magazine is difficult to remove because it holds the slide open, and must be removed against pressure of recoil spring

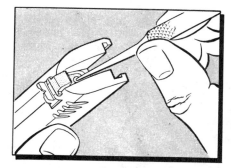

5 Firing pin (10) is retained by a small machined block in early guns, and by a sheet metal stamping in wartime models. To remove pin, simply push protruding end of it below surface of firing pin retainer (8), and pry retainer up and out as shown

The magazine, too, resembles the 1910 Mauser, in that it has elongated observation slots instead of holes. The floorplate will normally be stamped as shown, and is retained by a portion of the magazine follower spring.

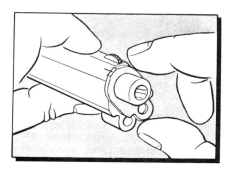

3 Barrel is retained by barrel bushing (1). First step in removing barrel, is to turn bushing about 30° until line on bushing coincides with line on slide (3). Then bushing can be pulled out of slide and off barrel

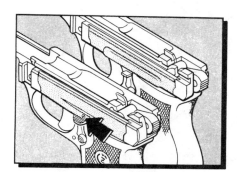

6 With side-plate (14) and grip (23) removed, operating parts can be easily removed. Early guns have a small side-plate screw (15) which must be loosened before plate can be slid up. Screw, if overly tightened, will bend side-plate and bind parts ∎

The Model 27 magazine has a pressed steel follower that again resembles the 1910 Mauser, but the offset notch that cuts through the follower and the back strap peg identify it as a Model 27.—E. J. HOFF-SCHMIDT.

CZ Model 50 Pistol

By E. J. HOFFSCHMIDT

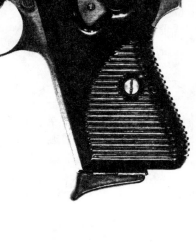

In 1948, the Czech arms factories were nationalized and shortly thereafter various new Czech commercial arms were introduce. One of these new guns was the CZ Model 50 self-loading pistol, developed in 1947-48 by Jan and Jaroslav Kratochvil and produced by Ceska Zbrojovka - Narodni Podnik, Strakonice (Czech Arms Factory, National Corporation, in Strakonice). Besides being sold commercially, this pistol is used by Czechoslovakian police. It is of blowback design, fires the universally popular .32 ACP cartridge and weighs 24-1/2 ounces. In size, general appearance and basic construction it is similar to the Walther Model PP. However these pistols differ from one another mechanically, especially in the lock mechanism.

Like several other modern self-loading pistols the Model 50 has a double-action lock mechanism. This makes it possible to safely carry the pistol with a cartridge in the chamber, the hammer uncocked and the safety catch disengaged and yet to quickly fire it by means of a long pull on the trigger. During firing, the exposed hammer is cocked by the movement of the slide in recoil, and a short pull on the trigger is required for subsequent shots.

Located on the left of the receiver in a position convenient for thumb operation, the safety catch is engaged when pivoted part way down. Lowering the cocked hammer is easily done by turning the safety downward past "SAFE". It is not dangerous to do this even with a loaded round in the chamber because the firing pin is blocked. No grip safety is provided, but a cartridge indicator projects from the left of the slide when the chamber is loaded.

The eight-round magazine is removed for loading by depressing the magazine catch on the upper left of the receiver. A takedown latch at the right front of the trigger guard permits easy field stripping. A combination hold-open latch and ejector holds the slide of the Model 50 to the rear when the last shot is fired.

Most parts are blued steel. The grips are grooved black plastic.

The Model 50 was discontinued some years ago, in favor of the newer Model 83.

Parts Legend

1. Slide
2. Extractor pin
3. Cartridge indicator
4. Rear sight
5. Extractor spring
6. Extractor
7. Firing pin
8. Firing pin lock spring
9. Firing pin lock
10. Recoil spring
11. Hold-open latch spring
12. Hold-open latch and ejector
13. Hold-open hinge pin
14. Left grip
15. Grip screw
16. Safety
17. Safety plunger
18. Safety spring
19. Hammer bolt
20. Sear spring
21. Sear
22. Hammer strut pin
23. Hammer
24. Hammer strut
25. Hammer spring
26. Spring retainer
27. Right grip
28. Trigger bar
29. Trigger spring
30. Trigger
31. Trigger pin
32. Trigger bar pin
33. Takedown catch spring
34. Takedown catch screw
35. Takedown catch
36. Magazine catch
37. Magazine catch spring
38. Sear pin
39. Sideplate
40. Hammer bolt nut
41. Receiver
42. Magazine
43. Barrel

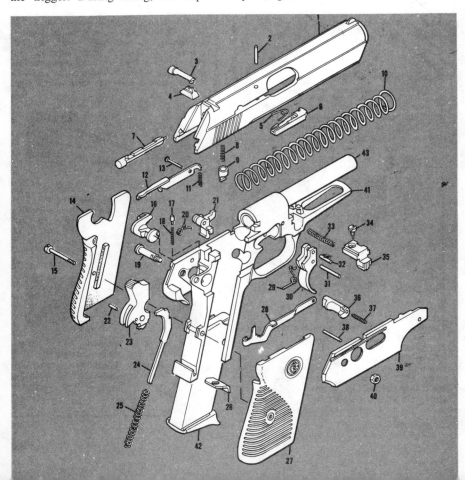

1 To field-strip the CZ Model 50, first remove the magazine (42) and clear the chamber. While pressing the takedown catch (35) to the left, pull the slide (1) back and lift it upward at the rear. Then ease the slide forward off the barrel (43) and remove the recoil spring (10).

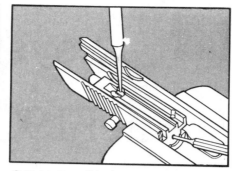

2 Hold the slide bottom side up in a vise. Depress the firing pin lock (9) with a punch and use a long thin punch from the front to push the firing pin (7) out. After the firing pin lock and spring are removed, drive out the extractor pin (2), and remove extractor (6), extractor spring (5), and cartridge indicator (3).

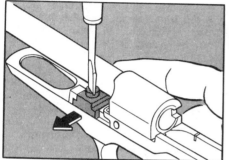

3 Push the takedown catch all the way to the left, and unscrew the takedown catch screw (34). In doing this, a screwdriver with a thin shank is required to clear the barrel. After removing the screw, take out the catch and spring to the right. The hold-open latch and ejector (12) and latch spring (11) can be removed by driving out the hold-open hinge pin (13) to the left. Do not remove these unless necessary.

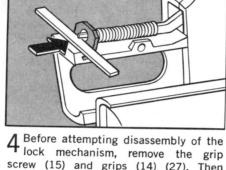

4 Before attempting disassembly of the lock mechanism, remove the grip screw (15) and grips (14) (27). Then carefully clamp the receiver (41) in a vise with padded jaws. Place a thin metal bar against the bottom of the spring retainer (26), and push on the bar until the retainer is free of the receiver. Then ease the bar back to original position and remove the hammer spring (25) from the hammer strut (24).

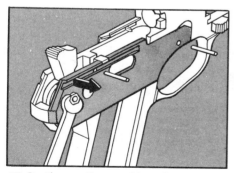

5 Continue disassembly of the lock mechanism by driving out the trigger pin (31) and sear pin (38), and use a small wrench to remove the nut (40) from the hammer bolt (19). Then push out the hammer bolt, lift the sideplate (39) from the receiver, and remove the trigger bar (28), trigger (30), hammer (23), and other lock parts.

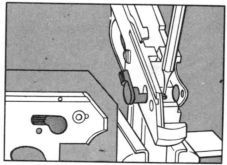

6 After removing the hammer, push the safety (16) out to left without rotating. Take care not to lose the safety plunger (17) and safety spring (18). Reassemble in reverse. In replacing the safety, use a small punch to hold the safety plunger depressed. In replacing the hammer bolt nut do not use excessive force and strip the threads. ∎

CZ Model 1922
Vest Pocket Pistol

PISTOL MAGAZINES

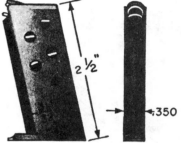

The Model 1922 vest pocket pistol is one of a number of interesting cal. .25 pistols turned out by Ceska Zbrojovka, Czechoslovakia. A. S., Prague. Unusual in design, the gun resembles a common cal. .25 pistol style, but it has no true slide. Instead, a bolt operates in a tunnel-like section formed of sheet metal. The frame is made of stamped and formed sheet metal that is pinned to a core, a clever design from a production point of view, but the thin-walled frame can be damaged easily if the gun is dropped.

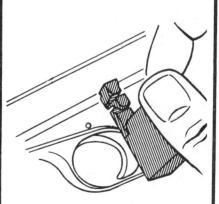

Like the rest of the gun, the magazine is well finished. The magazine floorplate is much heavier than normal and carefully pinned to the magazine walls. This is necessary because the floorplate is used as a takedown tool. Slide and barrel are retained by a square cross key. To disassemble the gun, this key must be pried out as shown. The front edge of the magazine floorplate is machined to a sort of screwdriver point to do the job.—EDWARD J. HOFFSCHMIDT

DAN WESSON MODEL W-12 REVOLVER

Illustrations By DENNIS RIORDAN
Text By LUDWIG OLSON

When viewed casually, the Dan Wesson Model W-12, .357 Magnum revolver appears to be of conventional, double-action, swing-out cylinder design. It is unusual, however, in that its barrel can be quickly and easily interchanged for others, of different lengths. The one-piece grip can also be interchanged for one of different shape and size.

This versatile solid-frame revolver is produced by Dan Wesson Arms, which was organized in 1968 at Monson, Mass. The late Daniel B. Wesson, who was the founder and president of the firm, was a great-grandson of Daniel B. Wesson of Smith & Wesson. Dan Wesson Arms, however, is not connected with S&W.

Barrels of six-inch, four-inch and 2-1/2-inch lengths are available for the Model W-12. To interchange them, the revolver is unloaded and a combination tool is used to unscrew the barrel nut. After the barrel nut and shroud are removed the barrel is unscrewed by hand. When installing a replacement barrel a shim, provided with the revolver, is used to obtain the proper clearance between the barrel and cylinder.

One-piece walnut grips of target, combat or "Michigan" styles are available. The latter was designed by two Michigan State Police officers. Also available is an inletted walnut blank for those who wish to shape their own grip.

The cylinder swings out to the left on a crane in the usual manner, but the latch is forward of the cylinder instead of to its rear. Pushing the ejector rod ejects all cartridges or fired cases simultaneously. The ejector rod is protected from damage by the barrel shroud - a desirable feature.

A simple, effective firing pin connector, which is pivoted on the trigger, transmits the hammer blow to the firing pin. When the trigger moves forward, the connector is lowered out of line with the firing pin so that a blow on the hammer will not cause the gun to fire.

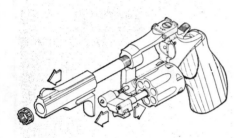

1 Before attempting disassembly, unload cylinder (50), and lower hammer (27). Use Wesson combination tool (or ⅝" double-hex box wrench) to unscrew and remove barrel nut (19). Slide off shroud (3), and unscrew barrel (20). Depress latch (22), and swing out crane (24) and cylinder. Pull cylinder-crane assembly forward from frame (18), and detach cylinder from crane. This is sufficient takedown for normal cleaning.

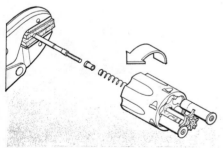

2 To disassemble cylinder parts, clamp knurled tip of ejector rod (48) between wooden blocks in vise or locking-jaw pliers. Insert two empty cartridge cases in opposite chambers, and use cases to unscrew cylinder from rod. This releases extractor (52), ejector rod bushing (49), and ejector spring (51).

3 Hole in underside of grip (34) gives access to grip screw (33). Remove screw with combination tool (5/32" Allen wrench), and pull grip downward from frame spike. Unscrew and remove sideplate screws (42) (47) with combination tool (5/64" Allen wrench). Lift sideplate (46) carefully; hand (35) is under spring tension and is easily displaced.

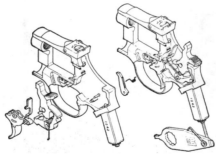

4 Unhook hand spring (39) from groove in rear of hand, and remove hand and spring. Cock hammer. Then tighten long sideplate screw into mainspring guide (44), through hole at bottom of frame spike. Pull trigger (40), and lower hammer with thumb. Draw long arm of trigger return spring (43) outward from trigger, and allow it to arc downward until the tension is relieved. Trigger and firing pin connector (25), hammer, trigger spring, and bolt (38) can then be lifted from frame.

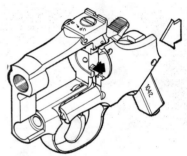

5 Assemble in reverse. Stub arm of trigger spring must be positioned to rear of frame-mounted hammer pivot pin. Install hand spring with shorter arm bearing on forward surface of firing pin connector and longer arm hooked into hand groove. Maintain fingernail pressure against tip of hand to prevent its escape while replacing sideplate. Hold sideplate flat against frame and slide forward into place.

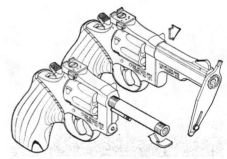

6 Clean barrel threads, rear barrel face, and forward face of cylinder before adjusting clearance. Place .006" shim gauge on cylinder face, and screw barrel inward until a very light drag is felt on shim, just enough to hold shim in position. Install shroud and barrel nut with shim in place, rechecking clearance after barrel nut has been tightened.

All springs in the Model W-12 are of piano wire, which is noted for its durability. Metal parts are steel with most exposed surfaces highly polished and blued. The hammer, trigger, top of the frame and the rib on the barrel shroud have a matte finish.

The well designed sights consist of a fully adjustable, square notch, rear and a Baughman quick-draw front. Windage and elevation adjustment screws in the rear sight have slots wide enough to accept a dime.

The Model W-12 was dropped in about 1974 in favor of improved models.

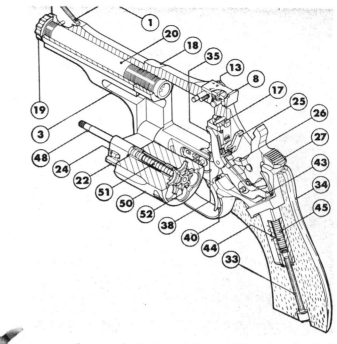

Cutaway indicates relative position of assembled parts. Cylinder is shown opened, hammer at full cock. Parts are number keyed to parts legend.

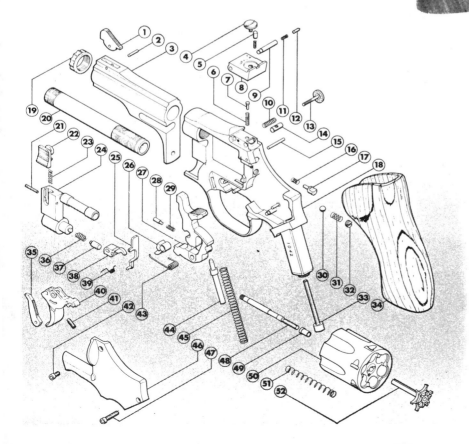

Parts Legend

1. Front sight
2. Front sight pin
3. Shroud
4. Elevation screw
5. Elevation click plunger
6. Elevation tension spring
7. Elevation tension plunger
8. Rear sight body
9. Hinge pin
10. Windage tension spring
11. Plunger spring (2)
12. Windage click plunger
13. Windage screw
14. Elevation nut
15. Firing pin retaining pin
16. Firing pin spring
17. Firing pin
18. Frame
19. Barrel nut
20. Barrel
21. Latch retaining pin
22. Latch
23. Latch spring
24. Crane
25. Firing pin connector
26. Strut
27. Hammer
28. Strut plunger
29. Strut spring
30. Cylinder aligning
31. Aligning ball spring
32. Aligning ball screw
33. Grip screw
34. Grip
35. Hand
36. Bolt spring
37. Bolt plunger
38. Bolt
39. Hand spring
40. Trigger
41. Trigger stop screw
42. Sideplate screw
43. Trigger return spring
44. Mainspring guide
45. Mainspring
46. Sideplate
47. Sideplate screw
48. Ejector rod
49. Ejector rod bushing
50. Cylinder
51. Ejector spring
52. Extractor

DERINGER'S POCKET PISTOL

By JAMES M. TRIGGS

HENRY DERINGER, JR., of Philadelphia, Pa., began manufacture of his famed single-shot muzzle-loading percussion pocket pistols in 1825 and limited production continued even after his death in 1868, when the firm was operated for a time by a son-in-law, Dr. Jonathan Clark.

However, the demand for all types of percussion pistols fell off sharply following the Civil War when the self-contained metallic cartridge came into common use. The Deringer was but one of many erstwhile popular percussion arms doomed by this development. In its heyday, the Deringer pistol was favored by individuals from all walks of life who desired a powerful yet easily concealed handgun. It was made in several calibers from .33 to .51, and with barrels ranging in length from less than 1" to more than 4".

Commonly sold in matched pairs, the genuine Deringer pistols had rifled barrels of wrought iron. Some were fitted with single-set triggers. The 2-line trademark DERINGER PHILADELᴬ was invariably stamped on the lockplate and breech. These pistols were not serially numbered, but the various parts were stamped with matching assembly numbers or letters. Like most well-made products, the Deringer pistols were subject to counterfeiting and some of this

was done by former employees of the Deringer firm. This resulted in litigation successful to Deringer, but the fact remains that the word Deringer (or Derringer) is today a proper noun commonly applied to any easily concealable short barrel pocket pistol of non-automatic type.

Deringer pistols figured in many notable homicides, the most famous being the assassination of President Abraham Lincoln by John Wilkes Booth.

The full story of the Deringer pistol is given in the book entitled *Henry Deringer's Pocket Pistol*, by John E. Parsons, published in 1952 by William Morrow & Co.

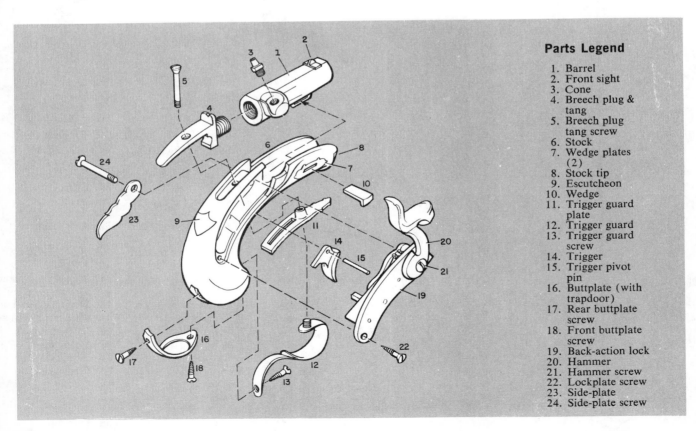

Parts Legend

1. Barrel
2. Front sight
3. Cone
4. Breech plug & tang
5. Breech plug tang screw
6. Stock
7. Wedge plates (2)
8. Stock tip
9. Escutcheon
10. Wedge
11. Trigger guard plate
12. Trigger guard
13. Trigger guard screw
14. Trigger
15. Trigger pivot pin
16. Buttplate (with trapdoor)
17. Rear buttplate screw
18. Front buttplate screw
19. Back-action lock
20. Hammer
21. Hammer screw
22. Lockplate screw
23. Side-plate
24. Side-plate screw

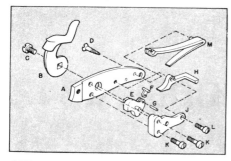

1 The conventional back-action lock is easily disassembled after removal from the stock. The lower end of the V mainspring (M) bears directly on the sear (H) and no sear spring is employed.

A) Lockplate
B) Hammer (20)
C) Hammer screw (21)
D) Lockplate screw (22)
E) Tumbler
F) Stirrup
G) Stirrup pin
H) Sear
J) Bridle
K) Bridle screws (2)
L) Sear screw
M) Mainspring

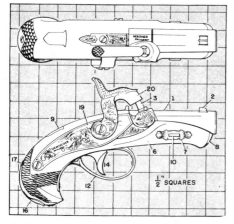

2 The scale drawing shows right side and top detail of the assembled Deringer pistol and is a reference in identifying genuine H. Deringer pistols of this type. Minor variations in style of engraving occur; however, the engraving shown is most typical of this arm.

Disassembly Procedure

Place hammer (20) at half-cock position and unscrew side-plate screw (24) from left side of stock. Unscrew lockplate screw (22) and tap left side of stock gently to loosen lockplate. Lift lock assembly out right side of stock. To remove barrel (1), drift wedge (10) out of stock. Unscrew breech plug tang screw (5) and lift barrel and breech plug assembly up out of stock. Trigger guard (12) and plate (11) can be removed from underside of stock after removing trigger guard screw (13). Trigger (14) is removed by drifting trigger pivot pin (15) out of stock. Buttplate is removed by unscrewing rear and front buttplate screws (17 & 18).

Removal of wedge plates (7), stock tip (8), escutcheon (9), and side-plate (23) from stock (6) is not recommended. Reassemble in reverse order. ∎

PISTOL MAGAZINES

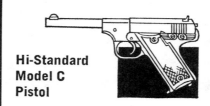

Hi-Standard Model C Pistol

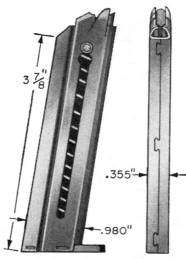

High Standard Mfg. Co. once felt there was a market for a sporting semi-automatic pistol chambered for the .22 short cartridge, and thus the Model C was developed. Although up to High Standard's usual good quality, it was not a commercial success.

The Hi-Standard Model C magazine is fully as wide as the normal .22 long rifle magazine, but is creased on the sides to limit its width for the .22 short cartridge.

The non-detachable floorplate is retained by 2 deep stab detents on either side of the magazine body. The creases that reduce the width of the magazine also serve to retain the floorplate.—E. J. HOFFSCHMIDT

PISTOL MAGAZINES

Korovin Cal. .25 Pistol

A medium-size arm, the Korovin cal. .25 pistol is turning up occasionally in the hands of the Viet Cong. Made in Russia's Tula Weapons Factory, it was sometimes issued to Russian doctors and nurses during World War II. Although fairly well made and finished, there is evidence of considerable hand fitting, a characteristic of early Soviet pistols. Korovin pistols are generally blued and have either checkered wood or black plastic grips bearing the letters TOZ in Cyrillic letters.

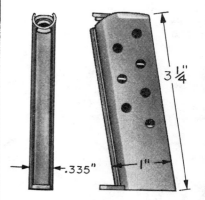

The Korovin is larger than most .25 automatic pistols, but this affords a better grip and a larger magazine capacity.

Korovin magazines are readily identified by the heavy crimped ridge on the front face, a construction feature imparting strength.

The follower is simply a flat piece of bent sheet metal, distinguished by its length and blunt tip.—E. J. HOFFSCHMIDT

Dreyse
Model 1907 Pistol

By E. J. Hoffschmidt

THERE was a period in Germany when any schoolboy could tell you that Nikolaus von Dreyse invented the famous Prussian needle gun. Though he died in 1867, his name was revered up through World War I and numerous guns designed long after his death carried his name. One is the Schmeisser-designed Dreyse Model 1907 pistol, manufactured by the Rheinische Metallwaren and Maschinenfabrik of Soemmerda, Germany.

The Dreyse is an awkward pistol, due in part to the fact that it was developed near the beginning of the automatic pistol era. A few years after the gun was first marketed, Europe was swamped by the 1910 series of Browning, Mauser, Sauer, and Walther pocket pistols. The better designs of these weapons soon overshadowed the Dreyse. Although it was manufactured up to World War I, the Model 1907 was superseded by the Rheinmetall pistol after World War I. During the short time it was in production, numerous machining changes were made. Around 1912 the gun was redesigned and scaled up to handle the 9 mm. Luger cartridge. The 9 mm. pistol was used to a limited extent during World War I, but the German Army never liked a blow-back-operated gun for such a powerful cartridge.

Although the grip design and general outline of the Model 1907 leave a great deal to be desired, it has a few interesting features. The most notable is the frame design. Unlike most common automatics, the sear mechanism can be inspected by removing a large side-plate. The frame is hinged and can be tipped up by moving a button at the back of the receiver. This action does not expose the barrel as in the Smith & Wesson and Le Francais pistols. It is helpful in clearing a jam, but it does not simplify the cleaning problem.

When the gun is cocked, a pin that can be easily seen or felt protrudes from the end of the slide. In spite of its seemingly complicated exterior, the operating parts are simple and fairly rugged.

Parts Legend

1. Slide
2. Extractor
3. Bolt head
4. Firing pin
5. Cocking indicator
6. Firing pin spring
7. Recoil spring
8. Recoil spring follower
9. Barrel extension
10. Ejector screw
11. Ejector
12. Sear spring cap
13. Sear spring
14. Right grip
15. Grip screw
16. Frame
17. Magazine
18. Magazine catch spring
19. Magazine catch
20. Magazine catch pin
21. Side-plate
22. Side-plate screw
23. Left grip
24. Grip screw
25. Safety catch
26. Side-plate screw
27. Hinge screw
28. Trigger bar
29. Trigger
30. Trigger spring
31. Sear
32. Disconnector
33. Frame latch
34. Frame latch spring
35. Safety catch spring

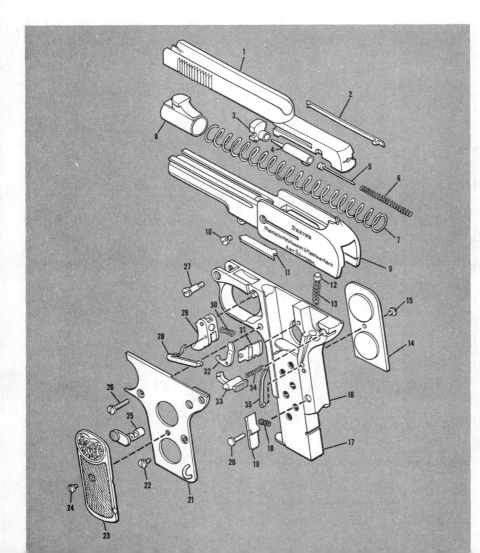

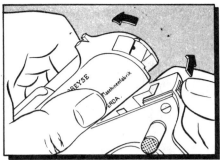

1 To disassemble: Remove magazine and clear chamber. Open action by pushing frame latch (33), on end of frame, to right and lifting up barrel extension (9) as shown. The gun will not come apart as it is hinged by a screw above the trigger guard

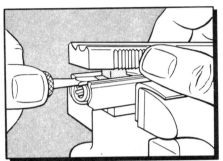

2 To avoid injuring knuckles it is best to clamp barrel extension of pistol in vise to simplify removal of slide. Depress recoil spring follower (8) with blade of small screwdriver until lug on follower clears notch in slide. Lift up serrated end of slide as shown, then ease follower off barrel, remembering it is under extremely heavy spring tension

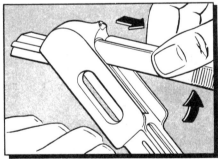

3 After recoil spring follower (8) and recoil spring (7) have been removed, push slide back as far as possible. Lift serrated portion and slide it free of barrel extension

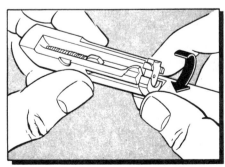

4 To remove firing pin (4) first lift out extractor (2), then rotate bolt head (3) as shown until rounded portion is free of retaining cut in slide. It may be necessary to tap the bolt head with a soft hammer to start it ∎

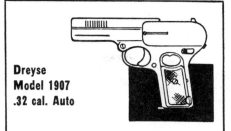

Dreyse Model 1907 .32 cal. Auto

PISTOL MAGAZINES

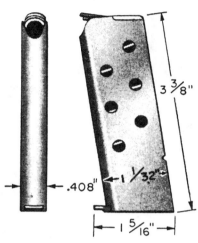

.32 caliber Dreyse pistols are a drug on the market. The gun's weird outline and lack of outstanding features have made it unpopular in America. It has an awkward grip and very high sights, making the gun difficult to shoot with any accuracy. Actually, it is made of excellent materials and usually well-finished. Most of the guns in this country are World War I souvenirs which had been issued as sidearms to special German troop units.

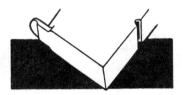

The tip of the magazine floorplate is the best clue to the identity of a Dreyse magazine. This tip is machined to a thinner cross-section as shown in the illustration. The other obvious clue is the magazine latch notch cut into the backstrap.

The follower is stamped from sheet steel and resembles that of other common magazines but the feed lips are somewhat weaker than most, since the wide bolt clearance notch at the top of the backstrap does not leave any metal for support.—E. J. HOFFSCHMIDT.

LeFrancais Cal. .25 Policeman Model

PISTOL MAGAZINES

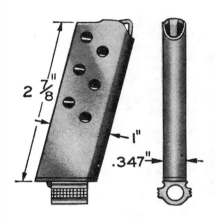

LeFrancais automatic pistols are very original in design. Unlike the average pocket pistol, the slide is not pulled back to load the chamber. The barrel tips up to accept the first round. This makes the gun easier to load and clean, and allows it to be used as a single-shot pistol. These pistols have a trigger action more like a revolver than an automatic. The trigger action is separate from the recoil action and the gun is cocked and fired by trigger pull alone. LeFrancais pistols are very well made and finished. An extractor is not provided, and is unnecessary as the cases are blown out by recoil. Two types of Policeman pistols are known. The obvious difference is in the magazines. The second model is shown here.

Late-type LeFrancais magazines have the distinctive follower shown here. The follower has a long guide bar at the front end and is stamped from a heavy piece of sheet steel. Observation holes are found only on the right side of the magazine.

The most distinctive feature of this magazine is the loop on the floorplate to hold the first round. This round is usually inserted by hand into the chamber of the upraised barrel.—E. J. HOFFSCHMIDT

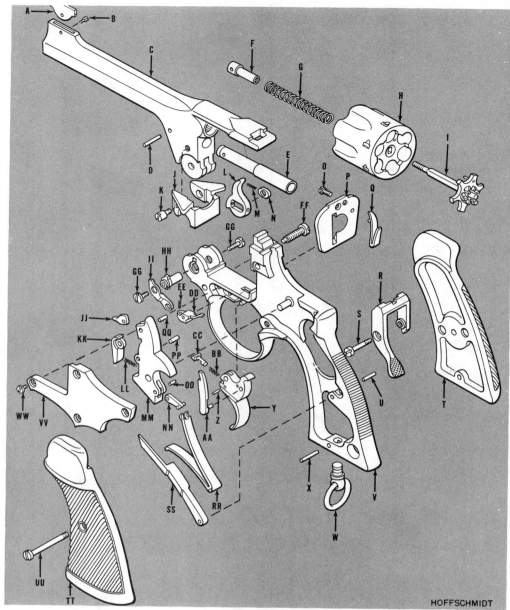

LEGEND

A—Front sight blade
B—Front sight screw
C—Barrel
D—Axle retaining pin
E—Cylinder axle
F—Extractor nut
G—Extractor spring
H—Cylinder
I—Extractor
J—Cylinder retaining cam
K—Cylinder cam screws
L—Extractor lever
M—Extractor lever spring
N—Extractor lever roller
O—Recoil plate screw
P—Recoil plate
Q—Barrel latch spring
R—Barrel latch
S—Barrel latch screw
T—Right-hand grip
U—Mainspring lever pin
V—Frame
W—Lanyard ring
X—Grip pin
Y—Trigger
Z—Stop operating catch pin
AA—Hand
BB—Stop operating catch spring
CC—Stop operating catch
DD—Cylinder stop
EE—Cylinder stop spring
FF—Cam lever screw
GG—Hinge pin screw
HH—Hinge pin
II—Cam lever
JJ—Hammer nose
KK—Hammer catch
LL—Hammer catch spring
MM—Hammer
NN—Hammer swivel
OO—Hammer swivel pin
PP—Catch retaining pin
QQ—Nose retaining pin
RR—Mainspring
SS—Mainspring lever
TT—Left-hand grip
UU—Grip screw
VV—Sideplate
WW—Sideplate screw

HOFFSCHMIDT

Enfield Revolver No. 2 Mk 1 and Mk 1*

By E. J. Hoffschmidt

The Enfield No. 2 , Mk I revolver, chambered for the .38-200 (or .38 S&W) cartridge, was adopted by the British army in 1932 to replace an older .455-in. caliber, Webley-pattern revolver, the Mk VI. The more recent No. 2, Mk I* - a double-action only modification of the original mechanism - was introduced in 1938.

Enfield No. 2 revolvers, the mainstay service handgun of British armed forces during World War II, were originally devised, as a simplification of a Webley and Scott design, by the Royal Small Arms Factory at Enfield Lock. The two revolvers, the No. 2, Mk I beginning in 1932, and the No. 2, Mk I* beginning in 1938, were introduced as replacements for the older .455-in caliber revolvers previously is service.

The No. 2, Mk I and Mk I* are basically the same revolver. The major dif-

ference between them is that the Mk I* has a double-action only mechanism, and lacks the full-cock notch and thumb-cocking hammer spur of the Mk I.

Webley & Scott "Mark IV" revolvers are often mistaken for Enfield No. 2 guns (particularly the No. 2, Mk I), but they are actually quite different both in design and in method of manufacture. While both were used during World War II, Enfields were made at the government arsenal at Enfield and Mark IV revolvers were made by Webley & Scott, Ltd. in their Birmingham plant. Even though the guns look a great deal alike, the Enfield is the simpler of the two from a repair standpoint. By removing the sideplate of the Enfield the operation of the parts can be studied. Not so with the Webley, as the parts are

installed through openings in the frame.

The majority of Enfield revolvers in this country have a wartime finish. Plenty of tool marks show, but the quality of steel was maintained throughout the war. In spite of the awkward appearance, these top-break revolvers are faster to load and extract than any other type of revolver. But, there are drawbacks. The cylinder can be knocked out of line should the gun be dropped while in the open position. And, closing the Mk I while the hammer is at full cock may cause damage to the hand which protrudes from the frame when the revolver is cocked and can be struck by the ratchet.

Enfield revolvers remained in service until 1957, when the British armed forces adopted a version of the Belgian, 9mm GP-35 (the Browning Hi-Power) designated L9A1.

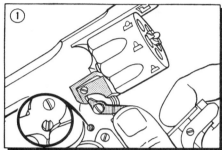

The first point in stripping the No. 2 revolver is to remove the cylinder (H). Remove the cam lever screw (FF). The screw slot is wide enough for a coin. Open the gun as far as it will go and push up on the cam lever (II) as shown. Lift the cylinder off the axle

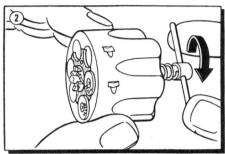

Before removing the extractor (I), put a few empty cartridges in the cylinder (H) to prevent the tiny locating pin from shearing off. Run a nail or punch through the hole in extractor nut (F) and unscrew it as shown. Lift out the extractor (I) and extractor spring (G)

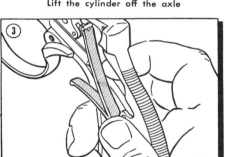

After the barrel latch (R), the sideplate (VV), and the grips have been removed, the mainspring (RR) may be pushed out of its seat as shown and unhooked from the hammer swivel (NN). Needless to say, this should not be attempted with the hammer at full cock (Mk 1 only)

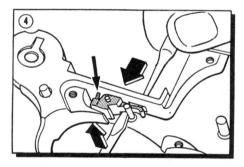

The only other delicate part in this gun is the cylinder stop spring (EE). Care must be taken not to deform it when removing the cylinder stop (DD). To remove the stop, it is necessary to depress it below the surface of the frame while prying it up off its pin

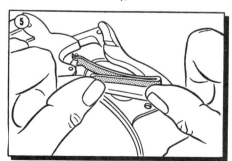

When re-assembling the gun, the mainspring is the only part that presents any difficulty. Squeeze the mainspring as shown. Insert the closed end into its seat in the frame. Then push the hammer swivel (NN) into its cutout in the mainspring (RR)

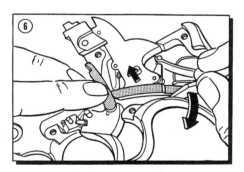

The hand (AA) is kept forward by the pressure of the mainspring lever (SS). To replace the hand (AA), it is necessary to pry the mainspring lever up until it is opposite its notch in the hand. Then push the hand in over the mainspring lever

---

Webley & Scott Self-Loading Pistol Mark I 1913

PISTOL MAGAZINES

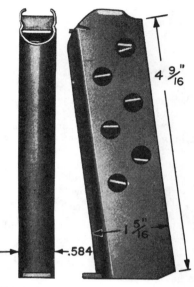

The design of Webley & Scott pistols may be a bit awkward by modern standards, but they are well made of the best materials. The cal. .455 Mark I 1913 pistol is a fairly common example. It has a man-sized grip and a business-like appearance.

According to official British publications, the Mark I magazine was manufactured with 2 locking notches so that the pistol could be used as a single-loader with the full magazine held in reserve. The half-moon notches and the clipped off floorplate are distinctive features.

The oddly shaped lips also identify this big magazine. The backstrap is cut away so the magazine will clear the slide hold-open, which is held out of action with cartridges in the magazine.—E. J. HOFF-SCHMIDT

ERMA .22 PISTOL

By DENNIS RIORDAN

The Luger pistol is extremely popular with both collectors and shooters. For many years there was a demand for a .22 rimfire version of this pistol and between the World Wars the Erma-Werke, in Germany, introduced a .22 caliber Luger conversion unit. In 1964 Erma brought out a .22 pistol that has the same general size and appearance as the German Model 1908, 9 mm Luger. However, these pistols differ from each other mechanically and in several other respects.

Chambered for the .22 Long Rifle cartridge, the Erma pistol weighs 36 ounces and has a 4-9/16" barrel. Its toggle-joint breech mechanism resembles that of the Luger, but the barrel does not recoil. The toggle mechanism retards the opening of the breech to some extent, and the pistol is thus of retarded-blowback type.

A manual safety on the left of the frame is pivoted down for engagement. With the safety in this position the word "GESICHERT" (safe) on the frame is exposed. The magazine holds eight rounds and can be removed by depressing the magazine catch on the left side behind the trigger. Many metal parts, including the frame, are die-cast non-ferrous alloy with a black finish. The breechblock, barrel liner and small parts are steel and the grips are checkered brown plastic.

In 1967, a redesigned version of this pistol, designated Model EP, was introduced. It features checkered walnut grips and an improved trigger mechanism and firing mechanism. Unlike the older version made for use with high-speed ammunition only, the improved pistol fires both high speed and standard velocity cartridges.

A long-barrel version of the Erma was also brought out in 1967. Called the Navy Model ET, this pistol has an 11-3/16" barrel and fired high speed and standard velocity .22 Long Rifle cartridges. It is equipped with a fully adjustable rear sight,

checkered walnut grips and fore-end, and the improved trigger mechanism and firing mechanism.

In 1978 a further improvement, the KGP-22 was introduced.

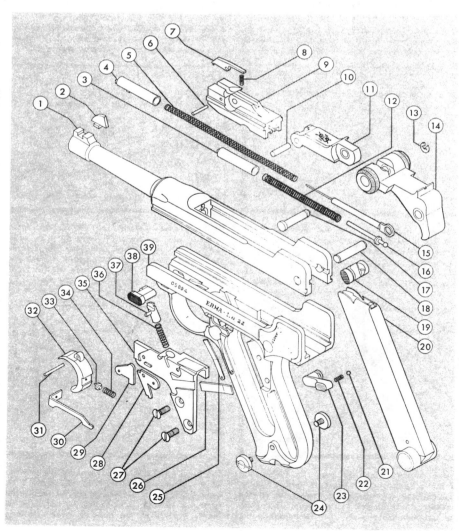

106

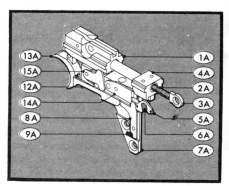

Parts Used in Model EP and Navy Model ET Only

1A. Breechblock
2A. Firing pin spring
3A. Ejector
4A. Firing pin assembly
5A. Safety ring
6A. Safety
7A. Sear housing
8A. Sear release
9A. Sear release spring

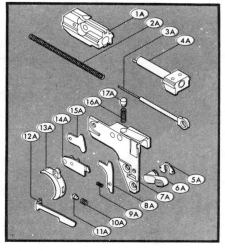

10A. Trigger bar plunger spring
11A. Trigger bar plunger
12A. Trigger bar
13A. Trigger
14A. Sear
15A. Disconnector
16A. Sear spring
17A. Sear plunger

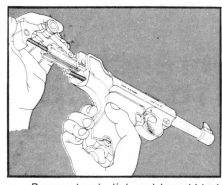

3. Remove toggle link and breechblock assembly to the rear. Take the recoil spring (12), recoil spring guide (16), and recoil spring sleeve (3) from rear of frame (39).

PARTS LEGEND

1. Barrel and receiver
2. Front sight
3. Recoil spring sleeve
4. Firing pin
5. Firing pin spring
6. Extractor pin
7. Extractor
8. Extractor spring
9. Breechblock
10. Breechblock pin
11. Front toggle link
12. Recoil spring
13. Toggle axle lockwasher
14. Rear toggle link
15. Firing pin spring guide and ejector
16. Recoil spring guide
17. Toggle axle pin
18. Receiver axle pin
19. Magazine catch
20. Magazine
21. Safety ball
22. Safety spring
23. Safety
24. Grip screws (2)
25. Magazine catch spring
26. Safety bar
27. Sear housing screws (2)
28. Sear lever
29. Disconnector
30. Trigger bar
31. Trigger pin
32. Trigger
33. Trigger plunger
34. Trigger spring
35. Sear housing
36. Sear spring
37. Sear
38. Locking bolt
39. Frame
Note: Grips are not shown

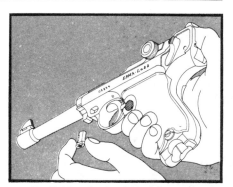

1. To field strip the Erma pistol, remove the magazine (20) and clear the chamber. Cock the pistol by pulling the rear toggle link (14) up and to the rear. Push the barrel and receiver assembly forward with the thumb as shown, and remove the locking bolt (38) to the left.

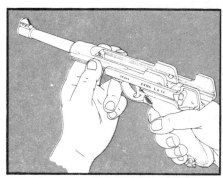

4. Slide the barrel and receiver (1) forward off the frame. Remove the firing pin spring (5), firing pin spring guide and ejector (15), and firing pin (4) from the breechblock (9). This completes field-stripping.

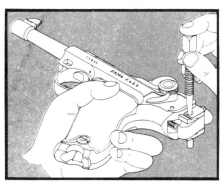

2. Release thumb pressure on rear toggle link, and allow the barrel and receiver assembly to spring rearward. Drift out the receiver axle pin (18).

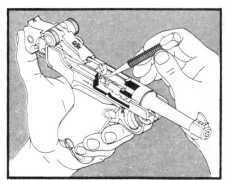

5. Reassemble in reverse. In replacing the toggle link and breechblock assembly of the older-version pistol, depress tip of sear with a punch. ∎

exploded views:
The Feinwerkbau
M-65

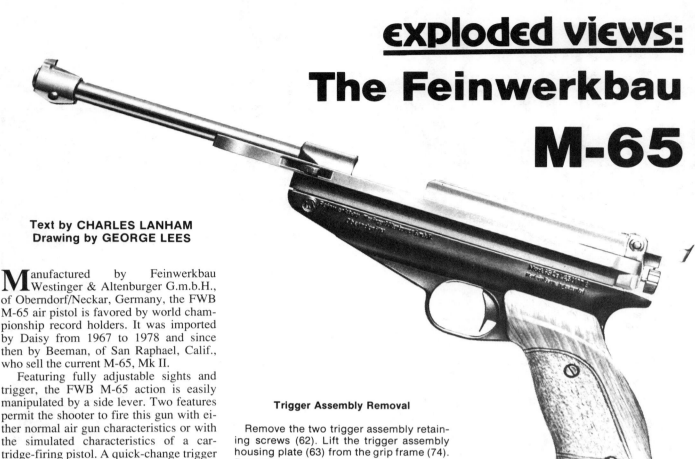

Text by CHARLES LANHAM
Drawing by GEORGE LEES

Manufactured by Feinwerkbau Westinger & Altenburger G.m.b.H., of Oberndorf/Neckar, Germany, the FWB M-65 air pistol is favored by world championship record holders. It was imported by Daisy from 1967 to 1978 and since then by Beeman, of San Raphael, Calif., who sell the current M-65, Mk II.

Featuring fully adjustable sights and trigger, the FWB M-65 action is easily manipulated by a side lever. Two features permit the shooter to fire this gun with either normal air gun characteristics or with the simulated characteristics of a cartridge-firing pistol. A quick-change trigger adjustment can give a light or a relatively heavy pull at will, and a recoil stop can be activated to increase felt recoil. A safety mechanism prevents the gun from being discharged when the action is open.

Disassembly Instructions

Make sure pistol is not cocked. Remove grip screws (78), grips (79, 80) and the two front grip attachment screws (77). With a short or ball-type 3 mm (.118″) Allen wrench, remove both rear grip frame attachment screws (75) and lock washers (76). The grip frame (74) containing the trigger assembly may now be separated from the barrel and piston housing (1).

Front Sight Assembly Removal

Clamp inverted barrel and piston housing (1) in a vise. The front sight base retaining pin (5) must be drifted out left to right. The front sight base (2) can now be pulled off to the front. In reassembly, be sure to insert the retaining pin (5) in reverse fashion to insure the front sight being at the 12 o'clock position.

Rear Sight Removal

Remove windage adjustment screw "E" ring (33) and thrust washer (33A). With thumb pressure against the rear sight base (36), turn windage adjustment screw (32) clockwise until free of the assembly. Do not lose the windage adjustment screw detent ball (34) or its spring (35). Assemble in reverse order.

Trigger Assembly Removal

Remove the two trigger assembly retaining screws (62). Lift the trigger assembly housing plate (63) from the grip frame (74). Reassemble in reverse manner.

Further takedown is not necessary or recommended for ordinary cleaning. Should it be required, proceed as follows:

Free the slot of the cocking lever pivot screw (30) and remove. Depress the cocking lever latch (9) and unhook the front of the cocking lever (29). Swing the cocking lever assembly with retracting lever (27) and pin (28) from the rear of the mainspring retainer (31) sufficiently to allow the front of the retracting lever (27) to be removed from its seat in the compression chamber (19). With barrel and piston housing (1) gripped in a padded vise, loosen the main spring retainer screw (12). Carefully take up the spring strain with a block of wood held against the main spring retainer (31) while lifting the retainer screw (12) from the assembly. Ease the mainspring retainer (31) containing the rear sight assembly and the outer piston spring(s) (25 & 26) from the barrel and piston housing.

To remove the rear recoil guide (13), the piston (22) with ring (23) and buffer (24), take the rear "E" ring (16) and spacing washer(s) (14) from the rear recoil guide pin (15) and drift it toward the muzzle enough to free the front "E" ring. Remove this "E" ring, slide the rear recoil guide pin (15) out to the rear. Use caution not to distort the front spacing washers (14), and note sequence for reassembly.

Further disassembly of the shooting mechanism is accomplished by clamping the inverted barrel and piston housing (1) in a padded vise. Remove all the "E" rings from one side of the assembly. Remove the front locking slide retaining pin (47) with

attached "E" ring. Unhook the locking slide spring (46) from the locking slide (45). With a .450″ long slave pin of less than .118″ dia., push the retaining pin (47) for the compression chamber pawl (49) and trigger pull change lever (50) from the assembly. When the slave pin is in place, these parts with associated springs (46 & 53), plunger (54), detent and screw (52 & 51), will spring free and may be removed as a unit. Push out the trigger pull connector (55), retaining pin (47) with its "E" ring and remove the trigger pull connnector (55). Push out sear connector (56) and retaining pin (47) with its "E" ring. A small pick may be used to lift the locking slide (45) enough to slide it forward and free of the assembly. The sear connector (56) may now be picked free of the assembly in a similar manner. Disconnect piston sear catch spring (60) where it attaches to the recoil release pawl (61). With a .450″ long slave pin, push out the interlock (57) and recoil release pawl retaining pin (47). Make sure that the interlock tension spring (58) is caught by the slave pin. Using another slave pin of similar size, push the retaining pin (47) for the piston sear catch (59) from the assembly. Now the interlock (57), piston sear catch (59), recoil release pawl (61) and the two springs may be removed from the assembly as a unit. The compression chamber (19) can now be slid rearward and removed.

Reassemble in reverse order.

Parts Legend

1. Barrel and piston housing
2. Front sight base
3. Front sight insert
4. Front sight insert retaining screw
5. Front sight base retaining pin
6. Recoil guide (front)
7. Recoil guide pin (front) (2 required)
8. Recoil guide pin "E" ring (4 required)
9. Cocking lever latch
10. Cocking lever latch retaining screw
11. Cocking lever latch spring
12. Main spring retainer screw
13. Recoil guide (rear)
14. Recoil guide spacers (as required)
15. Recoil guide pin (rear)
16. Recoil guide pin "E" rings (2 required)
17. Recoil lock
18. Recoil lock screw
19. Compression chamber
20. Barrel seal
21. Compression chamber buffer

22. Piston
23. Piston ring
24. Piston buffer
25. Piston spring (outer)
26. Piston spring (inner) Not present in all models
27. Piston retracting lever
28. Piston retracting lever pin
29. Cocking lever
30. Cocking lever pivot screw
31. Mainspring retainer
32. Windage adjustment screw
33. Windage adjustment "E" ring
33A. Thrust washer
34. Windage adjustment screw detent ball ball
35. Windage adjustment screw detent ball tension spring
36. Rear sight base
37. Rear sight depth adjustment plate
38. Rear sight elevation adjustment spring
39. Rear sight elevation adjustment spring retaining screw
40. Elevation adjustment screw
41. Elevation adjustment detent ball spring
42. Elevation adjustment detent ball
43. Elevation adjustment screw limiting clip
44. Rear sight depth adjustment screw
45. Locking slide
46. Locking slide spring
47. 3 mm x 21.5 mm pin (6 required)

48. "E" rings for above (12 required)
49. Compression chamber pawl
50. Trigger pull change lever
51. Change lever fine adj. screw
52. Change lever spring seat
53. Change lever spring
54. Change lever spring plunger
55. Change lever connector
56. Sear connector
57. Interlock
58. Interlock tension spring
59. Piston sear catch
60. Piston sear catch spring
61. Recoil release pawl
62. Trigger assembly retaining screws (2 required)
63. Trigger assembly housing plate
64. Pull-off adjustment screw
65. Pull-off adjustment/trigger sear housing
66. Trigger sear
67. Trigger sear spring
68. Trigger sear retaining pin
69. Trigger sear/pull-off adjustment housing retaining pin
70. Trigger spring
71. Trigger retaining pin
72. Trigger
73. Trigger stop adjustment screw
74. Grip frame
75. Grip frame attachment screws (rear) (2 required)
76. Grip frame attachment screws (rear) lock washer (2 required)
77. Grip frame attachment screws (front) (2 required)
78. Grip screws (2 required)
79. Grip panel, left
80. Grip panel, right

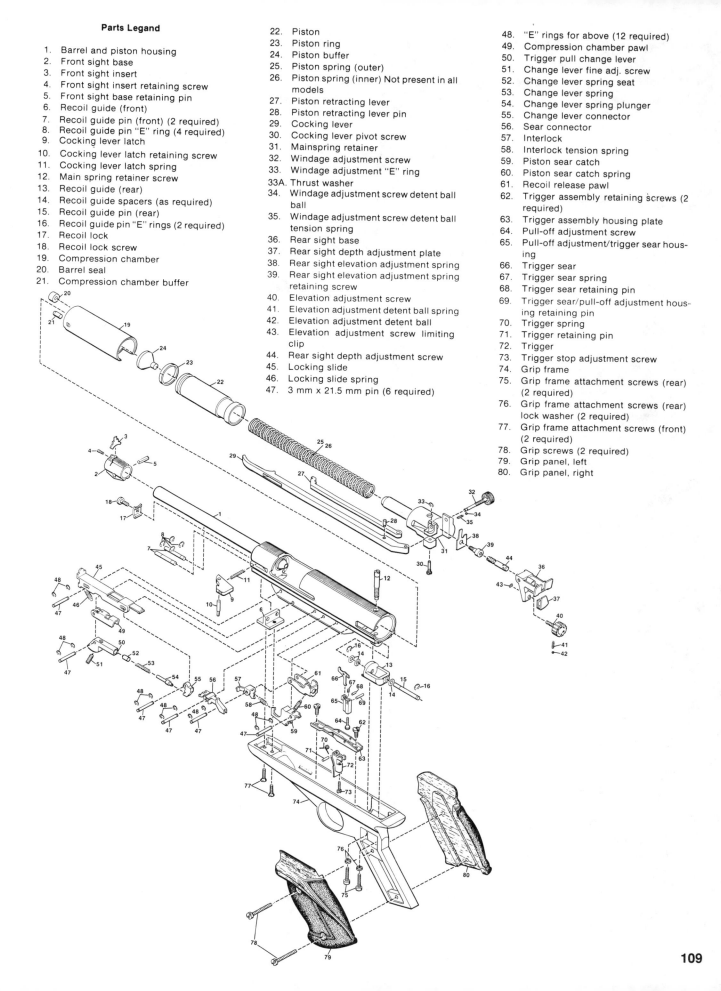

French Model 1935-A Pistol

By DENNIS RIORDAN

Bᴇᴛᴡᴇᴇɴ the World Wars, the French experimented with several different automatic pistols in an effort to find a suitable replacement for their 8 mm. Model 1892 Service revolver. This culminated in adoption of the 7.65 mm. Model 1935-A automatic pistol.

Based on the Browning short-recoil system and the designs of French engineer Charles Petter, this pistol was developed and produced by the Societe Alsacienne de Constructions Mecaniques, better known as S.A.C.M. It has an 8-round magazine, weighs 26 ozs., and fires a 7.65 mm. Long cartridge that is underpowered for military handgun use by U.S. standards. The muzzle

Parts Legend

1. Front sight
2. Cartridge indicator
3. Cartridge indicator spring
4. Cartridge indicator pin
5. Extractor pin
6. Extractor
7. Extractor spring
8. Slide
9. Safety
10. Barrel link pin
11. Barrel link (2)
12. Barrel
13. Firing pin spring
14. Firing pin
15. Right grip
16. Grip screw bushing (4)
17. Grip screw (4)
18. Trigger
19. Trigger bar pin
20. Trigger bar/disconnector
21. Trigger bar spring
22. Trigger pin
23. Magazine safety
24. Magazine safety screw
25. Magazine catch
26. Hammer strut
27. Hammer pin
28. Hammer strut pin
29. Hammer
30. Magazine
31. Sear
32. Sear pin
33. Sear housing/ejector
34. Sear pressure plate
35. Hammer spring
36. Hammer strut nut
37. Left grip
38. Frame
39. Magazine catch spring
40. Magazine catch nut
41. Slide stop catch
42. Slide stop
43. Recoil spring guide tip
44. Recoil spring ring
45. Recoil spring
46. Recoil spring guide pin
47. Recoil spring guide

velocity of the 88-gr. round-nose jacketed bullet is 1160 feet per second. Muzzle energy is 263 ft.-lbs.

During firing, the barrel and slide are locked together in the first 3/16″ of rearward travel. The rear of the barrel then pivots down to unlock, and the slide continues to the rear alone. This system is similar to that of the U.S. M1911 Colt .45 pistol.

Other features similar to that of the M1911 Colt are the slide stop and magazine catch on the left of the frame.

Located on the upper left of the slide, the safety shows considerable originality in design. Instead of locking the hammer in cocked position, it can be turned to safe with the hammer cocked or lowered. When on safe, it blocks the hammer from contacting the firing pin, and the hammer can be safely lowered by pulling the trigger. Also, the safety thumbpiece projects above the slide when the safety is engaged. This serves as a signal that the pistol is on safe.

Another safety device is a loading indicator that projects up from the slide when the chamber is loaded. There is also a half-cock position of the hammer and a magazine safety that prevents firing when the magazine is removed. A grip safety is not provided.

The well-shaped grips are checkered black plastic.

The pistol can be field-stripped quickly and easily without use of tools. Instead of the recoil spring being separate, it is of captive type and forms an assembly with the spring guide. This greatly facilitates field-stripping and reassembly. The hammer, sear, and several other lock parts are also combined in an assembly that can be easily removed from the frame.

Sights are simple and rugged. The square-notch rear sight is integral with the slide, and the square-top front sight can be driven laterally. There is no means of adjusting elevation.

This well-designed pistol was used by France during World War II, and some were used by Germany after the French defeat early in the War. In the 1950's it was replaced by a new French pistol in 9 mm. Luger caliber, and many Model 1935-A pistols were sold in the U.S. as military surplus.

The black painted finish of the metal parts gives the Model 1935-A a cheap appearance. However, the pistol is well-made and reliable. Its chief drawback is that it fires the 7.65 mm. Long cartridge which leaves much to be desired for military use and is not generally available except from surplus arms firms and dealers in collector cartridges.

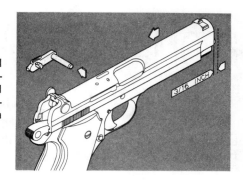

1. To field strip the French Model 1935-A pistol, remove the magazine (30) and clear the chamber. Pull the slide (8) 3/16″ to the rear, and remove the slide stop (42) to the left. Push the slide forward off the frame (38).

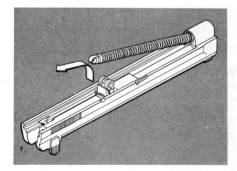

2. With the slide held bottom up, grasp the recoil spring and guide assembly, and remove it up and to the rear. Remove the barrel (12) in a similar manner. This completes field stripping.

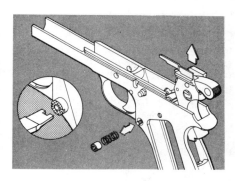

3. For further disassembly, grasp the upper part of the lock assembly, and lift it upward out of the frame. Remove the grip screws (17), grip screw bushings (16), and grips (15), (37). Grind a square notch in a screwdriver blade, and use this tool to unscrew the magazine catch nut (40). The magazine catch spring (39) comes out to the left, the magazine catch (25) to the right.

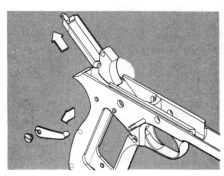

4. Remove the magazine safety screw (24) and magazine safety (23). Drift out the trigger pin (22) to the right. Then lift the trigger and trigger bar assembly from the top of the frame.

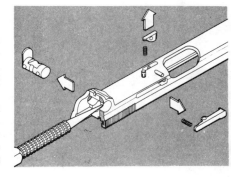

5. Push firing pin (14) forward with a thin punch, and pull the safety (9) from the left of the slide. Ease firing pin and firing pin spring (13) rearward out of the slide. Drift out the cartridge indicator pin (4) to the right, and remove the cartridge indicator (2) and indicator spring (3). Drift extractor pin (5) out through top of slide, and remove extractor (6) and extractor spring (7). Reassemble in reverse taking care that the extractor pin does not project from the lower surface of the slide. ∎

FROMMER STOP AUTOMATIC PISTOL

By DENNIS RIORDAN

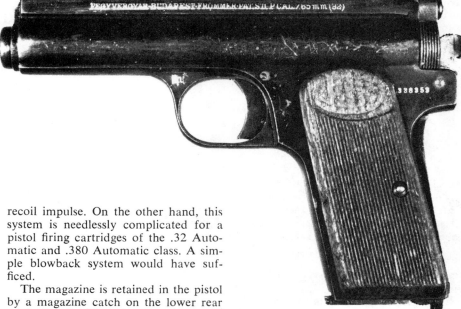

Pistols chambered for the .32 Automatic cartridge are commonly of blowback design. An exception is the Frommer Stop automatic pistol which operates on the long-recoil system. Developed by Rudolf Frommer, a Hungarian arms designer, this pistol was produced by the Small Arms and Machine Works, Inc., Budapest, Hungary. It was introduced commercially about 1911 or 1912, and was offered in .380 Automatic as well as .32 Automatic calibers. During World War I, it was extensively used in .32 Automatic caliber by the Austro-Hungarian Army and police. Many found their way to the U.S. later.

The long-recoil system of the Frommer is rather complex. During firing, the bolt mechanism and barrel are locked together and recoil as a unit. This compresses the recoil spring and bolt return spring above the barrel. At the end of recoil, the bolt is held to the rear by a catch. The barrel then unlocks from the bolt and is driven forward by the recoil spring. As the barrel nears its front position, the bolt is released and is pushed forward by the bolt return spring.

An advantage of this system is that the barrel mass is used to help resist the recoil impulse. On the other hand, this system is needlessly complicated for a pistol firing cartridges of the .32 Automatic and .380 Automatic class. A simple blowback system would have sufficed.

The magazine is retained in the pistol by a magazine catch on the lower rear of the handle. Magazine capacity in .32 caliber is seven rounds. The small external hammer has a rounded spur, and the only safety is the grip safety projecting from the rear of the handle.

Workmanship and finish of this 21-oz. pistol are generally excellent, although the serrated wood grips are rather crudely finished. Grip and balance are very good.

Although complicated, this pistol functions quite well. There is also a small version of the long-recoil Frommer pistol called the Frommer Baby. It is mechanically similar to the Stop model. Both the Stop and Baby models gave way in the 1920's to a Frommer-designed pistol based on the Browning blowback system.

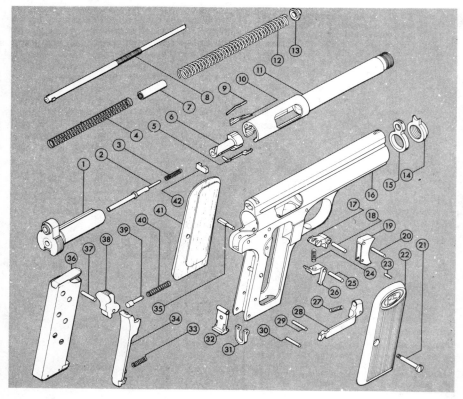

PARTS LEGEND

1. Bolt body
2. Firing pin
3. Firing pin spring
4. Bolt return spring
5. Extractor
6. Bolt head
7. Recoil spring guide sleeve
8. Recoil spring guide
9. Ejector spring
10. Ejector
11. Barrel and extension
12. Recoil spring
13. Barrel nut retainer
14. Barrel nut
15. Barrel guide
16. Frame
17. Bolt catch
18. Bolt catch pin
19. Trigger
20. Trigger pin
21. Grip screw
22. Right grip
23. Trigger bar pin
24. Sear spring
25. Sear pin
26. Sear
27. Trigger spring
28. Trigger bar
29. Magazine catch pin
30. Grip safety pin
31. Lanyard loop
32. Magazine catch
33. Grip safety spring
34. Grip safety
35. Disconnector pin
36. Magazine
37. Hammer pin
38. Hammer
39. Hammer plunger
40. Hammer spring
41. Left grip
42. Rear sight

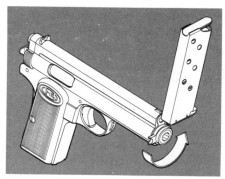

1 To field-strip the Frommer, remove magazine (36) and clear the chamber. Depress barrel nut retainer (13) with a corner of the magazine and unscrew barrel nut (14). Ease off pressure on barrel nut retainer and barrel guide (15) and remove them. Remove recoil spring (12).

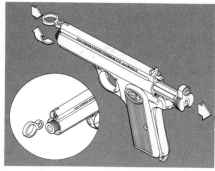

2 Top of barrel guide is slotted for use as a tool. Fit slot over cross lug at end of recoil spring guide (8). Push guide rearward, and rotate ¼ turn. Cock hammer (38) and pull bolt body (1) out to rear. Rotate bolt head (6) clockwise to separate from body.

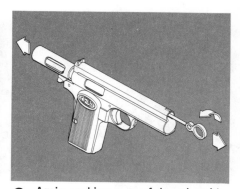

3 Again making use of barrel guide, rotate recoil spring guide an additional ¼ turn to release it from frame (16). Ease guide out forward. Push barrel (11) rearward to remove from frame. This completes field-stripping.

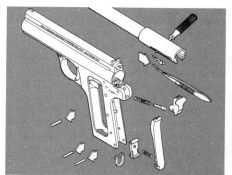

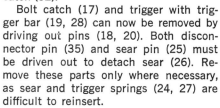

4 For further disassembly, use a small screwdriver to flex ejector spring (9) outward slightly. Grasp spring with a tweezers and slide out rearward; then, remove ejector (10). Unscrew grip screw (21) and remove grips (22, 41). Lower hammer. Drive out hammer pin (37) to release hammer with its plunger (39) and spring (40). Remove grip safety (34), spring (33), and lanyard loop (31), by driving out the grip safety pin (30). Drive out magazine catch pin (29) to free the catch (32).

Bolt catch (17) and trigger with trigger bar (19, 28) can now be removed by driving out pins (18, 20). Both disconnector pin (35) and sear pin (25) must be driven out to detach sear (26). Remove these parts only where necessary, as sear and trigger springs (24, 27) are difficult to reinsert.

Bolt head (6) is staked on both sides of extractor (5). The mushroomed edges must be filed down to disassemble these parts and the bolt head restaked on assembly. This should not be attempted without good cause.

7 Cutaway shows relationship between assembled parts. Bolt has been pulled fully to rear, unlocking bolt head, cocking hammer, and compressing bolt return spring. Parts are number keyed to parts legend. ■

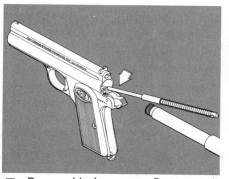

5 Reassemble in reverse. Depress bolt catch with tip of recoil spring guide when inserting barrel so that catch clears barrel threads.

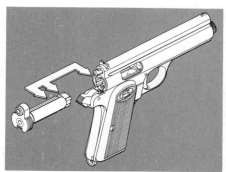

6 Bolt head must be turned so that its smaller locking lug aligns with rib on bolt body and groove in barrel extension when these parts are reassembled.

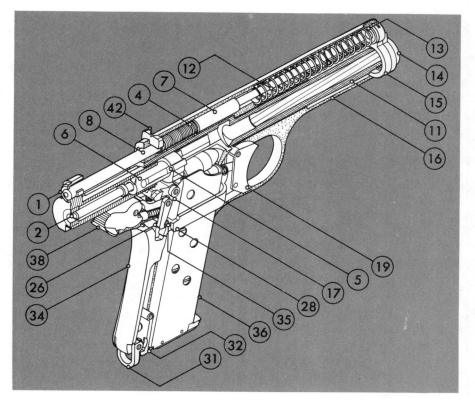

EXPLODED VIEW:

The Glisenti M1910

T HE Glisenti pistol was originally patented in 1905 by the Societa Siderurgica Glisenti in Brescia, Italy. Early pistols were chambered for the .30 Luger (7.63 mm) cartridge, but in 1909 the gun appeared in 9 mm caliber, was adopted by the Italian Military and eventually named the Pistola Automatica M910.

The Glisenti will chamber conventional 9 mm Luger ammo, but was not designed to handle it. The 9 mm ammo as made in Italy developed considerably less pressure than 9 mm German-made ammo of the same period, and the usage of commonly available 9 mm Luger ammo in the Glisenti is not recommended.

In 1911 a simplified version was put out by Metallurgica Bresciana Tempini (which accounts for the MBT molded into the grips of some guns). While the Brixia, as the revised gun was called, and the Glisenti are similar in appearance, their parts are not interchangeable. ∎

BY EDWARD J. HOFFSCHMIDT

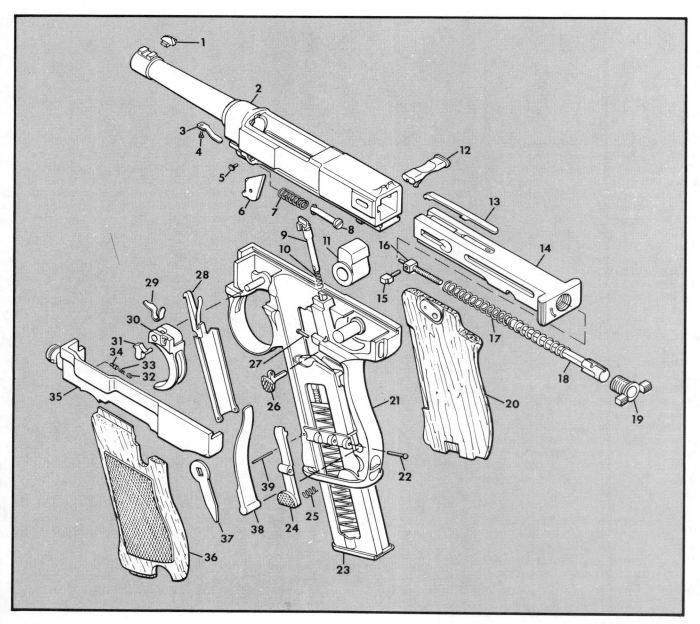

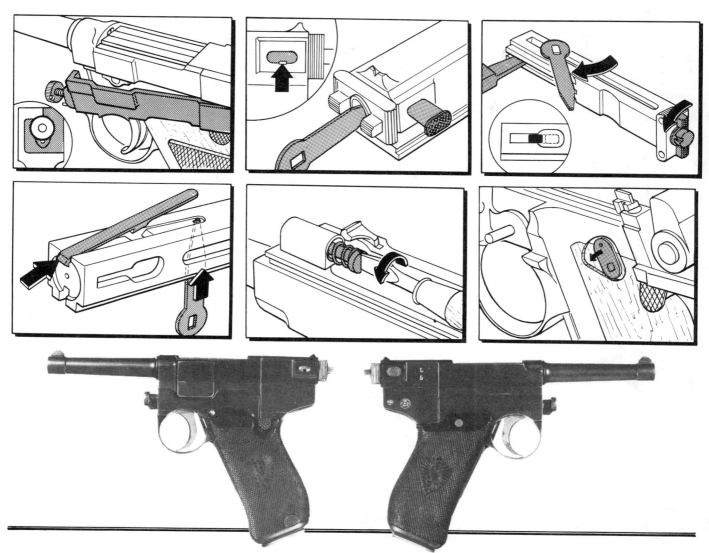

Disassembly Procedure

Step 1. Exposing the operating mechanism only requires removing the side plate (35). To do this, first remove the magazine (23) and clear the chamber. Push in the plunger (34), turn the large knurled screw (40) until it stops, then lift off the side plate, the left grip (36) and the disassembly tool (37). Push the barrel and receiver assembly to the left until it is free of the guide rib in the frame, then lift it up.

Step 2. The bolt assembly (14) is held in the receiver (2) by a cross key (12). To remove it, push up on the small spring (shown in the inserted drawing), push the key out from left to right and withdraw the bolt (14). To replace the bolt, push the firing pin in as far as it can go. It may be necessary to trip the sear to get it far enough forward to allow the cross key to clear the firing pin spring (17). Use a screwdriver or the disassembly tool to push the firing pin (18) forward.

Step 3. The firing pin guide (15) also acts as the sear and must be removed before removing the firing pin (18). It has a left hand thread and must be turned in the direction indicated by the arrow, using the disassembly tool as a wrench. Before attempting to remove the guide, insert a thin blade into the bolt and push back the firing pin until the guide is centered in the wide opening (note inserted drawing). When the guide is out, unscrew the safety catch (19) as shown and remove the firing pin (18), firing pin head (16) and firing pin spring (17).

Step 4. The disassembly tool is used to remove the extractor (13). After the firing pin has been removed, insert the tool into the small elongated slot in the bolt as shown. Push the tail of the extractor up slightly until it is just clear of the bolt (14); then tap it lightly on the front or claw end and it will spring free of the bolt.

Step 5. A separate barrel return spring (7) is incorporated into the underside of the receiver. The spring is rigidly assembled to the spring guide (8) so the assembly must be removed as a unit by inserting a small screwdriver into the screw slot on the spring guide. Push the plunger forward, rotate it 90° and ease the assembly out.

Step 6. To remove the right grip (20), first remove the magazine and rotate the small plate on the grip as shown. When the plate is free of the cut in the frame, the right hand grip can be lifted off.

Parts Legend

1. Front sight	21. Frame
2. Barrel & receiver	22. Magazine catch pin
3. Sear spring	23. Magazine
4. Screw	24. Magazine catch
5. Sear pin	25. Magazine catch spring
6. Sear	26. Hold open catch
7. Barrel return spring	27. Hold open catch pin
8. Barrel spring guide	28. Grip safety
9. Ejector & hold open catch	29. Trigger spring
10. Hold open spring	30. Trigger
11. Locking block	31. Disconnector
12. Cross key	32. Setscrew
13. Extractor	33. Spring
14. Bolt	34. Plunger
15. Firing pin guide	35. Side plate assembly
16. Firing pin head	36. Left grip
17. Firing pin spring	37. Disassembly tool
18. Firing pin body	38. Recoil spring
19. Safety catch	39. Grip safety pin
20. Right grip	40. Takedown screw

Glock 17
9 MM Pistol

A DOPTED as a service sidearm by the Austrian and Nor-wegian armies and under consideration by a number of U.S. law enforcement agencies, the Glock 17 semi-automatic pistol presents a number of novel features.

Utilizing a polymer receiver and several polymer/steel components, the Glock 17 has as its only "manual" safety a pivoting lever that protrudes through the face of the trigger. When the trigger is depressed by a shooter in the usual manner, the safety lever pivots and its rear portion moves up into the trigger body and out of contact with the frame, allowing the trigger to move back freely and effect discharge. A spring-loaded firing pin safety plunger is designed to block firing pin movement and prevent accidental firing if the pistol is dropped and lands muzzle-first.

Another polymer composition part of the Glock 17 is its magazine, designed to hold up to 17 9 mm rounds and equipped with individual cartridge "witness holes" on its back. Expanded capacity magazines (capable of holding two additional

BY DOUG WICKLUND

cartridges) for the Glock 17 can easily be recognized by their angled floorplates.

The disassembly procedures utilized with the Glock 17 also apply to the Glock 17L "Competition" or Glock 19 "Compact" pistols.

More information about the Glock 17 pistol can be found in the May 1986 *American Rifleman*.

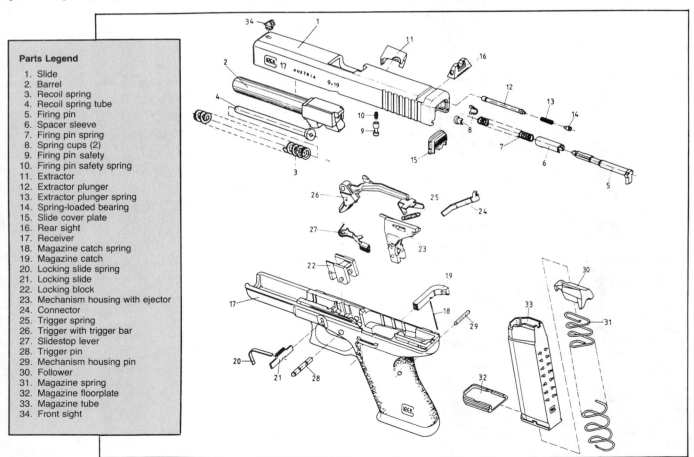

Parts Legend

1. Slide
2. Barrel
3. Recoil spring
4. Recoil spring tube
5. Firing pin
6. Spacer sleeve
7. Firing pin spring
8. Spring cups (2)
9. Firing pin safety
10. Firing pin safety spring
11. Extractor
12. Extractor plunger
13. Extractor plunger spring
14. Spring-loaded bearing
15. Slide cover plate
16. Rear sight
17. Receiver
18. Magazine catch spring
19. Magazine catch
20. Locking slide spring
21. Locking slide
22. Locking block
23. Mechanism housing with ejector
24. Connector
25. Trigger spring
26. Trigger with trigger bar
27. Slidestop lever
28. Trigger pin
29. Mechanism housing pin
30. Follower
31. Magazine spring
32. Magazine floorplate
33. Magazine tube
34. Front sight

Disassembly Instructions

Clear the pistol by removing the magazine, retracting the slide and checking the chamber and magazine well.

Pulling the trigger on an empty chamber, draw the slide back 1/4″ and pull down both sides of the locking slide (21) (**Fig. 1**). While holding the locking slide down, push the barrel/slide assembly forward off the frame. With the slide assembly resting upside down on a firm surface, lift the recoil spring tube (4) and recoil spring (3) out of the semicircular notch on the barrel (2). Tilt the barrel up and lift out for removal.

This completes basic field-stripping for the Glock 17 pistol. Further disassembly is not recommended by Glock, Inc., unless performed by a competent, factory-trained gunsmith. For those who elect to go further, we pass along our experience in full disassembly.

Two trigger positions are possible with a Glock 17 pistol: cocked (with the trigger forward) and uncocked (with trigger back).

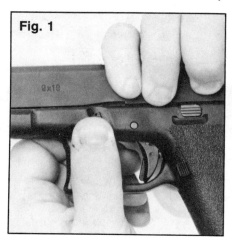

Fig. 1

Slide Disassembly

Using a pin punch, push down the spacer sleeve (6) towards the muzzle end of the slide and pull the slide cover plate (15) down, restraining the spacer sleeve and the spring-loaded bearing (14) within. The firing pin assembly and extractor plunger (12) with its spring (13) can then be pulled out. To break down the firing pin assembly, use the muzzle of the barrel to hold the spacer sleeve (**Fig. 2**). Depress the firing pin spring (7) and remove the spring cups (8) and the spacer sleeve.

To remove the extractor (11), push down on the firing pin safety (9) and pry out the extractor. The firing pin safety can then be lifted out with its spring (10).

The elevation-adjustable or fixed rear sight (16) can be removed by drifting out with a non-marring punch. The front sight (34) is factory staked in place and should not be removed except for replacement.

Frame Disassembly

Using a pin punch, remove the trigger pin (28) and the mechanism housing pin (29), pushing from left to right. Pull the slide stop lever (27) with its spring to the rear for removal. Prying up on the mechanism housing (23), lift

it out with the attached trigger (26) and trigger bar. Twist the trigger bar extension forward and up to detach from the mechanism housing. (**Fig. 3**). Separate the trigger spring (25) from the housing.

Pry up on the locking block (22) for removal. Press the locking slide spring (20) down and push the locking slide (21) to the left or the right to remove. The locking slide spring can then be lifted out.

To remove the magazine catch (19), use a screwdriver to raise the magazine catch spring (18) out of its groove in the magazine well and pull the spring out from the top using a pair of pliers. The magazine catch can be then pushed out to the right.

Disassemble the Glock 17 magazine by squeezing the magazine tube (33) in the center part of each side near the magazine floorplate (32). Simultaneously, push the floorplate off the tube, holding a finger over the top of the opening to prevent the spring from escaping.

Reassembly is in reverse order. When replacing the slide-stop lever (27), be sure the spring is correctly oriented. Insert an empty magazine to check that the lever is acted upon by the follower. ∎

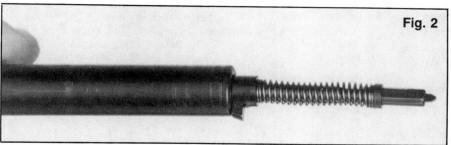

Fig. 2

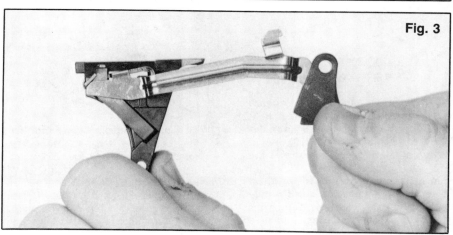

Fig. 3

HAENEL-SCHMEISSER MODEL I

Illustrations by DENNIS RIORDAN
Text by LUDWIG OLSON

1 To field-strip the pistol, engage safety (28) on safe, and remove and unload magazine (20). Replace magazine and disengage safety. Draw slide (5) fully rearward to clear chamber. Pull trigger (26), and re-engage safety on safe. Lock slide half open by pulling it back and lifting safety into slide notch. Remove magazine, and engage cutout on its bottom rear with annular groove on exposed tip of recoil spring guide (10). Pull guide forward and down until it locks. Lift out barrel (1).

4 Unscrew grip screw (9), and remove grips (8) (24). Drift out magazine catch pin (30), and remove magazine safety (15). Rotate magazine catch (31) forward into magazine well to unhook from sear spring housing (19). Remove magazine safety, magazine safety spring (16), and magazine catch spring (32) from their frame recesses with tweezers. Raise sear spring housing with flat punch to allow removal of safety. (During reassembly, safety must be installed in engaged position.)

2 Grasp recoil spring guide from below, maintaining contact between magazine and guide with thumb pressure from above. Raise guide into alignment and ease to rear. Draw slide slightly rearward to unlock from safety, and ease slide forward off frame (12). Remove recoil spring (11) and guide from frame. Then, remove firing pin (6), mainspring (7), signal pin (21), and spring (22) from slide. This completes field-stripping for normal cleaning.

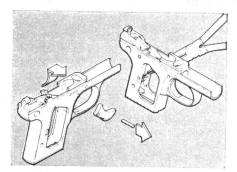

5 Drift out trigger pin (25), rotate bottom of trigger forward into guard, and remove. Twist trigger bar (27) slightly, so that its upper surface clears top of frame. Pull bar out of its frame recess into magazine well, and remove. Rotate trigger bar spring (29) forward into magazine well, and remove from its fixed frame pin with longnose pliers.

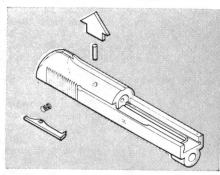

3 To disassemble further, drift extractor pin (2) upward out of slide, releasing extractor (3) and spring (4).

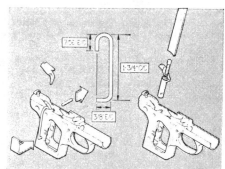

6 Bend a piece of 3/32" brazing rod as shown. Place upper end of rod atop head of sear spring plunger (18), depressing the plunger so that lower end of rod may be inserted into frame hole for magazine catch pin. Drift out sear pin (14), and remove sear (13). If necessary to remove spring housing, make a concave cut at end of 3/16" wide flat wood stick, and use stick to depress sear spring plunger. Remove brazing rod tool, and then ease out plunger and sear spring (17). Wear glasses and keep face clear. Reassemble in reverse.

A semi-automatic pistol small enough to be carried in a vest pocket was designed by John Browning and introduced by the Belgian firm Fabrique Nationale in 1906. The great success of this compact cal. .25 ACP handgun resulted in the development of many other vest-pocket semi-automatic pistols, among them the Haenel-Schmeisser Model I.

Designed by Hugo Schmeisser, the Haenel-Schmeisser Model I pistol was produced by the C. G. Haenel firm, Suhl, Germany. This blowback-operated handgun chambered for the cal. .25 ACP cartridge was brought on the market in the early 1920's. It is generally similar in appearance to the Browning vest-pocket pistol introduced in 1906, but differs considerably from the Browning in mechanical details.

The Haenel-Schmeisser Model I has a spring-driven firing pin as in the Browning vest-pocket pistol, and the firing pin also serves as the ejector. When the pistol is cocked, a signal pin projects from the rear of the frame. There is no ejection port in the slide as in the Browning. Instead, the upper front of the slide is cut away so that the breech is exposed when the slide is to the rear.

Located on the upper left side of the frame behind the grip, the safety is of half-turn type. The magazine cannot be removed unless the safety is engaged on safe. Also, the safety cannot be turned forward to the fire position with the magazine removed from the pistol. This unusual arrangement accomplishes the same thing as the conventional magazine safety of many other semi-automatic pistols, but is slower since it requires operation of the manual safety.

Overall length of the pistol is 4½", and weight unloaded is 13½ ozs. The magazine holds six rounds. Metal parts are blued, and the black hard rubber grips are checkered and bear the interlocked letters "HS". Workmanship and finish are excellent.

This pistol should not be confused with the Haenel-Schmeisser Model II pistol which is smaller and lighter than the Model I. Both models were discontinued at about the time of World War II. ∎

7 Cutaway indicates relative position of assembled parts. Pistol is shown cocked and unloaded, with safety disengaged. Parts are number keyed to parts legend.

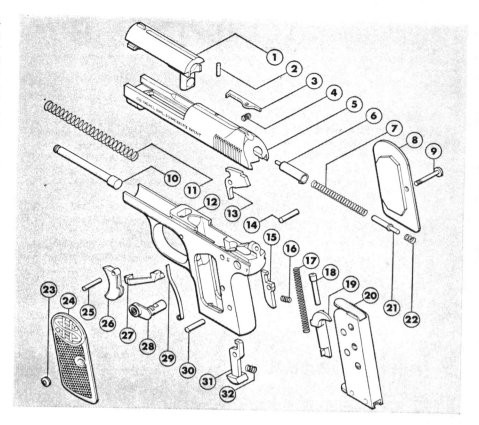

PARTS LEGEND

1. Barrel
2. Extractor pin
3. Extractor
4. Extractor spring
5. Slide
6. Firing pin
7. Mainspring
8. Right grip
9. Grip screw
10. Recoil spring guide
11. Recoil spring
12. Frame
13. Sear
14. Sear pin
15. Magazine safety
16. Magazine safety spring
17. Sear spring
18. Sear spring plunger
19. Sear spring housing
20. Magazine
21. Signal pin
22. Signal pin spring
23. Grip escutcheon
24. Left grip
25. Trigger pin
26. Trigger
27. Trigger bar
28. Safety
29. Trigger bar spring
30. Magazine catch pin
31. Magazine catch
32. Magazine catch spring

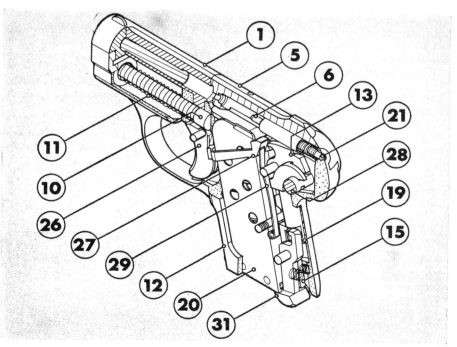

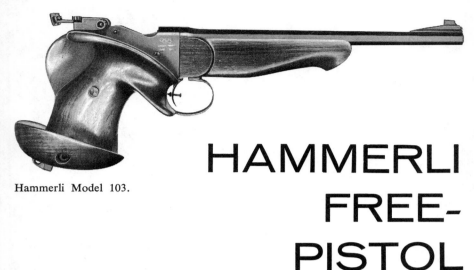

Hammerli Model 103.

HAMMERLI FREE-PISTOL

By EDWARD J. HOFFSCHMIDT

The free-pistol is designed specifically for precision slow-fire target shooting. It is free of practically all restrictions usually placed on international-competition firearms, hence the name free-pistol. Choice of barrel length, sight radius, trigger pull weight, and grip shape are practically unlimited.

One of the most popular guns of this type is the Hammerli that, from World War II until the last 10 years, swept the international competitive field and established an enduring reputation for accuracy and reliability.

Basically the Hammerli is a .22 rimfire, single-shot Martini-action pistol. The set trigger can be adjusted to give an

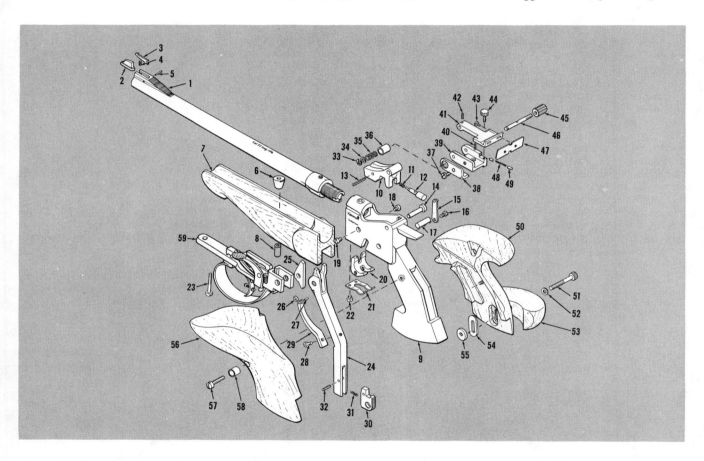

Parts Legend

1. Barrel
2. Front sight blade
3. Front sight latch
4. Sight latch spring
5. Latch hinge pin
6. Barrel lug
7. Forestock
8. Bushing
9. Frame
10. Breechblock
11. Firing pin spring
12. Firing pin
13. Firing pin retaining pin
14. Breechblock hinge pin
15. Hinge pin retaining spring
16. Spring retaining screw
17. Cross pin
18. Right extractor screw
19. Left extractor screw
20. Extractor
21. Extractor spring
22. Extractor spring screw (2)
23. Front guard screw
24. Lever
25. Hammer
26. Spring roller
27. Roller pin
28. Mainspring retaining screw
29. Mainspring
30. Lever latch
31. Latch spring
32. Latch pin
33. C-washer
34. Washer
35. Spring
36. Nut
37. Sight retainer screw
38. Retainer plate
39. Sight base
40. Sight leaf spring
41. Sight leaf
42. Retainer pin
43. Sight blade screw
44. Sight elevating screw
45. Windage screw
46. Sight leaf hinge
47. Sight blade
48. Detent spring
49. Detent (2)
50. Right grip
51. Heel support screw
52. Washer
53. Heel support
54. Elongated washer
55. Nut
56. Left grip
57. Grip screw
58. Bushing
59. Trigger assembly

extremely light pull. Since slow-fire 50-meter International matches are generally fired over a three-hour period, a shooter must be able to relax his grip frequently. Hammerli free-pistol grips are designed for just that. When a shooter buys a Hammerli, the company asks that he provide a sketch of his hand and information on whether he shoots with his arm extended or bent in the European manner. The resulting grip will fit like a glove. However, if the shooter wishes to shape his own, the grip can be supplied unfinished.

The Martini-type action of the Hammerli gives the rigidity and short hammer throw necessary in any super accurate gun. The action also allows for easy loading and has a powerful extraction system.

The frames of earlier Hammerli free-pistols were machined from bar stock, a costly procedure. With the advent of investment casting, Hammerli chose this method to produce the frame and some internal parts.

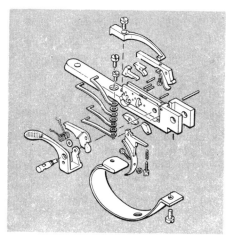

The trigger mechanism is the heart of the cal. .22 Hammerli free-pistol. It is carefully adjusted at the factory and can be adjusted to a very light pull. The exploded view of the trigger mechanism gives some idea of its complexity and why it should be disassembled and adjusted only by factory trained gunsmiths.

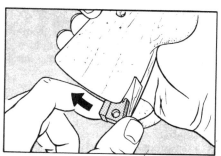

1 The Hammerli has a miniature Martini action. To drop the breechblock (10), squeeze the lever latch (30) at rear underside of the grip. When the lever (24) is moved forward, it cocks the hammer (25), drops the breechblock, and actuates the extractor (20).

The Hammerli Models 101, 102 and 103 were replaced in February 1963 by the Models 104 and 105. Mechanical refinements and changes made since then have led to the current Models 150 (with mechanical set trigger) and 152 (with electric trigger).

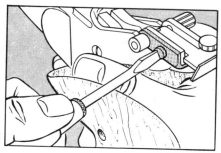

2 Two methods of rear sight attachment are used by Hammerli. The later type shown here is attached by a sight retainer screw (37) and a retainer plate (38). When the screw is loosened, the rear sight slides off the integral sight mount. The earlier type uses 2 screws to retain the sight. These are under the leaf and tapped into the sight mount. The leaf must be raised upright to get at these screws.

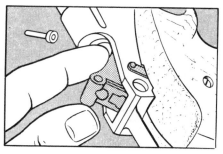

3 Occasionally it is necessary to remove the breechblock (10) for cleaning. To remove it, lift the hinge pin retaining spring (15) slightly and push it forward and clear of the breechblock hinge pin (14). Push out the hinge pin. Depress front of the breechblock (10) and lift it out. It may be necessary to move the loading lever a bit to free it from the breechblock.

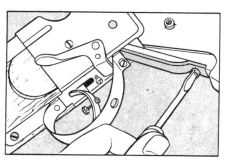

4 The cross pin (17) retains the rear of the trigger guard, the lever (24), and the hammer (25). Before attempting to remove it, loosen the mainspring retaining screw (28); this relieves tension on the cross pin (17). When cross pin is out, the trigger mechanism can be removed intact by removing front guard screw (23). ∎

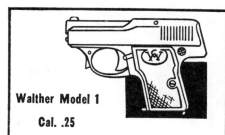

Walther Model 1

Cal. .25

PISTOL MAGAZINES

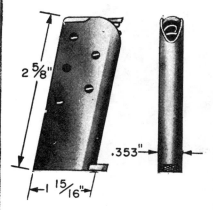

In 1908, Carl Walther founded his famous line of pistols with the .25 cal. Model 1. This little vest-pocket gun, although well made, shows none of the ingenious design features found in later Walther pistols. The safety catch is a cross button, awkward to operate, and the takedown system leaves much to be desired. Apparently it was difficult to sell or manufacture, for in 1909 it was superseded by the more compact Model 2.

Model 1 magazines are well made but have little to set them apart from other .25 cal. pistol magazines. The best point of recognition is the thick floorplate with checkering on the end, as shown.

Also the magazine catch notch is deeper and much higher up on the back strap than usual.—E. J. HOFFSCHMIDT

THE HAMMERLI WALTHER OLYMPIA

By E. J. Hoffschmidt

LEGEND

A—Slide
B—Extractor
C—Extractor plunger
D—Extractor spring
E—Firing pin housing pins
F—Firing pin retaining pin
G—Rear sight
H—Rear sight adjusting screws
I—Rear sight base
J—Firing pin housing
K—Firing pin spring
L—Firing pin
M—Right-hand grip
N—Muzzle brake
O—Muzzle brake set screw
P—Front sight
Q—Front sight set screw
R—Weight-retaining screws
S—Barrel and receiver
T—Ejector
U—Trigger stop set screw
V—Trigger spring
W—Trigger
X—Trigger bar
Y—Hammer
Z—Hammer strut pin
AA—Sear pin
BB—Sear
CC—Sear spring
DD—Sear spring pin
EE—Hammer strut
FF—Hammer spring
GG—Hammer spring seat
HH—Magazine
II—Trigger guard plunger
JJ—Plunger spring
KK—Trigger guard pin
LL—Safety catch
MM—Trigger guard
NN—Magazine catch
OO—Magazine catch spring
PP—Trigger pin

QQ—Trigger stop pin
RR—Trigger stop screw
SS—Recoil spring
TT—Front weight
UU—Recoil spring guide

VV—Secondary weight
WW—Weight retaining screws (long)
XX—Small weight
YY—Grip screw
ZZ—Left-hand grip

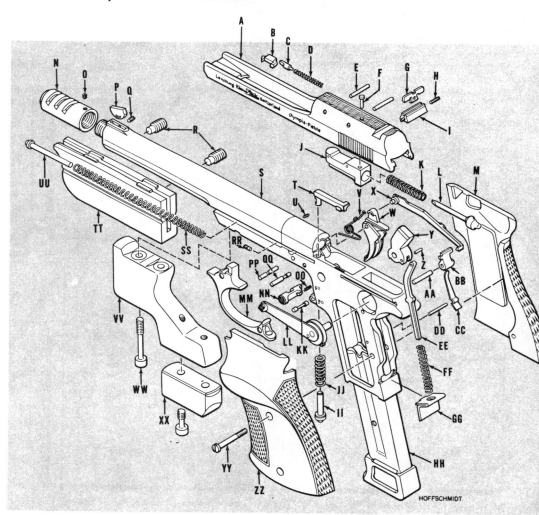

The 1936 Olympic games in Berlin witnessed the beginning of an amazing record for consistent accuracy. In that year the top five shooters in the Olympic rapid-fire matches all used the new Walther Olympia .22 rimfire self-loading pistol. From then until it was eclipsed by italian designs and by newer guns from Walther, the Olympia was the overwhelming choice of International target shooters.

The end of World War II saw Germany out of the gun business so Fritz Walther packed up and moved to Switzerland. There he sold both his services, as a design engineer and consultant, and the manufacturing rights to the Olympia to Hammerli Arms Co., of Lenzburg. By so doing Walther picked the right firm to carry on the Olympia production, for Hammerli guns have been renowned for their accuracy and workmanship for a long, long time.

From the end of World War II until about 1963, two models of the Hammerli/Walther Olympia were made. One, the Special Olympia, had a 9-1/2-inch barrel and a trigger pull of 1-1/2 pounds.

The other, the Standard Olympia had a 7-1/2-inch barrel and a trigger pull of at least 33 ounces.

The pistol is one of few designed expressly for target shooting. The adjustable grip, the trigger pull, the sear mechanism, all were designed for one purpose — to allow the shooter to make the highest possible score over a demanding course of fire.

On the early model Hammerli Olympia pistols the front sight is adjustable for elevation and rear sight is adjustable for windage. More recent versions, however, have rear sights that are more familiar to American shooters, that is, they are fully adjustable for elevation and windage. The addition of a slide hold-open latch and a buffer spring also improve the pistol a great deal. Like its Walther predecessor, the Hammerli Olympia was made for either .22 Short or .22 Long Rifle ammunition. While the rimfire ammunition does not have the kick of larger-caliber centerfire ammunition, it is powerful enough to get the gun off the target. The muzzle brake and weights are added to combat

this thrust. A muzzle brake of this type tends to keep the barrel down. While the weights have the same effect, they perform another function, too. The weights have a steadying influence allowing the gun to be swung more easily from target to target during Olympic rapid-fire strings.

Since the pistol is blowback operated, there is no locking mechanism to make the takedown procedure involved. The only point in the takedown that might be called unorthodox is the method used to remove the recoil spring and recoil spring guide from the pistol's receiver. The front end of the receiver has to be sprung away from the barrel a bit to free the end of the spring guide from its stop in the receiver. This is accomplished driving a brass wedge or screwdriver between the barrel and the front of the receiver. While this may seem to be deforming the receiver, it is nevertheless, the method used at the factory. The receiver is spread so little that it does not harm the gun.

Remove the magazine and check chamber to be sure the gun is empty. Remove the weights. Pull down on the front of the trigger guard (MM), push it to the side until it catches on a lip in the receiver (S). Draw the slide to the rear, lift it up off the receiver, and ease it forward over the barrel

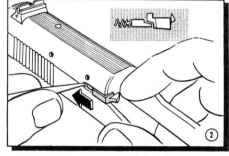

The extractor (B) is retained by a spring-loaded plunger (C). Using a small screwdriver, push the plunger back into the slide (A). If the slide is turned on its side, the extractor will then drop out. Ease up on the plunger (C) and it will come out with its spring (D)

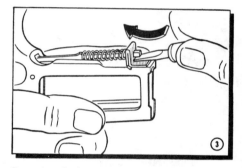

Removing the hammer spring seat (GG) is a bit tricky. First pull the trigger and ease the hammer to fired position, to take the tension off the hammer spring (FF). Push up hard as shown at the same time; lift the seat free from its notch in the receiver

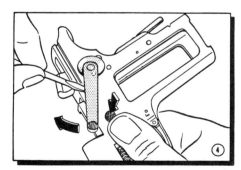

To remove the safety, lower the hammer (Y) to fired position. Depress the magazine catch (NN), lift the catch (LL) a bit as shown, to prevent it scratching the finish, and rotate it up over the edge of the receiver to the position illustrated. The catch will then spring free of the receiver

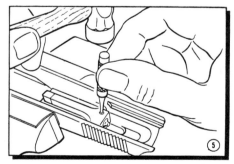

A spare firing pin (L) and firing pin spring (K) are supplied with each new gun. To remove the old parts, hold the slide (A) upside down in a vise, and tap the firing pin retaining pin (F) out, as shown. The firing pin and spring can then be lifted out of the slide

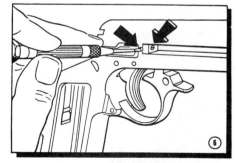

The trigger pull on the Olympia is not adjustable, but the amount of travel can be limited. The trigger stop screw (RR) can be reached only with a long thin screwdriver, but its set screw (U) can be reached from the outside, as shown

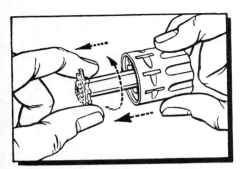

1 Remove center pin (1) and cylinder (2) from frame. Remove extractor (3) after pushing it out of cylinder as far as possible with center pin and rotating it ½ turn in either direction, then withdrawing

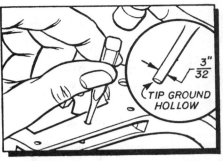

2 Drive out guard and sear pin (4) and front guard pin (12). These pins are knurled on one end and care should be taken to drive them out from the **left** and replace them from the **right**. Use proper size punch to avoid burring pin holes

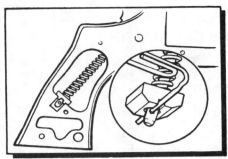

3 Remove grip screws (18) and grips (19). Remove mainspring assembly (20a) by moving hammer back toward cocked position until hole at bottom of mainspring guide (21) protrudes beneath mainspring seat (22). Secure mainspring by placing piece of wire through hole. Release hammer and drop out mainspring

Harrington & Richardson Model 922

By James M. Triggs

LEGEND

1. Center pin
2. Cylinder
3. Extractor
4. Guard and sear pin
5. Trigger guard
6. Sear spring
7. Sear
8. Cylinder stop
9. Cylinder stop spring
10. Center pin plunger spring
11. Center pin plunger
12. Trigger and front guard pins (2)
13. Trigger
14. Lifter
15. Lifter pin
16. Lever and spring assembly
17. Trigger spring
18. Grip screws (2)
19. Grips (2)
20a. Mainspring assembly
20. Mainspring
21. Mainspring guide
22. Mainspring seat
23. Hammer screw
24. Hammer screw stud
25. Hammer
26. Barrel retaining pin
27. Barrel
28. Front sight
29. Mainframe
30. Grip pins (2)

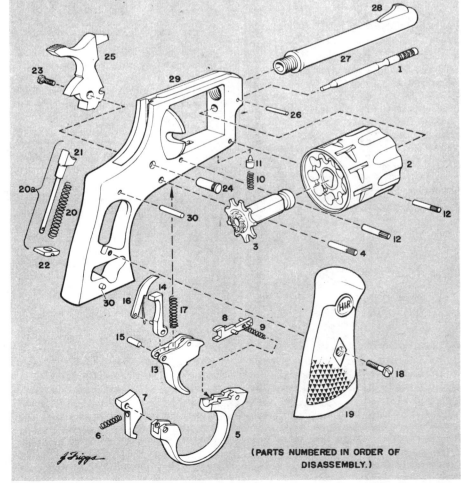

(PARTS NUMBERED IN ORDER OF DISASSEMBLY.)

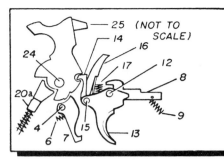

4 Remove trigger guard (5), cylinder stop (8), and stop spring (9), sear (7), sear spring (6), center pin plunger spring (10), plunger (11), from mainframe. Drive out trigger pin (12) and remove trigger assembly [trigger (13), trigger spring (17), lifter (14), lifter pin (15), lever and spring assembly (16)]. Diagram shows relative position of these parts assembled. Remove hammer screw (23) and gently drive out hammer screw stud (24) using care not to damage stud threads. Remove hammer (25). Removal of barrel should not be attempted except by a gunsmith

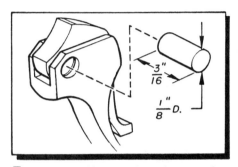

5 In reassembling, replace hammer first. Sear spring, sear, and trigger guard must be assembled before installation in frame, using slave pin through sear and trigger guard. Length of slave pin should not exceed width of trigger guard. Cylinder stop spring must be inserted into stop spring hole in trigger guard before assembling guard to frame

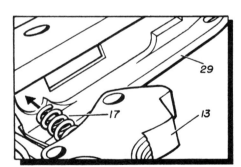

6 When reinstalling trigger assembly, end of trigger spring must be in line with spring seat in bottom of trigger guard slot in frame. Guide lifter into position between hammer and frame with small screwdriver and press trigger assembly up into frame until pin holes line up. Secure by replacing trigger pin (12). Trigger guard, sear, and cylinder stop assembly is secured by replacing front guard pin (12) and guard and sear pin (4). The slave pin holding sear and guard for assembly should be driven out when replacing guard and sear pin (4). Note: By making extra long slave pins with finger loops it is possible to speed up preliminary assembly and disassembly operations when adjustments are required. When functioning is satisfactory, install permanent pins — ∎

Little Tom Cal. .25 ACP

PISTOL MAGAZINES

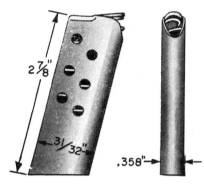

The Little Tom pistol is among the earliest double-action pistols produced. Made in Austria by the Wiener Waffenfabrik, it incorporates a number of unusual features. Aside from the double-action mechanism, the method of loading is novel. Unlike most other automatics, the magazine is loaded into the frame from the top through the slide opening. This was done to keep the loading procedure similar to the military Steyr Model 1911 pistol. The Steyr loads through the top only; the cartridges are on a stripper clip and not in a magazine like the Little Tom.

Little Tom magazines can be recognized by their brass color and lack of finger grip of any sort on the magazine floorplate. The small retaining notch on the back strap near the floorplate is another identifying mark.

Unlike most other common automatics, the slide must be locked back to remove or replace a magazine. The magazine cannot be removed through the bottom of the grip. It must be pushed upward through the slide opening as shown.—E. J. HOFFSCHMIDT

PISTOL MAGAZINES

Llama 9 mm./.38 Extra Long Model

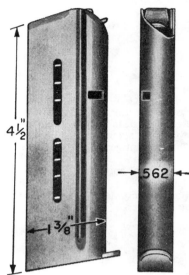

The firm of Gabilondo & Co. of Elgoibar, Spain, has built almost the entire line of Llama semi-automatic pistols on the Colt M1911A1 design. Models range from a small .22 to a full-size .45. The Llama "Extra Long" model is similar to the M1911A1, except that the barrel and slide are about ⅝″ longer. It shoots the Spanish military cartridge, the 9 mm. Largo, or the .38 Super Automatic cartridge.

Llama 9 mm./.38 magazines can be recognized by the 2 long observation slots in the right side. The step-shaped follower that actuates the hold-open catch is another reference.

The floorplate is generally unmarked, but the magazine body can be further recognized by the 2 long cartridge guide ribs indented into the sides.—E. J. HOFFSCHMIDT

H & R MODEL 929 "SIDE-KICK" REVOLVER

By JAMES M. TRIGGS

Parts Legend

1. Frame
2. Barrel
3. Front sight
4. Barrel retaining pin
5. Rear sight leaf
6. Rear sight screws (2)
7. Front trigger guard pin
8. Trigger pin
9. Rear trigger guard and sear pin
10. Hammer screw stud
11. Hammer screw
12. Hammer
13. Mainspring guide
14. Mainspring
15. Mainspring seat
16. Trigger
17. Lever and spring assembly
18. Lifter
19. Lifter pin
20. Sear
21. Sear spring
22. Trigger spring
23. Cylinder stop assembly
24. Trigger guard
25. Swingout arm assembly
26. Center pin spring
27. Extractor spring
28. Center pin
29. Center pin guide
30. Center pin head
31. Center pin head pin
32. Swingout arm pivot pin
33. Cylinder
34. Extractor

The Harrington & Richardson Model 929, "Side-Kick", double-action revolver was introduced in 1956. A solid frame design, with a swing-out cylinder, the Model 929 is chambered for .22 Short, Long or Long Rifle ammunition. Cylinder capacity is nine cartridges. There were minor changes in the design of the revolver, made before H&R closed its doors in 1986. In 1988, a new firm, New England Firearms Co., resumed production of many of H&R's old products, including a revolver similar to the Model 929.

Disassembly Procedure

Check revolver to be sure it is unloaded. Remove swingout arm pivot pin (32) from front end of frame (1). Pull hammer (12) back to lower cylinder stop, swing out cylinder and extractor assembly (33 & 34) with swingout arm assembly (25). Disassembly of extractor (34) from cylinder is not recommended and is unnecessary for normal cleaning.

Drift out front trigger guard pin (7) and rear trigger guard and sear pin (9) from *left to right*. Remove trigger guard (24) with cylinder stop assembly (23) and sear (20) with sear spring (21).

Remove grip screws and grips (not shown). Cock hammer (12) and place a nail or small pin through hole in lower end of mainspring guide (13) where it protrudes through mainspring seat (15). Release hammer and drop mainspring, guide, and seat assembly out of frame.

Drift out trigger pin (8) from *left to right* and drop trigger (16), trigger spring (22), lever and spring assembly (17), lifter (18) and lifter pin (19) out of frame. Remove hammer screw (11) and drift hammer screw stud (10) out of frame from *left to right*. Remove hammer (12) from top of frame. Reassemble in reverse. Note that all pivot pins are knurled at their right ends and should be replaced in frame from right to left with knurls at right.

Phantom of the Model 929 revolver shows the relationship of all interior lock mechanism parts when assembled in the frame. Lever and spring assembly (17) pivots on a pin set into the left side of the lifter (18). ∎

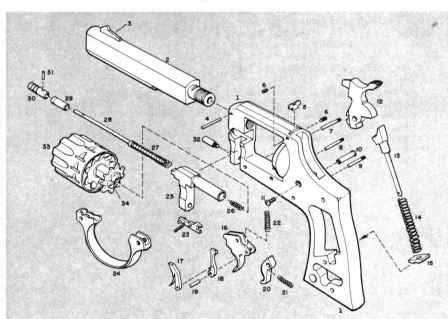

Note: Grips and 2 grip screws are not shown.

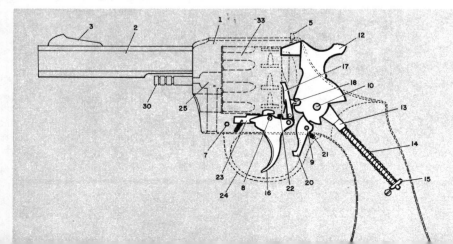

H&R SELF-LOADING PISTOL

INTRODUCED in 1916 by Harrington & Richardson of Worcester, Mass., the H & R cal. .32 self-loading pistol was based on design patents held by the English gunmaking firm of Webley & Scott. The Webley & Scott version of this pistol featured an outside hammer, but the model offered by H & R was a true hammerless, striker-fired arm.

The H & R cal. .32 pistol was one of the first American-made pocket pistols to have a magazine safety or disconnector to prevent firing of the gun when the magazine was removed. However, this feature was subsequently abandoned, so H & R pistols of this type will be found both with and without the magazine safety device.

Mechanical details of interest in this pistol include the cartridge indicator pin on the extractor which extends above the top of the slide when there is a cartridge in the chamber and the thumb safety which is pushed upward rather than downward to disengage it. The latter procedure is contrary to usual practice in pocket automatic pistols.

Production of the H & R cal. .32 self-loading pistol was discontinued in 1939. Approximately 40,000 were made.

By E. J. HOFFSCHMIDT

LEGEND:

1. Barrel
2. Slide
3. Bolt face retainer pin
4. Slide endplate
5. Detent spring
6. Endplate detent
7. Firing pin
8. Spring guide
9. Firing pin spring
10. Right grip
11. Slide return block
12. Recoil spring
13. Spring guide
14. Bolt face
15. Extractor
16. Extractor spring
17. Front guard pin
18. Trigger pin
19. Trigger guard hinge screw
20. Sear
21. Sear pin
22. Sear stop pin
23. Grip safety stop pin
24. Sear spring follower
25. Sear spring
26. Grip safety hinge pin
27. Grip safety
28. Spring plunger
29. Magazine safety spring
30. Trigger bar detent
31. Magazine safety pin
32. Magazine safety
33. Magazine
34. Magazine catch
35. Magazine catch spring
36. Magazine release button
37. Magazine catch pin
38. Trigger bar
39. Left grip
40. Grip screw
41. Thumb safety
42. Safety catch detent
43. Detent spring
44. Trigger spring plunger
45. Trigger spring
46. Trigger
47. Trigger stop pin
48. Trigger guard
49. Frame

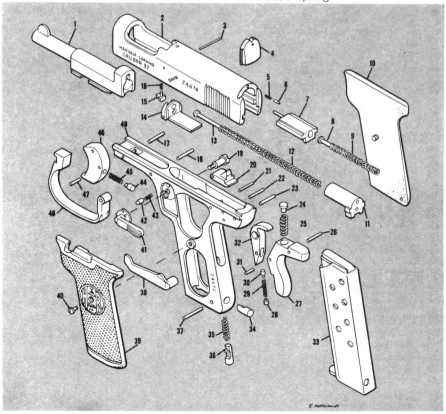

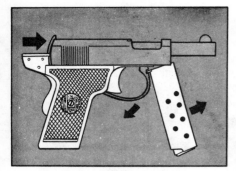

1 Takedown of the cal. .32 H&R pistol is not difficult. The barrel (1) is retained by the front of the trigger guard (48). The guard has a notch to allow the toe of the magazine floorplate to be used as a lever in disassembly. Pull trigger guard down slightly as shown, and push barrel and slide off. When reassembling, it is not necessary to pull down the guard. The cam on the underside of the barrel will push the trigger guard down.

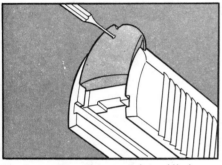

2 Once the slide endplate (4) is removed, the firing pin (7) and recoil spring (12) can be removed. To remove slide endplate, the endplate detent pin (6) must be depressed with a thin punch while the endplate is pushed up. Take care when the endplate is removed to prevent the slide return block (11) from flying out.

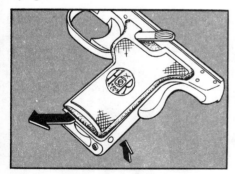

3 The left hard rubber grip (39) is easily broken if removed improperly. First remove the grip screws (40). Remove the right grip (10) and the magazine (33). Put thumb safety (41) in up or "off" position. Through the magazine well, push the lower end of the left grip. When free of the magazine catch pin (37), slide it down and out from under the edge of the thumb safety. Do not force.

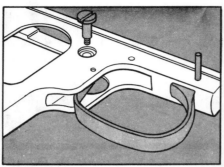

4 The H&R sear mechanism is unique in that there is no mechanical connection between trigger (46) and trigger bar (38). To remove the trigger, it is first necessary to remove the trigger stop pin (47). There is a small hole in the right side of the frame. If a thin punch is inserted through the frame hole when the trigger is at rest, the trigger stop pin can be driven out. Then the trigger pin (18) can be removed.

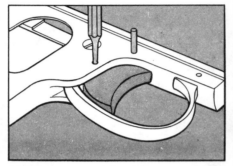

5 When reassembling trigger guard (48), insert the front tang into the frame with the front guard pin (17) out. Push the rear end of the guard into place and insert the trigger guard hinge screw (19) through the frame and through the hole in the trigger guard. Then pull the front tang down slightly and drive the front guard pin (17) into place.

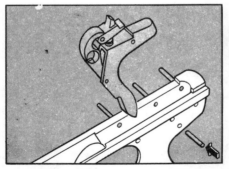

6 The sear (20), sear spring (25), sear spring follower (24), grip safety (27), magazine safety (32), and magazine safety spring assembly parts (28) (29) (30), must all be assembled together as shown and held together with the magazine safety pin (31). This assembly can then be easily installed in the frame as a unit. Line up the grip safety hinge pin (26) and then drive in the others. ∎

Harrington & Richardson .32 Cal. Auto

PISTOL MAGAZINES

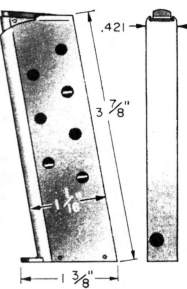

At first glance this little pistol is a dead ringer for the Webley Metropolitan Police pistol, except that the H&R is hammerless and has a squeeze safety. While it is a simple, effective pocket pistol, automatics have never proved as popular as revolvers, so H&R stopped its manufacture quite some time ago. The gun features a cartridge indicator and a magazine safety that prevents it firing when the magazine is removed. These, plus 2 manual safeties, make the gun an excellent house or pocket pistol.

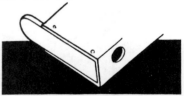

H&R magazines are sturdily made. The floorplate is pinned to the magazine body as shown. They can be best identified by the large magazine catch hole in the backstrap near the floorplate.

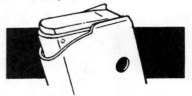

The shape of the magazine follower is another key to the identity of the H&R clip. It has a built-up double-step magazine follower. The rear third of the follower tapers down flush with the backstrap.—E. J. HOFF-SCHMIDT.

The H&R Premier Revolver

BY PETE DICKEY

THE history of Harrington & Richardson's Premier revolvers is a bit hazy despite their popularity proven by the vast numbers that are still to be found in all parts of this country and elsewhere.

The revolver was first noted in this research in the 1895 Montgomery Ward catalog, where it already had the Premier name but was offered (at $4) only in .32 S&W cal. with 3″ barrel and nickel plating. It continued in production at least until World War II in the five-shot .32 version, joined by a seven-shot .22 Long Rifle model. Both calibers could be had with blue or nickel finishes in 2″, 3″, 4″, 5″ and 6″ barrels, with oversized target stocks as an option.

At one time or another, there were variants available such as the ''Police Premier,'' like the illustrated standard model but lacking the hammer spur, and the ''Hammerless,'' that actually had a semi-circular hammer concealed by a contoured plate pinned into the top rear of the frame.

The disassembly/assembly guide given here can be applied to all the above models and will be also useful for the larger-framed H&R break-open pocket revolvers of the period.

Most of these larger revolvers were made for the .32 S&W Long (six-shot) or .38 S&W (five-shot), with various barrel lengths and spurred, spurless and concealed hammers. Many names were applied to them, including ''Automatic,'' ''Automatic Ejecting,'' ''Auto Ejecting,'' ''Police Automatic,'' ''Hammerless'' and ''Heavy Hammerless.''

An excellent history of the variations of the larger revolvers appeared in the April, 1984, *American Rifleman*.

Disassembly Instructions

Lift up the barrel catch (9), swing the barrel unit fully down and unscrew the cylinder counterclockwise.

Remove the hinge screw (32) to separate barrel and frame units and free the extractor hook (30) and its spring (31).

The barrel catch (9) and its screw (12) are removed after first taking out the catch spring (10) and spring screw (11) from the underside of the top strap. This is done with an angled or thin-shanked screwdriver bypassing the cylinder quill (13) that should be left in place. (Fig. 1) If quill removal is necessary, its pin (14) must be drifted out and great care taken in removing the fragile quill with padded pliers.

The cylinder can be stripped by grasping the extractor extension (15) with padded pliers and turning counterclockwise. This releases the extractor (5) and its spring (16).

For frame stripping, remove the stocks (8) and, with the hammer down, push the mainspring (33) out from its seat in the butt. Drift out front and rear guard pins (6 & 7) and remove trigger guard (3), noting the position of the trigger spring (26) in front of the guard

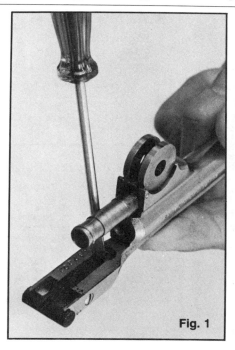

Fig. 1

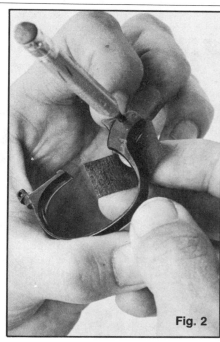

Fig. 2

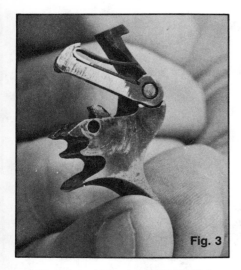

Fig. 3

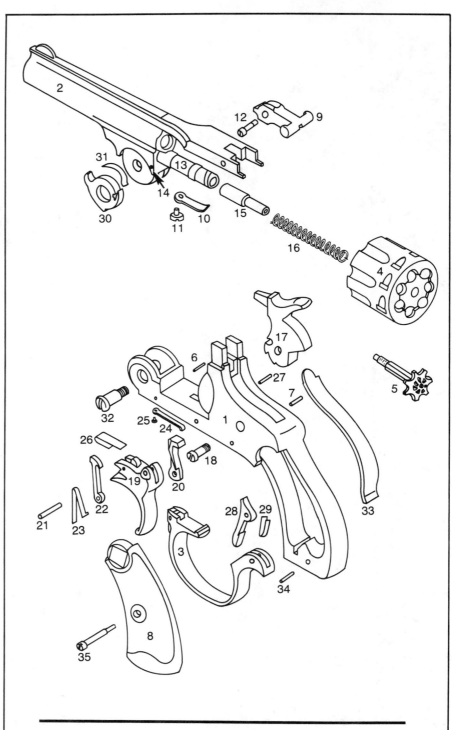

and the sear and its spring (28 & 29) that are positioned in the rear slot of the guard.

It is probably well to prepare the guard/sear/sear spring for reassembly at this point, as these components will require a "slave pin." A common lead pencil can be trimmed with a knife so that its lead is exposed for about ½". The lead is carefully pushed in to pin guard and sear together, and then trimmed flush with the guard sides. The sear should now be pushed down into the rear of the guard and held there with a strip of tape. **(Fig. 2)**

The trigger pin (27) is drifted out and the hammer screw (18) removed to permit removal of the trigger assembly and hammer. Position of the trigger, lifter, lifter pin, hand and hand spring (19-23) should be noted if these parts are to be separated. **(Fig. 3)**

Finally, the cylinder stop and screw (24 & 25) are removed from the front of the trigger guard slot in the frame.

Reassembly is generally accomplished in reverse order, but some manipulation of parts is necessary.

After replacing the cylinder stop and its screw, screw the hammer in place in the down position. Then start the trigger assembly (19-23) in through its frame slot, making sure the hand and lifter go in front of the hammer. A small screwdriver may be used to push the lifter forward so that it can spring back and enter its circular notch in the front of the hammer. The trigger pin is then inserted.

With the frame inverted, facing forward and held in the left hand, the trigger spring is placed with its long arm in the upper notch of the forward positioned trigger.

The front tab of the trigger guard assembly, that has been preassembled with tape and graphite slave pin as described, is now angled into its seat in the frame by retracting the trigger sufficiently to permit its passage. After the rear of the guard has been centered and pressed home, the two guard pins are inserted.

When the rear guard pin is correctly in place, the graphite slave pin will be driven out. The tape holding the sear can now be removed. The remaining parts replacements are made in straightforward manner with the rounded end of the mainspring seating in the rear hammer notch.

Parts Legend

1. Frame	12. Catch Screw
2. Barrel	13. Quill
3. Trigger Guard	14. Quill Pin
4. Cylinder	15. Extractor Extension
5. Extractor	16. Extractor Spring
6. Front Guard Pin	17. Hammer
7. Guard/Sear Pin	18. Hammer Screw
8. Stocks (pr.)	19. Trigger
9. Barrel Catch	20. Lifter
10. Barrel Catch Spring	21. Lifter Pin
11. Catch Spring Screw	22. Hand
	23. Hand Spring

24. Cylinder Stop	
25. Cylinder Stop Screw	
26. Trigger Spring	
27. Trigger Pin	
28. Sear	
29. Sear Spring	
30. Extractor Hook	
31. Hook Spring	
32. Hinge Screw	
33. Mainspring	
34. Stock Pin	
35. Stock Screw	

Heckler & Koch P9S Pistol

BY ROBERT W. HUNNICUTT

THE introduction of Heckler & Koch's P9S in 1972 helped open the U.S. market for a new kind of pistol — the ultramodern military/police semiautomatic. The manufacturing techniques used in the P9S and its successors like the P7 and VP 70Z are vastly different from those used in the making of familiar sidearms like the M1911 Colt or Walther P38.

The P9S, like the German G3 rifle and its civilian version, the HK91, is made almost entirely of precision steel stampings from automatic machinery. Hand fitting is minimized by extensive use of alloy stampings and plastic parts.

Like most H&K products, the P9S operates on the delayed blowback principle, with the delay provided by roller bearings which protrude through two holes on either side of the bolt. The bearings rest in recesses in the barrel extension. The barrel is fixed to the frame and does not move during firing.

When the P9S is fired, the bearings hold the action shut until they are rolled from their recesses. This keeps the slide forward until the bullet has left the barrel. The bolt and slide assembly continues to the rear to the limit of its travel, ejecting the spent case and cocking the hammer. As the slide moves forward, it strips the top cartridge from the magazine and inserts it in the chamber for firing.

On final closing of the breech, the bolt face stops on contact with the rear of the chamber and the slide continues forward a short distance, causing the angled surfaces of the locking piece to force the roller bearings out into the recesses of the barrel extension. The pistol is ready for another shot.

Among the P9S's advanced features is the lever on the left side of the grip, which performs several functions. It is raised to lock the slide open, and pressed down to release the slide. When the pistol is uncocked, it can be cocked for a single-action shot by firmly pressing down on the lever. The gun can be uncocked by pressing down on the lever, pulling the trigger while maintaining pressure on the lever and gradually releasing the lever. This operation should be performed only with the safety applied.

When the pistol is cocked, a small pin protrudes from the end of the slide. A loaded chamber is indicated by a raised extractor. The pin and extractor can be seen by day or felt at night, making it easy to determine the condition of the P9S at any time.

The P9S safety is located on the left side of the slide. When it is pulled down, the white dot shows, indicating the gun is safe. When it is pushed up, a red dot shows the gun is ready for firing.

Disassembly Instructions

Remove the magazine by pressing the magazine catch to the rear and withdrawing the magazine. Retract the slide to insure the chamber is empty.

Release the slide, allowing it to return to the forward position. Hold the pistol in one hand, using the thumb of the other hand to press the barrel clamp inside the trigger guard upward and push the slide/barrel assembly forward and lift it up and off the receiver. This may be done while the pistol is cocked or uncocked, on safe or off **(Fig. 1)**.

The barrel may be removed from the slide by pushing it forward against the pressure of the recoil spring, then lifting the rear of the barrel when it comes free of engagement with the bolt head. The barrel can then be allowed to come to the rear and out **(Fig. 2, 3)**.

The bolt head may be removed by using the barrel extension tang as a tool **(Fig. 4)**. The tang is inserted at the right rear of the bolt head, between the bolt head and the slide rail. The bolt head locking catch is depressed, freeing the bolt head from the bolt proper. The bolt head may now be lifted out of the slide. Further disassembly

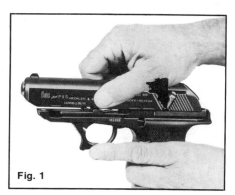

Fig. 1

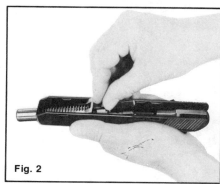

Fig. 2

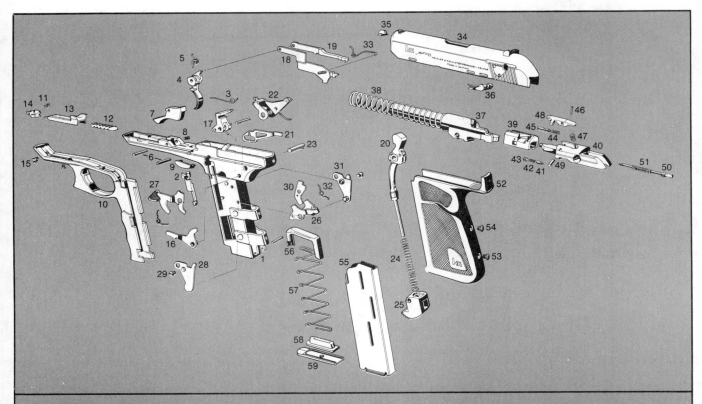

Parts Legend

1. Receiver
2. Catch
3. Spring for catch
4. Trigger
5. Trigger spring
6. Cylindrical pin
7. Barrel clamp
8. Compression spring for barrel clamp
9. Insert piece
10. Trigger guard
11. Lens head countersunk screw
12. Elastic buffer
13. Buffer housing
14. Support
15. Threaded insert
16. Safety latch
17. Catch lever, assembled
18. Pull bar

19. Trigger bar
20. Hammer
21. Indicator pin
22. Disconnector, assembled
23. Axle for hammer
24. Compression spring for shank
25. Magazine catch
26. Angle lever
27. Cocking lever
28. Bearing plate, left
29. Countersunk screw for bearing plate
30. Intermediate lever
31. Bearing plate, right
32. Elbow spring for cocking lever, angle lever and intermediate lever
33. Spring for pull bar
34. Slide with sights
35. Front sight
36. Safety catch
37. Barrel
38. Compression spring for barrel

39. Bolt head, complete
40. Bolt head carrier
41. Catch bolt
42. Compression spring
43. Set screw
44. Compression spring for locking catch
45. Pressure pin
46. Pin
47. Compression spring for locking catch
48. Locking catch
49. Cylindrical pin
50. Firing pin
51. Compression spring
52. Grip
53. Lens head countersunk screw
54. Lens head countersunk screw
55. Magazine housing
56. Follower
57. Follower spring
58. Support for follower spring
59. Magazine floor plate

---

for cleaning or maintenance is not required.

Assembly Instructions

Reassembly is accomplished by reversing the disassembly procedure. The tang of the barrel extension must be used to reassemble the bolt head to the bolt proper. After the barrel is reassembled in the slide, the slide should be seated muzzle end first to the forward end of the frame so the front guide lugs on the slide can engage the corresponding recesses. Lower the rear of the slide onto the frame and pull it to the rear. Then let it snap forward under the power of the recoil spring. The pistol is reassembled.

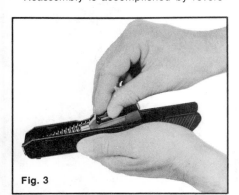

Fig. 3

Fig. 4

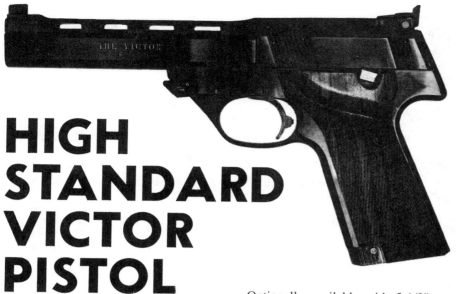

HIGH STANDARD VICTOR PISTOL

Among the first impressions gained in handling the Hi-Standard Victor self-loading pistol is that it is designed to win matches. This well balanced target pistol chambered for the .22 Long Rifle cartridge weighs 50 ounces unloaded, a feature that aids in steady holding. Also contributing to steady holding are the large, checkered walnut grips with the left one having a thumb rest for right-handed shooters. Left-hand grips, with the thumb rest on the right grip are available at the buyer's option.

The Victor is one of several pistols in High Standard's "Military" Model 107 series. Introduced in 1972, this highly accurate arm has a grip shape and angle generally similar to that of the U.S. M1911A1 service pistol. This eases the transition between the two pistols for match shooters.

Optionally available with 5-1/2" or 4-1/2" barrels, the blowback operated Victor has an internal hammer and a 10-shot detachable magazine. The magazine catch in the lower front part of the grip frame must be pulled forward to release the magazine. Another desirable feature is that the slide remains open after the last shot has been fired. the slide can be released by depressing the slide lock lever on the right side of the frame.

The trigger mechanism is of two-stage design with a light, crisp letoff. Overtravel is eliminated easily by adjusting a socket-headed stop screw on the trigger face, and weight of pull is adjustable by turning a screw in the upper rear of the frame. Good trigger control is provided by the 3/8"-wide, gold-plated trigger the thumb operated safety, on the left side of the frame, is also gold plated. Most other exposed metal surfaces have either a blued or a blackened finish.

Both front and rear target-style sights are mounted on a ventilated rib which extends from the muzzle to the upper rear of the pistol, above the slide. The 1/8" wide, square blade front sight is on a ramp base integral with the barrel. The square notch, fully adjustable rear sight is affixed to the opposite end of the same ramp and features positive click detents in its adjustments. Direction of sight movement is indicated on the movable leaf.

As with many other High Standard self-loading pistols, the barrel assembly of the Victor can be detached after depressing the barrel takedown plunger in the front of the frame. With the plunger fully engaged, the barrel is held firmly in the frame, an important requirement for good accuracy. The bottom of the barrel is drilled and tapped for attachment of barrel weights. A two-ounce weight is furnished with the 4-1/2" barrel at no extra cost.

A highly successful design, the Victor was well liked by target shooters nationwide. It remained in production until High Standard ceased manufacturing operations in 1985.

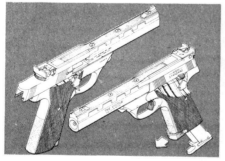

1 Begin disassembly by pushing safety (52) upward into safe position. Pull magazine catch (68) forward and remove magazine (73). Draw slide (19) fully to rear, checking visually that chamber is empty. Raise slide lock lever (40), and ease slide forward slightly until held open by slide lock.

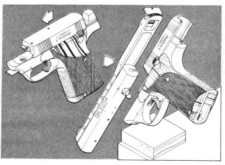

2 Place a wooden block at the edge of a sturdy table. Depress barrel takedown plunger (32) against the block, holding gun muzzle down with barrel at 45° angle to the table top. Grasp pistol firmly with one hand on barrel and the other on grip. With takedown plunger fully depressed, pull barrel assembly upward out of frame. Draw slide slightly rearward to release slide lock, and guide slide forward off the frame. No further disassembly is required for normal cleaning and lubrication.

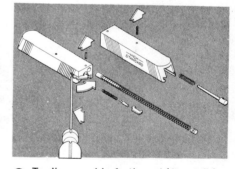

3 To disassemble further, drift out firing pin retaining pin (18) through top of slide to release firing pin (22) and firing pin spring (21). On replacement, face notch in firing pin head to right side of slide. Insert point of ice pick or awl between extractor (14) and extractor plunger (15), and depress the plunger well into the slide. Rotate forward end of extractor toward center of breech face and remove. Then, ease out plunger and extractor spring (16). Drift out driving spring plug pin (17) through top of slide. Place thumb firmly against driving spring plug (11) in breech face and withdraw punch. Then, ease plug, driving spring (12), and plunger (13) from slide.

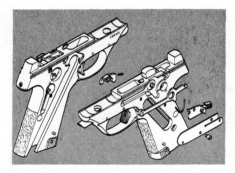

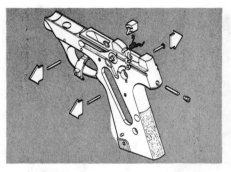

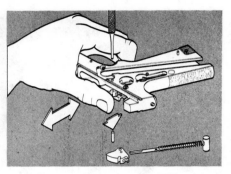

4 Unscrew grip screws (29), and remove grips (23) (67). Use caution in removing right grip to avoid dislocation of slide lock lever and loss of its tiny spring (39). Remove slide lock lever and spring carefully. Move safety downward to fire position, pull trigger (55) while holding hammer (44), and ease hammer fully forward with thumb. Unscrew and remove side plate screw (65), side plate (66), and safety. Unseat and remove sear bar spring (58). Push down rear end of sear bar (53) to disconnect it from sear (47). Hold frame left side down, and shake out sear bar.

5 Unscrew and remove sear adjustment screw (62), and shake out its plunger (61). When replacing plunger, its notched end must straddle legs of sear spring (45). Drift sear pin (42) out to right and remove sear. Drift out sear spring pin (59) and remove sear spring. Drift out trigger pin (56), rotate trigger ¼ turn, and pull downward from the frame.

6 Drift out hammer pin (57) with a 3/16" pin punch. Grasp frame as shown, and apply pressure to hammer with thumb. Withdraw punch, and ease hammer outward. Remove hammer strut (63), ring (64), and hammer spring (72). Push hammer strut anchor pin (48) out through side of frame. In reassembling these parts, insure that offset hammer spring seat in the anchor pin lies toward right side of frame, and that hammer strut contacts the hammer strut pin (41) contained within hammer. Reassemble in reverse, making sure that hammer is cocked before replacing slide. After pistol is reassembled, retract slide and let it snap forward against barrel several times to insure that barrel is locked firmly.

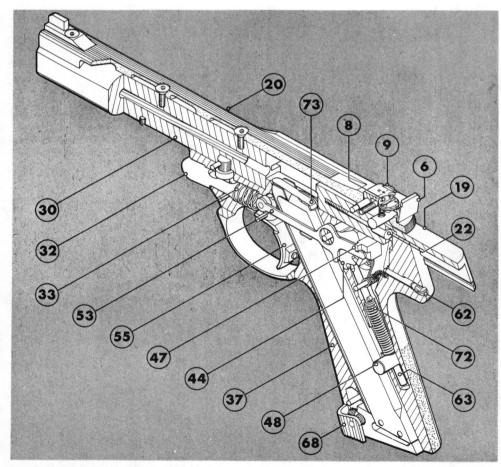

7 Cutaway indicates relationship between assembled parts. Slide is shown retracted and held open by slide stop. Parts are number keyed to parts legend.

PARTS LEGEND

1. Rib screw, short (2)
2. Sight elevation spring (2)
3. Elevation plunger
4. Elevation detent plunger
5. Elevation ball (2)
6. Sight leaf
7. Windage spring
8. Elevation adjustment screw
9. Windage screw
10. Rib screw, long
11. Driving spring plug
12. Driving spring
13. Driving spring plunger
14. Extractor
15. Extractor plunger
16. Extractor spring
17. Driving spring plug pin
18. Firing pin retaining pin
*19. Slide
*20. Rib
21. Firing pin spring
22. Firing pin
23. Grip, right
24. Sight leaf pivot pin
25. Windage detent plunger spring
26. Windage detent plunger
27. Sight, rear cross member
28. Grip washer (2)
29. Grip screw (2)
*30. Barrel
31. Barrel filler screw (2)
32. Barrel takedown plunger
33. Barrel takedown plunger spring
34. Barrel stud retaining pin
35. Barrel takedown plunger pin
36. Barrel stud

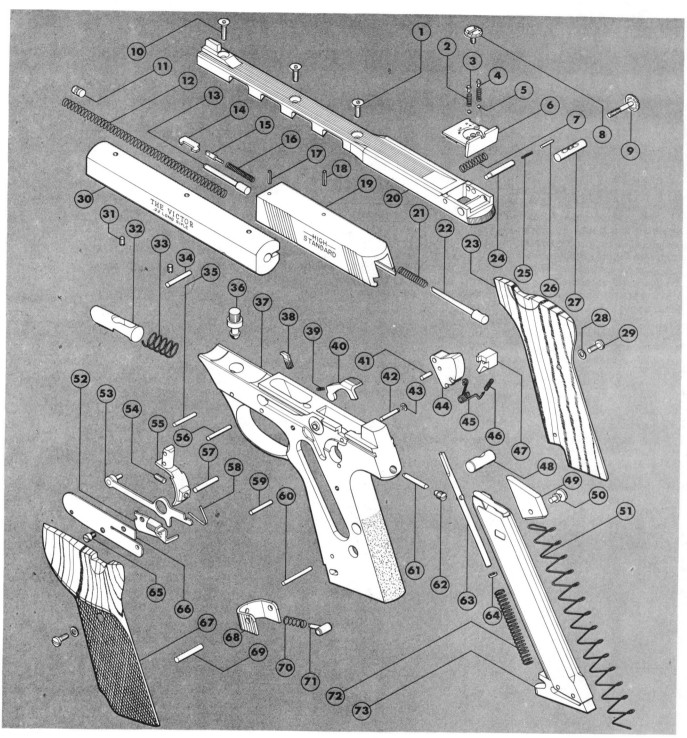

37. Frame	50. Magazine button	63. Hammer strut
*38. Ejector	51. Magazine spring	64. Hammer strut ring
39. Slide lock spring	*52. Safety	65. Side plate screw
40. Slide lock lever	*53. Sear bar and trigger pull pin assy.	66. Side plate
41. Hammer strut pin	54. Trigger stop screw	67. Grip, left
42. Sear pin	*55. Trigger	68. Magazine catch
43. Sear pin retaining ring	56. Trigger pin	69. Magazine catch roller pin
*44. Hammer	57. Hammer pin	70. Magazine catch spring
45. Sear spring, adjustable	*58. Sear bar spring	71. Magazine catch roller and spring guide assy.
46. Sear spring leg retainer	59. Sear spring pin	72. Hammer spring
*47. Sear	60. Grip alignment pin	73. Magazine, complete
48. Hammer strut anchor pin	*61. Sear adjustment screw plunger	* High Standard recommends factory fitting of
49. Magazine follower	*62. Sear adjustment screw	replacement part.

HI-STANDARD DURA-MATIC PISTOLS

By JAMES M. TRIGGS

The Hi-Standard Model M-100 Dura-Matic pistol was introduced in 1954 by the Hi-Standard Manufacturing Corp., Hamden, Conn., and was dropped from production in 1969.

Made to sell at a moderate price, this pistol is a blowback-operated striker-fired pistol is chambered for the economical .22 Long Rifle cartridge, regular or high speed. It was designed for informal target shooting or plinking. A choice of 4-1/2" and 6-1/2" barrel lengths was available. The sights were fixed but the rear sight could be drifted to the right or left to adjust for windage. The magazine has a capacity of 10 cartridges.

Pushing the cross-bolt safety to the left, or "ON", position locks the slide shut and also immobilizes the striker pin. When the striker mechanism is cocked a red dot on the rear of the striker is visible at the rear end of the striker sleeve.

An improved barrel locking system for this pistol was introduced in 1957. It was then re-designated M-101.

The J.C. Higgins Model 80 self-loading pistol once sold by Sears & Roebuck was mechanically identical to the M-101.

Parts Legend

1. Barrel*
2. Front sight
3. Barrel set screw
4. Frame*
5. Barrel lock plunger pin*
6. Ejector
7. Ejector pin
8. Sear bar
9. Barrel lock plunger*
10. Barrel lock ball*
11. Barrel lock ball spring*
12. Striker sleeve
13. Striker sleeve screw
14. Striker sleeve screw locking pin
15. Sear plunger
16. Sear spring
17. Safety detent
18. Sear
19. Sear pin
20. Trigger
21. Trigger pin
22. Trigger pull pin
23. Trigger spring
24. Magazine catch spring
25. Magazine catch
26. Magazine catch pin
27. Barrel nut lock washer*
28. Barrel nut*
29. Trigger guard
30. Trigger guard screw
31. Trigger guard screw lock washer
32. Safety*
33. Grip bolt
34. Grip bolt washer
35. Grip
36. Magazine assembly (not shown)
37. Slide
38. Extractor
39. Extractor plunger
40. Extractor spring
41. Rear sight
42. Slide spring
43. Striker pin (firing pin)*
44. Striker spring

Parts marked * are not interchangeable between M-100 and M-101 models.

Disassembly Procedure

Press in magazine catch (25) and withdraw magazine from grip (35). Draw slide (37) rearward and lock open by moving safety (32) to left. Safety acts as slide lock [safety is "on" when red enamel on right end of safety is *not* visible—safety locks striker pin (43) and slide]. Check chamber to be sure pistol is unloaded before proceeding with disassembly.

To remove barrel (1), depress barrel lock plunger (9) on front right side of frame (4). Unscrew barrel nut (28) and pull barrel up and out of its seat in frame. Slots in barrel nut permit use of coin or screwdriver for tightening or loosening nut. Barrel of M-101 is removed by unscrewing nut (28). A barrel lock is not provided in this model.

Move safety (32) to right, or "off" position, to release slide (37) and draw slide forward until its rear end is about ½" forward of rear of frame. Then, while holding the slide, pull the trigger to disengage sear plunger (15) from striker pin (43). Draw slide off frame and remove slide spring (42), striker pin (43), and striker spring (44) from rear of slide. Note striker pin and spring rest inside of slide spring and that flat surface of striker pin faces slot in bottom of slide.

To remove grip from frame, unscrew grip bolt (33), and remove bolt and its washer (34) from bottom of grip.

The above constitutes sufficient disassembly for normal cleaning purposes. Lock parts within frame are easily removed, but disassembly further than that given here is not recommended except for repair or replacement of parts. Reassemble in reverse. ∎

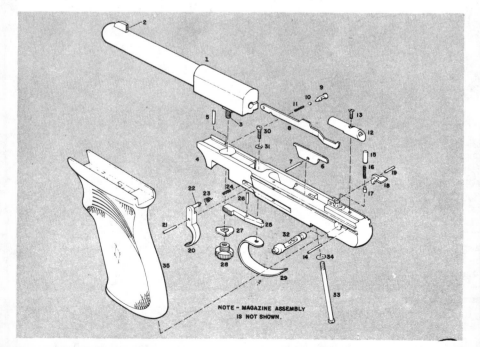

NOTE - MAGAZINE ASSEMBLY IS NOT SHOWN.

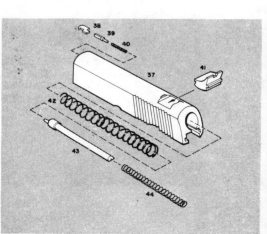

HI-STANDARD MODEL D-100

By JAMES M. TRIGGS

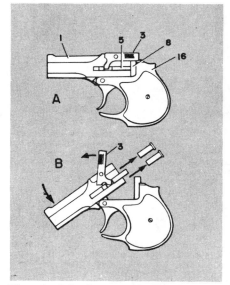

The High Standard Model D-100 pistol was introduced in 1962. Manufactured by the High Standard Manufacturing Corp., of Hamden, Conn., the Model D-100 has two, over-under, enbloc barrels that tip down for loading. It is chambered for the .22 Long Rifle cartridge and the lock mechanism is of hammerless, trigger cocking type with a ratchet to discharge the cartridges alternately. The breech of the D-100 is opened by lifting the stirrup hinged at the top of the barrel assembly. The barrels can then be tipped down to expose the breech. Lifting the stirrup to its upward limit cams the extractor to the rear and if done smartly throws the cartridges cases clear. The D-100 and its .22 WMR stablemate, D-101 remained in production until High Standard ceased manufacturing operations in 1985.

Disassembly Procedure

Lift stirrup (3) and tip barrel (1) to expose breech. Be sure pistol is unloaded.

Remove grip screws (39) and grips (38). Cover plate (37) over left side of housing (16) is removed by removing cover plate screw (20). Action is then exposed and is readily disassembled. Lift out actuator (34), taking care not to lose actuator spring (35). Compress hammer spring (31) to permit removal of spring, hammer strut (33), and abutment (30) assembly from housing. Hammer (18) assembly may be removed intact from housing.

Barrel (1) assembly can be removed from frame (8) by removing barrel pivot pin (9). Extractor (5) is removed from barrel to rear. Remove stirrup pivot pin (2) and remove stirrup (3) from barrel.

Due to simplicity of design of Model D-100, removal of grips and cover plate is sufficient disassembly for normal cleaning. Disassembly of hammer components from housing is not recommended unless for repairs. Reassemble in reverse.

The pistol is shown with breech locked and ready to fire (A), and with breech opened (B). Note that lifting the stirrup (3) moves extractor (5) to rear. Closing barrel will automatically retract extractor and lock stirrup over frame.

Parts Legend

1. Barrel
2. Stirrup pivot pin
3. Stirrup
4. Stirrup roller
5. Extractor
6. Stirrup plunger spring
7. Stirrup plunger
8. Frame
9. Barrel pivot pin
10. Trigger
11. Trigger spring
12. Trigger pivot pin
13. Hammer safety block
14. Hammer safety block spring
15. Hammer safety block pin
16. Housing
17. Hammer pivot screw
18. Hammer
19. Hammer pivot sleeve
20. Cover plate screw
21. Striker
22. Striker pivot pin
23. Striker spring
24. Striker spring spacer washer
25. Striker spring retaining pin
26. Hammer strut pin
27. Hammer pawl
28. Hammer pawl pin
29. Hammer pawl spring
30. Hammer spring abutment
31. Hammer spring
32. Hammer strut washer
33. Hammer strut
34. Actuator
35. Actuator spring
36. Ratchet
37. Cover plate
38. Grips (2) (left grip only is shown.)
39. Grip screws (2) ∎

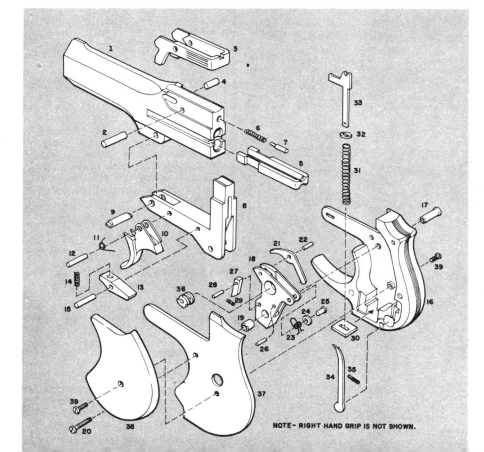

NOTE- RIGHT HAND GRIP IS NOT SHOWN.

LEGEND

A—Recoil spring stop
B—Recoil spring
C—Recoil spring guide
D—Extractor
E—Extractor plunger
F—Extractor spring
G—Recoil spring stop
pin
H—Extractor pin
I—Slide
J—Assembly lock screw
K—Firing pin spring
L—Firing pin
M—Rear sight
N—Assembly lock
plunger
O—Assembly lock
P—Firing pin retaining
screw
Q—Mainspring guide
R—Mainspring
S—Slide stop
T—Slide stop plunger
U—Slide stop spring
V—Takedown latch
W—Sear pin
X—Hammer pin
Y—Hammer strut pin
Z—Hammer
AA—Hammer strut
BB—Sear plunger
CC—Sear spring
DD—Frame
EE—Magazine
FF—Magazine catch
GG—Magazine catch
spring
HH—Magazine catch pin
II—Safety catch screw
JJ—Safety catch
KK—Side plate
LL—Trigger bar spring
MM—Trigger bar
NN—Sear
OO—Trigger
PP—Trigger pin
QQ—Pull pin
RR—Trigger spring
plunger
SS—Trigger spring
TT—Barrel pin
UU—Barrel
VV—Grip screw
WW—Left-hand grip

HOFFSCHMIDT

HI-STANDARD
MODEL HB

By E. J. Hoffschmidt

For years, until shortly before the firm closed its doors in 1985, High Standard manufactured the widest range of .22 rimfire self-loading pistols of any handgun maker.

Not only did High Standard produce a great variety of guns, they kept pace with the times and demands of shooters and handgun enthusiasts.

High Standard started production of their first pistol during the great depression. This gun, the Model B, looked a great deal like the defunct Hartford pistol produced between 1929 and 1930. But, it was well made and priced a good deal below its competitors, so it caught on.

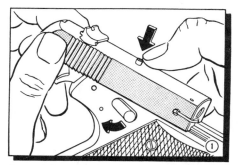

Remove the magazine, check the chamber to be sure it is empty. Pull the slide (I) to the rear until it stops. Depress the assembly lock plunger (N) and push the slide forward. Now depress the takedown latch (V) and pull the slide back off the frame

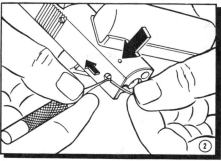

To remove the extractor (D), first remove the extractor retaining pin (H). Then insert a thin screwdriver or pointed tool, as shown. Push the extractor plunger (E) back into the slide. Now remove the extractor (D) by rotating it in toward the firing pin

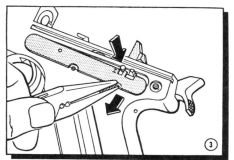

Never remove the takedown latch (V) while the slide (I) is on the frame, as it would cause a condition that is difficult to remedy. The side plate (KK) retains the takedown latch (V) on some models and must be removed as shown, to free the latch

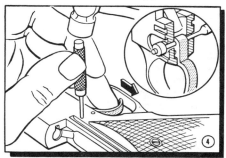

The trigger (OO) can be removed only after the pull pin (QQ) has been driven out. Insert a thin drift pin into the hole above the trigger pin. Move the trigger a bit until the drift is seated in the hole in the trigger. Drive out the pull pin (QQ), then the trigger pin (PP)

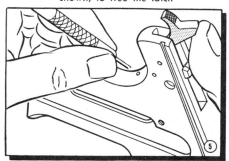

Because the mainspring is powerful, it must be kept in check when removing the hammer (Z) and sear (NN). To do so, cock the hammer and insert a thin pin into the hole in the back strap. Release the hammer and drive out the hammer pin (X) and the sear pin (W)

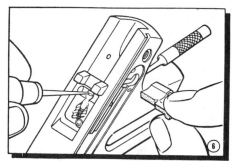

To replace the sear, push the sear spring (CC) and plunger (BB) back into the frame far enough to be caught through the opening for the takedown lever. While holding the plunger as shown, replace the sear (NN) and sear pin (W)

Following the Model B, High Standard kept up a steady stream of variations to delight the market and confuse the gunsmith.

The Model HB, shown here, is really the original Model B with a external hammer added. It makes an ideal plinking pistol for it is comparatively small and compact. Its external hammer is an excellent safety feature, since you can tell at a glance whether the gun is cocked. As a target gun it suffers from a short grip, but as a fishing or hunting companion the reverse angle on the grip makes for easy removal from a coat or trouser pocket. With a 4-1/2-inch barrel it weighs only 31 ounces, light enough to stick in your pocket and forget about. Like other, current, .22 caliber pistols, Hi-Standards are blowback operated, since the .22 cartridge does not develop enough pressure to require a more involved lock breech mechanism. Hi-Standard pistols are generally well made and finished. While they are easy to repair, care must be taken in ordering parts, since in the hammer gun series there are three different hammers and five different sears.

It's interesting to note, and a problem for proofreaders, that "High Standard" refers to the company and "Hi-Standard" refers to the guns.

PISTOL MAGAZINES

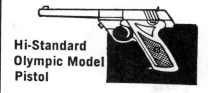

Hi-Standard Olympic Model Pistol

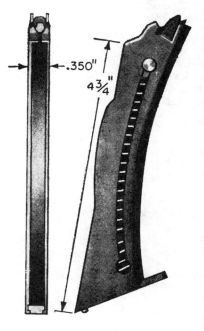

The oddly-shaped magazine shown was made for the early Hi-Standard Olympic Model pistol chambered for the .22 short cartridge. For production reasons, the opening in the gun frame was made for the .22 long rifle magazine.

To compensate for this, the magazine lips and follower were reduced in length for the .22 short cartridge.

The floorplate is detachable to facilitate cleaning interior of the magazine.—E. J. HOFFSCHMIDT

139

Hi-Standard Sentinel Revolver

By Thomas E. Wessel

The Hi-Standard Sentinel, introduced in 1955 by the High Standard Manufacturing Corp., of Hamden, Conn., met the demand for an moderately priced, 9-shot, swing out cylinder, double-action revolver chambered for economical .22 rimfire cartridges. The Sentinel remained in High Standard's line until about 1974.

Modern in concept when introduced, the Sentinel featured a light weight frame of aluminum alloy with a barrel and cylinder of steel. It was designed for use with either regular or high-speed .22 Short, Long or Long Rifle cartridges, with chambers counterbored to surround the cartridge rims. Hammer and trigger are of case-hardened steel and virtually unbreakable coil springs are used throughout.

The hammer is of the rebounding type and the lock mechanism incorporates an automatic safety block to prevent accidental discharge should the gun be dropped on a hard surface.

The front sight is of the square-blade Patridge pattern. The square-notch rear sight can be adjusted for windage by tapping it form side to side in its transverse slot.

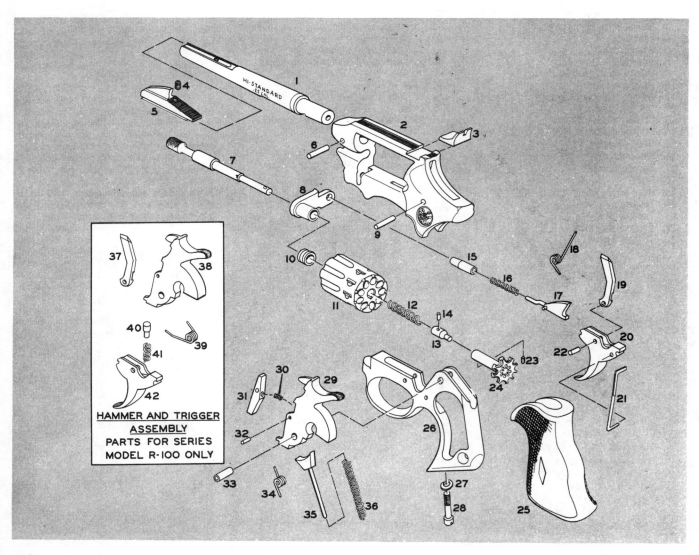

HAMMER AND TRIGGER ASSEMBLY
PARTS FOR SERIES
MODEL R-100 ONLY

The Sentinel was offered with 2-3/8", 4", and 6" barrel lengths and in several finishes including nickel plate and anodized turquoise, gold and pink as well as the traditional blue. Grips were of brown or white checkered plastic, with the latter also available in smooth finish to simulate ivory.

For several years, Sears, Roebuck & Co. sold a variant of the Sentinel under its own brand name.

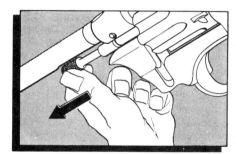

1 To swing out cylinder (11) for loading, pull ejector rod (7) forward and thence left. This is also first step for disassembly

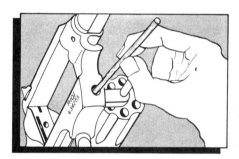

2 Next insert a small hardwood dowel into hole in front portion of frame (2) to depress link pivot pin (15). Pull cylinder assembly left until wood dowel prevents any further movement left. Withdraw dowel and place thumb over hole in frame. This will prevent cylinder stop spring (16) and link pivot pin from flying out of the hole as cylinder assembly is separated from the frame

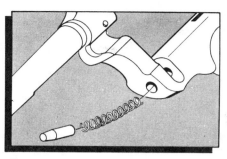

3 Up-end the revolver and shake out the link pivot pin and cylinder stop spring

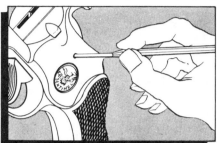

4 Loosen or remove grip screw (28) and drift out hammer pivot pin (9) with small flat-nosed punch. Entire trigger guard (26) and assembly may now be removed from frame. All internal parts are now exposed. Exercise care when executing this portion of the disassembly that cylinder stop (17) does not drop out and become lost

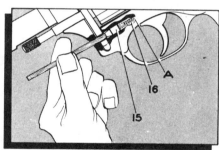

5 Reassembly is accomplished in reverse order. When reinserting the cylinder stop spring (16) insure that it slides onto arm portion (A) of cylinder stop; otherwise it becomes jammed and may be deformed ∎

Parts Legend

1. Barrel
2. Frame
3. Rear sight
4. Front sight set screw
5. Front sight
6. Barrel pin
7. Ejector rod
8. Crane
9. Hammer pivot pin
10. Cylinder bushing
11. Cylinder
12. Cylinder lock plunger spring
13. Cylinder lock plunger
14. Cylinder lock plunger pin
15. Link pivot pin
16. Cylinder stop spring
17. Cylinder stop
18. Hand spring
19. Hand
20. Trigger
21. Hammer safety stop
22. Trigger pivot pin
23. Ejector alignment dowel

24. Ejector
25. Grip
26. Trigger guard
27. Grip lock washer
28. Grip screw
29. Hammer
30. Hammer pawl spring
31. Hammer pawl
32. Hammer pawl pin
33. Hammer sleeve
34. Trigger spring
35. Hammer spring guide
36. Hammer spring

Hammer and trigger parts specific to Model R-100

37. Hand
38. Hammer
39. Hand spring
40. Trigger spring plunger
41. Trigger spring
42. Trigger

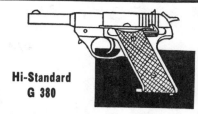

Hi-Standard G 380

PISTOL MAGAZINES

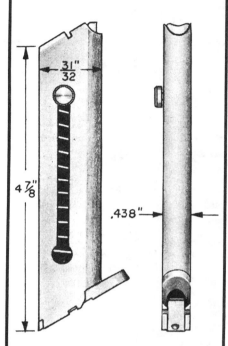

In 1947, Hi-Standard brought out a cal. .380 ACP pistol. It was blowback-operated and followed the lines of the then-current G-series of cal. .22 pistols. It did not become popular since it was too large for a pocket pistol, too expensive for a plinker, and not a target pistol. Like other Hi-Standard pistols, the G 380 is well made and finished. The magazine is built a great deal like the normal cal. .22 magazine, except it is about 20% thicker.

The G 380 magazine has a removable floorplate which allows its disassembly for easy cleaning.

The follower is unusual in design and unlike that of any other large-caliber pistol magazine. Stamped from sheet metal, its cross section resembles a railroad rail. The 3-piece construction of the backstrap is also unusual and is another good point of identification.—EDWARD J. HOFFSCHMIDT

HI-STANDARD SUPERMATIC TROPHY PISTOL

By Thomas E. Wessel

In the late summer of 1958 High Standard Manufacturing Corp., of Hamden, Conn. introduced four, 10-shot detachable magazine, .22 rimfire, self-loading pistols featuring detachable barrels and improved lockwork to provide crisp and uniform sear disengagement. These guns were designated Supermatic Trophy, Supermatic Citation, Olympic citation and Supermatic Tournament. The first three guns were regularly available with 10", 8" and 6-3/4" barrels. The fully adjustable rear sight is mounted on the slide of the 6-3/4"-barreled version, whereas the rear sight is mounted on the breech ring of the 8" and 10" barrels. The detachable barrel stabilizer minimizes muzzle jump, thereby aiding in quicker recovery of aim between shots. Screw adjustments are provided to vary weight of trigger pull and amount of backlash. The frame straps are grooved.

The Supermatic Trophy and Citation models are chambered for the .22 Long Rifle cartridge and conversion units are available to permit use of .22 Short cartridge. the Olympic Citation is chambered for .22 Short and is convertible to .22 Long Rifle by means of a factory installed conversion unit. The Supermatic Trophy is the deluxe model, featuring high polish blue finish, checkered walnut grips and gold plated trigger and safety button. Lettering is gold inlaid. The other models have checkered plastic grips, and triggers, and safety buttons are finished blue. Walnut grips are available at extra cost in lieu of the plastic grips.

The Supermatic Tournament, offered in .22 Long Rifle only, was available with 4-1/2" or 6-3/4" barrel. The lockwork is substantially identical to that of the other models, but does not incorporate trigger pull adjustment. The barrels are not equipped with integral or detachable stabilizers. The fully adjustable rear sight is mounted on the slide. Grips are of checkered plastic with walnut available at extra cost.

Disassembly procedure for the four guns, all of which had been discontinued in favor of more advanced models by the 1970s, is substantially the same. High Standard ceased manufacturing operations in 1985.

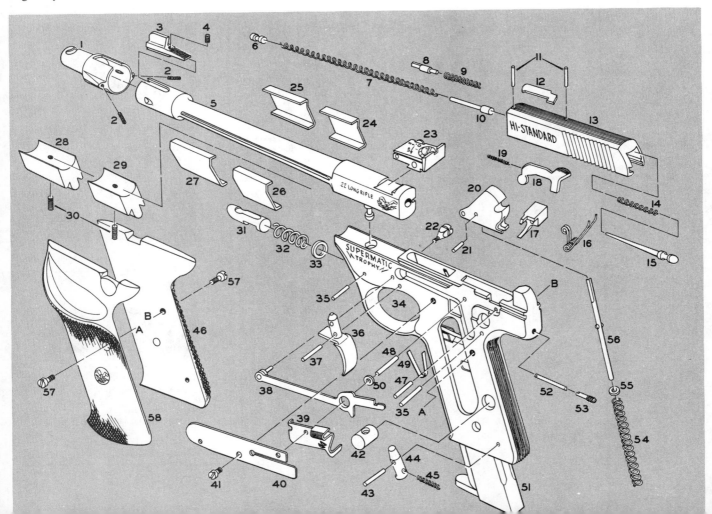

1 To disassemble Supermatic Trophy pistol, first press magazine catch (44) and withdraw magazine (51). Pull back slide (13) and lock it in place by pushing up slide lock lever (18). At same time inspect gun to insure that no cartridge remains in chamber. Next, move safety (39) to "On" position. This locks hammer (20) and sear (17), disconnects trigger (36), and completely separates sear bar (38) from sear. Grasp pistol as shown (left-handed persons should use a reversed grip) and depress barrel takedown plunger (31) with thumb. Lift barrel (5) out of its bedding with a straight upward motion. If, after extensive shooting, it becomes difficult to remove barrel by thumb pressure alone, press takedown plunger against a padded but solid object

Parts Legend

1. Stabilizer
2. Stabilizer set screw (2)
3. Front sight
4. Front sight screw
5. Barrel
6. Driving spring plug
7. Driving spring
8. Extractor plunger
9. Extractor spring
10. Driving spring plunger
11. Driving spring plunger pin (2)
12. Extractor
13. Slide
14. Firing pin spring
15. Firing pin
16. Sear spring
17. Sear
18. Slide lock lever
19. Slide lock spring
20. Hammer
21. Hammer strut pin
22. Anti-backlash screw
23. Adjustable rear sight
24. Right bracket, short barrel weight
25. Right bracket, long barrel weight
26. Left bracket, short barrel weight
27. Left bracket, long barrel weight
28. Long barrel weight
29. Short barrel weight
30. Barrel weight screw (2)
31. Barrel takedown plunger
32. Barrel takedown plunger spring
33. Anti-backlash detent washer
34. Frame
35. Barrel takedown plunger pin
36. Trigger
37. Trigger pin
38. Sear bar and trigger pull pin assembly
39. Safety
40. Side plate
41. Side plate screw
42. Hammer strut anchor pin
43. Magazine catch pin
44. Magazine catch
45. Magazine catch spring
46. Right handgrip
47. Sear pin
48. Hammer pin
49. Sear bar spring
50. Safety spacer washer
51. Magazine
52. Sear adjustment screw plunger
53. Sear adjustment screw
54. Hammer spring
55. Hammer strut ring
56. Hammer strut
57. Grip screw (2)
58. Left handgrip

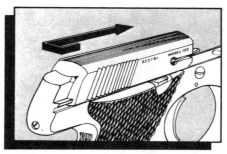

2 Continue disassembly by pulling back slide a short distance to release slide lock and ease slide forward off frame (34)

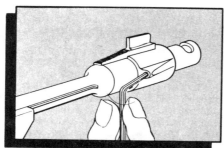

3 For top performance stabilizer (1) should be removed and cleaned every 300 rounds. Clean with tool furnished by manufacturer. Remove stabilizer by inserting proper-size Allen wrench (provided with gun) into stabilizer set screws (2) and back them off until they are clear of engaging slots in muzzle end of barrel. Stabilizer will then slide off

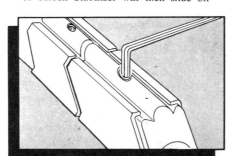

4 Forward weight and balance of gun may be adjusted by inserting proper-size Allen wrench (also provided with gun) into barrel weight set screw or screws (30) and loosening until either or both weights are movable within brackets (24 through 27). The weight may then be moved forward or backward as barrel groove permits. When optimum balance is achieved, tighten set screws with the wrench into detents provided

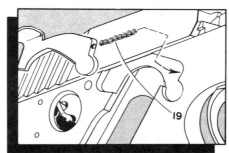

5 Should it become necessary to remove right grip (46) for replacement or exposure of working parts, slide lock lever (18) comes out very easily. Care must be exercised not to lose slide lock spring (19) as it is very small and hardly noticeable. When reinserting slide lock, make sure that this spring is properly seated in its hole in frame (34) ∎

PISTOL MAGAZINES

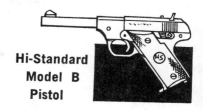

Hi-Standard Model B Pistol

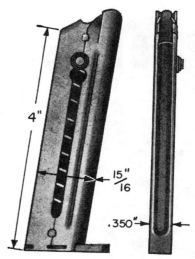

The Model B was one of the first of the long line of Hi-Standard automatic pistols. It differs from later models in that it was designed more as a plinker than a serious target pistol. During World War II a number were purchased by the Army and Navy for training purposes.

Model B magazines can be readily identified. The seam of the magazine is on the same side as the loading button. The weld marks at the top and bottom of the seams are typical of Hi-Standard Model B magazines.

Other points of identity are the 2 long stab marks which retain the floorplate, and the depression stamped into the back strap.—E. J. HOFFSCHMIDT.

HUNGARIAN
MODEL 1937 PISTOL

By E. J. HOFFSCHMIDT

Introduced in 1937, the Hungarian Model 1937 (M37) automatic pistol was chambered for either the .32 ACP or the .380 ACP. Action is of Browning blowback design with exposed hammer. Magazine is detachable.

Slides of prewar M37 pistols are generally marked "FEMARU-FEGYVER-ES. GEPGYAR R.T. 37M." Translated this means Metalware, Small Arms and Machine Works, Inc. Model 37. Following the German occupation, this Budapest firm was integrated into the German war economy and the M37 pistol in cal. .32 ACP was adopted by the Germans as a substitute standard military pistol. Slide markings were changed to "Pistole M37, Cal. 7.65 mm." plus the "jhv" code and a 2-digit numeral to indicate year of manufacture. On many guns the inscription "Kal." is found instead of "Cal."

M37 pistols made under German supervision have a manual safety in addition to the grip safety. The manual safety is lacking on prewar M37 pistols.

1 To strip the M37, first step is to be sure gun is unloaded. Pull slide (2) to rear until slide stop (38) engages rear notch as shown. Rotate barrel (8) and pull it out of slide. Then release slide stop, ease slide off frame, and remove magazine.

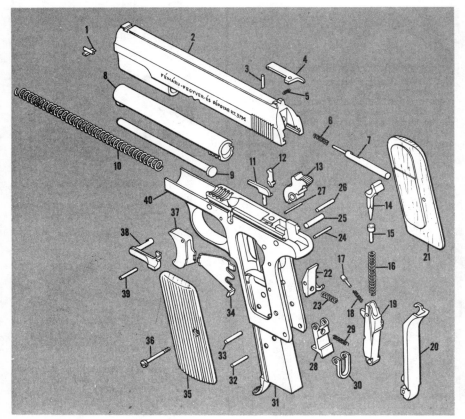

Parts Legend

1.	Front sight	21.	Right grip
2.	Slide	22.	Sear
3.	Extractor pin	23.	Sear spring
4.	Extractor	24.	Housing
5.	Extractor spring		retaining pin
6.	Firing pin spring	25.	Hammer pin
7.	Firing pin	26.	Sear pin
8.	Barrel	27.	Disconnector & ejector pin
9.	Recoil spring guide	28.	Magazine latch
10.	Recoil spring	29.	Latch spring
11.	Ejector	30.	Lanyard loop
12.	Disconnector	31.	Magazine
13.	Hammer	32.	Lanyard pin
14.	Hammer strut	33.	Magazine catch and housing pin
15.	Spring follower	34.	Trigger bar
16.	Hammer spring	35.	Left grip
17.	Plunger	36.	Grip screw
18.	Trigger spring	37.	Trigger
19.	Hammer spring housing	38.	Slide stop
20.	Grip safety	39.	Trigger pin
		40.	Frame

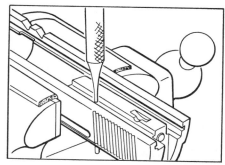

2 A single pin (3) retains firing pin in slide and acts as extractor hinge pin. Hold slide in padded vise as shown and drive pin out. Remove firing pin (7), firing pin spring (6), extractor (4) and extractor spring (5).

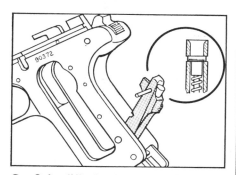

3 Only difficult piece to reassemble is hammer spring (16). A slave pin is employed to retain the hammer spring (16) and plunger (15). This slave pin is a short wire or nail that holds assemblies in place until proper pin is inserted. Correct pin (24) is driven through frame and knocks out slave pin.

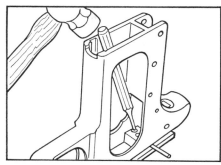

4 Disconnector (12) and ejector (11) are retained by cross pin (27) through frame. Remove pin and disconnector will drop out; however, ejector must be driven out as shown. When reinstalling cross pin, be sure it is in slightly below the surface to prevent retarding slide motion.

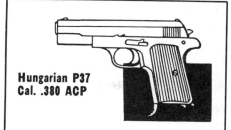

Hungarian P37 Cal. .380 ACP

PISTOL MAGAZINES

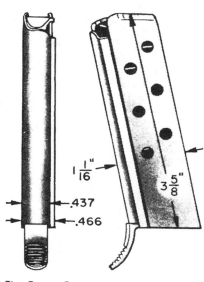

$1\frac{1}{16}''$ .437 .466 $3\frac{5}{8}''$

The Femaru-Fegyver, better known as the Hungarian P37, is an extremely well-made little blowback automatic. It is compact, simple, and rugged, and is generally found in .380 ACP or .32 ACP cal. It features a grip safety and an excellent takedown system. The finger extension on the magazine is standard equipment and gives the gun a very comfortable grip.

Like the rest of the gun, the magazine is heavily made. The floorplate is machined from a solid piece, and is usually engraved as shown.

The most distinctive feature of the magazine is the heavy guide rib found on the left side. This guides a projection on the magazine follower, and also guides the magazine into the grip.—E. J. HOFFSCHMIDT

PISTOL MAGAZINES

Model 1902 Cartridge Counter Luger

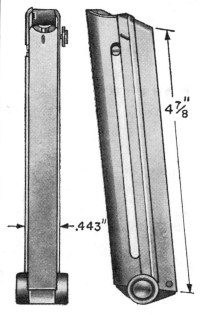

$4\frac{7}{8}''$ .443''

Probably the most desirable of all Luger pistols is the Model 1902 with the cartridge counter in the left grip. The magazine has a pointer on the left side that enables the shooter to see at a glance the number of rounds left in the magazine.

These magazines can be recognized by the small pointer button that protrudes from a slot in the left side. The pointer is pinned to the magazine follower. The dimple on the upper end of the back strap is found on some early Luger magazines, but seems to be peculiar to the counter magazine.

The magazine bottom is wood, with small metal inserts in either side of the finger rests. These inserts are also found on early Swiss Luger magazines.—E. J. HOFFSCHMIDT

145

I.J. Model 1900 and U.S. Revolver

BY PETE DICKEY

U.S. Double Action

I.J. Model 1900 Double Action

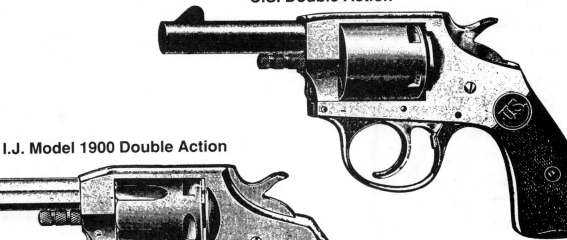

Iver Johnson's Arms & Cycle Works of Fitchburg, Mass., made the Model 1900 as an improved successor to its double-action "Bulldog" revolver line that had started in the 1880s. It was made from the model date until World War II and, for much of that time, was run concurrently with a mechanically identical version intended for catalog houses and others demanding a lower price.

The I.J. MODEL 1900 (so-marked with the address on the top-strap) had an octagonal barrel and fluted cylinder with the familiar Owl Head logo on the stocks; its cheaper running mate was round-barrelled and lacked the flutes. It bore no Iver Johnson identification, and its top-strap was marked only U.S. REVOLVER CO. MADE IN U.S.A. with the initials U.S. in a circle on its stocks.

The 1900 and U.S. models were produced by the millions, but the total quantity is not known. The factory claimed an annual output of nearly half a million in good years, and the low price insured sales even through the Great Depression. After the war, the remaining parts of the 1900 were assembled, but the last of them seem to have been completed and sold by 1946.

The tremendous popularity of the small, solid-framed "pin-ejectors" lay in their simplicity and affordability. The prices ran from $2 or $3 at the turn of the century through $5 or $6 during the depression to $11 for the postwar "cleanup," and the U.S. versions were usually somewhat cheaper.

A surprising number of nickel-plated or blued variations of the two brands were available during the manufacturing span. The original caliber choices were: .22 Long Rifle (seven shots), .32 rimfire (five), .32 S&W (five) and .38 S&W (five). In time the .32 rimfire was dropped, and a larger six-shot version chambered for the .32 S&W Long was added. The standard barrel length for all calibers was 2½", but 4½" or 6" barrels were also regularly offered, as were oversized hard rubber "target" stocks or pearl stocks and hinged loading gates, all at extra cost.

The 1900-series solid-framed revolvers were succeeded in the early 1960s by the similar Model 50 Iver Johnson that took advantage of formed wire springs and employed a rod ejector and a loading gate as standard equipment.

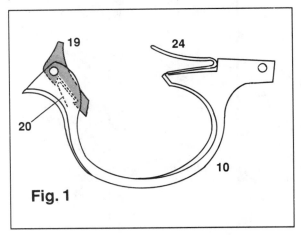

Fig. 1

Disassembly Instructions

Depress the cylinder latch (4); withdraw the cylinder pin (3) and remove the cylinder (2) from the right side of the frame (7).

Drift out rear guard/sear pin (12) and front guard pin (11). Work trigger guard (10) out of frame carefully, noting position of sear (19) and sear spring (20) at the trigger guard's rear and the trigger spring (24) at its front (Fig. 1). In the now-exposed frame recess ahead of the trigger spring will appear the end of the revolver's only coil spring, the cylinder friction spring (8)

The friction spring and stud (9) can be withdrawn, and drifting out the cylinder latch pin (5) will permit removal of the latch and its spring (6).

Remove the stock screw and stocks and pry out the bottom of the mainspring (18). Then remove the hammer screw (14) and drift out the trigger pin (23).

Work the trigger assembly (15, 16, 17 & 22) and the hammer down through the frame and push forward on the lifter (17) to disengage it from the hammer (13); then lift the hammer from the top of the frame. Note carefully the position of the trigger assembly components (Fig. 2)

Reassembly is done in reverse order, and the use of a slave pin in the sear/trigger guard assembly simplifies the procedure. ■

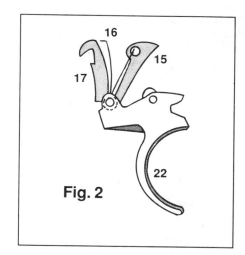

Fig. 2

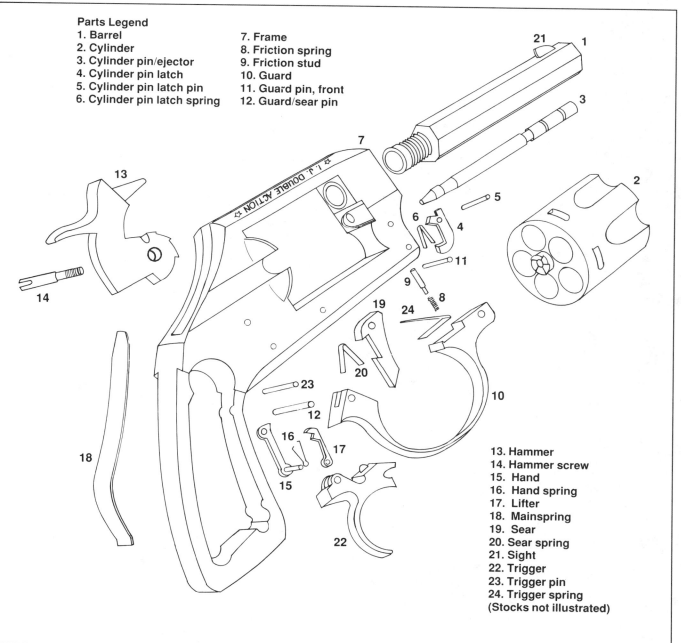

Parts Legend
1. Barrel
2. Cylinder
3. Cylinder pin/ejector
4. Cylinder pin latch
5. Cylinder pin latch pin
6. Cylinder pin latch spring
7. Frame
8. Friction spring
9. Friction stud
10. Guard
11. Guard pin, front
12. Guard/sear pin

13. Hammer
14. Hammer screw
15. Hand
16. Hand spring
17. Lifter
18. Mainspring
19. Sear
20. Sear spring
21. Sight
22. Trigger
23. Trigger pin
24. Trigger spring
(Stocks not illustrated)

Iver Johnson Model 50 Revolver

By JAMES M. TRIGGS

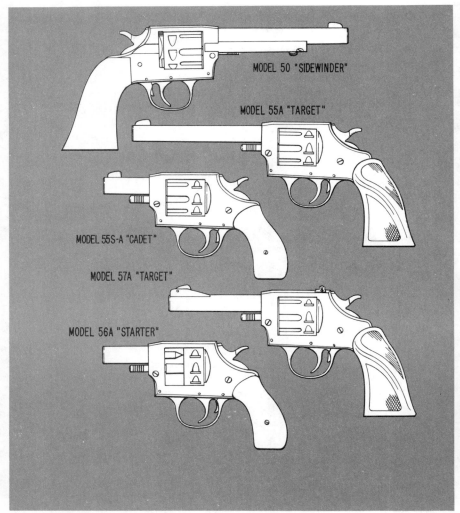

MODEL 50 "SIDEWINDER"

MODEL 55A "TARGET"

MODEL 55S-A "CADET"

MODEL 57A "TARGET"

MODEL 56A "STARTER"

Introduced in 1961, and produced until 1980, the Iver Johnson Model 50, "Sidewinder", was a .22 rimfire revolver designed for informal target shooting.

A solid frame, double-action, the Model 50 features rod ejection, a hinged loading gate and a western style walnut grip. Barrel length is 6 inches. Sights are fixed. The eight-shot capacity cylinder has counterbored chambers to enclose the cartridge heads. A flash shield on the front of the cylinder diverts powder gases forward and away from the shooter. The trigger mechanism includes a half-cock safety which permits cylinder rotation for loading and unloading. Deep checkering on the hammer spur facilitates cocking.

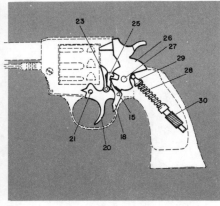

1 All Iver Johnson revolvers in the Model 50 series are shown here for comparison. Basic mechanism of all versions is the same and main differences in parts are in barrels, calibers, cylinders, sight arrangements, and grip styles.

2 Basic lock mechanism of the Model 50 Sidewinder and other Model 50 series Iver Johnson revolvers is shown in this phantom view. The small trigger spring (22), sear spring (19), and lever spring (24) are omitted for clarity.

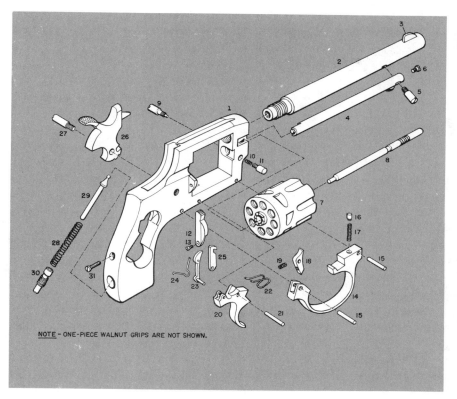

NOTE - ONE-PIECE WALNUT GRIPS ARE NOT SHOWN.

Parts Legend

1. Frame
2. Barrel
3. Front sight blade
4. Ejector assembly
5. Ejector tube screw
6. Ejector lock screw
7. Cylinder
8. Center pin
9. Center pin catch nut
10. Center pin catch spring
11. Center pin catch screw
12. Loading gate
13. Loading gate screw
14. Trigger guard
15. Trigger guard pins (2)
16. Cylinder friction stud
17. Cylinder friction stud spring
18. Sear
19. Sear spring
20. Trigger
21. Trigger pin
22. Trigger spring
23. Lever
24. Lever spring
25. Lifter
26. Hammer
27. Hammer screw
28. Mainspring
29. Mainspring plunger
30. Mainspring adjusting screw
31. Grip screw
32. Grip, one-piece (not shown)

Disassembly Procedure

Basic mechanism of Models 50, 55A, 55S-A, 56A, and 57A is the same and disassembly for all Model 50 series Iver Johnson revolvers is essentially the same. Press in center pin catch screw (11) at right of frame and withdraw center pin (8) to front. Open loading gate (12). Rotate cylinder (7) until rear end of barrel can slip through slot in flash control rim at front of cylinder. Remove cylinder to right. Remove grip screw (31) and pull off one-piece grip. In revolvers with small 2-piece grips, remove transverse grip screw.

Unscrew mainspring adjusting screw (30) until it stops. Remove hammer screw (27). Hold trigger (20) back and remove hammer (26) through top of frame. Remove mainspring (28) and mainspring plunger (29) through top of frame. Remove mainspring adjusting screw through cutout in frame.

Drift out trigger guard pins (15) and pull trigger guard (14) from bottom of frame with sear (18), sear spring (19), cylinder friction stud (16) and cylinder friction stud spring (17).

Drift out trigger pin (21) and remove trigger (20) with lifter (25), lever (23), and springs (22, 24). Loading gate is removed after unscrewing loading gate screw (13). Ejector assembly (4) is removed from barrel by removing ejector tube screw (5) and ejector lock screw (6), then sliding forward to disengage slotted rear end of tube from frame.

In reassembling lock mechanism parts, replacement of trigger guard in frame can be facilitated by using a short slave pin to secure sear and sear spring in place. When trigger guard pins are replaced through frame, slave pin will be pushed out.

Reising .22 Cal. Auto Pistol

PISTOL MAGAZINES

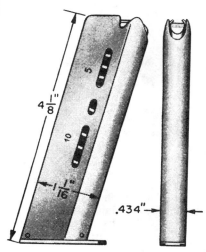

The Reising .22 cal. pistol embodied several interesting features, but could not compete with less expensive and more compact .22 cal. pistols. It was unusual in that the barrel could be tipped up to load like a single-shot pistol, or could be fired like a normal .22 automatic feeding from the magazine. It was a good shooter because of long sighting radius and comfortably-shaped grip. Magazines, like the rest of the gun, are well made and free of toolmarks. There are 2 types of magazines found; one has long observation slots on the side, and the other a row of holes.

Reising magazines are generally marked as shown, but if unmarked can be identified by their keyhole-shaped cross section instead of the usual rectangular cross section. Then, too, the floorplate is tapered from heel to toe.

The magazine lips are very carefully formed and are unusually strong. Another point of recognition is the rounded bolt clearance cut in the backstrap of the magazine.—E. J. HOFF-SCHMIDT

Iver Johnson Model 66 Revolver

Manufactured by Iver Johnson's Arms & Cycle Works, Fitchburg, Mass., from 1958 to 1980, the Model 66 "Trailsman" revolver was a 6"-barrel, single-shot, double-action revolver chambered for the .22 Long Rifle cartridge. Of top-break, or tipping-barrel, design, the Trailsman featured fully adjustable sights and a rebounding hammer. The chambers were counterbored to enclose cartridge heads and the front face of the cylinder had a flash shield to divert powder gases forward and away from the shooter. Cartridges or fired cases were ejected manually by depressing the ejector rod under the barrel. The 6"-barrel Model 66 was optionally available with one piece plastic, or walnut, grip.

From 1960 until 1964 the Model 66 was offered with a 2-3/4" barrel under the designation "Trailsman-Snub" (Model 66S). The Model 66S was chambered for the .32 S&W and .38 S&W, centerfire cartridges (cylinder capacity, five rounds) as well as in .22 rimfire.

From 1962 until 1964 the Trailsman .22 was offered with a 4-1/2" barrel in addition to the standard 6" length.

By JAMES M. TRIGGS

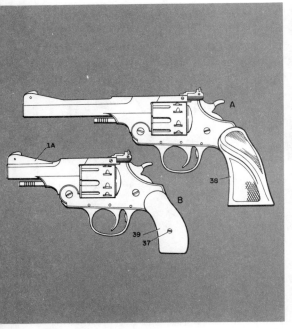

1 Note that the 2¾" barrel Snub Model 66S (B) is provided with the smaller two-piece grips (39) and single transverse grip screw (37). The standard model (A) with 6" barrel has one-piece grip with thumb rest (38). Grip is secured by a single screw (36).

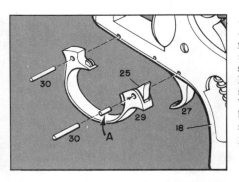

2 In reassembling lock mechanism, replacing trigger guard (29) in frame is facilitated by using a small slave-pin (as shown at ('A')) to secure sear and sear spring (25, 26) in rear of trigger guard. Make the slave-pin of brass rod or wood, slightly shorter than width of trigger guard. With slave-pin in place, trigger guard can be replaced in frame (18) with sear and spring and trigger guard pins (30) replaced. As rear trigger guard pin is drifted into frame, it will push slave-pin out.

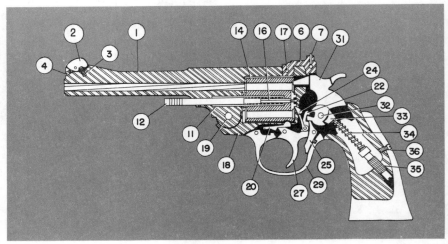

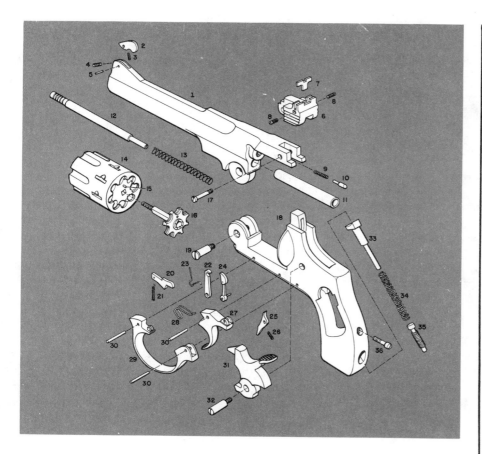

Davis-Warner "Infallible" .32 Cal. Auto.

PISTOL MAGAZINES

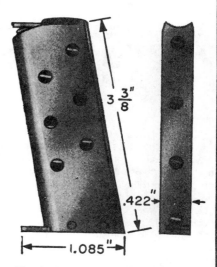

3 3/8"

.422"

1.085"

Parts Legend

1. Barrel, 6"
1A. Barrel, 2¾"
2. Front sight blade
3. Front sight spring
4. Front sight adjusting screw
5. Front sight pin
6. Barrel catch
7. Rear sight blade
8. Rear sight adjusting screws (2)
9. Barrel catch spring
10. Barrel catch plunger
11. Quill
12. Ejector rod
13. Extractor spring
14. Cylinder

15. Extractor pin
16. Extractor
17. Barrel catch screw
18. Frame
19. Joint screw
20. Cylinder stop
21. Cylinder stop spring
22. Lifter
23. Lever spring
24. Lever and pin
25. Sear
26. Sear spring
27. Trigger
28. Trigger spring
29. Trigger guard
30. Trigger and guard pins (3)

31. Hammer
32. Hammer screw
33. Mainspring plunger
34. Mainspring
35. Mainspring adjusting screw
36. Grip screw (for large grips)
37. Grip screw (for small grips
38. Grips (large, one-piece)
39. Grips (small, two-piece)
(Tang plug screw (not shown)

Disassembly Procedure

To separate barrel assembly from frame (1, 18) remove joint screw (19) and pull barrel off joint. Rear sight and barrel catch assembly (6) can be removed by unscrewing barrel catch screw (17) from left side of top strap of barrel, taking care not to allow ejection of barrel catch spring and plunger (9, 10). Cylinder (14) can be removed by holding up barrel catch and pulling cylinder to rear off quill (11). Complete disassembly of cylinder, extractor (16), and ejector rod (12) assembly is unnecessary for normal cleaning purposes and is not recommended.

Remove grip screw (36) and pull grip off frame. Unscrew mainspring adjusting

screw (35) until it stops. Remove hammer screw (32). Hold trigger (27) back and remove hammer (31) through top of frame. Remove mainspring plunger (33) and mainspring (34) through top of frame. Unscrew and remove mainspring adjusting screw through cutout in frame. Drift out trigger guard and trigger pins (30). Remaining lock parts are easily removed from frame. Reassemble in reverse order. Be sure that barrel catch is held up in unlocked position when replacing cylinder on quill to avoid damaging cylinder finish.

Note: Hammer must be in fired position when opening or closing revolver or lever will be damaged.   ■

Though the Davis-Warner "Infallible" was made in 2 distinct variations, it is a comparatively scarce American pocket pistol. This is probably due to the fact that it was a clumsy, bulky design. When compared with its contemporaries, the Colt, Remington, or Mauser, it had very little to recommend it. In shape and workmanship, it resembled some of the lesser known Belgian pocket pistols such as the Melior or the Feil. It is generally found either blued or with a mottled-color finish, and always in .32 cal. ACP.

While Davis-Warner magazines resemble most common .32 pistol magazines in outline, the row of holes and the notch in the backstrap are distinctive features.

Another distinctive feature is the overlay construction used to make the magazine. This construction leaves an edge of sheet metal showing along the backstrap.—E. J. HOFF-SCHMIDT

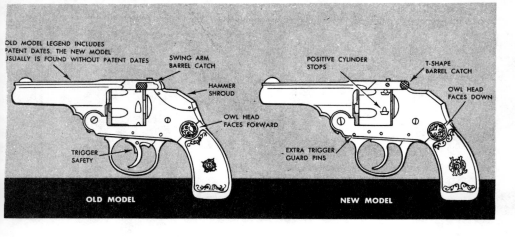

OLD MODEL LEGEND INCLUDES PATENT DATES. THE NEW MODEL USUALLY IS FOUND WITHOUT PATENT DATES

SWING ARM BARREL CATCH

HAMMER SHROUD

OWL HEAD FACES FORWARD

TRIGGER SAFETY

OLD MODEL

POSITIVE CYLINDER STOPS

T-SHAPE BARREL CATCH

OWL HEAD FACES DOWN

EXTRA TRIGGER GUARD PINS

NEW MODEL

hammer spring was changed to an adjustable coil spring. The simplified extractor cam was made more reliable by replacing the fragile flat spring with a coil spring.

The greatest source of trouble in the old model was the lack of a positive cylinder stop which resulted in lead being shaved from the bullet as it passed from the cylinder to the barrel. This difficulty was overcome in the new model.

Production of Iver Johnson top-break revolvers, both visible hammer and hammerless models, had all but ceased by the time of World War II.

Iver Johnson Top-Break Revolver

By E. J. Hoffschmidt

Around the turn of the 20th century top-break revolvers were as common, in the average American home, as can openers are today. For less than $2.00, a person could buy a solid frame revolver in .22, .32 or even .38 (usually rimfire) caliber. In 1902, Sears, Roebuck & Co., offered the more sophisticated Iver Johnson top-break revolvers at $3.50 for a .32 or .38 S&W, blue-finish, exposed hammer model, and $4.00 for the hammerless version of the same gun.

Iver Johnson top-break revolvers were made in barrel lengths from two inches to six inches and with several styles of grip, all available at added cost. Iver Johnson also made a less expensive line of top-breaks, marked "U.S.".

For years Iver Johnson advertisements pictured the hammering of a top-break hammer to prove its safety. While this sort of safety test is not particularly good for the gun, it was a selling point.

The safety hammer mechanism is a very clever design. When the hammer is down, it does not touch the firing pin. It rests against the frame and is cut away around the firing pin area. When the trigger is pulled or the hammer cocked, the lifter is brought up behind the firing pin. When the trigger actuates the sear, the hammer is released and strikes the lifter, which transmits the blow to the firing pin.

There is quite a difference in design between "new" and "old " models of the Iver Johnson top-break. Both guns feature the safety hammer mechanism, but most of the internal parts are unique to one model or the other. The gun illustrated is a visible hammer version of the "old" model. New models are easily recognized by the simple round barrel catch and the two additional frame pins. Internally the new model features a separate cylinder latch that allows a more positive stop. The flat

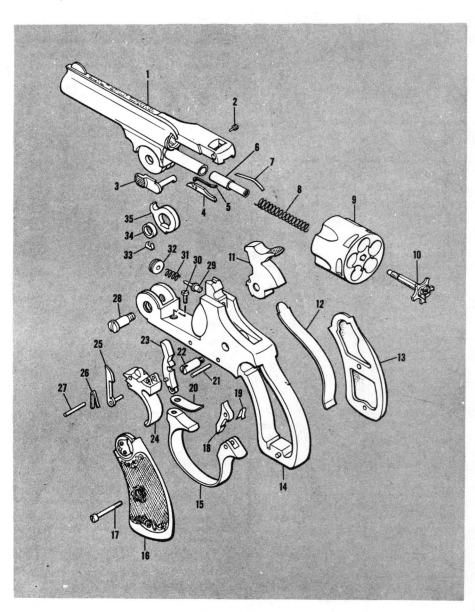

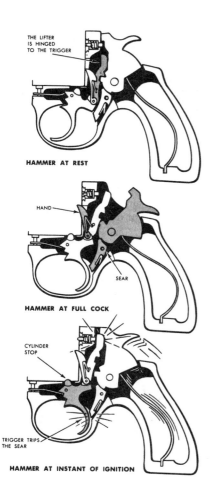

THE LIFTER IS HINGED TO THE TRIGGER

HAMMER AT REST

HAND

SEAR

HAMMER AT FULL COCK

CYLINDER STOP

TRIGGER TRIPS THE SEAR

HAMMER AT INSTANT OF IGNITION

Parts Legend

1. Barrel assembly
2. Barrel catch screw
3. Barrel catch
4. Barrel catch spring cover
5. Barrel catch spring
6. Extractor stem
7. Cylinder friction spring
8. Extractor spring
9. Cylinder
10. Extractor
11. Hammer
12. Hammer spring
13. Right grip
14. Frame
15. Trigger guard
16. Left grip
17. Grip screw
18. Sear
19. Sear spring
20. Trigger spring
21. Trigger guard pin
22. Hammer screw
23. Lifter
24. Trigger
25. Hand
26. Hand spring
27. Trigger pin
28. Hinge screw
29. Firing pin
30. Trigger guard screw
31. Firing pin spring
32. Firing pin bushing
33. Extractor spring
34. Extractor bushing
35. Extractor cam

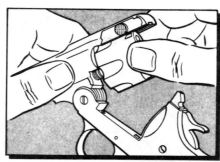

1 To remove cylinder (9) of old model, open gun far enough for extractor to snap back into cylinder. Pull back on cylinder and revolve it counterclockwise to free it from the barrel

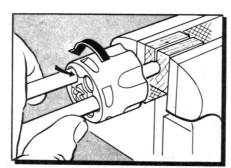

2 To remove extractor (10), hold extractor stem (6) in a padded vise. Insert a few empty cases part way into chambers and turn cylinder counterclockwise. It may be necessary to insert a pair of brass rods as shown to afford a better grip on cylinder

3 To remove firing pin (29), grind an old screwdriver into a 2-pronged tool. Stone prongs to fit into holes in firing pin bushing (32). Screw out bushing and remove firing pin and firing pin spring (31)

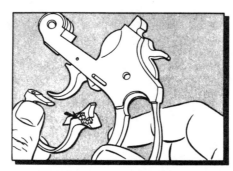

4 Reassembling the top-break can be simplified by using slave pin. Assemble parts outside gun with pin (arrow) slightly shorter than trigger guard width. Insert assembly in frame and drive pin through frame, to drift slave pin out other side ▬

Fiala Repeating Pistol

PISTOL MAGAZINES

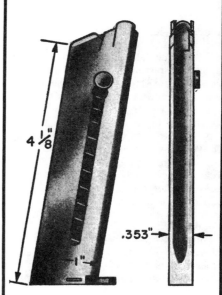

4 1/8"

.353"

1"

Maj. Anthony Fiala's weapon looks like a semi-automatic pistol, but in reality it is a repeater. After each shot the slide has to be actuated by hand. The barrel is removable. The gun was sold with short barrel for a pocket arm, a medium-length barrel for target shooting, and a long barrel for use with shoulder stock which could be screwed to the grip to make a rifle. The gun was never very popular, and therefore is not common.

While Fiala magazines look a great deal like early Hartford or Hi-Standard pistol magazines, they have a distinctive rounded backstrap which makes them easy to spot.

Another point of identity is the odd stab marks used to retain the floorplate.—E. J. HOFFSCHMIDT

JAPANESE TYPE 26 REVOLVER

By E. J. HOFFSCHMIDT

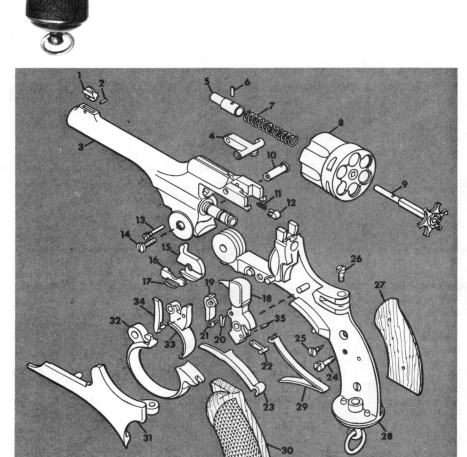

DURING the 26th year of Emperor Meiji's reign (Christian year 1893), the Japanese Army adopted the Type 26 9 mm. revolver. Designed and produced in Japan, this weapon was the standard Japanese Army handgun until replaced about 1914 by the Nambu automatic pistol. It remained in service as substitute standard after the Nambu was adopted, and was used to some extent during World War II.

The top-break system of the Type 26 is similar to that of several older Smith & Wesson revolvers. To open for loading and unloading, the latch at the top rear of the barrel is lifted, and the barrel is pivoted down. As the barrel pivots down, all 6 cartridges are extracted and ejected automatically and simultaneously.

In lockwork design, the Type 26 closely resembles the Austro-Hungarian Rast & Gasser Model 98 revolver. An excellent feature is that the sideplate can be pivoted open easily to expose the mechanism, and the lock parts can be removed for cleaning and lubrication without use of tools.

Firing requires a long pull of the trigger. The hammer has no full-cock notch and thus lacks a spur for thumb-cocking. This system, satisfactory for military purposes, is also used in the British No. 2 Mark I* Enfield service revolver. It is, however, not suitable for precision target shooting, even though the trigger action of the Type 26 is extremely smooth.

Simple and well made, this revolver has checkered wood grips and a lanyard swivel. It is marked on the right of the frame with the serial number, symbol of the manufacturing arsenal, and Japanese numerals and letters which stand for 26 Year Type.

The Type 26 was brought to the U.S. by returning servicemen in considerable numbers and is encountered frequently. The 9 mm. cartridge for it, however, is rare. Of straight-case rimmed type, it has a round-nose, lead bullet, propelled by smokeless powder. Other identifying features are the lack of a headstamp and the unusually thin rim.

The takedown of the revolver is illustrated; the assembly is in reverse order.

PARTS LEGEND

1. Front sight	10. Barrel hinge pin	18. Hammer	27. Right grip
2. Front sight pin	11. Latch spring	19. Strut	28. Frame
3. Barrel	12. Latch spring plunger	20. Strut spring	29. Mainspring
4. Latch	13. Latch screw	21. Strut screw	30. Left grip
5. Extractor bearing	14. Hinge pin screw	22. Hammer stirrup	31. Sideplate
6. Extractor bearing pin	15. Extractor cam	23. Rebound lever	32. Trigger guard
7. Extractor spring	16. Extractor release	24. Rebound lever screw	33. Trigger
8. Cylinder	17. Release tension spring	25. Right grip screw (2)	34. Hand
9. Extractor		26. Sideplate hinge screw	35. Hammer stirrup pin

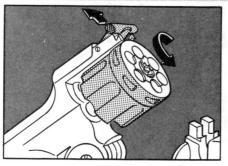

1 To disassemble, first lift the latch (4), pivot the barrel (3) down, and remove any cartridges from the cylinder (8). Then, while holding latch up, unscrew the cylinder counterclockwise.

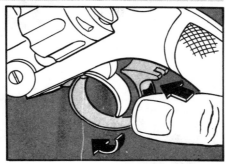

2 Push forward slightly on the rear of the trigger guard (32) to unlatch it, and then pivot the trigger guard down. This unlocks the sideplate so it may be opened.

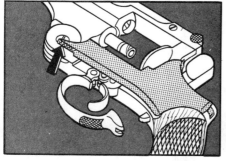

3 Grasp the lower front of the sideplate (31) where it is knurled, and pivot it rearward to expose the lock mechanism. Lift off the left grip (30) and remove the trigger guard.

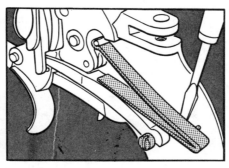

4 Hold the rear of the mainspring (29) firmly, lift it away from the frame (28) slightly or pry outward gently with a small screwdriver, ease it upward, and disengage from the hammer stirrup (22). Lock parts can now be easily removed.

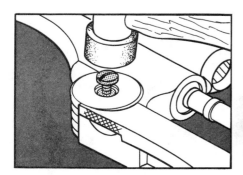

5 Unscrew the hinge pin screw (14) about ⅛", and tap it lightly with a mallet to partially drive out the barrel hinge pin (10). Then completely remove the screw and hinge pin, separate the barrel from the frame, and take out the extractor cam (15), extractor release (16), and release tension spring (17).

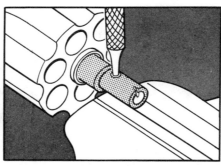

6 Locate the extractor bearing pin (6). Rest the bearing on vise jaws and drive out the pin with a drift punch and hammer. Then remove the bearing, extractor spring (7), and extractor (9) from the cylinder. The latch, latch spring (11), and latch spring plunger (12) can be removed from the barrel after turning out the latch screw (13). ∎

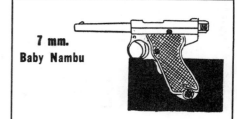

7 mm. Baby Nambu

PISTOL MAGAZINES

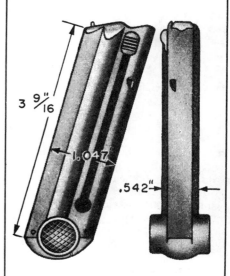

3 9/16"

1.047"

.542"

Baby Nambu pistols are scarce, but spare magazines and ammunition are even scarcer. This little weapon is almost a dead ringer for the larger Model 1914 Japanese Nambu pistol. It is extremely well made and fires a 7 mm. cartridge that is also a scaled-down version of the 8 mm. Jap pistol round. Except for size, the magazines are made exactly like the larger Model 1914 pistol.

Baby Nambu magazines can be recognized by the heavy aluminum floorplate that also acts as a finger grip to remove the magazine. As in its big brother, the finger grips are diamond checkered and pinned to the magazine body.

The Baby Nambu magazine is sturdy with heavy feed lips, and incorporates a button on the follower for easy loading. The follower is machined from solid material.—E. J. HOFF-SCHMIDT

JAPANESE TYPE 94 PISTOL

By E. J. HOFFSCHMIDT

D ESIGNED by Kijiro Nambu, the Type 94 (1934) Japanese Service pistol was chambered for the rimless 8 mm. Nambu Japanese service cartridge. This bottleneck cartridge was also used in Japanese Type 14 (1925) semi-automatic Service pistols and in Japanese submachine guns. A Nambu-designed semi-automatic pistol introduced about 1904 was also adapted for this round.

The recoil-operated Type 94 pistol has a device to lock barrel and slide together until the bullet has cleared the barrel and gas pressure has subsided. The detachable magazine housed in the grip holds 6 cartridges.

Safety devices on this arm are (1) a manual safety which locks the external sear and trigger bar and (2) a safety activated by the magazine catch mechanism. When the magazine catch button on the left side of the frame is depressed and the magazine is withdrawn from the grip, a bar rises to engage a detent notch in the rear of the trigger and thus block rearward movement of the trigger.

Other mechanical features of note in the Type 94 pistol include an independent spring-loaded firing pin, an internal, concealed hammer, and a lanyard ring attached to the rear of the frame. Grip plates are commonly of coarsely checkered black plastic, but smooth wood grips are also found on this arm.

A unique and potentially dangerous feature of the Type 94 pistol is that it can be fired by depressing the front end of the external sear and trigger bar which lies exposed in a slot milled in the left side of the frame. Also, the safety mechanism is not reliable.

The average Type 94 pistol is roughly machined and finished, showing hasty wartime manufacture.

Parts Legend

1. Front sight
2. Slide
3. Extractor
4. Breechbolt
5. Firing pin spring
6. Firing pin
7. Recoil spring
8. Recoil spring collar
9. Barrel
10. Crossbolt
11. Locking block
12. Hammer
13. Hammer roller pin
14. Hammer roller
15. Hammer spring
16. Sear hinge pin
17. Magazine catch
18. Right grip
19. Grip screw
20. Disconnector
21. Disconnector pin
22. Disconnector spring
23. Trigger spring
24. Trigger
25. Trigger screw
26. Sear spring
27. Sear and trigger bar
28. Magazine catch nut
29. Magazine catch spring
30. Magazine operated safety
31. Magazine safety spring
32. Hammer screw
33. Safety catch
34. Frame
35. Magazine
36. Left grip
37. Grip screw

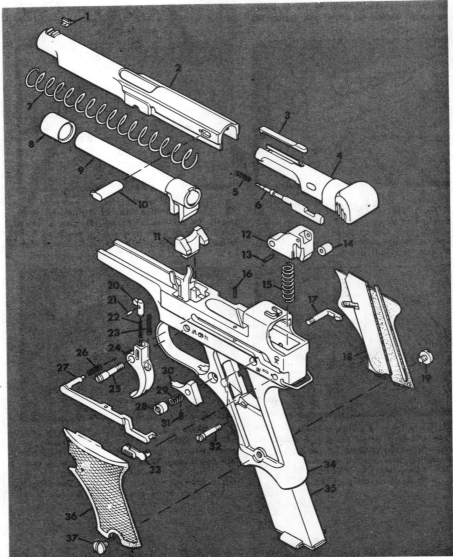

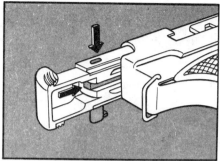

1 The first step in disassembling the Type 94 pistol is to pull the slide to the rear over an empty magazine. The slide (2) and the breechbolt (4) will be held to the rear. Push the firing pin (6) forward until it is flush with the shoulder in the slide; this will free the crossbolt (10). The crossbolt can then be pushed out of the slide from right to left as shown.

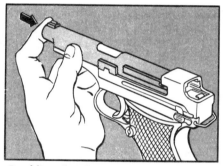

2 After the breechbolt has been re-moved, the slide may stay in place. To remove the breechbolt first take out the magazine (35). Then, holding the gun as shown, push the barrel (9) back while holding the slide. This action unlocks the slide and permits it to be eased off the front of the frame (34).

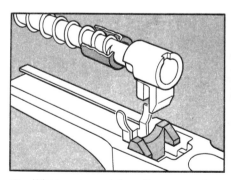

3 When reassembling the gun, place the locking block (11) in the frame correctly so that the yoke on the barrel can fit over the curved surface of it. The barrel must be installed in the frame before putting the slide back on. The recoil spring collar (8) must be installed with the solid face toward the chamber.

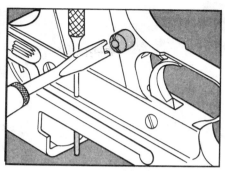

4 The magazine catch nut (28) is some-times peened or riveted to the shaft of the magazine catch (17). It can be unscrewed with a screwdriver ground to the shape shown or, if difficulty is en-countered, with the aid of pliers or a vise.

After removing left grip screw (37) and left grip (36), drift out sear hinge pin (16) from bottom. Remove trigger screw (25) and disengage trigger (24).

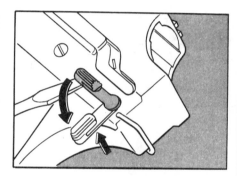

5 The safety catch has a detent on the inner face which retains the catch in the "on" or "off" position. The safety catch (33) blocks only the sear. To re-move the safety catch, remove the left grip (36), lift the catch out of engagement with frame, and swing it down. The safety catch can then be lifted out.

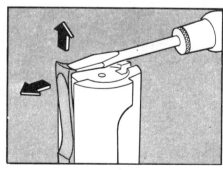

6 The extractor (3) is of simple design. The tail is dove-tailed into the top of the breechbolt. To remove the extractor, with a screwdriver push the front of the extractor outward far enough for the pro-jection on the extractor to clear its seat in the bolt. When it is free, pry the extractor out as shown. ■

Nambu Pattern 94
8 mm. Automatic

PISTOL MAGAZINES

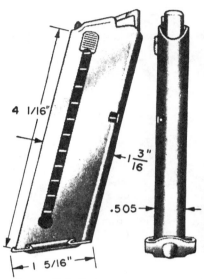

4 1/16"

1 3/16"

.505

1 5/16"

Some call it Pattern 94, others call it the Jap "Suicide" pistol. Regardless of what you call it, it is best as a decoration. These pistols are generally poorly made and poorly finished. The name Suicide pistol stems from the faulty design of the sear mechanism. The sear is exposed on the left side of the gun, making it possible to fire the gun with-out pulling the trigger. Contrary to the rest of the gun, the magazine is well designed and made of heavy gauge steel. The maga-zines were chrome-plated or blued.

Nambu 94 magazines can generally be rec-ognized by the loading button and groove on the right side, and by the absence of observa-tion holes on the left side, but most of all by the oddly-shaped floorplate that facili-tates its removal from the gun.

Since the follower is machined from a bar of solid steel, it is heavy enough to deform the magazine lips if the loading button did not stop it well below the lips.— E. J. HOFFSCHMIDT

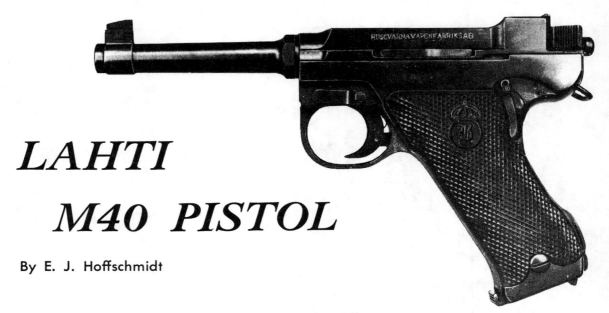

LAHTI

M40 PISTOL

By E. J. Hoffschmidt

Gun designer Aimo Johannes Lahti of Finland developed a wide range of firearms for his native land—from automatic pistols to aircraft cannons. Today he is best known for an automatic pistol adopted as the L35 by Finland and, in slightly modified form, as the M40 by Sweden.

While the Finnish L35 Lahti is virtually unknown here, the Swedish M40 version is far more common. A number of these guns, marked Husqvarna Vapenfabriks A. B., were imported and sold in the U. S. around 1949 and 1950.

The Lahti is a heavy, rugged gun and mirrors the conditions it was de-

signed for. The operating parts are strong and well designed for the extreme cold encountered along the Finnish and Swedish frontiers. The serrations on the slide are deep and tapered so that the slide can be retracted easily with a heavily gloved hand. The large trigger guard and protruding safety

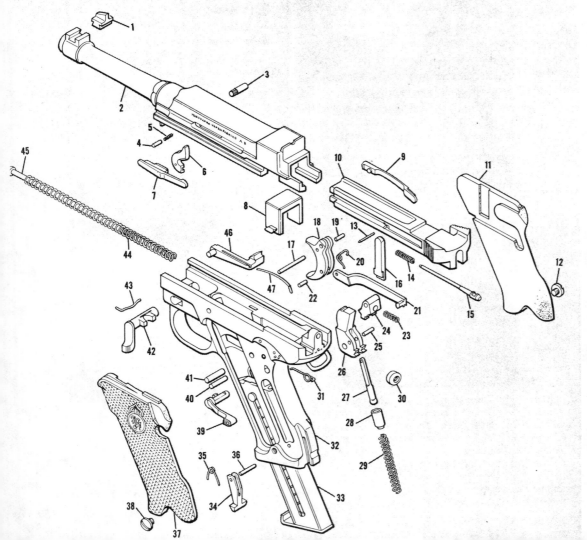

Parts Legend

1. Front sight
2. Barrel and barrel extension
3. Accelerator stop pin
4. Accelerator retainer
5. Accelerator retainer spring
6. Accelerator
7. Ejector
8. Locking block
9. Extractor
10. Slide
11. Right grip
12. Grip screw
13. Firing pin retainer pin
14. Firing pin spring
15. Firing pin
16. Disconnector
17. Trigger pin
18. Trigger
19. Trigger spring pin
20. Trigger spring
21. Trigger bar
22. Trigger bar pin
23. Sear spring
24. Sear
25. Hammer strut pin
26. Hammer
27. Hammer strut
28. Hammer spring plunger
29. Hammer spring
30. Spring guide nut
31. Trigger bar spring
32. Frame
33. Magazine
34. Magazine catch
35. Magazine catch spring
36. Magazine catch pin
37. Left grip
38. Grip screw
39. Safety catch
40. Sear pin
41. Hammer pin
42. Takedown catch
43. Takedown catch spring
44. Recoil spring
45. Recoil spring guide
46. Hold-open catch
47. Hold-open catch spring

catch were also designed for gloved-hand operation. The cold weather also influenced mechanism design.

Even though the gun shoots the powerful 9 mm. Luger cartridge, Lahti added an accelerator to aid the operating mechanism. The accelerator in L35 and M40 pistols is a lever pivoted to the barrel extension. As the barrel, barrel extension, and slide recoil to the rear, the locking block is cammed free of the slide. At this instant the lower portion of the accelerator strikes the receiver wall and this blow is transmitted to the unlocked slide, throwing it back with great force. When the slide counter-recoils, it pushes the accelerator back into place.

An excellent grip and a long, fixed sighting radius make the gun a fine shooter. When equipped with its Luger-type shoulder stock, it becomes a formidable carbine.

An unfavorable feature of this pistol is that it will fire with its locking block removed. A check should therefore be made before firing to make sure locking block is present.

Under an excellent blue job, the Swedish-made Lahti shows a great deal of rough machining and hand finishing. Fortunately this does not detract from the reliability and accuracy of the gun, since critical operating parts and bore are well finished.

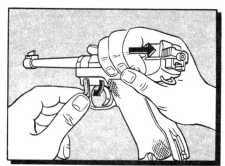

1 The Lahti takedown is simple. First remove magazine and clear chamber. Hold barrel extension (2) back as shown, or push the muzzle against a hard surface; at same time rotate takedown catch (42). Barrel assembly is now slid forward off receiver

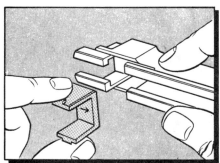

2 After barrel and barrel extension are free of receiver, push locking block (8) up and withdraw slide (10). When replacing locking block, be sure arrow on underside of block is facing forward toward barrel

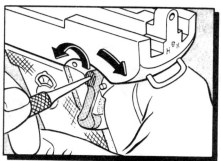

3 Safety catch (39) must be removed before attempting removal of left grip. Insert a thin punch into hole in serrated portion of safety. Pry it back slightly, enough to swing it over stop pin in frame. Rotate it to horizontal position and pull it out

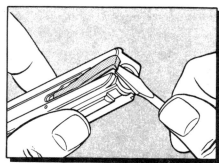

4 Extractor (9) is long and flexible. It is removed by inserting a small screwdriver under lip to push it free of locking hole in slide (10), then prying it out of its seat

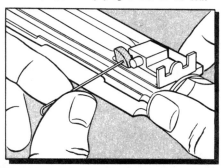

5 The accelerator (6) is designed for easy removal. Simply rotate accelerator until small hole in its side lines up with spring-loaded retainer pin (4). Push a thin piece of wire or paper clip through hole to depress spring. Lift out accelerator

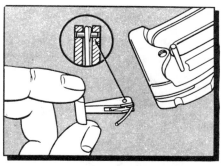

6 Some Lahti parts are difficult to reassemble without the aid of short slave pins. To replace magazine catch (34) and spring (35), use a short pin to hold them together until in position. Incoming magazine pin will drive short pin out other side and spring will remain in its place ■

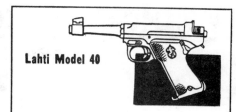

Lahti Model 40

PISTOL MAGAZINES

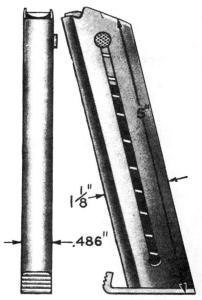

A few years ago a number of 9 mm. Lahti pistols were imported into America from Sweden. The Swedish gun is a slight modification of the original Finnish design. As handguns go, it is big and bulky but the grip is excellent. It is a locked breech recoil-operated design that will handle any of the various loadings of the 9 mm. Luger cartridge. In spite of the fact that Sweden was not a combatant in World War II, the guns usually show signs of hasty machining with numerous tool marks evident on Swedish Lahtis. The Finnish gun and Swedish copy are so similar that magazines are interchangeable.

Lahti magazines can usually be recognized by the rugged cast aluminum follower and Luger-type magazine button. The magazines are large, strong, and generally well made.

The floorplate is probably the best point of recognition. It is made from a flat steel stamping and affords an excellent grip when removing the magazine from the gun.—E. J. HOFFSCHMIDT

159

exploded views:

LE FRANCAIS 9mm BROWNING LONG PISTOL

DRAWING BY E. J. HOFFSCHMIDT
TEXT BY TECHNICAL STAFF

Variously known as the Model 1928, the Armee Model, and the Le Francais Military Model, this pistol was made by Manufrance of St. Etienne, France from 1928 to 1938 to a quantity of around 4000.

This Le Francais is blowback operated, and quite similar in appearance and function to the more common and smaller Manufrance-made Le Francais pistols in 6.35 mm (.25 ACP) and 7.65 (.32 ACP).

The 9 mm Browning Long cartridge is more impressive in nomenclature than in ballistics, being little more effective than the standard .380 ACP. By modern standards it would be considered underpowered for a military load. It was never made in the U.S., and today is seldom encountered.

The Armee Model/M1928, despite its name, ingenious design and high quality, was never officially adopted by the French.

The M28 operates on the "double action only" system; a long trigger pull being necessary to cock and release the striker. It is impossible to avoid this long pull and fire the pistol in "single action" mode. The pistol lacks any manual safety.

Another significant design feature of the Le Francais is the "pop-up" barrel which is activated by a lever on the right side of the frame (or by the removal of the magazine). This makes the loading of the chamber easy, and eliminates the need for an extractor or slide serrations. The clip on the bottom of the magazine holds a single cartridge which is used for quick chamber loading.

Disassembly of the M28 is simple, once the procedures are known, and requires no tools. The M28 is one of those few pistols that utilizes no screws in its construction — not even a grip screw. ∎

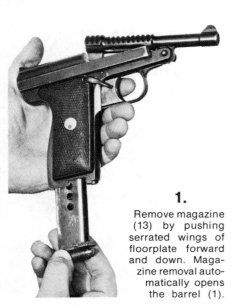

1.
Remove magazine (13) by pushing serrated wings of floorplate forward and down. Magazine removal automatically opens the barrel (1).

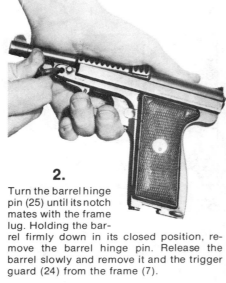

2.
Turn the barrel hinge pin (25) until its notch mates with the frame lug. Holding the barrel firmly down in its closed position, remove the barrel hinge pin. Release the barrel slowly and remove it and the trigger guard (24) from the frame (7).

3.
Push the slide cap (6) in and turn it counterclockwise one-quarter turn. Remove slide cap, firing pin (5), main spring (4) and firing pin rebound spring (3). Slide (2) may now be removed by pulling its front end upward slightly.

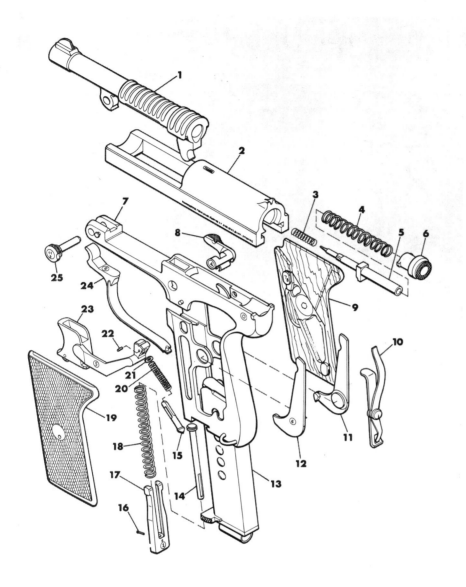

Parts Legend

1. Barrel
2. Slide
3. Firing pin rebound spring
4. Mainspring
5. Firing pin
6. Slide cap
7. Frame
8. Barrel lever
9. Right grip
10. Barrel lever spring
11. Right recoil lever
12. Left recoil lever
13. Magazine
14. Recoil spring guide
15. Trigger strut
16. Recoil link pin
17. Recoil link
18. Recoil spring
19. Left grip
20. Trigger spring
21. Trigger spring washer
22. Trigger strut pin
23. Trigger
24. Trigger guard
25. Barrel hinge pin

4.
Slide right and left grips (9 & 19) straight up and remove them.

5.
Push the frame down with the recoil link (17), which pro-trudes from the bottom front of the grip, bearing on a hard surface. With pressure on pt. 17, the recoil levers (11 & 12) can be removed. The trigger assembly (23) can now be lifted from the frame, as can the barrel lever spring (10).

6.
By pressing the sides of the recoil link together, it and the recoil spring assembly (18) can be withdrawn. The barrel lever (8) will now be free and can be removed, thus completing disassembly. Reassemble in reverse order.

LE FRANCAIS POCKET MODEL PISTOL

Illustrations by DENNIS RIORDAN
Text by LUDWIG OLSON

A number of semi-automatic pistols feature a double-action lock mechanism which permits the pistol to be carried safely uncocked with chamber loaded, and fired quickly like a double-action revolver simply by pulling the trigger. This desirable feature and several others are incorporated in the Le Francais Pocket Model cal. .25 ACP semi-automatic pistol introduced about 1914 by Manufrance (Manufacture Francaise d'Armes et Cycles de Saint Etienne), St. Etienne, France.

The double-action lock mechanism of this blowback-operated pistol is simple and ingenious. Pulling the trigger forces back the firing pin and compresses the mainspring. While moving back, the upper rear part of the trigger follows a cam surface in the frame. This causes the trigger to move down near the end of its rearward travel and release the firing pin which is driven forward by the mainspring to fire the cartridge. When the trigger is released, it is pushed forward by the trigger spring. The firing pin is held slightly rearward by the firing pin rebound spring, but is uncocked. Since the firing pin is not cocked except when the trigger is pulled, a safety lock is unnecessary and not provided.

Another desirable feature of this well-designed arm is its tip-up barrel which permits loading and unloading

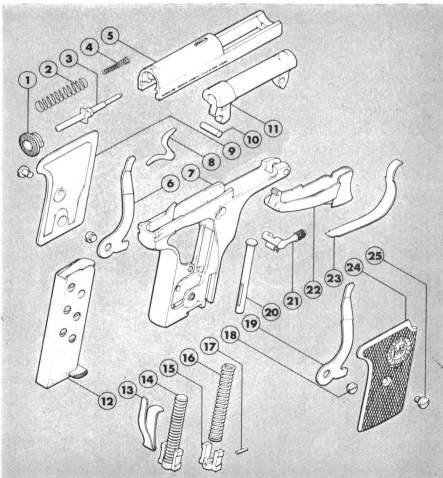

PARTS LEGEND

1. Slide cap
2. Mainspring
3. Firing pin
4. Firing pin rebound spring
5. Slide
6. Left recoil lever
7. Frame
8. Trigger spring
9. Left grip
10. Barrel pin
11. Barrel
12. Magazine
13. Barrel lever spring
14. Recoil spring assembly
15. Recoil link
16. Recoil spring
17. Recoil link pin
18. Recoil lever screw (2)
19. Right recoil lever
20. Recoil spring guide
21. Barrel lever
22. Trigger
23. Trigger guard
24. Right grip
25. Grip screw (2)

the chamber without retracting the slide. This makes the pistol easy to operate, even for weak women. The barrel pivots open under spring pressure when the barrel lever on the right side of the frame is depressed. It also pivots open automatically when the magazine is removed. Unloading the chamber after the magazine is removed is thereby not forgotten, and no magazine safety is required.

Well made and finished, this compact arm with blued finish and checkered hard-rubber grips weighs only 11¾ ozs. unloaded, and has a seven-round magazine. In the early version of this pistol, the magazine is detached by pulling it slightly forward and then down. The later version has a conventional thumb-operated magazine release in the lower rear of the frame. Also, the rear part of the frame is more slanted in the late version than in the early to give an improved grip.

Extraction in this pistol is by blow-back force only, and an extractor is not provided. Despite this, functioning is reliable. Accuracy is excellent for a pocket pistol.

There also are larger Le Francais blowback-operated pistols in calibers .25 ACP and .32 ACP. The Policeman Model in cal. .25 ACP has a domed mainspring housing at the rear of the frame and a longer barrel than the Pocket Model. A blowback-operated Military Model in cal. 9 mm. Browning Long was introduced about 1928, but was discontinued shortly before World War II. ■

1 Takedown of Le Francais begins with removal of magazine (12). To do this, pull forward and down on knurled wings extending from sides of magazine bottom. Barrel (11) automatically tips up as magazine is withdrawn. Remove any cartridge from chamber. Pivot barrel fully upward, and lift slide (5) up and forward off frame (7). Later versions of this pistol have a conventional butt-mounted magazine catch, but takedown procedures are similar to above.

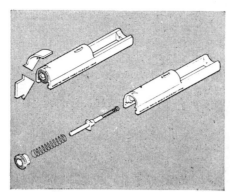

2 Press slide cap (1) forward into slide, rotate ¼ turn counterclockwise, and ease out to rear. Remove mainspring (2), firing pin (3), and rebound spring (4). This completes field stripping for normal cleaning.

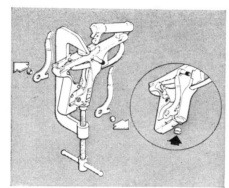

3 To disassemble further, unscrew grip screws (25) and remove grips (9) (24). Cut a short section of ¼" copper tubing, and tighten against recoil link (15) with clamp or vise to slightly compress recoil spring (16). Unscrew recoil lever screws (18), and remove recoil levers (6) (19). These levers are offset slightly to provide clearance for trigger (22), and must be replaced with offsets facing outward.

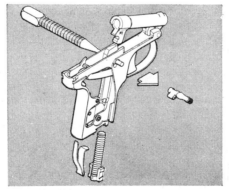

4 Release clamp, and remove recoil spring assembly (14) and barrel lever spring (13). Move barrel lever (21) to down (released) position, and push out of frame with punch. Straight leaf of barrel lever spring must seat within barrel lever's notched lug during reassembly.

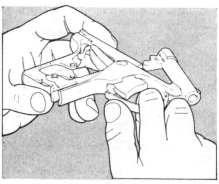

5 Holding pistol in left hand, pull rear of trigger guard (23) out of frame with right forefinger, keeping the guard bowed with pressure from right thumb and middle finger. Release pressure and rotate guard forward out of frame. Barrel can now be removed by driving out its pin (10).

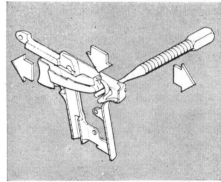

6 Insert a punch between trigger and trigger spring (8), and flex the spring rearward to disengage from trigger. Press down on rear of trigger to unlatch from frame and slide trigger forward and out. Remove trigger spring. The late version of this pistol has a coil-type trigger spring.

7 Cutaway indicates relative positions of assembled parts. Magazine has been removed, causing barrel to tip up. Parts are number keyed to parts legend.

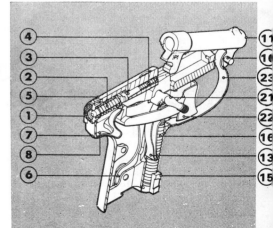

Absence of ejector and extractor permitted simple breech construction. Note fixed firing pin in percussion mechanism and rear sight notch in loading gate

Large trigger guard permitted firing with gloved hand. It extends above muzzle to form front sight

Liberator Pistol

By M. D. Waite

THE arming of partisan or other resistance forces within Nazi-occupied territories became a major problem to the Allies during World War II, especially since the production of such armament was carried out in addition to that for normal troop requirements. U. S. Army Ordnance, through its vigorous research and development program, made many significant contributions towards this little publicized effort, not the least of which was development and production of the rather unique 'Liberator' pistol.

The demand for this gun originated with the Office of Strategic Services (OSS), as that organization was vitally interested in arming resistance forces in Europe. OSS specifications called for a cheap but effective gun weighing one pound, and they wanted a million of them in a hurry!

The basic design for an effective .45 caliber single-shot pistol was soon formulated by Army Ordnance and the contract was let to the Guide Lamp Corporation, who completed tooling and production of the million guns in the record time of *thirteen weeks*. Final deliveries were made during the month of August, 1942. The ultimate cost of each unit was a little over $2.00 and the guns were constructed entirely of non-strategic materials. Each gun was individually packaged in a sturdy, paraffin-coated, cardboard box. Included were an instruction sheet, a wooden ramrod, and ten rounds of .45 ACP ammunition stored in the butt of the gun. With the exception of the 4-inch smoothbore, seamless steel tubing barrel and die-cast percussion mechanism, the gun is constructed throughout of sheet steel stampings and a few small steel pins and coil springs. The various parts are held together by a combination of folded seams, rivets, spot and acetylene welds. The net result is a very crude-looking weapon, but it was nevertheless a significant contribution towards the Allied war effort, based upon the theory that "some gun is better than none at all."

A study of the instruction sheet reveals that this is a very simple weapon to operate even though it lacks both an extractor and ejector. ◆ ◆ ◆

Firing sequence instruction sheet shows every phase of gun operation

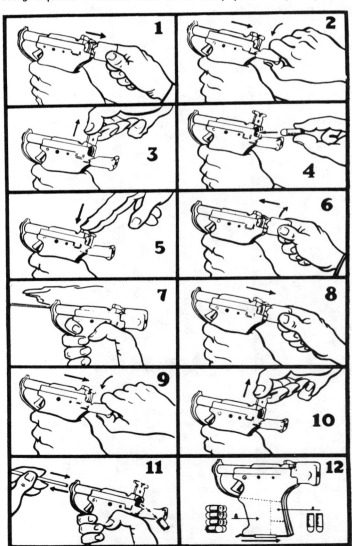

The Luger Pistol

By James M. Triggs

IN 1893 the German firm of Ludwig Loewe offered what was destined to become the first commercially-successful self-loading pistol chambered for a high-velocity smokeless powder cartridge. Known as the Borchardt, after its American inventor Hugo Borchardt, this new pistol featured a revolutionary toggle breech mechanism designed in principle by Sir Hiram Maxim of Maxim machine gun fame.

Although well received, the Borchardt pistol had a relatively short production life, thanks to design improvements effected by Georg Luger and patented by him in 1900. Although preserving the toggle-breech principle and removable-clip magazine, Luger's redesign was drastic in concept. The resultant pistol was lighter, neater, easier to manufacture, and possessed improved handling and pointing qualities.

The first Luger pistol to be produced in quantity was the 7.65 mm. cal. Model 1900, which featured a unique grip-safety device to prevent accidental discharge unless the piece was actually grasped in normal firing position.

Switzerland, in 1901, became the first nation to adopt the Model 1900 Luger pistol as an official service arm. It is interesting to note that U. S. Ordnance also in 1901 purchased 1000 Model 1900 Luger pistols for a subse-

LEGEND

1. Front sight
2. Barrel
3. Receiver
4. Ejector
5. Receiver axle
6. Trigger bar spring
7. Trigger bar
8. Trigger bar plunger pin
9. Trigger bar plunger spring
10. Trigger bar plunger
11. Coupling link
12. Coupling link pin
13. Rear toggle link
14. Toggle axle
15. Toggle axle pin
16. Forward toggle link
17. Breechblock
18. Breechblock pin
19. Extractor pin
20. Extractor spring
21. Extractor
22. Firing pin
23. Firing pin spring
24. Firing pin spring guide
25. Frame
26. Hold-open latch
27. Hold-open latch spring
28. Magazine catch
29. Recoil lever
30. Recoil lever pin
31. Mainspring
32. Mainspring guide
33. Locking bolt
34. Locking bolt spring
35. Trigger plate
36. Trigger lever pin
37. Trigger lever
38. Trigger
39. Trigger spring
40. Magazine catch spring
41. Safety bar
42. Safety catch
43. Safety pin
44. Grip (2—right-hand grip not shown)
45. Grip screw (2)
46. Magazine (shown partially withdrawn)

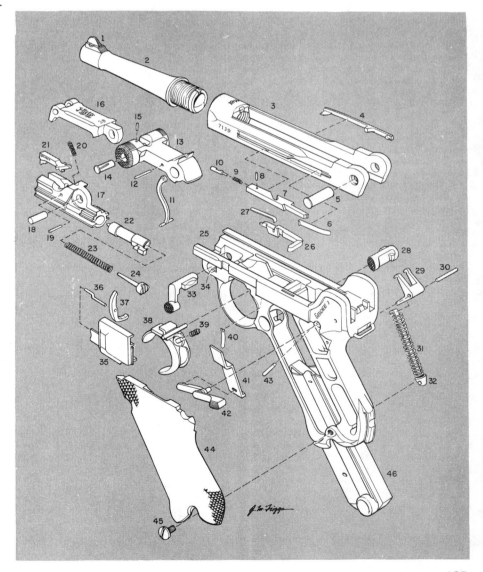

quent field trial which resulted in ultimate rejection of the design.

In 1902, Deutsche Waffen und Munitionsfabriken (DWM), manufacturer of the Luger pistol, offered the Model 1902 chambered for a new 9 mm. cal. rimless cartridge.

Designated the 9 mm. Parabellum, this new development was destined to become the world's most widely used pistol and submachine gun cartridge.

The Model 1902 was subsequently improved to become the Model 1904, adopted in 1904 by the German Navy. Although chambered for the 9 mm. Parabellum cartridge, it had the same grip safety, toggle lock, and flat mainspring of earlier models. The year 1904 also saw the introduction of the Luger carbine with extra-long barrel, wooden forearm, and detachable shoulder stock.

In 1906 DWM offered the improved Model 1906, which featured a coiled
(text continued on next page)

DISASSEMBLY PROCEDURE OF RECEIVER AND FRAME

In disassembling receiver (3), ejector (4) is removed by inserting blade of small screwdriver under rear end of ejector in recess provided in the receiver wall and prying up gently. Reassemble ejector by sliding it back into position from the rear until it snaps into place. Pry up forward end of trigger bar spring (6) with screwdriver blade and slide spring forward and out of its slot. Trigger bar (7) may be lifted out of its recess in left side of receiver with the fingers.

In disassembling frame, grips are removed by unscrewing the two grip screws (45). Trigger (38) can be lifted out of frame with the fingers, using care not to lose trigger spring (39) which is seated at the top of trigger. Magazine catch spring (40) may be pressed sideways out of its recess in frame with tip of small screwdriver. Magazine catch (28) may now be dropped out of right side of frame. Locking bolt (33) may be removed with the fingers. In reinserting locking bolt, it will be necessary to overcome tension from locking bolt spring (34) which is installed in frame inside locking bolt hole. Removal of this spring is not recommended unless necessary for replacement. Hold-open latch (26) and spring (27) are removed by lifting rear end of latch slightly and pressing *down* and to the rear on latch, disengaging latch and spring assembly from frame. Safety catch (42) and safety bar (41) are removed by drifting out safety pin (43) from inside of frame. Disassembly of recoil lever (29), mainspring (31), and mainspring guide (32) should be left to a competent gunsmith. Strong compression of mainspring will project guide with considerable force if lower end of guide is carelessly slipped out of its seat. While it is possible to reassemble mainspring and guide to recoil lever by hand, it is extremely difficult, requiring considerable effort.

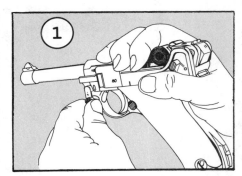

1 Remove magazine and check to be sure the pistol is unloaded. Using the left hand, push the assembled barrel and receiver to the rear about 1/4" to relieve tension on the recoil spring. Hold it in that position with the fingers of the right hand, as shown. With the left hand rotate the locking bolt (33) 90 degrees clockwise to free the trigger plate.

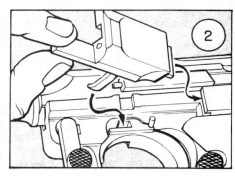

2 Lift out trigger plate assembly (35) from frame, as shown. When reassembling pistol, trigger lever (37) in trigger plate must fall into its slot in trigger (38) and small lip at rear of trigger plate must be inserted underside of frame in recess provided.

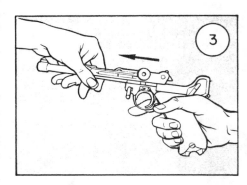

3 Slide complete barrel, receiver and breech assembly forward and out of frame as shown. During this operation, note the position of the coupling link (11) with relation to the recoil lever (29) in rear of frame for reference in reassembly.

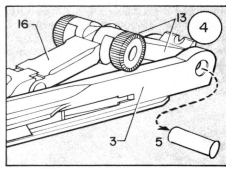

4 Grasp knurled knobs of rear toggle link (13) and pull upward buckling rear and forward toggle links (13 & 16) to relieve tension. Press receiver axle (5) from right to left out of the receiver. Toggle and breechblock assembly can now be withdrawn from rear of receiver.

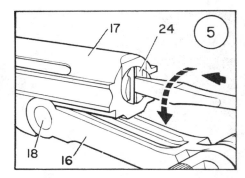

5 Invert toggle and breechblock assembly and insert a screwdriver blade in slot in firing pin spring guide (24) in rear of breechblock (17). Press guide in about 1/16" and turn counterclockwise 1/4 turn and allow firing pin spring guide and firing pin spring (23) to come out, taking care not to allow compressed firing pin spring to escape. Firing pin (22) can now be dropped out rear. Extractor (21) may be removed by holding thumb over top of breechblock and extractor and drifting out extractor pin (19), allowing extractor to pop up. Lift extractor out and extractor spring (20) may now be lifted out of its seat.

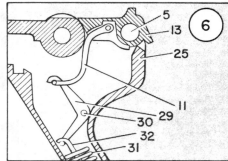

6 The above steps complete normal field stripping necessary for cleaning and lubrication. Reassembly is accomplished in reverse order. When replacing barrel, receiver and breech assembly on frame, be sure coupling link (11) drops into its proper place in front of inclined upper arms of recoil lever (29). The proper relationship of these parts, when assembled is shown here.

rather than a flat mainspring. This was the first of the so-called New Model Lugers and all earlier versions were thus automatically grouped in the Old Model category. The Model 1906 was equipped with a grip safety but lacked the toggle locking device found on earlier models.

Despite relatively early adoption by the German Navy, the German Army waited until 1908 to adopt what became known as the Pistole 08 or Model 1908 Luger pistol. Of coiled mainspring type, the Model 1908 was of 9mm Parabellum caliber and lacked the grip safety feature. Early Model 1908 Lugers were not fitted with the hold-open device subsequently adopted.

Shortly after the Army's acceptance of the Pistole 08, an additional manufacturing facility was established in Erfurt, Germany, at the Royal Arsenal. All Luger pistols issued to German forces during the World War I period were manufactured by DWM or at Erfurt. During and after World War I a flood of war-souvenir Luger pistols were brought to the U.S. by returning servicemen. A few dealers succeeded in obtaining good quality Lugers for the U.S. market.

After World War I the firm of Simson & Company, located in Suhl, Germany, furnished the Luger pistols to the new 100,000-man German *Reichswehr* authorized by the Versailles Treaty. This contract was completed in 1932. In 1930, production of Luger pistols was resumed by the Mauser firm in Oberndorf, Germany, with production continued during World War II.

The firm of Heinrich Krieghoff also made a quantity of Luger pistols for the German Luftwaffe during the 1930s.

German production of Luger pistols was terminated when World War II ended (though some were assembled from existing parts and transferred to the various occupying powers). For a time in the 1970s, and again in the 1980s, Mauser produced a limited number of Swiss 1929 variants, standard P.08 models and Luger carbines.

In addition to German production, Luger pistols have been made by the Swiss federal arsenal at Bern and by Vickers Ltd., in England (which, evidence suggests, was a marking for guns made in Germany and delivered by the British to Dutch buyers). In 1992, Mitchell Arms of Santa Ana, California undertook to produce an American made "Luger", known as the "American Eagle", and available in both regular and stainless steel.

These instructions were prepared with the standard P.08 pistol as an example. They can be used to disassemble any Luger pistol regardless of maker or variant. Those pistols having grip safeties may differ slightly in details of disassembly of parts from the pistol's frame.

The late James M. Triggs was a well known writer-illustrator and collector of antique firearms.

Luger 9 mm. & .30 Cal. Auto

PISTOL MAGAZINES

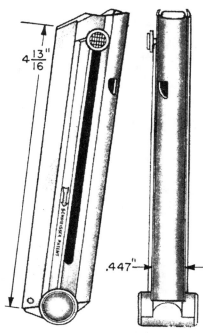

Luger magazines are numerous, but their quality varies. While the early stamped magazines with their wooden plugs are adequate, magazines made before and during World War II are far stronger. The best of these late magazines were machined from steel extrusions by Haenel. Some are marked as shown.

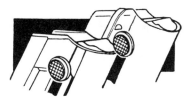

The machined magazines can be recognized by the smooth panels on the sides of the feed lips. Sheet metal magazines have ribs of folded sheet metal running from the base plug to the feed lips.

The base plug that identifies the Luger magazine was generally made from wood until the early 1930's. Later magazines will be found with either aluminum, zinc, or plastic base plugs.—E. J. HOFFSCHMIDT

MAB Model D

PISTOL MAGAZINES

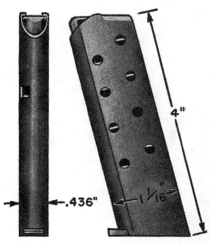

MAB (Manufacture d'Armes de Bayonne) pistols are probably the best known of the relatively few French guns in this country. The Model D was first produced around 1933. Production was continued under German supervision after France surrendered. After World War II, they were imported by Winfield Arms Co. under the trade name 'WAC'. While the gun is rather large for the cal. .32 ACP cartridge, it represents the thinking of a large segment of the Central European military establishment—that the .32 ACP is sufficient for a military side arm. The pistol is well finished but sometimes poorly fitted, especially the guns made under German occupation. The mechanism is simple and incorporates a thumb safety, a grip safety, and a magazine safety that prevents the gun from firing when the magazine is removed.

MAB clips can be identified by their long slender appearance, since they hold 9 rounds. The odd, straight feed lips and hole in the front strap for the magazine catch are other prominent characteristics.

Most MAB magazines are stamped as shown, but the stamping was omitted or done very lightly on late wartime guns. The long, narrow floorplate with grooved front edge is another point of recognition.—EDWARD J. HOFFSCHMIDT

Liliput 4.25mm Automatic

By E. J. Hoffschmidt

I⸱ᴛ's small and expensive. This description could fit many objects, but in this case it describes the 4.25 mm. Liliput automatic pistol. It's small—only 3½ inches long and weighs only six ounces. It's expensive—ammunition is so scarce that it sells for one or two dollars a round.

These Liliput pistols were first manufactured in 1925 by the firm of August Menz of Suhl, Germany. In spite of its eye appeal, not too many were sold, partly due to the depression in Germany around this time, and partly due to the fact that its tiny cartridge is not a very potent one. Yet the gun is not a toy, for it fires a 14-grain jacketed bullet at approximately 800 feet per second and will penetrate about 1½ inches of soft pine. The report is almost as loud as that of a .25 automatic pistol cartridge.

Like most pistols under 9 mm. caliber, the Liliput is a straight blow-back operated gun, which means that the slide and barrel are not locked together at the instant of firing. When the cartridge is fired, the slide is driven back, ejecting the empty cartridge case and chambering a fresh round from the magazine on the return trip.

These tiny automatics were well made, and finely finished, and the design is simple and reliable. All metal parts are made from steel. The barrel is machined as an integral part of the frame. The rest of the operating parts are simple shapes that can be easily reproduced in case of loss or breakage. The repair procedure is simple. Since the operating parts are not inside the frame, they can be removed by simply taking off the right-hand grip. 🌀 🌀 🌀

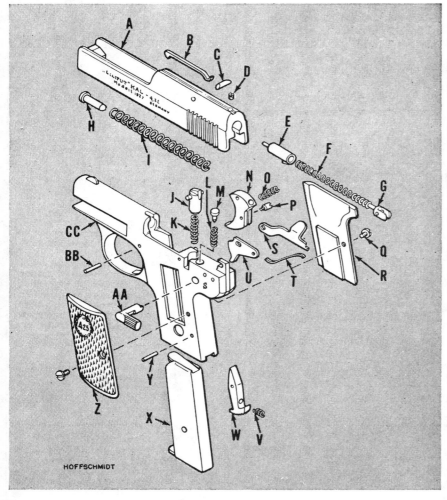

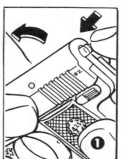 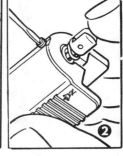

When 'taking down' the Liliput, first remove the magazine. Then check to be sure that the gun is empty, pull back the slide as far as it will go, and push in on the end of the firing pin spring guide (G). Lift the rear end of the slide and run it forward off the receiver

The only part that presents any problem is the firing pin. The spring guide retaining screw (D) is all that holds it in. Remove it and you get the spring guide, the firing pin spring (F), and firing pin (E). The other parts can be lifted off frame after removal of right-hand grip

HOFFSCHMIDT

LEGEND

A	Slide	K	Sear Spring	T	Trigger Bar Spring
B	Extractor	L	Safety Catch Spring	U	Rear Operating Lever
C	Extractor Retaining Pin	M	Safety Catch Plunger	V	Magazine Catch Spring
D	Spring Guide Retaining Screw	N	Trigger	W	Magazine Catch
E	Firing Pin	O	Trigger Spring	X	Magazine
F	Firing Pin Spring	P	Trigger Bar Pivot Screw	Y	Magazine Catch Pin
G	Firing Pin Spring Guide	Q	Grip Screw	Z	Left-Hand Grip
H	Recoil Spring Guide	R	Right-Hand Grip	AA	Safety Catch
I	Recoil Spring	S	Trigger Bar	BB	Trigger Pin
J	Sear			CC	Frame

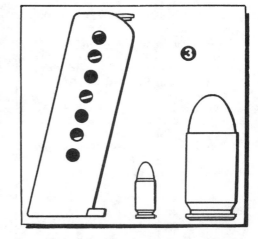

Some idea of the Liliput's size can be gained by comparing the magazine and a cartridge with a standard .45 caliber automatic pistol cartridge

The Makarov Pistol

By E. J. HOFFSCHMIDT

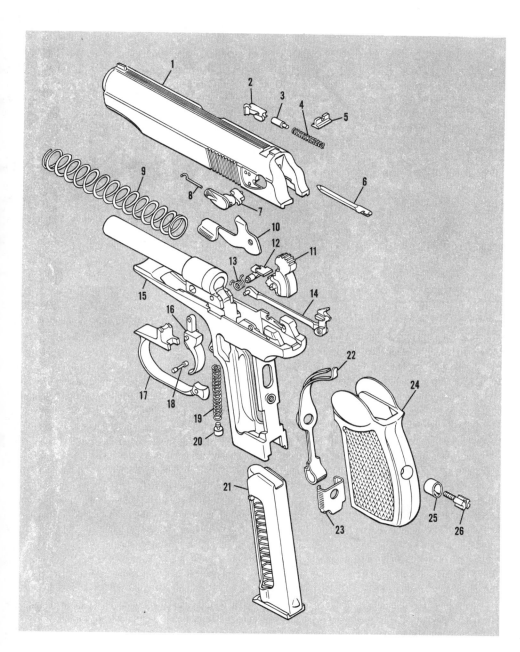

THE 9 mm. Makarov blowback-operated automatic pistol is one of many new weapons adopted by Russia since World War II. The pistol is generally similar in appearance and basic design to the German Model PP Walther pistol. It is called PM *(Pistolet Makarov)* by the Russians in accordance with their current weapons designation system which includes abbreviations of weapons type and designer's name.

Parts Legend

1. Slide
2. Extractor
3. Extractor plunger
4. Extractor spring
5. Rear sight
6. Firing pin
7. Safety
8. Safety detent spring
9. Recoil spring
10. Ejector and slide stop
11. Hammer
12. Sear
13. Sear and slide stop spring
14. Trigger bar assembly
15. Receiver and barrel assembly
16. Trigger
17. Trigger guard
18. Trigger guard pin
19. Trigger guard spring
20. Spring plunger
21. Magazine
22. Hammer and trigger spring
23. Spring retainer
24. Grip
25. Grip screw detent bushing
26. Grip screw

The lock mechanism of this pistol is of double-action type, and the hammer is exposed. The safety, on the left of the slide, is engaged in safe position when horizontal. A slide stop is provided on the left side above the grip. The bore is chrome plated. The one-piece plastic grip extends around the back of the receiver.

This pistol fires a rimless, straight-case cartridge midway between the .380 ACP and 9 mm. Luger in size and power. The round-nose bullet weighs 94 grs., and muzzle velocity is 1033 f.p.s. (feet per second).

The Makarov is also made and used by East Germany. The pistol shown is of East German manufacture.

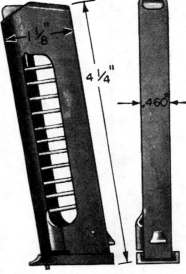

1 To field strip, first remove the magazine and clear the chamber. Put the safety (7) in fire position. Pull down on the front of the trigger guard (17) until it clears the receiver (15). Pull the slide (1) to the rear, lift the slide up, and ease it forward off the receiver.

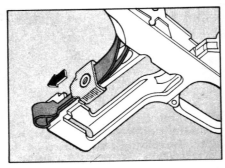

4 Remove grip screw (26). Grip (24) can be slid off receiver. This will expose the hammer and trigger spring (22). This spring acts as the magazine catch, hammer spring, and trigger spring. To remove, pull down on spring retainer (23) until free; then lift spring off boss in receiver.

The 9 mm. Makarov PM pistol is an interesting Soviet design. Body of its well-made magazine seems to be a thin-walled extrusion with long observation slots on both sides.

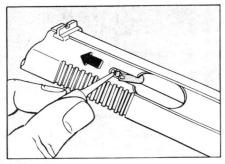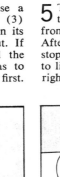

2 To remove the extractor (2), use a thin punch to push the plunger (3) back into the slide. Turn the slide on its right side. Extractor should drop out. If not, rotate the extractor in toward the firing pin hole or in such a way as to remove the tail section from the slide first.

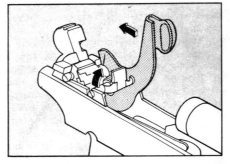

5 The next step is to unhook the tail of the sear and slide stop spring (13) from the ejector and slide stop (10). After the spring is free, rotate the slide stop up as shown. Then use it as a lever to lift the sear (12) out of its hole in the right of the frame.

The sturdy sheet metal follower has a projection extending out through an opening on the left side of the magazine. This projection actuates the hold-open catch when magazine is empty. It also serves as a stop to prevent the follower from pressing upward against the magazine lips.

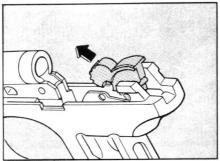

3 The firing pin (6) is retained by the safety (7). To remove the safety, push it up beyond the safe position. It can be rotated as shown only when the slide is held to the rear or off the gun completely.

6 The hammer (11) is one of the last parts to be removed. It can be removed in only one position. Rotate the hammer forward as shown, and pull it forward free of the receiver. ∎

The floorplate is detached by depressing the spring that extends through it. Other identity points are the projections on the lower end of the backstrap and lower left side of the body.—E. J. HOFFSCHMIDT

MAUSER HSc POCKET PISTOL

By E. J. Hoffschmidt

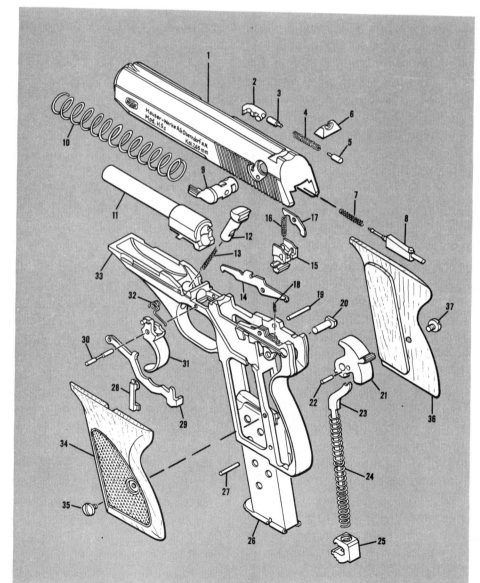

The Mauser HSc was a late-1930s vintage attempt by the Mauser firm to produce a pistol to compete with the Walther Model PP. Far from simply building on the earlier Mauser Model 1910 pistols, the HSc was an entirely new design that featured a double-action trigger mechanism.

In that same respect, the HSc is a far cry from Mauser's earlier, intricate and carefully machined military pistols. Internal parts were stamped wherever possible and music wire springs replace expensive machined and forged types. The result was a simple, rugged pistol, well suited for mass production and salable at a competitive price.

The HSc is a natural pocket pistol with no sharp edges to hang up in the user's clothing. The gun has an excellent grip and a fairly good double-action trigger pull. The design has one drawback for a person with a large hand. If the gun is gripped and fired hurriedly, there is a good chance that the hammer will catch a fold of skin between the shooter's thumb and forefinger as it is forces back to the full cock position. Aside from this, the gun reflects the design skill that made the Mauser name famous. Many of the operating parts perform two or more functions. For instance, a simple, stamped bar, pinned to the frame, acts as a magazine safety, slide hold-open device and ejector. Another part, the cartridge feed cam, positions the top round in the magazine for chambering, puts tension on the sear spring, and acts as a retainer for the hammer hinge pin. Such clever designing kept the number of parts to a minimum without loss of efficiency.

Slide Release

The slide release system is a carryover from the 1910 pocket pistol. When the last shot is fired, the slide stays locked to the rear. It can be released to return to battery only by partially withdrawing the magazine and pushing it back into place again — the presumption being that this would be done when exchanging an empty magazine for a full one. Thus, if a loaded magazine is inserted with the slide to the rear, the slide will automatically run forward, chambering a cartridge.

Another clever feature is the operation of the safety. When applied, it locks the tail of the firing pin into the top of the slide.

Mauser/Oberndorf production of the HSc ended at the end of World War II. The French, however, assembled a few using captured machinery and Heckler & Koch made a variant of the HSc, the HK4, from the mid-1960s until about 1984.

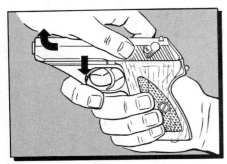

1 To take down the HSc, remove magazine and clear chamber. Pull hammer back to full cock and put safety catch down over red dot. Hold down notched catch inside front of trigger guard. At same time pull slide forward and upward until it is free of frame

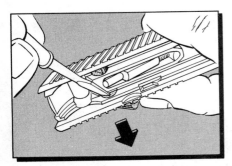

3 The safety catch (9) is held in place by a detent (5) and spring (4) that also actuate extractor. To remove firing pin (8) or safety catch, lift end of firing pin to position shown. Turn safety to a position halfway between 'on' and 'off' positions and push safety out with a screwdriver as shown. Remove extractor and detent parts

Parts Legend

1. Slide
2. Extractor
3. Extractor plunger
4. Extractor spring
5. Safety detent plunger
6. Rear sight
7. Firing pin spring
8. Firing pin
9. Safety catch
10. Recoil spring
11. Barrel
12. Takedown latch
13. Takedown latch spring
14. Magazine safety
15. Sear
16. Sear spring
17. Cartridge feed cam
18. Magazine safety spring
19. Sear hinge pin
20. Hammer hinge pin
21. Hammer
22. Strut pin
23. Hammer strut
24. Hammer spring
25. Magazine catch
26. Magazine
27. Magazine catch pin
28. Disconnector
29. Trigger bar
30. Trigger pin
31. Trigger
32. Trigger spring
33. Frame
34. Left grip
35. Grip screw
36. Right grip
37. Grip screw

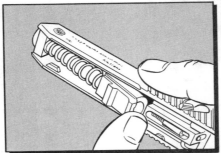

2 To remove barrel, hold slide as shown. Push chamber end of barrel forward and upward until it clears bolt face. If barrel is held too tightly in slide, use a block of wood or magazine floorplate to lever it out

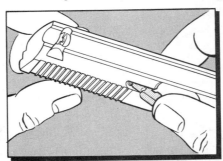

4 To replace safety catch, back firing pin (8) and spring (7) into slide. Lift firing pin tail as in disassembly. Install safety and push firing pin down into place. Replace detent part and push extractor in and back until it seats itself properly in slide

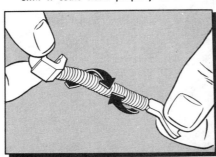

5 When magazine catch pin (27) is removed, magazine catch (25), hammer strut (23), and spring (24) come out as an assembly. This assembly can be taken apart by giving magazine catch a quarter turn. Great care must be taken when assembling or disassembling these pieces since they are under heavy spring tension

6 To remove takedown latch (12), hold frame as shown. Use a screwdriver or block of wood to push down latch and rotate it clockwise 180°. Care must be taken to prevent latch from flying out since it is under heavy spring tension——————————■

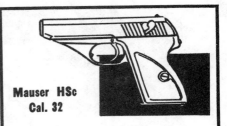

Mauser HSc Cal. 32

PISTOL MAGAZINES

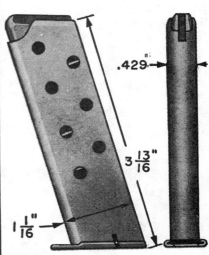

The Mauser HSc cal. .32 double-action pistol saw wide service during World War II and was carried by many German officers. It was first manufactured in the early 1930's, and production continued through World War II. Prewar guns can be recognized by their fine finish and the Mauser trademark on the magazine. Wartime guns usually lack the fine finish, but are still among the best pocket pistols yet designed.

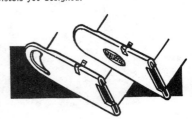

There are 2 common varieties of floorplates: the flat prewar with Mauser trademark and the wartime with a depression on the front edge. Floorplates with finger extensions are uncommon. The cutout on the floorplate allows the magazine catch to hold on the backstrap and not exert pressure on the floorplate.

Mauser HSc magazines have the carefully machined follower that has given them a reputation for reliability. The long cut down the back of the follower and magazine backstrap is another point of identification. — E. J. HOFFSCHMIDT

MAUSER
Military Pistol

By E. J. Hoffschmidt

THE 1890's can rightly be called the beginning of the automatic pistol era. During these years, gun designers such as Borchardt, Mannlicher, Schwarzlose, Browning, and Mauser focused their mechanical ingenuity on self-loading pistols. Probably the most remarkable of these early designs was Paul Mauser's Model 1896 Military Pistol. Few handguns can match its remarkable success and world-wide distribution. This unique design contains no pins and only one screw, the grip screw. All internal parts that require a pin or pivot are machined from solid stock so the pin is integral with the part.

During the half century that the gun was in production, several models were offered. These range from the odd 6-shot pistol to the selective-fire Model 712. Although never officially adopted by the German Army, Mauser pistols were widely carried by German officers during World War I, and to a limited degree in World War II. The World War I pistol is the most common; it has a 5½" barrel and is chambered for the 7.63 mm. Mauser cartridge. To simplify wartime ammuni-

E. J. HOFFSCHMIDT *is an artist-illustrator.*

tion problems, these guns were also chambered for the 9 mm. Luger cartridge. These can be recognized by the big red "9" carved into the grips.

In 1930 Mauser made a change in the safety catch operation. On previous pistols it was necessary to pull back the hammer with one hand and engage the safety with the other. The new universal safety of 1930 made it possible to apply the safety with the gun hand only. The only other major change came when Mauser dropped the rifle-style magazine and changed to a removable sheet-metal magazine which can be loaded in the gun from a stripper clip like a military rifle, or outside the gun like any normal pistol magazine. The sear mechanism was changed to incorporate a selector switch that allowed optional semi- or full-automatic fire. Manufacture was eventually stopped because the gun became too expensive to produce. It was subsequently replaced by cheaper and more modern designs.

Mauser military pistols were widely copied in Spain and China. Some are excellent copies and operate reliably. Others reflect only the distinctive Mauser outline with lock mechanism differing from the original.

PARTS LEGEND

1. Barrel and barrel extension
2. Extractor
3. Bolt
4. Bolt stop
5. Firing pin spring
6. Firing pin
7. Recoil spring
8. Trigger spring
9. Magazine plunger
10. Trigger
11. Rocker plunger
12. Mainspring
13. Mainspring plunger
14. Bolt locking block
15. Sear arm
16. Sear
17. Sear spring and hammer pivot
18. Hammer
19. Lock mechanism frame
20. Lock frame stop
21. Safety
22. Rocker coupling
23. Receiver
24. Lanyard ring
25. Left-hand grip
26. Grip screw
27. Follower spring
28. Follower
29. Magazine floorplate

1 With point of a bullet, press up magazine plunger (9) and slide floorplate (29) forward. Remove follower (28) and spring (27). Then cock hammer. Press up lock frame stop (20) as shown. Pull barrel extension assembly (1) off rear of receiver (23)

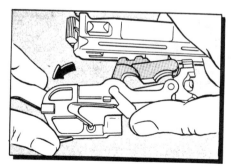

2 After barrel extension assembly is free of frame, pull down on rear of lock mechanism frame (19) to free it from barrel extension. Remove locking block (14). Handle lock work carefully to prevent frame stop (20) and sear (16) dropping out of place

3 To remove firing pin (6), use a small screwdriver to push in firing pin as far as it will go and give it a ¼-turn clockwise. Remove pin and push bolt stop (4) forward and out to right. Recoil spring (7) can now be removed

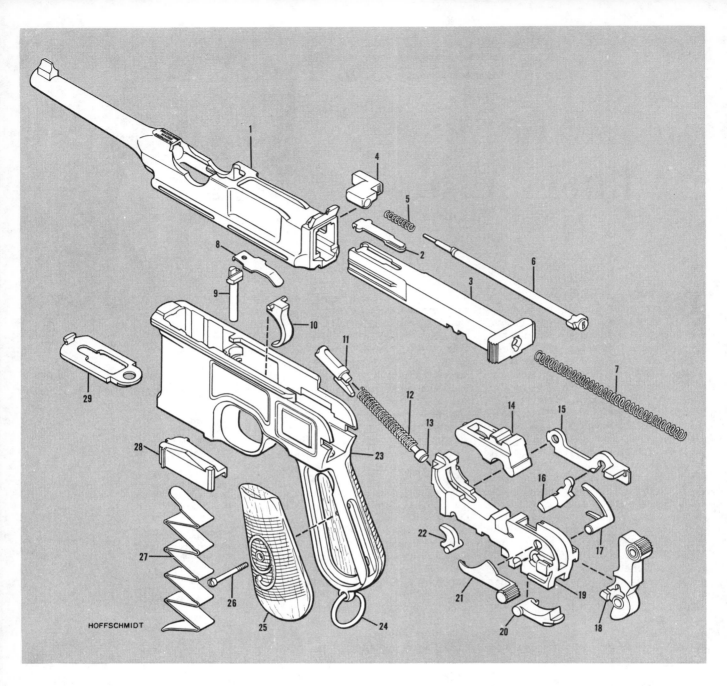

29

8

9

10

11

12

13

14

15

16

17

18

19

20

21

22

23

24

25

26

27

28

1

4

5

2

3

6

7

HOFFSCHMIDT

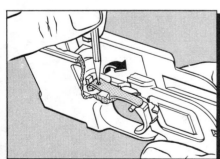

4 To remove trigger (10) and magazine plunger (9), trigger spring (8) must be removed first. To do this, use a tool with a small hook to lift spring free of plunger (9). At same time, push it toward butt until free

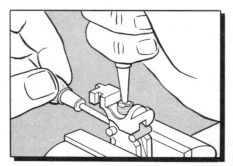

5 Care must be taken when removing rocker coupling (22) since it is under heavy spring tension. First lower hammer. Hold lock mechanism in a vise and press down on plunger (11). At same time push rocker coupling (22) through as shown

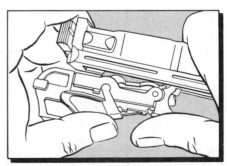

6 To reassemble gun, install bolt (3) and firing pin, etc. Turn barrel extension upside down and drop locking block (14) over its projection. Cock hammer and press down on forward end of lock mechanism until the tail of locking block (14) snaps into rocker coupling (22) ───────■

174

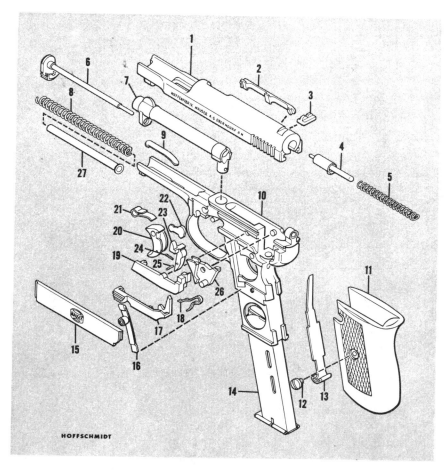

LEGEND

1. Slide
2. Extractor
3. Rear sight
4. Firing pin
5. Firing pin spring
6. Takedown rod
7. Barrel
8. Recoil spring
9. Takedown rod catch
10. Receiver
11. Grip
12. Grip screw
13. Magazine catch
14. Magazine
15. Side-plate
16. Safety catch release
17. Safety catch
18. Trigger bar spring
19. Trigger bar
20. Trigger
21. Trigger spring
22. Disconnector
23. Trigger sear
24. Trigger sear spring
25. Trigger sear pin
26. Ejector and hold-open catch
27. Recoil spring guide

HOFFSCHMIDT

MAUSER POCKET PISTOL 1910

By E. J. Hoffschmidt

THIS Mauser pistol was extremely popular in the United States in the '20's, having been brought back by returning World War I doughboys. They were also imported in quantity and sold for less than contemporary American automatic pistols.

The first model of the 1910 pistol was made in .25 ACP caliber. While larger than the average .25 caliber pistol, its excellent design and workmanship, and large magazine capacity made it an immediate success. The early model had hard rubber grips and a rather weak extractor. These defects were corrected shortly after the gun appeared on the market. The extractor design was changed completely and a wrap-around walnut grip replaced the hard rubber grip.

Shortly before World War I, Mauser brought out a scaled-up version to shoot the .32 ACP cartridge. This design remained static until a revised model was put on the market in 1934. The major change was in the grip, for while the Model 1934 retained the wrap-around grip, the back edge was curved to give the gun a more comfortable feel.

As pocket pistols go, the Mauser Model 1910 is unusually accurate and easy to shoot. This is due to the fact that it sits low in the hand and has a grip ample enough for the average hand. When the last shot is fired, the slide remains open, and if a loaded magazine is inserted, the slide will automatically run forward and chamber the first round in the magazine. To close the slide on an empty magazine, first pull the clip out about ½ inch, then push it home again. This will release the slide stop and the slide will fly forward. It is also possible to release the slide by snapping it a bit further to the rear and releasing it quickly. This method is not recommended, and should be used only when a magazine is not available. It will not work every time, and causes excessive wear on the hold-open mechanism.

The gun contains some interesting features. For instance, when the firing pin is cocked, the end of it protrudes

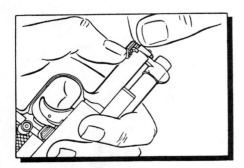

1 To field strip the gun, first remove the magazine and pull back the slide until it stays open. Depress the protruding portion of the takedown rod catch (9) and turn the takedown rod (6) until it is free of the lug on the receiver

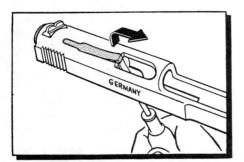

3 There are two types of extractors. The early type shown narrows down a short distance from its tail. This tail fits into a T-slot in the slide. Use a small screwdriver to lift the projection on the front end of the extractor free of the slide before attempting to pry it forward as shown

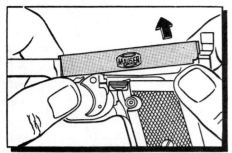

5 To observe the operating parts, the sideplate (15) can be pushed up and out of its grooves in the receiver. To remove operating parts, it is necessary to remove the grip (11). Do this carefully to prevent the safety catch parts (16), (17), (18) jumping out when they are free of the grip

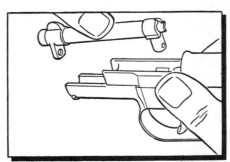

2 Withdraw the takedown rod (6) from the receiver (10). The barrel (7) can now be lifted out of its seat in the receiver. Replace the magazine and ease the slide (1) off the front of the receiver. Pull the trigger while easing the slide off to release the firing pin spring

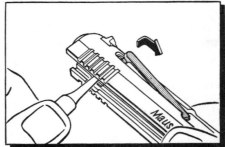

4 The later type extractor can be recognized by its straight outline and by the hole in the underside of the slide. The tail of the extractor must be pushed out of this hole with a thin punch and then pushed forward as shown

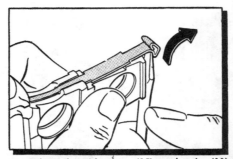

6 When the side-plate (15) and grip (11) have been removed, all the operating parts can be easily removed except the hold-open catch (26). The hold-open catch can be removed after the magazine catch (13) is removed. To remove the magazine catch, push it up clear of the receiver and pry it forward as shown

from the back of the slide. It can be easily seen in the daytime or felt in the dark. Another feature is the magazine disconnector that prevents the gun firing when the magazine is not in the gun. The thumb safety has a rather novel method of operation that locks the slide closed and also prevents it being accidentally released while the gun is being taken from the pocket. To engage the thumb safety simply push the thumbpiece down toward the button in the grip. To release it, press the button and the safety will snap back to 'fire' position.

While the gun features the usual fine Mauser workmanship, its internal design leaves a bit to be desired. The flat trigger spring and trigger bar spring are the source of some trouble, since they break easily if not carefully removed. Another bad feature is the strong magazine catch spring. This spring is usually so stiff that it causes the magazine catch to score the magazine when it is inserted. It also at times causes damage to the magazine floorplate.

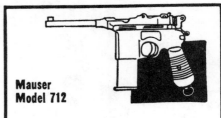

Mauser Model 712

PISTOL MAGAZINES

The original Mauser military pistol, designed before the turn of the century, was modernized in the 1930's to utilize a box magazine. The Model 712, as the revised gun was called, was sold in America up until World War II. It is strictly a semi-automatic pistol, firing the powerful 7.63 mm. Mauser cartridge. (A full-automatic version, the Model 711, which turns up occasionally, is classed as a machine gun under the 1968 Gun Control Act.) The Model 712 is an excellent piece but extremely awkward to handle because of its long magazine hanging down in front. High production costs and the advent of more modern designs caused production to stop. The gun was offered with 10- and 20-shot magazines.

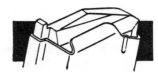

The 20-shot magazine is massive. The follower is milled from a heavy steel forging and highly polished.

The big Mauser trademark on the detachable floorplate is another point of recognition. The 10-shot magazine is of the same construction but only about half as long.—EDWARD J. HOFFSCHMIDT

Mauser W.T.P. Old Model

By E. J. Hoffschmidt

IN the 1920's all major German gun companies and many minor ones turned out vest-pocket pistols. Mauser brought out their W.T.P. or Westen-Taschen-Pistole (vest-pocket pistol), but it was not the most popular. The average German shopping for a vest-pocket gun usually chose the smallest and least expensive. Mauser was neither.

The W.T.P. is well made and finished. While not the smallest of its type, it is very compact. The grip is comfortable, and the safety catch is convenient and locks both sear and slide. Frame grip section is square and a thick hard rubber grip is used to fill out the area to a comfortable shape. This made the frame easier to machine but also made the grip susceptible to breakage. When the new model was introduced in 1938, the frame was forged to proper contour and conventional flat grips were screwed to the sides.

The W.T.P. has a magazine safety that prevents the gun from being fired with magazine removed. The firing pin spring guide projecting from the back of the slide locks the firing pin retainer and serves as a cocking indicator. It cannot be pressed inward when the gun is cocked.

When the last shot has been fired, the slide is held open by the magazine follower. When the magazine is removed, the slide snaps closed. The magazine must be removed against recoil spring tension. While the old model is a reliable gun, the new model that replaced it is a far better design.

Parts Legend

1. Slide
2. Extractor pin
3. Extractor
4. Firing pin retainer
5. Firing pin
6. Firing pin spring
7. Firing pin spring guide
8. Barrel
9. Recoil spring guide rod
10. Recoil spring
11. Disconnector
12. Magazine disconnector
13. Disconnector spring
14. Sear pin
15. Sear spring
16. Sear
17. Trigger lever
18. Trigger bar
19. Magazine catch
20. Grip
21. Grip screw
22. Frame
23. Magazine
24. Takedown catch spring
25. Takedown catch
26. Safety catch
27. Trigger pin
28. Trigger

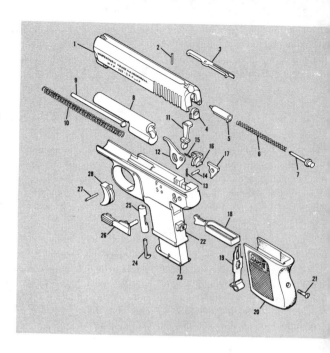

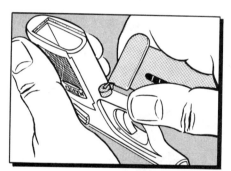

1 The takedown catch (25) runs through frame and locks barrel to frame. To strip gun, simply push in and down on takedown catch spring (24). This will disengage barrel and allow barrel and slide to be stripped off front of frame

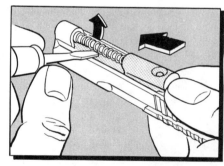

2 To remove barrel (8) and recoil spring (10) from slide, push barrel forward and upward. Ease it out of slide since it is under spring tension. When reassembling barrel and recoil spring, it may be necessary to lift spring and recoil spring guide rod (9) as shown to help align the rod

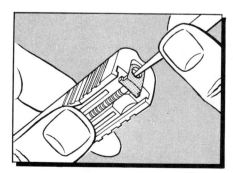

3 To remove firing pin (5), push firing pin spring guide (7) in with a punch. When it is clear of the firing pin retainer (4), push the retainer down as shown and ease out firing pin spring, and spring guide

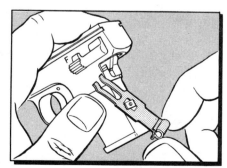

4 After grip (20) has been removed, the combination magazine catch (19) must be removed to expose sear parts. To do this rotate the spring 90° until square cutout on spring lines up with lug on frame, and lift off spring

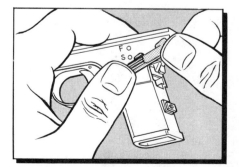

5 When safety catch (26) is removed it frees sear parts. To remove safety, it is necessary to first remove the grip. Safety can then be pushed down lower until it snaps free of frame. To reassemble, push it in until it is flat against frame, then push it up toward 'fire' position ∎

NAMBU
Type 14 Pistol

By E. J. Hoffschmidt

SEVEN years before we adopted the Model 1911 Colt Automatic, the Japanese high command issued a directive permitting Japanese officers to purchase and carry the Nambu pistol. While Col. Kijiro Nambu's pistol physically resembled the Luger pistol, it was an original design and not a direct copy of an existing arm. This early model, with its characteristic offset recoil spring and front-operated grip safety, was eventually modified.

The revised design, known as the Type 14 (1925), is far more common, for it was widely used by the Japanese during World War II and by Chinese Communist troops in Korea. There are two common varieties of the Type 14. The early model has a small trigger guard and usually lacks a magazine safety. The later model, with large winter trigger guard, invariably has a magazine safety. While the two Type 14's may look alike, many of the working parts are not interchangeable; for instance, the breech bolt on the early model is machined to take a long firing pin that stops short of the bolt lock, while the large trigger guard model has a short firing pin that passes through a notch in the bolt lock. Many round type trigger guards do not have the cutouts in the back strap or trigger projection necessary to operate in a frame equipped with a magazine safety.

Since the winter trigger guard version seems to be the most common, we will take a closer look at it. The Type 14 Nambu is a locked breech, recoil-operated pistol. It fires an 8 mm. bottleneck cartridge that looks a great deal like the .30 Luger cartridge but has a larger base. This cartridge, which fires a jack-

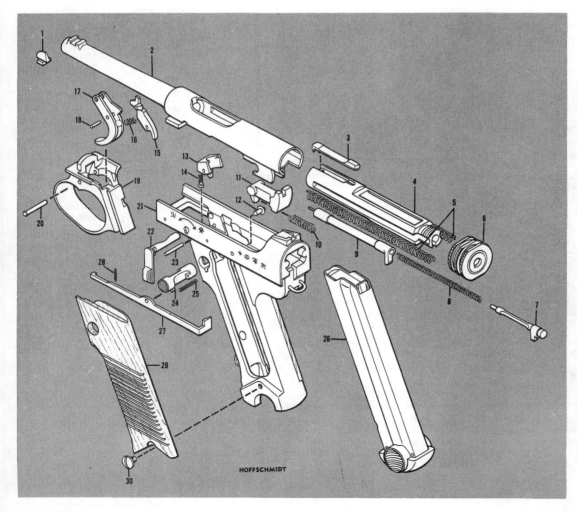

PARTS LEGEND

1. Front sight
2. Barrel and barrel extension
3. Extractor
4. Bolt
5. Recoil springs
6. Cocking piece
7. Firing pin extension
8. Firing pin spring
9. Firing pin
10. Locking block spring
11. Locking block
12. Trigger bar hinge pin
13. Magazine safety
14. Magazine safety spring and plunger
15. Trigger sear
16. Sear spring
17. Trigger
18. Trigger sear pin
19. Trigger guard
20. Trigger hinge pin
21. Receiver (frame)
22. Safety catch
23. Magazine safety hinge pin
24. Magazine catch
25. Magazine catch spring
26. Magazine
27. Trigger bar
28. Trigger bar spring
29. Left grip
30. Grip screw

HOFFSCHMIDT

eted 102-gr. bullet at about 900 f.p.s., is not too powerful.

Because of its well-shaped grip and excellent balance, the Type 14 points far more naturally than most military automatic pistols. These features, plus the mild recoil, make the gun pleasant to shoot.

The Type 14 has several bad features. First is the awkward operation and position of the safety catch, which cannot be operated with the shooting hand. Second, the magazine follower holds the breech open, which makes magazine removal difficult. The magazine of the large trigger guard model is even more difficult to remove because of a friction spring in the front strap. This device was furnished to prevent the magazine from dropping out if the magazine catch was accidentally released. The worst feature of the gun is the fact that it can be assembled without the locking block. If the gun were fired in this condition, it might injure the shooter and damage the gun.

Quality of workmanship varies a great deal. Prewar guns were well made and finished, but wartime production guns are usually poorly finished.——■

Nambu Pattern 14 8 mm. Automatic

PISTOL MAGAZINES

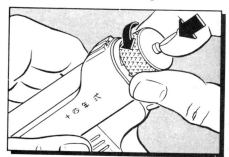

1 To field strip gun, first remove magazine. Then pull back bolt to clear chamber, but not enough to cock weapon. Ease bolt forward. Press in firing pin extension (7) protruding through cocking piece (6) and unscrew cocking piece. Shake out firing pin spring (8)

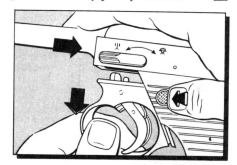

2 Rotate safety catch (22) to fire position as shown. Press magazine catch (24) in as far as it will go. Hold back barrel extension (2) or press muzzle against a solid surface. Pull down hard on trigger guard (19) until it is free of frame and lift barrel extension (2) out of frame

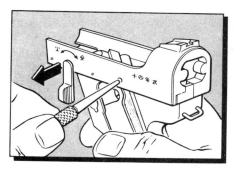

3 To remove safety catch (22) first remove left grip (29). Use a small punch to push out trigger bar hinge pin (12). This will allow trigger bar (27) and trigger bar spring (28) to drop out. Rotate safety catch to down position and pull it out of frame

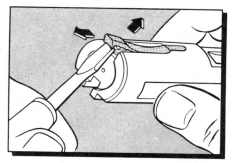

4 The method of retaining the extractor is a great deal like that of the Model 1900 Luger. To remove extractor (3), use a small screwdriver to push front free of retaining hole in bolt (4), then pry it forward, out of bolt

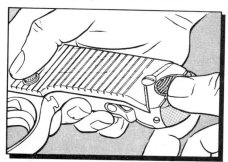

5 On early Type 14 pistols a loaded magazine will drop out of the gun if magazine catch is accidentally pushed. To prevent this, a friction spring was riveted to front strap of grip. This spring bears on magazine and holds it until deliberately pulled out

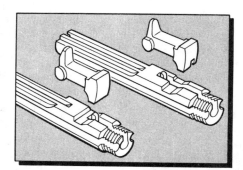

6 Although early and late Type 14's may look alike, parts are not necessarily interchangeable. The early type has a solid bolt lock and a long firing pin. The later, more common type, has a much shorter firing pin (9) and a grooved locking block (11) that allows the short firing pin to pass through it

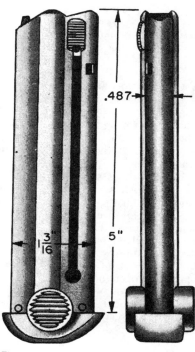

The Pattern 14 (1925) Nambu magazine is so distinctive that it is hard to miss it. Like all Japanese pre-war guns, the Nambu is well made and finished. It shoots a special 8 mm. bottle-neck cartridge that resembles a .30 cal. Luger.

The magazine is easily recognized by the heavy cast base with the serrated finger grips. This magazine should not be confused with the Model 1914 Nambu magazine. The finger grip on the 1914 magazine is checked, not serrated as on the Pattern 14.

Another distinctive feature of the Nambu Pattern 14 magazine is the loading button that depresses the follower for easy loading.
—E. J. HOFFSCHMIDT

Ortgies
Pocket Pistol

By E. J. Hoffschmidt

O RTGIES pistols are among the most common of the early German pocket pistols. They were extremely popular in Germany and central Europe in the 1920's-30's and large numbers were exported to the Americas during this period.

Heinrich Ortgies set up shop during 1919 in Erfurt, Germany. His guns, produced within the framework of the Versailles Treaty, were not classified as military weapons. The cal. .32 model was well received because of its compact design and low price. In 1920, the Deutsche Werke of Erfurt took over the production of the Ortgies. The cal. .32 pistol was followed by the smaller scale cal. .25 model. Around 1922 they brought out the cal. .380. At this point the design changed a bit and many of the .380 (9 mm. short) Ortgies will be found with an additional thumb-operated safety catch. Somewhere around 1926, production ceased.

Although the design contains 4 hinge pins, there is not a screw in the gun. The grips are retained by a clever spring-loaded catch. The barrel is rigidly fixed to the frame but can be easily removed for cleaning or replacement. It is interesting to note that the Ortgies does not have a fixed ejector. After the extractor has pulled the case from the chamber, the firing pin protrudes through the bolt face to eject it.

The cal. .25, cal. .32, and some models of the .380 have only one safety catch. This safety is of the squeeze type and protrudes only when the firing pin is cocked. Although the disconnector design is very clever it subjects the end of the disconnector to appreciable wear.

Due to the simple blowback action, takedown procedure is easy and uncluttered. The gun can be reassembled just as easily once the trick of restraining the firing pin assembly is known.

E. J. HOFFSCHMIDT *is an artist-illustrator and amateur gunsmith*

Parts Legend

1. Slide
2. Extractor pin
3. Extractor
4. Extractor spring
5. Firing pin spring guide
6. Firing pin spring
7. Firing pin
8. Right grip
9. Grip safety
10. Magazine catch
11. Magazine catch spring
12. Grip latch
13. Magazine
14. Grip safety hinge pin
15. Magazine and grip latch hinge pin
16. Left grip
17. Takedown catch
18. Takedown catch spring
19. Trigger spring plunger
20. Trigger spring
21. Trigger
22. Trigger pin
23. Frame
24. Barrel
25. Recoil spring
26. Disconnector
27. Disconnector spring
28. Sear
29. Sear spring

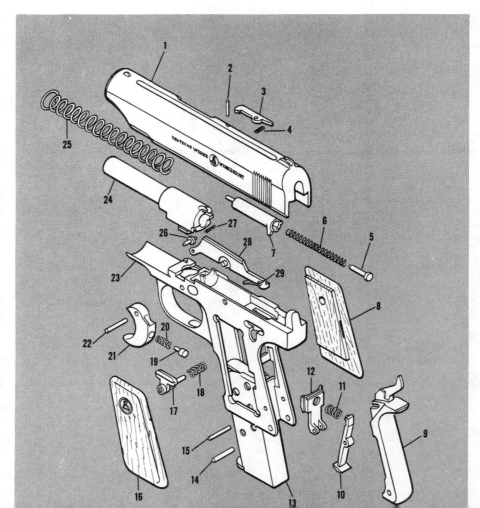

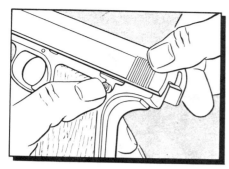

1 Remove magazine (13). Pull slide (1) back until slide serrations line up approximately with end of frame as shown. Push in takedown catch (17) and lift end of slide free of frame. Push slide forward off barrel

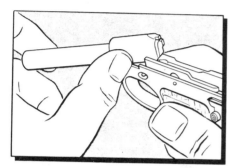

2 To remove barrel (24) for cleaning or repair, grasp barrel (24) and frame (23) as shown. Twist barrel counterclockwise until it is at right angles to frame and lift up

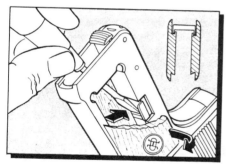

3 To remove grips, insert a screwdriver into magazine well and push grip latch (12) in toward backstrap. At same time pry or push up back edge of grips and rotate them free of undercut on front edge of grip

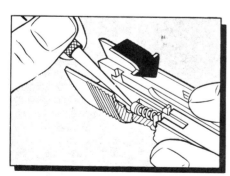

4 Ortgies reassembles easily once firing pin (7) is held in check. Push firing pin spring (6) and guide (5) into firing pin until end of guide can be pushed into its notch in top of slide. Hook slide over barrel, pull it to rear and downward——

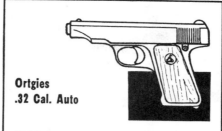

Ortgies .32 Cal. Auto

PISTOL MAGAZINES

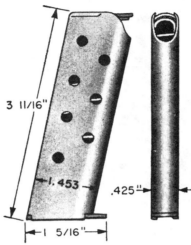

Ortgies automatics are one of the commonest German pocket pistols in the Americas. They were imported into North and South America in great quantities before World War II. Aside from being very compact guns, the pistols have few notable features. Finish is generally excellent and takedown is simple—once you get the knack of it. Ortgies were made in .25, .32, and .380 cal. Only the .32 cal. magazine is illustrated here, since it is by far the most common.

Ortgies magazines are generally stamped as shown with the Deutsche Werke insignia and the caliber. At times, the same insignia and caliber markings will be found on the side of the magazine. The large tabs that retain the floorplate are another key to identification.

Even though the follower is formed of sheet steel, the magazine is very well made. Though the guns are normally blued, the magazines are almost always chrome- or nickel-plated.—E. J. HOFFSCHMIDT.

Rheinmetall Cal. .32 Pocket Pistol

PISTOL MAGAZINES

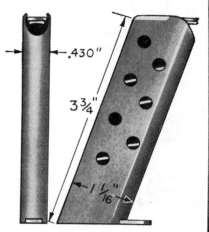

After World War I, the German Rheinmetall firm found its Dreyse pocket pistol to be outclassed by the postwar designs. So the Rheinmetall pocket pistol was brought out to replace the Dreyse. While not too popular, the Rheinmetall was a unique design with a very simple takedown, plus one of the simplest sear mechanisms and disconnectors yet designed. The outline is clean without sharp projections to snag in the pocket. Although well finished on the outside, the internal machining and finish are not good.

Rheinmetall magazines are not easy to distinguish, except that they are usually nickel-plated and have observation holes only on the right side; the left side is blank. The magazine follower is sheet metal and the cutout in the backstrap has a slight concavity.

The floorplate is generally longer and thinner than average. The fact that the extension portion of the floorplate is necked down may be of some help in identifying this magazine.—EDWARD J. HOFFSCHMIDT

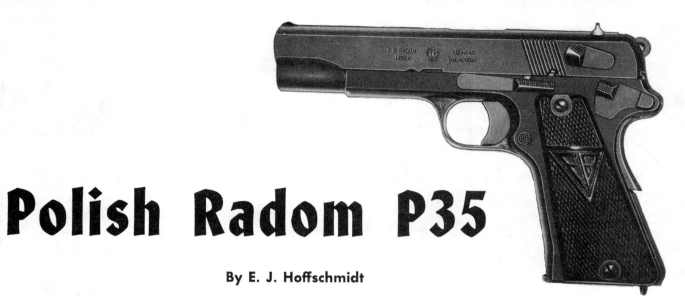

Polish Radom P35

By E. J. Hoffschmidt

LEGEND

A—Slide
B—Rear sight
C—Extractor
D—Firing pin spring
E—Firing pin
F—Magazine catch spring guide
G—Magazine catch spring
H—Magazine catch
I—Hammer strut pin
J—Hammer
K—Hammer strut
L—Grip safety
M—Trigger
N—Sear spring
O—Main spring cap
P—Main spring
Q—Main spring retainer pin
R—Main spring housing
S—Magazine
T—Main spring housing pin
U—Grip screw bushing
V—Left-hand grip
W—Grip screw
X—Take-down latch
Y—Sear and disconnector pin
Z—Hammer pin
AA—Slide stop
BB—Frame (receiver)
CC—Recoil spring
DD—Slotted recoil spring guide
EE—Spring guide retainer pin
FF—Auxiliary recoil spring
GG—Recoil spring stop
HH—Recoil spring guide
II—Barrel
JJ—Hammer lowering catch
KK—Hammer catch operating spring
LL—Firing pin retainer plate
MM—Disconnector
NN—Sear

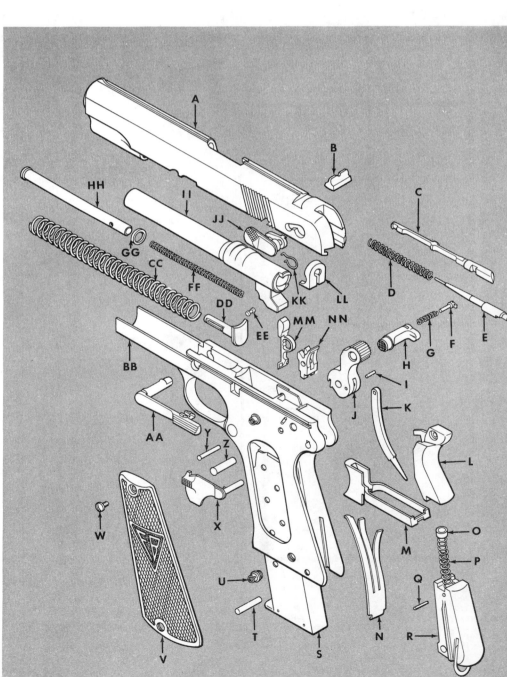

IT IS interesting to note that in almost every country that the German armies overran, they were faced with weapons designed by the ingenious John Browning. Poland was no exception, for it was there that the Germans had their first run-in with the 9 mm. Radom P35 automatic pistol.

In 1935, with the help of Fabrique Nationale engineers, Poland started production of what might be termed a modernized version of the Colt 1911 automatic pistol. The guns were manufactured at the government arsenal at Radom in central Poland. Like the vast majority of pre-war European guns, they were well made and finely finished. Pre-war pistols can be recognized easily by the large Polish eagle crest that is engraved on the slide; also, by the absence of the tool marks that are found on war-time P35's. These pre-war guns are rather scarce, since most of the guns that found their way over here were manufactured under German occupation. Many of the occupation guns were manufactured without the take-down latch, making the gun rather difficult to field-strip.

The gun weighs 2 pounds, 3 ounces, is 8 1/32 inches long, and is strong enough to handle any of the Service 9 mm. Luger cartridges manufactured today or used during World War II.

Radom pistols closely resemble the Colt 1911 or, even more, the Colt Commander with its round hammer and short spur on the grip safety. The main mechanical difference is the use of a captive recoil spring and the barrel locking device. The gun has a locked action that is unlocked by recoil like the .45 automatic, but, in place of the link at the breech end, there is substituted a cam projection to unlock the barrel from the slide.

The use of a captive recoil spring is one of the best features of this gun. It is pre-loaded and fixed to a recoil spring guide, making it very easy to remove or install. Another novel feature of the Radom P35 is the hammer lowering device. A large thumb catch is found on the left side of the slide, back near the hammer. If you wish to lower the hammer when it is cocked, press the thumb catch down hard. The hammer will fall but will not fire the cartridge in the chamber because the thumb catch moved the firing pin out of the way before tripping the hammer.

Another novel but deceiving feature is the take-down latch. This latch is often mistaken for a safety. It is in no way a safety; it merely locks the slide back for disassembly.

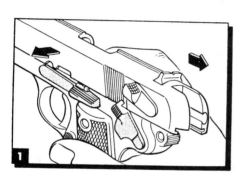

Remove the magazine, draw back the slide far enough to put on the take-down latch (X). Pull forward on the exposed end of the recoil spring guide (HH) to relieve the tension on the slide stop (AA). At the same time, push out the slide stop. Release the take-down latch and draw the slide assembly off the front of the receiver. (If pistol has no take-down latch, retract the slide, depress hammer-lowering catch, and ease slide forward until catch engages notch on hammer.)

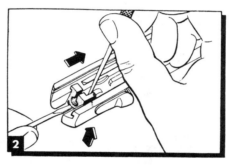

To remove the firing pin (E), first remove the firing pin retainer plate (LL). Due to the split construction, the retainer plate sometimes gets wedged into the slide. So, insert a thin-bladed screwdriver as shown. Push in the firing pin (E) with a thin punch far enough to catch the shoulder on the pin and hold it out of the bushing, while prying the retainer plate down and out of the slide.

To remove the extractor (C), pull out the recoil spring assembly (CC through HH) and disengage the barrel (II) from the slide. Remove the firing pin retainer plate (LL). Using a small screwdriver, press the extractor (C) outward toward the outside of the slide, pressing rearward at the same time. Remove the extractor through the rear of the slide.

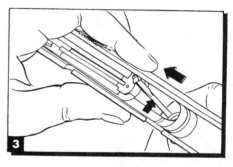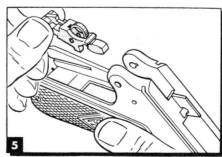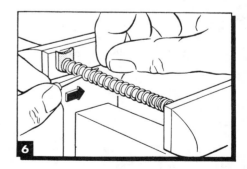

To remove the take-down latch (X), first cock the hammer. Hold the receiver (BB) as shown to depress the grip safety (L). Pull the take-down latch out slightly and turn it up as shown. To remove the latch, it may be necessary to wiggle it or move the safety slightly to free the pin. When the latch is removed, the grip safety (L) will drop free.

The sear (NN) and disconnector (MM) will drop out when the sear and disconnector pin (Y) is removed. To reassemble, place the pieces together as shown. Drop the tail of the disconnector into the hole in the receiver (BB). If the bearing holes in the parts do not line up with the hole in the receiver, pull the trigger a bit. This will usually line up the holes.

The recoil spring on this gun must be removed as an assembly. To disassemble the recoil spring group (CC through HH), squeeze the assembly slowly in a vise until the slotted recoil spring guide (DD) is in as far as it can go. Now, using a thin punch, push out the spring guide retainer pin (EE). It may be necessary to spread the coils of the spring to remove the pin.

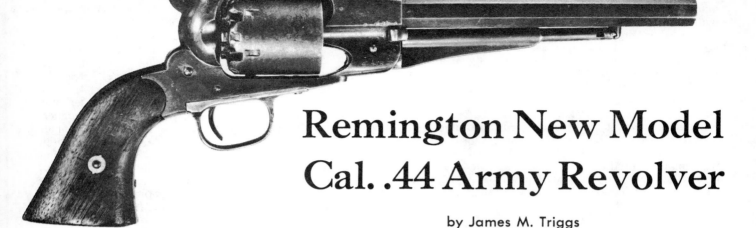

Remington New Model Cal. .44 Army Revolver

by James M. Triggs

Parts Legend

1. Main frame
2. Barrel
3. Front sight
4. Barrel stud
5. Cylinder pin
6. Cylinder
7. Nipples (6)
8. Loading lever screw
9. Loading lever
10. Latch pin
11. Latch
12. Latch spring
13. Front plunger link pin
14. Plunger link
15. Rear plunger link pin
16. Plunger
17. Trigger and cylinder stop spring

18. Trigger and cylinder stop spring screw
19. Cylinder stop
20. Trigger
21. Trigger and cylinder stop screw
22. Hammer
23. Hammer screw
24. Hammer roll
25. Hammer roll pin
26. Hand and hand spring assembly
27. Hand screw
28. Grip screw
29. Grips (2)
30. Grip pin
31. Mainspring set screw
32. Mainspring
33. Trigger guard
34. Trigger guard screw

THE cal. .44 6-shot Remington New Model Army percussion revolver, introduced in 1863, was a Civil War U. S. martial arm second only to the Colt in importance. Upon discontinuance of production in 1875, a total of over 140,000 had been manufactured. For the military it was furnished in blue finish, with casehardened hammer and oil-finished walnut grips. The oval trigger guard is of brass. The commercial version of the New Model was blue finished with varnished walnut grips. It was also available plated or engraved

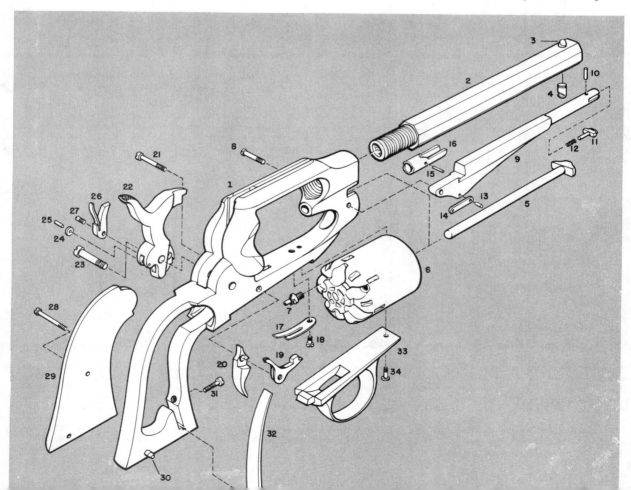

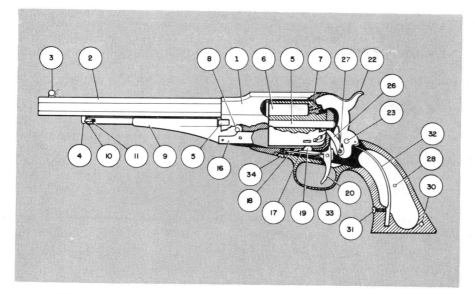

The sectional drawing shows all parts of the assembled revolver

and with pearl or ivory grips at extra cost.

With its 8″ octagon barrel the New Model weighs 2 lbs. 14 ozs. It represents one of the highest developments of the percussion revolver. A noteworthy design feature is the provision of hammer recesses between the nipples which permitted it to be carried safely fully loaded with hammer down. It was regularly used with combustible cartridges but was also conveniently loaded with loose powder and ball.

The cal. .36 6-shot Remington New Model Navy revolver, also introduced in 1863, is mechanically similar and was regularly furnished with 7⅜″ full octagon barrel. Total weight is 2 lbs. 10 ozs. Military and commercial versions were finished to same specifications as the Army revolver. Over 32,-000 of the cal. .36 revolver were produced from 1863 until its discontinuance in 1888.

DISASSEMBLY PROCEDURE

Pull backward on latch (11) and drop loading lever (9) down. Draw cylinder pin (5) out to front. Cylinder (6) may be withdrawn from main frame (1) to right by pulling back hammer slightly. Remove loading lever screw (8) and pull loading lever (9) and plunger (16) assembly to front and out of main frame. Remove grip screw (28) and grips (29). Loosen mainspring set screw (31) and tap mainspring (32) out of its seat in frame. Remove trigger guard screw (34) and drop trigger guard (33) out bottom of frame. Trigger and cylinder stop spring screw (18) and spring (17) may be removed from bottom of frame. Remove trigger and cylinder stop screw (21) and pull trigger (20) and cylinder stop (19) out from bottom of frame. Remove hammer screw (23) and pull hammer down from bottom of frame far enough so that

head of hand screw (27) on left side of hammer is exposed. Remove hand screw and pull hand and spring assembly (26) down and out bottom of frame. Hammer may now be removed from top of frame. Reassembly is accomplished in reverse order.

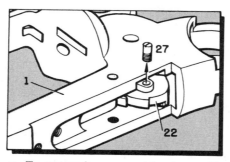

1 To remove hammer and hand assembly from main frame, remove hammer screw (23) and pull hammer (22) down and out bottom of frame until head of hand screw (27) is exposed. Removal of hand screw will allow removal of hand and spring assembly (26) from bottom of frame. Pull hammer back up into frame and remove from top of frame

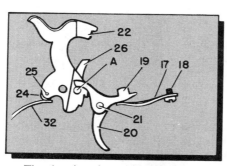

2 The drawing shows the relationship of lock mechanism parts from right when assembled inside frame. Note that cylinder stop cam (A) is integral with hammer and removal should not be attempted ■

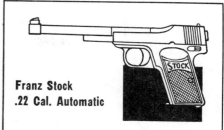

**Franz Stock
.22 Cal. Automatic**

PISTOL MAGAZINES

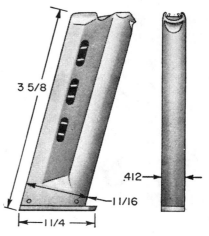

In between wars Franz Stock of Berlin turned out a few interesting pistols. They were made in either .22 or .32 cal. The .22 cal., shown here, while rather scarce contains one or two worthwhile features. The most noteworthy of these is the magazine design. Since .22 cal. bullets (for rimfire cartridges) are not jacketed there is a tendency to shave some lead or deform the bullets during feeding. To overcome this and also to eliminate usual machined guide ramp below the barrel, Stock rounded the front edge of the magazine to act as a cartridge guide.

Stock .22 cal. magazines have the typically German keyhole-shaped cross section. The floorplate is fitted and pinned as shown, making the magazine very sturdy. Although the guns were blued the magazines were usually chromeplated.

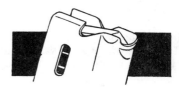

The long observation slots found only on one side of the magazine are an identifying feature, plus the odd-shaped magazine mouth with its rounded cartridge guide.—E. J. HOFFSCHMIDT.

REMINGTON DOUBLE DERRINGER

By James M. Triggs

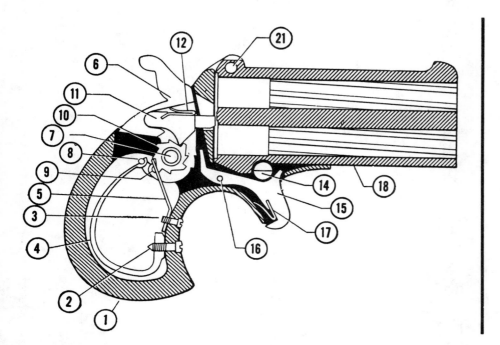

LEGEND

1. Frame
2. Mainspring screw
3. Firing pin ratchet spring screw
4. Mainspring
5. Firing pin ratchet spring
6. Hammer
7. Hammer pin
8. Hammer stirrup
9. Hammer stirrup pin
10. Firing pin ratchet
11. Firing pin
12. Firing pin spring
13. Barrel lock screw
14. Barrel lock
15. Trigger
16. Trigger pin
17. Trigger spring
18. Barrels
19. Ejector
20. Ejector screw
21. Barrel hinge screw
22. Grips (2)
23. Escutcheons (2)
24. Grip screw

THE fact that over 150,000 were eventually manufactured attests to the long-time popularity of the famous .41 caliber Remington Double Derringer pistol. Patented on December 12, 1865, and first offered in 1866, this stubby little 11-ounce three-inch barrel gun was invented in 1864 by William Elliot, a gun designer employed by Remington in 1861. It was *not* designed by Henry Deringer (note the one 'r' in Henry's name), inventor of the equally famous single-shot Deringer pistol. Like the original muzzle-loading D e r i n g e r, Elliot's superposed-barrel breech-loading gun owed its effectiveness to its relatively large caliber. The .41 rimfire cartridge with its blunt-nosed 130-grain lead bullet backed by ten grains of blackpowder was more than adequate.

The Remington Double Derringer,

production of which was discontinued in 1935, is of particular interest to arms collectors since it was offered in a varied assortment of finishes running the gamut from plain blue with hard rubber grips to elaborately engraved versions with ivory, walnut, or pearl grips. Guns plated with silver, gold, or nickel are also frequently encountered in both standard and custom 'presentation grades.

Early Double Derringers are marked (in capital letters) on top of barrel: "E. Remington & Sons, Ilion, N.Y., Elliot's Patent Dec. 12, 1865." Later models are marked (in capital letters): "Remington Arms Co., Ilion, N.Y." or "Remington Arms-UMC Co., Ilion, N.Y.".

DISASSEMBLY PROCEDURE

Turn barrel lock (14) to forward position and swing barrel up to determine that pistol

is unloaded. Remove barrel hinge screw (21) and separate barrel (18) from frame (1). Ejector (19) may be slid out of its slot on left-hand side of barrel after first removing ejector screw (20).

Unscrew grip screw (24) and remove grips (22) from frame. Pull hammer (6) all the way back to cocked position and slip blade of screwdriver between mainspring (4) and inside of frame. Holding mainspring compressed with blade of screwdriver, release hammer slowly at same time shaking or tapping frame slightly to allow hammer stirrup (8) to fall free of its seat at end of mainspring. Unscrew mainspring screw (2) and firing pin ratchet spring screw (3) and remove mainspring (4) and firing pin ratchet spring (5) from frame.

Hammer (6), with firing pin ratchet (10) and firing pin and spring (11 and 12) intact, can be removed from top of frame after drifting out hammer pin (7). The ratchet (10) and firing pin and spring (11

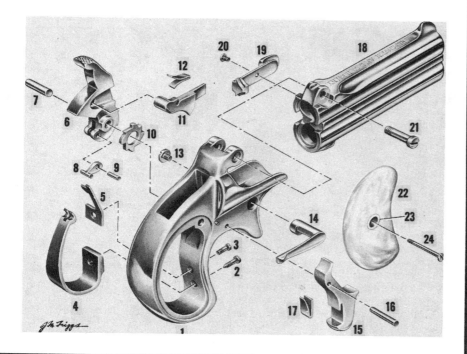

J.H. Triggs

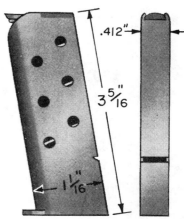

and 12) are easily pulled free of hammer with the fingers. Although not normally disassembled except for replacement, hammer stirrup (8) can be removed by drifting out its retaining pin (9).

Unscrew barrel lock screw (13) and remove barrel lock (14) from right-hand side of frame. Drift out trigger pin (16) and remove trigger (15) and spring (17) intact from top of frame. The small pin projecting from right-hand side of frame between trigger pin hole and hammer pin hole is a retaining or detent stud for the barrel lock and is permanently installed in frame.

Reassemble pistol in reverse order. To reinstall mainspring, replace mainspring and mainspring screw in frame. Replace hammer assembly through top of frame and fit hammer stirrup (8) to end of mainspring (4). Compressing mainspring by use of a screwdriver blade between mainspring and rear of frame will allow hammer to be pressed into position and will line up hammer pin hole in hammer and frame, per-

mitting reentry of hammer pin.

The pistol is shown on page 38 in a profile cross-section with action in fired position, and barrel (18) locked to frame (1) by action of the barrel lock (14). When hammer (6) is drawn back to its rearmost position, the sear end of trigger (15) will engage lower notch on hammer holding it in cocked position until trigger is depressed. As hammer is drawn back, firing pin ratchet spring (5) holds firing pin ratchet (10) in a fixed position. At hammer's rearmost position, lower arm of firing pin (11) drops into cut in ratchet (10)—in this case the deeper cut which allows firing pin to drop into lower barrel chamber on firing.

As hammer falls, ratchet (10) is turned one notch clockwise by forward movement of lower arm of firing pin (11). On again cocking hammer above process is repeated except that arm of firing pin will now rest in more shallow cut in ratchet, thus raising firing pin so that on firing it will drop into upper chamber of barrel.————

REMINGTON MODEL XP-100 PISTOL

Illustrations by JOHN F. FINNEGAN
Text by LUDWIG OLSON

The Remington Model XP-100 single-shot pistol is distinguished by its unorthodox appearance. Designed for hunting varmints and small game, this bolt-action handgun was introduced in 1963. It fires the .221 Remington Fire Ball center-fire cartridge loaded with a 50-gr., pointed soft-point bullet. The muzzle velocity is 2650 f.p.s. (feet per second), which is exceptionally high for a handgun. Muzzle energy is 780 ft.-lbs.

Chiefly responsible for the unusual appearance of this pistol is the rear position of the action, mostly behind the grip. Other features contributing to the unusual appearance are the ventilated barrel rib, long fore-end extending almost to the muzzle of the 10-13/16″ barrel, peculiar forward bend of the bolt handle, and the large flare around the base of the grip.

As with many modern bolt-action rifles, the bolt of the XP-100 has dual-opposed, integral locking lugs which engage shoulders in the receiver ring. The extractor and plunger-type ejector are in the bolt head. A loading groove is milled in the receiver floor. The cartridge is dropped into this groove, and is chambered by closing the bolt.

Cocking is accomplished by cam ac-tion chiefly when the bolt is turned open. The firing pin fall is only ¼″. This short fall and the strong mainspring give fast lock time.

The trigger mechanism is of single-stage design with a light, clean pull. It is screw-adjustable for sear engagement and overtravel after removing the stock. A long bar which Remington calls the trigger link connects the trigger assembly with the sear mechanism at the lower rear of the receiver.

A telescope sight can be fitted to this pistol easily since the receiver top is drilled and tapped for scope mounts. Also, the thumb-operated safety is on the right side of the receiver tang where it does not interfere with low mounting of a scope. The barrel rib is fitted with a flat-top blade front sight and a fully-adjustable, square-notch open rear sight, but the full performance capabilities of the pistol are not realized unless a scope sight is used.

Made of DuPont "Zytel" structural nylon, the walnut-color stock has black wavy streaks which simulate wood grain. Inlaid in the grip bottom and fore-end sides are diamond-shaped, white plastic inlays. The fore-end tip and trigger guard are black plastic. Both sides of the grip are checkered. A thumb rest on each side gives a comfortable grasp for both right- and left-handed users, and facilitates a two-hand hold.

While this pistol is unusual in appearance, it is accurate, reliable, and well suited for its intended purpose. ■

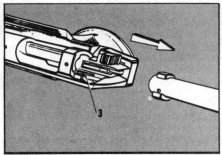

1 To disassemble the pistol, push safety (26) forward, open bolt (2), and remove any cartridge from chamber. Pull bolt rearward until bolt stop (3) is engaged. Push bolt stop downward with small screwdriver or similar tool. Then, pull bolt rearward out of pistol.

2 Hold firing pin head (D) in padded vise. Pull bolt forward and insert washer between firing pin head and bolt plug (A). Then, unscrew firing pin assembly from bolt. Place a metal sleeve (⅜″ diameter, ⅞″ long, with 3/16″ hole through it lengthwise) over front of firing pin (B), and screw bolt plug back into bolt until washer is released. Drive out firing pin cross pin (C) with close-fitting drift punch, and remove firing pin head. Unscrew bolt plug carefully as it is under force of mainspring (E). Remove bolt plug and mainspring from firing pin.

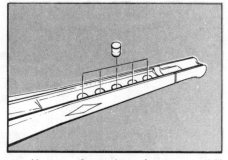

3 Unscrew forward receiver screw (12) and rear receiver screw (15). Remove stock (40). With stock removed, cal. .38 lead bullets can be placed in holes in fore-end to increase weight of pistol. Reassemble in reverse. During reassembly of firing mechanism, place metal sleeve over front of firing pin, reassemble mainspring and bolt plug on firing pin, and screw bolt plug into bolt. Then, replace firing pin head and firing pin cross pin on firing pin. While unscrewing bolt plug, insert coin between bolt plug and firing pin head, complete unscrewing plug, and remove metal sleeve.

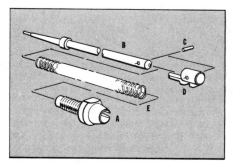

FIRING PIN ASSEMBLY

A. Bolt plug
B. Firing pin
C. Firing pin cross pin
D. Firing pin head
E. Mainspring

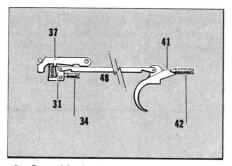

4 Sear block stop screw (34) adjusts engagement of sear block (31) to sear safety cam (37). This engagement should be about .020". Trigger adjusting screw (42) on forward end of trigger housing (46) can be screwed in or out to regulate play of trigger (41).

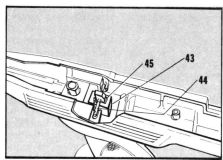

5 Trigger balance (43) must be positioned with large angle on bottom pointing forward. Both ends of trigger balance pin (44) must seat in slots of stock. Trigger balance spring (45) encircles pin on both sides of balance. Ends of spring engage against stock wall to hold balance under tension forward and central in stock. Trigger balance engages through opening in trigger link when stock is reassembled to action.

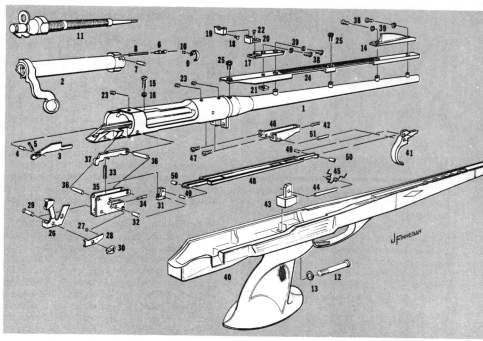

PARTS LEGEND

1. Barrel assembly
2. Bolt assembly
3. Bolt stop
4. Bolt stop pin
5. Bolt stop spring
6. Ejector
7. Ejector pin
8. Ejector spring
9. Extractor
10. Extractor rivet
11. Firing pin assembly
12. Forward receiver screw
13. Forward receiver screw washer
14. Front sight
15. Rear receiver screw
16. Rear receiver screw washer
17. Rear sight base
18. Rear sight elevation screw
19. Rear sight eyepiece
20. Rear sight leaf
21. Rear sight nut
22. Rear sight windage screw
23. Receiver plug screw (3)
24. Rib
25. Rib screw (2)
26. Safety assembly
27. Safety detent ball
28. Safety detent spring
29. Safety pivot pin
30. Safety snap washer
31. Sear block assembly
32. Sear block pin
33. Sear block spring
34. Sear block stop screw
35. Sear housing
36. Sear pin (2)
37. Sear safety cam
38. Sight screw (4)
39. Sight washer (4)
40. Stock assembly
41. Trigger
42. Trigger adjusting screw
43. Trigger balance
44. Trigger balance pin
45. Trigger balance spring
46. Trigger housing
47. Trigger housing screw (2)
48. Trigger link
49. Trigger link pin (2)
50. Trigger link roller (2)
51. Trigger pin

A rotary ratchet/firing pin allowed the Remington-Elliot to fire its four or five chambers. A four-shot version is shown.

Remington-Elliot Repeaters

BY JOHN KARNS

In 1861 the firm of E. Remington & Sons brought out its first fixed cartridge handgun that collectors now call the Zig-Zag derringer.

It was a six-shot .22 Short ring-trigger "pepperbox" with straight index slots and diagonal grooves on the rear of its revolving barrel cluster. The grooves guided the cluster in its rotation and account for the pistol's name.

This was only the first of three William H. Elliott-patented ring-trigger pistols that Remington made, and it was soon replaced by the more common Remington-Elliots with non-rotating barrels here described.

The "new" .22 and .32 rimfire Remingtons, advertised as "Elliot's Pocket Repeaters," were introduced in 1863 and differed from the Zig-Zag in that their barrel clusters did not revolve but depended on a rotating firing pin assembly for repetitive firing.

Production is said to have continued until 1888 (Flayderman estimates a total production of about 25,000 pieces including both calibers), but the last factory listing noted in this research appeared in an 1876 flyer. There, in very small print, the five-shot .22 was listed at $8 (blue), $8.50 (nickel-plated frame) and $9 (full plate). Engraving was available for $4 extra and ivory or pearl stocks could be had, instead of the standard hard rubber, at premiums of $4 and $6 respectively.

The four-shot .32 cal. version was listed in the same finishes at $.50 more, with the engraving and fancy stock options priced the same.

The .22 and .32 each work in the same way. Sliding the barrel latch forward allows the barrel cluster to be tipped down for loading or manual extraction.

A forward stroke of the index finger in the trigger's ring sets the mechanism for firing.

This engages the hand with the front notch of the hammer to permit a double-action trigger pull. As the trigger is set in the ready position and pulled rearward, the hammer is rotated down, compressing the mainspring as the pawl engages and rotates the firing pin assembly to the next chamber.

As the trigger nears full stroke the connecting link lifts the hand and releases the hammer, completing the firing sequence. The trigger, once moved forward to the ready position, can be released without firing by depressing the connecting link located between the ring-trigger and the guard spur. This raises the hand to disengage the hammer notch and permits the trigger to be retracted to its rearward position for safe carrying.

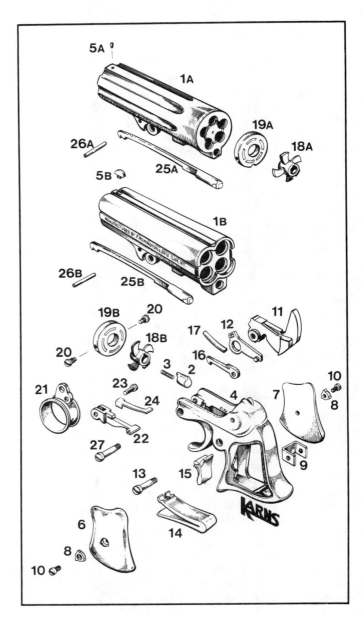

Disassembly Instructions

Pull out the sliding latch (25) and pivot the barrel cluster down to insure the gun is not loaded.

Remove the left grip panel screw (10) to detach both panels (6&7) and their retainer (9).

Next remove the trigger screw (27) that will free the barrel cluster (1) from the frame (4).

To remove the sliding latch (25) drift out its retaining pin (26) and slip the latch forward out of its recess in the barrel cluster.

Now remove both recoil plate screws (20) and invert the gun to cause the recoil plate (19), ratchet (18), firing pin (2) and its spring (3) to be displaced.

Next depress the mainspring (14). Note: This "V" style spring is very strong and a mainspring vise or locking grip pliers may be required to accomplish this (**Fig. 1**). With the mainspring (14) depressed, disengage the front cover plate (15) from the mainspring hooks and remove it from the grip frame. Slowly release the compressed mainspring and remove it to the front and out.

Now the hammer screw (13) may be easily removed to release both the hammer and trigger link assemblies. Raise the hammer assembly (11, 12, 16 & 17) to disengage the lug of the sear connecting link (22) from the hand (12) and withdraw the trigger assembly (21, 22, 23 & 24) down and out. Now the hammer assembly may be lifted out of the frame. This completes disassembly. Note the relationship of these assemblies as they are removed from the frame to facilitate reassembly. Complete disassembly of either the trigger or hammer sub-groups is not recommended unless repair or replacement is required. Both the pawl and the sear connecting link are staked in place. (**Fig. 2**).

Reassembly Tips

Both the hammer and trigger sub-groups must be assembled and installed in the frame together. First insert the hammer into the frame from the top and hold the pivot area above the barrel channel. Now position the pawl with its spring over the elevated pivot area on the left side of the hammer and lower it into the recess in the frame. Next insert the trigger assembly into the frame from the bottom and engage the lug on the connecting link in the hole in the hand as it is lowered into the frame. Now insert the hammer and trigger screws to retain their respective sub-assemblies in position to facilitate further reassembly (**Fig. 3**). Position the mainspring in the grip frame from the front. With a mainspring vise compress the spring to insert the front cover in its slot in the front of the grip frame and engage the hammer. Now, while supporting the cover in this position, slowly release the mainspring to allow the lower edge of the cover to engage the mainspring hooks.

With the firing pin and its spring positioned in the ratchet, insert this assembly into the face of the frame. Install the recoil plate with the oval notch down in the center of the frame. Align the holes in the recoil plate with frame and install retaining screws.

Insert the sliding latch in the channel of the barrel cluster and install its retaining pin. Next withdraw the trigger screw to mount the barrel assembly on the frame. Align the holes in the trigger, barrel and frame and reinsert the trigger screw. Replace the right grip panel and the grip panel retainer. Be sure the retainer is positioned so that it does not interfere with the hammer or the mainspring. Install the left grip panel last because the clockwise rotation of the screw will prevent the retainer from rotating up against the hammer which could restrict its throw and prevent the gun from firing. This completes reassembly. ∎

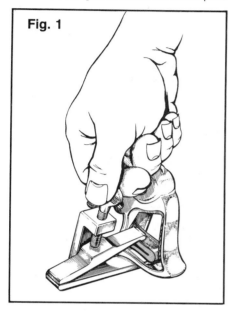

Fig. 1

Parts Legend

1A. Barrel cluster .22
1B. Barrel cluster .32
2. Firing pin
3. Firing pin spring
4. Frame
5A. Front sight bead .22
5B. Front sight blade .32
6. Grip panel (left)
7. Grip panel (right)
8. Grip panel escutcheons (2)
9. Grip panel retainer
10. Grip panel screws (2)
11. Hammer
12. Hammer connecting hand
13. Hammer screw
14. Mainspring
15. Mainspring front cover
16. Pawl
17. Pawl spring
18A. Ratchet .22
18B. Ratchet .32
19A. Recoil plate .22
19B. Recoil plate .32
20. Recoil plate screws (2)
21. Ring trigger
22. Sear connecting link
23. Sear rivet
24. Sear spring
25A. Sliding latch .22
25B. Sliding latch .32
26A. Sliding latch pin .22
26B. Sliding latch pin .32
27. Trigger screw

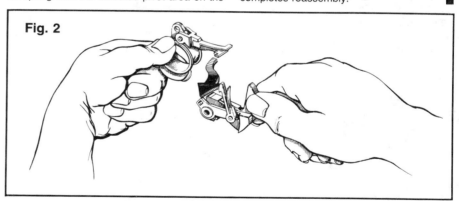

Fig. 2

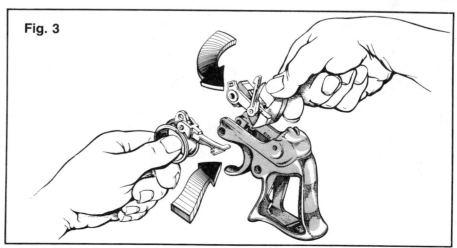

Fig. 3

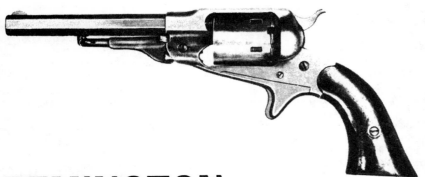

REMINGTON NEW MODEL POCKET REVOLVER

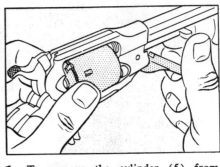

1 To remove the cylinder (5) from either percussion model or cartridge model, pull hammer back to half cock position. Pull loading lever (27) down far enough to allow cylinder pin (3) to be withdrawn. When pin is all the way forward, push cylinder out from left to right. If cylinder will not come out, check to see if loading lever is down too far. If it is, it may have pushed the rammer into one of the chambers

By EDWARD J. HOFFSCHMIDT

THE Civil War proved the effectiveness of the metallic cartridge over the cap-and-ball system. Not long afterward the major gun companies revised their lines and adopted the new rimfire cartridges. Remington began by converting their military revolvers to handle metallic cartridges. In most cases the conversions were such that the gun could not be readily converted back to shoot loose powder and ball or combustible cartridges.

The Remington New Model Pocket Revolver conversion is unique in this respect. It started out as a cal. .31 percussion arm. For conversion to metallic cartridges, a clever 2-piece cylinder was designed. It consisted of a 5-shot cylinder bored through from end to end, and a back-plate. The cylinder was counterbored to recess the heads of the cartridges. A back-plate that contained the cylinder rotating ratchet was loosely pinned to the end of the cylinder. The plate was machined to allow the hammer to hit only the rim of the cartridge. Safety notches were provided between the firing notches. When the gun was

loaded, the hammer rested on one of the safety notches.

Since the conversion retained the rammer assembly, it was a simple matter to switch back to cap-and-ball loading. The shape of the hammer was such that the lower portion fired the percussion caps, while the upper lip fired the metallic cartridge, depending on which cylinder was installed.

The New Model Pocket Revolver was first marketed around 1863 and proved fairly popular. The conversion system worked so well that the gun was offered as a combination gun until around 1888.

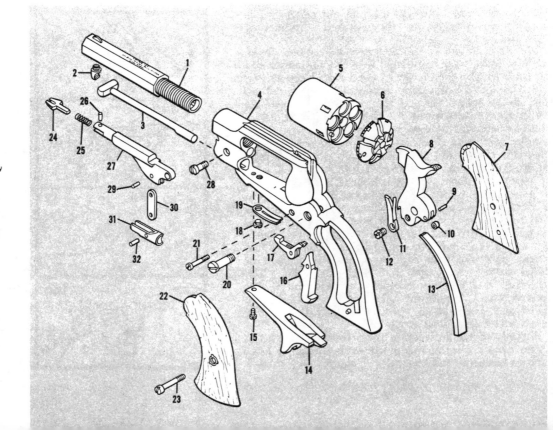

Parts Legend

1. Barrel
2. Rammer latch
3. Cylinder pin
4. Frame
5. Cylinder
6. Cylinder back-plate
7. Right grip
8. Hammer
9. Roller pin
10. Roller
11. Hand
12. Hand retaining screw
13. Mainspring
14. Trigger guard
15. Trigger guard screw
16. Trigger
17. Cylinder stop
18. Trigger spring screw
19. Trigger spring
20. Hammer screw
21. Trigger screw
22. Left grip
23. Grip screw
24. Loading lever latch
25. Latch spring
26. Latch pin
27. Loading lever
28. Lever screw
29. Lever link pin
30. Link
31. Rammer
32. Rammer link pin

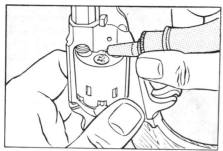

2   To load the cap-and-ball model, first fire a cap on each nipple to clear it. Then hold gun as shown, and throw a charge of FFg blackpowder into the chamber; place a cal. .31 ball on top and rotate the chamber under the rammer. Never, under any circumstances, load the gun with smokeless powder

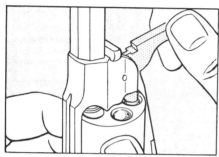

3   When the ball is under rammer (31), pull down loading lever (27) until it presses ball well below edge of chamber. If ball protrudes it will interfere with rotation of cylinder. After all balls are in place, fill remaining area around balls with heavy grease. This will act as a lubricant and prevent a flashover from setting off adjoining chambers. When all is ready, put caps on nipples and drop hammer until it rests in safety notch.

The cartridge version was loaded by removing back-plate (6) and inserting 5 rimfire cal. .32 cartridges. The plate was then replaced and cylinder put back in frame

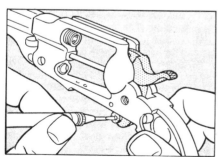

4   The Remington New Model Pocket Revolver is relatively easy to disassemble; but before attempting it, it is wise to place a few drops of penetrating oil on the screws. After trigger guard (14), hammer screw (20), and mainspring have been removed, push hammer down. This will expose screw (12) that retains hand (11). Remove this screw and hand, then hammer can be removed through top of frame (4) ∎

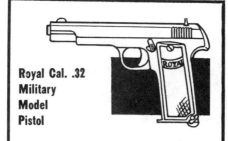

Royal Cal. .32 Military Model Pistol

PISTOL MAGAZINES

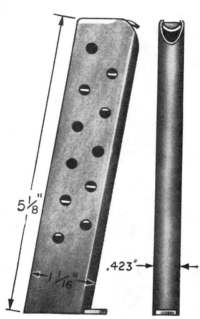

5⅛″

.423″

1 1/16″

The Royal automatic is one of a great number of Spanish imitations of the Browning-Colt pocket pistols. In an effort to make a cal. .32 pocket pistol into an acceptable military gun by European standards, the barrel was lengthened and the magazine capacity increased. The result was an oversized pocket pistol with a 12-shot capacity. Royal pistols are rather crudely machined and finished, but are sturdy. The magazines can be recognized readily by the fact that they are approximately 30% longer than the average pocket pistol magazine.

The follower is about the only distinctive feature of the magazine aside from its length. The tip of the sheet metal follower is generally bent over to facilitate loading and feeding of the cartridges.—EDWARD J. HOFFSCHMIDT

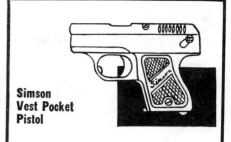

Simson Vest Pocket Pistol

PISTOL MAGAZINES

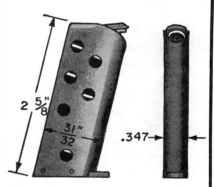

2 ⅝″

31/32″

.347

Simson and Co. of Suhl, Germany, made just about every type gun at one time or another. They made Mauser military rifles and fine sporters, combination guns, and shotguns. They also turned out an interesting little cal. .25 vest pocket pistol of simple design, and very well made. The odd design of the slide puts it high above the shooter's hand so that there is no pinching of the skin between thumb and forefinger, as happens with some of the small pocket automatics. The one serious drawback is the top ejector which can throw the empties up into the shooter's face when the gun is fired from the hip.

Simson clips are made similar to the magazine of the average European cal. .25 pistol. They are not generally marked, but can be partially identified by the thick sheet steel follower with long chisel-like bevel on the front edge.

The floorplate is not removable but is pinned to the magazine sides with 2 small cross pins as shown. The only other recognizable point is the large witness hole near the floorplate which is out of line with all other holes.—EDWARD J. HOFFSCHMIDT

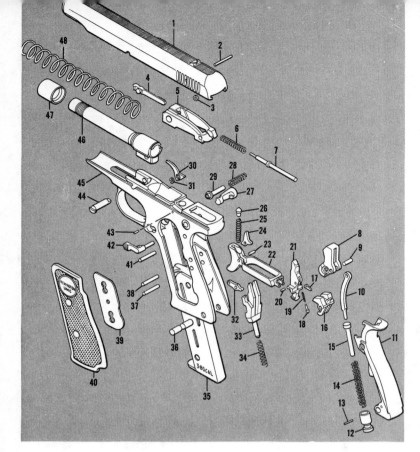

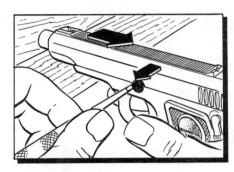

1 To field-strip the Remington, first remove the magazine and empty the chamber. Then push the slide (1) back far enough to align the cut in the slide with the head of the barrel lock pin (44). Push on the end of the pin to start it and pry it out the rest of the way with a screwdriver or the magazine floorplate tip

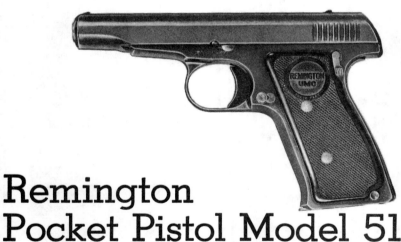

LEGEND

1. Slide	25. Trigger spring
2. Cocking roll pin	26. Trigger spring plunger
3. Cocking roll	27. Magazine lock
4. Extractor	28. Magazine lock spring
5. Breech bolt	29. Magazine lock follower
6. Firing pin spring	30. Ejector
7. Firing pin	31. Ejector spring
8. Hammer	32. Sear lock lever
9. Mainspring rod pin	33. Sear lock
10. Mainspring rod	34. Sear lock spring
11. Grip safety	35. Magazine
12. Mainspring plug	36. Grip safety pin
13. Plug retaining pin	37. Sear lock lever pin
14. Mainspring	38. Sear lock pin
15. Mainspring plunger	39. Stock plate (2)
16. Sear	40. Left-hand stock
17. Disconnector lever	41. Sear pin
18. Disconnector spring plunger	42. Safety lever
19. Disconnector spring	43. Ejector pin
20. Disconnector pin	44. Barrel lock pin
21. Disconnector	45. Receiver
22. Trigger	46. Barrel
23. Trigger pin	47. Action spring bushing
24. Trigger lever	48. Action spring

Remington Pocket Pistol Model 51

By E. J. Hoffschmidt

IT is too bad that Remington stepped out of the pistol business, for their handguns were, and still are, acclaimed far and wide. Their Civil War revolvers were the best of their time, and the little .41 caliber over-and-under derringer blasted itself into history.

Many of these Remington pistols command high prices today, but the Model 51 does not fall into this category. The Model 51 was worked out by John D. Pedersen, designer of the "Pedersen Device" of World War I fame, and the Pedersen semi-automatic rifle. The design incorporates a number of noteworthy features, best of which is the grip outline. This shape was settled on only after hundreds of experiments had been carried out to determine the best grip for the average hand. Since the pistol sits very low in the hand, it has an excellent balance and instinctive pointing ability.

The Model 51 has a full set of safety features. It has a grip safety, a thumb safety, and a magazine safety. The grip safety has a three-fold job, for it acts as a cocking indicator, since it pro-trudes from the grip only when the gun is cocked. It also acts as a hold-open device. When the slide is pulled all the way back, and the grip safety is not interfered with, the disconnector is held up in front of the breech bolt, preventing the slide running forward. When the grip safety is squeezed, it allows the disconnector to drop out of the path of the slide. If there is a cartridge in the magazine, it will chamber it but will not fire it until the trigger is pulled.

Unlike most common pocket automatics, the gun is not a true blowback. It is operated by cartridge setback or by what is sometimes called impinging action. The breech bolt is separate and not a fixed part of the slide. It is locked into a recess in the frame but can recoil in a straight line for a short distance. When the cartridge is fired, the bolt recoils at a high speed, striking the slide. The slide moves to the rear under the impact, lifting the breech bolt free of the locking recess in the frame. It returns during counter recoil, chambering the incoming round, and drops the

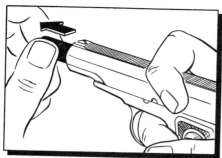

2 Pull back the slide again as shown, and at the same time pull the muzzle of the barrel forward. This will release the slide and barrel (46) from the receiver (45). To reassemble, push the slide assembly back on the receiver until it is stopped by the disconnector (21). Pull the trigger, depress the disconnector, and the slide can be pushed into final position

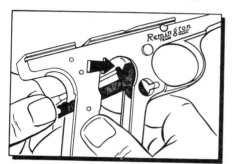

3 The trigger (22) will come out easily during disassembly, but putting it back requires the aid of a small screwdriver. Put the trigger assembly into the frame as shown. Then depress the trigger lever (24) until it can pass under the top surface of the trigger opening in the receiver

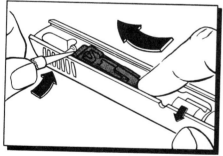

4 To remove the breech bolt (5) and firing pin (7), pull the barrel forward about ⅝ inch. Rotate it counterclockwise until it locks into the slide. Push the breech bolt to the rear and lift up the end as shown. Lift it free of the slide and the firing pin, and the firing pin spring (6) will drop down through the barrel

breech bolt back into its locking recess in the frame. This system makes the gun more pleasant to shoot than straight blowback designs.

Model 51 pistols were first marketed around 1918 and discontinued during 1935. They were made in .32 and .380 ACP calibers, and were well made and well finished. It is interesting to note that even with its outstanding design, a Model 51 could be purchased for $15.75 when the Colt Pocket Model sold for $20.50 and the Smith & Wesson .32 automatic for $33.50.———■

Remington Model 51 Auto

PISTOL MAGAZINES

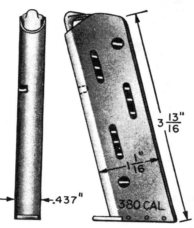

The Remington Pocket Pistol Model 51 is one of the best which has been produced in America. It is extremely compact and well designed, with a grip second to none in its class. The delayed blowback action and the gun's natural pointing abilities make it a pleasure to shoot. Model 51's were made in .32 and .380 cals. The only drawback is the rather awkward method of takedown, and the fact that the sights are rather small and difficult to find in a hurry.

Remington magazines are always marked with their caliber, either .32 or .380. They can also be identified by the convex backstrap on the rear edge of the magazine. The long observation holes in the left side are another guide point.

In keeping with the general excellence of design, the magazine follower is a carefully formed piece of pressed metal. Another point of recognition is the rectangular magazine catch hole in the front edge.—E. J. HOFFSCHMIDT

PISTOL MAGAZINES

Remington .380 Hammer Model Pocket Pistol

During the early stages of its development, an external hammer version of the J. D. Pedersen-designed Remington pocket pistol was produced in limited quantity. While these guns are rare, magazines for them turn up occasionally.

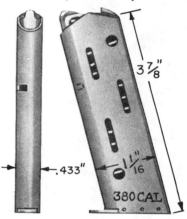

The early hammer model pistol had the same fine grip and finish that characterized the subsequent production arm, the Model 51 hammerless. Although externally similar, there were significant internal design differences in the two pistols.

One of the most notable of these is in the magazines. The magazine for the external hammer pistol has the ejector in the left magazine lip, a design feature dropped in the hammerless production model.

Points of identification in the hammer model magazine are the integral ejector, the elongated slots and holes in the sides, and the ".380 CAL" marking.—E. J. HOFFSCHMIDT

exploded views:

Rossi Princess Revolver

BY PETE DICKEY

Close to a million Rossi .22 Princess revolvers have been made by Amadeo Rossi S.A., of Sao Leopoldo, Brazil, since 1957. The prime market for these seven-shot double-actions has been Brazil and some Central American countries, but when they were imported from late 1965 through 1968 by the now defunct firm of Firearms International Corp., almost 60,000 came into the United States.

Because of its size, importation of what became known here as the Rossi "Ladysmith" ceased after the passage of the 1968 Gun Control Act.

The GCA's import regulations flatly prohibited further U.S. importation of any revolver frame of less than 4½" when measured lengthwise, parallel to the bore line. The Rossi came up 1/4" short.

Had the Zamak frame been made longer, the little double-action revolver would still not have met the BATF's factoring criteria which stipulate that a revolver must accrue 45 "points" to qualify for importation and must have certain "safety" standards. With its transfer bar mechanism, the Rossi easily met the safety standards, but it fell far short on the arbitrary and mysterious point system.

It needed a 4½" barrel length to gain even a single point. The standard barrel lengths were 3" and the more popular 2" (which GCA prohibited regardless of frame size or points).

It got no points for its die cast frame, despite the fact that such a frame in a center-fire revolver passed the BATF-sponsored endurance "tests" with flying colors. Had the frame been of investment cast steel, it would have garnered 15 points; had it been investment cast of aluminum — 20 points.

Since the revolver was a nickel-plated .22 designed primarily for the tackle box or knapsack, it lacked target hammer, trigger, sights and grip plates. Again, no points.

The Long Rifle chambering of the revolver (three points) and its weight, worth a point per ounce to the BATF, gave the 3"-barreled Rossi its final score — a disheartening grand total of 14.

The importers, who sat on a mountain of backorders, were furious that the Rossi could no longer come in, but Rossi couldn't have cared less. The firm had already twice tried to discontinue the Princess in order to concentrate on more profitable and conventional steel-framed .22s, .32s and .38 Spls., which are now imported by Interarms of Alexandria, Va. Rossi's South and Central American customers, however, simply wouldn't permit it to die.

The Princess was an excellent product for its price and purpose. It was cataloged in 1968 at only $38.25, complete with a handsome presentation case. Externally it greatly resembled the .22 Long Smith & Wesson "Ladysmith" (Hand Ejector Third Model), which accounted for its sales appeal, but inside it employed coil springs, a floating firing pin and the excellent Iver Johnson-type transfer bar safety system.

It is noteworthy that in the United States, from 1902 to 1921, only some 26,000 of the "classic" S&W .22 Hand Ejectors in all models were made. More than double this number of Rossis were sold here in only a fifth of that time. ∎

Disassembly Instructions

Begin disassembly by pulling the cylinder lock cap (10) forward and swing the cylinder out to the left. Remove the front side-plate screw (4) which serves to retain the cylinder yoke (12).

Slide the yoke, which holds the cylinder (17) and its parts, forward out of the frame (1). (Fig. A)

Fig. A

Remove both the grip screws (19) and grip plates (20 & 21). Now the three remaining side-plate screws (5, 6 & 7) can be taken out and the side-plate itself (3) will be free. If it is relatively loosely fitted to the frame, it may fall free or may be dislodged by holding the revolver right-side-down and tapping on the grip portion of the frame with a plastic mallet. If it is tightly fitted, it may be necessary to pry it from its

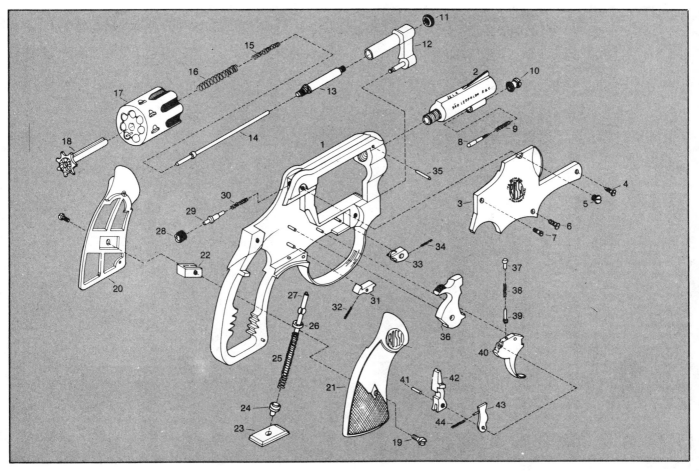

Parts Legend

1. Frame	9. Cylinder lock spring	18. Extractor	27. Mainspring rod	36. Hammer
2. Barrel	10. Cylinder lock cap	19. Grip screws (2)	28. Firing pin cup	37. Trigger plunger
3. Side-plate	11. Extractor rod cap	20. Left grip plate	29. Firing pin	38. Plunger spring
4. Front plate screw	12. Yoke	21. Right grip plate	30. Firing pin spring	39. Plunger spring seat
5. Top plate screw	13. Extractor rod	22. Grip plate spacer	31. Sear	40. Trigger
6. Bottom plate screw	14. Cylinder pin	23. Mainspring plate	32. Sear spring	41. Transfer bar pin
7. Rear plate screw	15. Cylinder pin spring	24. Mainspring stop	33. Cylinder stop	42. Transfer bar
8. Cylinder lock	16. Extractor spring	25. Mainspring	34. Cylinder stop spring	43. Hand
	17. Cylinder	26. Mainspring collar	35. Barrel pin	44. Hand spring

seat with a suitable bar. In either event, great care must be taken to protect the nickel plating. (Fig. B)

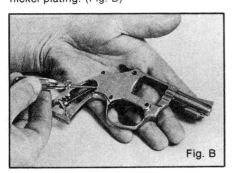

Fig. B

The side-plate removal will expose all the parts of the firing mechanism and, for complete cleaning and maintenance, no further stripping of the frame is necessary.

If it is required that the hand (43) be removed, simply lift it and its spring (44)

straight off its permanently mounted frame stud.

Hammer removal necessitates that the mainspring rod (27) be first pushed down against spring pressure (Fig. C), to free it

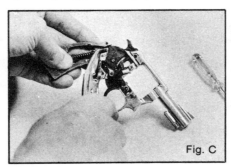

Fig. C

from its seat in the hammer. It is then lifted from the frame. Then the hammer (36) can be partially retracted and lifted from its frame stud. (Fig. D)

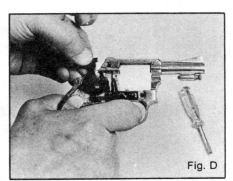

Fig. D

The firing pin (29) may be removed by unscrewing the slotted firing pin cup (28), which will free the firing pin and its spring. Other frame parts removal is obvious, and reassembly is done in reverse order.

Parts for the revolver are still available from Bob's Gun Shop, Box 2332, Hot Spring, Ark. 71901.

Legend

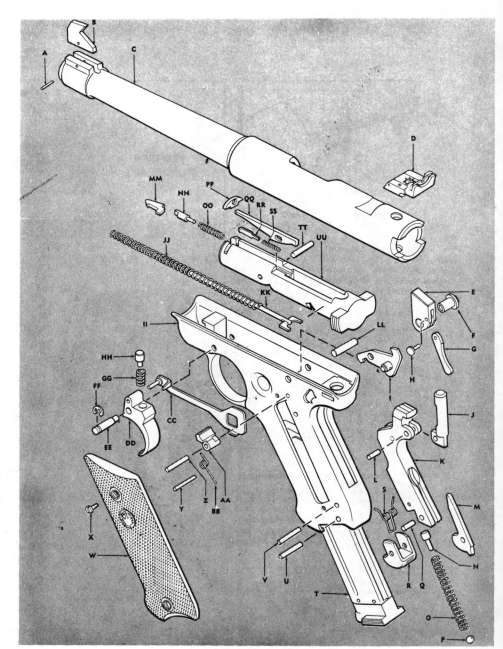

A—Front sight retaining pin
B—Front sight blade
C—Barrel and receiver assembly
D—Micro rear sight
E—Hammer
F—Hammer bushing
G—Hammer strut
H—Hammer strut pin
I—Safety catch
J—Bolt stop pin
K—Main spring housing
L—Bolt stop pivot pin
M—Housing latch
N—Main spring plunger
O—Main spring
P—Detent ball
Q—Housing latch pivot pin
R—Magazine catch
S—Magazine catch spring
T—Magazine
U—Magazine catch pivot pin
V—Magazine catch stop pin
W—Left hand grip

X—Grip screw
Y—Sear spring stop pin
Z—Sear pivot pin
AA—Sear
BB—Sear spring
CC—Disconnector
DD—Trigger
EE—Trigger pivot pin
FF—Trigger pin lock washer
GG—Trigger spring
HH—Trigger spring plunger
II—Frame
JJ—Recoil spring
KK—Recoil spring guide pin
LL—Hammer pivot pin
MM—Extractor
NN—Extractor plunger
OO—Extractor spring
PP—Recoil spring support
QQ—Firing pin
RR—Rebound spring support
SS—Rebound spring
TT—Firing pin stop
UU—Bolt

THE RUGER .22 AUTOMATIC

By E. J. Hoffschmidt

LATE in January of 1949, Southport, Connecticut saw the birth of a new gun company. This happy occasion was the result of months of hard work on the part of Bill Ruger, designer, and the late Alex Sturm, business man. The result of this work was a new Ruger .22 automatic pistol of rather interesting design. Production was begun in a small shop in Southport and the first guns were shipped in October of 1949. By the end of the year over 1,100 guns had been produced and the company was well on its way in the gun field.

About 2,500 pistols were manufactured before the first change of any significance was made. Somewhere between guns number 2,500 and 2,800, the bolt and firing pin were changed to facilitate production. This change did away with the hand fitting that was necessary in the early guns. In 1950 after the standard model had won its spurs, the firm introduced the Mark 1, a target model of the standard gun. The Mark 1 is basically the same as the standard model, with the exception of the heavy barrel and the target sights.

The standard model Ruger resembles a famous military automatic in outline and balance, but the resemblance ends there. The Ruger was designed with modern mass production methods in mind. The gun makes use of numerous well-designed stamped and screw machined parts. The frame of the Ruger .22 Automatic is manufactured in a rather novel manner. Two sides are stamped and pressed to shape, one right hand, and one left hand. These sides are then carefully welded together at the joint to form a complete frame. This procedure is excellent from a manufacturing point of view as it makes for a lightweight receiver and keeps costly machinery time to a minimum; but this procedure also has a drawback. Care must be taken when holding the receiver in a vice, for repairs. Do not apply too much pressure to areas on the receiver that lack cross numbers. Due to the manufacturing procedure used on the Ruger, the barrel and receiver are considered as an assembly. The barrel is screwed tightly against the face of a blank receiver. The barrel and receiver assembly is then machined as a unit.

The Ruger .22 is a blow-back operated automatic pistol. It has proved itself to be an accurate and reliable weapon as well as a target gun. The take-down procedure is simple but a few points must be observed when stripping the gun; be sure the hammer is down resting on the firing pin and the hammer strut (G) is in position to engage the main spring plunger (N) in the main spring housing (K). If strut is not in place, bolt cannot be drawn back. ◊ ◊ ◊

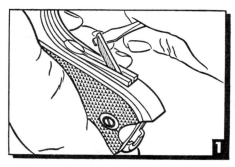

Remove magazine, pull bolt all the way back, release it and snap the trigger to uncock the hammer before attempting to disassemble the gun. Use a piece of plastic or a screw driver to pry the housing latch (M) open fully, then swing main spring housing (K) outward.

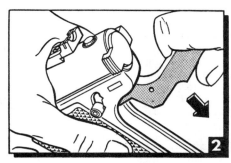

Pull main spring housing (K) down hard, as shown, to disengage bolt stop pin (J) from the receiver. With bolt stop pin removed, the bolt assembly may be withdrawn for cleaning. To disengage barrel and receiver (C) from the frame (II), grasp the barrel and pull it forward

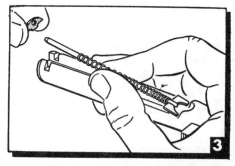

Assembly of bolt requires care, as recoil spring (JJ) is heavily compressed. It can easily be pried out under control, but to replace it hold the recoil spring compressed on spring guide pin (KK), as shown. Slip recoil spring support (PP) on the spring guide and ease it down into bolt.

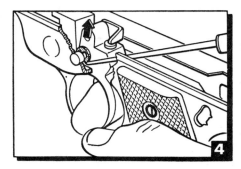

All pins except the staked pins in the main spring housing and the trigger pivot pin (EE) can easily be removed. Before removing the trigger pin, we must pry out the lock washer (FF) that holds the pin in place. Use a long thin rod to pry it upward. The pin can now be pushed out from left to right.

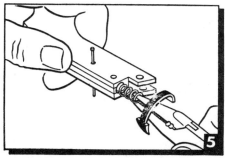

The simplest way to replace the main spring (O) or main spring plunger (N) without special tools is to drill an .062" hole through the main spring housing (K). Insert a wire nail and wind the spring in around it, below the surface, to support the detent ball (P) while pinning the housing latch (M) into place.

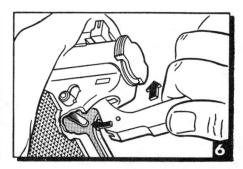

To reassemble, replace bolt. Lay receiver on the frame, ends flush. Push receiver back until it locks into the frame. Hold gun so that hammer rests on firing pin; push the bolt stop pin up through bolt and receiver. Swing main spring housing (K) down to engage the hammer strut. Snap the housing latch shut.

exploded views:

RUGER BEARCAT

BY STEPHEN K. VOGEL

INTRODUCED in 1958, the diminutive Bearcat revolver was a significant departure from earlier Ruger single-action models. Blackpowder enthusiasts will immediately recognize the similarity between the Bearcat's one-piece cylinder/grip frame construction and that of the 1861 Remington percussion revolver. The lockwork of the Bearcat is, however, typically Ruger and incorporates the music wire coil springs and Ruger patent coil spring/plunger cylinder latching mechanism found in the Single-Six and Blackhawk revolvers. Designed for use with standard .22 rimfire cartridges, the Bearcat revolver is dimensioned accordingly.

During its 15-year (1958 to 1973) production history, the design of this revolver remained virtually unchanged. The major difference between the 1958 Bearcat and its final evolution, the Super Bearcat, lies in the frame material. The original Bearcat frame was made of aircraft-quality aluminum. The Super Bearcat frame was constructed of a chrome molybdenum steel alloy.

Disassembly of the Bearcat revolver is simple and straightforward. With the exception of steps which require the compression of springs (i.e., removal and replacement of the trigger guard), no force is required to take apart or reassemble these guns. To avoid damage to the screws or finish (and a substantial reduction in collector value), properly fitting screwdrivers must be used. ∎

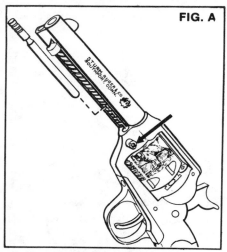

1. Check that revolver is unloaded by retracting hammer (16) two clicks to loading notch, opening loading gate (12) and, while manually rotating cylinder (36), examining each chamber.
2. Depress base pin latch body (7-arrow) and remove base pin (10) and cylinder (36). (Fig. A)

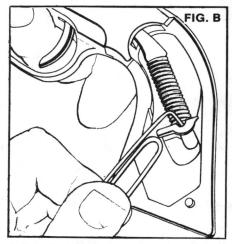

3. Remove ejector housing screw (4), ejector housing (3), rod assembly (5) and spring (6).
4. Remove grip panels (40). Bring hammer (16) to full cock and insert small wire or pin in hole in hammer strut (18). Depress trigger (32) and push hammer fully forward. Do not remove hammer strut (18) and hammer spring (19) at this time. (Fig. B)

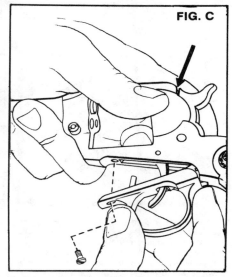

5. Retract the hammer two clicks, remove trigger guard screw (43) and pull trigger guard (42) down and forward until free of trigger. Note position of trigger (32), cylinder latch spring (39) and plunger (38). (Fig. C)

Parts Legend

1. Barrel
2. Front sight
3. Ejector housing
4. Ejector housing screw
5. Ejector rod assembly
6. Ejector spring
7. Base pin latch body
8. Base pin latch nut
9. Base pin latch spring
10. Base pin
11. Frame
12. Gate assembly
13. Gate detent plunger
14. Gate detent spring
15. Gate retaining screw
16. Hammer
17. Hammer pivot
18. Hammer strut
19. Hammer spring
20. Hammer spring seat
21. Hammer plunger
22. Hammer plunger pin
23. Hammer plunger spring
24. Pawl
25. Pawl spring
26. Pawl screw
27. Pawl spring plunger
28. Firing pin
29. Firing pin rebound spring
30. Recoil plate
31. Recoil plate cross pin
32. Trigger
33. Trigger pivot
34. Trigger spring
35. Trigger spring plunger
36. Cylinder
37. Cylinder latch
38. Cylinder latch plunger
39. Cylinder latch spring
40. Grip panel
41. Grip panel screw
42. Trigger guard
43. Trigger guard screw

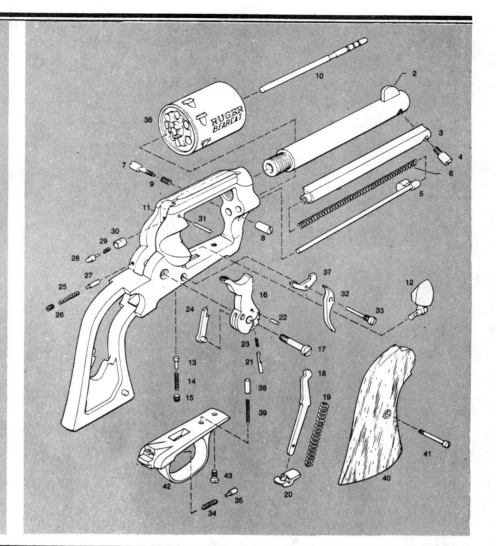

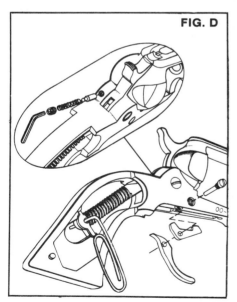

6. With 1/16″ hex wrench, remove pawl screw (26), spring (25) and plunger (27) (Fig. D insert). Remove trigger pivot (33), trigger (32) and cylinder latch (37). (Fig. D)

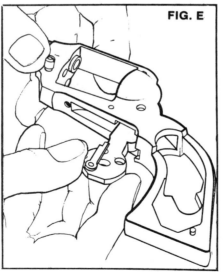

FIG. E

7. Remove the hammer pivot (17) and (without removing the pin or clip holding them together) take from the grip frame the hammer strut (18), spring (19) and seat (20) assembly. Remove hammer (16) and pawl (24). (Fig. E)

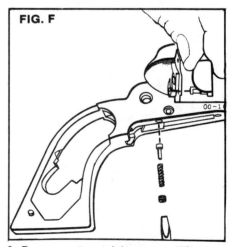

FIG. F

8. Remove gate retaining screw (15), gate detent spring (14) and gate detent plunger (13). This will free the gate assembly (12) which can be pulled forward from its seat in the frame. (Fig. F)

Further disassembly should be attempted only by a competent gunsmith, and reassembly is accomplished by reversing the above procedures.

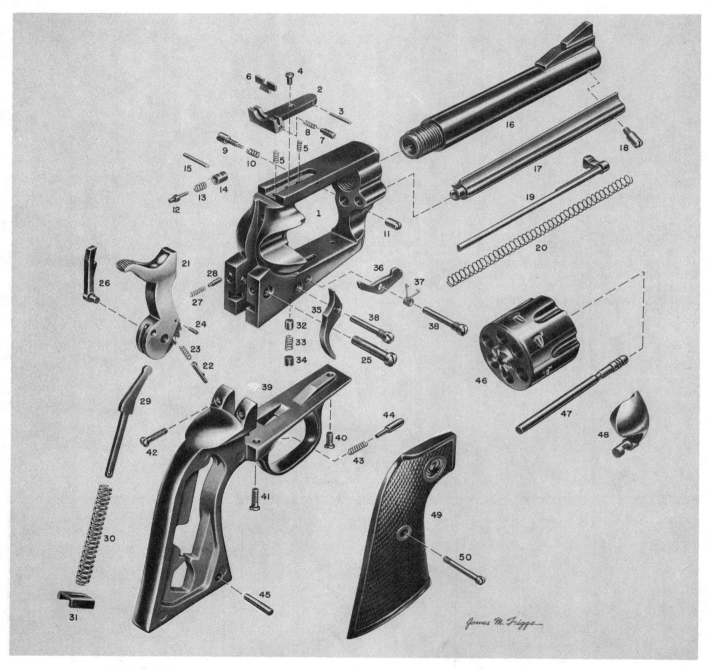

LEGEND

1. Cylinder frame
2. Rear sight
3. Rear sight pivot pin
4. Rear sight elevation screw
5. Rear sight elevation springs (2)
6. Rear sight leaf
7. Rear sight leaf (windage) screw
8. Rear sight leaf spring
9. Base pin latch
10. Base pin latch spring
11. Base pin latch nut
12. Firing pin
13. Firing pin spring
14. Recoil plate
15. Recoil plate retaining pin
16. Barrel
17. Ejector housing
18. Ejector housing screw
19. Ejector rod assembly
20. Ejector spring
21. Hammer
22. Hammer plunger
23. Hammer plunger spring
24. Hammer plunger retaining pin
25. Hammer pivot screw
26. Pawl
27. Pawl spring
28. Pawl spring plunger
29. Hammer strut
30. Mainspring
31. Mainspring seat
32. Gate detent plunger
33. Gate detent spring
34. Gate spring screw
35. Trigger
36. Cylinder latch
37. Cylinder latch spring
38. Trigger and latch pivot screws (2)
39. Grip frame
40. Front grip frame screw
41. Lower grip frame screws (2)
42. Rear grip frame screws (2)
43. Trigger spring
44. Trigger spring plunger
45. Grip pin
46. Cylinder
47. Base pin
48. Gate
49. Grip panels (2)
50. Grip screw

Revolver | By James M. Triggs

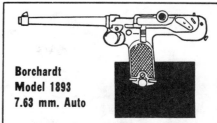

Borchardt Model 1893 7.63 mm. Auto

PISTOL MAGAZINES

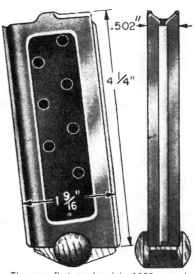

First announced in August 1955, the Ruger Blackhawk single-action revolver in .357 Magnum caliber bears a strong resemblance to the original Colt Single Action Army and Frontier revolver, Model of 1873. Designwise, however, the Blackhawk is a modernized version of its Colt counterpart. The incorporation of virtually unbreakable coil springs in the lockwork is a significant improvement. The ingenious one-piece grip frame of lightweight alloy, massive frame and fully adjustable rear sight are features to delight any shooter. Simplicity of the original Colt design was a strong selling point with the frontiersman and the same holds true for the modern Blackhawk.

In 1973 the original Blackhawk was replaced by a "New Model Blackhawk", featuring a transfer-bar between the hammer and the firing pin. Subsequently the Ruger factory undertook a program to modify older Blackhawks to incorporate the new mechanism.

DISASSEMBLY

Pull hammer (21) to half-cock, press in base pin latch (9) from left, and withdraw base pin (47) from cylinder frame (1). Open loading gate (48) and withdraw cylinder (46).

Remove grip panels (49) and cock hammer fully. Insert a nail or pin into the small hole at the lower end of the hammer strut (29). This pin will confine the mainspring (30) when the hammer is released. Remove the five grip frame screws (40, 41, 42) which fasten the grip frame (39) to the cylinder frame. In separating the grip frame from the cylinder frame, take care to prevent loss of the pawl spring (27) and plunger (28) which are located in a hole in the rear of the cylinder frame, adjacent to the upper left rear grip frame screw hole.

Remove the hammer pivot screw (25)

and the hammer from the cylinder frame. Remove the trigger pivot screw (38) and trigger (35). With a small screwdriver free the fixed leg of the cylinder latch spring (37). Remove the cylinder latch pivot screw (38), cylinder latch (36), and spring (37). Remove trigger spring (43) and plunger (44) from hole in grip frame, taking care not to deform the spring. Hammer plunger (22) and spring (23) may be removed from the hammer by drifting out the small retaining pin (24). Unscrew base pin latch (9) and remove base pin latch nut (11) and spring (10). The gate (48) may be removed from the cylinder frame by removing the gate spring screw (34) and dropping out the gate detent spring (33) and gate detent plunger (32).

To disassemble the rear sight assembly drift out the rear sight pivot pin (3) and remove the rear sight elevation screw (4). Remove the rear sight (2) from the cylinder frame using care not to lose the elevation springs (5). The rear sight leaf (6) and spring (8) may be removed by unscrewing the rear sight leaf windage screw (7).

Remove the ejector housing screw (18) and withdraw the ejector assembly from the barrel (16) and cylinder frame. The ejector rod assembly (19) may now be removed from the ejector housing (17).

The recoil plate (14), firing pin (12), and firing pin spring (13) are held in the cylinder frame by the recoil plate retaining pin (15). Disassembly of the recoil plate and firing pin is not recommended and should be attempted only by an experienced gunsmith. Removal of the hammer plunger (22) and spring (23) from the hammer is likewise not recommended. Although the above is a complete stripping procedure, it should be emphasized that, due to the rugged simplicity of the Ruger design, such a complete dismantling is seldom if ever necessary.

Reassembly is accomplished in the reverse order. ■

The gun, first produced in 1893, was designed by an American, Hugo Borchardt. Although clumsy, it was the first commercially successful self-loading or automatic pistol. Borchardt automatics were made by the Loewe Arms firm of Berlin and later at the famous DWM plant. Borchardt magazines are as distinctive as they are scarce. They bear a resemblance to the Luger magazine, which is natural, since the Luger is a development of it. The Borchardt cartridge is famous in its own right, since it was the forerunner of the powerful 7.63 mm. Mauser pistol cartridge.

Borchardt magazines have numerous distinctive features, but probably the most striking is the wooden magazine floorplate, with its large convex buttons to aid in its removal from the gun. The magazine is also a good deal wider than the average pistol magazine.

The follower is different from any other common magazine in that it is concave and fits around the base of the cartridge. Another striking feature is the large stiffener and guide rib on the front and rear surfaces. —E. J. HOFFSCHMIDT.

The late James M. Triggs was a well known writer-illustrator and collector of antique firearms.

Note—Although many Blackhawk .357, .44 Magnum, and .22 Single-Six revolver parts are interchangeable, it is advised that the owner of any of these three guns consult the Ruger factory parts list when ordering parts.

RUGER'S
HAWKEYE

BY JAMES M. TRIGGS

Ruger introduced the Hawkeye, rotating block, single shot pistol in 1963, in response to the rapid growth of handgun hunting in the U.S. Desiring an inexpensive entry into the hunting handgun market, Ruger modified a single-action revolver, replacing the cylinder with a latched, rotating breechblock having an internal firing pin. The Hawkeye was chambered for the .256 Winchester Magnum cartridge, Its 8-3/8 -inch barrel was drilled and tapped at the factory for telescopic sight mounts. Although the Hawkeye was well made, neither it nor the cartridge ever gained much popularity. The Hawkeye was only produced for one year.

Standard Ruger revolver frame is fitted with a rotating breechblock which has an inertia firing pin. After rotating breechblock, cartridge is loaded directly into the barrel.

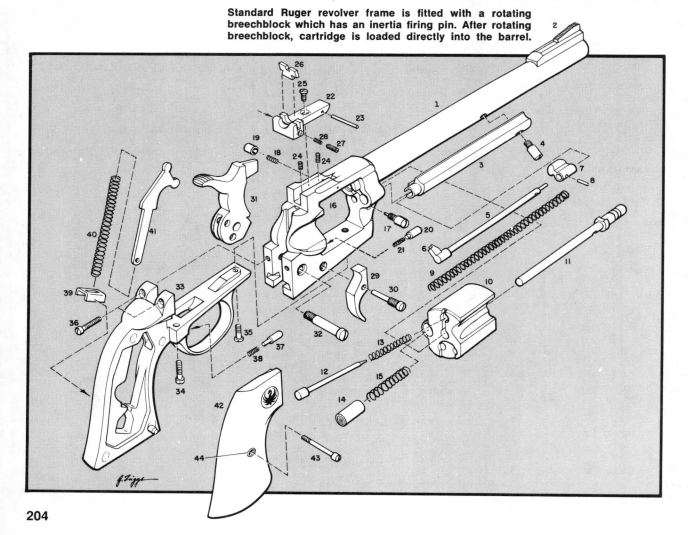

Single Shot

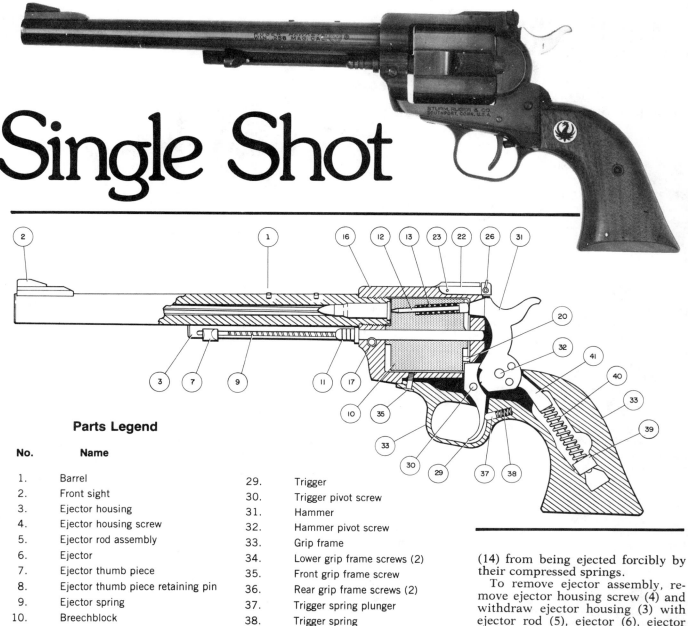

Parts Legend

No.	Name
1.	Barrel
2.	Front sight
3.	Ejector housing
4.	Ejector housing screw
5.	Ejector rod assembly
6.	Ejector
7.	Ejector thumb piece
8.	Ejector thumb piece retaining pin
9.	Ejector spring
10.	Breechblock
11.	Base pin
12.	Firing pin
13.	Firing pin spring
14.	Breechblock lock plunger
15.	Breechblock lock plunger spring
16.	Cylinder frame
17.	Base pin latch
18.	Base pin latch spring
19.	Base pin latch nut
20.	Detent plunger
21.	Detent plunger spring
22.	Rear sight body
23.	Rear sight pivot pin
24.	Rear sight springs (2)
25.	Rear sight elevation screw
26.	Rear sight blade
27.	Rear sight windage screw
28.	Rear sight windage screw spring
29.	Trigger
30.	Trigger pivot screw
31.	Hammer
32.	Hammer pivot screw
33.	Grip frame
34.	Lower grip frame screws (2)
35.	Front grip frame screw
36.	Rear grip frame screws (2)
37.	Trigger spring plunger
38.	Trigger spring
39.	Mainspring seat
40.	Mainspring
41.	Hammer strut
42.	Grip panel
43.	Grip panel screw
44.	Escutcheon (in right grip panel)

Disassembly Procedure:

To open breechblock (10), press in breechblock lock plunger (14) at left of cylinder frame (16) and rotate breechblock counter-clockwise. Check chamber to be sure pistol is unloaded. To remove breechblock (10) from cylinder frame (16), press in base pin latch (17) at left of cylinder frame and pull base pin (11) forward as far as possible. Roll breechblock (10) out to left side of cylinder frame taking care to prevent firing pin and breechblock lock plunger (14) from being ejected forcibly by their compressed springs.

To remove ejector assembly, remove ejector housing screw (4) and withdraw ejector housing (3) with ejector rod (5), ejector (6), ejector spring (9) and ejector thumb piece (7) toward front of pistol.

Remove grip panel screw (43) and grip panels from grip frame (33). Pull hammer (31) back to a fully cocked position and insert a small close-fitting nail or pin through hole in lower end of hammer strut (41) where it protrudes below the mainspring seat (39). Release hammer (31). Remove grip frame screws (34, 35, 36) and drop grip frame (33) from cylinder frame (16), taking care not to lose trigger spring (38) and trigger spring plunger (37). Remove compressed mainspring (40), hammer strut (41) and mainspring seat (39) as a unit from grip frame (33). Remove hammer pivot screw (32) and remove hammer (31) from cylinder frame (16). Remove trigger pivot screw (30) and drop out trigger (29). Reassemble in reverse order.

RUGER SECURITY-SIX REVOLVER

Illustrations by DENNIS RIORDAN
Text by LUDWIG OLSON

THE Ruger Security-Six double-action revolver is the result of imaginative designing and modern production techniques. This solid-frame handgun with side-swing cylinder and simultaneous ejection was introduced in 1970. It is offered in .38 Special and .357 Magnum chamberings and with choice of fixed or adjustable target-style sights.

Trim, compact, and strong, this six-shot revolver with four-in. barrel weighs 33 ozs. unloaded and measures 9¼" long overall. It is also available with 2¾" and six-in. barrels. To quote the manufacturer: "It is a handsome, rugged holster revolver—compact in the overall, yet massive enough to properly be designated as a heavy duty revolver for the rigors of police and military service."

Among several desirable features of the Security-Six is that it can be disassembled easily for cleaning and lubrication without use of special tools. After turning out the grip screw with a cartridge rim, coin, or screwdriver, the grips, lockwork, and cylinder assembly can be removed. Except for windage- and elevation-adjustment screws in the rear sight of the target version, the only screw in this revolver is the grip screw.

Unlike most other handguns, the frame, crane, hammer, trigger, trigger guard, and several smaller parts of the Security-Six are produced from chrome-molybdenum steel investment castings. The barrel is a machined forging and the cylinder, which rotates to the left, is machined from bar stock. All springs are of durable coil type. The frame is not fitted with a sideplate as in many other revolvers. This aids strength.

Integral with the barrel are an ejector rod housing and a raised grooved barrel rib. Pinned to the front of the rib is a Baughman-style quick-draw front sight.

In pleasing contrast with the blued finish of the other metal parts, sides of the hammer and trigger are polished bright. The grips are oil-finished American walnut, each fitted with a small circular Ruger medallion of white metal. Cut checkering in a diamond-shaped area on the grips is nicely executed.

An excellent safety feature of this revolver is the system of transmitting the hammer blow to the spring-loaded firing pin by means of a transfer bar. The hammer nose rests on the frame, and the transfer bar does not align with the firing pin until the trigger is fully to the rear. This prevents accidental firing should the gun be dropped with the hammer down, or should the hammer be struck when down and with the trigger forward.

Another excellent safety feature is that the hammer cannot be cocked when the cylinder has been swung out, and the cylinder cannot be opened when the hammer is cocked. The cylinder assembly is released to swing out to the left by depressing the cylinder release button in the left recoil shield of the frame.

Handling and pointing qualities of this well-made reliable revolver are excellent, and its overall precision is very good. Its double-action trigger pull is satisfactorily smooth, without excessive buildup of resistance when the trigger pressure is increased. The single-action pull weighs approximately three lbs., and has very little creep.

The Security-Six is well made and finished throughout, and its design shows considerable ingenuity. ■

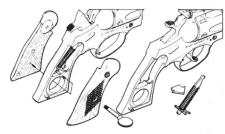

1 Determine that revolver is unloaded before attempting disassembly. Unscrew grip screw (48) with coin or cartridge rim, and remove grips (42) (47). Cock hammer (24) with thumb. Insert disassembly pin (43), stored in left grip, through hole at bottom of hammer strut (19). Pull trigger, lower hammer with thumb, and remove mainspring/hammer strut assembly from grip frame.

2 Pull trigger fully to rear and remove hammer pivot assembly (20). Keeping trigger fully depressed, roll hammer forward and lift straight upward from frame.

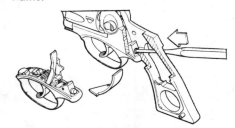

3 Working through frame opening, depress trigger guard plunger (60) with punch. Pull rear of trigger guard (57) downward and remove from frame. In the field, trigger guard plunger may be depressed by rounded head of hammer strut.

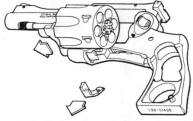

4 With the gun on its right side, press crane latch (37) and open cylinder (34). Draw cylinder/crane assembly forward and out of frame. Remove cylinder latch (38).

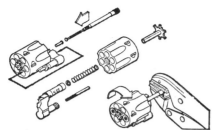
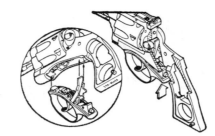
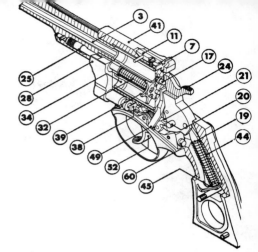

5 If cylinder/crane assembly must be taken down, clamp knurled head of ejector rod (25) between wood blocks in vise or locking jaw pliers. Insert empty cartridge cases in opposite chambers and unscrew cylinder, turning clockwise. (Assembly is secured with left-hand threads.) When cylinder is fully unscrewed, squeeze crane (28) and cylinder together and remove from ejector rod. All parts may then be separated.

To reassemble cylinder/crane assembly, replace cylinder latch spring and plunger (29) (30) within crane pivot. Insert ejector rod washer (31) and ejector spring (32) within cylinder axle, making sure that the washer seats squarely upon its shoulder. Assemble ejector (39), cylinder, and crane. Slide center pin spring (26) over center pin rod (27) and insert through threaded end of ejector rod. Holding cylinder/crane assembly tightly together, replace center pin lock (33) and ejector rod assembly, turning ejector rod counter-clockwise to start its thread. Tighten in vise, as before.

6 Assemble rest of gun in reverse order. When installing trigger guard assembly, locate transfer bar (49) and pawl (56) ahead of their internal frame shoulders, and enter lug at front of guard within its frame seat. Pivot assembly upward into contact with frame. Determine that transfer bar is situated to rear of internal crossbar of frame latch, and snap guard home. Pulling trigger will cycle cylinder, if assembly is correct. When replacing mainspring assembly, position mainspring seat (45) with offset hammer strut hole to rear.

7 Cutaway indicates relationship between assembled parts. Gun is shown unloaded, with all springs at rest. Crane latch has been omitted for clarity; its crossbar would lie between center pin lock and transfer bar. Parts are number keyed to parts legend.

PARTS LEGEND

1. Front sight
2. Front sight cross pin
3. Barrel
4. Front latch cross pin
5. Front latch spring
6. Front latch
7. Rear sight blade
8. Rear sight elevation screw
9. Rear sight pivot pin
10. Rear sight elevation spring (2)
11. Rear sight
12. Rear sight windage spring
13. Rear sight windage screw
14. Recoil plate cross pin
15. Recoil plate
16. Firing pin rebound spring
17. Firing pin
18. Hammer dog pivot pin
19. Hammer strut
20. Hammer pivot assembly
21. Hammer dog
22. Hammer dog spring plunger
23. Hammer dog spring
24. Hammer
25. Ejector rod
26. Center pin spring
27. Center pin rod
28. Crane and crane pivot assembly
29. Cylinder latch spring
30. Cylinder latch plunger
31. Ejector rod washer
32. Ejector spring
33. Center pin lock
34. Cylinder
35. Crane latch spring plunger
36. Crane latch spring
37. Crane latch
38. Cylinder latch
39. Ejector
40. Crane latch pivot
41. Frame
42. Grip panel (left) complete
43. Disassembly pin
44. Mainspring
45. Mainspring seat
46. Grip panel dowel
47. Grip panel (right) complete
48. Grip panel screw
49. Transfer bar
50. Trigger spring
51. Trigger bushing
52. Trigger
53. Trigger pivot pin
54. Pawl spring
55. Pawl plunger
56. Pawl
57. Trigger guard
58. Trigger guard plunger cross
59. Trigger guard plunger spring
60. Trigger guard plunger

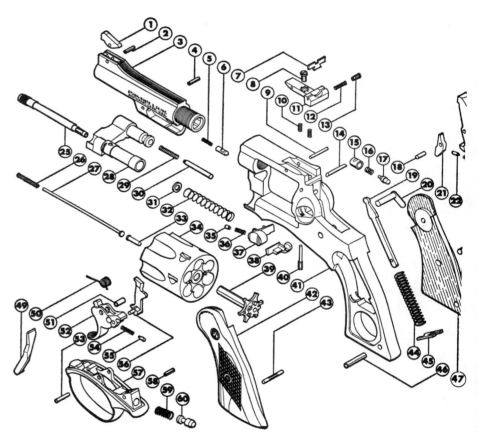

In early 1954 Strum, Ruger & Co., of Southport, Conn., began production of their Single-Six, a .22 rimfire, six-shot, single-action rod ejecting revolver. Patterned after the Colt Single Action Army, the Ruger Single-Six answered the demand for a high-quality, western style, single-action revolver chambered for the economical .22 rimfire cartridge. It was not designed for competitive shooter, but rather for plinking at informal targets of opportunity encountered afield or along a trap line. This is not to disparage the accuracy of the Single-Six as it is quite capable of target accuracy within the limitations of its sights. The blade front sight is fixed but the rear sight can be ad-

By Thomas E. Wessel

justed for windage by tapping it sideways in its dovetail slot. There is no provision for adjusting elevation.

The salient design feature of the Single-Six is the use of virtually unbreakable music wire springs throughout the lock mechanism. Breakdowns due to spring failure are, thus, unlikely.

For a short period in the mid-1950s, the Single-Six was made with a lightweight alloy frame that, with a total weight of 22 ozs., gave a considerable weight saving over the 35-oz. conventional steel frame guns. There was also a "Buntline", 9-1/2" barrel version. Single-Sixes were first offered in .22 Winchester Magnum Rimfire in 1959 and interchangeable cylinder models appeared a short time later.

The year 1956 also saw the introduction of a short-lived, engraved version of the Single-Six. These "presentation" models had polished alumunum grip

Ruger Single-Six Revolver

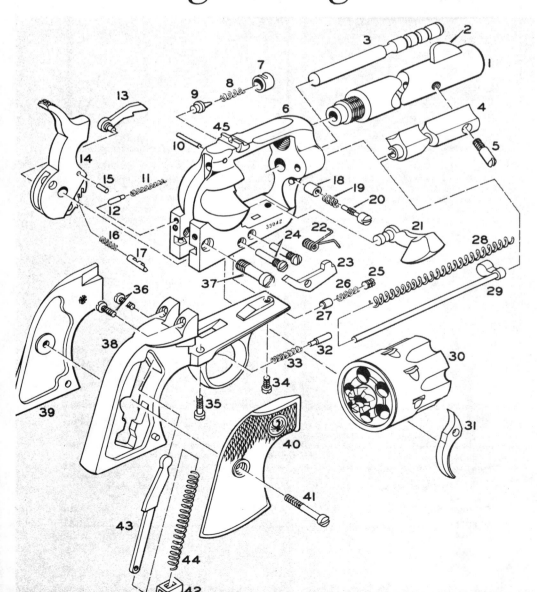

Parts Legend

1. Barrel
2. Front sight
3. Base pin
4. Ejector housing
5. Ejector housing screw
6. Cylinder frame
7. Recoil plate
8. Rebound spring
9. Firing pin
10. Recoil plate pin
11. Pawl spring
12. Pawl plunger
13. Pawl
14. Hammer
15. Hammer plunger pin
16. Hammer plunger spring
17. Hammer plunger
18. Base pin nut
19. Base pin nut latch spring
20. Base pin latch
21. Gate assembly (contoured)
22. Cylinder latch spring
23. Cylinder latch
24. Pivot screw (2)
25. Gate spring screw
26. Gate detent spring
27. Gate detent plunger
28. Ejector spring
29. Ejector rod assembly
30. Cylinder
31. Trigger
32. Trigger plunger
33. Trigger spring
34. Grip frame screw, front
35. Grip frame screw, lower (2)
36. Grip frame screw, rear (2)
37. Hammer pivot screw
38. Grip frame
39. Grip panel, left
40. Grip panel, right
41. Grip panel screw
42. Mainspring seat
43. Hammer strut
44. Mainspring
45. Rear sight

frames with other parts being of blue-finished steel. The two-piece grips were of varnished walnut

In 1973 the Single-Six underwent a major change with the incorporation of a transfer bar, to preclude accidental discharge, into the mechanism. Concurrently Ruger changed the model's name to "Super Single-Six" and undertook a program to convert existing Single-Sixes to the new lock mechanism.

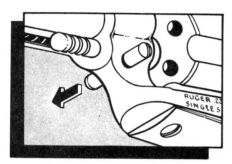

1 To remove cylinder (30), first remove any cartridges, position hammer on loading notch, and open gate (21). Next, press base pin nut (18) on left side and withdraw base pin (3). Cylinder may now be removed from right side.

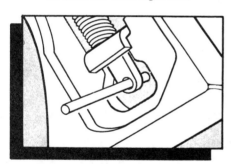

2 To further disassemble, remove grip panel screw (41), and lift grip panels (39) and (40) away from grip frame (38). Bring hammer to full cock and insert nail or pin into small hole in lower end of hammer strut (43). Next, depress trigger and move the hammer forward. The nail will keep mainspring (44) compressed

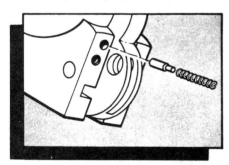

3 Continue disassembly by removing the 5 screws—2 (35), 2 (36), and (34)—which hold grip frame to cylinder frame (6). In separating grip and cylinder frames, take care to prevent loss of pawl spring (11) and plunger (12). These parts are located in a hole drilled in left rear face of cylinder frame, adjacent to rear left grip frame screw hole

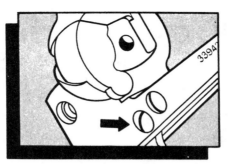

4 Remove hammer pivot screw (37) and hammer. Remove trigger pivot screw (24-arrow) and trigger (31)

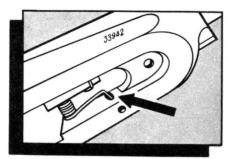

5 With a small screwdriver, free fixed leg of cylinder latch spring (22) from its anchoring hole in left inside wall of cylinder frame. Remove cylinder latch pivot screw (24), cylinder latch (23), and cylinder latch spring (22)

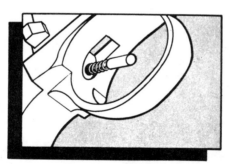

6 Trigger spring (33) and plunger (32) are positioned in a hole in grip frame at rear of trigger guard bow. Innermost coil of trigger spring is enlarged to prevent loss during disassembly and reassembly. Care should be exercised in removing plunger and spring to prevent deformation of spring

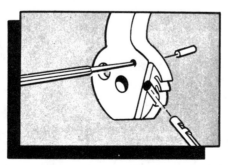

7 Hammer plunger (17) is retained in hammer by a small pin (15) which may be removed by means of a small flat-nosed punch. Reassembly of arm is accomplished in reverse order ∎

French 1935A MAS .32 Automatic

PISTOL MAGAZINES

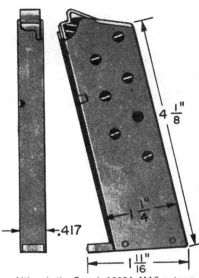

Although the French 1935A MAS automatic pistol is not particularly well known or appreciated in this country, it is nevertheless an interesting weapon. This gun is a copy of a 9 mm. pistol designed by a Swiss engineer named Petter. It fires a rather odd cartridge that resembles a long .32 automatic pistol cartridge. Contrary to general practice the pistol is finished in a baked enamel. While this finish tends to cheapen the appearance of the MAS, it is practical for it is much more rust resistant than the standard blue finish.

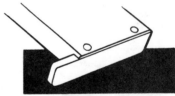

Magazines for the 1935A MAS can usually be identified at a glance by their shape. They look long enough to handle a 9 mm. but are far too narrow to accept one. Another point of note is the way in which the magazine floorplate is pinned to the magazine sides.

Other points of identity are the double step in the follower, the rounded shape of the slide clearance notch in the back strap of the magazine, and the observation holes in both sides.—E. J. HOFFSCHMIDT

209

Sauer & Sohn Model 38 Pistol, Cal. .32 ACP

By E. J. Hoffschmidt

War-production gun without safety catch

EXCEPT for short periods between wars, the German firm of J. P. Sauer & Sohn has been making fine guns continuously for more than 200 years. In 1751 they started with flintlock fowling pieces and ended up in 1945 producing semi-automatic pistols and Mauser rifles.

When the Russians occupied the German gun center of Suhl, they turned arms manufacture over to the East Zone Communists. Production was resumed under a state cooperative called MEWA. The firms were given new names such as Ernst-Thälmann-Werk VEB (C. G. Haenel), Jagdgewehr-und Lehrenbau VEB (Greifelt and Co.), Fortuna-Werk VEB (J. P. Sauer & Sohn). The Sauer management finally left the East Zone, and in March 1951 set up shop in Düsseldorf and Eckernförde in West Germany. They are currently making business machines, shotguns, and 3-barrel guns.

During the early 1930's, the Walther firm startled the German gun trade with their double-action pistols. Not to be outdone, Sauer began work on the Model H. While retaining some of the lines of the old Sauer Behördenmodell, the new gun was designed for mass production. Many of the operating parts were stampings or die castings. Machining of the slide was simplified

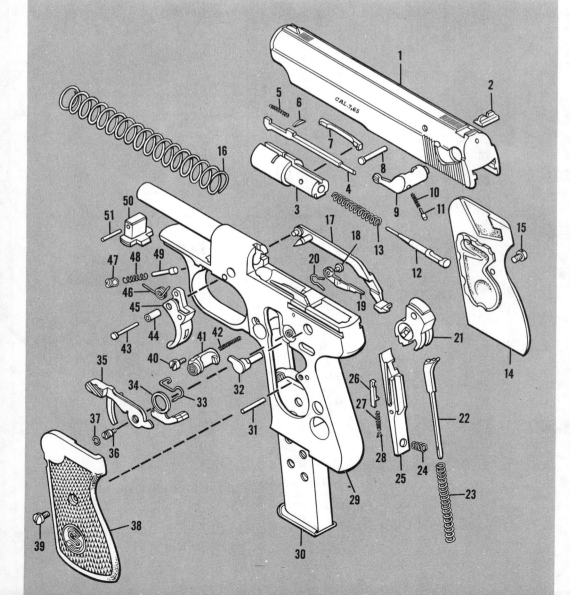

Parts Legend

1. Slide
2. Rear sight
3. Breechblock
4. Cartridge indicator
5. Indicator spring
6. Spring retainer
7. Extractor
8. Block retainer pin
9. Safety catch
10. Safety detent spring
11. Safety detent
12. Firing pin
13. Firing pin spring
14. Right grip
15. Grip screw
16. Recoil spring
17. Trigger bar
18. Magazine safety retainer
19. Magazine safety bar
20. Safety spring
21. Hammer
22. Hammer strut
23. Hammer spring
24. Sear spring
25. Sear
26. Sear disconnector
27. Disconnector spring
28. Spring retainer
29. Frame
30. Magazine
31. Sear hinge pin
32. Hammer extension
33. Cocking lever spring
34. Hammer lever
35. Cocking lever
36. Lever hinge screw
37. Retainer ring
38. Left grip
39. Grip screw
40. Magazine catch screw
41. Magazine catch
42. Magazine catch spring
43. Trigger pin
44. Trigger bushing
45. Trigger
46. Trigger spring
47. Spring retainer
48. Detent spring
49. Takedown detent
50. Takedown latch
51. Latch crosspin

by making the breech a separate piece and pinning it to the slide.

Unlike its contemporaries, the Model H, or Model 38 as it is better known, features an enclosed hammer. With the aid of an ingenious lever, the internal hammer can be cocked for single-action fire. This lever also allows the hammer to be eased down from full cock. If the lever is pushed down when the hammer is cocked, it releases the hammer, allowing it to be lowered as in a pistol with an outside hammer. Another interesting feature is the indicator pin, which protrudes from the end of the slide when a cartridge is in the chamber. The Model 38 has 2 safeties: a magazine safety that prevents firing when the magazine is removed, and a slide safety. The slide safety is handy and simple. It blocks the hammer and locks the trigger mechanism.

Like most other late German pocket pistols, the Sauer Model 38 is found in 2 types—the pre-war gun with fine finish and excellent workmanship, and the crude but serviceable wartime product. The bulk of the Sauers in the U. S. seem to be of the later wartime production, usually without the slide safety.

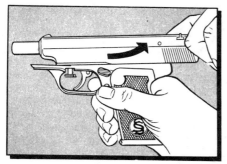

1 To disassemble, remove magazine and clear chamber. Pull down latch (50) in upper portion of trigger guard. Pull slide (1) to rear and lift it up. Ease slide forward off barrel

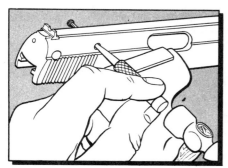

2 To remove breechblock assembly, drive out retainer pin (8). It must be driven from right to left. Breechblock can now be driven forward out of slide exposing firing pin (12), extractor (7), and cartridge indicator (4)

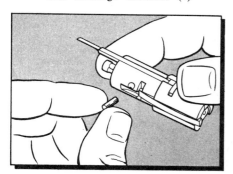

3 When reassembling breechblock, install extractor and indicator pin. Firing pin should be held in place by a short slave pin which is pushed out when retainer pin is driven in. This will prevent damage to spring and firing pin

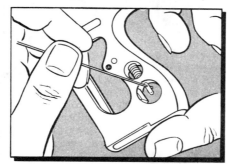

4 To disassemble sear mechanism, bring hammer back to full cock. Hammer strut (22) will extend through hole in frame exposing a small cross-drilled hole. Slip a piece of wire through to hold hammer strut and hammer spring. Sear mechanism can now be easily removed

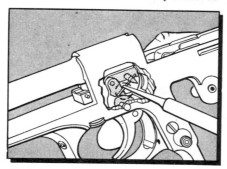

5 When trigger bar (17) is reinstalled, long tail of trigger spring (46) must push up on pointed pin on trigger bar. To do this, hold spring down with a thin punch thrust through large hole on left side of frame (29)

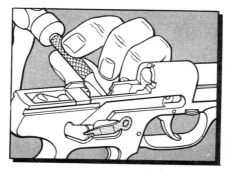

6 Magazine safety retainer (18) is staked to frame but sometimes it is necessary to remove it. To do this, hold gun in a vise and tap out from inside. It must be restaked when replaced ∎

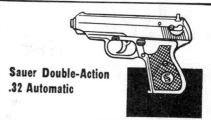

Sauer Double-Action .32 Automatic

PISTOL MAGAZINES

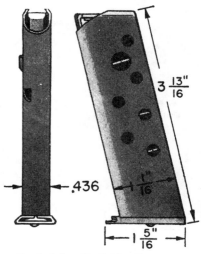

Shortly before World War II, J. P. Sauer and Sohn brought out an advanced double-action automatic pistol to compete with the new Walther, Mauser, and Bergmann designs. The gun has a fine balance and contains numerous excellent features. It has an internal hammer that can be cocked for single-action shooting or lowered to uncocked position by an outside thumb lever. A magazine disconnector that prevents the gun from firing when the magazine is out is another noticeable feature.

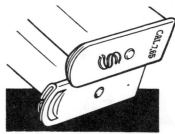

The unusual folded sheet metal floorplate, or the solid plate with the serrated front edge and the take-down buttons are characteristic of the Sauer double-action magazine. These magazines are seamless and have the observation holes only in the left-hand side, and since they are retained by a cross latch the magazines have a retaining notch in the right front side.

Another distinguishing feature of the double-action Sauer is the small protrusion (or pin) pressed out of the right side of the magazine. This protrusion operates the magazine disconnector.—E. J. HOFFSCHMIDT

SAUER MODEL 1930 PISTOL

By E. J. HOFFSCHMIDT

MANUFACTURED by the German arms firm of J. P. Sauer & Sohn, the Sauer Model 1930 cal. .32 ACP pistol was first offered in 1930. Of simple blowback-operated, striker-fired design, the Model 1930 pistol is a development of an earlier Sauer pistol introduced in 1913. Detachable magazine of the Model 1930 pistol holds 7 cartridges.

There is a close resemblance between the earlier version and the Model 1930 pistol, but they can be readily distinguished by differences in frame design. Front grip strap of the earlier pistol is straight, whereas that of the Model 1930 curves forward at the base to provide a support for the little finger. Frame of the Model 1930 pistol extends beyond the rear face of the slide cap, whereas the slide cap of the earlier model overhangs the frame slightly.

As a further refinement of the Model 1930 pistol, the Sauer firm introduced their Behorden Model (Authority Model), also chambered for the .32 ACP cartridge. Apparently aimed at possible municipal government markets, the Behorden Model features a trigger safety, magazine safety, manual safety, and optional cartridge signal pin device in the slide cap. With the exception of the manual safety, none of these auxiliary safety devices are present in the Model 1930 pistol. Model 1930 and Behorden Model pistols were optionally available with steel or aluminum frames and slides. Minor changes were made in their internal mechanisms during course of manufacture. Sauer Model 1930 and Behorden Model pistols were superseded by the Sauer Model 38 double-action pistol.

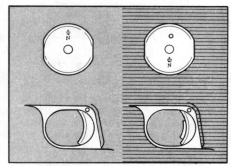

1   Slide cap and trigger details of Model 1930 (l.) and Behorden Model pistols. Trigger safety of Behorden Model pistol extends from face of trigger. Cartridge signal pin protrudes from upper hole in slide cap of Behorden Model pistol when cartridge is in chamber.

2   To disassemble Model 1930 pistol, first remove magazine and be certain chamber is unloaded. Pull back slide (1) about an inch until safety catch (29) engages slide. Depress rear sight and unscrew slide cap (4) from slide. Remove breech-block assembly (7). Then release safety and ease slide off front of frame.

3   Safety catch should be removed before disassembling gun internally. First remove grips, then rotate safety catch 180° until hinge pin portion is clear of undercut in frame. Do not let safety catch detent pin (27) and detent spring (28) fly out when safety catch is withdrawn. To replace, depress the safety catch detent pin with thin piece of brass and push into frame.

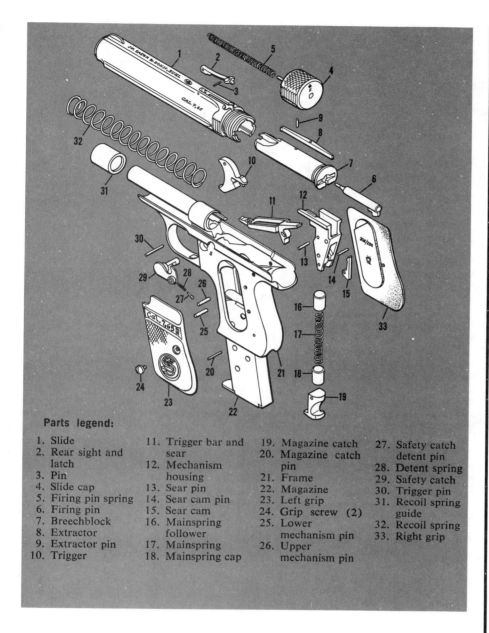

Parts legend:

1. Slide	11. Trigger bar and sear	19. Magazine catch
2. Rear sight and latch	12. Mechanism housing	20. Magazine catch pin
3. Pin	13. Sear pin	21. Frame
4. Slide cap	14. Sear cam pin	22. Magazine
5. Firing pin spring	15. Sear cam	23. Left grip
6. Firing pin	16. Mainspring follower	24. Grip screw (2)
7. Breechblock	17. Mainspring	25. Lower mechanism pin
8. Extractor	18. Mainspring cap	26. Upper mechanism pin
9. Extractor pin		27. Safety catch detent pin
10. Trigger		28. Detent spring
		29. Safety catch
		30. Trigger pin
		31. Recoil spring guide
		32. Recoil spring
		33. Right grip

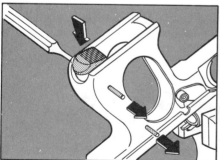

4 The pins in the Model 1930 Sauer pistol are tapered and should be removed from right to left. In reassembly, install mainspring (17), mainspring follower (16) and mainspring cap (18) last. Hold pistol in padded vise jaws and push in magazine catch. Use a thin punch to hold and align magazine catch (19) in frame while inserting magazine catch pin (20).

5 Mechanism housing (12) has several functions: ejector, cartridge guide, slide guide, and it also contains the sear mechanism. To remove unit, drive out lower and upper mechanism pins (25, 26) and lift free of trigger. Take care to prevent mainspring assembly (16, 17, 18) from flying out. To replace, be sure trigger bar and sear (11) are pointing down. ∎

PISTOL MAGAZINES

Webley & Scott 9 mm. Pistol

The Webley & Scott 9 mm. Browning automatic pistol was used by a number of police organizations throughout the British Commonwealth. This is a straight blowback-operated pistol without delay device in the mechanism. The powerful cartridge requires a heavy slide and strong recoil spring to prevent premature opening of the slide.

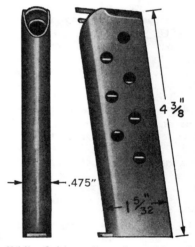

While finish and workmanship of the pistol is first class, the design leaves something to be desired. The outside hammer is difficult to thumb back for a rapid first shot and the grip angle makes shooting awkward. The magazine is well made, but has little to distinguish it from other common types.

The magazine follower is simply a bent piece of sheet metal. Magazine lips are slightly rounded to conform with contour of the cartridges.

An obvious point of recognition is the magazine catch hole in lower end of backstrap.—E. J. HOFFSCHMIDT

SAVAGE
Model 1910 Pocket Pistol

By E. J. Hoffschmidt

THE early 1900's was the golden age of automatic pistol development, with all leading American and European companies experimenting with both military and pocket types. The Savage Arms Co. was no exception, their first effort being a cal. .45 ACP pistol for the U. S. Army trials of 1907. At the same time they adapted E. H. Searle's locking system to a pocket pistol. The system enabled Savage to build a light compact gun that lies low in the hand and points naturally. With the Searle system, the barrel has to turn as the breechblock moves to the rear. But while the bullet is going through the barrel, the work of spinning the bullet resists this rotation of the barrel, which helps to hold the breech closed until the bullet has left the barrel. In the cal. .32 and .38 models there is no true mechanical lock.

The Savage has the largest magazine capacity of any popular pocket pistol. The cal. .32 model has a 10-round magazine capacity while the cal. .380 has a 9-round capacity. The magazines hold the cartridges in a staggered double row, and are very strongly made.

An interesting feature is the method used to retain the grips, as no screws are necessary. The hard rubber grips are slid into corresponding dovetail slots in the frame, with projections on the inside of the grips snapping into grooves in the frame to utilize the natural resilience of the hard rubber.

In spite of its features and excellent workmanship, the Savage has its drawbacks. The position of the cocking lever and strength of the firing pin spring make it almost impossible for the average shooter to cock the gun with the shooting hand only. Another feature subject to criticism is the unusual sear mechanism built into the breech plug, which does not have a half-cock position. Thus, the firing pin is either all the way forward or at full cock. This makes it, for practical considerations, impossible to carry the gun with a cartridge in the chamber and hammer down as the hammer is directly connected to the firing pin and the firing pin contacts the cartridge primer when the hammer is down. If there is a round in the chamber, the only safe way to carry the gun is at full cock with safety catch on. Even though the trigger mechanism has a disconnector, the guns are more prone to going automatic than any other pocket pistol. If the trigger pull is lightened too much, or dirt and fouling build up between the sear and the breechblock, these pistols have been known to fire as the slide slams forward.

The gun illustrated is the 1908 type, more popularly called the Model 1910. It was made in cals. .32 ACP and .380 ACP, in a number of variations. There were hammerless models, models with grip safeties, and some with hold-open devices. In 1917 the gun was revised and the grip and hammer reshaped. These Savage pistols are notable for their design and unsurpassed workmanship.

E. J. HOFFSCHMIDT *is an artist-illustrator with years of experience with firearms.*

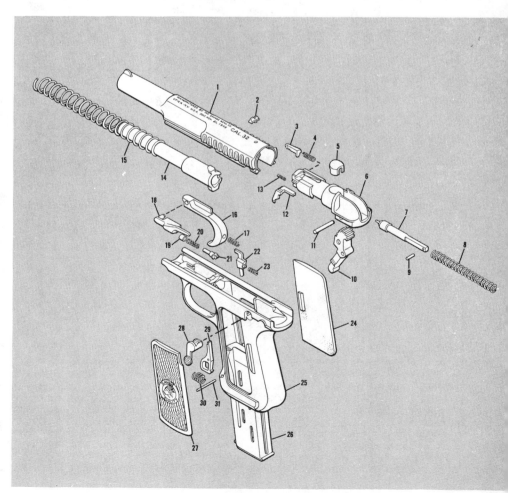

1 To take down the Savage, first remove magazine and clear chamber. Pull back slide and put safety catch (28) on. Grasp cocking lever and breech plug as shown, squeeze, and rotate plug ¼ turn. Plug assembly can now be pulled free of slide

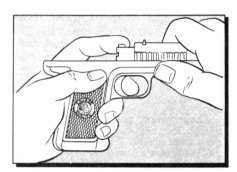

2 After removing breech plug (6), hold back trigger and release safety. Ease slide off front of frame (25); when reassembling, hold barrel as shown and push slide to rear until it can be held back by safety catch (28)

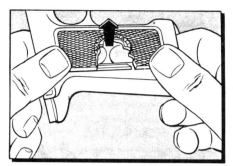

3 Grips are retained by dovetail slots in top and bottom of frame. To remove them, insert first finger of each hand into magazine well as shown and push at center of grip. Resiliency of the hard rubber grip will allow it to snap out without breaking

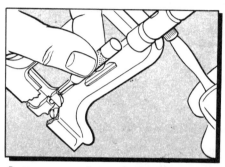

4 To remove safety catch (28), it is necessary to first drive out ejector (22). After grips are removed, insert a thin punch or nail set as shown, and gently tap ejector stem out. Put safety catch in 'fire' position to prevent damage to safety catch spring (23)

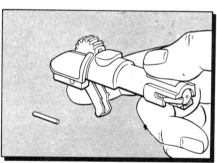

5 To disassemble breech plug (6), drive out cocking lever hinge pin (11). Then cock cocking lever (10) to raise firing pin retainer (5). Remove retainer and pull out cocking lever and firing pin assembly

6 After cocking lever and firing pin assembly have been removed, rotate sear (12) upward so that its tail drops into breech plug hollow far enough to lift it out. Extractor (3) can easily be pushed out as shown———

Parts Legend

1. Slide
2. Rear sight
3. Extractor
4. Extractor spring
5. Firing pin retainer
6. Breech plug
7. Firing pin
8. Firing pin spring
9. Firing pin hinge pin
10. Cocking lever
11. Cocking lever hinge pin
12. Sear
13. Sear spring
14. Barrel
15. Recoil spring
16. Trigger
17. Trigger spring
18. Sear trip
19. Sear trip lifter
20. Sear trip spring
21. Sear trip catch
22. Ejector
23. Safety catch spring
24. Right grip
25. Frame
26. Magazine
27. Left grip
28. Safety catch
29. Magazine catch
30. Magazine catch spring
31. Magazine catch pin

Savage Model 1917 Automatic

PISTOL MAGAZINES

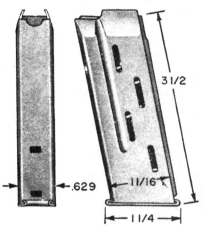

When the Savage Arms Co. stepped out of the pistol business in 1928, the gun world lost a source of interesting weapons. Their pocket pistols worked on the so-called hesitation blowback system as differed from the usual straight blowback system found on most pocket pistols. Savage pocket pistols were produced in several models and in either .32 or .380 cal. Shown here is the magazine for the Model 1917. The gun can be identified by its spur hammer and unusually wide grip. Well made and with large magazine capacity, Savage pistols were among the best pocket pistols of their day.

Savage magazines are almost twice as thick as the usual .32 automatic since they carry a staggered double row of cartridges. They are rarely marked but some will be found with a serial number. The illustration shows the unusual method of retaining the magazine floorplate.

These magazines are well made and resemble a small-scale version of the Browning Hi Power. The feed lip is very stiff and strong with a long tapering slope on either side to prevent the staggered row of cartridges from jamming.—E. J. HOFFSCHMIDT.

SAVAGE MODEL 101 PISTOL

By JAMES M. TRIGGS

This single-shot pistol was introduced in 1960 and remained in production until 1969. It generally resembles the traditional frontier-type single-action revolver, but the cylinder is actually a dummy and merely shrouds the rear end of the barrel. The barrel and dummy cylinder swing to the right to expose the breech for loading or ejection. The rod ejector is actuated by pressing a thumb button under the left side of the barrel near the muzzle. The hammer is of rebounding type. The Independent spring-loaded firing pin is pinned in the rear of the frame. The mainspring is of coil type.

The frame and dummy cylinder of the Model 101 are of die-cast alloy. The barrel and other parts are steel. The grips are laminated, walnut-colored wood, impregnated with plastic.

Parts Legend

1. Frame
2. Barrel & cylinder assembly
3. Front sight
4. Cylinder pivot pin
5. Detent housing
6. Detent plunger spring
7. Detent plunger
8. Cylinder pivot pin bushing
9. Firing pin
10. Firing pin spring
11. Recoil plate

12. Recoil plate retaining pin
13. Rear sight
14. Hammer
15. Hammer pin
16. Mainspring plunger
17. Mainspring
17A. Mainspring trunnion
18. Trigger spring plunger
19. Trigger spring
20. Trigger
21. Trigger pin

22. Ejector assembly
23. Ejector spring
24. Ejector rod assembly
25. Ejector tube
26. Ejector tube guide
27. Ejector tube plug
28. Ejector tube screw
29. Grip, right (left grip not shown)
30. Grip screws (2) (right screw only shown)

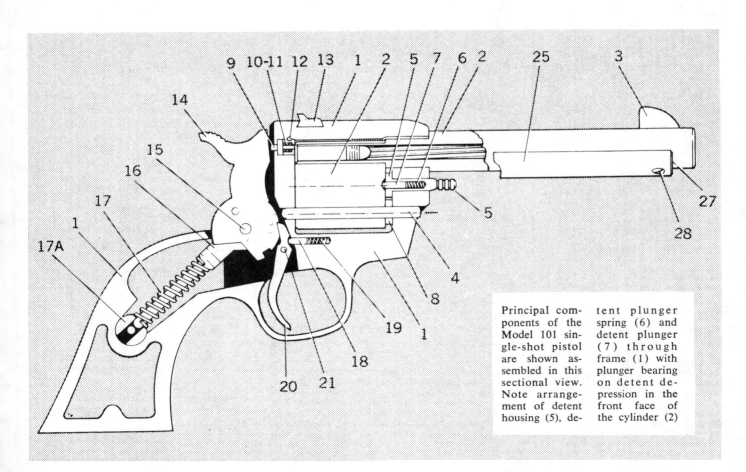

Principal components of the Model 101 single-shot pistol are shown assembled in this sectional view. Note arrangement of detent housing (5), detent plunger spring (6) and detent plunger (7) through frame (1) with plunger bearing on detent depression in the front face of the cylinder (2)

Disassembly Procedure

Check action to be sure pistol is unloaded. Remove grip screws (30) and grips (29) from frame (1). Drift out hammer pin (15) from left to right and drive mainspring trunnion (17A) out of frame from left to right. Remove mainspring (17), pull back on trigger (20), and lift hammer (14) out top of frame with mainspring plunger (16). Drift out trigger pin (21) from left to right, taking care not to allow escape of compressed trigger spring (19) and trigger spring plunger (18). Trigger (20) may now be removed from frame.

With barrel and cylinder assembly (2) in firing position, drift out cylinder pivot pin (4) toward muzzle by inserting punch through hammer slot in rear of frame. Remove cylinder pivot pin bushing (8).

To remove barrel and cylinder assembly from frame, follow procedure carefully. *Do not rotate cylinder in frame after removing cylinder pivot pin. Take care to guide cylinder to allow detent plunger (7) to pass between dummy chamber holes in front face of cylinder.* With detent plunger clear of cylinder, remove entire assembly from frame. Follow same procedure in reassembly of barrel and frame.

Note: If detent plunger (7) is allowed to enter any of the dummy chamber holes in front face of cylinder, it will be impossible either to complete disassembly or to re-assemble barrel and cylinder assembly to frame without cutting or drilling out detent housing (5) in order to remove detent plunger (7) from front of cylinder.

After removing barrel and cylinder assembly from frame, withdraw detent plunger (7), detent plunger spring (6), and detent housing (5) to rear. Removal of firing pin assembly is accomplished by drifting out recoil plate retaining pin (12) and removing firing pin (9), firing pin spring (10), and recoil plate (11) to front. Ejector assembly is removed by unscrewing ejector tube screw (28) and separating ejector components after unscrewing ejector assembly (22) from ejector rod assembly (24). Reassemble pistol in reverse. ∎

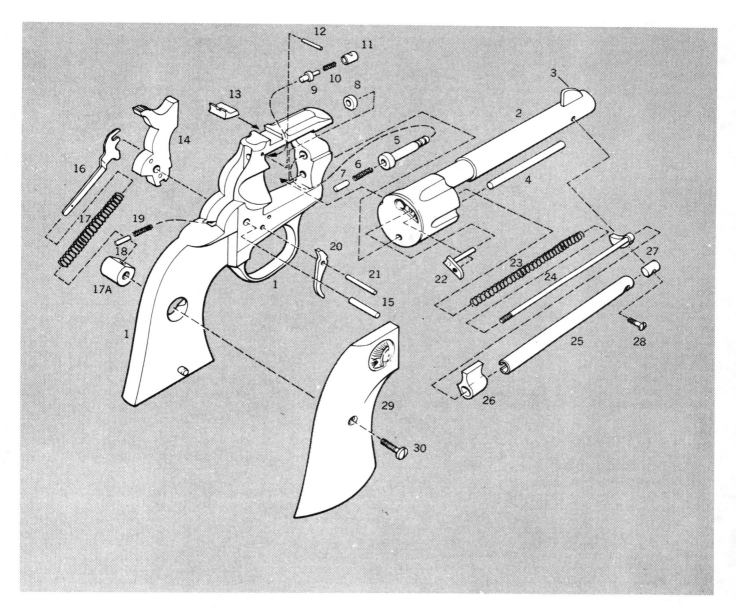

Legend

A—Front sight
B—Slide
C—Extractor
D—Extractor spring
E—Rear sight
F—Firing pin spring
G—Firing pin
H—Firing pin retainer plate
I—Extractor hinge pin
J—Barrel
K—Recoil spring assembly
L—Slide stop operating spring
M—Trigger spring
N—Trigger hinge pin
O—Trigger
P—Trigger bar pin
Q—Trigger bar
R—Sear
S—Sear pressure plate
T—Sear and hammer housing
U—Sear spring
V—Hammer hinge pin
W—Hammer
X—Hammer strut pin
Y—Hammer strut
Z—Hammer spring
AA—Spring retainer nut
BB—Spring retainer lock nut
CC—Sear hinge pin
DD—Pressure plate stop pin
EE—Magazine disconnector screw
FF—Magazine disconnector
GG—Grip screw
HH—Right-hand grip
II—Magazine catch pin
JJ—Magazine catch
KK—Magazine
LL—Left-hand grip
MM—Safety catch
NN—Slide stop
OO—Receiver

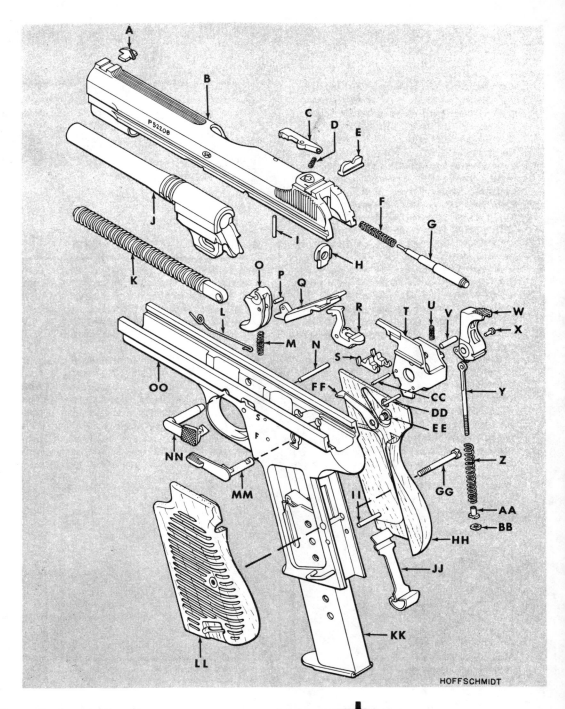

HOFFSCHMIDT

SIG-
Neuhausen Pistol

By E. J. Hoffschmidt

The same workmanship displayed in Swiss watches and machinery is carried over into the firearms they make. One of the most interesting of the latter is the SP47/8 SIG, known now as the SIG-Sauer P-210. This gun was used for some years as the service sidearm of the Swiss, and Danish armies and by the West German Border Patrol. It was designed to replace earlier Luger pistols, revolvers, and other SIG designs. The oldest arms factory in Switzerland, the Schweitzerische Industrie-Gesellschaft (SIG) in Neuhausen/Rheinfalls is the originator of the pistol, manufacture of which was transferred to SIG-Sauer in the mid-1980s.

A quick glance at the P-210 suggests the Browning and P-38 lines. The grips resemble those of the P-38 and the gun uses the Browning type of locked breech, but there the resemblance stops. The sear, hammer and trigger mechanisms are entirely different.

A number of novel features are incorporated into this pistol. First of all the slide is guided back and forth far more rigidly and accurately than on any other current self-loading pistol. this is due to the long tracks that run the full length of the top of the receiver. Secondly, the hammer and sear mechanism can be removed

TECHNICAL DATA			
	Parabellum		*Long Rifle*
Caliber	9 mm.	7.65 mm.	.22
Barrel length	4-¾″	4-¾″	4-¾″
Number of grooves	6	4	6
Right-hand twist, one turn in	9-⅞″	9-⅞″	17-¾″
Magazine capacity: Cartridges	8	8	8
Weights:			
Weapon without magazine	31-¾ ozs.	32 ozs.	29-¾ ozs.
Empty magazine	3 ozs.	3 ozs.	3-⅓ ozs.
Length of line of sight	6-½″	6-½″	6-½″
Overall length	8-½″	8-½″	8-½″
Muzzle velocity f.p.s.	1150	1200	670

as an assembly for cleaning or repair. The design incorporates an excellent, two-stage trigger and a magazine disconnector that prevents the gun from firing when the magazine is removed. Last, but not least, is the captive recoil spring. this prestressed spring assembly can be removed easily without fear of losing an eye or deforming the spring.

The early SIG pistols were made in 9 mm Parabellum or 7.65 mm Luger. A .22 rimfire conversion kit consisting of a barrel, recoil spring magazine, and lightened slide, was also available. Popular in Europe, a 4 mm conversion was also offered.An overall length of 8-1/2 inches and a weight of 34-1/2 ounces make the P-210 feel and handle like a target pistol.

Strong enough to handle ammunition made for any World War II and current submachine gun, the P-210 will handle mixed magazine loads of American, German, Swiss and English 9 mm cartridges without trouble.

While takedown procedure is simpler in some respects than that for the M1911A1 pistol, it could be improved by provision of a latch to hold the slide in a position from which the slide stop can be pushed out. Grip removal is tricky, too. After removing the grip screw, insert a long thin knife blade under the grips and spread them. The grips must be spread in this manner because an undercut projecting into the frame prevents the grips from being lifted off in the usual manner.

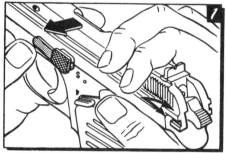

Remove the magazine (KK) and put the gun on safe. Grasp the gun with the right hand as shown, move the slide back enough to line up the first serration on the slide (B) with the edge of the receiver (OO). Now push the slide stop (NN) through from right to left

Strip the slide assembly off the receiver (OO). The sear and hammer assembly can now be lifted out as a unit. To strip this assembly, remove the hammer spring retainer (AA) and lock nut (BB) to relieve the tension on the hammer (W). Now pins (CC), (DD), and (V) may be driven out if necessary

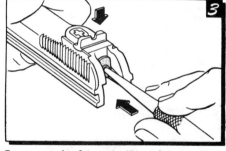

To remove the firing pin (G) and spring (F), it is necessary to depress the end of the firing pin below the surface of the firing pin retainer plate (H). Use the slide stop or a small diameter punch to depress the firing pin, then push the retainer plate down as shown

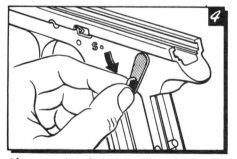

After removing the grips, (LL) and (HH), the safety (MM) can be rotated below the "F" engraved in the receiver until it springs free. It may be necessary to lift the safety out of the detent hole alongside the "F", before attempting to rotate it downward

The slide stop spring (L) is the only part that is difficult to remove. It is necessary to pry it up and over the pin in the receiver as shown. Then push it toward the hammer until the end of the spring is out of its notch in the receiver

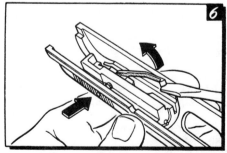

The extractor in the 9 mm. or 7.65 mm. can be removed by driving out pin (I). To remove the .22 conversion unit extractor, it is necessary to pry it up to a vertical position, as shown, to free it. Now, with the aid of a thin punch, push the loose pin across the slide into the hole left by the extractor and the firing pin can be removed

LEGEND

1. Barrel
2. Bushing retaining pin
3. Pivot screw
4. Recoil spring rod
5. Spring rod bushing
6. Recoil spring
7. Recoil spring cap
8. Cap retaining pin
9. Extractor
10. Extractor plunger
11. Extractor spring
12. Bolt (slide)
13. Firing pin retaining pin
14. Firing pin spring
15. Firing pin
16. Ejector
17. Ejector spring
18. Extractor pin
19. Bolt release catch spring
20. Bolt release catch spring plunger
21. Bolt release catch
22. Trigger guard
23. Trigger guard pivot
24. Frame
25. Upper backstrap screw
26. Hammer
27. Hammer strut pin
28. Hammer strut
29. Sear
30. Sear plunger pin
31. Sear plunger spring
32. Sear plunger

33. Sear hinge pin
34. Mainspring plunger
35. Mainspring
36. Plunger retaining pin
37. Safety catch spring
38. Safety catch plunger
39. Safety catch
40. Backstrap
41. Sear spring
42. Notch plate
43. Safety slide
44. Lower backstrap screw
45. Magazine catch plunger
46. Magazine catch spring
47. Magazine catch
48. Magazine
49. Magazine catch pin
50. Sear spring pin
51. Notch plate pin
52. Hammer pin
53. Grip safety spring
54. Grip safety
55. Trigger plunger
56. Trigger plunger spring
57. Trigger plunger pin
58. Trigger
59. Left-hand grip
60. Grip screw

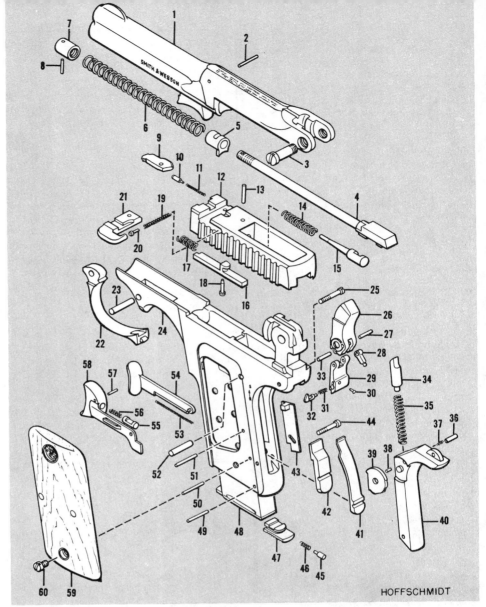

HOFFSCHMIDT

Smith & Wesson .35 Cal. Auto Pistol

By E. J. Hoffschmidt

To some readers, the title of this article may look like a misprint, but the .35 caliber automatic was an unfortunate reality to Smith & Wesson.

In the early 1900's, pocket pistols were selling like 'hotcakes'. Most of the larger American gun companies were producing a variety of .25, .32, and .380 caliber automatics. About 1913, Smith & Wesson took the plunge, but instead of following the trend, they brought out not only a new gun, but a new cartridge, too!

The gun itself was based on a patent by C. P. Clement of Belgium, and, like other Smith & Wesson products, was beautifully made and finished.

The design had less to recommend it than that of many of its foreign and American contemporaries. For instance, while the gun had numerous safety features, the two main safeties were awkwardly placed. The manual safety is a small wheel which projects from the backstrap, making it almost impossible to remove or apply with the gun held in firing position. If the squeeze safety had been placed in the backstrap, it would have operated almost automatically, but since it was in front, it took a conscious effort to release it. The recoil spring disconnecting catch is another feature that is novel but cumbersome. Since the slide is very light, a

heavy recoil spring is necessary to snub its high recoil speed. This spring makes the gun very difficult to cock. Therefore the gun was so made that by pressing the catch on the slide crosswise, the recoil spring is disconnected from the slide. Then the internal hammer can be cocked and a fresh cartridge chambered without working against the heavy recoil spring. This feature is excellent if you are thoroughly familiar with the gun or not too familiar with other automatics, as it takes a conscious effort to cock and load as compared with other common pocket automatics. The above features seem to make the gun a good safe house pistol, but not

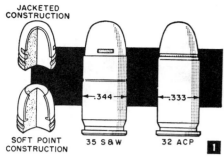

Except for the unusual construction of the bullets and the few thousandths increase in diameter, the .35 Smith & Wesson cartridge could pass for a .32 automatic. The idea was to make a jacketed bullet that would operate through a magazine without deforming, yet have only the lead touch the rifling to decrease barrel wear. Ballistically, the .32 ACP is a bit more powerful

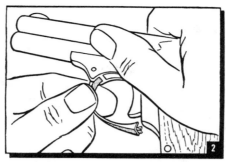

The takedown system is the best feature of the Smith & Wesson .35 automatic. Simply pull down on the rear of the trigger guard as shown. When free, swing it forward and lift up the front end of the barrel. The gun can then be cleaned from the breech without fear of losing any parts

Smith & Wesson
.35 Cal. Auto

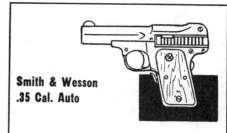

PISTOL MAGAZINES

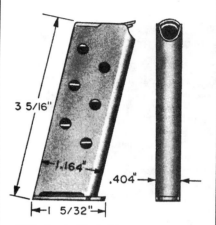

While the Smith & Wesson .35 cal. automatics were beautifully made and finished, the odd caliber is considered the main reason for its downfall. Produced between 1913 and 1921, it was never very popular. Actually, it is a better gun to have around the house than for on-the-person use. The safeties are awkward and the recoil spring very strong, making it difficult to pull back the slide unless the spring disconnecting latch is used.

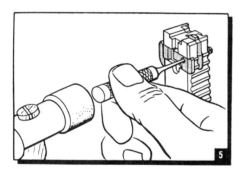

Unlike most pocket pistols, when the grip screws (60) are removed, the grips (59) remain fixed tightly to the frame. Since they are riveted to a metal plate that is dove-tailed into the frame, the grip (59) must be pushed off as shown. Never try to pry them free; it will ruin them

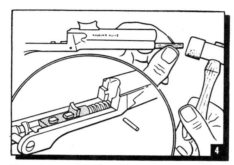

Since the recoil spring (6) is part of a captive assembly, it cannot fly out when the bushing retaining pin (2) is removed. When removing the spring rod bushing (5), replace the pivot screw (3) to prevent the assembly being damaged when it is driven out. Then, with a wooden dowel, drive the assembly out as shown

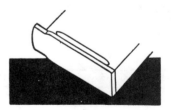

The Smith & Wesson .35 cal. magazine is no larger than the conventional .32 cal. magazine and will readily interchange with the rare Smith & Wesson .32 automatic. It is difficult to identify, since it is not marked, but it features the long crimp above the floorplate. This is characteristic of only the Smith & Wesson magazine.

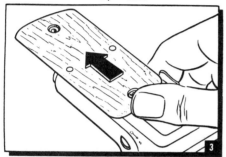

The extractor pin (18) is the key to the bolt (12) takedown. It must be driven out through the hole in the bolt release catch (21) with a thin punch. With this pin out, the extractor (9), its spring (11) and plunger (10), and the bolt release catch (21) with its spring (19) and plunger (20), will be free

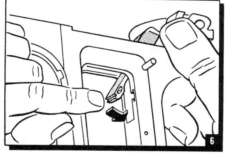

After the hammer (26) and sear (29) have been pinned together, insert the hammer into the frame through the magazine opening. Insert the hammer pin (52) and swing the sear back into the frame as shown. Do not try to insert the assembly through the backstrap opening

With the possible exception of the nearness of the witness holes to the back of the magazine, there is little else to distinguish it from the average .32 cal. magazine.—E. J. HOFFSCHMIDT

one to be carried for defense. The operating procedure is too slow. So, in spite of its famous name, and the flawless workmanship, only a little over 8,000 pistols were sold between 1913 and 1921, when production was stopped.

There are at least two common variations. In the earlier model, the magazine latch works from side to side, but in the later guns, it works from front to rear, or in the conventional manner.

The takedown procedure for cleaning is simple, but beyond that care must be taken since the gun has several tiny spring-loaded parts.

The .35 caliber ammunition is scarce, since it has not been manufactured since 1940. The gun will feed, fire, and eject .32 caliber ACP ammunition. The cases will bulge, but usually not enough to rupture. ■

exploded views:

S&W Bodyguard Revolvers

BY JAMES S. McLELLAN

The aluminum-frame Model 38 Bodyguard was introduced in mid-1955. Its heavier twin, the steel-frame Model 49, came along in 1959.

THE S&W Bodyguard was developed for law enforcement agencies that required a revolver with a protected hammer that would not catch on clothing but would be exposed enough for single-action cocking. To accomplish this, the factory designed a new J frame that extended even with the hammer spur, and a new low-profile hammer with more surface area.

The first Bodyguard (Model 38 Airweight) was made with an aluminum frame. Since the revolver was to be carried in the pocket by law enforcement personnel, the factory felt it was important to keep the weight to a minimum. This was the first airweight model made by S&W.

The first Model 38s were made in August, 1955, beginning at serial number 66,000 in the J-frame series. The first-year production revolvers (2422 units) were manufactured in what the collectors classify as the four-screw side-plate variation; i.e., an additional screw on the upper area of the plate.

In 1959, after receiving an inquiry from the Massachusetts State Police, S&W began to produce the Model 49 with steel frame. Production began in July, 1959, with serial number 163,051.

The Models 38 and 49 are now available in blue or nickel finish with 2″ barrels. In the past, a few Model 49s were manufactured with a 3″ barrel, and a stainless steel cylinder Model 49 was once produced to meet the requirements of the Michigan State Police. ∎

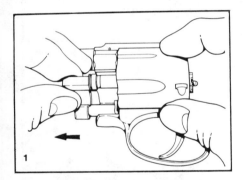
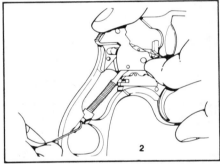
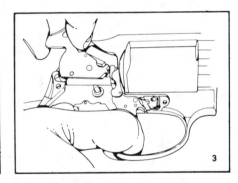
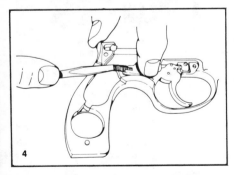
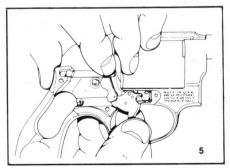
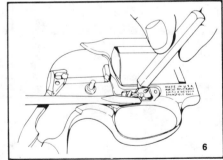

Disassembly Instructions

1. Remove stocks by loosening stock screw (9). Leaving screwdriver in place, push the screw in against the right stock (32). This will release that stock without damaging the frame. Remove left-hand stock (10) by tapping gently with screw-driver through the frame (30). Remove yoke screw (57). Hold cylinder (6) in open position and draw the yoke (8) forward out of the frame. Insert a dummy or empty cartridge in one of the chambers to protect extractor pins, then grasp the extractor rod (3) in a vise. Never put the knurled end into the vise. Now turn the cylinder clockwise to unscrew the extractor rod.

2. Remove round head side-plate screw (56) and flat head side-plate screw (55). Loosen side-plate (54) by tapping the side of the backstrap with a nylon hammer. Hold the front of the side plate to prevent dropping it. The hammer block (53) may drop out when you remove the side-plate, as it rides in a slot in the plate. If it does not, remove it. Cock the hammer (36) and insert

222

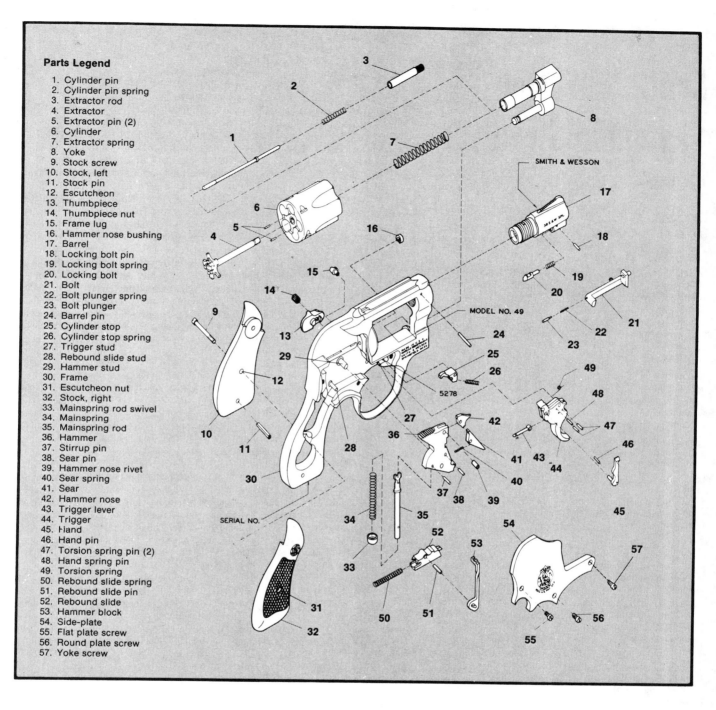

Parts Legend

1. Cylinder pin
2. Cylinder pin spring
3. Extractor rod
4. Extractor
5. Extractor pin (2)
6. Cylinder
7. Extractor spring
8. Yoke
9. Stock screw
10. Stock, left
11. Stock pin
12. Escutcheon
13. Thumbpiece
14. Thumbpiece nut
15. Frame lug
16. Hammer nose bushing
17. Barrel
18. Locking bolt pin
19. Locking bolt spring
20. Locking bolt
21. Bolt
22. Bolt plunger spring
23. Bolt plunger
24. Barrel pin
25. Cylinder stop
26. Cylinder stop spring
27. Trigger stud
28. Rebound slide stud
29. Hammer stud
30. Frame
31. Escutcheon nut
32. Stock, right
33. Mainspring rod swivel
34. Mainspring
35. Mainspring rod
36. Hammer
37. Stirrup pin
38. Sear pin
39. Hammer nose rivet
40. Sear spring
41. Sear
42. Hammer nose
43. Trigger lever
44. Trigger
45. Hand
46. Hand pin
47. Torsion spring pin (2)
48. Hand spring pin
49. Torsion spring
50. Rebound slide spring
51. Rebound slide pin
52. Rebound slide
53. Hammer block
54. Side-plate
55. Flat plate screw
56. Round plate screw
57. Yoke screw

SMITH & WESSON

MODEL NO. 49

a paper clip through the hole in the mainspring rod (35). Release hammer so compressed mainspring (34) and rod can be removed as shown.

3. Push thumbpiece (13) to the rear and pull trigger (44) to its full rearward position. This will cock the hammer. While holding the trigger rearward, lift the hammer straight out of the frame as shown.

4. Remove rebound slide (52) and spring (50) by raising slide halfway up on stud (28) with screwdriver as shown. Change position of screwdriver to flat edge and push in on spring. Allow spring to release *slowly*. Note that the screwdriver and finger prevent spring from flying off.

5. To remove trigger (44) and hand (45),

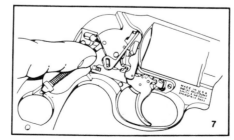

use left index finger to hold the hand out of the slot in the frame while the thumb and middle finger of the right hand lift trigger straight off the trigger stud (27).

6. Push cylinder stop (25) down from the

top, then use a drift pin to hold it down while the screwdriver lifts it straight up off its pin. Be careful to contain the spring to prevent loss.

7. Reassemble in reverse order, making sure parts are inserted level. Be sure trigger lever (43) is inside frame and can be inserted into front of rebound slide assembly. Hold trigger rearward when installing hammer. Hook top of mainspring rod on stirrup pin (37), then cock hammer to relieve compression so you can remove paper clip. Be sure hammer block is laid in its "up" position. Install side-plate front and top undercuts first, then seat it by tapping lightly with a nylon hammer on the screw holes.

Smith & Wesson Centennial Revolver

By James M. Triggs

In 1888 Smith & Wesson introduced an internal hammer, double-action revolver, a great stride in handgun design for personal defense. It was a pistol that guarded against accidental discharge and it embodied all the best features of Smith & Wesson's already famous line of revolvers. The Safety Hammerless

The late James M. Triggs was a well known writer-illustrator and collector of antique firearms.

"New Departure" was of hinged frame de sign and was made to chamber a relatively mild blackpowder cartridge.

After World War II, it became obvious that there was still a demand for a so-called hammerless revolver. Smith & Wesson was receiving orders for an arm of that type but was also keenly aware that a newly designed gun, similar in purpose to the New Departure must be sturdy enough to handle modern am-

munition with a fair margin of safety.

As a result, S&W decided to produce an entirely new gun. It was named the "Centennial", because its introduction, in 1953, closely coincided with the company's 100th anniversary. The Centennial remained in production for 21 years, until 1974.

The Centennial was of solid frame design, capable of handling standard .38 Special cartridges of its time, and in it are combined the outstanding features of its older counterpart. While in production, the Centennial It was available with a steel frame or optionally with a lightweight alloy frame, known as the "Centennial Airweight".

The Centennial was immediately and enthusiastically accepted by two groups of users — law enforcement officers, especially detectives, who found it an excellent sidearm for undercover or off-duty use, and plain "John Q. Citizen", private individuals who wanted a safe, effective handgun for personal defense. The Centennial was a good answer to both requirements. The introduction, in

PARTS LEGEND

1. Frame
2. Bolt
3. Bolt plunger
4. Bolt plunger spring
5. Thumbpiece
6. Thumbpiece screw
7. Extractor
8. Cylinder
9. Dowel pin (2)
10. Extractor spring
11. Center pin
12. Center pin spring
13. Yoke
14. Extractor rod
15. Locking bolt
16. Locking bolt spring
17. Locking bolt pin
18. Barrel
19. Barrel pin
20. Safety lever
20A. Safety lever pin
20B. Safety lever lock pin (in storage hole)
21. Safety lever spring
22. Stock pin
23. Safety latch
24. Safety latch pin
25. Rebound slide spring
26. Rebound slide
27. Cylinder stop
28. Hammer
29. Hammer nose rivet
30. Hammer nose
31. Sear
32. Sear pin
33. Sear spring
34. Mainspring rod
35. Mainspring
36. Mainspring swivel
37. Trigger
38. Trigger lever
39. Hand
40. Hand torsion spring
41. Hand torsion spring pins (2)
42. Trigger lever pin
43. Side-plate
44. Flat head side-plate screw (1)
45. Large head side-plate screw
46. Small head side-plate & yoke screws (2)
47. Stock screw
48. Stock (2)

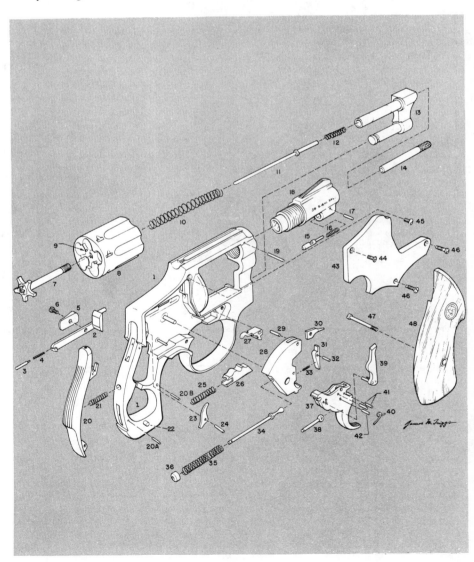

the mid- and late 1960s, of successfully powerful, self-loading pocket pistols spelled the end for the Centennial.

DISASSEMBLY PROCEDURE

Disassembly of the S&W Centennial follows generally that of other S&W revolvers. Remove the stock screw (47), stocks, and side-plate screws (44, 45, 46) and, holding the gun with the side-plate up, tap the frame gently with a wooden or fiber hammer until the side-plate works loose. Prying off the side-plate usually results in burring its edges and damaging the finish. The cylinder and yoke assembly are removed by swinging out the cylinder and pulling the yoke forward and out of the frame.

Remove the mainspring assembly as detailed in Fig. 2. Remove the rebound slide (26) and spring (25) by lifting the rear of the slide up and free of the pin in the frame. Care should be taken in this operation to prevent the compressed spring escaping once it is free from its pin.

The remaining interior parts of the revolver are easily removed. The safety lever (20) and spring (21) may be removed by gently drifting out the safety lever pin (20A). The safety latch (23) may be removed by drifting out its pin (24) also. Note that all S&W Centennial revolvers are supplied with a lock pin (20B) carried in a recess in the frame adjacent to the base of the mainspring. Installation of the lock pin in order to deactivate the safety lever is detailed in Fig. 3. ————■

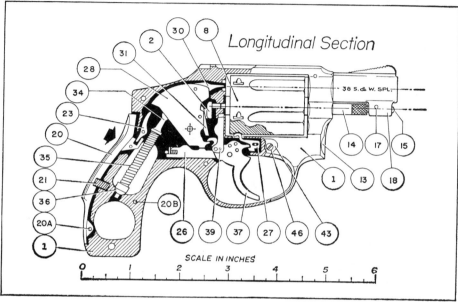

Longitudinal Section

38 S. & W. SPL.

SCALE IN INCHES

1 The working parts of the Centennial revolver. This mechanism is basically the same as that of other Smith & Wesson revolvers with the exception of hammer and the safety lever feature. This revolver also differs from other S&W arms in that it does not have a hammer block. In order to fire the revolver, the grip must be held firmly enough to depress the safety lever (20) as shown by the arrow. Depressing the safety lever moves the upper arm of the safety latch back and out of the

path of the rear face of the hammer as it is retracted when the trigger is pulled. If the safety lever is not fully depressed, its interlocking lug which engages the lower arm of the safety latch (23) will hold the upper arm of the latch under the hammer, preventing the hammer from coming back to a firing position. The drawing shows the safety lever extended (not depressed) with the safety latch blocking the hammer. Note that this arm is fired only double-action

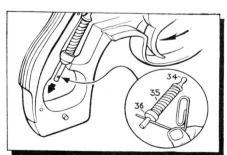

2 The mainspring can be removed by pulling back on the trigger until the small hole at the base of the mainspring rod (34) clears the mainspring swivel (36). Insert a straightened paper clip or other small pin in this hole, holding the mainspring (35) compressed and lift the entire mainspring assembly clear of the frame

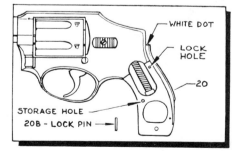

WHITE DOT
LOCK HOLE
20
STORAGE HOLE
20B - LOCK PIN

3 To deactivate the safety lever (20), remove the lock pin (20B) from storage hole in frame, and insert in lock hole in the frame above the lug of the safety lever while pressing the lever in to its depressed position. There is a white dot on the top of the safety lever which is visible when the lever is in its 'safe' position. The dot is not visible when the lever is pressed in for firing or locked in by the lock pin

French MAS
Model 1935S

PISTOL MAGAZINES

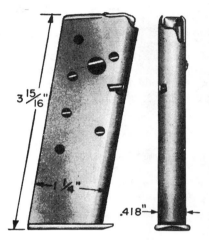

$3\frac{15}{16}$"

1 ¼"

.418"

It is unfortunate that French military automatic pistols are chambered for the uncommon 7.65 mm. Long pistol cartridge. Ammunition is so scarce that these interesting guns are not fully appreciated. The Model 1935S was manufactured at the government arsenal at St. Etienne. It is an excellent gun, with a simple rugged mechanism and a grip that is second to none. These guns are generally finished with a blue-black paint that is far more rust resistant than the common blued finish.

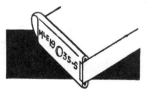

Like the rest of the gun, the 1935S magazine is usually marked as shown. Unlike the magazine of the 1935A Model, the floorplate is removable. Press in the center button and the floorplate can be slid off the front of the magazine.

The follower is made from a sheet-steel stamping and the left side of the magazine is cut down to allow the follower to operate the hold-open latch. The small half-round protrusion on the left-hand side operates the magazine safety.—E. J. HOFFSCHMIDT

Smith & Wesson Escort

BY DENNIS RIORDAN

Introduced in March, 1970, the Model 61 Smith & Wesson Escort is a small, lightweight autoloading pistol for the .22 LR cartridge. It is blowback operated with a 2⅛" barrel fixed in its aluminum frame. The grips and follower for the five-round magazine are made of molded plastic. The pistol is 4¹³/₁₆" long and weighs 14 ozs.

There are four versions. The original Model 16 carries serial numbers from B1,001 to B7,800. In May, 1970, a trigger block magazine safety was added and the result called the Model 61-1. The serial number range of this version is B7,801—B9,850. One lot was made with serial numbers from B1—B500. These low-numbered guns are not first production of the Model 61 but a special run of the Model 61-

1. In September, 1970, a nut was added to secure the muzzle end of the barrel in the frame. This is the Model 61-2. Serial numbers range from B9,850—B40,000. In July, 1971, a forged aluminum frame which extends upward to hold the recoil spring guide tube replaced the earlier cast frame. The serial number range is B40,001—B65,438. This final version illustrated here is known as the Model 61-3. The four versions are identified by the model number stamped at the bottom of the grip behind the serial number.

The Model 61 was officially discontinued in March, 1973. Limited quantities were assembled from existing parts until February, 1974. Total production of all versions was nearly 65,000.

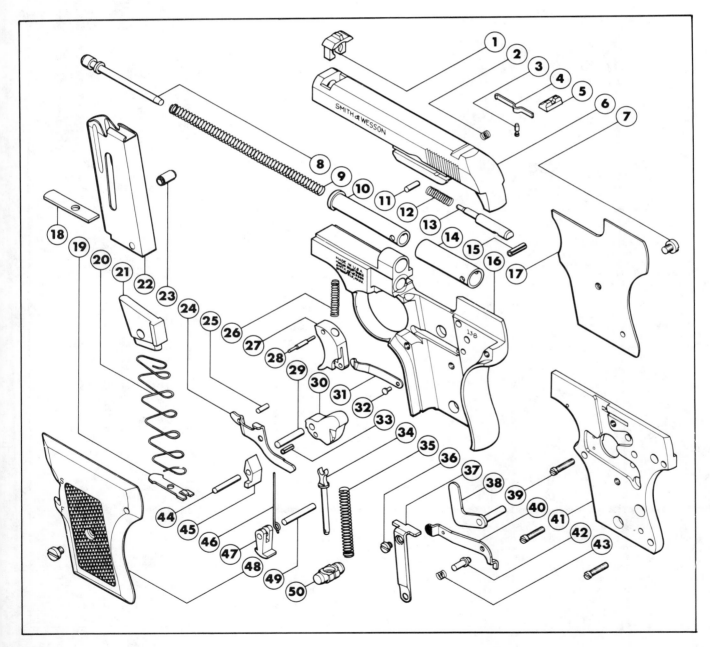

Parts Legend

1.	Front sight	18.	Magazine buttplate	35.		Mainspring
2.	Extractor spring	19.	Magazine spring plate	36.		Ejector screw
3.	Extractor pin	20.	Magazine spring	37.		Ejector
4.	Extractor	21.	Magazine follower	38.		Disconnector
5.	Rear sight	22.	Magazine tube	39.		Side-plate screw (3)
6.	Slide	23.	Magazine follower pin	40.		Manual safety lever
7.	Stock screw (2)	24.	Trigger bar	41.		Side-plate
8.	Recoil spring guide	25.	Trigger bar pin	42.		Indicator plunger
9.	Recoil spring	26.	Trigger bar spring	43.		Indicator plunger spring
10.	Recoil spring guide tube	27.	Trigger	44.		Sear pin
11.	Firing pin retaining pin	28.	Trigger pin	45.		Sear
12.	Firing pin spring	29.	Hammer pin	46.	Spring, magazine catch and sear	
13.	Firing pin	30.	Hammer			
14.	Retainer tube	31.	Trigger block	47.		Magazine catch
15.	Recoil spring stop pin	32.	Trigger block rivet	48.		Stock-left hand
16.	Frame	33.	Stirrup pin	49.		Magazine catch pin
17.	Stock-right hand	34.	Stirrup	50.		Mainspring retainer

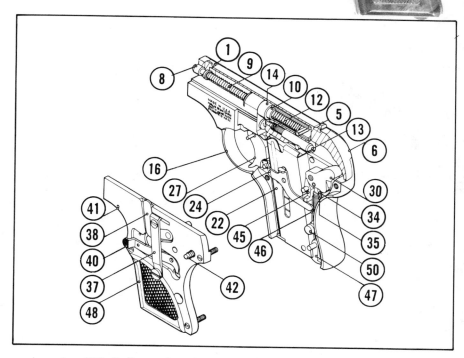

Disassembly Procedure:

The Model 61 may be field stripped without tools. The front sight (1) is the key to disassembly. Remove the magazine and pull back the slide (6) to insure there is no cartridge in the chamber. Release the slide and press inward on the end of the recoil spring guide (8) which projects above the muzzle. Lift out the front sight while holding the spring guide in.

Pull the recoil spring (9) and guide out of the slide. The slide may then be removed by moving it to its extreme rearward position, then lifting it straight up off the frame. Further disassembly is not required for routine cleaning.

To strip the frame, place the assembly right side down on a bench. Remove the left stock screw and lift off the stock. Withdraw the indicator plunger (42) and spring (43). Unscrew the ejector screw (36) and lift off the ejector (37). Remove the disconnector (38) and safety lever (40). Unscrew the side-plate screws (39) and remove side-plate (41) by grasping at the top and bottom, working it off slowly and evenly. Do not allow the four frame pins or the mainspring retainer (50) to come out. It may be necessary to hold them down with a punch.

To disassemble the trigger mechanism, insert a straightened paper clip through the hole near the tip of the stirrup pin (33). Thumb back the hammer (30) and trip the sear (45), using the paper clip to check the

mainspring (35). Pull out the trigger (27), trigger bar (24), and spring (26) as an assembly. Unhook the torsion spring (46) from the sear. The remaining parts are easily removed from the frame.

In reassembly, it may be necessary to align the hammer pin (20) and mainspring retainer (50) with the side-plate holes by using a punch inserted between the side-plate and frame. Be sure the torsion spring (46)

which operates the magazine catch and sear is installed with the loop toward the rear.

To disassemble the magazine, pass a punch through the hole in the buttplate (18) to depress the spring plate (19). Slide out buttplate and ease out spring plate and spring (20). Remove follower (21) by pushing out follower pin (23) after aligning it with disassembly hole in right side of magazine tube. ∎

The first Smith & Wesson "Masterpiece", the K-22, was introduced in 1940, just in time to have its production suspended during World War II.

In 1947, the Masterpiece line was reintroduced, in .22 rimfire, .32 S&W Long and .38 Special, designated K-22, K-32 and K-38. In 1949, in answer to demands from target shooters, the K-38 was offered in a heavyweight version featuring an cylindrical, ribbed barrel of 6" length. The revised design brought the weight of the .38 Special revolver up to that of its .22 and .32 stablemates so that a shooter could switch from one gun to another without a change in the feel and handling qualities. Target stocks and a target hammers were available at added cost.

The Masterpieces were fine revolvers, but were overtaken by technology, particularly the introduction of self-loading pistols to the country's target ranges. The K-32 was discontinued in 1974, the K-38 was dropped in 1981, and the .22 Magnum version of the K-22 disappeared in 1986. In 1992, only a cosmetically much-changed version of the .22 rimfire retains the "Masterpiece" name.

Smith & Wesson revolvers are comparatively simple to repair, mainly because they will operate without the sideplate, allowing a full view of what makes them tick. Malfunctions can then be seen and corrected. But, removing the sideplate can be difficult at times. The factory recommends that the gun be held with the sideplate up and the rear tang of the frame tapped lightly with a wooden or leather-faced mallet until the sideplate is jarred free.

Of course the grips must be removed before attempting this. These, too, must not be pried off. Instead, loosen the grip screw until the head clears the stock. Then use the screw to push the right-hand stock free. The left-hand stock can then be removed by tapping lightly through the frame from the right.

By E. J. Hoffschmidt

Smith & Wesson K38 Heavyweight Masterpiece

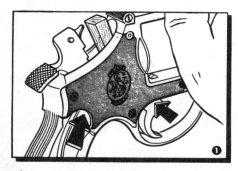

After removing the sideplate screws (39, 40, 41, 41a), tap the frame lightly with a wood or leather mallet to jar the sideplate (38) loose. If it is rusted in, it must be wedged up with a hard wood wedge and pried out evenly to prevent damage to plate or frame pins

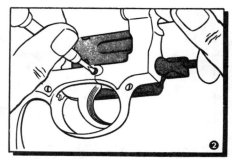

To remove the cylinder assembly, unscrew the small head plate screw (40). Then swing out the cylinder assembly and ease it forward out of the frame. This screw is sometimes filed on the end to give a close fit; be sure to replace it in the same position when reassembling

When removing the mainspring (53), remove the strain screw (51) and push the spring out of its slot. To replace the mainspring, hook it to the hammer stirrup (46), and spring it into place over a piece of ¼-inch dowel as shown and tighten the strain screw (51)

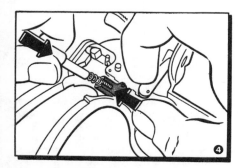

The rebound slide (49) and spring (50) can be removed by lifting the rear section free of the stud in the frame. Keep a cloth over the gun to trap the spring and prevent injury. Replace it by pushing the spring (50) inside the rebound slide (49) and down behind the frame stud

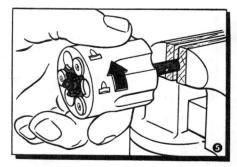

The extractor may be removed by holding the extractor rod (5) between wooden jaws in the vise and turning the cylinder as shown. Keep a few empty cartridges in the chamber to prevent strain on the cylinder spline and extractor-guide pins, Post-1959 guns have a left-hand thread

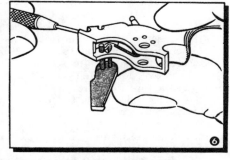

When replacing the hand (44) in the trigger (36), it is necessary to hold up the tail of the hand spring (45) with a small screwdriver while the hand pin is pushed into place as shown. The trigger and hand are then put in the gun as an assembly

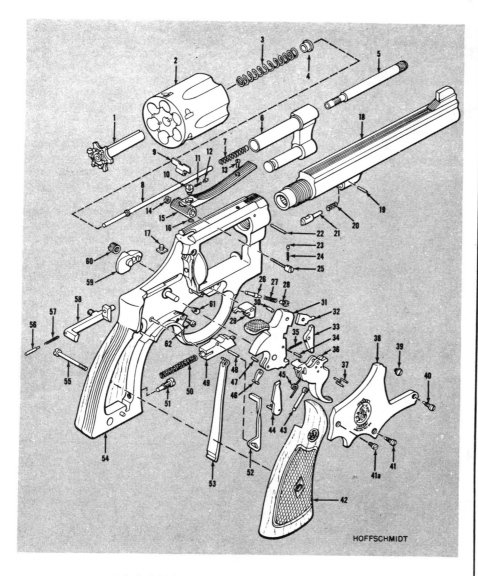

HOFFSCHMIDT

LEGEND

1. Extractor
2. Cylinder
3. Extractor spring
4. Extractor rod collar
5. Extractor rod
6. Yoke
7. Center pin spring
8. Center pin
9. Sight slide
10. Sight elevating nut
11. Sight leaf plunger spring
12. Sight leaf plunger
13. Sight leaf screw
14. Windage screw nut
15. Sight leaf
16. Windage screw spring clip
17. Sight elevating stud
18. Barrel
19. Locking bolt pin
20. Locking bolt spring
21. Locking bolt
22. Barrel pin
23. Sight leaf plunger
24. Sight leaf plunger spring
25. Windage screw
26. Cylinder stop plunger
27. Cylinder stop plunger spring
28. Cylinder stop screw
29. Cylinder stop
30. Hammer nose rivet

31. Hammer
32. Hammer nose
33. Sear
34. Sear pin
35. Sear spring
36. Trigger
37. Trigger pins
38. Sideplate
39. Large head plate screw
40. Small head plate screw
41. Small head plate screw
41a. Small flat head plate screw
42. Stock, right-hand
43. Trigger lever
44. Hand
45. Hand spring
46. Hammer stirrup
47. Hammer stirrup pin
48. Rebound slide pin
49. Rebound slide
50. Rebound slide spring
51. Strain screw
52. Hammer block
53. Mainspring
54. Frame
55. Stock screw
56. Bolt plunger
57. Bolt plunger spring
58. Bolt
59. Thumbpiece
60. Thumbpiece nut
61. Trigger stop
62. Trigger stop screw

Polish Radom
Cal. 9 mm. Luger

PISTOL MAGAZINES

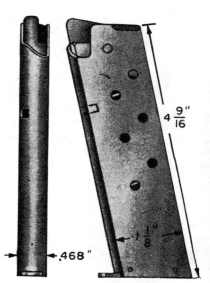

In 1935, Poland began production on what might be called a modernized version of the Colt 1911 automatic. This was the P-35, better known as the Radom. Pre-World War II Radoms were beautifully made and finished, but with the coming of World War II the guns deteriorated. Wartime pressure eliminated the shoulder stock and the hold-open latch, as well as the fine finish. The Radom, however, remains a strong, reliable design.

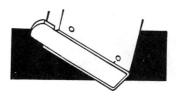

Like the rest of the gun, the Radom magazines are strong and well made. The magazines are generally not marked, but can be identified by the location of the magazine catch slot and the shape of the floorplate. The floorplate is riveted to the magazine sides as shown.

The shape of the follower is distinctive. The front edge usually protrudes well up beyond the magazine lips. The follower is pressed from sheet steel and presents a solid appearance.—E. J. HOFFSCHMIDT

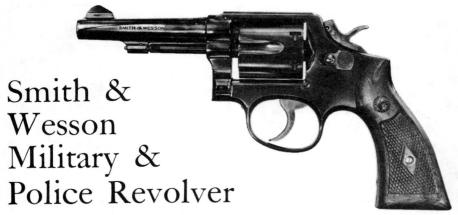

Smith & Wesson Military & Police Revolver

By James M. Triggs

DURING the Spanish-American War, Smith & Wesson, Springfield, Mass., was tendered a government contract for 3000 cal. .38 double-action revolvers, of which 2000 were for the Navy and 1000 for the Army. The war ended before delivery of a single gun had been made, but the contract was not canceled, and first deliveries were eventually made early in 1899. Designated the .38 Hand Ejector, Military & Police Model, this revolver was the first cal. .38 side-swing model to be made by Smith & Wesson. It was chambered for the .38 Colt long cartridge. The military version was made with 6½" barrel and walnut grips. The commercial model had hard rubber grips and 4" barrel.

The improved Model 1902 M&P introduced in that year was chambered for the new cal. .38 S&W Special cartridge, and also featured a front lock for the extractor rod.

The Model 1905 that superseded the Model 1902 also incorporated significant improvements. By 1942 over 1,000,000 M&P's had been manufactured. Under pressure of wartime need, Smith & Wesson in April 1942 began production of the Victory Model M&P with gray sandblasted finish. Serial numbers were preceded by the letter 'V' and a new numbering series was begun. In December 1944 an improved hammer block was instituted and serial numbers were preceded by the letters 'VS' to indicate incorporation of this feature in the lock mechanism. With the coming of peace, and cancellation of government contracts, Smith & Wesson resumed production of commercial

Parts Legend

1. Frame
2. Barrel
3. Barrel pin
4. Yoke
5. Extractor rod
6. Center pin spring
7. Center pin
8. Extractor rod collar
9. Extractor spring
10. Cylinder
11. Extractor
12. Bolt
13. Bolt plunger spring
14. Bolt plunger
15. Thumbpiece
16. Thumbpiece nut
17. Locking bolt
18. Locking bolt spring
19. Locking bolt pin
20. Side-plate
21. Side-plate screws, roundhead (2)
22. Side-plate screw, large head (discontinued)
22A. Side-plate screw, flathead
23. Cylinder stop plunger
24. Cylinder stop plunger spring
25. Cylinder stop screw
26. Cylinder stop
27. Strain screw
28. Stock pin
29. Rebound slide spring
30. Rebound slide
31. Rebound slide pin
32. Mainspring
33. Hammer block
34. Hammer
35. Hammer nose
36. Hammer nose rivet
37. Stirrup
38. Stirrup pin
39. Sear
40. Sear pin
41. Sear spring
42. Trigger
43. Trigger lever
44. Trigger lever pin
45. Hand spring torsion pins (2)
46. Hand torsion spring
47. Hand
48. Stocks
49. Stock screw

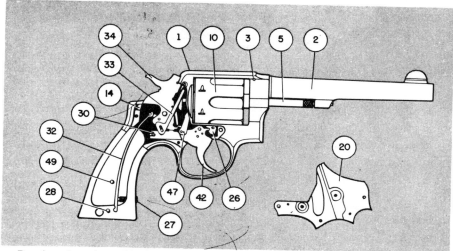

Drawing of revolver with side-plate removed shows proper relationship of interior parts

M&Ps, but continued the serial number sequence begun in 1942. Serial numbers were preceded by the letter "S".

Production of the "S" series continued until March 1948, when the factory completed its second million Military & Police revolvers The prefix was changed to a "C" at that time and to a "D" upon completion of another million revolvers in 1967.

Still a best seller, the present-day S&W Military & Police revolver is known as the Model 10. Its variants include the Model 13, in .357 Magnum, and the stainless steel Model 65, among others.

The late Jim Triggs was a writer-illustrator and well known gun collector.

DISASSEMBLY PROCEDURE

Swing out cylinder, then loosen forward side-plate screw (21) and withdraw cylinder and yoke assembly from frame. Withdraw yoke (4) from cylinder assembly. On older guns with knobbed extractor rod, yoke cannot be removed from cylinder assembly until extractor rod has been removed as in next step.

To disassemble cylinder assembly insert several empty cases in cylinder to prevent strain on extractor (11), then grip extractor rod (5) with pliers (pad jaws) and turn cylinder until extractor rod is free of extractor. Guns made from 1899 to 1960 have a right-hand thread; those after 1961 a left-hand thread. Withdraw extractor rod, yoke, extractor rod collar (8), extractor spring (9), center pin (7) with center pin spring (6), and extractor.

Remove stock screw (49) and stocks (48).

Remove side-plate screws (21 [2], 22, 22A). Side-plate (20) is loosened by tapping opposite surface of frame sharply with a wood or fiber hammer until it can be removed from frame. Attempts to pry out side-plate will deform its edges and those of frame cut.

Mainspring (32) is easily removed by loosening strain screw (27). All interior parts of lock mechanism are now easily removed for cleaning or replacement. However, for normal cleaning purposes, it is seldom necessary to carry disassembly beyond removal of side-plate. The accompanying drawings point out some methods for further disassembly.

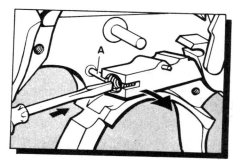

1 To remove rebound slide (30), pry up rear end of slide with blade of small screwdriver but do not allow spring to clear end of rebound slide stud (A) in frame. Compress rear end of rebound slide spring (29) with screwdriver blade as shown and draw rebound slide up off stud (A), taking care not to let compressed spring escape. In replacing rebound slide in frame, spring must again be compressed inside slide so that it will clear stud before slide can be pressed down into position. Note that the stud (A) and other pivot studs in frame are permanently installed and their removal should not be attempted

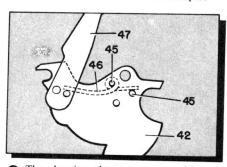

2 The drawing shows proper position of hand (47) installed in trigger (42). Hand can be removed from trigger by pulling it free. When replacing hand in trigger, take care that hand torsion spring (46) is in correct position with respect to hand spring torsion pins (45) in trigger and small torsion pin installed in hand ∎

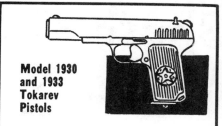

Model 1930 and 1933 Tokarev Pistols

PISTOL MAGAZINES

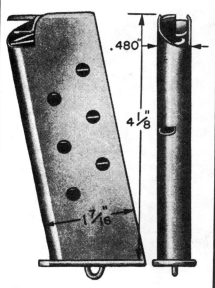

.480"

4 1/8"

1 7/16"

Tokarev pistols are basically of Browning design, but lack any safety except for the half-cock. They are only fairly well machined and the parts are not always interchangeable. This is true of the magazines. For best results the magazine number should match the pistol serial number. Tokarevs fire the powerful bottleneck 7.62 mm. Russian and 7.63 mm. Mauser pistol cartridges. They are not as well made as most German and U. S. automatics, but are powerful and reliable.

Tokarev magazines can be recognized by their relatively small width and large front-to-rear dimension. The step in the sheet metal follower is another identifying point.

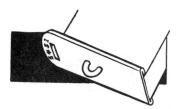

These magazines are usually numbered on the front lip of the floorplate. The lanyard loop and rectangular floorplate retaining stud are typical features.—E. J. HOFFSCHMIDT

Smith & Wesson Model 39

By James M. Triggs

The Model 39 Smith & Wesson, introduced in August 1954, is the first centerfire, self-loading pistol of double-action type designed and made for the commercial market by an American firm. Earlier commercial self-loading pistols featuring a double-action mechanism were of European manufacture. Perhaps the most noteworthy of these is the German Walther 9 mm Heeres (Army) Pistol designed in 1937 and subsequently adopted as an official German Service pistol, designated Pistole 38. The P.38 was produced in great quantities by German firms during world War II, and its double-action capability appeals to those who feel the revolver to be a more reliable combat arm than the self-loading pistol. When a cartridge misfires in a double-action revolver the user has but to pull the trigger to place a *fresh round* under the hammer. With the self-loading pistol the user must pull back the slide to eject the faulty cartridge or hand cock the hammer (if the gun has an exposed hammer) before he can again pull the trigger.

The late Jim Triggs was a writer-illustrator and well known gun collector

The shooter equipped with a double-action pistol, in such an instance, is in a somewhat more favorable position should a cartridge fail to fire, for he has only the pull the trigger to deliver a second blow to the cartridge. A secondary advantage of the double-action mechanism is that the pistol can be safely carried with a cartridge in the chamber, hammer down and safety "OFF" and yet be fired merely by a deliberate pull on the trigger.

Smith & Wesson made the basic Model 39, with an aluminum alloy frame (a steel-frame Model 39 was available between 1954 and 1966) from 1954 until 1981, at which time it was modified and redesigned Model 439, for the standard gun and 639 for a stainless steel version. Current pistols in the series are cataloged using a four-digit designator beginning with "39".

DISASSEMBLY PROCEDURE

Remove magazine and verify that pistol is unloaded. Put safety in "fire" (upper) position. While pressing *in* on right hand end of slide stop (21), draw slide (1) to rear until recess in lower left side is aligned with forward end of slide stop. Pull slide

stop out of frame from left and pull slide forward off the frame (20). With slide upside down, compress recoil spring (15) and lift out recoil spring guide assembly (16) with spring. Remove barrel bushing (17) by rotating its lower portion to left side of slide and draw it forward out of slide. Remove barrel (18) by grasping rear bottom end of barrel and drawing up and outward from slide to the rear. Further disassembly is not recommended as pistol may be properly cleaned and lubricated when thus field-stripped.

To reassemble pistol, replace barrel in slide and replace barrel bushing. Replace recoil spring and recoil spring guide assembly, making sure that recoil spring guide bushing is engaged in small radius cut in barrel lug and properly centered. Failure to center properly will leave recoil spring guide protruding from barrel bushing after assembly. Replace slide on frame, depressing ejector (29) and sear release lever (25) in turn so slide will travel to the rear over them. When slide stop cut on slide is aligned with slide stop hole in frame, insert slide stop and allow slide to return to forward position. Replace magazine. The numbered illustrations at right detail the steps in field-stripping the pistol.

To disassemble slide assembly, press rear end of firing pin (13) in as far as possible with a small punch and grasp forward end of firing pin with a pair of pliers and hold. Turn manual safety thumbpiece (19) half way between "fire" and "safe" positions and press right end of manual safety into slide, withdrawing it from slide from the left. Hold thumb over rear end of firing pin and release grip on pliers. Remove firing pin (13) and firing pin spring (14). Manual safety plunger (10) and spring (9) may be removed from rear end of extractor (8).

Continued on page 237

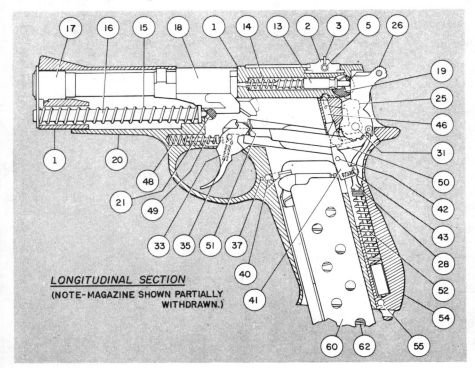

LONGITUDINAL SECTION
(NOTE—MAGAZINE SHOWN PARTIALLY WITHDRAWN.)

Specifications

SMITH & WESSON MODEL 39 DOUBLE-ACTION AUTOMATIC PISTOL

MECHANISM TYPE: Autoloading, double action
CALIBER: 9 mm. Parabellum (Luger)
WEIGHT: 28 ozs. with magazine
RIFLING: 6 groove, right twist
BARREL LENGTH: 4"
OVER-ALL LENGTH: 7½"
MAGAZINE CAPACITY: 8 rounds
SIGHTS: Front, fixed; rear, adjustable for windage
SIGHT RADIUS: 5½"

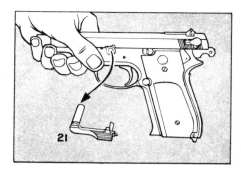

1 Slide is held rearward firmly with slide stop hole in frame aligned with cut in slide to allow removal of the slide stop (21)

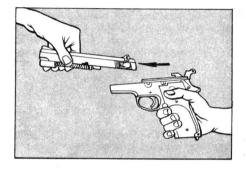

2 Slide assembly is withdrawn toward front and off frame assembly

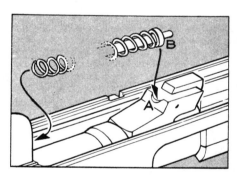

3 Remove recoil spring and guide assembly from underside of slide. Note radius cut in barrel lug at "A" which receives rim of recoil spring guide "B"

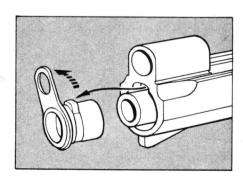

4 With slide upside down, turn barrel bushing (17) counterclockwise about 45° and withdraw from front of slide. Lift barrel lug upward and draw barrel out of slide to rear

PARTS LEGEND

1. Slide
2. Rear sight leaf
3. Rear sight slide
4. Rear sight windage nut
5. Rear sight windage screw
6. Rear sight windage screw plunger
7. Rear sight windage screw plunger spring
8. Extractor
9. Manual safety plunger spring
10. Manual safety plunger
11. Ejector depressor plunger spring
12. Ejector depressor plunger
13. Firing pin
14. Firing pin spring
15. Recoil spring
16. Recoil spring guide assembly
17. Barrel bushing
18. Barrel
19. Manual safety
20. Frame assembly
21. Slide stop
22. Slide stop plunger pin
23. Slide stop plunger spring
24. Slide stop plunger
25. Sear release lever
26. Hammer
27. Stirrup pin
28. Stirrup
29. Ejector
30. Ejector spring
31. Sideplate assembly
32. Trigger pin

33. Trigger
34. Trigger plunger pin
35. Trigger plunger
36. Trigger plunger spring
37. Magazine catch plunger
38. Magazine catch plunger spring
39. Magazine catch nut
40. Magazine catch
41. Sear
42. Sear pin
43. Sear plunger
44. Sear plunger spring
45. Sear plunger pin
46. Disconnector
47. Disconnector pin
48. Drawbar plunger spring
49. Drawbar plunger
50. Drawbar
51. Trigger play spring (assembled to drawbar)
52. Mainspring
53. Mainspring plunger
54. Insert
55. Insert pin
56. Frame studs (4—assembled to frame)
57. Slide stop button (assembled to frame)
58. Stocks (right hand not shown)
59. Stock screws (4)
60. Magazine tube
61. Magazine follower
62. Magazine spring
63. Magazine buttplate catch
64. Magazine buttplate

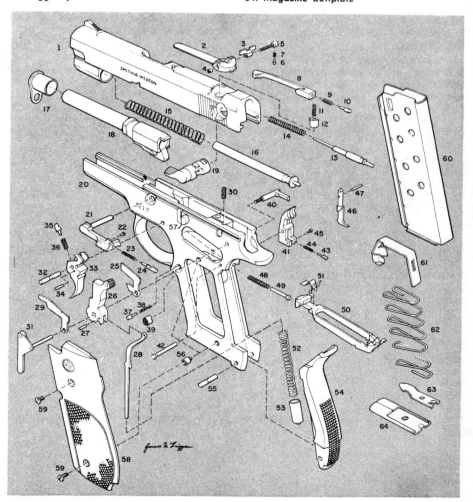

233

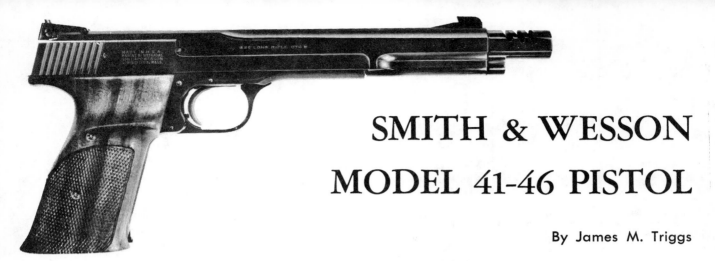

SMITH & WESSON
MODEL 41-46 PISTOL

By James M. Triggs

THE Smith & Wesson Model 41 cal. .22 long rifle semi-automatic target pistol, introduced in 1957, was the culmination of a development program begun in 1941. A pilot model was shown that year to shooters at Camp Perry, but U. S. entrance in World War II halted further work on this project which was not resumed until after the war. Production was eventually scheduled for 1950, but the outbreak of the Korean War in that year again resulted in a postponement, and it was not until late 1957 that Model 41's finally began coming off the assembly line.

Designed to be shot on an out-of-the-box basis, the Model 41 has all the extra refinements appreciated by top-flight competitive shooters. These include a wide trigger adjustable for weight of pull, adjustable trigger stop, fully adjustable rear sight, cocking in-dicator pin, muzzle brake, and checkered walnut target grips with thumb-rest. Both front and rear sights are mounted on the barrel assembly to eliminate the possibility of a sight alignment error which is sometimes present in guns having the rear sight mounted on a separate breechblock.

The Model 41 was initially made with 7⅜″ barrel only. Total weight is 43½ ozs. with muzzle brake, barrel

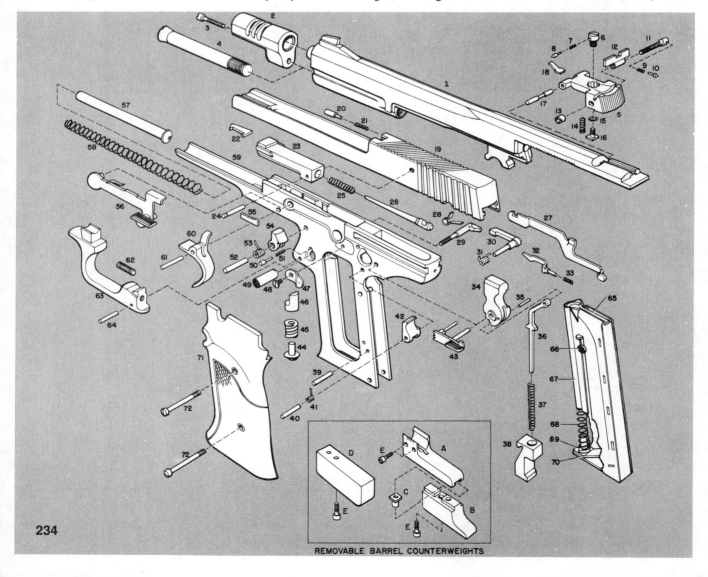

REMOVABLE BARREL COUNTERWEIGHTS

weight, and magazine in place. A set of three, accessory counterweights totaling 16-1/2 ounces, for attachment to the barrel assembly, is, available.

In the fall of 1959 an interchangeable five-inch barrel was offered so that the Model 41 could be purchased with either barrel length. Currently the Model 41 comes with either the original barrel length or an optional 5-1/2", heavy barrel. Weight of the short-barreled Model 41 is 44-1/2 ounces.

From late 1959 until 1968, a lower-price and somewhat simplified version of the Model 41, known as the Model 46, was offered. The Model 46 was made without the muzzle brake, cocking indica-tor and integral trigger adjusting device, and with plain rather than high-luster blue finish. Also, the Model 46 lacked the grooving on top of the barrel and on the front strap, and checkering on the head of the magazine release. Standard Model 46 grips were of Nylon rather than walnut. A detachable, two-ounce counterweight for attachment under the barrel was furnished as an extra.

Disassembly and assembly procedures for the Model 46 are the same as those for the Model 41.

1 Pull slide (19) all the way back until it locks open. Press in magazine catch nut (49) and remove magazine. Pull trigger guard (63) down while holding finger over top of barrel assembly to prevent it falling off when trigger guard is down. Remove barrel assembly (1) from frame (59)

2 Pull slide (19) backward and raise rear of slide slightly. Slide may now be moved forward and off receiver and recoil spring (58) may be removed. This is sufficient disassembly for normal cleaning purposes. Removal of grip screws (72) and grips (71) will allow complete disassembly of parts inside frame. After reassembling slide (19) to frame (59), lock slide in its rearward position by holding back while pressing upwards on slide stop (56). Barrel is then easily added

Parts Legend

1. Barrel assembly
2. Muzzle brake
3. Muzzle brake screw
4. Barrel weight
5. Rear sight
6. Rear sight elevating nut
7. Rear sight elevating nut plunger spring
8. Rear sight elevating nut plunger
9. Rear sight windage screw plunger spring
10. Rear sight windage screw plunger
11. Rear sight windage screw
12. Rear sight slide
13. Rear sight windage nut
14. Rear sight elevating spring
15. Rear sight spring clip
16. Rear sight elevating stud
17. Rear sight pivot pin
18. Rear sight pivot clip
19. Slide
20. Extractor plunger
21. Extractor spring
22. Extractor
23. Bolt
24. Bolt pin
25. Firing pin spring
26. Firing pin
27. Trigger bar
28. Trigger bar spring
29. Magazine catch
30. Magazine disconnector assembly
31. Magazine disconnector spring
32. Indicator
33. Indicator spring
34. Hammer
35. Stirrup pin
36. Stirrup
37. Mainspring
38. Mainspring retainer
39. Mainspring retainer pin
40. Sear pin
41. Sear spring
42. Sear
43. Manual safety assembly
44. Pawl cam plunger
45. Pawl cam spring
46. Pawl cam
47. Manual safety spring plate
48. Manual safety spring plate screw
49. Magazine catch nut
50. Magazine catch plunger
51. Magazine catch spring
52. Pawl pin
53. Pawl & trigger spring
54. Pawl
55. Trigger pull adjusting lever
56. Slide stop & ejector assembly with slide stop spring
57. Recoil spring guide
58. Recoil spring
59. Frame
60. Trigger
61. Trigger pin
62. Trigger stop screw
63. Trigger guard
64. Trigger guard pin
65. Magazine follower
66. Magazine pin
67. Magazine tube
68. Magazine spring
69. Magazine spring plunger
70. Magazine buttplate
71. Grips (2)
72. Grip screws (2)
Removable barrel counterweights
A. Counterweight upper section, steel or aluminum
B. Counterweight middle section
C. Counterweight nut
D. Counterweight lower section
E. Counterweight screws

Walther Model 9 .25 Cal. Auto

PISTOL MAGAZINES

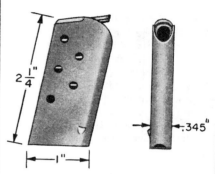

The .25 cal. Walther Model 9 automatic pistol is one of the smallest and most compact pistols ever manufactured, yet the gun fits the average hand very well and the safety can be easily reached and operated. The rear end of the firing pin protrudes when the gun is cocked, indicating its position even in the dark.

Model 9 magazines can be recognized by the lack of a pull-out tab on the floorplate. In its place there is a notch in the front edge for a fingernail. Another point is the large hole near the bottom of the magazine, and the small protrusion stamped opposite this hole on the right side of the magazine.

The feed lips are not at all distinctive; they look exactly like any one of a dozen common automatic magazines. The follower is a flat stamping that is adequate but not remarkable.
—E. J. HOFFSCHMIDT

SMITH & WESSON MODEL 52 PISTOL

By JAMES M. TRIGGS

DESIGNED expressly for target shooting, the Smith & Wesson Model 52 semi-automatic pistol was introduced in 1962. It is chambered for the .38 S&W Special cartridge loaded with flush-seated wadcutter bullet. The magazine will not accept cartridges longer than 1.19", and capacity of the magazine is 5 rounds only.

The Model 52 is of locked-breech type and its basic design stems from the Model 39 double-action pistol introduced by the same maker in 1954. The lock mechanism of the Model 52 can be adjusted for double-action use by tightening the double-action lockout screw. However, this increases initial trigger slack which many shooters consider objectionable. This pistol will not fire with magazine removed. A feature of interest to the target shooter is that this pistol may be dry-shot with impunity as the engagement of the safety interposes a solid block between hammer and firing pin.

The rear sight is of modern design with click adjustments for both windage and elevation. Each click moves point of impact approximately ¾" in elevation and ½" in windage at 50 yds.

Disassembly Procedure

Press in magazine catch nut (46) on left side of frame (28) and withdraw magazine (60) from butt. Check chamber to be sure pistol is unloaded. Place manual safety (17) in fire or upper position.

While pressing to left on right end of slide stop (30), pull slide (1) rearward until recess on lower left side of slide is lined up with forward end of slide stop. Pull slide stop out of frame to left and draw slide forward off frame.

Invert slide and, while compressing recoil spring (7) with fingers, lift out recoil spring guide assembly (8). Place barrel bushing wrench (29) over notches on barrel bushing (2), depressing barrel bushing plunger (4). Turn bushing counterclockwise, removing it from slide. Lift rear end of barrel (6) and withdraw barrel from slide to rear.

To reassemble, replace barrel in slide. Replace barrel bushing and plate, turning bushing to a firm fit aligning closest notch to plunger. When replacing recoil spring guide assembly and spring, be sure that guide bushing part of guide assembly (8) is engaged in small radius cut in barrel lug and properly centered. Replace slide in frame, depressing ejector (39) so slide will travel over it to rear. Align slide stop cut in slide with slide stop hole in frame and insert slide stop from left side of frame. Return slide to forward position and replace magazine, completing the reassembly procedure.

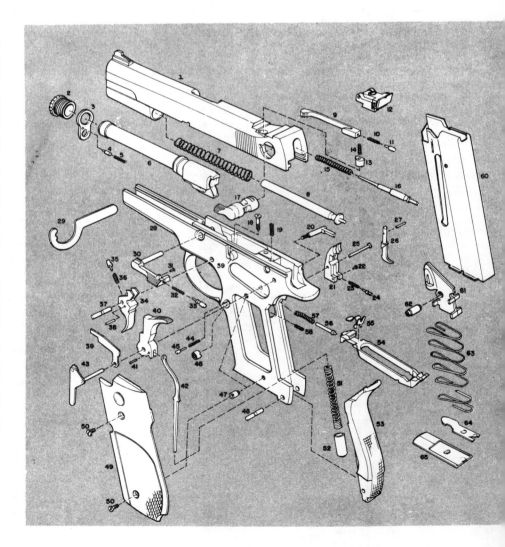

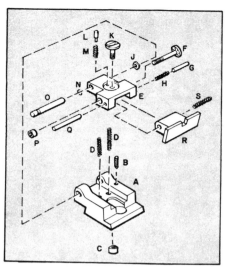

Rear Sight Assembly Parts Legend

A. Base
B. Lock screw
C. Elevation nut
D. Elevation springs
E. Body
F. Windage screw
G. Windage plunger
H. Windage plunger spring
J. Wavy washer
K. Elevation screw
L. Elevation plunger
M. Elevation plunger spring
N. Spring clip
O. Pivot pin
P. Windage nut
Q. Traverse pin
R. Slide
S. Windage spring

1 To elevate rear sight, turn top elevating screw (K) to left (counterclockwise). To depress, turn screw (K) to right (clockwise). To move sight to right, turn windage screw (F) to right (clockwise). To move sight to left, turn windage screw (F) to left (counterclockwise)

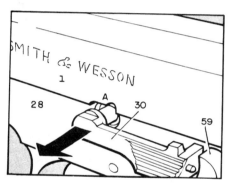

2 Hold slide (1) rearward in position shown with recess in slide aligned with forward end of slide stop (30) as shown at A. Press right end of slide stop into frame and withdraw slide stop from the left side

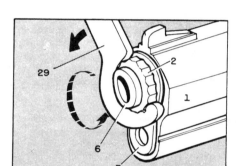

3 Place wrench (29) over notches on barrel bushing (2), compressing barrel bushing plunger (4) with wrench simultaneously. Turn bushing to left to unscrew from the slide

Extractor may be removed by lifting it forward to clear hook and pressing to rear.

To reassemble slide assembly, place extractor in its recess, with extractor hook forward. Press extractor down sufficiently to straighten slight bend and press forward to engage lug in slide cut. Replace manual safety plunger and spring in rear of extractor. Insert firing pin and spring from rear of slide and press rear of firing pin into slide as far as possible and hold from front with pliers as described above. Insert manual safety in left of frame, pressing in until right end of manual safety contacts manual safety plunger (10). Release grip on pliers holding firing pin. Depress manual safety plunger and spring and depress manual safety to the right and into position.

To disassemble frame assembly, remove stocks (58) by removing the four stock screws (59). Drive out insert pin (55) and remove insert (54) and mainspring. Lift out sideplate assembly (31). Lift out hammer (26) and stirrup (28). Remove ejector (29) and ejector spring (30) and sear release lever (25). Push sear pin (42) out from right side of frame, allowing sear (41) to drop out. Drive trigger pin (32) out from left side, allowing drawbar (50) to slide back toward rear of frame. Let disconnector (46) drop out and pull drawbar out from rear. Tip frame to vertical position butt down, allowing drawbar plunger (49) and spring (48) to drop out. Push trigger (33) upward and forward out of frame. Place frame on right side so magazine catch body is supported. Using a drift pin or small punch, press down on magazine catch plunger (37) and hold. Turn magazine catch nut (39) counterclockwise and remove.

To reassemble frame assembly, insert magazine catch body in frame. Support frame on solid surface and replace magazine catch spring and plunger. Depress plunger and assemble magazine catch nut. Turn until shank of magazine catch body is slightly below surface of nut. Release plunger and let it snap into notch. Insert trigger downward through top of frame. Insert drawbar plunger and spring into hole in frame forward of trigger. Insert drawbar through rear of frame, engaging drawbar plunger. Hold drawbar in position, and with frame bottom side up, insert disconnector. Grasp trigger and work drawbar all the way forward so that rear of drawbar is *under* foot of disconnector. Insert trigger pin. Insert sear and sear pin, taking care that headed end of sear pin is at left side of frame. Hold trigger back and insert stirrup and hammer. Release trigger. Insert ejector spring in hole at top of frame and ejector in place. Insert side plate stud in hole in left side of frame through ejector and partially through hammer. Insert sear release lever at right of hammer and press sideplate stud the rest of the way through hammer, sear release lever, and right side of frame. Place top of insert in frame and swing base into place with stirrup in mainspring and mainspring seated in plunger (53). Drive in insert pin and replace stocks and stock screws. –■

Parts Legend

1. Slide
2. Barrel bushing
3. Barrel bushing plate
4. Barrel bushing plunger
5. Barrel bushing plunger spring
6. Barrel
7. Recoil spring
8. Recoil spring guide assembly
9. Extractor
10. Extractor spring
11. Extractor spring plunger
12. Rear sight assembly (see Fig. 1.)
13. Ejector-depressor plunger
14. Ejector-depressor plunger spring
15. Firing pin spring
16. Firing pin
17. Manual safety
18. Double action lockout screw
19. Ejector spring

20. Magazine catch
21. Sear
22. Sear plunger pin
23. Sear plunger spring
24. Sear plunger
25. Sear pin
26. Disconnector
27. Disconnector pin
28. Frame
29. Barrel bushing wrench
30. Slide stop
31. Slide stop plunger pin
32. Slide stop plunger spring
33. Slide stop plunger
34. Trigger
35. Trigger plunger
36. Trigger plunger spring
37. Trigger pin
38. Trigger plunger pin
39. Ejector & magazine depressor
40. Hammer
41. Stirrup pin
42. Stirrup

43. Side plate assembly
44. Magazine catch spring
45. Magazine catch plunger
46. Magazine catch nut
47. Frame stud (4)
48. Insert pin
49. Stock, left (Right stock not shown.)
50. Stock screws (4)
51. Mainspring
52. Mainspring plunger
53. Insert
54. Drawbar
55. Trigger play spring
56. Drawbar plunger
57. Drawbar plunger spring
58. Trigger stop screw
59. Slide stop button
60. Magazine tube
61. Magazine follower
62. Magazine pin
63. Magazine spring
64. Magazine buttplate catch
65. Magazine buttplate

exploded views:

Smith & Wesson Model 59

BY JAMES S. McLELLAN

In 1954, Smith & Wesson introduced their, and America's, first double-action, semi-automatic pistol. Their Model 39 9mm was an immediate success on this market and continues to enjoy wide popularity here and abroad.

It lacked one feature that many modern pistol shooters consider worthwhile and that some consider mandatory — a large capacity magazine. The Model 39 used a single column magazine with a capacity of eight rounds.

S&W responded to requests for greater magazine capacity by bringing out, in 1971, the Model 59. Essentially, it is the Model 39 with a double-column magazine capable of holding not eight but 14 9mm cartridges.

To accommodate this larger magazine, the grip contour of the pistol was made straighter than the somewhat curved Model 39. The grip material was changed from walnut to relatively thin nylon to keep the total grip thickness down to a reasonable size and yet remove any chance of splitting. ∎

S&W's Model 59 is most commonly found with the rear sight as illustrated but recently the sight has been changed to include protective wings on either side.

Disassembly Instructions

1. Place the manual safety (13) in low or "safe" position; remove the magazine by pressing the magazine release button (62) on the left side of the frame at the rear of the trigger guard and draw the magazine from the butt. Retract the slide (23) and inspect the chamber to make sure the pistol is not loaded, then put the safety in the upper or "fire" position.

2. While pressing the protruding shaft of the slide stop (53), draw the slide (23) back until the recess in the lower left side of the slide is lined up with the forward end of the slide stop. Pull the slide stop completely from the frame.

3. Remove the slide by pulling it forward and off the frame (44).

4. Hold the slide upside down, compress the recoil spring (16) and lift out it and the recoil spring guide (60).

5. Remove the barrel bushing (3) by rotating its lower portion toward the left side of the slide and pulling it forward from the slide.

6. Remove the barrel (2) by lifting its rear end back and out of the slide. No further disassembly is recommended by the factory. Reassembly is accomplished in reverse order.

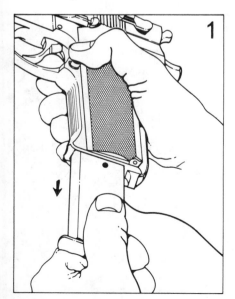
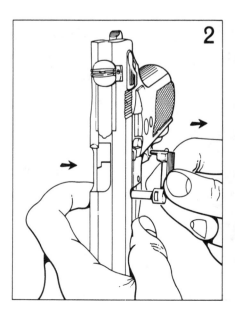
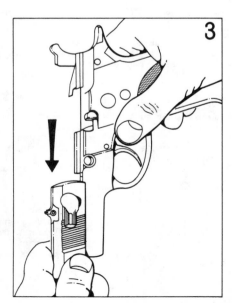

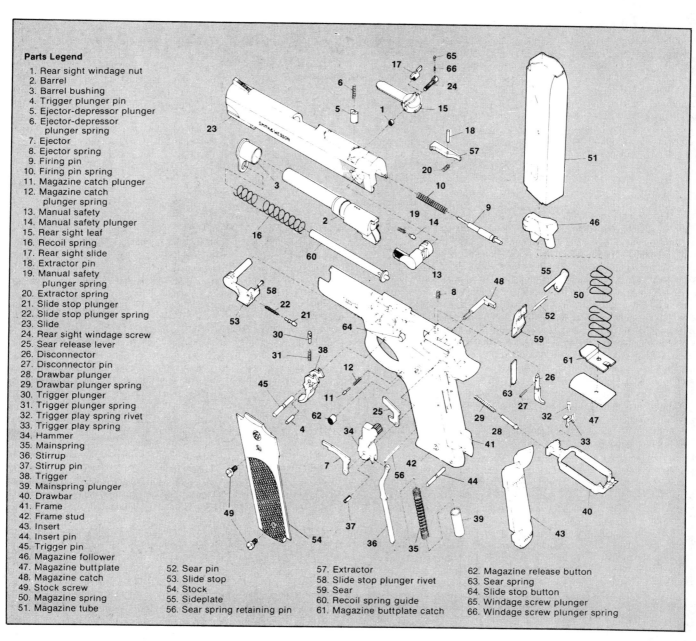

Parts Legend

1. Rear sight windage nut
2. Barrel
3. Barrel bushing
4. Trigger plunger pin
5. Ejector-depressor plunger
6. Ejector-depressor plunger spring
7. Ejector
8. Ejector spring
9. Firing pin
10. Firing pin spring
11. Magazine catch plunger
12. Magazine catch plunger spring
13. Manual safety
14. Manual safety plunger
15. Rear sight leaf
16. Recoil spring
17. Rear sight slide
18. Extractor pin
19. Manual safety plunger spring
20. Extractor spring
21. Slide stop plunger
22. Slide stop plunger spring
23. Slide
24. Rear sight windage screw
25. Sear release lever
26. Disconnector
27. Disconnector pin
28. Drawbar plunger
29. Drawbar plunger spring
30. Trigger plunger
31. Trigger plunger spring
32. Trigger play spring rivet
33. Trigger play spring
34. Hammer
35. Mainspring
36. Stirrup
37. Stirrup pin
38. Trigger
39. Mainspring plunger
40. Drawbar
41. Frame
42. Frame stud
43. Insert
44. Insert pin
45. Trigger pin
46. Magazine follower
47. Magazine buttplate
48. Magazine catch
49. Stock screw
50. Magazine spring
51. Magazine tube

52. Sear pin
53. Slide stop
54. Stock
55. Sideplate
56. Sear spring retaining pin

57. Extractor
58. Slide stop plunger rivet
59. Sear
60. Recoil spring guide
61. Magazine buttplate catch

62. Magazine release button
63. Sear spring
64. Slide stop button
65. Windage screw plunger
66. Windage screw plunger spring

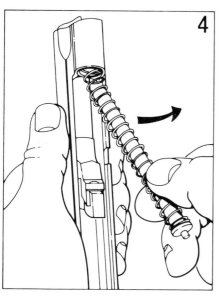

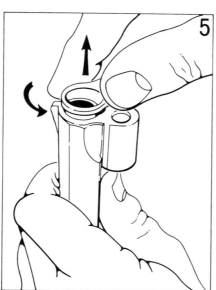

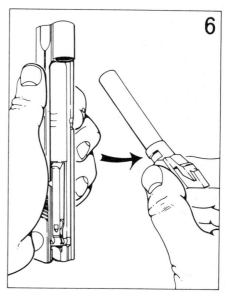

Smith & Wesson Model 29

BY JAMES S. McLELLAN

IN the years immediately following World War II, experimenters had been developing ever more powerful loads for the .44 Spl. cartridge. It was natural that a more powerful counterpart to that round should be developed in the same way that the .357 Mag. evolved from the .38 Spl.

Smith & Wesson and Remington agreed to take the plunge, and on Dec. 29, 1955, the first .44 Mag. revolver was completed. The earliest models were available in blue or nickel finish, with 4″ or 6″ barrels. S&W was flooded with requests for a long-barreled .44 Mag., and on April 10, 1958, a drawing for an 8⅜″ barrel was completed. Production on the long-barrel version started soon thereafter.

The Model 29 commanded premium prices during the mid-1970s after it was featured in the popular film *Dirty Harry,* making it among the most popular of S&W's many revolvers.

The N-framed Smith & Wesson Model 29 enjoyed a massive burst of popularity in the 1970s when it was featured in *Dirty Harry.*

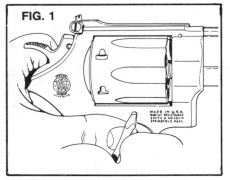

FIG. 1

Disassembly Instructions

1. First remove the stocks by loosening the stock screw. Leaving the screwdriver in place, push the screw into its hole against the right stock half. This will release that stock without damaging it or scratching the frame. Then invert the gun and remove the left panel by gently tapping with a screwdriver or punch through the frame. Remove the yoke screw (**Fig. 1**). This is a fitted screw, so keep it

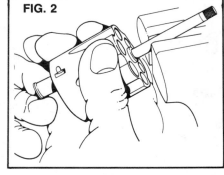

FIG. 2

separate by placing it in a hole in one of the stock halves.

2. Remove yoke and cylinder by opening the cylinder and placing the gun on its right side. Hold the cylinder in its open position while drawing the yoke forward out of the frame.

3. Insert a dummy cartridge in one of the charge holes to protect the extractor pins, then grasp the extractor rod in a vise (**Fig. 2**). Now turn the cylinder clockwise to unscrew the

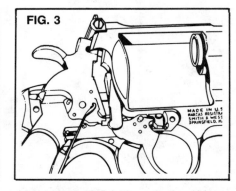

FIG. 3

extractor rod. Model 29s and other N-frame revolvers made before 1960 have a right-hand thread, so the cylinder should be turned counterclockwise.

4. Remove round head side-plate screw and flat head side-plate screw. The flat head screw fits under the stocks. Then loosen the side-plate by tapping the side of the backstrap with a nylon hammer . Hold the front of the side-plate to prevent dropping it.

5. The hammer block will likely drop out when

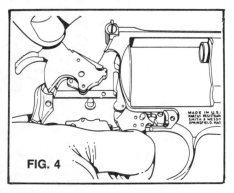

FIG. 4

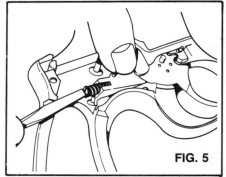

FIG. 5

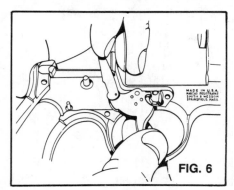

FIG. 6

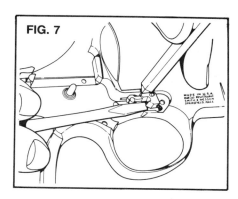

FIG. 7

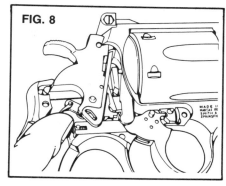

FIG. 8

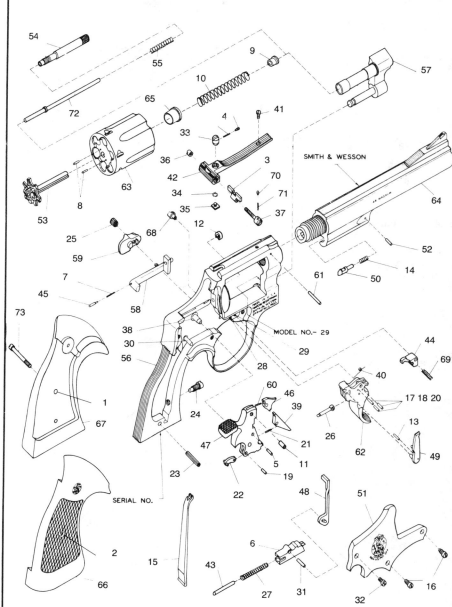

SMITH & WESSON

MODEL NO.— 29

SERIAL NO.

you remove the side-plate, as it rides in a slot on the side-plate. If it doesn't, remove it. Loosen the mainspring strain screw in the frontstrap. Then the foot of the mainspring can be pushed to the right and removed (**Fig. 3**).

6. Push the thumbpiece bolt to the rear and pull the trigger to its full rearward position. This will cock the hammer. While holding the trigger rearward, lift the hammer straight out of the frame (**Fig. 4**).

7. Remove the rebound slide and spring by raising the slide halfway up on the stud with a screwdriver (**Fig. 5**). Change the position of the screwdriver to the flat edge and push in on the spring. Allow the spring to release *slowly*. Note that the screwdriver and finger prevent the spring from flying off.

8. To remove the trigger and hand, use the left index finger to hold the hand out of the slot in the frame while the thumb and middle finger of the right hand lift the trigger straight off the trigger pin (**Fig. 6**).

9. Push the cylinder stop down from the top, then use a drift pin to hold it down while the screwdriver lifts it straight up off its pin (**Fig. 7**). Be careful to keep the spring from flying off. The adjustable sight can be removed by removing the screw at the front of the sight leaf and sliding the assembly to the rear.

10. Reassemble in reverse order. Be sure the trigger lever is inside the frame and can be inserted into the front of the rebound slide assembly. Hold the trigger rearward when installing the hammer. Hook the top of the mainspring on the hammer stirrup first (**Fig. 8**), then slide its foot into the frame and tighten the strain screw. Be sure the hammer block is in its "up" position. Install the side-plate front and top undercuts first, then seat it by tapping lightly with a nylon hammer on the screw holes. ∎

Parts Legend

1. Escutcheon
2. Escutcheon Nut
3. Rear Sight Slide
4. Rear Sight Assembly
5. Sear Pin
6. Rebound Slide
7. Bolt Plunger Spring
8. Extractor Pin
9. Extractor Rod Collar
10. Extractor Spring
11. Hammer Nose Rivet
12. Hammer Nose Bushing
13. Hand Pin
14. Locking Bolt Spring
15. Mainspring
16. Plate Screw, Crowned
17. Hand Spring Pin
18. Hand Spring Torsion Pin
19. Stirrup Pin
20. Trigger Lever Pin
21. Sear Spring
22. Stirrup
23. Stock Pin
24. Strain Screw
25. Thumbpiece Nut
26. Trigger Lever
27. Rebound Slide Spring
28. Trigger Stud
29. Cylinder Stop Stud
30. Rebound Slide Stud
31. Rebound Slide Pin
32. Plate Screw, Flat Head
33. Rear Sight Elevation Nut
34. Rear Sight Spring Clip
35. Rear Sight Elevation Stud
36. Rear Sight Windage Nut
37. Rear Sight Windage Screw
38. Hammer Stud
39. Sear
40. Hand Spring
41. Rear Sight Leaf Screw
42. Rear Sight Leaf
43. Trigger Stop Rod
44. Cylinder Stop
45. Bolt Plunger
46. Hammer Nose
47. Hammer
48. Hammer Block
49. Hand
50. Locking Bolt
51. Side Plate
52. Locking Bolt Pin
53. Extractor
54. Extractor Rod
55. Center Pin Spring
56. Frame
57. Yoke
58. Bolt
59. Thumbpiece
60. Hammer Nose Spring
61. Barrel Pin
62. Trigger
63. Cylinder
64. Barrel
65. Gas Ring
66. Right Stock
67. Left Stock
68. Frame Lug
69. Cylinder Stop Spring
70. Rear Sight Plunger
71. Rear Sight Plunger Spring
72. Center Pin
73. Stock Screw

S&W New Departure Safety Hammerless Revolver

By James M. Triggs

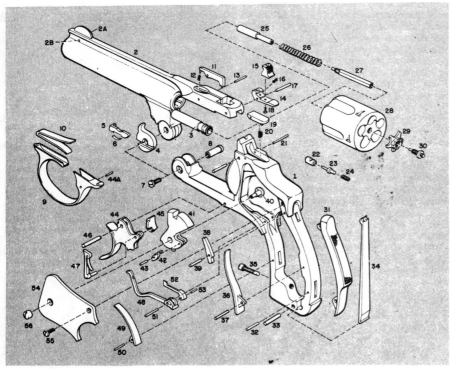

Parts Legend

1. Frame	29. Extractor
2. Barrel	30. Extractor stud
2a. Front sight	31. Safety lever
2b. Front sight pin	32. Safety lever pin
3. Base pin	33. Stock pin
4. Extractor cam	34. Mainspring
5. Extractor cam latch	35. Strain screw
6. Extractor cam latch spring	36. Latch spring
7. Joint pivot screw	37. Latch spring pin
8. Joint pivot	38. Latch
9. Trigger guard	39. Latch pin
10. Trigger spring	40. Hammer stud
11. Cylinder catch	41. Hammer
12. Cylinder catch spring	42. Stirrup
13. Cylinder catch pin	43. Stirrup pin
14. Barrel catch	44. Trigger
15. Barrel catch thumbpiece	44a. Trigger stop pin
16. Barrel catch spring	45. Sear
17. Barrel catch pin	46. Trigger pin
18. Barrel catch thumbpiece screw	47. Hand & hand spring
19. Barrel catch plate	48. Cylinder stop
20. Barrel catch plate spring	49. Cylinder stop spring
21. Barrel catch plate pin	50. Cylinder stop spring pin
22. Firing pin bushing	51. Cylinder stop pin
23. Firing pin	52. Split spring
24. Firing pin spring	53. Split spring pin
25. Extractor post	54. Side-plate
26. Extractor spring	55. Side-plate screw
27. Extractor rod	56. Hammer stud nut
28. Cylinder	

I N 1887, Smith & Wesson, Springfield, Mass., introduced their 5-shot Safety Hammerless top-break revolver. It was initially offered only in cal. .38 S&W with choice of blue or nickel finish and barrel lengths of 3¼", 4", and 5".

The editorial announcement of this new arm, in the April 1887 issue of *The Rifle*, predecessor of THE RIFLEMAN, stated that the new S&W Safety Hammerless represented a 'new departure' in revolver design. Apparently this phrase appealed to Smith & Wesson as it was subsequently used in designating this model in factory literature.

The Safety Hammerless revolver in cal. .32 was introduced in February 1888 and was also available in blue or nickel finish with barrel lengths of 3" and 3½". The frame and other parts were made to smaller scale than the cal. .38 revolver. Subsequently this model was also offered with 2" barrel.

Smith & Wesson advertisements in 1887 issues of *The Rifle* mentioned proposed production of the Safety Hammerless in cal. .44, but this model was never commercially available.

The mechanical features of the Safety Hammerless revolver were not particularly unique even in 1887. It was not the first hammerless self-cocking revolver, nor was it the first top-break or hinged-frame type. In retrospect, the only unique feature was the grip safety which prevented cocking and firing of the gun until the safety lever had been depressed. The trigger pull was extremely heavy but S&W capitalized on this by claiming that this made the gun safe around small children lacking the strength to fire the gun. It was also claimed that guns of this design were less liable to accidental discharge. However, the only apparent real advantage was the absence of an exterior hammer liable to snag in the pocket when the gun was withdrawn hurriedly.

Interesting lock feature

An interesting feature of the lock mechanism provided a definite hesitation or stopping point just prior to sear disengagement. Then, slight additional pressure on the trigger discharged the revolver without dislodging the sights from point of aim. It was thus possible to shoot slow-fire reasonably accurately.

In late 1888 or early 1889 the Ordnance Dept. purchased one cal. .38 Safety Hammerless revolver. Also purchased at the same time was one cal. .38 Colt New Navy Pattern double-action revolver. The sample guns were turned over to an Ordnance Board for test and evaluation. After subjecting the 2 guns to strenuous tests the board recommended purchase and field test of limited quantities of both guns to determine which was the more serviceable for military purposes. One hundred each of the S&W and Colt revolvers were purchased and 96 of each were issued to troops for a 14-month trial period. Upon completion of the trials these guns were turned over to an Ordnance Board convened Jan. 16, 1892. The Board's findings were in favor of the Colt revolver, which in modified form was subsequently adopted. The Safety Hammerless revolver was rejected largely because its mechanism was considered delicate. It also proved difficult to open when rusty or dusty. It had 10 more parts than the Colt and was more difficult to disassemble and assemble.

Despite its failure of adoption as a military weapon, the Safety Hammerless enjoyed considerable popularity as a commercial arm. Two models of the cal. .32 revolver were made. The first model was manufactured from February 1888 until September 1900 with serial numbers running from 1 to 91,417. Production of the second model started in September 1900 with gun 91,418 and ended with gun 242,880 in October 1922.

Five models of the cal. .38 Safety Hammerless were produced according to the following schedule:

1st Model   1-   5000 Jan. 1887-July 1888
2nd Model 5,001- 42,483 July 1888-Aug. 1890
3rd Model 42,484-116,002 Aug. 1890-Dec. 1898
4th Model 116,003-190,064 Dec. 1898-Apr. 1907
5th Model 190,065-261,493 Apr. 1907-June 1940

Production span of the Safety Hammerless revolver was 53 years.

DISASSEMBLY PROCEDURE

To dismount barrel from frame, break action and remove joint pivot screw (7). Punch out joint pivot (8) to right. Pull barrel (2) free of frame (1). Extractor cam (4) and extractor cam latch (5) can now be slipped free of joint. Remove cylinder (28) complete by pressing cylinder catch (11) on top strap of barrel and unscrewing cylinder and extractor assembly from base pin (3). (Note: Not all S&W Safety Hammerless revolvers have this cylinder catch and cylinder removed in the same manner.) Removal of base pin (3) from barrel is not recommended. Cylinder catch assembly (11) and barrel catch assembly (14-20) are easily removed by drifting out the respective pins (13, 17, 21). Remove barrel catch thumbpiece screw (18) to separate catch assembly.

To disassemble lock mechanism, remove grips and unscrew side-plate screw (55) and hammer stud nut (56). Ease side-plate (54) up out of frame gradually by prying gently and tapping reverse side of frame with a fiber or wooden hammer. Unscrew strain screw (35) and withdraw mainspring (34) from frame. Safety lever (31), latch (38) and latch spring (36) are removed by drifting out pins (32, 37, 39). Drift out trigger pin (46). Trigger guard (9) is removed by springing rear portion of guard toward the front and pulling downward and out of frame. Drift out cylinder stop pin (51) and work hammer (41) back until it can be lifted out of frame. Manipulate trigger and cylinder stop assembly in frame until hand (47) can be lifted out of frame. Drop trigger and cylinder stop out bottom of frame. Remove sear (45) through side-plate hole in frame. Reassemble in reverse.

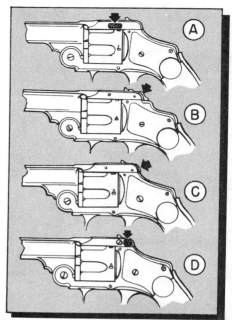

1 This drawing shows the 4 major variations of the Safety Hammerless revolver: **A**—First Model with Z-bar barrel catch operated by pushing bar in top strap from left to right. **B**—Second Model, opened by pushing down on checked thumbpiece protruding from rear of top strap of barrel (this is the model illustrated in the exploded drawings). **C**—Third Model, opened by pushing down on checked flat thumbpiece on top of strap. **D**—Fourth Model, opened by lifting T-shaped barrel catch with knurled buttons on each side. The Fifth Model is identical with the fourth except that the front sight is forged integrally with the barrel rather than a separate piece as on the preceding models

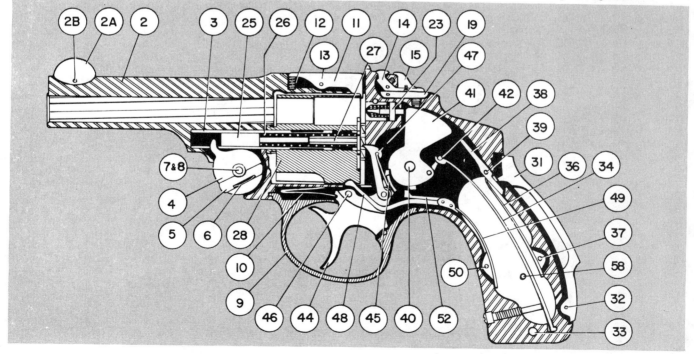

2 This detailed longitudinal-section of the revolver reveals the working mechanism with all parts in proper relationship. The revolver is shown with the lock mechanism in fired position. Note that the safety lever (31) is out, allowing the top end of the latch (38) to stand out in the way of the hammer (41), preventing the hammer from coming back far enough to fire. When the safety lever is pressed in, the top of the latch moves back against the inner wall of the frame, leaving the hammer clear to come all the way back to fire

Smith & Wesson Number 1 Revolver By James M. Triggs

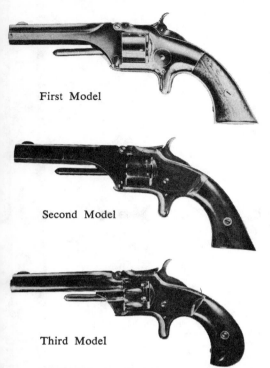

First Model

Second Model

Third Model

IN 1857 Smith & Wesson of Springfield, Mass., introduced the first American metallic cartridge revolver which was also the first with cartridge chambers bored through the cylinder from end to end under the Rollin White patent of Apr. 3, 1855, No. 12,648. This 7-shot revolver, designated Number 1, was chambered for a unique Smith & Wesson designed cal. .22 rimfire cartridge still manufactured today as the .22 short. The early round was primed with fulminate of mercury and featured a 3-gr. powder charge behind a 30-gr. lead bullet. While ballistically poor, this cartridge and revolver combination proved immediately popular. Eventually certain improvements were effected and in 1860 the Second Model of the Number 1 revolver was introduced. In 1868 the Third Model of the Number 1 revolver supplanted the Second Model. It too proved popular until production was discontinued in 1879.

The late Jim Triggs was a writer-illustrator and well known gun collector.

All told there were 254,958 Number 1 revolvers manufactured, with the Third Model accounting for 128,528 of this total.

A note of caution regarding these old S&W 'tip-up' revolvers: while the length of the cylinder is too short to permit use of modern .22 long or long rifle cartridges, the .22 short will usually chamber satisfactorily. However, these revolvers were manufactured many years before the advent of smokeless powder and it would be unwise to fire them with modern smokeless powder ammunition.

Disassembly Procedure

While there are several minor variations in No. 1 S&W revolvers, disassembly procedure for all is substantially the same.

To tip up barrel, raise latch (34) and swing barrel (31) upward. Cylinder (9) is removed by drawing it straight forward.

To remove barrel from frame, unscrew barrel pivot screw (8). Ejector pin (32) is removed by unscrewing its screw (33). Remove barrel latch screw (36) and drop latch (34) out bottom of barrel lug. Barrel latch spring (35) will drop out after latch.

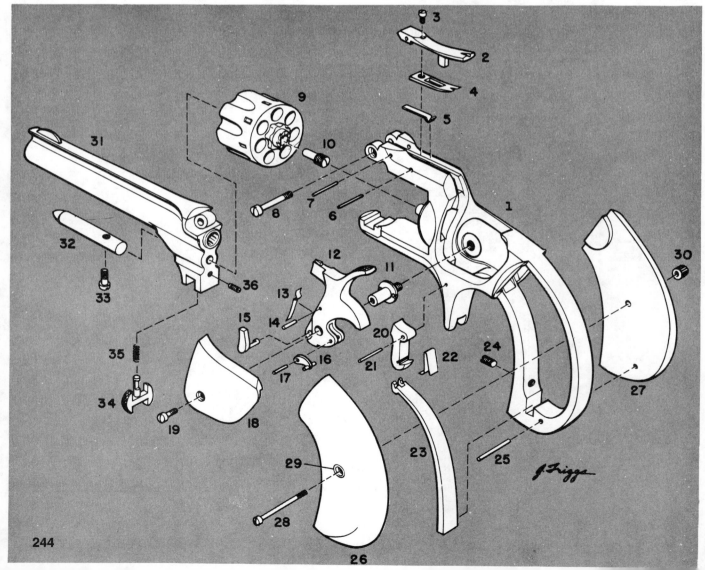

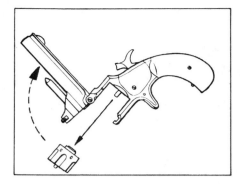

1 Pressing upward on barrel latch (34) releases barrel which tips upward as shown. Cylinder can be withdrawn from frame toward the front

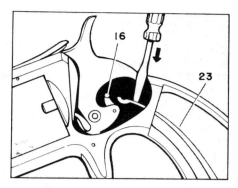

2 After loosening mainspring strain screw (24), mainspring (23) may be removed by pressing down on top end of spring at point shown to disengage stirrup (16) and lifting from frame with the fingers

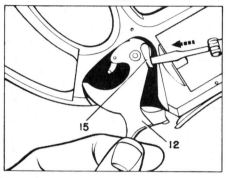

3 To remove hammer (12) from frame, hold hand (15) back and clear of its slot in frame with the tip of a small screwdriver or similar implement as shown and work hammer up off hammer stud

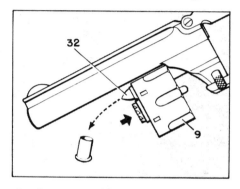

4 Empty cartridge cases are ejected by pressing reversed cylinder onto ejector pin (32)

To disassemble lock mechanism, first remove stock screw (28) and stocks (26 & 27). Remove sideplate screw (19). Hold frame with sideplate (18) downward and tap frame sharply with a wooden or plastic hammer until sideplate works loose and drops out of frame. Do not attempt to pry sideplate out. Unscrew mainspring strain screw (24) and press top end of mainspring (23) down with tip of screwdriver or similar tool until it disengages from stirrup (16). Mainspring (23) may be easily lifted out of frame. While holding tip of hand (15) back and clear of its slot in frame with tip of small screwdriver, work hammer (12) up off hammer stud (11) and out of frame (1) with fingers. Hammer

will frequently fit quite snugly to its stud and a few drops of penetrating oil may help in lifting it free. Hand and hand spring (13) as well as stirrup rarely need be removed from hammer except for replacement. Either of these parts may be easily removed by drifting out their respective pins (14 & 17). Inasmuch as a special spanner wrench will be required to remove hammer stud from frame, such removal is not recommended and should seldom if ever be necessary. Cylinder stop assembly and spring (2, 3, 4, 5) can be removed from top of frame by drifting out cylinder stop pin (7) and spring pin (6). Trigger (20) and spring (22) are easily removed from frame by drifting out trigger pin (21). Reassembly is accomplished in reverse order.

Parts Legend

1. Frame	19. Sideplate screw (screws into hammer stud)
2. Cylinder stop	20. Trigger
3. Cylinder stop screw	21. Trigger pin
4. Cylinder stop striker	22. Trigger spring
5. Cylinder stop spring	23. Mainspring
6. Cylinder stop spring pin	24. Mainspring strain screw
7. Cylinder stop pin	25. Stock pin
8. Barrel pivot screw	26. Stock, left hand
9. Cylinder	27. Stock, right hand
10. Cylinder stud	28. Stock screw
11. Hammer stud	29. Escutcheon
12. Hammer	30. Escutcheon nut
13. Hand spring	31. Barrel
14. Hand pin	32. Ejector pin
15. Hand	33. Ejector pin screw
16. Stirrup	34. Barrel latch
17. Stirrup pin	35. Barrel latch spring
18. Sideplate	36. Barrel latch screw

PISTOL MAGAZINES

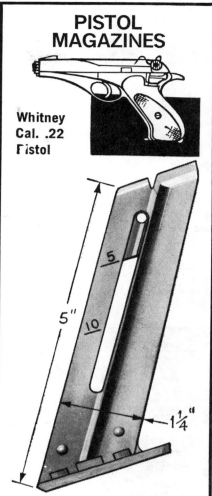

Whitney Cal. .22 Pistol

Although not a commercial success, the Whitney cal. .22 semi-automatic pistol has a number of unusual design features, the most notable of which is its die-cast aluminum frame. Most of the other parts are steel, as is the magazine.

Whitney magazines can be identified easily by the cartridge indicator number stamped on the right side of the body. The stepped arrangement of the feed lips is another identifying feature.

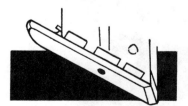

The floorplate and the large dents in the side of the magazine are notable points of identification.— E. J. Hoffschmidt

exploded views:

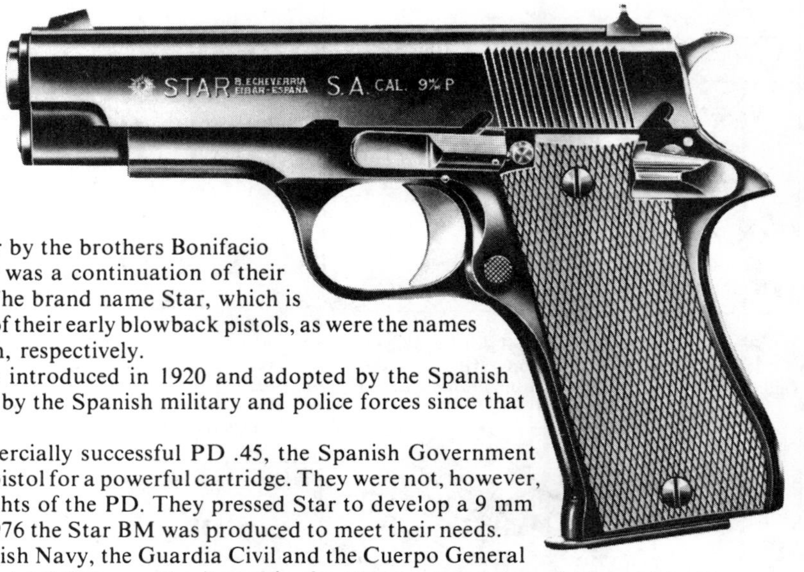

BY AGUSTIN GUISASOLA

Bonifacio Echeverria, S.A., was founded in 1905 in Eibar by the brothers Bonifacio and Julian Echeverria Orbea. In actuality, the company was a continuation of their father's small gunmaking firm Txantoya of that same city. The brand name Star, which is now the commonly used term for the firm, was used on some of their early blowback pistols, as were the names Izarra and Estrella, which mean Star in Basque and Spanish, respectively.

Star's first locked breech pistol, the Modelo Militar, was introduced in 1920 and adopted by the Spanish Guardia Civil. Star pistols in various models have been used by the Spanish military and police forces since that time.

In the early 1970s, while Star was developing their commercially successful PD .45, the Spanish Government showed interest in the concept of the PD — an ultra-compact pistol for a powerful cartridge. They were not, however, interested in the .45 ACP cartridge or the fully adjustable sights of the PD. They pressed Star to develop a 9 mm handgun smaller than the already small Model BKS and in 1976 the Star BM was produced to meet their needs. The steel-framed BM is now the official handgun of the Spanish Navy, the Guardia Civil and the Cuerpo General de Policia. It and a variation with aluminum frame, the Model BKM, are distributed in the U.S. by Interarms of Alexandria, Va.

Parts Legend

1. Barrel bushing
2. Slide
3. Extractor pin
4. Firing pin retaining pin
5. Extractor
6. Extractor spring
7. Rear sight
8. Firing pin spring
9. Firing pin
10. Magazine catch lock spring
11. Magazine catch
12. Magazine catch lock
13. Recoil spring guide
14. Recoil spring guide washer
15. Recoil spring
16. Barrel w/link and pin
17. Recoil spring guide head
18. Ejector
19. Interruptor
20. Trigger, assembly
21. Magazine safety
22. Sear
23. Sear spring
24. Hammer w/strut and pin
25. Hammer spring plunger
26. Hammer spring
27. Grip, right
28. Magazine, complete
29. Frame
30. Grip screws
31. Grip, left
32. Slide stop, assembly
33. Trigger pin
34. Ejector pin
35. Safety, thumb
36. Safety plunger
37. Safety plunger spring
38. Hammer pin
39. Sear pin

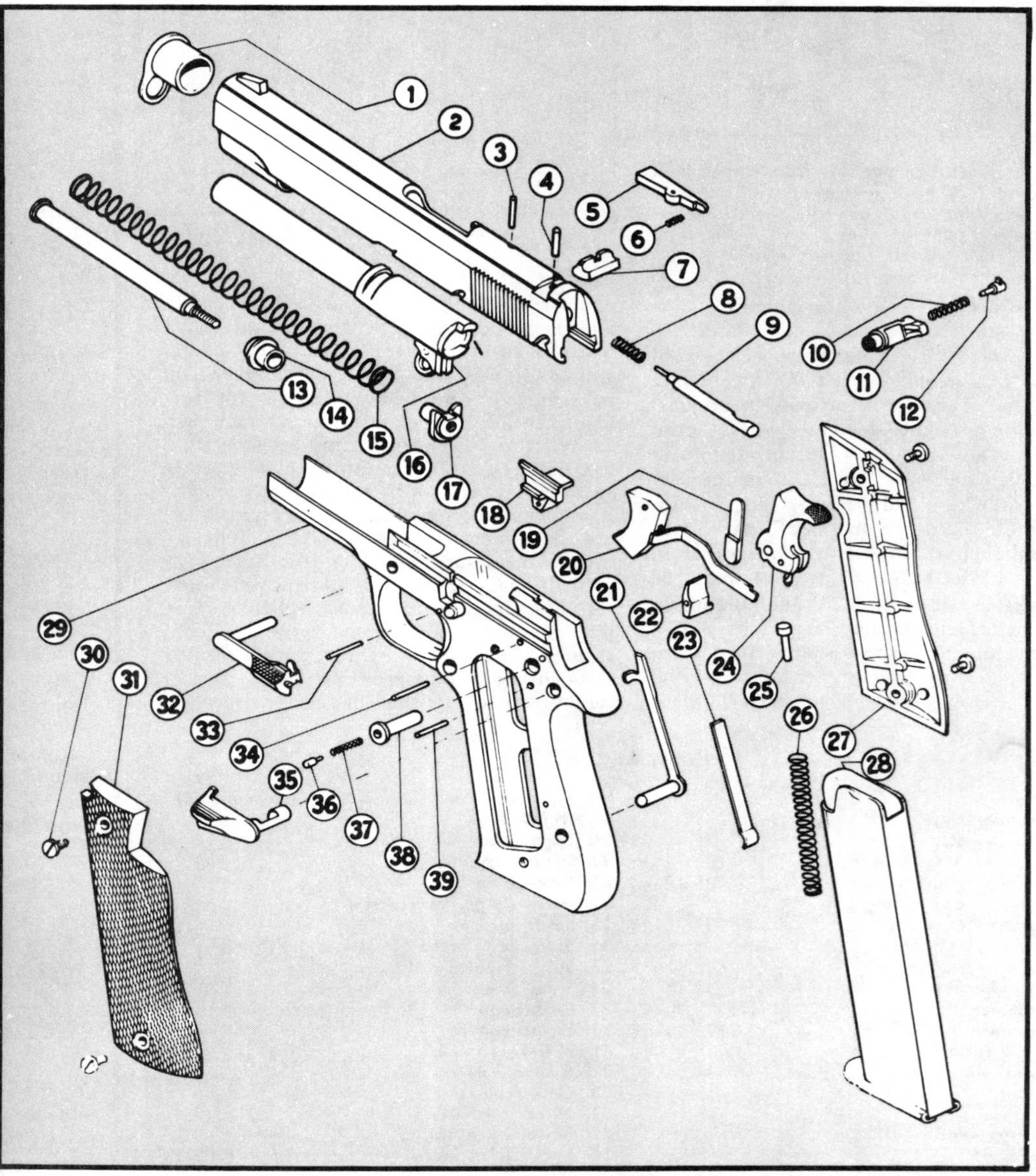

STAR BM/BKM PISTOLS

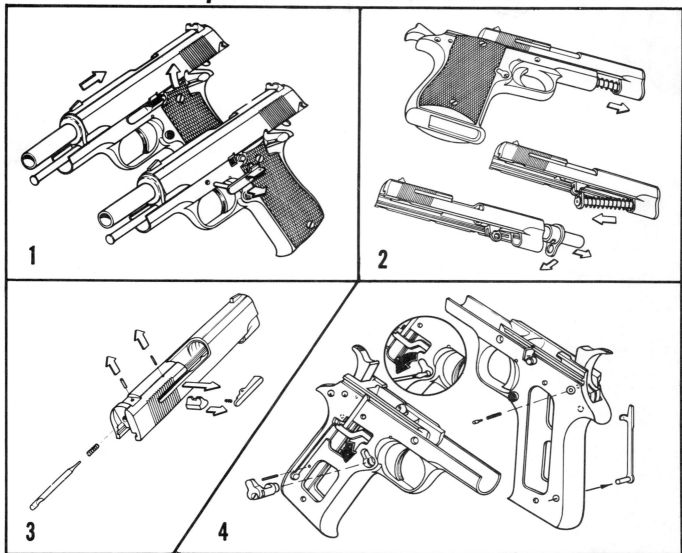

Disassembly Procedure

1. Check to be sure gun is unloaded by depressing magazine catch (11), removing magazine (28), retracting slide (2) and examining chamber to be sure it is empty. With slide still retracted, push up on the thumb safety (35) so that its hook engages in the slide notch just forward of the finger serrations. The slide will now remain in its rearward position and the slide (32) can be removed by pushing on its rod which protrudes from the right side of the frame.

2. Hold the slide by its serrations to limit the recoil spring pressure and depress the thumb safety to allow the slide to ride forward off the frame (29). Lift recoil spring assembly (13, 14, 15 & 17) and remove it from the slide. Turn barrel bushing (1) counterclockwise and pull it and the barrel (16) forward from the slide.

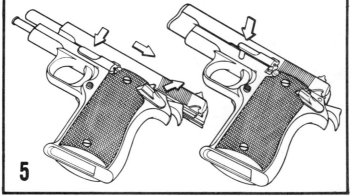

3. The slide itself can be stripped by using a brass punch to drift out the rear sight (7) from left to right. From the underside of the slide, using a suitable punch, drive up the firing pin retaining pin (4) and remove it, the firing pin (9) and its spring (8). Using the same punch, drift the extractor pin (3) up through

the slide and remove the extractor (5) and extractor spring (6).

4. Remove grip screws (30) and grips (27 & 31). The magazine safety (21) may be temporarily or permanently removed, if desired, by driving out its lower arm from the frame. Lower the hammer (the magazine must be inserted to do this if the

magazine safety is present) to simplify thumb safety removal. Rotate the thumb safety (35) to its vertical position and carefully "wiggle" it from the frame, being careful not to lose its plunger (36) and spring (37) which are small and under pressure. The magazine catch is taken out by depressing its knurled button and, with a small screwdriver, turning the magazine catch lock (12) counterclockwise out of its seat in the frame. The catch with its lock and spring may now be removed as an assembly (10, 11 and 12).

5. Reassembly is accomplished by reversing the above procedures, but before replacing the assembled slide on the frame, tilt the barrel link forward. After reinstalling the slide unit on the frame, align the barrel link hole with the slide stop hole in the frame before partially inserting the slide stop rod. Then lock the slide back with the thumb safety hook and fully seat the slide stop. ∎

Star "Super" Model Pistols

BY PETE DICKEY

Super SM .380 ACP

Super B 9 mm Luger

FROM 1946 until 1983, Star Bonifacio Echeverria of Eibar, Spain, made "Super" variations of its standard Browning/Colt M1911-type pistols in various sizes.

The standard Stars differed from the basic M1911 design mainly in that they had hammer-blocking thumb safeties, lacked grip safeties and had external extractors.

The Super Models added a quick takedown feature, a magazine safety and a loaded chamber indicator and, at one time or another, were made for seven different cartridges.

The first chambering was in 9 mm Bergmann Bayard, the Spanish service cartridge, in the 39-oz. Model Super M. These 9 mm/.38-marked pistols also worked well with .38 ACP or .38 Super ACP ammunition.

Soon the like-chambered but slightly thinner-slided Model Super A, the 9 mm Parabellum Model Super B and the 9 mm Browning Long Super C were being made at a 2-oz. weight saving together with the far smaller .32 ACP Super SI and .380 Super S at 22 ozs. each.

All, save the Super C that was made only on a trial basis, continued in manufacture until 1983.

In 1950 an even smaller .380, the Super D, was made, again on a trial basis, and in 1958 a very few .45 ACP cal. Super Ps were produced.

As a result of the capricious "point sytem" of the 1968 Gun Control Act, some Super Ss were fitted with screw-adjustable rear sights so as to be importable in the U.S. as the Super SM. This is the version shown, but all Super variations use similar parts arrangement and disassembly procedures.

In 1989 Star began to ship its final inventory of new Super B 9 mm Parabellums to its U.S. importer, Interarms of Alexandria, Va. (see June 1989, p. 55), and, at this writing, replacement parts, most of which will fit the Super Models A and M as well as the Super B, are available from that firm.

Fig. 1

Field Stripping

First depress the magazine catch (21) and remove the magazine assembly (35-39). Retract and release the slide (41) and ensure that the chamber is empty. Turn the takedown lever (34) counterclockwise and remove the slide assembly from the front of the frame (1) **(Fig. 1)**.

The slide assembly can then be stripped by lifting out the recoil spring (56) with its button and guide (54 & 55). This will free the barrel bushing (53) that is turned 45° to the left of the slide and then pulled out, thus allowing the barrel (40) to be removed from the front of the slide.

No further dismantling is necessary for normal cleaning or inspection but can be accomplished, if required, as follows:

Slide Disassembly

With a brass or plastic punch, drift out the rear sight or, in the case of the Super SM, the rear sight assembly (49-52). This will free the live-round indicator (48) and expose the top of the firing pin retaining pin (46). Now, with the slide inverted, drift out the firing pin retaining pin (46) as shown **(Fig. 2)**. The firing pin (45) and its spring (47) can now be removed. With the slide inverted, drift out the extractor pin (43), whose bottom is exposed about an inch forward of the firing pin retaining pin hole. It too is drifted from the bottom of the slide through the top. This completes slide disassembly, as the front sight is staked in place and normally should not be removed.

Frame Disassembly

Remove the four grip screws (60) and the grip plates (58 & 59); depress the magazine catch (21) and turn the slotted magazine catch lock (22) 90° counter-clockwise. Remove the magazine catch assembly (21-23).

Removal of the thumb safety (27) requires special care, as its plunger (28) is under pressure from its spring (29) and is easily lost. Hold the frame (1) left side up in the left hand and, placing the right thumb on the top of the thumb safety's platform, push it down until the plunger pops up to be retained by the thumb **(Fig. 3)**. Then swing the thumb safety up and, while pulling the hammer (4) back past its full-cock position, out of its recess. Rotate the takedown lever (34) so that it points straight down and pull it from its seat, thus freeing it and the slide stop (30), its plunger, spring and retaining screw (31-33).

To remove the magazine safety and its lock and spring (24-26), first temporarily reinsert the magazine. Then turn the slotted magazine safety lock (25) a quarter turn counterclockwise and remove the magazine, permitting the magazine safety to fall out.

Drift out the trigger pin (15) from left to right and remove the trigger (14) with its attached plunger spring, plunger and sear bar (16-18) to the rear. This permits removal of the interrupter (20) from its slot.

With the hammer (4) fully down and firmly retained by the thumb, drive out the hammer pin (9) and carefully remove the hammer that will be under pressure of its spring and plunger (7 & 8).

This is followed by the removal of the sear pin (11), the sear (10), the sear spring pin (13) and the sear spring (12). Note their positions for easy reassembly in reverse order. ■

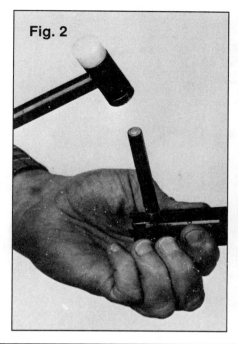

Fig. 2

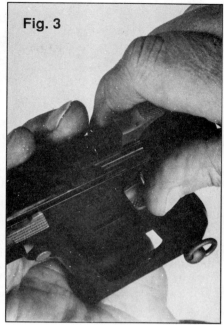

Fig. 3

Parts Legend

1. Frame
2. Ejector
3. Ejector pin
4. Hammer
5. Hammer strut
6. Hammer strut pin
7. Hammer spring
8. Hammer spring plunger
9. Hammer pin
10. Sear
11. Sear pin
12. Sear spring
13. Sear spring pin
14. Trigger
15. Trigger pin
16. Trigger plunger spring
17. Trigger plunger
18. Sear bar
19. Sear bar pin
20. Interrupter
21. Magazine catch
22. Magazine catch lock
23. Magazine catch lock spring
24. Magazine safety
25. Magazine safety lock
26. Magazine safety lock spring
27. Thumb safety
28. Thumb safety plunger
29. Thumb safety plunger spring
30. Slide stop
31. Slide stop plunger
32. Slide stop plunger spring
33. Slide stop plunger retaining screw
34. Takedown lever
35. Magazine
36. Magazine follower
37. Magazine spring
38. Magazine floorplate
39. Magazine floorplate catch
40. Barrel
41. Slide
42. Extractor
43. Extractor pin
44. Extractor spring
45. Firing pin
46. Firing pin retaining pin
47. Firing pin spring
48. Live round indicator
49. Rear sight blade
50. Rear sight sight screw
51. Rear sight base
52. Rear sight spring
53. Barrel bushing
54. Recoil spring button
55. Recoil spring guide
56. Recoil spring
57. Front sight
58. Grip plate, right
59. Grip plate, left
60. Grip screws (4)

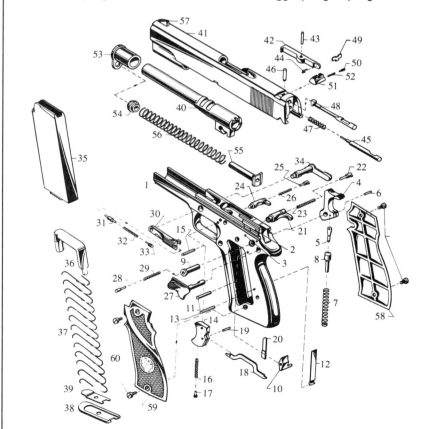

STAR MODEL BS PISTOL

Illustrations by DENNIS RIORDAN
Text by LUDWIG OLSON

WHEN the Colt Model of 1911 cal. .45 semi-automatic pistol was introduced, it set a new standard in handgun excellence. This rugged reliable autoloader met with great success in foreign countries as well as the U.S., and its basic features were used in various other semi-automatic pistols, among them the Star Model BS.

Produced by Star Bonifacio Echeverria, S.A., of Eibar, Spain, the Star Model BS pistol is chambered for the 9 mm. Luger cartridge. This autoloader for military, law-enforcement, and defense use is similar to the Model 1911A1 version of the Colt in size and appearance, and has the Colt short-recoil system in which the rear of the barrel pivots downward for unlocking. The lockwork in the Star, however, differs considerably from that of the Colt.

An obvious difference between these pistols is that the Star lacks a grip safety. Another obvious difference is that the extractor of the Star is exposed on the right side of the slide, and the Colt extractor is almost entirely concealed. Also, the extractor of the Star is actuated by a coil spring, while the Colt extractor is made of springy steel so that no separate spring is required.

Many other differences in these pistols are internal and therefore not apparent except when the guns are disassembled. These differences are in the firing pin, disconnector, ejector, and trigger mechanism. Also, the Star lacks grip screw bushings, and its slide stop spring and plunger are in the slide stop.

The thumb safety of the Star is on the upper left side of the frame, and locks the hammer and slide when engaged. When this safety is disengaged, a red dot on the frame is exposed. Other safety devices are a magazine safety to prevent the pistol from being fired when the magazine is removed, and the half-cock position of the hammer. The firing pin projects from the breech face when the hammer is down, and the only safe way to carry the pistol when the chamber is loaded is with the hammer cocked and thumb safety engaged.

As with the Colt, the magazine catch of the Star is on the left side of the frame. Magazine capacity is eight rounds. After the last shot is fired, the slide is locked open automatically by the slide stop.

When a fully-loaded magazine is inserted in the pistol with the slide closed, a tab-like portion of the cartridge follower projects through a slot in the magazine base to indicate the fully-loaded condition. Another desirable feature of the magazine is that it can be disassembled easily for cleaning and lubrication.

All metal parts are steel with a high-luster blue finish on most exposed surfaces. The grips are checkered brown plastic. Since this well-made pistol is primarily for military and law-enforcement use, it is fitted with fixed sights. It has a large comfortable grip, good balance, generally favorable handling qualities, and performs well.

There is also a lightweight version of this pistol called the Model BKS Starlight. Featuring a lightweight-alloy frame, the Starlight weighs 25 ozs. as compared with 37½ ozs. for the Model BS. Barrel length of the Starlight is 4¼″, while the Model BS has a 5″ barrel. Other Star pistols closely related to the Model BS are the Model A in cal. .38 Super Automatic and the Model P in cal. .45 ACP. These are similar to the Model BS except for caliber. Star pistols are imported by Interarms of Alexandria, Va.

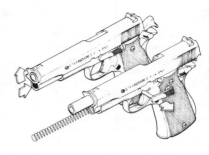

1 Depress magazine catch (11), and remove magazine (28). Draw slide (2) fully rearward to clear chamber and cock hammer (24). Release slide, and engage thumb safety (34). Depress knurled head of recoil spring plug (13), and rotate barrel bushing (1) clockwise (viewed from front) to its stop. Ease plug out of slide and remove. Release safety, and move slide rearward until rounded takedown notch on its left side aligns with lug on slide stop (31). Push inward on slide stop axle protruding from right side of frame (19), and withdraw slide stop to left.

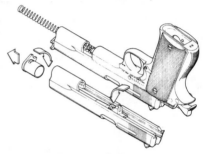

2 Turn pistol upside down, and move slide forward off the frame. Lift recoil spring guide (14), and remove to rear along with the recoil spring (15). Turn barrel bushing counter-clockwise to its stop and remove. Lift barrel (16) to unlock from slide, rotate barrel link fully forward, and draw barrel forward out of slide. This completes field stripping for normal cleaning and lubrication.

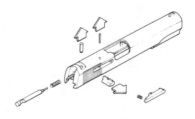

3 For further disassembly, drift extractor pin (3) out through top of slide to release extractor (5) and extractor spring (6). Rear sight (7) must be driven out before firing pin (9) can be removed. Use a brass punch, and remove sight from left to right. Drive firing pin retaining pin (4) upward, and withdraw firing pin and firing pin spring (8).

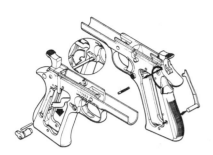

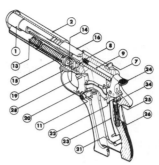

4 Unscrew grip screws (29), and remove grips (27)(30). Detach magazine safety (21) by drifting out its integral pin. Pull trigger, and lower hammer wih thumb. Turn thumb safety downward beyond fire position, and lift out safety plunger (35) and spring (36). Rotate safety upward beyond safe position and withdraw it to the left. Depress magazine catch flush with frame, and turn magazine catch lock (12) fully to left with a small screwdriver (inset). Remove entire magazine catch assembly. Drift out trigger pin (32) from left to right. Pull outward and downward on trigger w/sear bar (20) until the assembly can be removed through side of magazine well. Slide disconnector (18) downward out of frame.

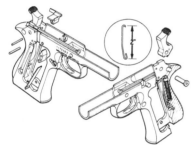

5 Drift out sear pin (38) from right to left, and remove sear (22) and sear spring (23). Drift ejector pin (33) out to the left, and lift off ejector (17). Bend a piece of 1/16" brazing rod as shown (inset). Attach loop of rod to fixed frame pin. Draw back the hammer, and insert hook of rod within cup of hammer spring plunger (25). Adjust hook so that hammer is free of spring tension when fully forward. Push out hammer pin (37) and withdraw hammer. If hammer spring (26) must be removed, depress spring plunger with tapered punch and remove the tool. Then, ease out the plunger and spring cautiously.

6 Assemble in reverse order. Before replacing the assembled slide, position the barrel link vertically. Start the slide on the inverted frame, align barrel link hole with slide stop hole in frame, and insert the slide stop. Move the slide further rearward to bring takedown notch opposite the slide stop lug, and fully seat the stop.

7 Cutaway shows how the parts interrelate. Barrel is shown locked to slide, hammer is at half-cock, and manual safety is disengaged. Parts are number keyed to the parts legend.

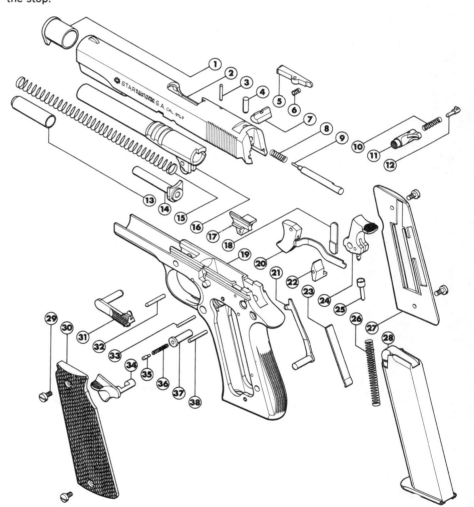

Parts Legend

1. Barrel bushing
2. Slide
3. Extractor pin
4. Firing pin retaining pin
5. Extractor
6. Extractor spring
7. Rear sight
8. Firing pin spring
9. Firing pin
10. Magazine catch lock spring
11. Magazine catch
12. Magazine catch lock
13. Recoil spring plug
14. Recoil spring guide
15. Recoil spring
16. Barrel w/link and pin
17. Ejector
18. Disconnector
19. Frame
20. Trigger w/sear bar, complete
21. Magazine safety
22. Sear
23. Sear spring
24. Hammer w/strut and pin
25. Hammer spring plunger
26. Hammer spring
27. Grip, right
28. Magazine, complete
29. Grip screws (4)
30. Grip, left
31. Slide stop, complete
32. Trigger pin
33. Ejector pin
34. Thumb safety
35. Safety plunger
36. Safety spring
37. Hammer pin
38. Sear pin

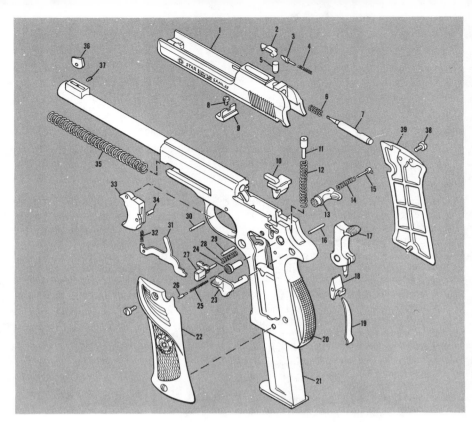

Since 1905 the firm of Bonifacio Echeverria, Eibar, Spain, has made a wide variety of handguns most of which have been sold under the "STAR" brand name. STAR guns range from small .25 ACP pistols up to a full-size, full-automatic version of the Colt M1911.

Firearms International Corp. began importing the STAR Model F, .22 rimfire series in 1948. Three barrel lengths were available, 4-1/4", 6", and 7", plus a so-called "Olympic" model, with weights and muzzle brake.

Well-made and accurate, the Model F had only one design drawback, the lack of a slide hold-open device to lock the slide to the rear following the last shot. Thus, those who would use the pistol on a target range had to develop the habit of carrying a block of wood or plastic to hold the slide back in compliance with the safety rules in force on most ranges. This lack continued to plague the design until it was discontinued in 1968. The problem was corrected, however, when the follow-on FM, FR and FRS models were introduced, with slide hold-open devices.

The Model F was an excellent design, that incorporated a number of interesting features, The takedown system, for example, is truly clever — press a button and lift off the slide.

The Model F has a very sturdy and well-designed magazine. The follower is an aluminum casting and the floorplate is removable for easy cleaning. Except for one or two small stamped parts, the Model F is machined from steel. Internal parts such as the hammer, sear and ejector are case-hardened for durability. The external finish and bluing are excellent, but some of the internal parts are not well finished. The Model F was suitable for small-game hunting or informal target shooting.

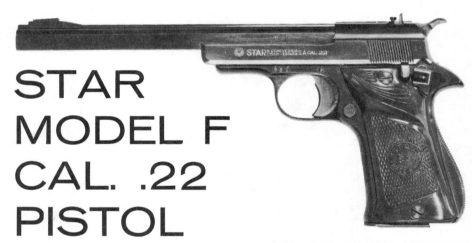

STAR MODEL F CAL. .22 PISTOL

By EDWARD J. HOFFSCHMIDT

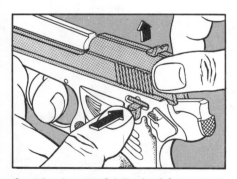

1 The Star Model F pistol has a comparatively simple takedown system. To strip the pistol, begin by first removing the magazine and clearing the chamber. Next push in the takedown catch (27 —lower arrow) and lift the rear of the slide upward (upper arrow). The slide (1) can now be stripped off the front of the barrel.

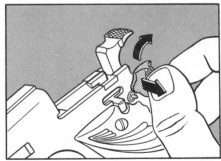

2 The safety catch (23) can best be removed when the hammer (17) is in fired position. Rotate the safety catch to vertical position and wiggle it free of the frame (20). If in the right position, the catch will come out easily; never force it out. Do not let safety catch detent plunger (26) and spring (25) fly out when catch is removed.

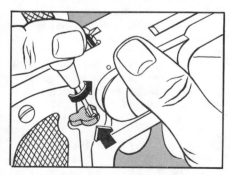

3 The magazine catch (13) is retained in exactly the same manner as in the Colt M1911 pistol. To remove the magazine catch, push it in as if removing the magazine. At the same time turn the magazine catch retainer (15) until it locks into the catch. Then the magazine catch, retainer, and spring can be removed as a single assembly.

Parts Legend

1. Slide
2. Extractor
3. Extractor plunger
4. Extractor spring
5. Firing pin retainer
6. Firing pin spring
7. Firing pin
8. Rear sight lock screw
9. Rear sight
10. Ejector
11. Hammer spring plunger
12. Hammer spring
13. Magazine catch
14. Magazine catch spring
15. Magazine catch retainer
16. Sear pin
17. Hammer
18. Sear
19. Sear spring
20. Frame and barrel
21. Magazine
22. Left grip
23. Safety catch
24. Hammer hinge pin
25. Plunger spring
26. Safety catch detent plunger
27. Takedown catch
28. Takedown spring
29. Ejector retaining pin
30. Trigger pin
31. Trigger bar
32. Trigger spring
33. Trigger
34. Trigger bar pin
35. Recoil spring
36. Front sight
37. Front sight screw
38. Grip screws (4)
39. Right grip

4 The firing pin (7) is retained by pin (5). Since this retainer pin is located under the rear sight (9), the rear sight must be removed in order to get at the pin. Simply loosen the sight lock screw (8) and push out the rear sight. Then, hold the slide in a vise padded to prevent marring finish and drive out the pin (5) as shown in the illustration. ∎

PISTOL MAGAZINES

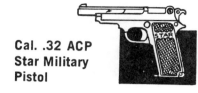

Cal. .32 ACP Star Military Pistol

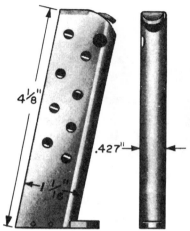

Star pistols have become fairly common in America since the end of World War II. The earlier models, such as the military pistol shown, are not as common as later imports. The military model is an original design bearing some resemblance to early Mannlicher pistols. The safety rotates to shield the firing pin so that the shooter can dry-fire. Like the rest of the gun, the magazines are crudely finished but serviceable.

The main point of recognition is the large hole in the upper right side of the magazine wall. This hole is for the magazine catch to hold the magazine in the gun. Another point of identity is the rounded follower which permits easier loading.

The floorplate, of typical Spanish design, is heavy and is pinned to the sides.—E. J. HOFFSCHMIDT

Star 9 mm. Auto Pistol

PISTOL MAGAZINES

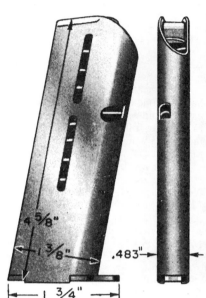

Some Star automatics look and feel like a Colt Model 1911A1 but the resemblance stops there. While these copies of the 1911A1 are not too well made or finished, they will handle any 9 mm. Luger load, but it is hard to say how long they would hold up with Schmeisser or Sten gun loads, since the parts show little evidence of heat-treating.

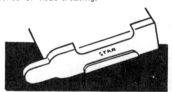

Many of these guns were sold to the Germans, and so often turn up with German proofmarks. Others were purchased from traveling salesmen by GI's fighting in France near the Spanish border.

Magazines for 9 mm. Star automatics are large and heavily constructed. They can be identified by the brand on the floorplate, or by the long observation slots in only one side of the magazine. Another clue is the method of locking the floorplate to the magazine body with tabs as shown. The follower is stamped from flat sheet steel and bent to a step shape. This allows the lower step to push up the hold-open latch when the last shot is fired.—E. J. HOFFSCHMIDT

exploded views:

STAR PD .45 PISTOL

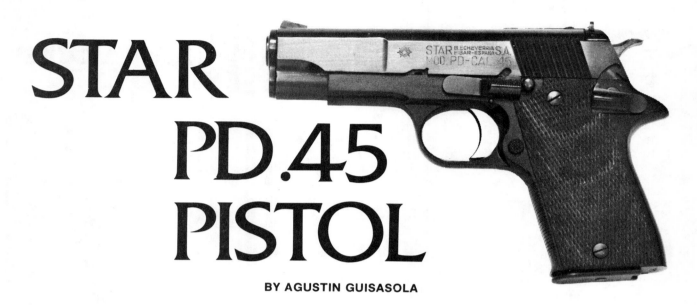

BY AGUSTIN GUISASOLA

Manufacture of .45 ACP cal. pistols is not a new undertaking for Star Bonifacio Echeverria of Eibar, Spain. In the 1920s, they made .45 ACP versions of their various Modelo Militar pistols for export. Later, their Model A pistol was made in that caliber, and by the 1950s they had produced a selective-fire pistol complete with wooden shoulder stock/holster (Model MD) and three pistols of the P series. The standard P lacked a magazine safety; the PS had one, and the rare Super-P

had a quick-takedown lever on the right side of the frame.

In 1975, after several years of development, the PD was introduced. It was designed specifically for the U.S. market but has since proved popular throughout the world. With its aluminum frame, the PD is considerably lighter, shorter and more compact than any of the other Star .45s, and is equipped with a fully adjustable rear sight. At present it is the only .45 being made by Star or being sold by the U.S. importers, Interarms of Alexandria, Va. ■

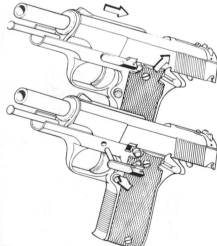

Fig. 1. Check to be sure gun is unloaded by depressing magazine catch (15), removing magazine (36), retracting slide (2) and examining chamber to be sure it is empty. With slide still retracted, push up on the thumb safety (43) so that its hook engages in the slide notch just forward of the finger serrations. The slide will now remain in its rearward position, and the slide stop (38) can be removed by pushing on its rod which protrudes from the right side of the frame.

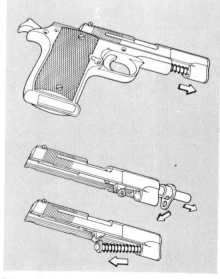

Fig. 2. Hold the slide by its serrations to limit the recoil spring pressure and depress the thumb safety to allow the slide to ride forward off the frame (37). Lift recoil spring assembly (18 to 24) and remove it from the slide. Turn barrel bushing (1) counterclockwise and pull it and the barrel (49) forward from the slide.

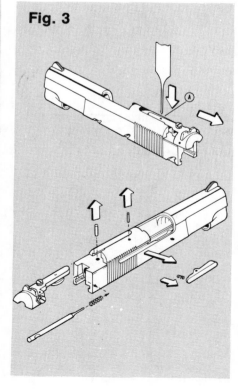

Fig. 3

PARTS LEGEND

1. Barrel bushing
2. Slide
3. Extractor pin
4. Firing pin retaining pin
5. Extractor
6. Extractor spring
7. Sight elevation spring
8. Sight windage spindle plunger
9. Sight windage spindle plunger spring
10. Sight windage spindle retaining pin
11. Sight slide
12. Sight windage spindle
13. Sight
14. Sight elevation screw
15. Magazine catch
16. Magazine catch lock spring
17. Magazine catch lock
18. Recoil spring
19. Recoil spring guide plug
20. Recoil spring guide washer
21. Recoil spring guide
22. Recoil spring guide washer
23. Recoil spring guide buffer
24. Recoil spring guide head
25. Firing pin spring
26. Ejector
27. Firing pin
28. Trigger assembly
29. Sear
30. Sear spring
31. Disconnector
32. Hammer spring plunger
33. Hammer assembly
34. Hammer spring

35. Grip, right
36. Magazine assembly
37. Frame
38. Slide stop assembly
39. Trigger pin

40. Slide stop button
41. Ejector pin
42. Safety plunger
43. Safety
44. Safety piunger spring

45. Hammer pin
46. Sear pin
47. Grip, left
48. Grip screw
49. Barrel with link and pin

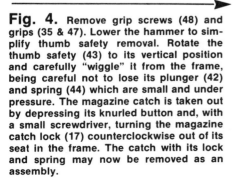

Fig 3. To strip the slide, first remove the rear sight assembly (7 to 14) by unscrewing the elevation screw (14) to its limit and then inserting a small punch in hole A. The entire sight assembly may now be pushed out to the rear. From the underside of the slide, using a suitable punch, drive up the firing pin retaining pin (4) and remove it, the firing pin (27) and its spring (25). Using the same punch, drift the extractor pin (3) up through the slide and remove the extractor (5) and extractor spring (6).

Fig. 4. Remove grip screws (48) and grips (35 & 47). Lower the hammer to simplify thumb safety removal. Rotate the thumb safety (43) to its vertical position and carefully "wiggle" it from the frame, being careful not to lose its plunger (42) and spring (44) which are small and under pressure. The magazine catch is taken out by depressing its knurled button and, with a small screwdriver, turning the magazine catch lock (17) counterclockwise out of its seat in the frame. The catch with its lock and spring may now be removed as an assembly.

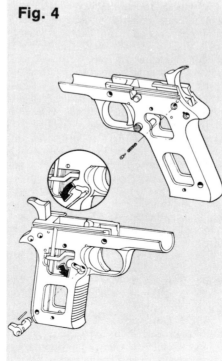

Fig. 4

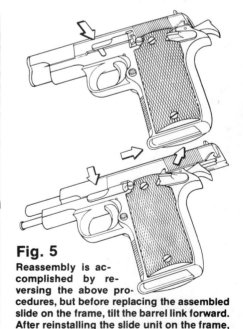

Fig. 5
Reassembly is accomplished by reversing the above procedures, but before replacing the assembled slide on the frame, tilt the barrel link forward. After reinstalling the slide unit on the frame, align the barrel link hole with the slide stop hole in the frame before partially inserting the slide stop rod. Then lock the slide back with the thumb safety hook and fully seat the slide stop.

STEYR MODEL 1912 PISTOL

By E. J. HOFFSCHMIDT

THE Steyr Model 1912 9 mm. automatic pistol, designed and produced by the Austrian Arms Co., Steyr, Austria was the principal Austro-Hungarian handgun during World War I. Introduced in 1911, it was adopted by the Austro-Hungarian Army in 1912.

Several references list this exposed-hammer pistol as a Model 1911 (some are marked "M.1911") while other sources call it Model 1912, the designation used by the Austro-Hungarian Army. Another name commonly used is Steyr-Hahn (Steyr-hammer). This unofficial designation distinguishes the pistol from the Austro-Hungarian Roth-Steyr Model 1907 hammerless pistol.

One chief characteristic of the Steyr Model 1912 is its short-recoil action with revolving barrel. During the period of high pressure, the barrel is locked to the slide. As the slide and barrel start back, the barrel is revolved about 60° on its long axis by a cam, and is unlocked. The slide continues its rearward motion alone.

Another principal feature is the non-detachable magazine in the grip. Accessible only from the top, it is loaded by using an 8-round strip clip, or inserting cartridges singly. After the last round is fired, the slide is locked back by the magazine follower.

The safety is on the left of the receiver. When pivoted upward, it locks both the hammer and slide. It is also used to lock the slide to the rear. This is done for loading singly, and unloading. Cartridges can be released from the magazine by depressing the cartridge release above the left grip.

Barrel length is 5⅛″, and over-all length is 8½″. Weight empty is 34 ozs., about average for a large 9 mm. military handgun. Large checkered walnut grips and the well-distributed weight make for favorable handling qualities. However, the grip is almost at a right angle with the line of bore, which is not good for natural pointing.

Functioning is reliable, and accuracy is sufficient for military use. Features which aid reliability are the well-enclosed action and non-detachable magazine. There are no fragile sheet metal magazine lips to become bent, and the magazine cannot be accidentally lost.

The 9 mm. Steyr cartridge for this pistol is not produced in the U.S., but is available from dealers in surplus military ammunition. Of straight-case rimless design, it has a 117-gr. full metal-jacketed bullet, driven at 1215 feet per second muzzle velocity. Muzzle energy is 385 ft.-lbs.

In addition to being used by Austria-Hungary, the Steyr Model 1912 was adopted by Rumania and Chile. It was also used by police units in Austria during World War II. Some of these specimens were converted to fire the 9 mm. Luger cartridge, and are marked "08", a German military designation for this round.

Sturdy and very well made, this pistol was produced in large quantity, but it never achieved widespread popularity. It was discontinued at the end of World War I.

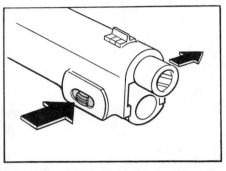

1 To field-strip the pistol, clear the magazine and chamber. Then depress the serrated end of the wedge spring, and push the wedge (2) out of the slide (4) and receiver (30).

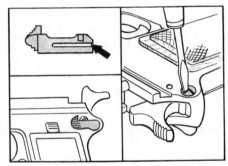

3 For further disassembly, lower the hammer (8), and remove any dirt from the slotted pin part of the safety (19). Then turn the safety so that it points forward, and use a punch or small screwdriver to push it to the left out of the receiver. Unscrew the hammer screw (18), and remove the hammer. Use a screwdriver to compress the upper rear of the recoil spring retainer (11), and push the retainer out forward. Then remove the recoil spring (13) and recoil spring caps (12) (14). Slightly depress the ejector and disconnector (9), and use a small screwdriver to gently pry out the trigger bar (7). Then lift out the ejector and disconnector. Turn out the grip and floorplate screw (22), slide the grips (21) and (31) out of the receiver, and remove the floorplate (23) with attached springs, the magazine spring (28), and magazine follower (27). Depress the cartridge release spring (20), turn it forward a quarter turn, and lift from receiver. Also remove the cartridge release (17). Driving out the trigger pin (16) and removing the trigger (15) completes disassembly of the receiver group.

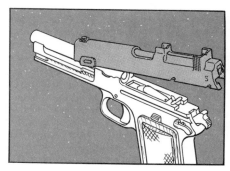

2 Pull the slide all the way back and lift it off the receiver. The barrel (10) can then be removed. In reassembly, the barrel must be positioned so the locking lugs are to the right.

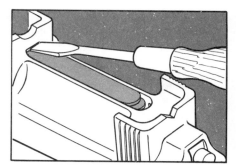

4 Place a screwdriver on the upper front of the extractor (3), and push down and forward. After the extractor is pushed forward, lift it at the rear to free the firing pin (6), and remove the firing pin and firing pin spring (5).

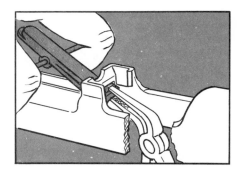

5 Use a needle-nose plier (one with bent jaws is preferable) to compress the extractor limbs at the front. Then push the extractor rearward until the lug on its upper limb is behind the loading port. Push the extractor hook upward with a brass punch or rod, and force the extractor rearward out of the slide. An aid in doing this is to put a pin or nail through the hole in the extractor to provide a finger grip. ∎

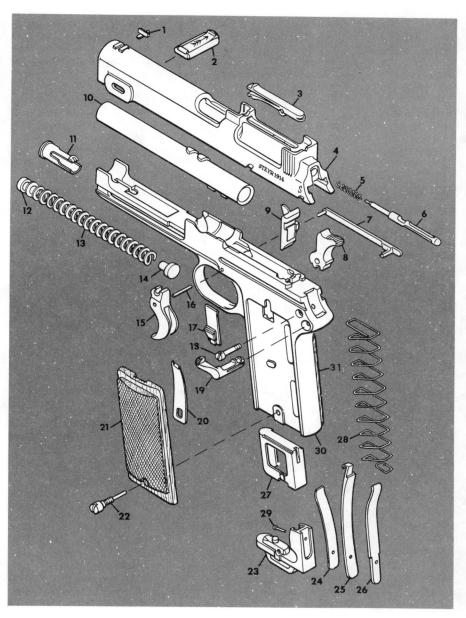

Parts Legend
1. Front sight
2. Wedge
3. Extractor
4. Slide
5. Firing pin spring
6. Firing pin
7. Trigger bar
8. Hammer
9. Ejector and disconnector
10. Barrel
11. Recoil spring retainer
12. Front recoil spring cap
13. Recoil spring
14. Rear recoil spring cap
15. Trigger
16. Trigger pin
17. Cartridge release
18. Hammer screw
19. Safety
20. Cartridge release spring
21. Left grip
22. Grip and floorplate screw
23. Floorplate
24. Disconnector spring
25. Sear and sear spring
26. Hammer spring
27. Magazine follower
28. Magazine spring
29. Spring retainer pin
30. Receiver
31. Right grip

Steyr Model SP Pocket Pistol

By E. J. HOFFSCHMIDT

The Steyr Model SP, .32 ACP double-action pistol was introduced in the late 1950s. Manufactured by Steyr-Daimler-Puch A.G., Steyr, Austria, the Steyr SP is a true double-action design. Since there is no provision in this pistol for single-action operation, the internal hammer does not stay cocked after each shot as in conventional self-loading pistols; the trigger must be pulled through its full cycle to cock and release the hammer for each shot. There is an inertia firing pin within the slide.

A unique feature of the Model SP pistol is the cross-bolt safety catch in the trigger. When pushed to the left with the trigger finger the catch engages the frame to block rearward movement of the trigger. The safety is disengaged by pressing the catch to the right with the thumbnail of the gun hand.

The magazine catch is in the butt of the pistol. Of sheet metal construction, the detachable box magazine holds seven, .32 ACP (cal. 7.65 mm) cartridges. When the last shot is fired the slide is held in the open position by the magazine follower. Partially withdrawing the magazine from the grip releases the slide, which is then free to go forward under pressure of the recoil spring. Few Steyr Model SPs were imported into the U.S. All importation stopped upon implementation of provisions of the 1968 gun Control Act.

Parts Legend

1. Barrel bushing
2. Slide
3. Rear sight
4. Extractor pin
5. Extractor
6. Extractor spring
7. Firing pin retaining pin
8. Firing pin bushing
9. Firing pin bushing lock screw
10. Firing pin spring
11. Firing pin
12. Recoil spring
13. Trigger pin
14. Sideplate screw
15. Hammer
16. Hammer strut pin
17. Hammer strut
18. Hammer spring
19. Hammer hinge pin
20. Magazine catch
21. Magazine catch pin
22. Right grip
23. Grip screw
24. Frame
25. Magazine
26. Left grip
27. Grip screw
28. Sideplate
29. Trigger spring retaining screw
30. Trigger spring
31. Trigger bar
32. Trigger spring follower
33. Trigger
34. Safety catch
35. Safety catch spring
36. Safety catch detent

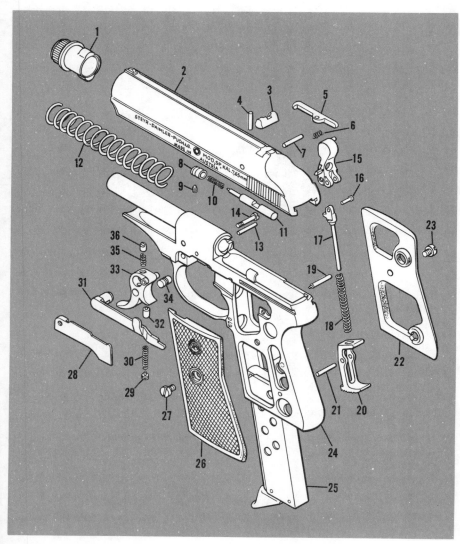

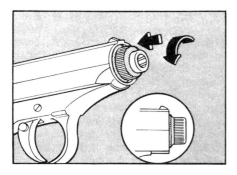

1 To take down the Steyr Model SP pistol, first remove the magazine, and pull back slide and examine chamber to be sure that it is empty. Push in barrel bushing (1) and turn about 15° counterclockwise until it is free to be eased off barrel. Then pull slide (2) to rear and lift it free of frame (24), and slide it off front of barrel.

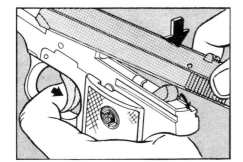

2 When reassembling pistol, put slide back over barrel and pull it back as far as possible. Pull trigger about half way back to partially cock hammer. Then push down on rear of slide until it engages grooves in frame. Install recoil spring (12) and barrel bushing. When barrel bushing is properly seated, it should be flush with end of barrel.

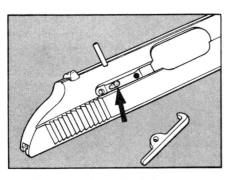

3 To remove firing pin, it is necessary to first remove extractor (5). Drive out extractor pin (4) and remove extractor and extractor spring (6). When extractor is removed, it exposes end of firing pin retaining pin (7) and also exposes a hole that can, if necessary, be of assistance in removing a stuck firing pin bushing (8) or in carrying off gases in event of a punctured primer.

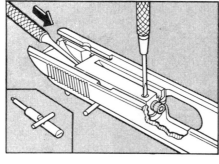

4 To remove firing pin, drive out firing pin retaining pin (7). Then loosen firing pin bushing lock screw (9). Firing pin (11) can now be pushed or tapped out through front of breech. It will in turn push out bushing and firing pin spring (10). Before reassembling firing pin, scribe or pencil a line across large end of pin parallel to flat on pin. Line is an aid in positioning flat to let firing pin retaining pin (7) pass through.

5 Safety catch (34) is a cross-bolt pin that blocks trigger when in "safe" position. To remove it, tap pin out of either side of trigger. Safety is retained by a V-shaped safety catch detent (36) and safety catch spring (35). When replacing safety, install spring and detent in hole in trigger. Hold detent down as shown and tap safety catch into place.

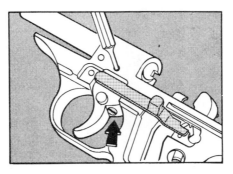

6 After sideplate screw (14) and sideplate (28) and grips have been removed, function of trigger can be studied or disassembled further. First drive out trigger pin (13). Trigger and trigger bar (31) can now be lifted out. To remove trigger bar, remove trigger spring retaining screw (29) on under side of trigger carefully, since it is under spring tension. Remove trigger spring (30) and trigger spring follower (32). Lift out trigger bar. ∎

Steyr Model 1908 Cal. .32 Auto. Pistol

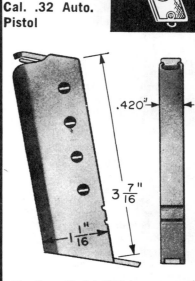

.420"

3 7/16"

1 1/16"

The Steyr Model 1908 is an unusual arm. Although a semi-automatic pistol, it can also be used as a single-loader. When the side-lever is depressed, the barrel flips up for loading. Early guns lacked extractors and depended on blowback to extract the empty cases. Although functioning was satisfactory without an extractor, one was added to later guns to improve their reliability.

Easiest point of recognition for a Steyr magazine is the reversed floorplate and the 2 notches in the back strap. When magazine is gripped by the upper notch, it is held clear of the slide so that the gun can be used as a single shot.

Magazine follower is a flat piece of sheet metal with slight bend at the tip to facilitate loading the magazine.
—E. J. HOFFSCHMIDT

STOEGER LUGER .22 By DENNIS RIORDAN

THE Luger pistol has enjoyed a long colorful history. Named after Georg Luger, its German designer, this famous handgun was developed in the late 1890's, and was produced by DWM (Deutsche Waffen und Munitionsfabriken; German Arms and Ammunition Co.), Berlin, Germany. Later, it was also produced in large quantity by Mauser and several other firms for various governments and commercial sales.

Many Lugers were imported into the U.S. chiefly by Stoeger Arms Corp. These pistols were in calibers 9 mm. Luger and 7.65 mm. Luger, both center-fire rounds. The supply of these commercial pistols was cut off by World War II, and the Luger was discontinued.

Popularity of the Luger has increased since the war, however, and in 1969 Stoeger introduced a U.S.-made version of this pistol chambered for the highly-popular .22 long rifle rimfire cartridge. The new pistol was developed by gun designer Gary Wilhelm.

Possessing the same general appearance as the German Army Model 1908 Luger pistol, the Stoeger Luger fires regular or high-velocity .22 long rifle ammunition. Barrel length of the Stoeger pistol is 4½", 9/16" greater than that of the Model 1908. Weight is 30¼ ozs., or only ¾ oz. less than the Model 1908. Magazine capacity is 11 rounds.

Mechanical design of the Stoeger Luger differs considerably from the center-

fire models. While the Stoeger Luger has a toggle-joint breech system resembling that of the center-fire models, the barrel is fixed in the frame and does not recoil. The action is of retarded-blowback design since opening of the breech is retarded to some extent by the toggle mechanism.

Unlike center-fire Lugers, the lock mechanism has a pivoting hammer powered by a coil spring in the handle. The recoil spring, also of coil type, is in the breechbolt. As in center-fire models, the safety is on the left of the frame. The pistol is optionally available at no extra cost with the safety on the right of the frame for left-handed users.

Materials in the Stoeger Luger are in

PARTS LEGEND

1. Bolt stop
2. Bolt stop pin
3. Bolt stop spring
4. Sear
5. Sear spring
6. Safety shoe
7. Hammer
8. Magazine guide pin (2)
9. Sear pin
10. Boltways block pin
11. Hammer spring washer
12. Front sight
13. Barrel
14. Barrel pin
15. Trigger pull pin
16. Trigger
17. Magazine catch anchor plate
18. Magazine catch anchor
19. Trigger pin
20. Trigger pin plunger spring
21. Trigger pin plunger
22. Safety detent plunger
23. Safety spring
24. Safety spring housing
25. Main frame pin
26. Magazine
27. Sear bar
28. Sear bar pin
29. Sear bar guide pin
30. Boltways
31. Magazine guide
32. Hammer strut pin
33. Hammer strut
34. Hammer spring
35. Hammer strut anchor plate
36. Right grip
37. Grip screw (2)
38. Front toggle pin, left hand
39. Front toggle
40. Front toggle pin, right hand
41. Frame
42. Toggle grip pin (2)
43. Toggle grip, left hand
44. Toggle link pin
45. Toggle grip, right hand
46. Rear toggle
47. Rear toggle spring
48. Sear bar retaining screw
49. Extractor
50. Extractor spring
51. Front toggle pin retaining pin (2)
52. Extractor pin
53. Firing pin retaining pin
54. Bolt
55. Magazine catch
56. Magazine catch plunger
57. Magazine catch spring
58. Magazine catch plunger guide
59. Magazine catch pin
60. Rear toggle pivot pin
61. Safety lever
62. Left grip
63. Firing pin spring
64. Drive spring
65. Drive spring guide
66. Firing pin
67. Boltways block
68. Takedown plunger spring
69. Takedown plunger

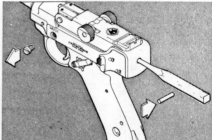

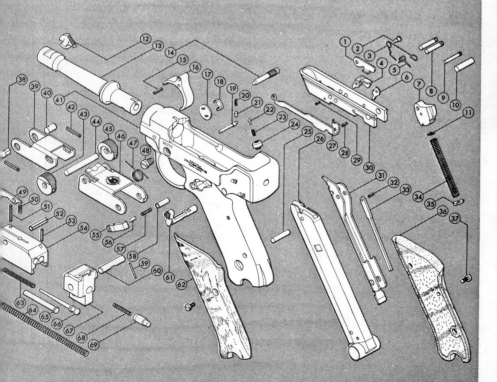

1 Disassemble pistol on a clean, well-lighted bench. Depress magazine catch (55) and remove magazine (26), checking that it is empty. Grasp toggle grips (43, 45) and pull back and up on toggle fully to clear chamber. Release toggle and replace magazine. Move safety lever (61) to fire position, and leave action cocked. Unscrew sear bar retaining screw (48) and grip screws (37). Remove grips (36, 62). Use pin punch to push out main frame pin (25). Then, depress takedown plunger (69). Action will rise slightly as takedown plunger clears frame (41).

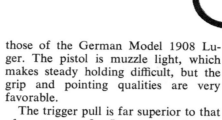

keeping with the current trend in gun construction. The frame is forged aluminum alloy instead of steel, and some parts are fabricated from sheet steel. There are also several plastic parts. The barrel, breechbolt, and other parts subject to great wear and stress are steel. Resin-impregnated checkered wood grips were used at first. These had the appearance of plastic, and this resulted in a change to epoxy-finished unchecked-ered walnut grips. The current-production Stoeger Luger also has an improved safety detent plunger and bolt stop pin

A highly-desirable feature is that most of the mechanism can be easily removed as a unit from the frame for cleaning and lubrication. After the mechanism is removed, the bore is accessible for cleaning from the breech end.

Handling qualities are similar to those of the German Model 1908 Luger. The pistol is muzzle light, which makes steady holding difficult, but the grip and pointing qualities are very favorable.

The trigger pull is far superior to that of most center-fire Lugers, and the pistol is reliable and accurate. A wide, square-top front sight and square-notch rear sight help make sighting accurate and easy. The sights are not screw-adjustable. However, the front sight can be driven laterally.

This pistol meets the need for a .22 rimfire handgun generally similar to center-fire Lugers in size, weight, and handling qualities, and is well suited for informal target shooting.

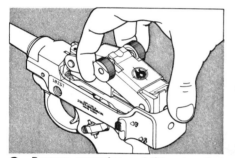

2 Remove magazine and lift out action assembly by pulling straight upward on toggle grips. Rest thumb over rear of frame to catch the spring-loaded takedown plunger as it emerges. Sear bar (27) may not release from trigger pull pin (15). If resistance is felt, move action laterally to free sear bar.

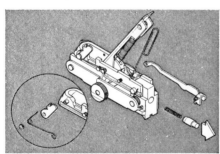

3 Remove takedown plunger and spring (68) so that they are not lost. No further disassembly is required for normal cleaning. If sear bar becomes separated from action assembly, place horseshoe shaped section of the bar in its notch on underside of boltways (30). Bend a small hook in a wire and use to lever the rearward arm of sear spring (5) around and over the sear bar pin (28). On older models, the bolt stop (1) and spring (3) were secured by a separate retainer. Should these parts become displaced, reassemble them over their pin in the order shown (inset).

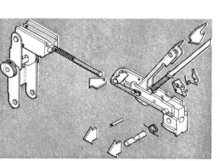

4 To disassemble action, turn assembly upside down and unhook arm of rear toggle spring (47) from boltways block pin (10). Push bolt (54) fully to the rear, in contact with boltways block (67). Push out rear toggle pivot pin (60) with punch. Swing toggle assembly downward and remove rear toggle spring. Ease bolt forward, holding drive spring (64) in alignment so that it is not kinked. Unhook sear spring and remove sear bar. Then, lower hammer (7) cautiously with thumb. Place cleaning rod section or other tube over tip of hammer strut (33), compress hammer spring (34), and pivot assembly clear of magazine guide (31). Drift out swaged pins traversing boltways so that their serrated ends emerge first. Assemble action group in reverse. Longest arms of rear toggle and sear springs bear on boltways block and sear bar pins respectively. Reset both springs with wire hook.

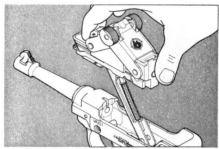

5 To reassemble the field-stripped pistol, first replace takedown plunger and spring. Notch in rear toggle pin must align with takedown plunger. Turn exposed ends of rear toggle pin if necessary. Grasp action between fingers and thumb, compressing drive and takedown plunger springs. Insert tail of magazine guide at rear of magazine well and ease assembly down into place. When fully seated, takedown plunger will snap into its frame recess. Ease toggle closed.

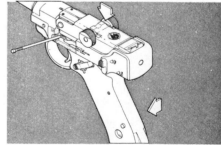

6 Replace magazine and depress rear toggle (46) to align main frame pin holes. Insert frame pin so that it protrudes equally through both sides of frame. Hold trigger (16) fully forward and seat sear bar over trigger pull pin, working through frame hole with the point of a nail. Replace sear bar screw and draw up snugly. Do not use force. Test function of safety and bolt stop. If satisfactory, replace grips and grip screws.

The Tokarev Pistol

By E. J. Hoffschmidt

Legend

A—Slide
B—Extractor retaining pin
C—Extractor
D—Extractor spring
E—Rear sight
F—Firing pin spring
G—Firing pin
H—Hammer
I—Hammer spring
J—Hammer mechanism housing
K—Sear spring
L—Sear
M—Disconnector
N—Spring retainer pin
O—Hammer pin
P—Sear pin
Q—Right hand grip
R—Magazine
S—Trigger return spring
T—Spring retainer pin
U—Left hand grip
V—Trigger
W—Magazine catch spring guide
X—Magazine catch spring
Y—Slide stop
Z—Frame (receiver)
AA—Recoil spring guide
BB—Recoil spring retainer
CC—Recoil spring
DD—Slide stop retainer clip
EE—Magazine catch
FF—Barrel link
GG—Barrel link pin
HH—Firing pin retainer pin
II—Barrel
JJ—Barrel bushing

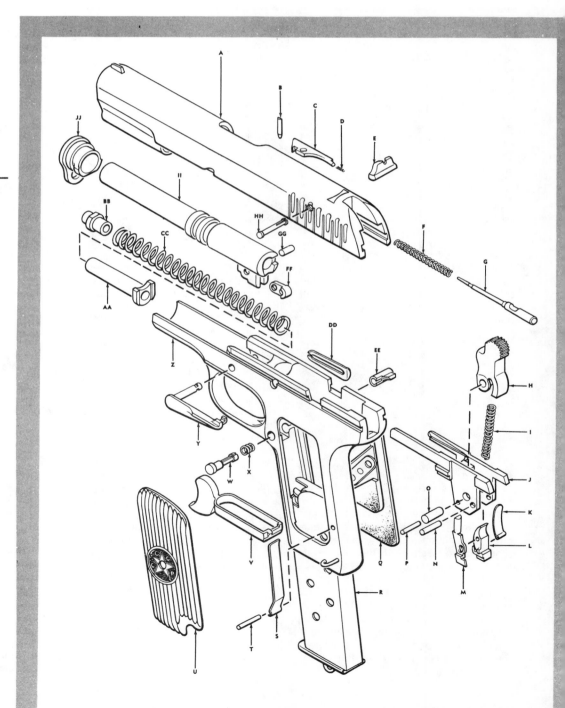

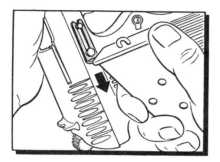

Figure 1—Remove the magazine. Draw back the slide to eject any cartridge in the chamber. Using the back edge of the bottom plate of the magazine as a tool, pull back hard on the slide stop retainer clip (DD) until it releases. Then push the slide stop (Y) through from right to left.

Figure 2—Draw the slide off the front of the frame slowly. As soon as the recoil spring is exposed, hold it up against the barrel to prevent it from bending out of the slide. While holding the recoil spring in place, grasp the recoil spring guide (AA) and push it toward the muzzle, while lifting it free of the barrel lug.

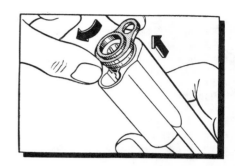

Figure 3—The barrel bushing (JJ) can now be turned 180 degrees and then lifted free of the slide. The barrel (II) can now be pulled out the front of the slide. This method of "take down" will be found much simpler than the one usually recommended for the take down of similar Browning type pistols.

THE TOKAREV automatic pistol Model 30 in 7.62 Russian or 7.63 Mauser caliber, like other products designed by the Russians during the 1930's, was made with an eye for ease of production. During that period, Russia was woefully lacking in machine tools; therefore every unnecessary machining operation was eliminated. It is interesting to note, also, that the Tokarev was designed around the time-proven Browning recoil-operated slide lock and stirrup type trigger. The net result was a simple, compact, and dependable automatic pistol, but without manual safety catches or any finely machined parts. I have yet to see a Tokarev automatic, either pre-war or post-war, that measures up to American machining standards.

The one really bad feature of the Tokarev in an otherwise good design, is the lack of a manual safety catch. If the gun is carried at full cock, the danger is obvious. If the gun is carried at half-cock, the awkward hammer shape makes it difficult to get the first shot off quickly. Another drawback, measured by American standards, is the small caliber. The 7.62 Russian or the .30 caliber Mauser, both of which may be fired in the Tokarev, is an excellent man-stopper when soft-point or hollow-point bullets are used, but with jacketed bullets it lacks the stopping power so necessary in a close combat weapon. The angle of the grip is a little too straight. The Tokarev lacks the fine feel of similar type Browning designs, such as the Colt .45 semi-automatic pistol.

In spite of all the above comments, the Tokarev contains some very interesting points. The most notable of these is the hammer mechanism. This mechanism can be lifted out as a unit after the slide has been removed. The unit not only houses the sear, disconnector, and hammer, but also acts as feed lips for the 8-round magazine. Since these lips are an integral part of the gun mechanism, they are not subjected to the rough treatment that magazine lips normally get. In the right side of the housing (part J), there is an inspection hole. Through here can be seen the operation of the hammer and sear. It is also possible to see any dangerous wear on the sear or sear notch in the hammer without disassembling the unit.

There is very little that can go wrong with the Tokarev, which weighs one pound fifteen ounces, measures 7-11/16 inches in overall length, and has a barrel 4-9/16 inches long. The weakest parts of the gun are the split pins used to retain the magazine catch and firing pins (parts HH and W). These pins have a tendency to break at the bottom of the slot unless they are squeezed together while being removed. The Tokarev grips are another headache. They are made of a resin composition which chips easily. All in all, the simplicity of the design and of the parts make this pistol an easy weapon to repair.

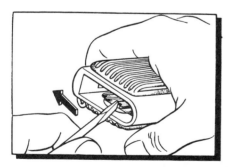

Figure 4—The grips on this weapon are held on with a latch arrangement. Holding the gun as shown a T-shaped piece of steel can be seen. Reach in with a screw driver and push the T-shaped piece toward the rear of the gun grip. The left-hand grip can now be removed by pushing against the inside surface. Do not attempt to pry the grip from the outside—the plastic is a very low grade and will chip along the edges.

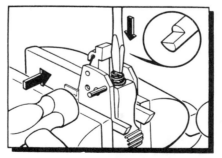

Figure 5—The hardest section on this gun to disassemble or assemble is the hammer group, but after removing the hammer spring retainer pin (N), the other pins may be removed easily. To reassemble, replace all parts but the hammer spring. Using a screw driver or tool shown in the insert, depress the spring (I) deep enough to allow the pin (N) to hold it. Then tap the pin all the way through.

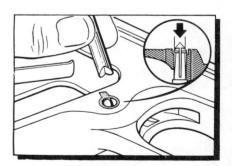

Figure 6—The firing pin and the magazine catch are retained by split pins. These split pins (HH) and (W) can be removed with the aid of the tool shown. This tool forces the pin to close up so that it may be pushed out easily. If an attempt is made to drive the pins out with a flat-end punch, they may be broken or badly deformed.

UNIQUE MILITARY AND POLICE PISTOL

By DENNIS RIORDAN

DURING World War II, the Germans used many substitute-standard small arms, among them the Unique Military & Police Model 7.65 mm. (.32 ACP) automatic pistol. Commonly called the Kriegsmodell (War Model), this blowback-operated pistol was designed and produced by Manufacture d'Armes des Pyrenees Francaises, Hendaye, France. It has a 9-round detachable magazine, and weighs 26½ ozs. The barrel is 3¼" long.

Of simple, straightforward design, this pistol has an exposed hammer with rounded spur. The safety is on the left of the frame above the trigger, and the hammer has a half-cock notch. When the chamber is loaded, the extractor projects from the slide and serves as a loading indicator. The magazine catch is on the bottom of the handle.

The grips are black plastic with vertical serrations. Each has a circular shield marked with the caliber and mag-

azine capacity. The marking on specimens made for German use is "7.65 M/M. 9 SCHUSS." On specimens made for French use, the marking is "7.65 M/M. 9 COUPS." There are also specimens with the grips bearing the interlocked letters "RF," presumably for Republique Francaise.

While this pistol is only fairly well made and finished, it is strong, serviceable, and sufficiently accurate for its intended purpose.

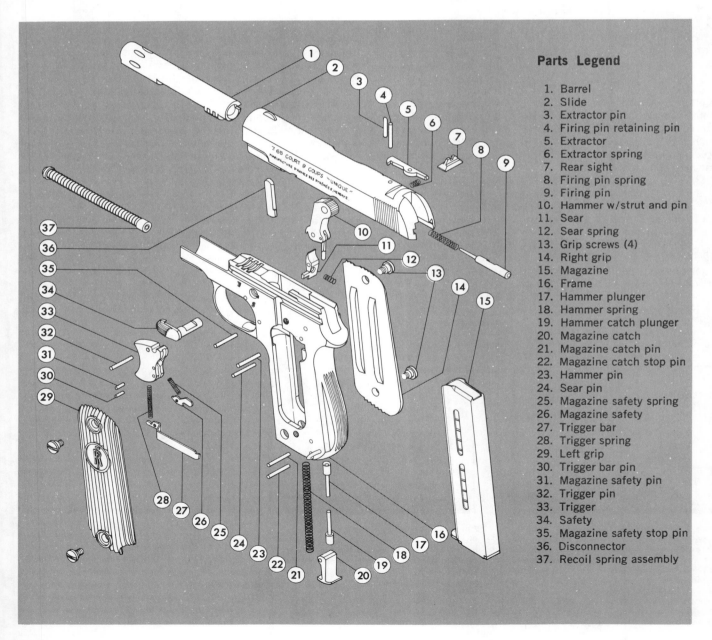

Parts Legend

1. Barrel
2. Slide
3. Extractor pin
4. Firing pin retaining pin
5. Extractor
6. Extractor spring
7. Rear sight
8. Firing pin spring
9. Firing pin
10. Hammer w/strut and pin
11. Sear
12. Sear spring
13. Grip screws (4)
14. Right grip
15. Magazine
16. Frame
17. Hammer plunger
18. Hammer spring
19. Hammer catch plunger
20. Magazine catch
21. Magazine catch pin
22. Magazine catch stop pin
23. Hammer pin
24. Sear pin
25. Magazine safety spring
26. Magazine safety
27. Trigger bar
28. Trigger spring
29. Left grip
30. Trigger bar pin
31. Magazine safety pin
32. Trigger pin
33. Trigger
34. Safety
35. Magazine safety stop pin
36. Disconnector
37. Recoil spring assembly

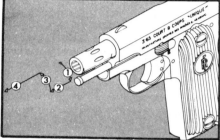

1 To field-strip the Unique Military & Police Model, remove the magazine (15) and clear the chamber. Pull the slide (2) to the rear, and engage the safety (34) with the front notch on the slide to lock the slide back. Rotate the barrel (1) clockwise 60° (step 1), pull it forward ¾″ (2), rotate it counterclockwise 60° (3), and pull forward (4) out of the slide.

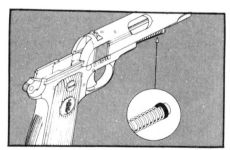

2 While holding the slide firmly, turn the safety downward, and ease the slide forward off the frame (16). Remove the recoil spring assembly (37). This completes field-stripping.

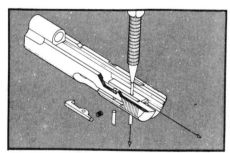

3 For further disassembly, place the slide bottom up in a vise with padded jaws. Drift out the extractor pin (3) and firing retaining pin (4), and remove the extractor (5), extractor spring (6), firing pin (9), and firing pin spring (8). Drift out retaining pins in the slide to the top; those in the frame from right to left.

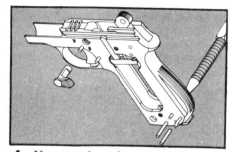

4 Unscrew the grip screws (13), and remove grips (14), (29). Rotate the safety a half turn from safe position and lift out of frame. Re-insert magazine, hold hammer (10), pull trigger (33), and ease hammer down. Place frame in a vise with padded jaws, and drift out magazine catch stop pin (22). While holding magazine catch (20), drift out magazine catch pin (21), and remove magazine catch, magazine catch plunger (19), hammer spring (18), and hammer plunger (17). Drift out hammer pin (23), and remove hammer with strut.

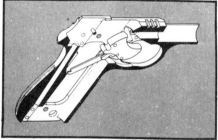

5 Drift out sear pin (24), and remove sear (11) and sear spring (12). Drift out magazine safety stop pin (35) and trigger pin (32). Pull trigger bar (27) inside of frame, and slide disconnector (36) down to remove it. Roll trigger assembly back and down through magazine well. Trigger assembly can be disassembled by drifting out trigger bar pin (30) and magazine safety pin (31) from right to left. Reassemble in reverse. Use a drift punch or slave pin to aid insertion of magazine catch pin. Head of extractor pin is shaped to match rounded top of slide. Drive this pin with a plastic hammer or wood block to avoid damaging it. Extractor pin and firing pin retaining pin must not project from bottom of slide or they will interfere with slide movement. ∎

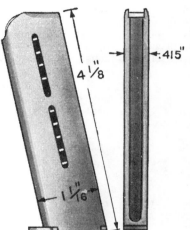

The only unique feature of the French Unique cal. .32 pistol is the marking on World War II guns made for the German Army. Legend on the slide states in French that the gun holds 9 cal. .32 cartridges. The grip marking gives the same information in German. The guns were usually crudely made and finished. The design is relatively simple, but parts are sturdy and the gun seems to function well.

Unique magazines are easily recognized by the depression in the backstrap which forms a pair of rails. This construction stiffens the backstrap and reduces friction when inserting the magazine. The long observation slots and rounded end of the follower are also good points of identification.

Sides of the magazine are bent over the floorplate to hold it in place.— E. J. HOFFSCHMIDT

U.S. MODEL 1842 PERCUSSION PISTOL

By EDWARD J. HOFFSCHMIDT

The Navy's Model 1842, Cal. .54 percussion pistol with six-inch round barrel was manufactured by N.P. Ames of springfield, Mass., and Henry Deringer of Philadelphia, Pa.

Those made by Ames are smoothbored and are dated 1842, 1843, 1844 or 1845, according to the year of manufacture. They are found both with and without brass blade front sights. Those made for Navy purchase are marked "U.S.N."

Others, made for the Treasury Department's Revenue Cutter Service, are marked "U.S.R."

Model 1842 Navy pistols made by Deringer are encountered with both smoothbore and rifled barrels, with the latter having both front and rear sights. Most Deringer guns are unmarked as to the year of production, but a few bear the date 1847.

Box-lock, or inside hammer, mech-

anisms are uncommon in U.S. martial arms' designs. The idea of the inside hammer was to prevent it from snagging when a sailor thrust a brace of pistols under his belt. this development led to a simplified lock mechanism in which the half- and full-cock notches were cut directly into the hammer and the need for a tumbler and tumbler screw was eliminated — as were the parts.

Another advanced feature of the 1842 Navy pistol was its internal hammer stop. This sturdy projection on the underside of the lockplate prevented the hammer from battering the nipple.

Model 1842 Navy pistols were handsome guns having all brass hardware with case hardened lockplates and hammers. Most barrels were lacquer browned, though some were tinned to prevent salt water corrosion.Relatively few Model 1842 Navy pistols were made. Estimates of the combined production of Ames and Deringer is fewer than 4,000 guns.

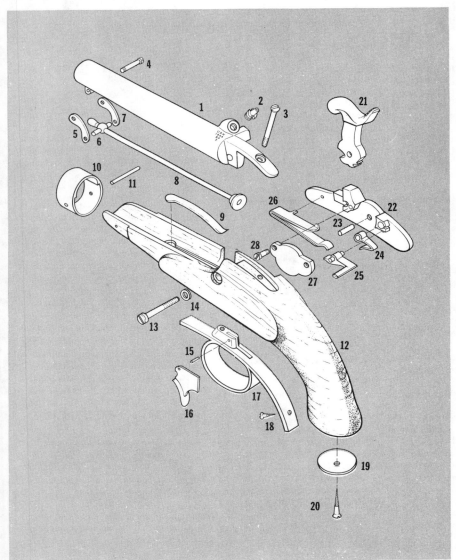

Parts Legend

1. Barrel
2. Cone
3. Barrel screw
4. Swivel screw
5. Left ramrod swivel
6. Ramrod guide
7. Right ramrod swivel
8. Ramrod
9. Ramrod spring
10. Band
11. Band cross pin
12. Stock
13. Lock retaining screw
14. Washer
15. Trigger pin
16. Trigger
17. Trigger guard
18. Trigger guard screw
19. Butt cap
20. Butt cap screw
21. Hammer
22. Lockplate
23. Hammer pin
24. Sear spring
25. Sear
26. Mainspring
27. Bridle
28. Bridle screws (2)

1 To remove the lockplate, first pull the hammer back to half-cock position to clear the cone (2). Loosen the lock retaining screw (13) a few turns and tap it gently with a plastic hammer. If the lock does not come out easily, tap the lockplate (22) lightly. This will help break the lock loose from rust and grime. Continue to loosen the retaining screw (13) and to tap it until the lock is free of the stock. Never attempt to pry the lockplate loose, as this may scar the stock

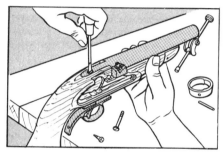

2 After the lock mechanism has been removed, the balance of the gun can be disassembled easily. First pull out the ramrod (8). Drive out the band cross pin (11), and carefully drive off the band (10) with a block of wood or plastic hammer. The barrel screw (3) holds the barrel (1) and the trigger guard (17) together and must be removed completely. Be sure the lock retaining screw is out of the stock, since it, too, retains the barrel

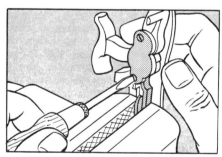

3 Before attempting to disassemble the lock, treat the screws with a good penetrating solvent. Take the tension off the mainspring (26) with an old spring clamp if one is available. If not, clamp the mainspring (26) in a vise as shown. Squeeze the mainspring just enough to relieve the pressure on the hammer. Remove the bridle screws (28) and lift off the bridle (27). Lift out the hammer (21). The mainspring is now free to pivot until the short end is free of its notch in the lockplate. Ease the mainspring out ∎

Old Model Sauer Automatic

PISTOL MAGAZINES

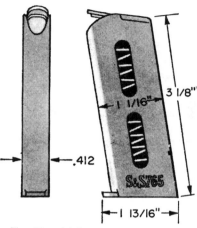

The old model Sauer & Sohn pistol is best known for its excellent finish, compact design, and simple takedown. This model was made in .25 and .32 caliber. Although it was popular in Europe and gave excellent service, it was replaced in 1930 by the Behoerdenmodell, which freely translated means the Authorities Model. The magazines of the two guns are not interchangeable because of the difference in angle and method of retaining them. Old model Sauer magazines are usually stamped with the initials "S&S" followed by the caliber.

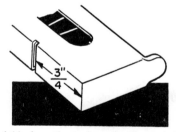

Aside from the trade mark, the most distinctive features of the old model magazines are the long observation slots on either side and the retaining notch on the back edge of the magazine.

The magazines have a flat sheet steel follower. While this follower serves the purpose, it would be better if it had been replaced by a pressed or solid follower. —E. J. HOFFSCHMIDT.

Sauer Model 1930

PISTOL MAGAZINES

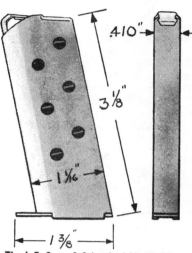

The J. P. Sauer & Sohn pistol Model 1930 is a streamlined version of the original model. It can be recognized by the well-shaped grip, the small safety trigger protruding from the regular trigger, and the large entwined "S" molded into the left grip. The model 1930, like its predecessors, is beautifully made. The design is good but slightly prone to jam due to the small ejection port. The magazine of the new model and the old model are not readily interchangeable because of the difference in the angle of the grip

Sauer magazines can be recognized by a number of features. The magazine base plate is usually stamped as shown and observation holes are only on the left side. The magazine has flush sides and turned-over tabs on the base plate. These tabs are inletted into the base plate, locking it securely in place.

Other distinguishing features of the Sauer magazines are the shape of the bolt clearance notch in the back of the magazine and the shape of the feed lips. The followers are usually bent from sheet steel.

—E. J. HOFFSCHMIDT.

U.S. Model 1842 Pistol

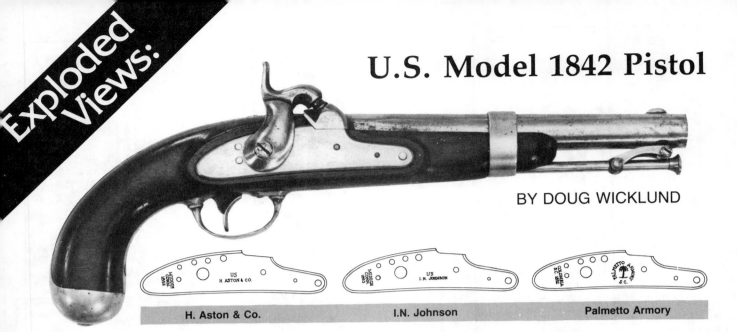

BY DOUG WICKLUND

H. Aston & Co.   **I.N. Johnson**   **Palmetto Armory**

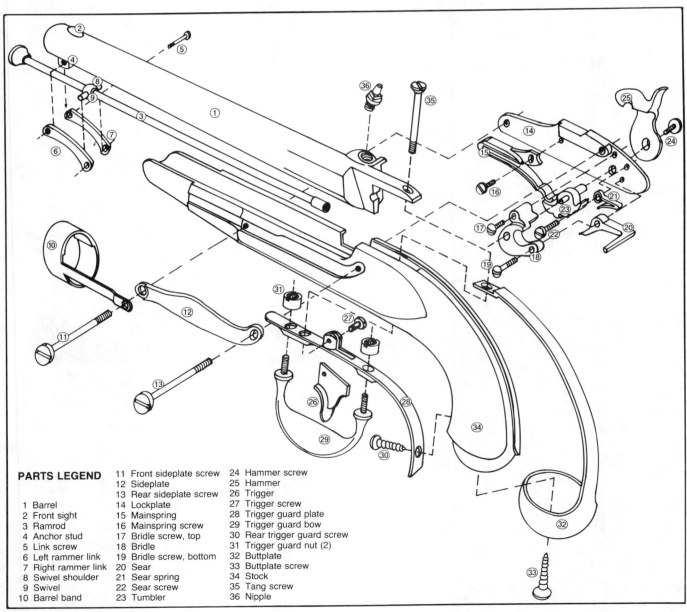

PARTS LEGEND

1 Barrel	11 Front sideplate screw	24 Hammer screw
2 Front sight	12 Sideplate	25 Hammer
3 Ramrod	13 Rear sideplate screw	26 Trigger
4 Anchor stud	14 Lockplate	27 Trigger screw
5 Link screw	15 Mainspring	28 Trigger guard plate
6 Left rammer link	16 Mainspring screw	29 Trigger guard bow
7 Right rammer link	17 Bridle screw, top	30 Rear trigger guard screw
8 Swivel shoulder	18 Bridle	31 Trigger guard nut (2)
9 Swivel	19 Bridle screw, bottom	32 Buttplate
10 Barrel band	20 Sear	33 Buttplate screw
	21 Sear spring	34 Stock
	22 Sear screw	35 Tang screw
	23 Tumbler	36 Nipple

THE U.S. Model 1842 .54 cal. percussion pistol with 8½″ barrel was manufactured by Henry Aston and Ira N. Johnson, both operating in Middletown, Conn. While the majority of pistols encountered are from either of these two contractors, pattern pistols were produced at Springfield Armory and a variant was made at the Palmetto Armory in South Carolina prior to the Civil War.

The graceful lines of earlier U.S. martial flintlocks (many of them later converted to percussion) were continued with this percussion smoothbore. Henry Aston, a former employee of Simeon North at Springfield Armory, received a contract for 30,000 pistols at $6.50 each on February 25, 1845. Specifications for the Model 1842 included all brass furniture, even to the blade front sight, and attachment of the trigger guard was by two spanner nuts instead of riveting as in earlier models. After the reorganization of Aston's company in 1850, his former employee, Ira N. Johnson, received an independent contract for 10,000 pistols at $6.75 each.

Date stamping on the barrel tang as well as the lockplate was commonly done by both makers of this 2-lb., 12 oz. pistol. Government inspection stamps are found usually on the barrel tang and on the left side of the stock near the sideplate. Original finishing called for all metal surfaces to be left bright except for the blued trigger.

Firing a half-ounce .54 cal. round ball, the Model 1842 provided a potent single-shot package in the Mexican War period, and the guns saw limited use as late as the Civil War. The rarer Palmetto Armory variation, produced by William Glaze & Co. in Columbia, S.C., can be characterized as a Model 1842 pistol with changes in both barrel and lockplate markings and saw service with Southern forces of this period.

While many other percussion firearms of U.S. military origin have been reproduced by foreign and domestic manufacturers, the Model 1842 has yet to get such attention.

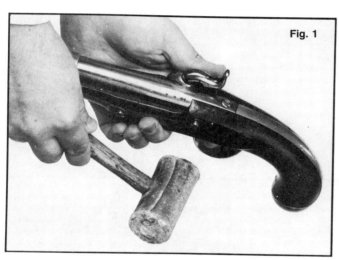
Fig. 1

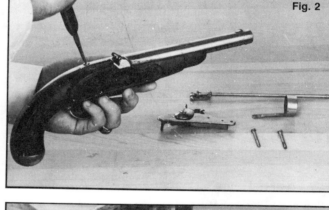
Fig. 2

Fig. 3

Fig. 4

Disassembly Instructions

After checking the bore for an unfired charge, the hammer (25) should be drawn back to the half-cock position so as to clear the nipple (36). Loosen the front and the rear sideplate screws (11 & 13) slightly. Once the screw heads have risen above the surface of the sideplate (12), a light, non-marring mallet can be used to gently tap them and free the lockplate (14). Prying the lockplate out from the other side may result in scarring of the surrounding wood (Fig. 1).

After the lockplate mechanism has been removed from the stock (34), pull out the ramrod (3). Unscrewing the link screw (5) will free the ramrod assembly. The barrel band (10) can be tapped off the stock using a wood drift. The barrel (1) is held in place by the tang screw (35) which terminates in the trigger guard plate (28) (Fig. 2).

To disassemble the lock mechanism, apply pressure to the mainspring (15) with a mainspring vise or a shop vise (Fig. 3). After removing the mainspring screw (16) the compressed mainspring can be withdrawn from the lockplate. After removing the bottom bridle screw (19) the sear can be taken out. Remove the top bridle screw (17) and the bridle (18). The hammer (25) is held in place by the hammer screw (24). Remove the sear spring screw (22) and the sear spring (21). Tap the tumbler (23) clear of the lockplate (Fig. 4). ■

Walther Model 4
exploded views: 7.65 mm

1.
2.
3.

BY E. J. HOFFSCHMIDT
Completed by Dennis Riordan

THE Carl Walther firm of Zella St. Basii, Germany, was among the earliest automatic pistol makers. They brought out Germany's first .25 cal. automatic pistol in 1908. In 1910 they introduced the .32 cal. Model 3, then, in the same year, enlarged the Model 3 and called it the Model 4.

While only in production for about 15 years, the Model 4 was revised several times, and over one hundred thousand were manufactured and used during WW I. Model 4 pistols were well liked by WW I German officers and a great number were still in use during WW II. They were small, well made, reliable, and had a very simple takedown system. Thousands of all versions of the Model 4 were brought home by returning GIs in 1945. Later, more thousands were imported by Interarms before the advent of the 1968 GCA, prohibiting the importation of such pistols.

As stated, the first Model 4 was simply a Model 3 pistol with a longer barrel and grip. The larger size made the pistol much more practical from a military standpoint. Increasing the magazine capacity to eight rounds (plus a round in the chamber) gave the Model 4 a nine-shot capability. Lengthening the barrel resulted in a longer sighting radius.

After the first few hundred guns, the slide was redesigned to simplify the takedown and lighten the pistol. The second version (shown in the exploded view) is probably the most common version of the Model 4. This second mechanical variation went through a bewildering number of different slide markings and minor changes. The shape of the ejection port was changed at various times and at some later date a rear sight was inserted into a dovetail slot cut into the slide.

Extensive military use in WW I pointed up the need for some design changes, so the Model 4 came again to the drawing board for the third and last major alteration. On earlier guns the trigger bar, that connects the trigger to the sear, was simply laid in an open slot milled into the frame. It was exposed to the elements and only retained by the left grip. The last revision of the Model 4 moved that trigger bar inside the frame so that it was no longer exposed. Slide serrations were changed from wide flat grooves to a series of 16 sharp "V" serrations.

The Model 4 was eventually replaced in the Walther line by the more modern designs of the late 1920s and '30s.

Second Variation

4.

270

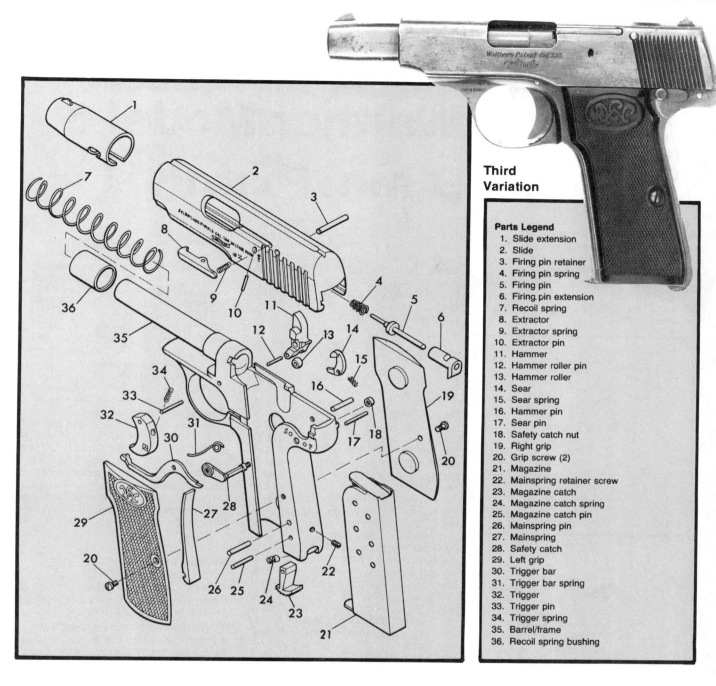

Third Variation

Parts Legend

1. Slide extension
2. Slide
3. Firing pin retainer
4. Firing pin spring
5. Firing pin
6. Firing pin extension
7. Recoil spring
8. Extractor
9. Extractor spring
10. Extractor pin
11. Hammer
12. Hammer roller pin
13. Hammer roller
14. Sear
15. Sear spring
16. Hammer pin
17. Sear pin
18. Safety catch nut
19. Right grip
20. Grip screw (2)
21. Magazine
22. Mainspring retainer screw
23. Magazine catch
24. Magazine catch spring
25. Magazine catch pin
26. Mainspring pin
27. Mainspring
28. Safety catch
29. Left grip
30. Trigger bar
31. Trigger bar spring
32. Trigger
33. Trigger pin
34. Trigger spring
35. Barrel/frame
36. Recoil spring bushing

Disassembly Procedure

1. Depress the magazine catch (23) and withdraw the magazine (21). Retract the slide (2) and check to be sure that the chamber is empty. Holding the grip in one hand, with the other push in the slide extension (1), turn it counterclockwise to its limit, when viewed from the muzzle end, and allow it to ride forward out of the slide under spring pressure. Remove it, the recoil spring (7) and the recoil spring bushing (36).

2. The slide (2) can now be drawn fully back, its rear lifted up, and the unit easily pushed forward off the barrel (35).

3. With a small drift punch on an angle, drive the extractor pin (10) down from the top of the slide (2) through its oval hole in the left side of the slide. A larger punch can be used to drive out the firing pin retainer (3) from left to right. This frees the firing pin (5), its spring (4), and extension (6).

4. Lower the internal hammer (11) by turning the safety (28) to its forward position, placing the thumb on the hammer to cushion its fall, and pulling the trigger (32). Remove the grip screws (20) and grips (19 & 29). This exposes most working parts and allows the manual depression of the trigger bar spring (31), freeing it from its notch in the bottom of the trigger bar (30) which may now be lifted from its recess in the trigger (32).

5. If further disassembly is required, loosen the mainspring retainer screw (22) and, holding the frame in a padded vise or on a soft wooden block, drive out the magazine catch pin (25) to remove the magazine catch (23) and its spring (24). The mainspring pin (26) and mainspring (27) can be similarly removed and, with a sturdy punch of the correct diameter and the safety (28) in 7 o'clock position, the hammer pin (16) can be drifted out, freeing the hammer (11) with its roller (13) and roller pin (12), the trigger bar spring (31), and safety (28). Drifting out the trigger pin (33) will free the trigger (32) and its spring (34). Removal of the sear pin (17) frees the sear (14) and its spring (15) and completes disassembly. Reverse procedure for reassembly.

exploded views:—

BY EDWARD J. HOFFSCHMIDT
Completed by Dennis Riordan

Walther Model 6
9 mm Pistol

WHEN Germany entered WWI, there was a critical need for military pistols. Walther's Models 1, 2, 3, 4 and 5 were pressed into service, but these pistols were in either .25 or .32 cal., not the standard 9 mm military caliber.

In an effort to supply a 9 mm Luger cal. pistol that could be produced faster than the Luger PO8 or the Mauser military pistol in 9 mm, Walther developed the Model 6. Basically, it was an overgrown Model 4. The barrel was longer, 4-13/16″ to be exact; the grip was longer by about one inch and the slide was lengthened by 2⅜″ to add more mass.

The Model 6 is a "blowback" operated pistol. The German description is more explicit; they call this mechanically unlocked system "mass-locked." The system differs from the locked breech systems, found on the Colt M1911, Luger, Mauser Model 1896 or the P38. On the Model 6, a heavy slide and a stiff spring compensate for the lack of a breech lock.

In order to shoot the Model 6, a loaded magazine is inserted into the butt. The slide is then drawn back and released. The heavy slide with its powerful return spring chambers the first round, thereby possibly creating a problem. Model 6 chambers seem to be very tight and the heavy slide may "press-fit" the first round into the chamber. Since the blowback design does not provide for any primary extraction, almost nothing short of firing the round or pushing it out with a rod will extract it. This defect may account for the Model 6 never having been officially adopted by the German army.

The Walther Model 6 was only made from 1915 to the end of the war,

and from the serial number range it appears that less than two thousand were made. Apparently, some pistols were exported after WWI because many of the known specimens have "Germany" stamped on the lower left hand of the slide.

On the left side the slide is marked Selbstlade-Pistole Cal. 9M/M, Walther's patent. Selbstlade-Pistole means self-loading pistol in English. The right hand side of the slide is marked Carl Walther, Waffenfabrik, Zella St. Bl. (the town of Zella St. Blasii). Proof marks are found on the right side of the frame, near the end of the barrel support, close to the trigger pin and near the muzzle on the right side of the barrel. The serial number is found at the juncture of the trigger guard and frame. The last three digits of the serial number were also stamped inside the slide just behind the firing pin. ∎

Disassembly Instructions

1. **Warning:** Since the Model 6 chambers are very tight, some brands of 9 mm cartridges may stick in the chamber, making it extremely difficult to open the slide. In this case, remove magazine (23), apply safety catch (26), insert a screwdriver tip beneath lip of extractor (5), and pry extractor outward to free it from the chambered round. Then the slide can be retracted and the round

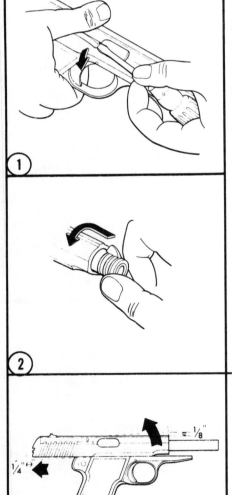

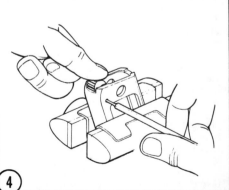

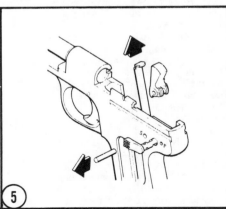

removed safely with a cleaning rod.

2. To field strip the pistol, depress magazine catch (22) and remove the magazine (23); then clear the chamber, allowing the slide (2) to close. Holding the gun in the left hand, push the slide extension (1) ⅛ inch into the slide, and turn it 20 degrees counterclockwise. Ease out slide extension and recoil spring (10). (In reassembly, line up the mark on the slide extension with the middle of the slide, push extension in and turn clockwise to lock.)

3. Pull the slide rearward until it stops. Lift its forward end ⅛″ and move the slide another ¼″ further to the rear, freeing it from its twin grooves in the frame (34). Now lift the rear of the slide and strip it from the frame by drawing it forward, over the barrel.

4. Remove the grip screws (19) and grips (18 & 28). Pull the trigger (30) while easing hammer (12) forward with thumb. Hold frame in a soft-jawed vise and drive out the magazine catch pin (24). As the magazine catch is under heavy spring pressure, press it downward, into the frame while removing pin punch, and grasp it firmly as it is eased out of the grip. Drive out sear pin (25) and remove sear (17), sear spring (16), and sear spring bushing (15).

5. The hammer pin (27) is tight, but it can be driven out. If an arbor press is not available, use a punch of almost the same diameter and a few drops of penetrating oil. Remove hammer (12), mainspring (20), and mainspring tube (11). Then the safety catch will come out easily.

6. Drive out trigger pin (31) and move trigger rearward; then pull trigger bar (29) straight out against pressure of trigger spring (33). Replace by easing the point of the trigger bar into the trigger slot, between the trigger spring plunger (32) and the fixed trigger cross pin. Then push forward until it snaps into place. Reassemble in reverse order.

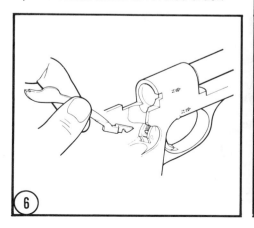

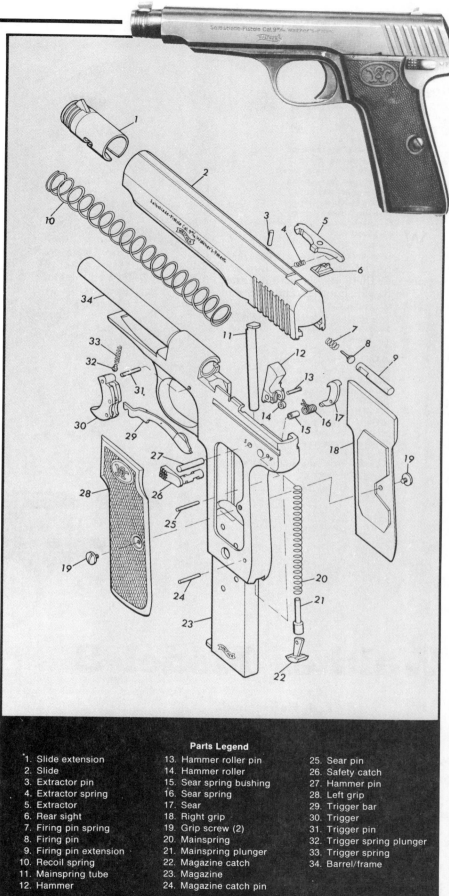

Parts Legend

1. Slide extension	13. Hammer roller pin	25. Sear pin
2. Slide	14. Hammer roller	26. Safety catch
3. Extractor pin	15. Sear spring bushing	27. Hammer pin
4. Extractor spring	16. Sear spring	28. Left grip
5. Extractor	17. Sear	29. Trigger bar
6. Rear sight	18. Right grip	30. Trigger
7. Firing pin spring	19. Grip screw (2)	31. Trigger pin
8. Firing pin	20. Mainspring	32. Trigger spring plunger
9. Firing pin extension	21. Mainspring plunger	33. Trigger spring
10. Recoil spring	22. Magazine catch	34. Barrel/frame
11. Mainspring tube	23. Magazine	
12. Hammer	24. Magazine catch pin	

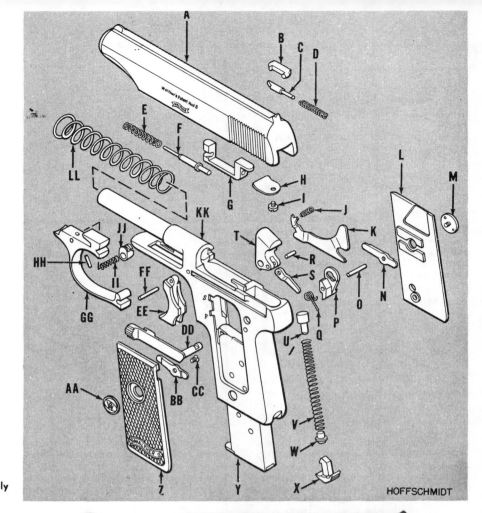

LEGEND

A—Slide
B—Extractor
C—Extractor plunger
D—Extractor spring
E—Firing pin spring
F—Firing pin
G—Firing pin housing
H—Retaining plate
I—Retaining plate screw
J—Trigger bar spring
K—Trigger bar
L—Right-hand grip
M—Right-hand grip screw
N—Right-hand grip retainer
O—Sear pin
P—Sear
Q—Sear spring
R—Hammer strut pin
S—Hammer strut
T—Hammer
U—Mainspring plunger
V—Mainspring
W—Magazine latch plunger
X—Magazine latch
Y—Magazine
Z—Left-hand grip
AA—Left-hand grip nut
BB—Left-hand grip retainer
CC—Left-hand grip screw
DD—Safety catch
EE—Trigger
FF—Trigger pin
GG—Trigger guard
HH—'Takedown' latch pin
II—'Takedown' latch spring
JJ—'Takedown' latch
KK—Receiver and barrel assembly
LL—Recoil spring

Walther Model 8

By E. J. Hoffschmidt

There was a time during the 1920's when most central European businessmen carried a .25 caliber automatic pistol. Europe was in the clutches of a depression and a compact handgun often came in handy for defense purposes.

Many German gunsmiths, to stay in business, turned to these popular inexpensive pistols. They stopped building fancy Drillings and expensive Mausers, and concentrated on a bewildering assortment of vest pocket pistols.

The Walther Model 8 was first marketed in 1920. Yet, in spite of being introduced in the midst of a depression, it caught on almost immediately, and by 1939 more than 200,000 had been sold. Stoeger sold them in America until World War II cut off the supply. The price ranged from $25 for the standard version and up to $92.50 for an engraved, gold-plated model in a presentation case.

When compared with later Walther pistols, such as the PP or PPK, the Model 8 contains nothing very startling in the way of mechanisms. Its popularity was due chiefly to its clean, compact design, to say nothing of the flawless workmanship evident on all pre-war Walther products. The gun is large enough to afford an adequate grip and has a nine-shot capacity, carrying eight in the magazine and one in the chamber. The Model 8 might be called a medium-sized .25 automatic, for while it is smaller than the Mauser Pocket Model .25 caliber, it is larger than the

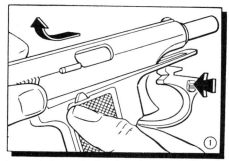

Remove the magazine, check the chamber to be sure it is not loaded. Push in the 'takedown' latch (JJ) on the right-hand side of the trigger guard, pulling the guard down as shown. Draw the slide to the rear, lift the end free of the frame, then ease it forward off the barrel

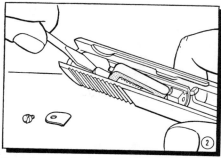

To take the firing pin (F) out of the late model, remove the retaining plate screw (I) and the retaining plate (H). The firing pin assembly can then be pried free of the slide. Since the retaining plate screw (I) is usually extremely tight, your screwdriver must fit the screw slot to prevent damage to the head

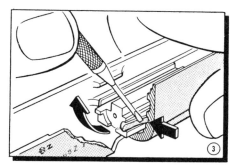

Removal of the early model firing pin presents a problem. It is necessary to pry the extractor free of its recess in the slide while prying up the front edge of the breechblock assembly, since the extractor retains the breechblock and a projection on it retains the firing pin

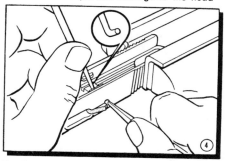

The late model extractor (B) is retained by a spring (D) and plunger (C). It may be easily removed by pushing back the spring-loaded plunger with a jeweler's screwdriver. Then, using a tool similar to the one illustrated, push the tail of the extractor out of the slide (A) from the inside

Unless a tool similar to the one shown is made, it is difficult to remove the blue medallion (grip screw, M) without damaging it. With this screw out, lift off the right-hand grip (L), remove the magazine (Y), and unscrew the left grip screw from the inside

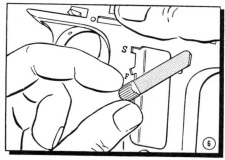

In order to remove the safety catch (DD), the grips must be removed. Next, ease the internal hammer (T) to the fired position. Press the safety in toward the receiver out of engagement with the notches, and revolve it to the position shown. Now it can be lifted free of the receiver

average vest pocket .25 automatic.

As in other Walther pistols, internal design changes were made without much fanfare, since at least two definite variations of the Model 8 are to be found. In the original Model 8 pistol, it was possible to pry the entire breechblock assembly out of its seat in the slide. This assembly carried the firing pin, firing pin spring, and extractor. The extractor tail acted as a firing pin retainer, and the extractor as a breechblock latch. While this system was simple, it had a tendency to loosen up after prolonged use. There is no record of when the gun was revised but the internal mechanism of the slide was changed a great deal. For one thing the breech face on the later model is an integral part of the slide. A firing pin housing is retained by a screw and plate. The extractor was moved into the slide similarly to the PP and PPK. But the rest of the gun was left unchanged, so if you want a Model 8 for protection, get the late model, since it is more rugged and easier to clean and repair.———————— ■

Walther Model 8 .25 Cal. Auto

PISTOL MAGAZINES

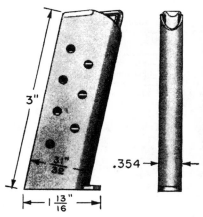

Should you find a magazine stamped Walther, that looks long enough to fit a .32 automatic but rattles around in a .32 frame, chances are you have a magazine for the .25 cal. Walther Model 8. This trim little pistol was very popular in Europe, and many Service pistol matches abroad have been won with it. As .25 cal. automatics run, the Model 8 is rather large, but this is not a serious drawback, since it gives the gun an excellent grip and a 9-round capacity. Like other pre-war Walther pistols, the Model 8's are beautifully finished and made of the best steels.

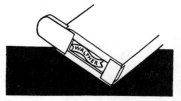

The unique method of inserting the Walther trademark into the magazine floor plate is characteristic of the Model 8. Its long, thin outline also sets it apart from the vast majority of other .25 automatic pistol magazines.

There is nothing especially distinctive about the follower or magazine lips of the Model 8, but some followers will be found with small raised ridges, as shown. Others will be found with plain flat followers.—E. J. HOFFSCHMIDT.

Walther Olympia Rapid-Fire Pistol

By E. J. HOFFSCHMIDT

Before World War II, the firm of Carl Walther of Zella-Mehlis, Germany, was foremost in the design and manufacture of Olympic-style rapid-fire pistols. After the war, the factory was taken over by the Russians and Walther then opened a new plant in Ulm/Donau, West Germany. By 1958 a new rapid-fire pistol had been designed and a limited number made for test. Production began around 1965 and by 1968 the Model OSP had evolved.

Parts Legend

1. Sight lock screw
2. Front sight
3. Barrel
4. Weight
5. Weight screw (2)
6. Receiver
7. Cocking piece
8. Bolt
9. Extractor pin
10. Extractor
11. Extractor spring
12. Firing pin retainer
13. Firing pin and spring
14. Recoil spring housing
15. Recoil spring
16. Recoil spring guide
17. Bolt stop
18. Plunger spring
19. Stop retaining plunger
20. Trigger assembly
21. Side plate screw
22. Side plate
23. Rear sight leaf assembly
24. Sight leaf pin
25. Click pin
26. Sight elevation screw
27. Rear sight base
28. Rear sight spring
29. Sight retainer screw
30. Washer
31. Sight retainer nuts
32. Safety catch spring
33. Magazine catch spring
34. Magazine catch bushing
35. Magazine catch
36. Safety catch
37. Magazine catch pin
38. Magazine
39. Barrel lock
40. Hold-open latch pin
41. Barrel lock stop screw
42. Barrel lock bushing
43. Lock nut pin
44. Lock nut
45. Spacer
46. Hold-open latch spring
47. Hold-open latch
48. Adjusting screw nut
49. Slide plate
50. Grip
51. Palm rest
52. Adjusting screw
53. Grip screw
54. Frame

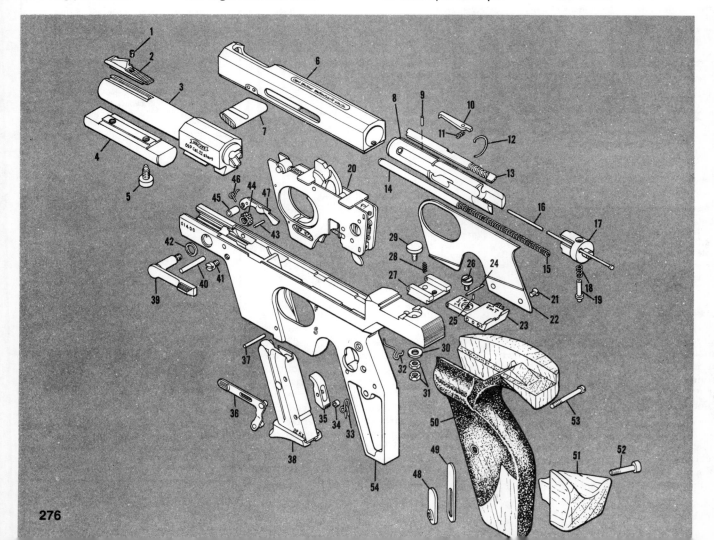

Despite its unorthodox outline, handling qualities of the Walther rapid-fire pistol are excellent. Its mechanism is similar in some respects to a blowback-operated .22 semi-automatic rifle in that the bolt operates inside the receiver to give an unbroken, stationary line of sight. There is no recoiling slide.

The rear sight is fully adjustable. Takedown is simple and the barrel can be quickly detached for cleaning. The fully adjustable trigger mechanism seats down inside the light alloy frame and can be easily removed as a unit. It consists of a sheet-metal housing containing the hammer, sear, and trigger.

The Walther rapid-fire pistol is an expensive, well-designed arm made for a specialized sport. It is not intended for the casual target shooter or plinker.

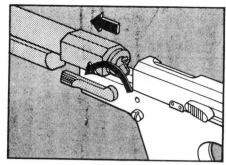

1 To disassemble pistol, first remove magazine (38) and clear chamber. Then pull trigger to drop hammer, since gun must not be cocked when disassembled. Rotate barrel lock (39) forward until it is horizontal as shown. Then pull barrel forward off frame (54). If lock is not horizontal, barrel (3) cannot be removed.

2 After barrel has been removed, receiver (6) and bolt assembly can then be lifted out. Lift end of receiver slightly and pull it forward until it is free of the frame. When reassembling the gun, it may be necessary to push the front of the receiver down tight against the frame to help seat barrel properly.

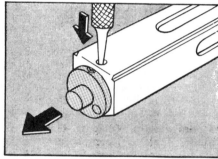

3 Bolt assembly is retained by a spring-loaded plunger (19) in bolt stop (17). To disassemble bolt, push in on plunger as shown and remove bolt stop. When recoil spring (15) and guide (16) are removed, cocking piece (7) can be pulled out through side of bolt and receiver. Balance of bolt assembly can then be removed.

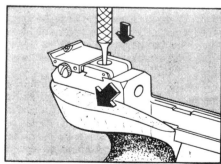

4 Grip (50) is a one-piece wrap-around type made of European walnut. Due to its design, there is a possibility that grip may shrink on the frame. To remove grip, take out grip screw (53). If grip does not slide off easily, strike it gently with heel of hand at point shown. If this does not work, remove rear sight elevation screw (26) and tap grip lightly with a punch small enough to fit through hole in frame.

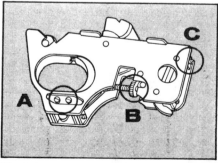

5 When receiver is removed, trigger assembly (20) can be lifted out. To free it, push it up from inside trigger guard and lift it by hammer. Trigger pull can be lightened or increased by turning knurled nut at (B). Screws at (A) are for adjusting position of trigger within trigger guard. Red-colored screw at (C) should not normally be touched. It repositions trigger bar if hammer fails to catch. ■

Walther P38 9 mm. Auto

PISTOL MAGAZINES

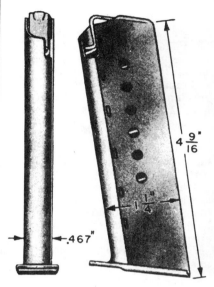

4 9/16"

.467"

1 1/4"

In spite of the poor finish and sloppy workmanship on many souvenir Walther P38's, the gun remains one of the best military automatics yet produced. The design incorporates numerous interesting features. It is double action; it has a cartridge indicator to show whether the chamber is loaded; and it has a simple takedown.

P38 magazines can be easily identified by the row of weld marks along the left front side. The push-button removable floorplate is another identifying mark. Early magazines are marked P38, but late models are often found unmarked.

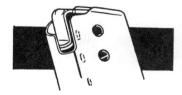

Other striking features are the double step in the magazine follower, and the cut in the side for engagement of the hold-open lever.—E. J. HOFFSCHMIDT

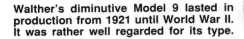

Walther Model 9 .25 ACP Pistol

BY JOHN KARNS

Walther's diminutive Model 9 lasted in production from 1921 until World War II. It was rather well regarded for its type.

THOUGH best known for its double-action police and military pistols (Models PP, PPK and P.38 etc.), the Carl Walther firm got its start in 1908 with its Model 1, a single-action .25 cal. vest-pocket pistol.

From 1908 until 1920 eight Walther pistols were introduced, all blowback-operated single-actions, and of them five were .25s. They were small, with an average weight of ll.3 ozs. and an average barrel and overall length of 2.5" and 4.7", respectively.

In 1920 the Model 9 came on the market and was, by far, the smallest of the lot, weighing less than 9 ozs. with a 2" barrel and an overall length of 3.9".

The standard pistol, referred to in Walther's 1936 catalog as the Model 9a, was blued with black composition grip plates and a six-round magazine. The Model 9b was listed as having an etched "engraving" panel on the slide with blue enamel/gold plate grip escutcheons. Full nickel, gold and silver plating were also offered, as was full engraving and mother-of-pearl or ivory grip plates.

The Model 9 was imported into the U.S. by Stoeger (at $20 for the standard grade in the 1940 *Shooter's Bible* for instance), and many were brought back to the U.S. by servicemen returning from World War II. The pistol went out of production during the war, but is still valued today as one of the smallest and best made pistols of its type.

Parts Legend

1. Disconnector bar
2. Ejector
3. Extractor
4. Firing pin
5. Firing pin spring
6. Firing pin spring guide
7. Frame & barrel assembly
8. Grip escutcheon (2)
9. Grip panel, left
10. Grip panel, right
11. Grip screw (2)
12. Grip screw bushing (2)
13. Latch retainer lever
14. Latch retainer pin
15. Magazine base
16. Magazine catch
17. Magazine catch spring
18. Magazine catch spring plunger
19. Magazine follower
20. Magazine housing
21. Magazine spring
22. Recoil spring
23. Recoil spring guide
24. Safety lever
25. Sear
26. Sear lever
27. Sear lever pin
28. Sear pin
29. Slide
30. Takedown latch
31. Takedown latch spring
32. Takedown latch spring plunger
33. Trigger
34. Trigger spring

Disassembly Instructions

Push back the magazine catch (16), remove the magazine (20), retract the slide (29) and check the chamber to insure that the pistol is not loaded. Depress the latch retainer lever (13) to release the takedown latch (30). Raise the rear of the slide about 20° to elevate the breechbolt face above the barrel (**Fig. 1**).

Pivot the slide assembly (29) forward and off the frame (7). Remove the firing pin (4), its spring and guide (5 & 6). The recoil spring (22) and its guide (23) may be removed from the recess in the frame below the barrel. This effectively field strips the pistol for general service and cleaning.

If complete disassembly is required, remove the grip screws (11) and detach both grip panels (9 & 10) to expose the frame and provide access to the components below.

Rotate the safety lever (24) to a vertical position. This cams the ejector post up to clear the safety retaining groove and frees the safety for removal. With the ejector (2) in this elevated position, it may be easily removed, if required. (**Fig. 2**).

Note: The fitted ejector post is notched with an elliptical cut to provide clearance for the takedown latch. This required cut makes the ejector post susceptible to damage if twisted or levered out. To avoid possible damage, invert the frame and secure the ejector body in a bench vise. To withdraw the ejector, pull straight up on the frame, avoiding all lateral stress.

Drift out the sear pin (28) to remove the sear group (25, 26 & 27). Note the relationship of these components as they are removed from the frame to facilitate reassembly. Complete disassembly of the sear

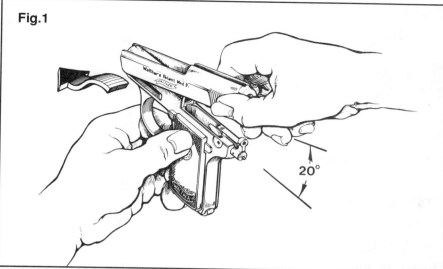

Fig.1

20°

sub-group is not recommended unless repair or replacement is required.

The takedown latch (30) may now be withdrawn from the rear of the frame. Exercise caution to avoid losing the takedown latch spring and plunger (31 & 32) contained in the latch. The latch retainer pin (14) may be drifted out to free the latch lever (13).

To remove the disconnector (1), lift its lower spring leg to clear the retaining stud in the frame. This allows the disconnector/trigger bar to be removed and frees both the trigger (33) and its spring (34) from the trigger guard.

The extractor (3) may be removed from the breech face by depressing the rear lug of the extractor and levering it forward through the access hole in the underside of the slide. (**Fig. 3**).

To remove the magazine catch (16), insert a small screwdriver through the bottom of the magazine well and depress the catch lug located inside the backstrap. This will

release the catch, its spring and plunger (16, 17 & 18).

The grip screw bushings (12) are staked in place from inside the magazine well and should be removed only if replacement or repair is required.

Reassembly Tips:

Reassemble the pistol in the reverse order with special attention given to the takedown latch and sear sub-groups which must be installed simultaneously. To initiate this, install the sear group in the frame, insert the safety and insure that its shaft passes through the sear lever. Install the takedown latch assembly in the rear of the frame and insert the sear pin to a sufficient depth to retain the latch in a takedown position. Then position the sear and sear lever to align their pivot holes with that of the frame and push the sear pin to a full engagement position to provide both a pivot for the sear group and a stop for the takedown latch. ∎

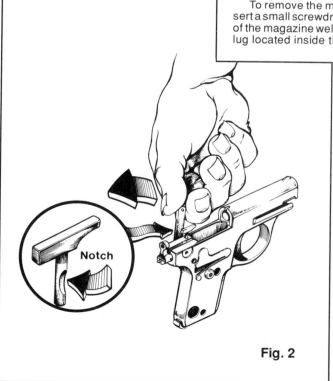

Notch

Fig. 2

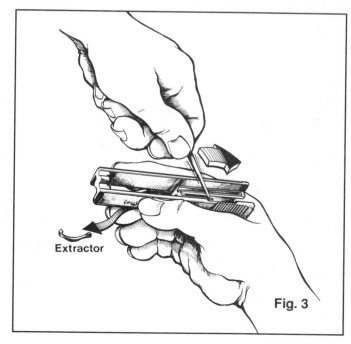

Extractor

Fig. 3

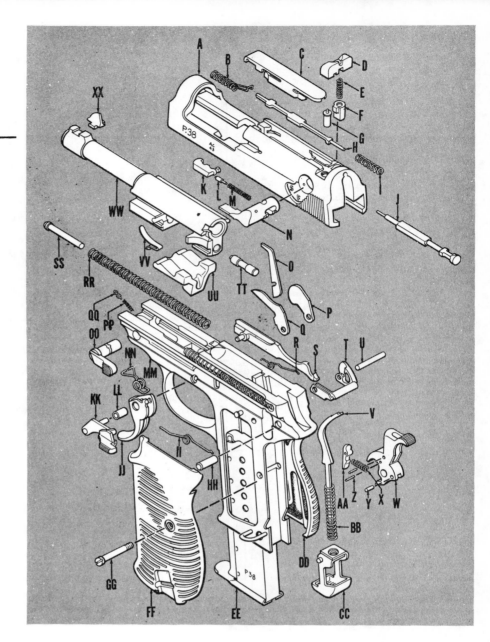

By E. J. Hoffschmidt

Legend

A—Slide
B—Firing Pin Spring
C—Firing Pin and Indicator Cover
D—Rear Sight
E—Automatic Firing Pin Lock Spring
F—Automatic Firing Pin Lock
G—Firing Pin Retainer Pin
H—Cartridge Indicator Pin
I—Cartridge Indicator Spring
J—Firing Pin
K—Extractor
L—Extractor Plunger
M—Extractor Plunger Spring
N—Safety Catch
O—Ejector
P—Firing Pin Lock, Lifter
Q—Safety Hammer Lowering Lever
R—Trigger Bar Spring
S—Trigger Bar
T—Sear
U—Sear Pin
V—Hammer Strut
W—Hammer
X—Hammer Lever Spring
Y—Strut Axle Pin
Z—Hammer Lever Pins

AA—Hammer Lever
BB—Hammer Spring
CC—Magazine Catch
DD—Right Hand Grip
EE—Magazine
FF—Left Hand Grip
GG—Grip Screw
HH—Hammer Pin
II—Slide Stop Return Spring
JJ—Trigger
KK—Slide Stop
LL—Trigger Bushing
MM—Frame (Receiver)
NN—Trigger Spring
OO—Barrel Retaining Latch
PP—Retainer Latch Plunger Spring
QQ—Retainer Latch Plunger
RR—Recoil Spring
SS—Recoil Spring Guide
TT—Locking Block Operating Pin
UU—Locking Block
VV—Locking Block Retainer Spring
WW—Barrel
XX—Front Sight

Walther P.38

D uring the 1930s Germany began a modernization program designed to give its armed forces the finest possible tools for war. This extensive program brought forth the famous, dual purpose 8.8 cm gun, the Schmeisser MP38 and MP40 submachine guns, and the MG34 and MG42 light machine guns. Among the best known military arms fielded during this period was the P.38 self-loading pistol.

The firm of Karl Walther, in Zella-Mehlis, Thuringia was given the task of designing a new self-loading pistol for the German army. The Model HP (*Heeres Pistole* — "Army" pistol), introduced in 1937, was the result of this effort. By 1938 the Model HP had been very slightly modified and accepted by the German army. Its official designation became P.38. This gave Germany one of the most modern pistols is service at the time.

Pre-war Walther HP and P.38 pistols

Push the safety catch (N) to safe position. Pull back the slide until the slide stop (KK) retains it. Remove the magazine. Revolve the barrel retaining latch (OO) until it stops. Release the slide stop and pull the slide and barrel assembly forward, off the receiver. Push in the exposed end of the locking block pin (TT) to separate the barrel from the slide

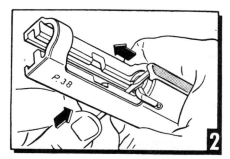

To check the firing pin (J) and the indicator pin (H), the cover must be removed. Hold the slide as shown to prevent the rear sight from falling out. Using a small screwdriver, push the indicator pin inside the slide and insert the blade as shown. A simultaneous push upward and forward will free cover (C) from slide

Remove automatic firing pin lock spring and lock (E and F), firing pin retainer pin (G), and indicator pin and spring (H and I). Safety catch must be in fire position before pushing out firing pin. With safety catch between safe and fire, pry out with screwdriver, as shown

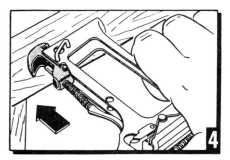

The first step in the disassembly of the trigger mechanism is to relieve the tension on the hammer. After removing the grips, hold the gun as shown. Push the magazine catch (CC) firmly against the edge of a solid bench. As soon as the pivot pin on the magazine catch is free of the frame, ease up on the pressure and remove the catch and hammer spring

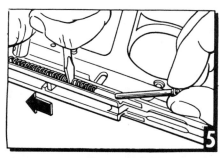

The recoil spring (RR) may be easily removed with the aid of a small screwdriver. Insert the screwdriver blade about 6 to 8 coils from the front of the spring guide (SS). Compress the recoil spring as far as possible and remove the guide. Ease up on the spring pressure carefully to prevent the spring from flying out

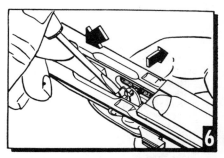

The trigger bar (S) is retained by the pressure of the trigger spring (NN) on a small notch in the portion of the bar that engages in the trigger. Use a small screwdriver to hold the trigger spring out of the notch as shown. Pry the trigger bar free with the other hand while the spring is held back

were manufactured and finished to the highest shop standards. this is not true of P.38s produced later during the war. Inferior materials, shoddy workmanship and outright sabotage by conscripted laborers combine to make some of the pistols produced during 1944 and 1945 dangerous to use.

When the P.38 is loaded with eight, 9 mm Parabellum cartridges in the magazine plus one in the chamber it is a formidable handgun. The overall length is 8-1/2 inches and a weight of 32 ounces give the gun the feel and instinctive pointing qualities of the Luger pistol.

The P.38 is a locked breech, short recoil operated pistol. At the moment of firing the barrel and slide are locked together. As they travel rearward, propelled by the recoil of the pistol, the end of the locking block operating pin that is part of the barrel assembly (TT) strikes the face of the frame of the pistol and cams the locking block (UU) down

and out of the locking recesses that are part of the slide (A). The barrel assembly stops against the frame and the slide continues to the rear extracting the fired case and ejecting it, cocking the hammer for the next shot and feeding the next cartridge from the magazine. The recoil springs (RR) then return the slide to its closed and locked position chambering the fresh cartridge.

It is interesting to note that U.S. foreign equipment summaries printed as late as December 1941, fail to mention the P.38 even though the 1939 Stoeger catalog listed the 9 mm HP at $75.00 with slightly higher prices for .38 Super and .45 ACP versions.

Must criticism has been heaped upon the P.38 by those who object to the use of sheet metal stampings. They forget that the P.38 was designed from a production point of view. A stamped part, when properly designed, will do the job just as well as apart machined from bar stock, and do it for less

cost. Another sore spot is the use of music wire, coil springs in place of forged flat springs. Again, the keynote is production. The coil springs used in the P.38 mechanism are quicker to produce and more durable and usually take up less room in a mechanism than do flat springs.

Manufacture of the Walther P.38 was interrupted at the end of World War II when the Walther plant and the plants of other contract makers fell into Allied hands. In the mid-1950s Walther re-established facilities at Ulm in what was then west Germany and re-instituted manufacture of the P.38, but with an aluminum alloy frame instead of steel. Shortly thereafter the west German army, the Bundeswehr, adopted the alloy-frame pistol as its "P1".

Though succeeded by more recent designs such as Walther's P5 and P88, the P.38 continues to be produced, imported into the U.S. by Interarms of Alexandria, Va.

WALTHER MODEL PP .22 CAL. PISTOL

To strip, remove the magazine and empty the chamber. Pull down the front end of the trigger guard (21) and push it to the right. It will rest against the frame and remain open. Pull the slide (1) to the rear as far as it will go. Lift up and ease it forward off the frame

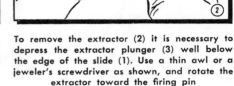

To remove the extractor (2) it is necessary to depress the extractor plunger (3) well below the edge of the slide (1). Use a thin awl or a jeweler's screwdriver as shown, and rotate the extractor toward the firing pin

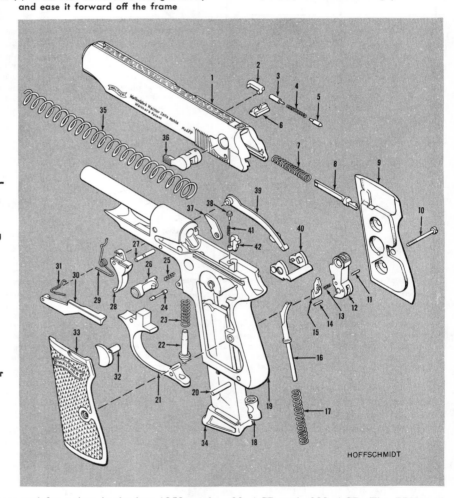

HOFFSCHMIDT

LEGEND

1. Slide	22. Trigger guard plunger
2. Extractor	23. Trigger guard spring
3. Extractor plunger	24. Trigger guard pin
4. Extractor spring	25. Magazine catch spring
5. Safety catch plunger	26. Magazine catch
6. Rear sight	27. Trigger pin
7. Firing pin spring	28. Trigger
8. Firing pin	29. Trigger spring
9. Right-hand grip	30. Ejector
10. Grip screw	31. Ejector spring
11. Sear pin	32. Hammer pin
12. Hammer	33. Left-hand grip
13. Sear spring	34. Magazine
14. Hammer strut pin	35. Recoil spring
15. Sear	36. Safety catch
16. Hammer strut	37. Hammer release
17. Hammer spring	38. Hammer block plunger
18. Hammer spring plug	39. Trigger bar
19. Frame	40. Cocking piece
20. Spring plug pin	41. Hammer block spring
21. Trigger guard	42. Hammer block

By E. J. Hoffschmidt

Most GIs who spent time in Europe during and after World War II came home with one or more products of the immense Walther plant at Zella-Mehlis, in Thuringia. It might have been a P.38 pistol, or a sporting or target rifle, or it might have been a Model PP or PPK in .32 or .380 ACP, or even a scarce model PP in .22 rimfire. Pre-war Walther guns were made of the finest materials and the finish was the best quality. They could be had in lightweight models with aluminum alloy frames at extra cost.

World War II put Walther out of busi-

ness and for a time in the late 1950s and early 1960s Walther pistols were made under license by *Manufacture de Machines du Haut-Rhin* the French firm, better known as *Manurhin*, in Mulhouse, France, and were so marked. U.S. importers include Thalson, on the west coast, and currently Interarms of Alexandria, Va. Walther Model PP pistols, today, are made by Karl Walther, Ulm/Donau, Germany and imported by Interarms. Others in the PP series, the PPK and PPK/S are made in the United States under Walther license. The PP is offered in .22 rimfire,

.32 ACP and .380 ACP. The PPK and PPK/S are available in .380 ACP only.

In addition to its double-action trigger mechanism, the Model PP features a number of enviable safety devices. Unfortunately, one of the best of these, the chamber loaded indicator had to be omitted from the .22 rimfire models. Some of the wartime .32 and .380 guns are without it, too, the parts omitted to save production effort.

The manual safety catch is the cleverest part of all. When the safety is put "ON" it rotates around the firing pin, lock-

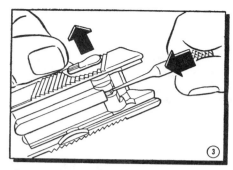

After the extractor spring (4) and safety catch plunger (5) have been removed, the safety catch (36) can be easily removed by first rotating it to the off position. Then, while pushing the firing pin deep into the slide, lift out the safety catch as shown

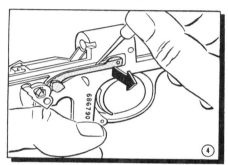

The trigger bar (39) should never be pried out. To remove it, first unhook the trigger spring (29) and push it into the frame. Pull the trigger as far as it will go and, using a small screwdriver, lift the trigger bar free of its slot in the frame

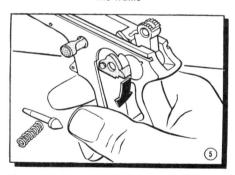

The magazine catch (26) is retained by the trigger guard plunger (22). To remove it, first remove the trigger guard pin (24). This will free the trigger guard plunger (22) and spring (23). The cocking piece (40) can be removed by rotating it as shown until it drops free of the frame

ing it to the rear and also placing itself in the way of the hammer. At the same time it drops the hammer onto a small block that prevents the hammer from striking the shrouded firing pin.

In spite of the intricate shapes of the operating parts, the design of the PP series of pistols is excellent and will give years of foolproof service. Any malfunctions on the part of .22 rimfire models can usually be traced to use of standard velocity ammunition instead of the high-speed ammunition for which the pistol was designed.

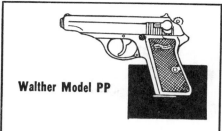

Walther Model PP

PISTOL MAGAZINES

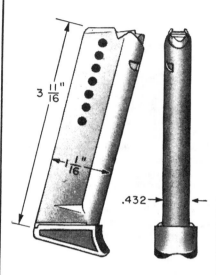

German-made magazines for the Walther PP and PPK are usually marked as such, but only when found in .32 or .380 cal. The .22 cal. magazines were rarely, if ever, marked with the model or caliber. The magazine shown here looks a good deal like a .32 cal. magazine, since it lacks the spring fingers usually found on the mouth of American .22 cal. magazines. While the PP is fairly common, it is rarely found in .22 cal. As a .22 cal. pistol, it is compact and handy but does not have the signal pin that protrudes when there is a round in the chamber, which is found on the .32 cal. model.

Walther PP magazines were made with or without the finger extension. The .22 cal. models can be readily identified by the key-hole-shape cross section, instead of the usual flat-sided rectangular shape.

The thick, double-stepped follower and the single row of holes are telltale marks of the Walther PP .22 cal. magazines. Notice, too, the odd shape of the magazine lips.—E. J. HOFFSCHMIDT

Walther Model PPK

PISTOL MAGAZINES
One of a series

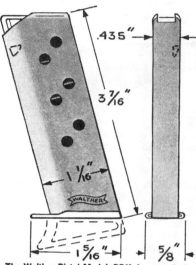

The Walther Pistol Model PPK is one of the last of a long series of automatic pistols produced by the Carl Walther plant in Zella Mehlis, Germany. Although PPK's were manufactured in .22 long rifle, .32 ACP, and .380 ACP, the .32 cal. is the most common caliber found in America. This pistol was renowned for its fine finish, excellent workmanship, modern design, and its safety features. Its double-action trigger pull provides the speed and safety of a revolver in carrying and getting off the first shot. An indicator pin, in the slide above the hammer, protrudes when there is a cartridge in the chamber.

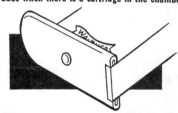

PPK magazines are easily identified by the retaining notch in the front edge of the magazine. Most small automatic pistols are retained by a catch at the bottom. The base plate construction and trade mark shown are common to the PPK. Many are found with plastic finger extension.

The square feed notch and straight feed lip help identify PPK magazines. The magazine follower is simply bent from a piece of sheet steel. Both sides of the magazine are punched with indicator holes.
—E. J. HOFFSCHMIDT

WEBLEY MARK IV REVOLVER

By DENNIS RIORDAN

Webley Mark IV .38 caliber revolver.

Webley & Scott Ltd., of Birmingham, England were, for the best part of a century, among the world's leading producers of handguns. they were particularly well known for their excellent top-break, double-action revolvers, offered both commercially and for use by British and Commonwealth military forces.

The Webley firm worked in close cooperation with the British War Office on handgun matters from 1887 until the 1920s. This close association ended about 1927, when the War Office chose its own, Enfield-designed revolver (see Page 104) over the Webley entant in a competition to provide a replacement for the .455"-caliber Webley revolvers then in use.

Despite the army's rejection, Webley introduced its Mark IV revolver, chambered for the .38 S&W cartridge, to the commercial market in 1929.

Like its heavy-caliber predecessors, the Webley & Scott Mark IV is a six-shot revolver of top-break design, with double-action lockwork and exposed hammer. A V-shaped mainspring drives the hammer and actuated the mainspring lever. As the trigger moves forward after each shot, the hammer rebounds to a safe position. The barrel is unlocked from the frame by by depressing the barrel catch on the left side of the frame. The barrel is then pivoted open for loading and unloading of the cylinder. Cartridges in the cylinder, fired and unfired, are extracted and ejected automatically as the barrel is opened.

In keeping with its simple, rugged mechanism, Mark IVs are fitted with fixed sights, the rear of which is integral with the barrel catch. The revolver weighs 27 ounces, unloaded, and has well proportioned, checkered plastic grips and a ring-type butt swivel. Exposed metal parts are blued and workmanship is generally excellent.

The Mark IV mechanism was used, not only for the Mark IV, but also for a "Target" versions in .22 rimfire or .38 S&W and a "Pocket" model in .32 and .38 S&W. The Target model had a six-inch barrel and adjustable sights. Pocket revolvers had three-inch barrels and came with either small grips, to enhance compactness, or as the "OP" (Overhand Pocket) variant, with a large grip and butt swivel. Standard Mark IVs were offered with a choice of four- or six-inch barrels.

The Webley Mark IV is similar in appearance to the Enfield No. 2 revolver with which it competed unsuccessfully for military adoption, but the two differ substantially in mechanical detail. The Enfield, for example, has a removable sideplate through wich access to the lockwork is gained. The Webley mechanism is contained within a solid frame.

Webley Mark IV revolvers did eventually gain military acceptance, during World War II when the War Office bought a substantial quantity of them to supplement supplies of handguns in service.

1 To field-strip the Mark IV, depress the thumb lever of barrel catch (10), open revolver fully, and remove any cartridges. Remove cam lever lock screw (38) with a coin. Rotate cam lever (39) upward and push it toward barrel (1). Lift cylinder (6) off its axle.

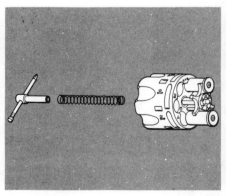

2 Place two empty cartridge cases in opposite chambers of cylinder. Insert a nail through hole in extractor nut (2) and use as a lever to unscrew nut. Remove extractor (7) and extractor spring (3). This is sufficient stripping for normal cleaning.

3 For further disassembly, unscrew hinge pin screw (46) and push hinge pin (42) out to left. Barrel and extractor lever (45) can now be removed and separated. Unscrew the two cylinder cam screws (5) and remove cylinder retaining cam (4).

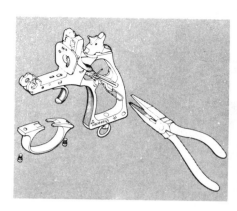

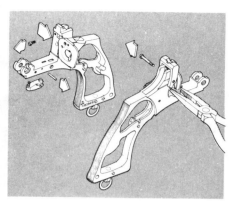

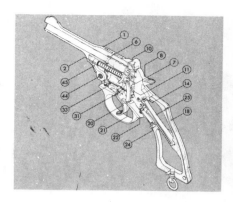

4 Unscrew grip screw (30) and remove grips (29), (16). Then, cock the hammer (8). Loop a paper clip around the mainspring (25), securing the wire by twisting with pliers. Pull trigger (20), and lower hammer with thumb. Unhook upper limb of mainspring from hammer swivel (14), and lift out mainspring. Relieve mainspring tension by pinching limb ends together with padded pliers and sliding loop of paper clip toward closed end of spring. Unscrew trigger guard screws (23) and remove trigger guard (22).

6 Compress barrel catch spring (9) against recoil shield (28) with padded pliers, meanwhile unscrewing barrel catch screw (37). Slide barrel catch and spring off to rear. Unscrew recoil shield screw (41), and drive recoil shield out to left. Use pin punch to drive out bolt pin (36). Bolt (33) and spring (35) fall free as punch is removed. Reassemble in reverse.

7 Cutaway shows revolver with parts at rest. Hammer is in rebound position, locked by mainspring lever; cylinder is secured by bolt. One chambered cartridge lies under the hammer. Forward portion of mainspring lever has been broken away for clarity. Parts are number keyed to parts legend.

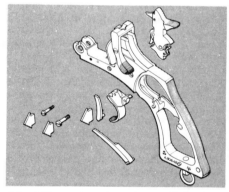

5 Lift mainspring lever (24) from notches in frame (18) and slide out to rear. Unscrew trigger screw (27), and pull trigger and hand (21) downward from the frame and separate. Unscrew hammer screw (26) and lift out hammer.

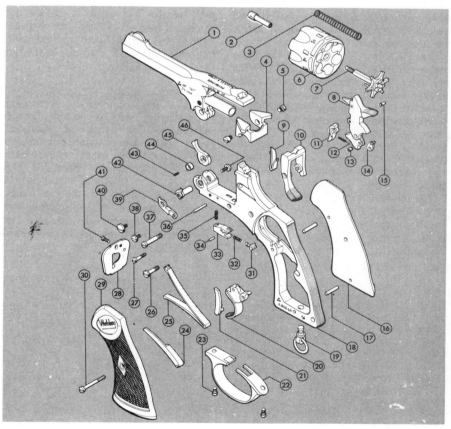

PARTS LEGEND
1. Barrel
2. Extractor nut
3. Extractor spring
4. Cylinder retaining cam
5. Cylinder cam screw (2)
6. Cylinder
7. Extractor
8. Hammer
9. Barrel catch spring
10. Barrel catch
11. Hammer catch
12. Hammer catch spring
13. Hammer swivel screw
14. Hammer swivel
15. Hammer catch screw
16. Right-hand grip

17. Grip pin (2)
18. Frame
19. Lanyard ring
20. Trigger
21. Hand
22. Trigger guard
23. Trigger guard screw (2)
24. Mainspring lever
25. Mainspring
26. Hammer screw

27. Trigger screw
28. Recoil shield
29. Left-hand grip
30. Grip screw
31. Bolt catch
32. Bolt catch spring
33. Bolt
34. Bolt catch pin
35. Bolt spring
36. Bolt pin

37. Barrel catch screw
38. Cam lever lock screw
39. Cam lever
40. Cam lever screw
41. Recoil shield screw
42. Hinge pin
43. Extractor lever spring
44. Extractor lever roller
45. Extractor lever
46. Hinge pin screw ∎

Webley Mark VI Revolver

BY JOHN KARNS

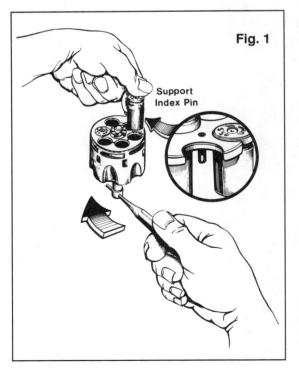

The tough top-break Mark VI served the British forces from 1915 into the 1950s. Many were imported to the U.S. market.

England's most famous handgun, adopted by the British government in 1915, has had several names. As late as 1940 its designer and prime manufacturer, Webley & Scott Ltd. of Birmingham, cataloged the commercial version as the "Mark VI .455 Service Model." It was offered with either 4" or 6" barrel, the latter being the government standard, and a 7 ½"-barrelled variation with an adjustable sight in the barrel latch that was listed as the "W.S. Bisley Target."

But the bulk of Webley's sales were to its government that first dubbed the gun "Pistol, Revolver Mark VI." This differentiated it from the similar but "bird's head"-gripped .455 cal. Webley Marks I through V that had been of British issue beginning in 1887.

In 1926, on the eve of the adoption of a smaller .38 cal. revolver designed by Webley but produced by the Royal Small Arms Factory at Enfield Lock (R.S.A.F.), the .455 was renamed "Pistol, Revolver No. 1 Mark VI" (the "Enfield" became "Pistol, Revolver .38 No. 2 Mark I").

Webley delivered more than 300,000 .455s in the World War I period, where they gained the reputation of being fine military handguns and the strongest break-open revolvers ever made. Following that war, between 1921 and 1926, R.S.A.F.-Enfield took up the military production of some 25,000 Mark VIs, and Webley continued some commercial assembly so that it was able to refurbish Mark VIs for its government at the outset of World War II.

The Mark VI was of standard issue until 1936 and then reclassified as "reserve standard" until 1948 when it was officially replaced in the army by the .38 Mark I and Mark I*. Despite this some Mark VIs were still noted in British service during the Korean conflict in the 1950s and may have had some semi-official use until 1957, when the adoption of the Browning Hi Power semi-automatic replaced revolvers in British service.

Some Marks VIs were permanently converted to .22 Long Rifle cal. for target work; others were fitted with .22 conversion kits.

Surplus .455s of all six Marks were imported into the U.S. in large quantities and, of these, many had about 1/16" of their cylinders and extractor ratchets faced off so that they would accept U.S. .45 Auto Rim cartridges or .45 ACP cartridges that could be used with pairs of the same half-moon clips made for Smith & Wesson and Colt M1917 revolvers.

Disassembly Instructions

Depress the thumb lever of the barrel latch (2) and pivot the barrel assembly down to insure that the revolver is unloaded and safe to service. Remove the cylinder cam lever lock screw (7). Lift the rear of the cam lever (6) to depress the cylinder cam (9) and allow the cylinder (5) to be lifted off the cylinder post. Remove the grip screw (25) and detach both grip panels (22 & 24). This field strips the revolver for general service and cleaning.

If complete takedown is required, support the extactor with wooden dowels or fired cases inserted into opposing chambers of the cylinder (**Fig. I**) to avoid damage to the extractor pin (18) as you loosen the extractor rod retainer. Insert a drift through the disassembly hole in the extractor rod retainer (15) and rotate counter-clockwise to remove. Lift both the rod and spring (15 & 16) out the face of the cylinder and remove the extractor/ratchet (17) to the rear.

Remove the cylinder cam lever screw (8) and lift off the cylinder cam lever (6) from the left side. Turn out the hinge pin screw (36) from the right side. Push the hinge pin (35) to the left through the frame (19) to free the barrel assembly (1). Note: exercise caution not to lose the extractor lever (11) housed in the pivot flange of the barrel assembly. If replacement or repair is required, the extractor lever may be disassembled by drifting out the cam pin (13) to release both the cam and its spring (12 & 14). Remove the right and left cylinder cam screws (10) to separate the cylinder cam (9) from the barrel pivot flange. The front sight blade (20) may be removed by turning out its retaining screw (21) to complete disassembly of the barrel group.

To remove the mainspring (38) set the hammer in a full cock position to compress the vee-spring before securing it with a vee-spring vise or locking grip pliers (**Fig. 2**). Lower the hammer to disengage the spring hooks from the hammer

Fig. 1

Support Index Pin

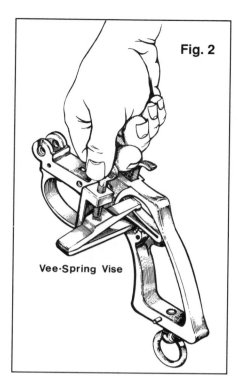

Fig. 2

Vee-Spring Vise

may be removed by drifting out the lower grip panel pin(23).

Remove the trigger guard and screws (47 & 48). Turn out the hammer pivot screw (32) and with the trigger depressed lift the hammer assembly (28) from its slot. If required, both the hammer catch/sear and the hammer swivel/stirrup (29 & 33) may be detached by removing their respective screws (30 & 34). Remove the trigger pivot screw (49) to free trigger assembly (43). Lift the pawl/hand (40) from its recess and remove the trigger catch spring screw (46) to detach both the spring and catch (45 & 44).

To remove the barrel latch (2), depress the latch spring (4) to relieve pressure while turning out the latch screw (3). Slide the latch down and back to clear the recesses in the sides of the frame. Lever the latch spring (4) from the retaining hole in the recoil plate. To complete disassembly, turn out the recoil plate screw (42) and drift the recoil plate laterally from its seat.

Reassembly Tips

Reassemble the revolver

in reverse order with special attention given to locating and seating the vee-springs. This operation is best accomplished by employing a vee-spring vise to control both compression and retention.

The use of a properly fitted slave-pin facilitates installing the trigger assembly in the frame (**Fig. 3**). ∎

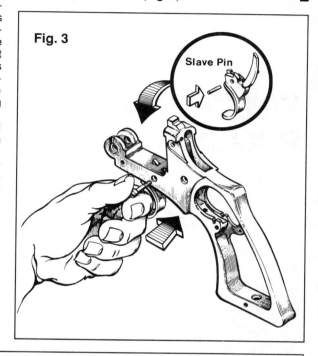

Fig. 3

Slave Pin

stirrup (33). Lift the secured mainspring to free the spur engaging the frame on the lower side. Raise the mainspring auxiliary lever (39) from its pivot point and remove to the rear. If required, the lanyard ring (37)

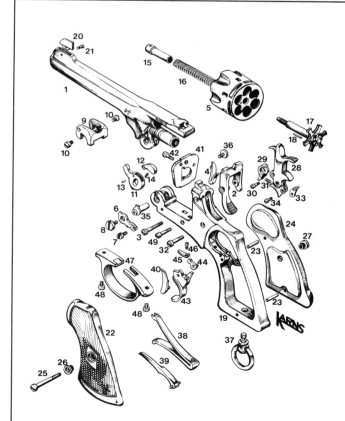

Parts Legend
1. Barrel
2. Barrel latch/rear sight
3. Barrel latch screw
4. Barrel latch spring
5. Cylinder
6. Cylinder cam lever
7. Cylinder cam lever lock screw
8. Cylinder cam lever screw
9. Cylinder cam
10. Cylinder cam screw (2)
11. Extractor lever
12. Extractor lever cam
13. Extractor lever cam pin
14. Extractor lever cam spring
15. Extractor rod retainer
16. Extractor spring
17. Extractor/ratchet
18. Extractor/ratchet index pin
19. Frame
20. Front sight blade
21. Front sight blade screw
22. Grip panel, left
23. Grip panel pin (2)
24. Grip panel, right
25. Grip screw
26. Grip screw escutcheon, left
27. Grip screw escutcheon, right
28. Hammer
29. Hammer catch/sear
30. Hammer catch screw
31. Hammer catch spring
32. Hammer pivot screw
33. Hammer swivel/stirrup
34. Hammer swivel screw
35. Hinge pin
36. Hinge pin screw
37. Lanyard ring
38. Mainspring
39. Mainspring auxiliary lever
40. Pawl/hand
41. Recoil plate
42. Recoil plate screw
43. Trigger
44. Trigger catch/cylinder stop
45. Trigger catch spring
46. Trigger catch spring screw
47. Trigger guard
48. Trigger guard screw (2)
49. Trigger pivot screw

WEBLEY METROPOLITAN POLICE PISTOL

By DENNIS RIORDAN

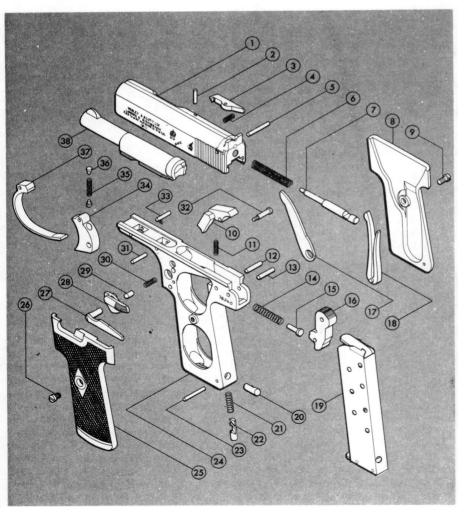

Parts Legend

1. Slide
2. Extractor pin
3. Extractor
4. Extractor spring
5. Firing pin retaining pin
6. Firing pin spring
7. Firing pin
8. Right grip
9. Right grip screw (long)
10. Sear
11. Sear spring
12. Sear pin
13. Hammer pin
14. Hammer spring
15. Hammer spring plunger
16. Hammer
17. Recoil arm
18. Recoil spring
19. Magazine
20. Magazine catch
21. Magazine catch spring
22. Magazine release button
23. Magazine catch pin
24. Frame
25. Left grip
26. Left grip screw (short)
27. Trigger bar
28. Safety
29. Safety detent
30. Safety detent spring
31. Trigger pin
32. Safety screw
33. Trigger guard pin
34. Trigger
35. Trigger Spring
36. Trigger spring plunger (2)
37. Trigger guard
38. Barrel

PRODUCED by Webley & Scott, Ltd., Birmingham, England, the Webley Metropolitan Police Model .32 caliber automatic pistol was designed by Webley works manager W. Whiting. First of the Webley automatic pistols, it was offered from 1906 to 1940 and was the official handgun of the London Metropolitan Police and many other police departments in the British Empire.

Typical of automatic pistols chambered for the .32 Automatic cartridge, the Metropolitan Police is blowback-operated, and the slide is mounted on the frame in the usual manner. However, the recoil spring is V-shaped and housed under the right grip, an unusual feature. Also, unlike most center-fire blowback-operated pistols, the barrel extends considerably forward of the slide.

In most other respects, this pistol is conventionally designed. The exposed hammer has a rounded spur, and the eight-round magazine is detached by pressing a release on the bottom of the handle. Metal parts are blued steel, and the grips are checkered hard rubber. The safety is on the frame above the left grip. It is conveniently located for the thumb. However, it is moved upward for disengagement which makes operation rather awkward.

The pistol weighs 20 ozs. unloaded. Well made, it is of simple design, functions reliably, and is very easy to field-strip. Another favorable feature is the large comfortable grip. However, the grip angle with line of bore is almost 90° which is not conducive to natural pointing. Also, the right grip piece is fragile and easily broken since it is hard rubber and thin where it houses the recoil spring.

Identifying markings are a crown above the letters "M.P." on the left of the slide. There is another .32 caliber Webley automatic pistol similar to the Metropolitan Police Model but without these markings. Also, the Metropolitan Police Model has a fixed rear sight that projects above the slide while the other pistol has a groove on the slide that serves as a rear sight.

1. To field strip, depress magazine release button (22) and remove magazine (19). Clear the chamber. Lower hammer (16) and move safety (28) down to safe position. Snap rear of trigger guard (37) forward and down. Then push slide (1) and barrel (38) forward off frame (24) and separate. This is sufficient takedown for normal cleaning.

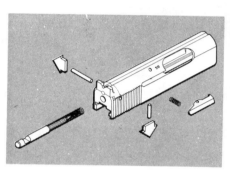

3. The grips are brittle and must be removed with care; never attempt to pry them off. Remove left grip screw (26) and rotate safety to its upward position. Magazine catch pin (23) protrudes through both sides of frame and fits grips snugly. Reach upward through bottom of magazine well and apply slight pressure in this area while working left grip (25) off with a back and forth motion. Use same procedure for right grip (8).

5. Pull trigger bar (27) out through left of frame. Push out trigger guard pin (33) and remove trigger guard. Push out trigger pin (31) to release trigger (34) along with its spring (35) and plungers (36).

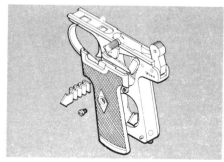

2. To strip slide, use punch to drive out firing pin retaining pin (5), and remove firing pin (7) and firing pin spring (6) to rear. Drive extractor pin (2) downward out of slide, and lift out extractor (3) and extractor spring (4).

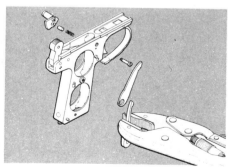

4. Remove recoil spring (18) with locking-jaw pliers or mainspring vise. Grasp spring as high as possible and compress just enough to allow removal. Lift off recoil arm (17) and loosen safety screw (32), releasing safety with its detent (29) and spring (30).

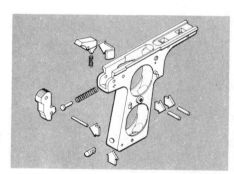

6. Drift out magazine catch pin (23) and depress magazine release button (22). Grasp protruding end of magazine catch (20) and pull it from frame. Ease out magazine release button and magazine catch spring (21). Push out sear pin (12). Pull sear (10) forward and down, and remove to the left. Be careful not to lose sear spring (11). Push out hammer pin (13), and lift out hammer (16), hammer spring (14), and plunger (15). Reassemble in reverse. A tapered punch is useful for aligning holes when replacing pins.

WHITNEY
.22
AUTOMATIC PISTOL

By JAMES M. TRIGGS

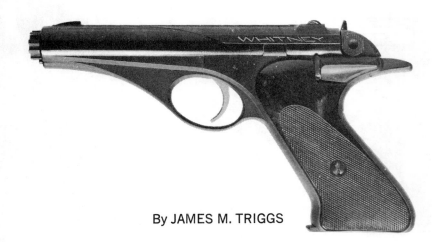

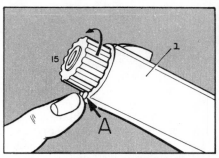

1 While holding barrel locking plunger (18) flush with face of frame as shown at "A", unscrew nut (15) counter-clockwise as indicated by arrow.

THE Whitney .22 long rifle semi-automatic pistol was introduced in 1956. It is blowback operated with detachable 10-round capacity magazine in the grip.

The action mechanism is a self-contained unit retained within the hollow aluminum alloy frame by a serrated nut threaded to the muzzle end of the barrel. By removing this nut the entire action assembly can be slid to the rear and out of the frame. A separate internal washer and key position and align the assembly within the frame.

The mechanical safety on the Whitney is engaged by pushing it down, not up. This is contrary to the usual practice with semi-automatic pistols.

The Whitney pistol was made by Whitney Firearms, Inc., of North Haven, Conn., which is no longer in business. There was no connection between this firm and the Whitney Arms Co. which ceased operations in 1888.

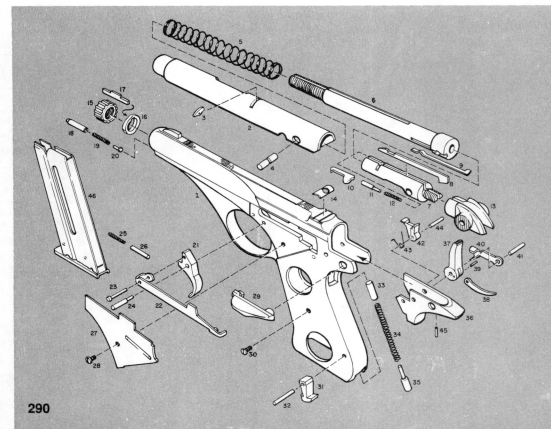

Parts Legend

1. Frame
2. Tube
3. Firing pin lock
4. Breech pin
5. Mainspring
6. Barrel
7. Breechblock
8. Firing pin
9. Ejector
10. Extractor
11. Extractor plunger
12. Extractor spring
13. Cocking piece
14. Rear sight
15. Nut
16. Barrel seat washer
17. Barrel key
18. Barrel locking plunger
19. Barrel locking plunger spring
20. Spring seat
21. Trigger
22. Sear bar
23. Trigger connector

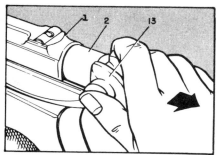

2 With hammer at full cock position, draw tube assembly out of frame (1) to rear by pulling back on cocking piece (13) as shown by arrow.

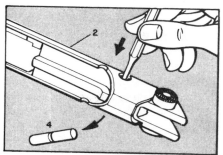

3 While pulling forward on barrel slightly to lessen tension on breech pin (4), push pin out of tube (2) with punch. (Underside of assembly is shown).

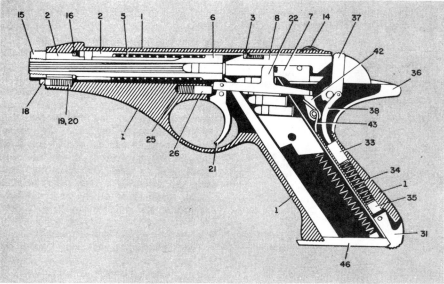

4 The longitudinal section shows the relative position of all parts. Pistol is shown here with a cartridge in the chamber and hammer uncocked.

24. Trigger pin
25. Trigger spring
26. Trigger spring plunger
27. Side plate
28. Side plate screw
29. Safety
30. Grip screws (2)
31. Magazine catch
32. Magazine catch pin
33. Hammer spring plunger
34. Hammer spring
35. Hammer spring seat
36. Action frame
37. Hammer
38. Strut
39. Strut pin
40. Magazine disconnector safety
41. Hammer pin
42. Sear
43. Sear spring
44. Sear pin
45. Safety lock pin
46. Magazine assembly
Note: Grips are not shown.

Disassembly Procedure

Remove magazine (46) and check chamber to be sure pistol is unloaded. Replace magazine and pull trigger. Remove magazine once more. Depress barrel locking plunger (18) flush with forward face of frame (1). Unscrew nut (15). Cock hammer (37) and pull tube (2), breechblock (7), and cocking piece (13) assembled out of frame to rear. Remove barrel seat washer (16) and barrel key (17) from front end of frame. Firing pin lock (3) may be removed by rapping inverted tube (2) sharply, causing it to drop out. Pull firing pin (8) out of breechblock (7). Pull barrel (6) forward slightly and push breech pin (4) out of barrel and tube. Remove breechblock (7) and barrel (6) from tube (2). Lift extractor (10) out of breechblock and remove extractor plunger and spring (11 & 12) from breechblock. Disassembly of ejector (9) from barrel is not recommended.

Reassembly is accomplished in reverse. Install barrel seat washer (16) and barrel key (17) on barrel (6) before barrel and tube (2) are replaced in frame (1). ∎

Walther Cal. .22 Sport Pistol

PISTOL MAGAZINES

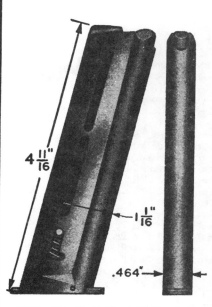

Shortly after World War I, Walther brought out their cal. .22 long rifle Sport pistol. Like all Walther guns, the workmanship was topnotch and it had an adjustable trigger pull. This gun was well liked, but its sale was limited since it was about 3 to 4 times as expensive as a pocket pistol in Germany. Magazine capacity was 12 rounds.

The magazine for this gun contains a novel retractable screwdriver that can be used to adjust the front sight screw or the trigger pull screw.

Unlike American cal. .22 pistol magazines, Walther did not find it necessary to use spring fingers to guide the cartridge. The magazine is very well made and rarely gives trouble.— E. J. HOFFSCHMIDT

Appendix

When setting out to disassemble a firearm, its owner is often challenged to find instructions for the procedure as it applies to the particular gun in question. As a partial solution to this problem, the list that follows contains the brand names and model designations of many pistols and revolvers, represented generally, but not specifically, in this book. These firearms are listed alphabetically with the page number in the book on which a mechanically and operationally similar firearm is described.

Keep in mind, when applying the directions for one firearm to the disassembly of another similar gun, that differences will exist and procedures may need adaptation if disassembly and reassembly are to be done successfully. Discretion, in this instance, may save an embarrassing trip to one's local gunsmith.

- A -
Albion Motors No. 2-series Revolvers, 104
AMT Lightning Pistol, 198
American Derringer, 186
American Derringer Corp. DA 38 Derringer, 137
Argentine "Hi-Power" Pistol, 40
Argentine Model 1916 Pistols, 56
Argentine Model 1927 Pistols, 56
Astra A-60 Pistol, 8
Astra Camper Pistol, 52
Astra Condor Pistol, 10
Astra Cub Pistol, 52
Astra Firecat Pistol, 80
Astra Model 41 Revolver, 6
Astra Model 44 Revolver, 6
Astra Model 45 Revolver, 6
Astra Model 200 Pistol, 80
Astra Model 1921 Pistol, 10
Astra Model 2000 Pistol, 52
Astra Model 3000 Pistol, 10
Astra Model 4000 Pistol, 10
Auto Ordnance M1911A1 Pistol, 56

- B -
Ballester-Rigaud Pistol, 12
Bauer .25 Pistol, 26
Berettas Model 950 Pistol, 18
Beretta Model 950BS Pistol, 18
Beretta Minx Pistol, 18
Beretta Jetfire Pistol, 18
Beretta Model 1923 Pistol, 20
Beretta Model 1931 Pistol, 20
Beretta Model 1932 Pistol, 20
Beretta Model 1935 Pistol, 20
Beretta Model 934 Pistol, 20
Beretta Model 935 Pistol, 20
Beretta Model 948 Pistol, 20
Bohmische Modell 27 Pistol, 94
Browning Buckmark Pistol, 32
Browning Challenger Pistol, 44
Browning Model 1903 Pistol, 36
Buffalo Single-action Revolver, 70
Butler Derringer, 69

- C -
CVA Philadelphia Derringer, 100
Charter Arms Undercoverette Revolver, 48
Charter Arms Off Duty Revolver, 48
Chinese "Mauser"-marked .32 ACP Pistols, 34
Colt Ace Pistols, 56, 60
Colt Agent Revolver, 76
Colt "Alaskan Model" Revolver, 64
Colt Army Special Revolver, 76
Colt Banker's Special Revolver, 76
Colt Buntline Scout, 70
Colt Challenger Pistol, 74
Colt Cobra Revolver, 76
Colt Commander Pistol, 56

Colt Commando Revolver, 76
Colt Deringer No. 4, 69
Colt Detective Special Revolver, 76
Colt Huntsman Pistol, 74
Colt Junior .25 Pistol, 52
Colt Models of 1900 to 1905 Exposed Hammer Pistols, 50
Colt Model 1917 D.A. Revolver, 76
Colt New Pocket Revolver, 67
Colt New Police Revolver, 67
Colt New Service Revolver, 76
Colt Officers ACP Pistol, 56
Colt Officer's Model Revolver, 76
Colt Open Top Percussion Revolvers, 84
Colt "Philippine Model" 1902 Revolver, 64
Colt Pocket Positive Revolver, 76
Colt Police Positive Revolver, 76
Colt Pony .380 Pistol, 246
Colt "Root's Patent" Revolver, 86
Colt Service Ace Pistol, 56, 60
Colt Targetsman Pistol, 74
Colt .38 Super Auto Pistol, 56
Colt Thunderer Revolver, 62
Colt U.S. Model 1889 Revolver, 67
Colt U.S. Model 1892 Revolver, 67
Colt U.S. Model 1894 Revolver, 67
Colt U.S. Model 1896 Revolver, 67
Colt U.S. Model 1901 Revolver, 67
Colt U.S. Model 1903 Revolver, 67
Colt USMC Model 1905 Revolver, 67
Crown City M1911A1 Pistol, 56
Czech Model 82 Pistol, 282
Czech P-64 Pistol, 282

- D -
Davis Derringer, 186
Dakota Single-action Revolver, 81
Deutsche Werke Pistol, 180

- E -
EAA Single-action Revlovers, 81
Egyptian Helwan Pistols, 16

- F -
FEG (Hungarian) B9R Pistol, 40
FEG (Hungarian) PJK-9HP Pistol, 40
French M.A.P.F. Pistols - Various, 264
F.I. Model D Pistol, 246
F.I.E. Best Pistol, 52
FN V.P. (Model 1906) Pistol, 80
Fegyvergyar 29M Pistol, 144
Fegyvergyar STOP Pistol, 112
Femaru Model 37M Pistol, 144
Frazier .25 Pistol, 26
Frommer M37 Pistol, 144

- G -
Gamba "HSc" Super Pistol, 171
German P.08 Pistol, 165